Abstract of Graves of Revolutionary Patriots

Volume 1

A-D

Patricia Law Hatcher

HERITAGE BOOKS
2007

HERITAGE BOOKS
AN IMPRINT OF HERITAGE BOOKS, INC.

Books, CDs, and more—Worldwide

For our listing of thousands of titles see our website at
www.HeritageBooks.com

Published 2007 by
HERITAGE BOOKS, INC.
Publishing Division
65 East Main Street
Westminster, Maryland 21157-5026

Copyright © 1987, 1988 Patricia Law Hatcher

Originally published by:
Pioneer Heritage Press
8040 Claremont Drive
Dallas, Texas 75228

Reprinted 2001, published jointly by:
Pioneer Heritage Press and
Willow Bend Books
65 East Main Street
Westminster, Maryland 21157-5026

The material in this book is an abstract of, and index to, information reported by the National Society Daughters of the American Revolution and published in their Annual Reports to the Smithsonian Institute, printed as Senate Documents (1900-1974), published by the Society in a separate volume (1975-1977) and published annually in the DAR magazine (1978-1987).

All rights reserved. No part of this book may be reproduced or transmitted in any form or by any means, electronic or mechanical, including photocopying, recording or by any information storage and retrieval system without written permission from the author, except for the inclusion of brief quotations in a review.

Library of Congress Catalogue Card Number 87-61590

International Standard Book Number: 978-1-58549-712-6

Acknowledgments

I particularly wish to acknowledge those thousands of ladies who, for over eight decades, have explored town cemeteries and country fields to locate the burial sites of those who fought or gave patriotic service in the American Revolution.

Thanks go to Lloyd DeWitt Bockstruck, head of the Genealogy Section, and his wonderful staff at the J. Eric Jonsson Central (Dallas Public) Library, who were both patient and encouraging and allowed me access to the Senate Document volumes; and fellow genealogists, DAR members and my family who aided and encouraged me.

I hope these volumes will aid those researching their families, and increase awareness of this patriotic activity performed by the Daughters of the American Revolution.

Preface

The source. Almost since its beginning, members of the National Society Daughters of the American Revolution have been locating the graves of Soldiers and Patriots of the American Revolution. The names and locations were first published in 1900 in the DAR's Annual Report to the Smithsonian Institution. Each year since then, additional names and locations, now numbering over 58,500, have been reported.

From 1900 to 1974 the list of graves located during the year (a "year" generally began in March or April) was included in the DAR's Annual Report to the Smithsonian Institution and published as a Senate Document (not the most accessible of publications). In 1975 this report was discontinued. The DAR published the lists for 1975, 1976 and 1977 in a separate volume (as they did for 1978–81). Beginning with 1978, the list of graves located has been published in the DAR Magazine, usually during the following year. These lists, except the earliest ones, are by state, so searching can be tedious.

Accuracy. The accuracy and amount of information varies considerably within and between years. Sometimes almost no specifics were given; sometimes even source citations were included. They are much more complete in later years, but the validity of the information can not be assumed and should be checked. During the years from 1901 through 1914, the grave reports were combined with other reports, and frequently were incomplete or confusing. These years were not abstracted or indexed for this book, because it appears that in 1915 many of these early reports were reviewed or resubmitted. In that year over 3000 names were published. A few apparent duplicates exist, but some of these are persons of the same name buried in the same cemetery, and a few others represent additional or corrected information.

The abstract. Names are spelled exactly as they were in the original documents. Alphabetizing is strict, so check all possible spellings. A few liberties were taken in abstracting grave locations, such as including information which may have appeared elsewhere in the report, correcting the spelling of county names, and occasionally researching and correcting obvious typesetting errors.

It was not possible to fit all of the information contained in each source listing onto the single line necessary to keep this series to a manageable size, so the facts most useful to the reader were chosen. The term "Fam cem" (family cemetery) was frequently used to replace such phrases as "Old Jones family burying place" if the patriot's surname was spelled the same, in order to allow for more details about the location.

The index. The number at the end of the line is the reporting year. For example, "45" indicates the grave was located between April 1, 1944 and April 1, 1945. If possible, check the original publication (see following page), which might contain additional information, such as the patriot's birth and death dates and places, the service record of the patriot, and more details on the grave location.

All volumes of the DAR Reports to the Smithsonian are available at the DAR Library in Washington, D.C. The genealogical section of the Dallas Public Library has most of the Senate Documents. The Genealogical Library in Salt Lake City has the 1975–1977 volume. Local DAR and genealogy collections may have copies of the publications. The Brigham Young University library has a card file based on the published work of the DAR which is being microfilmed by the Genealogical Library in Salt Lake City.

Using this book. While all of these reports are available at DAR headquarters, there is little if any information available there to link these references to specific sources of proof, to provide researchers with details as to why a grave was marked or to verify the listing of a located grave as indeed being that of a Revolutionary War patriot. Many listings, particularly the earlier ones, were not substantiated; **all information should be independently verified and proved before being submitted to any patriotic or hereditary society for application or other purpose.** For additional information and clarification on these listings, please contact the Office of the Historian General, NSDAR, 1776 D St., NW, Washington, DC 20006-5392 or the DAR Library at the same street address.

The ravages of time have caused the location of many graves to be lost today, and we should be grateful for this wealth of material.

Patricia Law Hatcher
Dallas, Texas 2001

Senate Documents. The Senate Documents that contained the DAR annual report and the list of located graves are part of the US Serial Set. The Serial Set is comprised of Senate and House Reports and Documents since 1789. They were issued in matching volumes (over 15,000 thus far) in tan bindings. Each book has a serial and volume number assigned to it.

Serial Set collections are maintained by depositories (there are some in every state, usually universities). Distribution of the Serial Set volumes has, unfortunately, not been consistent. Depository libraries may have some or all (or none) of the volumes indexed in these books. CIS (Congressional Indexing Service) are microfiching a set of every known Serial Set publication, therefore some libraries may have microfiche copies instead of bound volumes.

Locating these volumes can be a frustrating experience. To aid you I have listed below the serial and volume numbers opposite the index years from this book. To find out if a library has the one in which you are interested, contact the Government Documents section of the library and ask if they have the Serial Set; if they do, ask for the serial number and volume number listed below.

year	serial	volume	year	serial	volume
00	4044	16	45	10950	13
15	6924	14	46	11127	2
16	7119	6	47	11216	2
17	7324	14	48	11304	3
18	7601	6	49	11393	3
19	7782	4	50	11507	6
20	7783	5	51	11587	4
21	7973	7	52	11670	3
22	8163	4	53	11756	6
23	8234	2	54	11831	4
24	8399	7	55	11912	4
25	8542	4	56	11999	8
26	8701	10	57	12172	4
27	8848	5	58	12259	4
28	8985	2	59	12260	5
29	9200	3	60	12356	9
30	9337	5	61	12449	6
31	9504	6	62	12556	7
32	9661	7	63	12625	4
33	9787	5	64	12671	4
34	9901	7	65	12718	3
35	10000	2	66	12842	3
36	10094	5	67	12842-2	3-2
37	10173	1	68	(91-Sen Doc 102)	
37	10303	2	69	12939	
38	10448	2	70	12978	1
40	10468-A	23	71	12978	2
41	10572	12	72	(93-Sen Doc 54)	
42	10675	7	73	(93-Sen Doc 113)	
43	10772	8	74	(94-Sen Doc 117)	
44	10861	11			

Abbreviations

aban	abandoned	AL	Alabama
adj	adjoining	AR	Arkansas
Assoc	Association	CA	California
Bapt	Baptist	CAN	Canada
betw	between	CO	Colorado
Bur Gr	Burying Ground	CT	Connecticut
Bur Plot	Burial Plot	DE	Delaware
Cem	Cemetery	DC	Dist of Columbia
Ch	Church	ENG	England
Comm	Community	FL	Florida
Co	County	GA	Georgia
Cong	Congregational	IA	Iowa
Cr	Creek	ID	Idaho
Dist	District	IL	Illinois
Epis	Episcopal	IN	Indiana
Evang	Evangelical	KS	Kansas
Fam	Family	KY	Kentucky
Ft	Fort	LA	Louisiana
fr	from	ME	Maine
Hwy	Highway	MD	Maryland
Hist	Historical	MA	Massachusetts
Hnd	Hundred	ml	Michigan
is	Island	MN	Minnesota
Luth	Lutheran	Ms	Mississippi
Menn	Mennonite	MO	Missouri
Meth	Methodist	NH	New Hampshire
mi	miles	NJ	New Jersey
Morav	Moravian	NY	New York
Mt	Mount	NC	North Carolina
Mtg Hs	Meeting House	OH	Ohio
Natl	National	OK	Oklahoma
nr	near	OR	Oregon
NYC	New York City	PA	Pennsylvania
OPP	opposite	RI	Rhode Island
Pres	Presbyterian	SC	South Carolina
Prim	Primitive	TN	Tennessee
Priv	Private	TX	Texas
Prop	Property	VT	Vermont
Pt	Point	VA	Virginia
Rd	Road	W IND	West Indies
Ref	Reformed	WV	West Virginia
Rev	Reverend/Revolutionary	WI	Wisconsin
Rt	Route		
St	Saint/street		
Twp	Township		
Unit	United		
UCC	United Church of Christ		
UMC	United Methodist Church		

Abbe John	Enfield Cem, Enfield, CT 47
Abbe John III	Enfield St Cem, Enfield, CT 23
Abbe Richard Jr	Enfield St Cem, Enfield, CT 23
Abbe Richard Sr	King St Cem, Enfield, CT 23
Abbe Thomas	Enfield Cem, Enfield, CT 59
Abbey Abner	West Cem, Granby Co, MA 58
Abbey Hezekiah	Old Cem, Westminster, VT 42
Abbey John	Arkwright Cem, Pomfret, Chautauqua Co, NY 78
Abbey Thomas	Clam River Cem, Sandisfield, MA 56
Abbey Thomas Capt	Enfield St Cem, Enfield, CT 46
Abbot Abiel	Chester Hill Cem, Chester, MA 62
Abbot Abiel	South Parish Cem, Andover, Essex Co, MA 55
Abbot Abril	South Parish Bur Gr, Andover, Essex Co, MA 26
Abbot Asa	South Parish Bur Gr, Andover, Essex Co, MA 26
Abbot Benjamin Sgt	Old North Bur Gr, Concord, NH 41
Abbot Caleb	South Parish Bur Gr, Andover, Essex Co, MA 26
Abbot Ephram	South Parish Bur Gr, Andover, Essex Co, MA 26
Abbot George	South Parish Bur Gr, Andover, Essex Co, MA 26
Abbot Henry	South Parish Bur Gr, Andover, Essex Co, MA 26
Abbot Isaac	South Parish Bur Gr, Andover, Essex Co, MA 26
Abbot Jeduthun Capt	West Parish Bur Gr, Andover, Essex Co, MA 26
Abbot Jeremiah	South Yard, Wilton, NH 34
Abbot John	Bloomfield Cem, Greene Co, IN 24
Abbot John	Fairview Cem, Westford, MA 55
Abbot John	Old North Bur Gr, Concord, NH 41
Abbot John	South Parish Bur Gr, Andover, Essex Co, MA 26
Abbot John Capt	South Parish Bur Gr, Andover, Essex Co, MA 26
Abbot Johnathan Capt	West Parish Bur Gr, Andover, Essex Co, MA 26
Abbot Jonathan	South Parish Bur Gr, Andover, Essex Co, MA 26
Abbot Jonathan	West Brookfield Cem, Brookfield, MA 71
Abbot Jonathan Lt	West Parish Bur Gr, Andover, Essex Co, MA 26
Abbot Joseph	Old North Bur Gr, Concord, NH 41
Abbot Joseph	Stricklands Ferry, ME 20
Abbot Joshua Capt	Old North Bur Gr, Concord, NH 41
Abbot Nathan	South Parish Cem, Andover, Essex Co, MA 71
Abbot Nehimiah	South Parish Bur Gr, Andover, Essex Co, MA 26
Abbot Samuel	South Parish Bur Gr, Andover, Essex Co, MA 26
Abbot Timothy	South Parish Bur Gr, Andover, Essex Co, MA 26
Abbot William	South Parish Bur Gr, Andover, Essex Co, MA 26
Abbot William	Vale End Cem, Wilton, NH 34
Abbot Zebediah	South Parish Bur Gr, Andover, Essex Co, MA 26
Abbott Aaron	Bloomfield Cem, Richfield Springs, NY 34
Abbott Aaron	Bloomfield Cem, Herkimer Co, NY 41
Abbott Abel	South Yard, Wilton, NH 34
Abbott Amos Jr	West Concord Cem, Concord, Rockingham Co, NH 55
Abbott Asa	Priv Cem, nr Knox, Albany, NY 33
Abbott Benjamin	Churchyard, Hollis, NH 39
Abbott Benjamin	Edgewood Cem, Nashua, NH 40
Abbott Bigsby	Greenfield, NH 52
Abbott Charles	Sunbury Cem, Berkshire Twp, Delaware Co, OH 53
Abbott Daniel	Old Village Cem, Claremont, NH 50
Abbott Daniel	West Cem, Amherst, MA 56
Abbott David	West Parish Bur Gr, Andover, Essex Co, MA 26
Abbott Elias	Priv Cem, Northfield, NH 29

Abbott Elias Capt	Fam Cem, Northfield, NH	34
Abbott Elijah Triall	Dutch Ch, Rhinebeck Village, Dutchess Co, NY	21
Abbott Ephraim	North Bur Gr, Wayland, MA	56
Abbott Jeptha	Gloucester Co, NJ	32
Abbott Jeptha	Meth Cem, Aura, Gloucester Co, NJ	68
Abbott Jeremiah Lt	Conway Cem, Conway, NH	32
Abbott John	Abbott Yard, Maple St, North Berwick, ME	56
Abbott John	Bloomfield Cem, Bloomfield, Greene Co, IN	73
Abbott John	Old Bur Gr, Holden, MA	15
Abbott John	Priv plot, own plantation, West Union, Oconee Co, SC	80
Abbott John	Wilmington, DE	56
Abbott John Capt	Westfall Cem, Cayuga Co, NY	41
Abbott John Col	Westfall Cem, Cayuga Co, NY	41
Abbott John Pvt	Town Cem, Andover, ME	49
Abbott Joseph	Boscawen, NH	54
Abbott Joseph	Fam Cem, Franklin Twp, Brown Co, OH	55
Abbott Joseph	Fam Cem, OH	15
Abbott Joseph	Franklin Twp, Brown Co, OH	34
Abbott Joseph	Old Bur Gr, Lincoln, MA	55
Abbott Joseph	Old Cem, Lincoln, MA	55
Abbott Joseph	West Rumney Cem, Rumney, NH	36
Abbott Joshua	River Rd Cem, Bow, NH	32
Abbott Josiah	Cem nr Village, Colebrook, NH	32
Abbott Moses	Ye Olde Bur Gr, Bedford, MA	55
Abbott Nathan	[no cem named], CT	19
Abbott Nathaniel C	Village Cem, Rumney, NH	36
Abbott Nehemiah	First Cem, North Andover, Essex Co, MA	56
Abbott Nehemiah	Old Bur Gr, Lincoln, MA	55
Abbott Samuel	Meridian, Cato, NY	56
Abbott Sele	Cornwell-Tilden plot, New Lebanon, Columbia Co, NY	79
Abbott Solomon	Fam Cem, Cherokee Springs, Spartanburg Co, SC	80
Abbott Stephen	Abbott fam lot, North Berwick, ME	26
Abbott William	Kirkland Avenue Cem, Clinton, Oneida Co, NY	79
Abbott Zebediah	South Parish Cem, Andover, Essex Co, MA	55
Abeel Anthony	Fam Cem, Rt 23A, Catskill, Greene Co, NY	58
Abeel David	First Dutch Ref Ch Cem, New Brunswick, NJ	24
Abel Caleb	Trumbull, Lebanon, CT	56
Abel David	East Coy Cem, Pike, Wyoming Co, NY	80
Abel David	Fam Cem, Saratoga, NY	32
Abel Eliphalet	Exeter, Lebanon, CT	56
Abel Everitt	Old Bethel Cem, Fairfield Co, OH	64
Abel Isaac	Norwich Town Cem, Norwich, CT	18
Abel John	Perry Cem, Perry, Lake Co, OH	34
Abel John	Perry, OH	26
Abel Rufis Backus	Norwich Town Cem, Norwich, CT	18
Abel Simon	Goshen, Lebanon, CT	56
Abel Simon	Old Cem, nr Franklin, Delaware Co, NY	73
Abell Frederick	East Lempster Cem, East Lempster, NH	35
Abell Joshua	Center Cem, Goshen, MA	51
Abell Robert	Newman Cem, Rumford, East Providence, RI	36
Abell Robert	Newman Ch Cem, Rumford, RI	55
Abell Robert	Old Rumford Cem, Newman Ave, Rehoboth, MA	55
Abell Robert	Walnut St Cem, Brookline, MA	55
Abell Thomas	Old Fredonia Cem, Pomfret, Chautauqua Co, NY	15
Abendschon Samuel	Fam Cem, nr Mill Creek Bapt Ch, Botetourt Co, VA	73
Abendschon Samuel	Fam Cem, Botetourt, VA	58
Abercrombie Charles	Fam Cem, own land, Hancock Co, GA	25
Abercrombie Isaac	West Cem, Pelham, MA	40
Abernathy Buckner	Old Abernathy Cem, Giles Co, TN	57
Abernathy Buckner	Old Abernathy Cem, Giles Co, TN	59
Abernathy William	Fam Cem, 4 mi SE of Pulaski, TN	54

Abstract of Graves of Revolutionary Patriots 3

Able Joseph	Middletown Cem, Middletown, Jefferson Co, KY 73
Abney Dannett	Fam bur gr, Saluda Co, SC 15
Abney John	Mount Zion Cem, nr Haughton, Bossier Parish, LA 15
Abney Nathaniel	Joel Abney Cem, Saluda Co, SC 15
Abney Nathaniel	Old fam land, Saluda-Newberry Hwy, Edgefield, SC 59
Abney Paul	Barnes's Cem, Saluda Co, SC 15
Abney Paul	[no cem named], SC 15
Abney William	Fam bur gr, Saluda Co, SC 15
Aborn Daniel	Green Cem, Pawtuxet, Warwick, RI 36
Aborn James	Old bur gr, Marblehead, MA 45
Aborn John	Cole Cem, opposite Jim Smith Inn, Pawtuxet, Warwick, RI 36
Aborn Samuel	Cole Cem, opposite Jim Smith Inn, Pawtuxet, Warwick, RI 36
Aborn Samuel Jr	Cole Cem, opposite Jim Smith Inn, Pawtuxet, Warwick, RI 36
Abrams Gabriel	Priv Cem, Watson farm, McClellandtown, Fayette Co, PA 66
Abshire Josiah	East View Cem, Wadesboro, Anson Co, NC 49
Abstom John	Brownwood, TX 23
Abston John	[no cem named] 15
Ache John H	Resitville, PA 52
Achey Henrich	Manheim Twp, PA 49
Ackard Adam	Stone Ch, Rhinebeck, Dutchess Co, NY 21
Ackart Peter	Elmwood Cem, Schaghticoke, Rensselaer Co, NY 38
Acken John	Pres Ch Cem, Rahway, NJ 76
Acken Jonathan	Pres Ch Cem, Westfield, NJ 76
Acken Joseph	Pres Ch Cem, Westfield, NJ 76
Acken Robert	Westfield Cem, Westfield, NJ 24
Acker George	Old Pres Ch Cem, Preble, Cortland Co, NY 36
Acker Jacob Jr	Ziegel's Ch Cem, Breinigsville, Lehigh, PA 40
Ackerly John	Lakeville Rural Cem, Lake Grove, Suffolk Co, NY 77
Ackerly Phillip	Meth Ch Cem, Ronkonkoma, NY 34
Ackerman Abram	Paramus Ch Cem, Paramus, NJ 55
Ackerman Casparuis	Terry-Shear Cem, Coeymans, NY 58
Ackerman John	North Fork Cem, Middlebury Twp, Knox Co, OH 34
Ackerman John	North Fork, Middlebury Twp, Knox Co, OH 39
Ackers Joseph	Heil Cem, Greenville, Floyd, IN 66
Ackers Thomas Sr	Heil Cem, Greenville, Floyd, IN 66
Ackerson Cornelius	Sterling Valley, Sterling, NY 56
Ackerson Thomas	Ardera Cem, Ardera, NJ 30
Ackert Conraedt	Wurtemburg, Rhinebeck, Dutchess Co, NY 21
Ackert George	Stone Ch, Rhinebeck, Dutchess Co, NY 21
Ackert Martinus	St Paul's Cem, Rhinebeck, NY 70
Ackert Solomon	Community Ground, Rhinebeck, Dutchess Co, NY 21
Ackert Solomon	Dyer, Canton, CT 56
Ackhart Solomon	Dyer Cem, Canton, CT 55
Ackley Ahira	Fowler Ridge, Trumbull Co, OH 56
Ackley Elihu	Priv Cem, Edson Corners, NY 31
Ackley Gideon	Millington, East Haddam, CT 56
Ackley Hezekiah	New Preston Cem, New Preston, CT 55
Ackley Isaac Chalker	East Haddam, CT 56
Ackley Joel	Cem, Danby, NY 34
Ackley Joel	Rural Cem, Danby, NY 15
Ackley Nathaniel	East Hampton Cem, East Hampton, Middlesex Co, CT 72
Ackley Samuel	Rumford, ME 53
Ackley Simeon	Richmond Cem, MA 40
Ackley Thomas	Ellsworth Cem, Sharon, Litchfield Co, CT 66
Ackley William	Friendship Meth Epis Cem, nr Buena, NJ 25
Acree Crocamus	Bowers Cem, Roane Co, TN 24
Acree Crocamus	Bowers Cem, TN 23
Acres George	Warren Cem, Little Lakes, Warren, Herkimer Co, NY 41
Acres Jacob	Fairview Cem, Washington Co, TN 31
Acton Smallwood	Acton, Clark Co, KY 56
Acuff Jacob	St Thomas Epis Ch Cem, Montgomery Co, PA 59

Adair James	Brookville Cem, Brookville, IN 57
Adair James	Luth Cem, Brookville, IN 33
Adair James	Pres Cem, Poland, Mahoning Co, OH 34
Adair John	Adair Station, Knox Co, TN 24
Adair John	Adair's Station, TN 23
Adair John	Fam Cem, Adair Creek, Knoxville, TN 29
Adair John	Harrodsburg, KY 15
Adair John	State Cem, Frankfort, KY 15
Adair Joseph	Clinton, SC 26
Adair Morris	Guernsey Co, OH 53
Adair William	Old Caldwell place, Lebanon Rd, Danville, KY 27
Adam (serv of Gardner)	Walnut Street Cem, Brookline, MA 56
Adam Robert	Cross Creek Cem, Fayetteville, Cumberland Co, NC 80
Adams Aaron	Northbridge Center Cem, Whitinsville, MA 53
Adams Aaron	Temple Hill Cem, Geneseo, Livingston Co, NY 79
Adams Aaron	Temple Hill Cem, Geneseo, Livingston Co, NY 22
Adams Abel	St Andrews Cem, Bloomfield, CT 55
Adams Abel	Walnut Street Cem, Brookline, MA 56
Adams Abel Sr	Chelmsford, MA 52
Adams Abner	Pleasant Valley Cem, nr Hinman Hollow, Otsego Co, NY 71
Adams Abraham	Harlem Cem, Harlem Twp, Delaware Co, OH 46
Adams Abraham	Redding Cem, CT 46
Adams Amasa	Old Cem, Wethersfield, CT 56
Adams Andrew	Old Village Cem, Lancaster, NH 37
Adams Andrew	Old section, Cem nr center, Grafton, MA 49
Adams Andrew	West Litchfield Cem, West Litchfield, CT 17
Adams Ansel	Barnstable Cem, Barnstable, MA 62
Adams Asahel	Miami Cem, Liberty Twp, Trumbull Co, OH 34
Adams Asahel	Town Cem, Bristol, NH 29
Adams Barnabas	Lee Cem, Lee, MA 15
Adams Benjamin	Cavendish, VT 16
Adams Benjamin	Hopkinton, MA 48
Adams Benjamin	Meeting House Cem, Newington, NH 25
Adams Benjamin	Old Village Yard, New Ipswich, NH 29
Adams Benjamin	Wayland Cem, Old Sudbury Rd, Wayland, MA 55
Adams Buckley	Center Bur Gr, Lincoln, MA 55
Adams Chester	French Cem, Potter, Yates Co, NY 80
Adams Daniel	Old Bur Gr, Townsend, MA 56
Adams Daniel	Pentucket Cem, Haverhill, MA 28
Adams Daniel	Pentucket, Haverhill, MA 27
Adams Daniel Jenifer	Old Swedes Ch Cem, Wilmington, New Castle Co, DE 36
Adams Daniel Lt	Chippenhook Cem, Clarendon, VT 24
Adams Daniel Lt	Chippenhook Cem, Clarendon, VT 25
Adams Davenport	Center, New Marlborough, MA 56
Adams David	1 mi E of Ocmulgee, nr Glochville, GA 32
Adams David	Bapt Ch Cem, Charleston, SC 15
Adams David	Bethlehem Cem, Johnson Co, IN 43
Adams David	Centennial Cem, Gilsum, NH 32
Adams David	Forest Hill Cem, East Derry, NH 38
Adams David	Harlem Cem, Harlem Twp, Delaware Co, OH 46
Adams David	Harlem Twp, Delaware Co, OH 18
Adams David	Mud Meeting House, Mercer Co, KY 52
Adams David	Old Cem, Rindge, NH 36
Adams David	West of Morgantown, IN 16
Adams David	Westford Cem, Westford, Otsego Co, NY 71
Adams David	Zebulon Cem, Pike Co, GA 57
Adams David Maj Gen	Nr Monticello, Jasper Co, GA 35
Adams Ebenezer	Ancient Bur Gr, Kingston, MA 50
Adams Ebenezer	Becket Center, Becket, MA 56
Adams Ebenezer	Princes Hill Cem, Barrington, RI 36
Adams Ebenezer	Upper Red Hook, Dutchess Co, NY 21

Adams Ebenezer Sgt	Fam farm, Province Rd, Barnstead, NH	28
Adams Edmund	Forest Hill Cem, East Derry, NH	38
Adams Edward	Lower Cincinnatus Cem, Cincinnatus, Cortland Co, NY	36
Adams Eli	Nr Snow Hill, MD	56
Adams Eli	Parker Hill Cem, Springfield, VT	42
Adams Elias	Old Cem, Spencer, MA	56
Adams Elias	Opposite church, Newbury, MA	56
Adams Elihu	Union Cem, Holbrook, MA	31
Adams Elijah	Center Cem, Hubbardston, MA	26
Adams Elijah	Copps Hill Bur Gr, Boston, MA	55
Adams Elijah	Monroe Twp Cem, Licking Co, OH	34
Adams Elijah	Vedder Ch Cem, Gallatin, Columbia Co, NY	74
Adams Elijah	Vine Lake, Medfield, MA	56
Adams Elisha	Hopkinton, MA	53
Adams Ephraim	Center, Southwick, MA	56
Adams Ephraim Dea	Old Cem on Hill, Stoddard, Cheshire Co, NH	27
Adams Ephriam	Old Village Yard, New Ipswich, NH	29
Adams Ephriam Jr	Old Village Yard, New Ipswich, NH	29
Adams Evi	Deckertown Union Cem, Wantage Twp, Sussex Co, NJ	79
Adams Ezekiel	Opposite First Cong Ch, Hamilton, MA	56
Adams Ezekiel	Vine Lake, Medfield, MA	56
Adams Ezekiel Jr	Opposite First Cong Ch, Hamilton, MA	56
Adams Ezra	North Canton Cem, Canton, CT	55
Adams Francis	Ancient Bur Gr, Kingston, MA	50
Adams Francis	Mud Mtg Hs, Mercer Co, KY	52
Adams Francis	Northbridge Center Cem, Whitinsville, MA	53
Adams George	Martin Cem, 3 mi E of Greenville, Darke Co, OH	34
Adams Gershon	Vine Lake, Medfield, MA	56
Adams Gideon	Mount View Cem, West Pawlet, VT	48
Adams Gideon	West Pawlet Cem, VT	15
Adams Hedman	Butler Co, OH	56
Adams Henry	Old Cem, Freidensville, Lehigh Co, PA	40
Adams Isaac	Ancient Cem, West Boxford, MA	29
Adams Isaac	Phillips Cem, Jaffrey, NH	37
Adams Israel	Ancient Cem, West Boxford, MA	29
Adams Israel Jr	Old Hill Yard, Hill, NH	36
Adams Issacher	Old Cem, Hubbardston, MA	50
Adams Jacob	Huff farm graveyard, Southampton, Bedford Co, PA	80
Adams Jacob	Milford, NH	15
Adams James	Cold Water Cem, nr Cold Water Ch, Elbert Co, GA	34
Adams James	His prop (grave), Coldwater Cem (marker), Elbert Co, GA	25
Adams James	Krum Cem, Harlemville, Columbia Co, NY	71
Adams James	Mecklenburg Co, VA	56
Adams James	Old Cem, Lincoln, MA	55
Adams James	Wilmington & Brandywine, New Castle Co, DE	46
Adams James Lt	Forest Hill Cem, East Derry, NH	38
Adams Jedediah	Crowell Cem, Biddeford, ME	29
Adams Joel	East End Cem, East Aurora, NY	33
Adams Joel	Jarmany Hill Cem, Sharon, Hillsborough Co, NH	77
Adams Joel	St Johns Ch Cem, Congarees, SC	42
Adams John	Acton, MA	55
Adams John	Ancient Bur Gr, Kingston, MA	50
Adams John	Beach Plain, Sandisfield, MA	56
Adams John	Bean Yard, Center Harbor, NH	29
Adams John	Bean Yard, Moultonboro, NH	30
Adams John	Beech Plain Cem, Sandisfield, Berkshire Co, MA	79
Adams John	Canterbury, CT	52
Adams John	Center Cem, Chelmsford, MA	56
Adams John	Crossroads, Springport, NY	56
Adams John	Fairhaven, VT	31
Adams John	Fam Cem, nr Core Creek & Boone, Watauga Co, NC	71

Adams John	Fam Cem, Quincy, MA 57
Adams John	Lamington Pres Cem, Somerset Co, NJ 63
Adams John	Milton Cem, Milton, MA 46
Adams John	North Cem, Acton, MA 56
Adams John	Old Cem, Northbridge, MA 54
Adams John	Old Town Cem, opposite 1st Cong Ch, Newbury, MA 55
Adams John	Pres Ch Cem, Woodbridge, Middlesex Co, NJ 75
Adams John	Pres Ch Cem, Rahway, NJ 76
Adams John	Priv Post Rd, Old Greenwich, CT 55
Adams John	Rural Cem, betw Fly Creek & Toddsville, Otsego Co, NY 71
Adams John	Schwenksville Cem, Montgomery Co, PA 59
Adams John	Sherrill-Danner Cem, Hickory, Catawba Co, NC 57
Adams John	South Sutton Cem, Sutton, NH 37
Adams John	Tomb in Unitarian 1st Parish Ch, Quincy, MA 74
Adams John	West Bedford, OH 25
Adams John Capt	Old Rowe Cem, Rowe, MA 46
Adams John Corp	New London Cem, New London, NH 37
Adams John Lt	Old Cem, Brooklyn, PA 21
Adams John Lt	Old Town Cem, Stratham, NH 28
Adams John Sr	East Bloomfield Cem, East Bloomfield, NY 60
Adams Jonathan	Fam Cem, Marlboro Co, SC 60
Adams Jonathan	Medway, MA 56
Adams Jonathan	Millis, Millis-Medway, MA 56
Adams Jonathan	Old Cem, Sennett, NY 15
Adams Jonathan	Old Cem, Sennett, Cayuga Co, NY 41
Adams Jonathan	Vessel Rock Cem, Gilsum, NH 37
Adams Jonathan	West Medway Cem, Medway, MA 56
Adams Jonathan Capt	Forest Hill Cem, East Derry, NH 38
Adams Jonathan Jr	Millis, Millis-Medway, MA 56
Adams Joseph	Ancient Bur Gr, Kingston, MA 50
Adams Joseph	Center Cem, Chelmsford, MA 55
Adams Joseph	North Concord Cem, Concord, MA 55
Adams Joseph	Old Seceder Ch Cem, Mercer Co, KY 45
Adams Joseph	River St Cem, West Newton, MA 44
Adams Joseph	South St Cem, Fitchburg, MA 55
Adams Joseph	Town Cem, Grand Isle, VT 25
Adams Joseph	[no cem named], VT 25
Adams Joseph Rev	Old Town Cem, Stratham, NH 28
Adams Joshua	Old Bur Cem, Kingston, MA 62
Adams Josiah	Mendon Center Cem, Mendon, MA 46
Adams Josiah	Old Cem, Mendon, MA 55
Adams Lemuel	Old Milton Cem, Milton, MA 46
Adams Levi	Ludlow, VT 15
Adams Luke	Southington Cem, Hartford Co, CT 72
Adams Luther	Wilhoits Graveyard, 2 mi W of Jasper, IN 72
Adams Mathew	Hunterdon Co, NJ 56
Adams Mayhew	Childmark Cem, Martha's Vineyard, MA 55
Adams Micah	Millis, Millis-Medway, MA 56
Adams Micajah	Acuff Cem, Blountville, TN 37
Adams Micajah	Acuff's Chapel Cem, Kingsport, Sullivan Co, TN 73
Adams Moses	Dublin Cem, Dublin, Cheshire Co, NH 77
Adams Moses	Franklin, OH 26
Adams Moses	Medway Cem, Medway, MA 46
Adams Moses Rev	Acton, MA 55
Adams Nathan	Dummerston Center, Dummerston, VT 22
Adams Nathan	Vine Lake, Medfield, MA 56
Adams Nathaniel	Center Cem, Grafton, MA 49
Adams Nathaniel	Ft Griswold, Groton, CT 53
Adams Nathaniel	Opposite First Cong Ch, Hamilton, MA 56
Adams Newdigate	Princes Hill Cem, Barrington, RI 36
Adams Noah	Revolutionary Cem, Cavendish, VT 56

Abstract of Graves of Revolutionary Patriots

Adams Obediah	North Bellingham Cem, Bellingham, MA	46
Adams Oliver	Millis, Millis-Medway, MA	56
Adams Parmenio	Fam Cem, Plainville, Onondaga Co, NY	71
Adams Peter	Granary Cem, Boston, MA	46
Adams Peter	Talbot Cem, Taunton, MA	41
Adams Richard	Gilson Yard, Nashua, NH	30
Adams Robert	Altavista, VA	30
Adams Robert	Altavista, VA	29
Adams Robert Capt Jr	Ward Cem, Pittsylvania Co, VA	37
Adams Roderick	Walnut Grove Cem, Onondaga Hill, NY	32
Adams Salathiel	Forefathers Bur Gr, Chelmsford, MA	57
Adams Samuel	Boothbay, ME	55
Adams Samuel	Center Cem, Chelmsford, MA	56
Adams Samuel	Country Yard, Melvin, NH	29
Adams Samuel	Granary Cem, Boston, MA	46
Adams Samuel	Greene, Androscoggin Co, ME	18
Adams Samuel	Heart Pond Cem, Chelmsford, MA	57
Adams Samuel	Hitchcock Cem, Monroe Co, MI	55
Adams Samuel	Lamington Pres Cem, Somerset Co, NJ	63
Adams Samuel	Mud Mtg Hs, Mercer Co, KY	52
Adams Samuel	North Bellingham Cem, Bellingham, MA	46
Adams Samuel	Old 2nd Ward Cem, Cleveland, Cuyahoga Co, OH	55
Adams Samuel	Old Granary Bur Gr, Boston, MA	51
Adams Samuel	Old Mud Meeting House, Mercer Co, KY	45
Adams Samuel	Opposite First Cong Ch, Hamilton, MA	56
Adams Samuel	Plain, Sheffield, MA	56
Adams Samuel	South Bangor Cem, South Bangor, Franklin Co, NY	77
Adams Samuel	West Hill Cem, Williamstown, VT	40
Adams Samuel Capt	Old Center Cem, Jaffrey, NH	37
Adams Samuel Dr	Forest Hills Cem, Boston, MA	46
Adams Seth	Troy, PA	15
Adams Silas	Boyce Cem, Milton, NY	32
Adams Silas	Opposite church, Newbury, MA	56
Adams Smith	River St Cem, West Newton, MA	44
Adams Solomon Ens	New London Cem, west part, New London, NH	37
Adams Stephen	Colby Cem, Henniker, NH	31
Adams Stephen	Old Cem, West Medway, MA	48
Adams Stephen	Roses Brook Cem, Stamford, NY	35
Adams Steven	Swasey Yard, Meredith, NH	32
Adams Thomas	Greene Co, OH	45
Adams Thomas	Henrietta, Monroe Co, NY	33
Adams Thomas	Nicholson Cem, 8 mi N of Edgefield, SC	15
Adams Thomas	North Cemetery, Amherst, MA	56
Adams Thomas	Off Hartwell Rd, 3 mi fr Elberton, GA	32
Adams Thomas	Old Center Cem, Jaffrey, NH	37
Adams Thomas	Old Harmony Ch, nr Brewer's Mill, Elbert Co, GA	34
Adams Thomas	Old Harmony Ch, Elbert Co, GA	27
Adams Thomas	Old Town Cem, Medfield, Norfolk Co, MA	59
Adams Thomas	Old Town Cem, Medfield, Norfolk Co, MA	57
Adams Thomas	Village Cem, Surry, NH	35
Adams Thomas	Worden Cem, Halifax, VT	38
Adams Timothy	Cavendish Cem, VT	29
Adams Timothy	Old Town Cem, Medfield, Norfolk Co, MA	57
Adams William	Center Cem, Chelmsford, MA	55
Adams William	Forest Hill Cem, East Derry, NH	38
Adams William	French Creek Cem, Chautauqua Co, NY	63
Adams William	Newell Twp, Vermilion Co, IL	15
Adams William	Open Field, N of Danville, IL	15
Adams William	Raleigh City Cem, Wake Co, NC	49
Adams William	Somerset Co, MD	56
Adams William	West Alexander, PA	38

Adams William Capt	Old Cem, Arlington, MA 46	
Adams William Dr	Unionville Cem, Westchester Co, NY 35	
Adams William Jr	Hopkinton Cem, Hopkinton, MA 47	
Adams Winborn Lt Col	Stillwater Battlefield, NH 50	
Adamy Henry	Monroe St Cem, Cleveland, OH 15	
Adamy Henry	Monroe St Cem, Monroe & 32nd, Cleveland, Cuyahoga Co, OH 55	
Addington John	Ridgeville Cem, Randolph Co, IN 25	
Addis Simon	Elm Ridge Cem, Franklin Park, Somerset Co, NJ 33	
Addison Joseph	Cem, old Burts place, Edgefield, SC 15	
Addoms John	Fam Cem, Cumberland Head, Plattsburg, NY 56	
Adelman Philip	Houck Cem, Hilliar Twp, Knox Co, OH 53	
Adgate John Hart	Old Cem, Mahoning Ave, Warren, Trumbull Co, OH 34	
Adkins Isaiah	Union Hill, nr Mehoopany, PA 17	
Adkins John	North Charleston, NH 15	
Adkins John Sr	[no cem named], WV 29	
Adkson Thomas	Massacred nr mouth of Lechry Creek, Dearborn Co, IN 24	
Adriance Isaac	Ref Ch Cem, Hopewell Junction, NY 85	
Adriance Rem	Ref Ch Cem, Hopewell Junction, NY 85	
Adriance Rem	Ref Ch Cem, Hopewell Junction, NY 85	
Adriance Theodorus	Ref Ch Cem, Hopewell Junction, NY 85	
Adsit John	Bapt Ground, Stanford, Dutchess Co, NY 21	
Adsit John	Hillsdale, Albany, NY 56	
Adsit Samuel	Bapt Ground, lot #1, Stanford, Dutchess Co, NY 21	
Adsit Samuel Aject	McIntyre Cem, Stanford, NY 54	
Adsit Silas	Montgomery County Cem, Montgomery Co, NY 58	
Adye John	Gilead Cem, Bethel, VT 52	
Aear George	Luth Ch Cem, Red Hooks, NY 46	
Agan John	Pittstown Cem, Pittstown, Rensselaer Co, NY 34	
Agan Patrick	Raymerstown, Rensselaer Co, NY 35	
Agard John	[no cem named], OH 26	
Agard Joseph	Old Cem, Smithville Flats, NY 35	
Agard Joseph	Smithville Flats, NY 16	
Agard Noah	Fam Cem, Odessa, Schuyler Co, NY 77	
Agee James	Buckingham Co, VA 71	
Ager Benjamin	Lakeview, South Weymouth, MA 50	
Ager Jonathan	Lakeview, South Weymouth, MA 50	
Agnew David	Lower Marsh Creek Pres Ch Cem, Gettysburg, PA 56	
Agnew Samuel	Old Greenville Ch, nr Ware Shoals, SC 53	
Agor Charles	Cem back of fire house, Carmel, Putnam Co, NY 36	
Agor Charles	Old Bapt Cem, Carmel, Putnam Co, NY 57	
Agry Thomas	Hallowell Cem, Hallowell, ME 17	
Aiken –	Oak Hill Cem, Newnan, GA 26	
Aiken James	Forest Hill Cem, East Derry, NH 38	
Aiken James	Londonderry, NH 15	
Aiken James	St Peter's Ch Cem, Spencertown, Columbia Co, NY 79	
Aiken James Capt	Old Graveyard, South Bedford, NH 34	
Aiken James Dr	Second Pres Cem, Baltimore, MD 15	
Aiken John	Fam farm, Barnstead, NH 28	
Aiken John	Pisgah Cem, Hampshire Rd, Pisgah Hill, Maury Co, TN 75	
Aiken John Lt	Merrimac Cem, Merrimac, NH 40	
Aiken Jonathan	Londonderry Cem, Londonderry, NH 46	
Aiken Joseph	West Alexander, PA 38	
Aiken Phineas	Center Cem, Bedford, NH 34	
Aiken Samuel	Long Meadow Cem, Chester, NH 33	
Aiken Thomas	South Side, Wilkins Cem, Deering, Hillsborough Co, NH 61	
Aikens Nathaniel	Garfield Cem, Potsdam, NY 30	
Aikens Solomon	Barnard, VT 16	
Aikens Solomon	Massacred nr mouth of Lechry Creek, Dearborn Co, IN 24	
Aikman John	Harrison Twp, Preble Co, OH 56	
Ainsworth Ameriah	East Randolph Cem, Randolph, Orange Co, VT 72	
Ainsworth Daniel Jr	Fairview Cem, Bethel, Windsor Co, VT 72	

Ainsworth Darius	Norwich, Burlington, NY 56
Ainsworth Edward Lt	Old Village Cem, Claremont, NH 50
Ainsworth Laban Rev	Old Center Cem, Jaffrey, NH 37
Ainsworth Wyman	Fairview Cem, Bethel, Windsor Co, VT 72
Aitken Andrew Dr	Westminster Pres Cem, lot 53, Baltimore, MD 15
Akens James	Nr Newman, GA 15
Aker John	Freetown Corners Cem, Freetown, Cortland Co, NY 36
Akerman Barnet	North Cem, Portsmouth, NH 34
Akerman Benjamin	North Cem, Portsmouth, NH 34
Akerman Walter	North Cem, Portsmouth, NH 34
Akers Joseph L	Heil Cem, N of Greenville, Floyd Co, IN 71
Akers Peter	Moore farm, Valley Creek Rd, Culleoka, Maury Co, TN 73
Akers Thomas Sr	Heil Cem, N of Greenville, Floyd Co, IN 71
Akin John G	Warren Cem, Silver Springs, NY 35
Alban George	Two Ridges Cem, Island Creek Twp, Jefferson Co, OH 55
Alban George	Two Ridges Cem, Jefferson Co, OH 25
Albanugh Zachariah	Evans Cem, nr St Louisville, Licking Co, OH 34
Albaugh John William	Chapel Cem, Libertytown, Frederick Co, MD 77
Albee Abel	Vernon Grove Cem, Milford, MA 46
Albee Asa	Holton Cem, Erving, MA 30
Albee Benjamin	Huntoon Cem, Wiscasset, ME 51
Albee Ebenezer	Old Rockingham Cem, VT 48
Albee James Jr	Chestnut Hill Cem, Millville, MA 46
Albee John	Mendon Cem, Mendon, MA 56
Albee Jonathan	Kingfield, ME 22
Albee Jonathan	Lexington, ME 30
Albee Nathan	Vernon Grove Cem, Milford, MA 46
Albee Simon	Vernon Grove Cem, Milford, MA 46
Alben George	Two Ridges Cem, Jefferson Co, OH 34
Albergotti Anthony	St Helena's Ch Cem, Beaufort, SC 70
Albert Abraham	Old Cem, Tenth & Linden St, Allentown, Lehigh Co, PA 40
Albert Andrew	Bermudian Cem or Franklin Churchyard, NJ 50
Alberthal Nicholas	Shirks UMC Cem, East Hanover Twp, Lebanon Co, PA 83
Albertson Ephraim	Newton Union Sloan Cem, West Collingswood, NJ 50
Albertson Garrett	Union Chapel Cem, Warren Co, NJ 35
Albertson Isaac	Newton Union Sloan Cem, West Collingswood, NJ 50
Albertson Jacob Jr	Newton Union Sloan Cem, West Collingswood, NJ 50
Albertson Jacob Sr	Newton Union Sloan Cem, West Collingswood, NJ 50
Albertson Joseph C Sr	Newton Union Sloan Cem, West Collingswood, NJ 50
Albertson Josiah	Newton Union Sloan Cem, West Collingswood, NJ 50
Albie Ichabod	Lord Cem, Westmoreland, NH 25
Albin John	SE Corner Cem, Ebenezer, Yellow Springs Rd, Clark Co, OH 34
Albin William	Provident Cem, Greencastle, IN 52
Albott Bixby	West Parish Cem, Andover, Essex Co, MA 57
Albright Adam Jr	St James Luth Ch Cem, Phillipsburg, Warren Co, NJ 40
Albright Hendrick	Fam Cem, E of Mt Pleasant Cem, Cliff Rd, Albany Co, NY 66
Albright Hendrick	Luth Ch Cem, nr Bellemont, Alamance Co, NC 49
Albright Jacob	Albright Mem Ch Cem, Kleinfeltersville, Lebanon Co, PA 83
Albright Jacob	Fam Cem, E of Mt Pleasant Cem, Cliff Rd, Albany Co, NY 66
Albright Johannes	Fritz Cem, Little Oley, Berks Co, PA 78
Albright John	East Homer Cem, Homer, Cortland Co, NY 36
Albright John	Fam Cem, E of Mt Pleasant Cem, Cliff Rd, Albany Co, NY 66
Albright Joseph	Christ Union Ch Cem, Shoenersville, Lehigh Co, PA 40
Albright Joseph	Christ Union Ch, Schoenersville, Northampton Co, PA 22
Albright Ludwig	Brick Ch Cem, Whitsett, Guilford Co, NC 76
Albright Martin	Luth Ref Ch Cem, Schaefferstown, Lebanon Co, PA 83
Albright William	Brick Ch Cem, Whitsett, Guilford Co, NC 76
Albro Thomas	Allenton Cem, North Kingstown, RI 36
Alcorn George	West of Columbus, IN 48
Alcott Asa	Haven Bur Gr, Benton, Yates Co, NY 78
Alcott David	Mt Hope Cem, Athens, Greene Co, NY 76

Alcox James	Center Cem, Wolcott, CT 57
Alcox James	Southington, CT 29
Alcox John	Center, Wolcott, CT 56
Alcox John B	Center, Wolcott, CT 56
Alcox John Capt	Southington, CT 29
Alcox Samuel	Southington, CT 29
Alcox Solomon	Center, Wolcott, CT 56
Alden Austin	Gorham Cem, Gorham, ME 45
Alden Barnabas	Center Cem, Whately, MA 55
Alden Benjamin	Mayflower Cem, Duxbury, MA 50
Alden Benjamin	Stowe Cem, Stowe, VT 57
Alden Benjamin	Turner, ME 18
Alden Briggs	Mayflower Cem, Duxbury, MA 58
Alden Daniel	Ashland St Cem, Brockton, MA 15
Alden Daniel	School St Cem, Lebanon, NH 32
Alden David	Cem, Middlefield, Geauga Co, OH 34
Alden Eleazer	Summer St Cem, Bridgewater, MA 55
Alden Elijah	Plymouth St, Middleboro, MA 56
Alden Ichabod Col	Cherry Valley Cem, Otsego Co, NY 33
Alden Isaac	First Parish (Unitarian), East Bridgewater, MA 56
Alden Isaiah	Mayflower Cem, Duxbury, MA 50
Alden Israel	Mountain View Cem, Lester, Broome Co, NY 78
Alden Israel	West Otis, Otis, MA 56
Alden James Corp	Old Village Cem, Claremont, NH 50
Alden John	Trumbull, Lebanon, CT 56
Alden John Jr	Duxbury, MA 52
Alden Jonathan	First Parish, East Bridgewater, MA 56
Alden Jonathan	Miles Standish Cem, Duxbury, MA 62
Alden Joseph	Bridgewater, MA 55
Alden Joshua	South Parish, Bridgewater, MA 56
Alden Judah	Mayflower Cem, Duxbury, MA 50
Alden Mason Fitch	Overfield Cem, Meshoppen, Wyoming Co, PA 67
Alden Moses	Maple Side Cem, Alstead, NH 43
Alden Nathan	First Parish (Unitarian), East Bridgewater, MA 56
Alden Nathan	Old Cem, The Green, Middleboro, MA 50
Alden Noah	Bellingham Cem, Bellingham, MA 46
Alden Oliver	Summer St Cem, Bridgewater, MA 55
Alden Prince	Overfield Cem, Meshoppen, Wyoming Co, PA 67
Alden Samuel Jr	Mayflower Cem, Duxbury, MA 58
Alden Silas	Needham, MA 50
Alden Solomon	Great Woods Cem, Bridgewater, MA 50
Alden Thomas	Four Corners Cem, Leicester, VT 25
Alden Thomas	Four Corners Cem, Leicester, VT 24
Alden Wrestling	Mayflower Cem, Duxbury, MA 50
Alderfer Abraham	Lower Salford Mennonite Cem, Montgomery Co, PA 59
Alderfer Jacob	Lower Salford Mennonite Cem, Montgomery Co, PA 59
Alderfer Joseph	Lower Salford Mennonite Cem, Montgomery Co, PA 59
Alderman David	Brennen Cem, Bulloch Co, GA 64
Alderman John	Fam Cem, nr Delway, Sampson Co, NC 72
Alderman Timothy	Prob Brookfield Cem, Trumbull Co, OH 55
Aldrich Abel	Uxbridge, MA 53
Aldrich Abner	Killingly, CT 49
Aldrich Abner	North Cem, Richmond, NH 36
Aldrich Abraham	Mendon Center Cem, Mendon, MA 46
Aldrich Amasa	Mount Caesar Cem, Swanzey, NH 35
Aldrich Amos	Union Cem, Woonsocket, RI 36
Aldrich Augustus	Fam Cem, Woonsocket, RI 36
Aldrich Caleb	Fam Cem, Woonsocket, RI 36
Aldrich Caleb	Rand Cem, Northfield, NH 31
Aldrich David	Pound Hill Rd, North Smithfield, RI 36
Aldrich Ebenzer	North Cem, Westmoreland, NH 25

Aldrich Esek	Locust Grove Cem, Providence, RI	36
Aldrich George	North Cem, Westmoreland, NH	25
Aldrich Gustavus	Mendon Center Cem, Mendon, MA	46
Aldrich Israel	Isenois farm, Pound Hill Rd, North Smithfield, RI	36
Aldrich James	Ide farm, North Scituate, RI	55
Aldrich Joel	Fam Cem, Woonsocket, RI	36
Aldrich John	Fernwood Cem, Kingston Rd, South Kingston, RI	36
Aldrich Naaman	Fam Cem, Woonsocket, RI	36
Aldrich Noah	Smithville Cem, North Scituate, Providence Co, RI	31
Aldrich Richard	Town Cem, West Canaan, NH	29
Aldrich Samuel Jr	Isenois farm, Pound Hill Rd, North Smithfield, RI	36
Aldrich Seth Sr	Mendon Center Cem, Mendon, MA	46
Aldrich Silas	Mendon Center Cem, Mendon, MA	46
Aldrich Simeon	Fam farm, Louisquisset Pike, Lincoln, RI	36
Aldrich Thomas	Fam Cem, Woonsocket, RI	36
Aldrich Timothy	Mound or Foust Cem, Westfield Twp, Morrow Co, OH	53
Aldrich William	North Cem, Westmoreland, NH	25
Aldrich William	Sugar Hill, NH	26
Aldridge John	Rush Co, IN	55
Aler Thomas	Luth Cem, Reisterstown, MD	19
Alexander Abraham	Newport, VT	35
Alexander Abraham	Poplar Tent Pres Ch Cem, Cabarrus Co, NC	49
Alexander Abraham	Sugar Creek Pres Ch Cem #2, Mecklenburg Co, NC	49
Alexander Adam	Philadelphia Pres Ch Cem, Mecklenburg Co, NC	49
Alexander Adam Col	Old Rock Springs Cem, 7 mi E of Charlotte, NC	18
Alexander Agnes B	Indiana Univ, Bloomington, Monroe Co, IN	24
Alexander Agnes B	Indiana Univ Campus, Bloomington, Monroe Co, IN	72
Alexander Amos	Head of Christiana Cem, nr Newark, DE	51
Alexander Amos	Head of Christiana Cem, nr Newark, New Castle Co, DE	45
Alexander Archibald	Augusta Co, VA	56
Alexander Archibald	Epis Cem, New Castle, New Castle Co, DE	46
Alexander Archibald	Timber Ridge Cem, Rockbridge Co, VA	36
Alexander Charles	Fam Cem, nr Providence Pres Ch, Mecklenburg Co, NC	72
Alexander Dan	Pine Pole Cem, Union, MS	70
Alexander Eliphas	Indian Mound, Moravia, NY	56
Alexander Ezra	Polk Graveyard, Big Sugar Creek, Pineville, NC	50
Alexander Ezra Capt	Sugaw Creek Cem, Charlotte, Mecklenburg Co, NC	18
Alexander Gabriel	Marvin Cem, nr Taylorsville, Alexander Co, NC	49
Alexander George	Hunter's Cem, Cabarrus Co, NC	49
Alexander George	Spanker Luth Ch Cem, Bohlander farm, Montgomery Co, OH	55
Alexander Hezekiah	Second Sugaw Creek Cem, Charlotte, Mecklenburg Co, NC	18
Alexander Hezekiah	Sugar Creek Pres Ch Cem #2, Mecklenburg Co, NC	49
Alexander Hugh	Fleming Hill Cem, Cayuga Co, NY	41
Alexander Hugh	Galway Cem, Galway Village, NY	32
Alexander Hugh	Lowery Cem, nr Louisville, GA	32
Alexander Isaac Dr	Old Pres Ch Cem, Camden, SC	45
Alexander James	Brick Pres Ch, W Kishacoquillas Valley, Lewistown, PA	56
Alexander James	Concord Pres Ch, Hwy 90 2 mi W of Loray, Iredell Co, NC	77
Alexander James	Franklin, PA	56
Alexander James	Greenhill Cem, Union, Monroe Co, WV	42
Alexander James	Piney Grove Cem, Swannanoa, Buncombe Co, NC	49
Alexander James	Piney Grove Cem, nr Asheville, NC	40
Alexander James	Scotch Ridge, nr Martins Ferry, Belmont Co, OH	34
Alexander James	Union, Monroe Co, WV	30
Alexander James Jr	Fairview Cem, Greenville Co, SC	40
Alexander James W	Fam plantation, now Nelson Farms, Early Co, GA	59
Alexander John	Arel Cem, OH	15
Alexander John	Fairview Pres Ch Cem, nr Lawrenceville, Gwinnett Co, GA	62
Alexander John	Fam Cem, Cumberland Co, KY	49
Alexander John	Galway Cem, Galway Village, NY	32
Alexander John	Head of Christiana Cem, nr Newark, New Castle Co, DE	45

Alexander John	Lebanon Cem, Mifflin Twp, Allegheny Co, PA 71
Alexander John	Meeting House Hill Cem, Brattleboro, VT 25
Alexander John	Meeting House Hill Cem, Brattleboro, VT 24
Alexander John Ens	Mtg Hs Hill Cem, Brattleboro, VT 30
Alexander John Lt	Village Cem, Winchester, NH 36
Alexander John McKnitt	Hopewell Pres Ch Cem, Mecklenburg Co, NC 49
Alexander John McKnitt	Hopewell Ch Cem, Mecklenburg Co, NC 18
Alexander John McKnitt	Hopewell Cem, Charlotte, NC 57
Alexander Joseph	Old Cem, Cadiz, Harrison Co, OH 34
Alexander Joseph	St Paul's Cem, Odessa, New Castle Co, DE 46
Alexander Joseph	Sugar Grove Cem, NW of New Richmond, IN 59
Alexander Margaret C	Scotch Ridge Cem, nr Martin's Ferry, Belmont Co, OH 55
Alexander Nathaniel	Old City Cem, nr 1st Pres Ch, W Trade St, Charlotte, NC 49
Alexander Nathaniel	West Martinsburg, NY 16
Alexander Randal	Antrim, NH 15
Alexander Raynold	Fannette Twp, Cumberland Co, Path Valley, PA 58
Alexander Reuben Capt	Village Cem, Winchester, NH 36
Alexander Robert	Cutter's Cem, nr Newfield, NY 34
Alexander Robert	Goshen Cem, Gaston Co, NC 49
Alexander Robert	Priv Cem, Klein farm, Gladys, Campbell Co, VA 79
Alexander Roger	Anthony farm Cem, Ledyard, NY 69
Alexander Samuel	Fam Cem, Linville River, Ashford, Burke Co, NC 76
Alexander Seth	Village Cem, Winchester, NH 36
Alexander Stephen	Poplar Tent priv Cem, Cabarrus Co, NC 60
Alexander Walter	[no cem named], DE 45
Alexander Walter Capt	[no cem named], MD 19
Alexander William	Beachwood Cem, Cornersville, Marshall Co, TN 79
Alexander William	Effingham House, nr Manassas, Prince William Co, VA 48
Alexander William	Hermon Ch Cem, Greene Co, TN 57
Alexander William	His farm, nr Farmington, St Francois Co, MO 16
Alexander William	Lexington Cem, Lexington, VA 36
Alexander William	North Road Cem, Wilmot, NH 34
Alexander William	Reese's Chapel Cem, S of Columbia, Maury Co, TN 73
Alexander William	Shawnee Run, KY 52
Alexander William	Trinity Ch Cem, Wall St & Broadway, NYC, NY 64
Alexander William	Valley Cem, Londonderry, NH 35
Aley Abraham	Aley Ch Cem, Miami City, OH 25
Alford Benedict	Cem, N of Pope's Corners, Welshfield, Geauga Co, OH 34
Alford Elijah	[no cem named], OH 26
Alford Jacob	Ashpole Pres Ch Cem, Rowland, NC 70
Alford John	Griffin Cem, Canton, PA 16
Alford Nathaniel	Canton St Cem, Canton, CT 55
Alfree William	St Ann's Cem, Middletown, New Castle Co, DE 46
Algar Archibald	St James Epis Ch Cem, Edison, NJ 75
Alger Benjamin	Pine Grove Cem, Easton, MA 55
Alger Stoughton	Oneonta Plains Cem, Oneonta, Otsego Co, NY 71
Allbee Ichabod	North Westmoreland Cem, Westmoreland, NH 53
Allbee Jonathan	Lexington, ME 15
Allbright Adam	Barton, Tioga Co, NY 15
Allcock Joseph	North Cem, Portsmouth, NH 34
Alld Benjamin	Old Cem, Peterborough, NH 29
Alld Benjamin	Peterborough, NH 15
Allebach Abraham	Hunsberger Cem, Montgomery Co, PA 58
Alleman John	Nr Harrisburg, Dauphin, PA 54
Alleman Stophel	Old aban Cem, rear of Farmers' Hotel, Middletown, PA 21
Allen –	[no cem named], IL 19
Allen Aaron	Center Cem, Barkhamsted, CT 62
Allen Aaron	Village Cem, Walpole, NH 25
Allen Abel	Coot Hill Cem, Moriah, NY 33
Allen Abel	Old Town Cem, Walpole, MA 45
Allen Abel	West Hill Cem, Surry, NH 35

Allen Abijah	First Parish Cem, Braintree, MA	46
Allen Abner	Newman Cem, Rumford, East Providence, RI	36
Allen Adam	Coons Cem, Jamestown Pike, Milledgeville, Fayette Co, OH	34
Allen Adam	Jefferson Cem, Hwy 35, Jasper, Fayette Co, OH	57
Allen Adam	Koontz Cem, Fayette Co, OH	18
Allen Amasa Gen	Walpole, NH	16
Allen Amaziah	Old Rumford, Newman Ave, Rehoboth, MA	55
Allen Amos	Aban Cem, E of North Bergen, Genesee Co, NY	65
Allen Amos	North Bur Gr, Providence, RI	36
Allen Ananias	Bloomingburg Cem, Paint Twp, Fayette Co, OH	55
Allen Appollus	West Hill Cem, Sherburne, NY	16
Allen Archibald	Magnolia Cem, Magnolia Twp, Putnam Co, IL	81
Allen Asaph	Old Waterbury Center Cem, VT	36
Allen Asaph Dea	Old Waterbury Cem, Waterbury, VT	34
Allen Benjamin	Cem nr Schoolhouse Rd, Austerlitz, NY	71
Allen Benjamin	Charlestown, NH	16
Allen Benjamin	Downing-Winn Richmond plot, Hillsdale, Columbia Co, NY	42
Allen Benjamin	South Valley Cem, Roseboom, Otsego Co, NY	75
Allen Burgess	Old Cem, Silver Creek, Greene Co, OH	56
Allen Caleb	North Pawlet, Blossom Dist, VT	48
Allen Charles	North Bur Gr, Providence, RI	36
Allen Charles Jr	Fam Cem, Laurens Co, SC	70
Allen Daniel	Colonial Cem, Johnstown, NY	63
Allen Daniel	Delphi Cem, Pompey, Onondaga Co, NY	75
Allen David	Allen farm Cem, Person Co, NC	49
Allen David	[no cem named], CT	19
Allen David	Cem on Hinsdale farm, Hinsdale, NH	37
Allen David	East Windsor Cem, East Windsor, CT	31
Allen David	Edgartown Cem, Edgartown, MA	45
Allen David	Edgartown, MA	15
Allen David	Harkness Cem, Smithfield Twp, Bradford Co, PA	72
Allen David	High St Cem, Greenfield, MA	45
Allen David	Old Bur Gr, Fairfield, CT	70
Allen David	Old Cem, Washington Co, PA	38
Allen David	Scantic Cem, East Windsor, CT	27
Allen David	West Alexander, PA	38
Allen David S	West Franklin, Bradford Co, PA	53
Allen Diarca	Lebanon, NH	56
Allen Diarca	School St Cem, Lebanon, NH	27
Allen Ebenezer	Muscalonge Cem, Hounsfield, Jefferson Co, NY	39
Allen Ebenezer	North Cem, Middletown, CT	61
Allen Ebenezer	Westchester County Central Cem, Westchester Co, NY	35
Allen Ebenezer Hon	Newfane, VT	31
Allen Edward	North Bur Gr, Providence, RI	36
Allen Elihu	Robert's Cem, Wayne Twp, Ashtabula Co, OH	34
Allen Elihu	Timothy Ch Cem, St Arnold, Quebec, Can	57
Allen Elihu	Wayne Twp, Ashtabula, OH	56
Allen Elihu	Wayne, Ashtabula Co, OH	18
Allen Elijah	Bascom, Cem, Jacksonville, VT	34
Allen Elisha	Meeting House Cem, Princeton, MA	49
Allen Elnathan	Dana Cem, North Pomfret, VT	23
Allen Eluathan	Prospect Hill Cem, Brattleboro, VT	24
Allen Eluathan	Prospect Hill Cem, Brattleboro, VT	25
Allen Gen Amasa	Village Cem, Walpole, NH	25
Allen Gideon	Clark Cem, Providence, NY	32
Allen Gideon	Fam Cem, Springport, NH	15
Allen Gideon	Fam Cem, Springport Twp, Cayuga Co, NY	41
Allen Gilbert	Pres Cem, Morristown, NJ	32
Allen Hezekiah	Dover Cem, Dedham, MA	55
Allen Hezekiah	Willett Cem, Willett, Cortland Co, NY	36
Allen Humphrey	Beech Grove, Central Village Cem, New Bedford, MA	45

Allen Isaac	First Parish (Unitarian), East Bridgewater, MA	56
Allen Isaac	Phellis farm, E of Rosedale, Madison Co, OH	55
Allen Isaac	Rosedale Cem, Manchester, MA	55
Allen Isaac	West Franklin, Bradford Co, PA	53
Allen Isaac	Wolf Creek Cem, Parke Co, IN	25
Allen Isaiah	Rehoboth Cem, Rehoboth, MA	62
Allen Isham	Mosby farm Cem, Boone, KY	70
Allen Israel	Old Cem, Spencer, MA	55
Allen Jabez	Ausable Chasm, Peru, Clinton, NY	56
Allen Jacob	Ashwood Cem, nr Hunt School, Weymouth, MA	50
Allen Jacob	Meth Epis Cem, W of Davis Lane, Cincinnati, OH	56
Allen Jacob	Old Cem, East Bridgewater, MA	56
Allen Jacob	Old Cem, Manchester, MA	55
Allen Jacob	Pioneer Cem nr Lunken Airport, Columbia, Hamilton Co, OH	55
Allen Jacob	Prospect Cem, Mansfield, Tioga Co, PA	15
Allen James	Allen-Baker Fam Cem, Greenfield, Saratoga Co, NY	42
Allen James	Canton Cem, Canton, ME	30
Allen James	Fam Cem, Greenfield, NY	32
Allen James	Fam Cem, Hwy 14, nr Laurens, SC	75
Allen James	Old Ch Cem, 6 mi fr Waynesboro, Burke Co, GA	24
Allen James	Old Sapp place, nr Waynesboro, Burke Co, GA	22
Allen James	Priv fam Cem, Greenfield Center, NY	41
Allen James	South Parish, Bridgewater, MA	56
Allen James	Summer St Cem, Bridgewater, MA	55
Allen James	Turner, ME	18
Allen James Jr	Old Stone Ch, N of Staunton, Augusta Co, VA	36
Allen Jeremiah	North Ridge, NY	33
Allen Jeremiah	North Billerica, MA	55
Allen Jesse	Lake Wesauking Cem, Wysox Twp, Bradford Co, PA	72
Allen Jesse	Pond Hill Cem, Bradford Co, PA	53
Allen Jethro	Acushnet Cem, Fairhaven, MA	55
Allen Jethro	Hixville Corner, Dartmouth, MA	55
Allen Job	Rockaway, NJ	50
Allen John	Allen lot, Myricks, MA	51
Allen John	Barker Cem, Itaska, Broome Co, NY	78
Allen John	Bedminister Ref Cem, NJ	47
Allen John	Chester, Chester Dist, SC	56
Allen John	Clam River Cem, Sandisfield, MA	56
Allen John	Common Cem, Stockbridge, VT	59
Allen John	Connecticut Farms Cem, Union Co, NJ	32
Allen John	Greene, ME	20
Allen John	His farm, Kansas & State Hwy, McVeytown, Mifflin Co, PA	62
Allen John	Louisiana Cem, Louisiana, MO	15
Allen John	Maplewood Cem, Stockbridge, Windsor Co, VT	76
Allen John	Minot, ME	18
Allen John	Oak Hill farm, Quidnessett, North Kingston, RI	36
Allen John	Old Cem, Pawlet, VT	15
Allen John	Old Mettowee Cem, Pawlet, VT	48
Allen John	Soaptown, Highland Ave, Warren, SE of Loadstown, OH	24
Allen John	Sugarland Cem, N of Washington, Daviess Co, IN	72
Allen John	Union Brick Cem, Warren Co, NJ	38
Allen John	Waterboro, ME	50
Allen John	West Hartford, CT	38
Allen John	West Main St Cem, Norton, MA	55
Allen John	Young County Cem, Young, NC	61
Allen John Col	Treats Island, Eastport, ME	45
Allen John Jr	Ashly Cem, Rochester, MA	59
Allen John Maj	Paris Cem, Paris, Bourbon Co, KY	15
Allen Jonathan	Clam River Cem, Sandisfield, MA	56
Allen Jonathan	Enfield St Cem, Enfield, Hartford Co, CT	24
Allen Jonathan	Old Cem, East Bridgewater, MA	45

Abstract of Graves of Revolutionary Patriots

Allen Jonathan	Vine Lake, Medfield, MA	56
Allen Joseph	Ashwood Cem, nr Hunt School, Weymouth, MA	50
Allen Joseph	East Windsor Cem, East Windsor, CT	31
Allen Joseph	Free Cem, West Groton, NY	32
Allen Joseph	Mountain View Cem, New Concord, Columbia Co, NY	72
Allen Joseph	Old Cem, Burks Flat, Bernardston, MA	00
Allen Joseph	Scantic Cem, East Windsor, CT	27
Allen Joseph	Swan Point Cem, Providence, RI	36
Allen Joseph	Town Cem, West Tisbury, MA	45
Allen Joseph	Washington Hollow, NY	15
Allen Joseph	West Torrington Cem, Torrington, CT	55
Allen Joseph	Wilson Cem, Barre, VT	48
Allen Joseph Sr	East Windsor Cem, East Windsor, CT	31
Allen Joseph Viall	Princes Hill Cem, Barrington, RI	36
Allen Joshua	Maple Grove Cem, Walpole, MA	45
Allen Joshua Col	Haven Hill Cem, Rochester, NH	36
Allen Josiah	Dickerson Cem, 3 mi fr Cadiz, Harrison Co, OH	34
Allen Josiah	First Unitarian Parish, East Bridgewater, MA	56
Allen Josiah	Newell Cem, South Attleboro, MA	47
Allen Josiah	North Bur Gr, Wayland, MA	56
Allen Josiah	South Attleboro, MA	15
Allen Lemuel	Old Cem, Monument Square, Saugus, MA	45
Allen Matthew	Allen Yard, Nayat, Barrington, RI	36
Allen Matthew 3d	First Unitarian Parish, East Bridgewater, MA	56
Allen Micah	Mansfield, MA	55
Allen Moses	Alex Cem, Mount Pleasant, NJ	48
Allen Moses	Alexandria Cem, Mount Pleasant, NJ	24
Allen Moses	Brush Creek Bapt Cem, Brush Creek, Wilson Co, TN	85
Allen Moses	West Sheridan, NY	15
Allen Moses	Yellow Frame Cem, Warren Co, NJ	38
Allen Moses Dea	Madison Cem, Morris Co, NJ	33
Allen Nathan	Hubbard Hill Cem, Charlestown, NH	85
Allen Nathan	North Charlestown, NH	15
Allen Nathan Jr	Vine Lake, Medfield, MA	56
Allen Nathaniel	East Troy, PA	16
Allen Nathaniel	Old Cem, Summer St, Manchester, MA	55
Allen Nathaniel	Old Yard Cem, Weston, MA	55
Allen Nehemiah	Old Cem, beside Oakham Ch, Oakham, MA	45
Allen Nehemiah 2nd	West Pawley, VT	56
Allen Noah	Reed St, nr Aldrich farm, Rehoboth, MA	55
Allen Noah	Scantic Cem, East Windsor, CT	27
Allen Noah	Vine Lake, Medfield, MA	56
Allen Noah Ens	East Windsor Cem, East Windsor, CT	31
Allen Noah Sr	Old Center Cem, Tyringham, now Monterey, MA	57
Allen Oliver	Prob on battlefield, Ticonderoga, NY	54
Allen Oliver	Vine Lake, Medfield, MA	56
Allen Oliver H	Hudson City Cem, Hudson, Columbia Co, NY	74
Allen Othniel	Hockanum Cem, East Hartford, CT	19
Allen Pelatiah	Center Cem, Barkhamsted, CT	62
Allen Philip	Hixville Corner, Dartmouth, MA	55
Allen Philip	Mount Phillip Cem, Allen's Grove, WI	29
Allen Philip	Mt Hope Cem, Rochester, Monroe Co, NY	79
Allen Phineas	Fam Cem, Falconer-Frewsburg Rd, Poland, Herkimer Co, NY	77
Allen Phineas	Village Cem, Surry, NH	35
Allen Phineas	Vine Lake Cem, Medfield, MA	50
Allen Reuben	Murray Cem, Murray, NY	34
Allen Reuben	Sweden, NY	15
Allen Richard	Cem, Lexington, KY	26
Allen Richard	Garrard Co, KY	27
Allen Richard Sr	Fam Cem, N of Roaring River, Edwards Twp, Wilkes Co, NC	73
Allen Robert	Opequon Ch, Opequon, VA	56

Allen Rufus	Braceville, OH 56
Allen Samuel	Chippenhook Cem, Clarendon, VT 76
Allen Samuel	East Windsor Cem, East Windsor, CT 31
Allen Samuel	Eldridge Cem, Burlington, VT 35
Allen Samuel	Elm St Cem, Ansonia, CT 15
Allen Samuel	Fam bur gr, his estate, NJ 47
Allen Samuel	Fam Cem, Loyalville, PA 52
Allen Samuel	Millertown Cem, 1 mi fr Johnsonville, Rensselaer Co, NY 37
Allen Samuel	North Bur Gr, Providence, RI 36
Allen Samuel	Old Town Cem, Walpole, MA 45
Allen Samuel	Princes Hill Cem, Barrington, RI 36
Allen Samuel	Ringold Cem, Pulaski Co, KY 61
Allen Samuel	Scantic Cem, East Windsor, CT 27
Allen Samuel Lt	Chippenhook Cem, Chippenhook, VT 31
Allen Silas	Cem, Royalton, Fairfield Co, OH 34
Allen Silas	Center Cem, Heath, Franklin Co, MA 55
Allen Simeon	First Unitarian Parish, East Bridgewater, MA 56
Allen Simeon	Meeting House Cem, Princeton, MA 49
Allen Stephen	Evergreen Cem, Scipio, NY 56
Allen Stephen	Newman Cem, Rumford, East Providence, RI 36
Allen Stephen	Pond Hill Cem, Bradford Co, PA 53
Allen Thomas	Allen Yard, Nayat, Barrington, RI 36
Allen Thomas	East Readfield, ME 29
Allen Thomas	Elmwood Cem, Schaghticoke, Rensselaer Co, NY 38
Allen Thomas	Newman Cem, Rumford, East Providence, RI 36
Allen Thomas E	Brown Co Cem, Brown Co, OH 66
Allen Timothy	North Pawlet, VT 15
Allen Timothy	North Pawlet, Blossom Dist, VT 48
Allen Tobias	Village Cem, Prospect Harbor, ME 56
Allen Viall	Princes Hill Cem, Barrington, RI 36
Allen Walter	Old Friends Cem, Woonsocket, RI 36
Allen William	Agawam Center Cem, Agawam Center, MA 17
Allen William	Church Cem, Livingston, Columbia Co, NY 48
Allen William	Cong Ch Cem, Ashford, Windham Co, CT 71
Allen William	Family Cem, Benton, Scott Co, MO 81
Allen William	May's Lick Cem, Mason Co, KY 72
Allen William	Meth Ch Cem, Dahlonega, Lumpkin Co, GA 25
Allen William	Mt Hope Cem, Lumpkin Co, GA 49
Allen William	New Scotland Ch Cem, New Scotland, Albany Co, NY 75
Allen William	Newman Cem, Rumford, East Providence, RI 36
Allen Zachariah	Town St Cem, East Windsor, CT 27
Allen Zebadiah	Barre Cem, Barre, MA 46
Allenton John	Massacred nr mouth of Lechry Creek, Dearborn Co, IN 24
Aller Peter	Lebanon, NJ 55
Allere Bazelle	Randolph Co, IL 48
Allere Joseph	Randolph Co, IL 48
Allerton Isaac	Amenia Cem, Dutchess Co, NY 68
Allerton Jonathan	Lake Mills Allerton Cem, Gayhead, Greene Co, NY 58
Alley Ephraim	Conkling estate, Boothbay, ME 40
Alley Ephraim	Old Western Cem, Lynn, MA 55
Alley James	Eastern Cem, Lynn, MA 56
Alley John	Butler Twp, Franklin, IN 71
Alley John	Wetzel Co, WV 54
Alley Joseph	Union St, Lynn, MA 56
Alley Joshua	Conkling estate, Boothbay, ME 40
Alley Nathan	Union St, Lynn, MA 56
Alley Samuel	Fam Cem, Decatur Co, IN 63
Alley William	Indian Mound, Moravia, NY 56
Allin Thomas	Spring Hill, KY 52
Alling John	Mount Pleasant Cem, Newark, NJ 26
Alling Pruden	Hanover, NJ 49

Abstract of Graves of Revolutionary Patriots

Allis Ebenezer	Hill, Shelburne, MA 56	
Allis Lucius	Pumpkin Hollow Cem, Conway, MA 53	
Allis Moses	Laport, OH 56	
Allis Nathaniel	West Cem, Madison, CT 54	
Allis Russell	East Cem, Whately, Hampshire Co, MA 55	
Allis Stephen	Church Cem, Buckland, MA 56	
Allison Andrew	Fam farm, 3 mi SE of Indiana, PA 58	
Allison Benjamin	Country Cem, Green Twp, Gallia Co, OH 55	
Allison Francis	Old Pres Ch Cem, New London Twp, Chester Co, PA 75	
Allison Hugh	Greenlawn Cem, Marietta, OH 56	
Allison John	Cedar Hill Cem, nr Greencastle, PA 20	
Allison Joseph	Fam prop, Gordansville, Smith Co, TN 78	
Allison Joseph	Mt Repose Cem, Haverstraw, Rockland Co, NY 78	
Allison Matthew	Jacksonville, PA 15	
Allison Matthew	Mt Repose Cem, Haverstraw, Rockland Co, NY 78	
Allison Richard	Cem, SW part of Stonelick Twp, Clermont Co, OH 34	
Allison Richard	Now in Wesleyan Cem, Colerain Ave, Cincinnati, OH 56	
Allison Richard	Stonelick Twp Cem, Clermont Co, OH 40	
Allison Robert	Ramsayburg, Warren Co, NJ 36	
Allison Samuel	Forest Hill Cem, East Derry, NH 38	
Allison Theophilus	Perth Assoc Ref Pres Cem, Iredell Co, NC 49	
Allison William	Deer Creek Cem, Christian Twp, Pickaway Co, OH 34	
Allison William	Drowned lands, Goshen, NY 52	
Allison William	Massacred nr mouth of Lechry Creek, Dearborn Co, IN 24	
Allred John	Gray's Chapel Cem, Franklinville, Randolph Co, NC 69	
Allred William	Gray's Chapel Cem, Franklinville, Randolph Co, NC 69	
Allterton John	Nr county line, Portage Co, OH 56	
Allton John Jr	Sanger Yard, South Woodstock, CT 31	
Allwein Conrad	St Mary's Ch Cem, Lebanon, Lebanon Co, PA 83	
Allyn Benjamin Capt	Windsor, CT 15	
Allyn Eleazer Rev	Shiloh Cem, Shiloh, IL 44	
Allyn Elisha	Palisado Cem, Windsor, CT 55	
Allyn Ephraim	Church Cem, Goshen, CT 53	
Allyn Job	Windsor, CT 56	
Allyn John	Christian Lane, Berlin, CT 56	
Allyn John Capt	West Lane, Berlin, CT 56	
Allyn John Ens	Palisado Cem, Windsor, CT 55	
Allyn John Jr	Palisado Cem, Windsor, CT 55	
Allyn Joseph	Palisado Cem, Windsor, CT 55	
Allyn Nathan	[no cem named], OH 55	
Allyn Prior	Palisado Cem, Windsor, CT 55	
Allyn Samuel	Palisado Cem, Windsor, CT 55	
Allyn Samuel Capt	Wood Bur Gr, Stonington, CT 15	
Allyn Solomon	Old Bloomfield Cem, Bloomfield, CT 55	
Allyn Thomas	Old Bloomfield Cem, Bloomfield, CT 55	
Allyn William	Rehoboth Village, MA 55	
Almy Benjamin	Old Common Cem, Newport, RI 36	
Almy John	Lot on Fogland Rd, Tiverton, RI 36	
Almy Jonathan	Old Common Cem, Newport, RI 35	
Almy Peleg	Union Cem, Portsmouth, Newport Co, RI 78	
Almy Sanford	Fam Cem, top of Windmill Hill, Little Compton, RI 36	
Alrich Benjamin	Wilmington & Brandywine, New Castle Co, DE 46	
Alrich Jonas	Wilmington & Brandywine, New Castle Co, DE 46	
Alrich Lucas	Wilmington & Brandywine, New Castle Co, DE 46	
Alsop Benjamin	Fredericksburg, VA 30	
Alsop Benjamin	Fredericksburg, VA 29	
Alsop Benjamin Lt	Fam Cem, nr Fredericksburg, VA 34	
Alsop John	Frederick Co, MD 17	
Alsop John	Old homestead, Ledyard, NY 56	
Alspach Henry	Zions Red Ch, Orwigsburg, PA 49	
Alspach Philip	Zions Red Ch, Orwigsburg, PA 49	

Alspaugh John	Belzor Ch Cem, Fairfield Co, OH 56
Alspaugh Michael	Belzor Ch Cem, Fairfield Co, OH 56
Alston James	Ruckersville Meth Ch Cem, Elbert Co, GA 62
Alston John	SW of Winnsboro, nr Mossydale School, Fairfield Co, SC 40
Alston Phillip	House of Horsesho, 12 mi fr Carthage, NC 49
Alston Thomas	Bur gr, First Pres Ch, Woodbridge, NJ 25
Alston William Lt Col	Nr Elbert, Elbert Co, GA 34
Alter Jacob	Fam Cem, Buffalo Twp, Washington Co, PA 38
Alter John	Nr New Buffalo, PA 56
Althouse Johannes	Leidy's Old Cem, Montgomery Co, PA 59
Altizer Emera	7 mi fr river on Little River, VA 36
Altizera Emera	Altizer farm, Chestnut Ridge, Riner, Montgomery Co, VA 73
Altland Philip	Altland Mtg Hs Cem, Canal Rd, Paradise Twp, York Co, PA 75
Altman Anthony	Zion Ch Cem at Harrolds, nr Greensburg, PA 56
Altman Casper	Brush Creek Cem, North Huntington, Westmoreland Co, PA 76
Altman John Peter	Brush Creek Cem, North Huntington, Westmoreland Co, PA 76
Altman Philip	Priv Cem, fam farm, Blacklick Twp, Indiana Co, PA 56
Alton John	Fam Cem, Palmyra Twp, Knox Co, IN 69
Alverson Caleb	Hartford Ave, city line, Johnston, RI 36
Alverson John	Col Tillinghast farm, Johnston, RI 36
Alverson Uriah	Madison, NY 56
Alvey Thomas Green	Lamb Cem, Tobinsport, Perry Co, IN 77
Alvis Jesse	Mt Washington Cem, nr Pekin, Washington Co, IN 72
Alvord Eliphaz	Center Cem, Winchester, CT 59
Alvord Jeniel	Center Cem, Westhampton, MA 53
Alvord Job Capt	South Hadley, MA 15
Alvord John	Canton Twp, Bradford Co, PA 53
Alvord John	Greenfield Hill Cem, Fairfield, CT 62
Alvord Samuel	South Hadley, MA 15
Alvord Thomas Gould Jr	Atwater Cem, Homer, Cortland Co, NY 36
Alvord Thomas Gould Sr	Atwater Cem, Homer, Cortland Co, NY 36
Alward Benjamin	Pres Ch Cem, Basking Ridge, NJ 47
Amadon Joseph	Poestenkill Cem, NY 46
Amadon Samuel	Readsboro Cem, VT 46
Ambler Benjamin	St Matthew's Epis Cem, Bedford, NY 35
Ambler John	Grave obliterated, Pres Ch records, Truxton, NY 36
Ambler John	Spencertown, NY 48
Ambler Peter	Wooster Cem, Danbury, Fairfield Co, CT 62
Ambrose Hadley	Lasting Hope Cem, Columbia, Maury Co, TN 76
Ambrose Nathaniel	Ambrose Yard, Moultonborough, NH 29
Ambrose Samuel	Center Sandwich Cem, Sandwich, NH 31
Ambrose Samuel Rev	North Bur Gr, Sutton, NH 37
Amburn Samuel L	Union Cem, Stony Creek Twp, Randolph Co, IN 72
Amderson Cornelius	Rockaway, Morris Co, NJ 32
Ament Phillips	Meteer farm, Bethlehem & Hutchinson Rd, KY 52
Amerman Powell J	Parsell Cem, Owasco, Cayuga, NY 41
Ames Benjamin	South Parish Bur Gr, Andover, Essex Co, MA 26
Ames Benjamin Capt	South Parish Bur Gr, Andover, Essex Co, MA 26
Ames Bezar	Milton Cem, Milton, MA 62
Ames Burpee	Churchyard, Hollis, NH 39
Ames Daniel	West Bloodvill Cem, Milton, NY 32
Ames David	Fam Cem, nr home, Canterbury, NH 29
Ames David	Pine Ridge (Old) Cem, Hancock, NH 36
Ames David	Town Cem, Tamworth, NH 29
Ames Ebenezer	Church St Cem, Easton, MA 56
Ames Ebenezer	South Parish, Bridgewater, MA 56
Ames Elijah	Grant Cem, Potsdam, NY 30
Ames Elijah	Walton Cem, Pepperell, MA 56
Ames Elisha	Mehoopany, PA 17
Ames Isaac	Plainville Cem, Marshfield, MA 50
Ames Job	Ashland St Cem, Brockton, MA 15

Ames Jonathan	Plymouth, NY	16
Ames Joseph	South Parish, Bridgewater, MA	56
Ames Jotham	County farm nr Phoenix Mills, Middlefield, Otsego Co, NY	72
Ames Moses	Maplewood Cem, Marlboro, MA	50
Ames Nathaniel	Oregon Prairie Mount Cem, WI	29
Ames Phineas	South Dover Cem, Dover, ME	39
Ames Samuel	Cavendish, VT	16
Ames Samuel	Central South Water St Cem, Boscawen, NH	32
Ames Samuel	Fam Cem, Canterbury, NH	54
Ames Samuel	West Torrington Cem, Torrington, CT	55
Ames Samuel E	Copps Hill, Boston, MA	56
Ames Samuel Lt	Fam Cem, nr home, Canterbury, NH	29
Ames Seth	Village Cem, Dedham, MA	56
Ames Stephen	Cem, South Kirtland, Lake Co, OH	34
Ames Stephen	Kirtland, OH	26
Ames Stephen Jr	Town House Cem, North Groton, NH	35
Ames Timothy	Ashland St Cem, Brockton, MA	15
Amey George	Small Cem, nr aban rd, West Bath, NH	51
Amidon Ephraim	Canoe Brook Cem, Westmoreland, NH	25
Amidon Reuben	Brookside Cem, Barberville, Rensselaer Co, NY	41
Amiss Levi	Amissville, VA	56
Amlin John	Fam farm, on Whipple Run, Washington Co, OH	69
Ammerman Derrick	Old Town Bur Gr, Newburgh, Orange Co, NY	69
Ammerman Powell J	Parsell, Owasco, NY	56
Ammidon Phillip Col	Mendon Center Cem, Mendon, MA	46
Ammidown Jacob	Pine Ridge Cem, nr Navarino, Onondaga Co, NY	78
Ammidown Moses	Epis Ch Cem, Granville, Washington Co, NY	85
Ammon (Canedy's slave)	Race Course Cem, Lakeville, MA	57
Ammon Thomas	Bourbon Co, KY	45
Amonette John	Hazel Green, Madison Co, AL	15
Amos James	9 mi W of Sparta, GA	32
Amos Joseph	South Parish, Bridgewater, MA	56
Amos Mordecai	Connotton Cem, row 16, North Twp, Harrison Co, OH	56
Amrine Abraham	Fam Cem, Paris Twp, Union Co, OH	34
Amsden Abel	Amdsen Cem, Reading, VT	46
Amsden Abraham	Prob Ashtabula, OH	55
Amsden Elisha	Pumpkin Hollow Cem, Conway, MA	53
Amsden Isaac Capt	Seneca, NY	15
Amsden Joel	Depot Hill Cem, Henniker, NH	32
Amsden Noah	Union Cem, Livonia, NY	16
Anable Jacob	Opposite First Cong Ch, Hamilton, MA	56
Anable Robert Jr	Old Cem, Hamilton, MA	56
Anderson Abraham	Massacred nr mouth of Lechry Creek, Dearborn Co, IN	24
Anderson Absolon	On his farm, Ft Meade, MD	52
Anderson Archelaus	Littleville Cem, Chester, MA	62
Anderson Augustine	Morgan Co, OH	55
Anderson Baley	Fam Cem, Elysian Fields, Harrison Co, TX	75
Anderson Benjamin	Silver Spring Ch Cem, Cumberland Co, PA	17
Anderson Charles	Fam Cem, Calahan, Iredell Co, NC	76
Anderson Cornelius	Rockaway First Pres Ch Cem, Rockaway, Morris Co, NJ	79
Anderson David	Champlain prop, Spartansburg, SC	55
Anderson David	Cherry Valley Cem, Otsego Co, NY	34
Anderson David	Cross Creek Cem, Fayetteville, Cumberland Co, NC	80
Anderson David	Old Rice place, nr Waterloo, SC	15
Anderson Eliakim	Rockaway, Morris Co, NJ	32
Anderson George	Augusta Co, VA	56
Anderson Isaac	E of Pickering School, Schuylkill Twp, Chester Co, PA	75
Anderson Isaac	Valley Park, Montgomery Co, PA	17
Anderson Isaac	Vincent Cem, Butler Co, OH	34
Anderson Isaac Lt	Massacred nr mouth of Lechry Creek, Dearborn Co, IN	24
Anderson Jacob	Bethlehem, NJ	32

Anderson Jacob	Bryn Zyon Cem, Kent Co, DE	46
Anderson James	Buffalo Cem, Buffalo Twp, Washington Co, PA	68
Anderson James	Country Cem, nr Belfast, Highland Co, OH	34
Anderson James	Epis Cem, Georgetown, Sussex Co, DE	46
Anderson James	Fam Cem, Sandborn, Vigo Twp, Knox Co, IN	72
Anderson James	Fam farm, nr Rockville, MD	15
Anderson James	Hill Cem, Shelburne, MA	56
Anderson James	On his farm, nr Andersons Crossing, MD	52
Anderson James	Pres Ch Cem, Basking Ridge, NJ	47
Anderson James Arthur	Rootstown, Portage Co, OH	56
Anderson James Capt	Old Tennent Ch Yard, nr Freehold, NJ	48
Anderson Jeremiah	Fam Cem, Portchester, NY	35
Anderson John	Ch Cem, Lawrenceville, NJ	26
Anderson John	Fam Cem, 2 mi E of Dexter, Meigs Co, OH	55
Anderson John	Fam Cem, Long farm, Cumberland Twp, Greene Co, PA	56
Anderson John	Fam farm, Spring Valley, Greene Co, OH	56
Anderson John	Gaines Cem, Gaines, NY	31
Anderson John	Gaines Cem, Orleans Co, NY	34
Anderson John	Hill Cem, Shelburne, MA	34
Anderson John	Kine farm, nr Richland Ch, 2 mi fr Spring Valley, OH	51
Anderson John	Morison Chapel Cem, W Carter's Valley, Sullivan Co, TN	73
Anderson John	Pres Ch Cem, Rahway, NJ	76
Anderson John	Scotch Cem, West Charlton, NY	32
Anderson John	Valley Cem, Londonderry, NH	35
Anderson John	Windham Cem, Windham, NH	51
Anderson Joseph	Fam Cem, Portchester, NY	35
Anderson Joseph	Friendship Cem, nr Metcalf, Thomas Co, GA	66
Anderson Joseph	Randolph Co, IL	48
Anderson Joseph	Riverside Cem, Copenhagen, NY	16
Anderson Keneth	Old Cem, Shelbyville, TN	31
Anderson Kenneth	Richardson Cem, Dalton, GA	27
Anderson Lemuel	Old Cem, betw Fly Creek & Toddsville, Otsego Co, NY	71
Anderson Lewis	Old Bapt Cem, nr Carlisle, Warren Co, OH	34
Anderson Matthew	Pleasant St Cem, West Rutland, VT	55
Anderson Oliver	Slate Hill, nr Mercersburg, PA	56
Anderson R Clough Col	Soldiers' Retreat, KY	31
Anderson Richard Clough	Soldiers Retreat Cem, KY	62
Anderson Robert	Fincastle Pres Ch Cem, Fincastle, Botetourt Co, VA	73
Anderson Robert	Goodwill Cem, Montgomery, Orange Co, NY	78
Anderson Robert	Old Stone Ch Cem, nr Clemson College, SC	70
Anderson Robert	Otisfield Homestead Cem, Otisfield, Cumberland Co, ME	55
Anderson Robert	Tater Hill, East Haddam, CT	56
Anderson Robert	West Beaver Twp Cem, Columbiana Co, OH	55
Anderson Samuel	Union Cem, Westfield & Portland, Chautauqua, NY	77
Anderson Samuel	Venice, Butler Co, OH	53
Anderson Thomas	Long Meadow Cem, Chester, NH	33
Anderson Thomas	Moose Meadow, Willington, CT	29
Anderson Thomas	Old Newton Cem, Newton, Sussex Co, NJ	79
Anderson Timothy	Center Cem, East Hartford, CT	19
Anderson Turner	Henderson Co, KY	33
Anderson William	Akron Cem, Akron, NY	33
Anderson William	Cem, old part, Ashland Co, OH	34
Anderson William	Churchyard, Ware, MA	29
Anderson William	Fincastle Pres Ch Cem, Fincastle, Botetourt Co, VA	73
Anderson William	First Cem, Candia, NH	29
Anderson William	Hillsboro, IN	56
Anderson William	His estate, Anderson Bottom, Hampshire Co, WV	42
Anderson William	Nr Beltsville, Prince Georges Co, MD	52
Anderson William	Old Cem, Mahoning Ave, Warren, OH	24
Anderson William	Old Cem, Mahoning Ave, Warren, Trumbull Co, OH	34
Anderson William	St Paul's Ch Cem, Chester, PA	52

Anderson William C	Hert farm, nr Louisville, KY	24
Anderson William Col	Nr Roanoke, VA	31
Anderson Worsham	Lloyd farm, Mason Co, KY	39
Andre Nicholas	Old Cem, Apollo, PA	56
Andreas Ludwig	Old Morav Cem, Emaus, Lehigh Co, PA	40
Andreus Jeremiah	Noroton River Cem, Darien, CT	55
Andreus Samuel	Noroton River Cem, Darien, CT	55
Andrew Allen	Berlin Cem, nr Montpelier, VT	16
Andrew Charles	Maple Hill Cem, Shaftsbury, Bennington Co, VT	71
Andrew Henry	Pinehill Cem, Taunton, Bristol Co, MA	86
Andrew John	Anapolis, Jefferson Co, OH	25
Andrew Levi	Pleasant St Cem, Raynham, MA	55
Andrew Nathan	First Church, Boxford, MA	56
Andrew Sylvester	Maple Hill Cem, Shaftsbury, Bennington Co, VT	71
Andrews Abraham	Fam lot, Pontiac Rd, W of Reservoir Ave, nr Pontiac, RI	36
Andrews Allen	Berlin Corner Cem, Berlin Corner, VT	20
Andrews Andrew	Cedar Creek, 10 mi fr Fayetteville, NC	49
Andrews Arthur	Hopewell Cem, Boone Co, IN	72
Andrews Asa	Center Cem, Hartford, Trumbull Co, OH	55
Andrews Ashbel	First (Sadler) Cem, Saratoga, NY	32
Andrews Ashbul	Hadlyme, West Haddam, CT	56
Andrews Daniel	Danbury Quarter Cem, Winchester, CT	59
Andrews Daniel	Glastonbury Cem, CT	48
Andrews Daniel	Park Settlement, Candor, NY	34
Andrews Deliverance	Yellow Mtg Hs Cem, Stillwater, NY	32
Andrews Deliverance Dea	Yellow Mtg Hs Cem, Stillwater, Saratoga Co, NY	39
Andrews Ebenezer	Unitarian Ch Cem, Main St, Dighton, MA	55
Andrews Edmund	Old Cem, Carlisle, MA	55
Andrews Eli	Sangerfield Cem, Sangerfield, NY	32
Andrews Elijah	Berlin Cem, nr Montpelier, VT	16
Andrews Elijah	Berlin Corner Cem, Berlin Corner, VT	20
Andrews Elijah	Evergreen Cem, Fabius, Onondaga Co, NY	78
Andrews Elijah	Old Farmington Cem, Farmington, CT	62
Andrews Elisha	Fam Cem (priv), Berwick, ME	56
Andrews Elisha	Yellow Mtg Hs Cem, Stillwater, Saratoga Co, NY	39
Andrews Elkanah	Unitarian Ch Cem, Main St, Dighton, MA	55
Andrews Elnathan	Maploroot Cem, Washington, Coventry, RI	36
Andrews Ephraim	Turner, ME	18
Andrews Francis	Farm, nr Thompsonville, NY	30
Andrews George	Midland Cem, Westboro, MA	50
Andrews George	Pleasant St Cem, Raynham, MA	55
Andrews Hugh	Bethany Ch Cem, Hwy 21, 7 mi N of Statesville, NC	40
Andrews Hugh	Bethany Cem, 7 mi N of Statesville, Iredell Co, NC	49
Andrews Hugh	Old (aban) Pres Ch Cem, OH	34
Andrews Hugh	Old Pres Ch Bur Gr, Dayton, OH	55
Andrews Ira	Black Cem, VT	20
Andrews Ira	Black Cem, Berlin, nr Montpelier, VT	15
Andrews Issachar	Central Bur Gr, Carlisle, MA	55
Andrews James	Fam lot, Kent Rd, S of North Scituate Village, RI	31
Andrews James	North Shirkshire Cem, Conway, MA	53
Andrews James Jr	Fam lot, Kent Rd, S of North Scituate Village, RI	31
Andrews Jason	Greenridge Cem, Saratoga Springs, Saratoga Co, NY	39
Andrews Jeremiah	Rockland Cem, Scituate, Providence Co, RI	31
Andrews Jesse	Fairview Cem, New Britain, CT	55
Andrews John	Cem, Warren, PA	52
Andrews John	Fam tomb, Old Cem, Boylston Center, MA	36
Andrews John	Lord prop, Andrews Point, Warren, ME	63
Andrews John	Yellow Mtg Hs Cem, Stillwater, NY	32
Andrews John Jr	Yellow Mtg Hs Cem, Stillwater, Saratoga Co, NY	39
Andrews John Sr	Yellow Mtg Hs Cem, Stillwater, Saratoga Co, NY	39
Andrews Jonathan	Bingham, ME	16

Andrews Jonathan	Harper Cem, Bryant's Grove, Broome Co, NY 78
Andrews Jonathan	Hop Meadow Cem, Simsbury, CT 55
Andrews Jonathan	Pleasant Ridge, ME 17
Andrews Jonathan	Union Village Cem, Louisquisset Pike, N Smithfield, RI 75
Andrews Joseph	Cornwell-Tilden plot, New Lebanon, Columbia Co, NY 79
Andrews Joseph	Fairview Cem, New Britain, CT 55
Andrews Joseph	New Boston, NH 16
Andrews Joseph	New Boston Cem, New Boston, NH 28
Andrews Joseph	North Road Cem, Truxton, Cortland Co, NY 36
Andrews Joseph	Old Bur Hill, Marble Head, MA 55
Andrews Joseph	Old Essex Cem, MA 48
Andrews Joseph	Unitarian Ch Cem, Main St, Dighton, MA 55
Andrews Joseph	West Main St Cem, Norton, MA 55
Andrews Louden	Letts Cem, 6 mi S of Ionia, MI 21
Andrews Mark	Hope Cem, Perry, Wyoming Co, NY 64
Andrews Mark	Hope Cem, Perry, Wyoming Co, NY 80
Andrews Mark	Turner, ME 18
Andrews Miles	Greenridge Cem, Saratoga Springs, Saratoga Co, NY 39
Andrews Moses	Fairview Cem, New Britain, CT 55
Andrews Moses	Federal Street Cem, Greenfield, MA 00
Andrews Nathaniel	Midland Cem, Westboro, MA 50
Andrews Nehemiah	Center Cem, Barkhamsted, CT 62
Andrews Nehemiah	Maplehurst Cem, Guilford, VT 19
Andrews Nehemiah	Stockbridge Cem, Stockbridge, MA 47
Andrews Nehemiah	Stockbridge, MA 56
Andrews Ozias	Lindsey Cem, Richmond, MA 56
Andrews Reuben	Pleasant St Cem, Raynham, MA 55
Andrews Robert Capt	Fam tomb, Old Cem, Boylston Center, MA 36
Andrews Robert Capt	Old Cem, Boylston Center, MA 46
Andrews Robert Sr	Youngsville, PA 52
Andrews Samuel	Burlington Cem, Burlington, CT 62
Andrews Samuel	South Sutton Cem, Sutton, NH 37
Andrews Sperry	Wethersfield Cem, Wethersfield, NY 64
Andrews Squire	Old fam farm, Snake Hill Rd, Gloucester, RI 36
Andrews Stephen	Unitarian Ch Cem, Main St, Dighton, MA 55
Andrews Thomas	Midland Cem, Westboro, MA 50
Andrews Timothy	McGraw Cem, Cortland, Cortland Co, NY 36
Andrews Titus	Yellow Mtg Hs Cem, Stillwater, Saratoga Co, NY 39
Andrews William	Fam Cem, nr Hillsborough, Orange Co, NC 85
Andrews William	North Dixmont Cem, Dixmont, ME 28
Andrews William Capt	St Michael's Ch Cem, Marblehead, MA 36
Andrews Zaphaniah	North Bur Gr, Providence, RI 52
Andros Thomas	Unitarian Ch Cem, Main St, Dighton, MA 55
Andrus Clement	Austinburg, OH 56
Andrus David	East Trumbull Cem, Ashtabula Co, OH 34
Andrus David	East Trumbull Cem, E Trumbull, Ashtabula Co, OH 55
Andrus Elisha	Granville Center Cem, Grandville Twp, Bradford Co, PA 53
Andrus Elisha	Yellow Mtg Hs Cem, Stillwater, NY 32
Andrus Ethan	West Cem, Middlebury, VT 29
Andrus Jeremiah	Stockbridge Cem, Stockbridge, MA 47
Andruss John	Yellow Mtg Hs Cem, Stillwater, NY 32
Andruss Titus	Yellow Mtg Hs Cem, Stillwater, NY 32
Anewalt Valentine	Stone Church, Kreidersville, Northampton Co, PA 22
Anewalt Valentine	Zion's Stone Ch Cem, Kreidersville, Northampton Co, PA 40
Angel Daniel	Roger Hollow, Mehoopany, PA 17
Angell Abel	Rockland Cem, Scituate, Providence Co, RI 31
Angell Abraham	Cumberland Cem, Dexter St, Lonsdale, Cumberland, RI 36
Angell Andrew Capt	Smithville Cem, North Scituate, Providence Co, RI 31
Angell Benjamin	Fam Cem, North Scituate, Providence Co, RI 31
Angell Elisha	Fam bur gr, North Providence, RI 47
Angell Enoch Capt	North Bur Gr, Providence, RI 36

Angell Eseck	Angellville Cem, Angellville, Clinton Co, NY 73
Angell Ezekiel Jr	Angell lot, Georgiaville, Reservoir, Smithfield, RI 36
Angell Fenner	North Bur Gr, Providence, RI 36
Angell Gideon	Ballou Cem, Mendon Rd, Ashton, Cumberland, RI 36
Angell Israel Col	North Bur Gr, Providence, RI 36
Angell James	Centerdale, North Providence, RI 36
Angell Jesse	Grave on Aldrich estate, North Scituate, Scituate, RI 36
Angell John	Newman Cem, Rumford, East Providence, RI 36
Angell John	North Bur Gr, Providence, RI 36
Angell John	Sweetman Cem, Ballston, Saratoga Co, NY 76
Angell John Col	Angell lot, Arnold farm, Smithfield, RI 36
Angell Jonathan	Angell lot, Georgiaville, Reservoir, Smithfield, RI 36
Angell Joseph	Smithville Cem, North Scituate, Providence Co, RI 31
Angell Joshua	Chatham Center Cem, Chatham, Columbia Co, NY 79
Angell Nebediah	Manton Cem, Manton, Johnston, RI 36
Angell Pardon	Rockland Cem, Scituate, Providence Co, RI 31
Angell Samuel	North Bur Gr, Providence, RI 36
Angell William	Thompson Cem, Northumberland, Saratoga Co, NY 76
Angevine Anthony M	[no cem named], NJ 32
Angevine James	York Twp, Dearborn Co, IN 25
Angier Samuel	Thompson farm Cem, Framingham, MA 56
Angier Silas	Town Cem, Fitzwilliam, NH 32
Angle Daniel	Beach Ridge Cem, Lexington, Greene Co, NY 69
Angle William	Ramsayburg, Warren Co, NJ 36
Angle William	Ramsayburg Cem, Warren Co, NJ 38
Anglin Adrian	Stony Point Cem, Leesburg, Kosciusko Co, IN 70
Angst Daniel	Jacob's Ch, Pine Grove Twp, PA 49
Angst Michael	Pine Grove Twp, PA 49
Angst Nicholas	St Peter's Ch, Pine Grove, PA 49
Ankeny DeWalt	St Paul's Cem, nr Clearspring, Washington Co, MD 51
Ankeny Peter	Ankeny Square, Somerset, PA 59
Annabil Ebenezer	Bridgwater Town Hall, Washtenaw, MI 56
Annable Edward Dr	Marcellus, NY 35
Annable Robert	Old Cem, Manchester by the Sea, Manchester, MA 46
Annin James	Cayuga Village (Lakeview), Aurelius, NY 56
Annin Joseph	Cayuga Village Cem, Aurelius, NY 69
Annin William	Village Cem, Cayuga, Aurelius, NY 41
Annis Benjamin	Old Cem, Gustavus, Trumbull Co, OH 56
Annis Jacob	Lewis Cem, Ellery, Chautauqua, NY 63
Annis Jacob	North Thetford, VT 17
Annis Samuel	Grasmere Cem, Goffstown, NH 28
Annoble Joseph	Lothrop's Hill Meth Cem, Barnstable, MA 58
Antee Heinrich	Shalkop's Bur Gr, Montgomery Co, PA 59
Antere Michael	Randolph Co, IL 48
Antes John Henry Jr	Fam Cem, Williamsport, Lycoming Co, PA 78
Antes William	Old Pioneer, Canandaigua, NY 56
Anthoine Nicholas Jr	Knight Cem, Windham, ME 75
Anthony David	Lee's River & Wilbur Ave, on Hill, Somerset, MA 54
Anthony Douglass	Berry Cem, Manteo, Dare Co, NC 49
Anthony Edward	Wickes fam Cem, Westshore Rd, Warwick, RI 36
Anthony Gideon	New Woodstock Cem, New Woodstock, Madison Co, NY 82
Anthony Jacob	Henrietta, Monroe Co, NY 33
Anthony Jacob	River View Cem, Henrietta, Monroe Co, NY 79
Anthony John	Athens Twp, Bradford Co, PA 53
Anthony John	His estate, nr Galena, Kent Co, MD 51
Anthony John	Lee's River & Wilbur Ave, Somerset, MA 54
Anthony John	Walnut Hill, Evington, VA 37
Antisdel Simon	Town Ground, East Springfield, NY 15
Antisel Silas	Farm, South Ridge, Madison, Madison Co, OH 34
Antisel Silas	Farm, South Ridge, Madison, OH 26
Antisel Simon	Old Town Cem, Springfield, Otsego Co, NY 78

Antisell Perez	Farmington, Ontario Co, NY 56	
Antisell Simon	Middle Village Cem, Springfield, NH 52	
Antony Joseph	Wilkes Co, GA 56	
Appell Henry	Helderburgh Ref Ch, Guilderland Center, Albany Co, NY 66	
Apperson David	Blue Ridge (Ortman) farm, Greenwood, Albemarle Co, VA 74	
Apperson Richard	Oakley, old O'Hara place, Frankfort, KY 15	
Apperson William A	Fam Cem, nr East Bend, Surry Co, NC 81	
Apple Henry	St Johns Ch, Friedensburg, PA 49	
Applebee Thomas	Town Cem, Milton Mills, NH 27	
Applebey Thomas	Fam bur gr, Williams Rd, Smithfield, RI 40	
Applegate Andrew	First Pres Ch Cem, Cranbury, NJ 76	
Applegate Anthony	First Pres Ch Cem, Cranbury, NJ 76	
Applegate Bartholemew	Cedar Grove Meth Cem, Monmouth Co, NJ 26	
Applegate Bartholomew	Cedar Grove Cem, Cedar Grove Rd, Toms River, NJ 76	
Applegate Benjamin	Jefferson Co, KY 46	
Applegate Daniel	Cedar Grove Meth Cem, Monmouth Co, NJ 26	
Applegate Daniel	St Louis Cem, St Louis, MO 60	
Applegate Jacob	Cedar Grove Meth Cem, Monmouth Co, NJ 26	
Applegate James	Seceders Corners Ch Cem, Liberty Twp, Trumbull Co, OH 34	
Applegate John	Jefferson Co, KY 46	
Applegate John	Kirklin Cem, Frankfort, Clinton Co, IN 25	
Applegate Joseph	First Pres Ch Cem, Cranbury, NJ 76	
Applegate Joseph	Middlesex Co, NJ 54	
Applegate Richard	Jefferson Co, KY 46	
Applegate Samuel	Jefferson Co, KY 46	
Applegate Stacy	Jefferson Co, KY 46	
Applegate William	Mount Salem Cem, New Castle Co, DE 46	
Applegate Zebulon	New Richmond Cem, Clermont Co, OH 34	
Appleton Benjamin	Opposite First Cong Ch, Hamilton, MA 56	
Appleton Daniel	Old South Cem, Ipswich, MA 48	
Appleton Daniel	Pentucket Cem, Haverhill, MA 29	
Appleton Francis	Dublin Cem, Dublin, Cheshire Co, NH 77	
Appleton Isaac	Old Village Yard, New Ipswich, NH 29	
Appleton Oliver	Hamilton Cem, Hamilton, MA 45	
Appleton Oliver	Old South Cem, Ipswich, MA 48	
Appleton Samuel	Old South Cem, Ipswich, MA 48	
Appleton Samuel	Pentucket, Haverhill, MA 27	
Appleton Samuel	Pentucket Cem, Haverhill, MA 28	
Appleton Thomas	The Old Bur Gr, Ipswich, MA 46	
Appley Jacob	[no cem named], NY 39	
Arbogast Michael	Crabbottom Cem, Highland Co, VA 55	
Arbuckle Thomas	Country Cem, 2 mi NW of New Washington, Clark Co, IN 15	
Arbuckle Thomas	Washington Co, OH 45	
Arbuckle William	Fam Cem, nr Arbuckle, WV 50	
Arbuckle William Capt	Arbuckle Cem, Mason Co, WV 19	
Archbold John	Ridge Ch Cem, Archer Twp, Harrison Co, OH 56	
Archbold Thomas	Reynolds Cem, 2 mi NW of Decatur, Root Twp, Adams Co, IN 71	
Archbold Thomas	Ridge View Cem, Archer Twp, Harrison Co, OH 56	
Archer Benjamin	Keene Cem, NH 46	
Archer James	St John's Cem, Yonkers, NY 35	
Archer John	Cherryfield, ME 56	
Archer John	Grove Cem, Trumansburg, NY 31	
Archer John	Prosperity Cem, Prosperity, Washington Co, PA 68	
Archer John Maj	Church Hill, Harford Co, MD 30	
Archer Robert	Fam Cem, Princeton, IL 58	
Archer Stephens	Day's Run, WV 24	
Archer Thomas	Old Bur Gr, Suffield, Hartford Co, CT 24	
Archer Zachariah	Brick Cem, nr West Union, Clark Co, IL 15	
Archibald John	Statesville, NC 52	
Ardinger Christian	Riverview Cem, Williamsport, Washington Co, MD 77	
Arendall Nathan	Old fam Cem, Franklin Co, GA 41	

Argenbright Augustus	Trinity Ch Cem, Staunton, VA 36
Argesinger John	Johnstown Cem, Johnstown, NY 63
Argotey Villebas Don	Second St Louis Cem, New Orleans, LA 71
Armand Jean Pierre	Catholic Cem, Savannah, GA 39
Armantrout Frederick	Crawfordsville, Montgomery Co, IN 55
Armentrout Peter	Old Dutch Ch Cem, Rockingham Co, VA 62
Armentrout Philip	Old Dutch Ch Cem, Rockingham Co, VA 62
Armington Joseph	Newman Cem, Rumford, East Providence, RI 36
Armistead Anthony	Wilkinson Co, MS 44
Armistead Robert	Mt Pleasant Meth Ch Cem, Montgomery Co, TN 75
Armistead William	Cem 10 mi S of Whatley, AL 60
Armitage Enoch	Pennington, NJ 32
Armitage Enoch	Pres Ch Cem, Pennington, NJ 46
Armitage James	Upper Spruce Cr Pres Ch, Graysville, Huntingdon Co, PA 80
Armour Andrew	Greensboro, GA 52
Armour Gawen	Cem on the Hill, Windham, NH 28
Arms Consider	Peregrove Cem, Conway, MA 58
Arms Josiah	Brattleboro, VT 31
Arms Josiah	Meeting House Hill Cem, West Brattleboro, VT 45
Arms Susannah Willard	Meeting House Hill Cem, West Brattleboro, VT 45
Armsbury Jeremiah	Peck Cem, Arnold Mills, Cumberland, RI 36
Armstong Robert	Brick Union Cem, Fleming, KY 55
Armstrong Abel	Mount Tabor Cem, Salem Twp, Champaign Co, OH 55
Armstrong Abraham	[no cem named], OH 46
Armstrong Agness H	Alamance Pres Ch Cem, NC 49
Armstrong Alexander	Fam bur gr, Mercer Co, KY 45
Armstrong Alexander	Oregon Pike, KY 52
Armstrong Ambrose	School lands, Johnson Co, IN 50
Armstrong Bela	Hope Cem, Perry, Wyoming Co, NY 80
Armstrong Benoni	Wilcox Cem, Locke, Cayuga Co, NY 57
Armstrong David	Old Cem on the Plains, Windham, NH 26
Armstrong David	Plaingrove, Lawrence Co, PA 56
Armstrong Edward Lt	Pres Cem, White Clay Creek, New Castle Co, DE 46
Armstrong Ephriam	Norriton Pres Ch Cem, Montgomery Co, PA 59
Armstrong George	Lamington Pres Cem, Somerset Co, NJ 63
Armstrong George	Sandusky Co, OH 25
Armstrong George	Yellow Frame Cem, Warren Co, NJ 38
Armstrong George	York Twp, Clinton Co, OH 56
Armstrong Isaac	Cem, lot 27, Colestown, NJ 30
Armstrong Isaac	Fam Cem, Malta, Saratoga Co, NY 76
Armstrong Isaac	Jefferton Twp, Putnam Co, IN 24
Armstrong Isaac	Putnam Co, IN 16
Armstrong James	Mount Herman, Warren Co, NJ 35
Armstrong James	Revolutionary War Cem, Salem, Washington Co, NY 78
Armstrong James	Zion Ch Cem, Maury Co, TN 24
Armstrong James F	Riverview Cem, Trenton, NJ 28
Armstrong Jesse	Acotes Hill, Chepachet, Gloucester, RI 36
Armstrong John	Allin farm, State Pike, KY 52
Armstrong John	Carlisle, PA 15
Armstrong John	Cem on the Plains, Windham, NH 28
Armstrong John	Center Chapel, row 12 #11, Wells Twp, Jefferson Co, OH 55
Armstrong John	Granary Cem, Boston, MA 46
Armstrong John	Lower Brandywine Pres Ch, Centerville, DE 42
Armstrong John	North of McDowell, VA 56
Armstrong John	Old Cem, Washington Co, PA 38
Armstrong John	Pope Graveyard, Otego, Otsego Co, NY 72
Armstrong John	Stonewall Dist, Highland Co, VA 56
Armstrong John	Third Creek Ch Cem, Rowan Co, NC 51
Armstrong John	Yellow Frame Cem, Warren Co, NJ 38
Armstrong John Capt	North Cem, Dorchester, MA 46
Armstrong John Col	Priv bur gr, Clark Co, IN 15

Armstrong John Jr	Red Rock, NY 53
Armstrong Joseph	Norriton Pres Ch Cem, Montgomery Co, PA 59
Armstrong Joseph Col	Pres Ch Cem, Rocky Springs, PA 20
Armstrong Joseph Col	Rocky Springs Pres Ch Cem, 6 mi fr Chambersburg, PA 19
Armstrong Joshua	Richland Cem, nr Jerseyville, IL 31
Armstrong Matthew	Smith's Cem, below Belmont, NC 56
Armstrong Robert	Concord Cem, Menard Co, IL 26
Armstrong Robert	First Pres Ch Cem, Knoxville, TN 29
Armstrong Robert	Menard Co, IL 30
Armstrong Robert	Second St Cem, NY 33
Armstrong Samuel	Granary Cem, Boston, MA 46
Armstrong Solomon	Barker Cem, Barker, Broome Co, NY 78
Armstrong Thomas Maj	Frankfort Plains, NJ 24
Armstrong William	Crider Cem, nr Princeton, Caldwell Co, KY 73
Armstrong William	Lebanon Ch, Falling Spring, Augusta Co, VA 36
Armstrong William	McCarthy Cem, Oakland, MD 68
Armstrong William	Providence, KY 52
Armstrong William	Thyatira Pres Ch Cem, Rowan Co, NC 72
Armstrong William	Yellow Frame Cem, Warren Co, NJ 38
Armstrong William 1	Fam plantation, Carters Valley, Hawkins Co, TN 40
Armstrong William 2	New Providence Cem, Stony Point, TN 40
Arndt Abraham	Straw Ch Cem, Phillipsburg, Warren Co, NJ 40
Arndt Barnhard	Old Cem, Hecktown, Northampton Co, PA 21
Arndt Jacob	Fam Cem, nr Paubsville, PA 57
Arner Henry	Lutheran Cem, Petersburg, OH 56
Arner Jacob	Zionsville Luth Cem, Shimersville, Lehigh Co, PA 40
Arnett John	Lone grave in pine field, Sylvania, Screven Co, GA 75
Arnett John	Nr Sylvania, Screven Co, GA 34
Arnold Abimeleck	Union Cem, Unadilla, Otsego Co, NY 71
Arnold Anthony	Pocasset Cem, Cranston, RI 36
Arnold Aza	Old Friends Cem, Lincoln, RI 36
Arnold Burington	Bristol Ferry Cem, Portsmouth, RI 36
Arnold Caleb	Prob, NY 36
Arnold Christopher	Old fam Cem, Metropolitan Pkwy, West Warwick Downs, RI 36
Arnold Daniel	Ogden, NY 56
Arnold David	North Bur Gr, Providence, RI 36
Arnold David	Sand Lake, Rensselaer Co, NY 15
Arnold David	West Main St Cem, Norton, MA 55
Arnold Edmund	Fam lot, E of East Rd, N of Knotty Oak Ch, Coventry, RI 36
Arnold Edward	Mayflower Cem, Duxbury, MA 50
Arnold Elisha	Lime St Cem, Adams, MA 46
Arnold Elisha	Park Ave, Cranston, RI 36
Arnold Fenner	Nahaiwe, Great Barrington, MA 56
Arnold George	Colombo farm, Warwick Ave, Warwick, RI 36
Arnold George	Fairfield Cem, Fairfield Co, OH 59
Arnold Henry	Fam Cem S of Pontiac, Pawtuxet River Bank, W Warwick, RI 36
Arnold Israel	Highland Cem, Pawtuxet, Warwick, RI 36
Arnold Israel	Old Friends Cem, Lincoln, RI 36
Arnold Israel	Quaker Mtg Hs Bur Gr, Lincoln, RI 52
Arnold Jacob	Bethel Cem, Miami Co, OH 45
Arnold Jacob	Morristown, NJ 32
Arnold Jacob Col	First Pres Bur Gr, Morristown, NJ 24
Arnold James	Piscataway Cem, White Church, NJ 47
Arnold Jesse	Old fam Cem, Metropolitan Pkwy, West Warwick Downs, RI 36
Arnold John	5 mi E of Milledgeville, Baldwin Co, GA 36
Arnold John	Cherry Valley Cem, Otsego Co, NY 34
Arnold John	Cong Cem, East Haddam, CT 56
Arnold John	Highland Cem, Pawtuxet, Warwick, RI 36
Arnold John	New Pawtuxet Cem, Harrison Ave, Lakewood, Warwick, RI 75
Arnold John	Old fam Cem, adjoining Quaker Cem, Lincoln, RI 36
Arnold John	St Peter's Ch Cem, Perth Amboy, NJ 45

Arnold John Rice	Green, Pawtuxet, Warwick, RI 36
Arnold Jonathan	Elm St Cem, Braintree, MA 54
Arnold Jonathan	Meredith Cem, Meredith, Delaware Co, NY 71
Arnold Jonathan	Old fam Cem, adjoining Quaker Cem, Lincoln, RI 36
Arnold Jonathan Dr	Mount Pleasant Cem, St Johnsbury, VT 15
Arnold Joseph	Achley, East Haddam, CT 56
Arnold Joseph	Common Grave, Milford Cem, Milford, CT 56
Arnold Joseph	Farm, No 10, Lent Co, RI 56
Arnold Joseph	Sennett Old Cem, Sennett, NY 56
Arnold Joseph	Spring Hill Cem, Marlboro, MA 45
Arnold Joseph Jr	North Bur Gr, Providence, RI 36
Arnold Josiah	Fam Cem, Jefferson Twp, Pike Co, IN 72
Arnold Josiah	West Stockbridge Cem, West Stockbridge, MA 49
Arnold Luke	Old Friends Cem, Lincoln, RI 36
Arnold Moses	First Parish Cem, Braintree, MA 46
Arnold Moses	Quasset Yard, Woodstock, CT 29
Arnold Nathaniel	Old Wheelock, Putnam, CT 56
Arnold Oliver	Columbia Ave, off Fair St, Pawtuxet, RI 35
Arnold Oliver	Evergreen Cem, Rutland, VT 23
Arnold Oliver	Forest Home Cem, Waverly, NY 15
Arnold Peleg	Elmgrove Cem, North Kingston, RI 55
Arnold Peter	Old Roman Catholic Cem, Bedford Co, PA 80
Arnold Philip	Columbia Ave, off Fair St, Pawtuxet, RI 35
Arnold Richard	Fam plot, Harrison, Hamilton Co, OH 34
Arnold Richard	Glen Haven Cem, Harrison Co, OH 31
Arnold Richard	Harrison, OH 15
Arnold Robert	Morristown, NJ 32
Arnold Samuel	Hockanum Cem, East Hartford, CT 19
Arnold Samuel	Leeds, ME 18
Arnold Samuel	Union Cem, Weymouth, MA 62
Arnold Seth	Old Cem, Westminster, VT 42
Arnold Stephen	Arnold-Benscoter, Muhlenberg, PA 56
Arnold Stephen	East Clarendon Cem, Clarendon, VT 25
Arnold Stephen	East Clarendon Cem, Clarendon, VT 24
Arnold Stephen	Fam Cem, Wilton, Saratoga Co, NY 76
Arnold Stephen	Union Village Cem, Louisquisset Pike, N Smithfield, RI 75
Arnold Sylvanus	Morristown, NJ 32
Arnold Thomas	Selma, Dallas Co, AL 56
Arnold William	Mayflower Cem, Duxbury, MA 58
Arnold William	Mt Bethel Meth Epis Ch, Princeton, Laurens Co, SC 72
Arnold William	Union Village Cem, Louisquisset Pike, N Smithfield, RI 75
Arnot Henry Sr	Mt Hedding Cem, Lillydale, Monroe Co, WV 72
Arrauts Herman Lt	Cecil Co, MD 19
Arrauts Jacob Lt	Cecil Co, MD 19
Arrison Jeptha	Old Liberty Ch Cem, Liberty Twp, Delaware Co, OH 53
Arter John	Center Twp, Columbiana Co, OH 56
Arters Richard	Tidioute, PA 52
Arters William	Rock Hill Cem, Flushing Twp, Belmont Co, OH 56
Arthur Benjamin	Hillsboro Cem, Highland Co, OH 55
Arthur James	Old Town Cem, Crawfordsville, Montgomery Co, IN 55
Arthur James	Youngsville, PA 52
Arthur Joel	Fam Cem, nr Clay, OH 56
Arthur Richard	Westfield, MA 55
Artman John Justis	Jewett Center Cem, Jewett, Greene Co, NY 69
Arvin William	Wells Cem, Canaan, NH 36
Asbury Daniel	Rehobeth Meth Ch, Catawba Co, NC 59
Ash Fred	Floyd Co, KY 45
Ash James H	Old Christ Ch, Philadelphia, PA 48
Ash William	Old Hebron Ch Cem, Franklin Co, GA 41
Ash William	Symond's Cem, Franklin, NH 30
Ashbaugh Martin	Brush Creek Cem, North Huntington, Westmoreland Co, PA 76

Ashbrook Thomas	Old Secrest Cem, nr Romana, Owen Co, IN 72
Ashby Bladen	Clark farm, nr Middleburo, Wayne Co, IN 72
Ashby Jesse	Walton Creek Ch Cem, Centertown, KY 30
Ashcraft Daniel Capt	Baker Cem, southern Guilford, VT 19
Ashcraft Jedediah	Old Trinity Yard, Brooklyn, CT 30
Ashcraft Simon	Hammonton, NJ 15
Ashe Samuel	Rocky Point Cem, Pender Co, NC 60
Ashe William	Hebron Ch Cem, Franklin Co, GA 43
Asher Bartlett	Gass Cem, N of Gosport, Owen Co, IN 72
Ashley Abner	Bethany, NY 15
Ashley Abner	Old Tolland Cem, Tolland, CT 45
Ashley Alden	Old Waterford Cem, Waterford, Saratoga Co, NY 76
Ashley Benjamin Lt	Ashleyville Center, West Springfield, MA 15
Ashley Daniel Lt	West Claremont Bur Gr, Claremont, NH 50
Ashley David Lt	Ashleyville Center, West Springfield, MA 15
Ashley Israel Dr	Mechanic St, Westfield, MA 56
Ashley James	Battle area, Stone Arabia, NY 56
Ashley James	Steuben Cem, Steuben, OH 56
Ashley John	Ashleyville Center, West Springfield, MA 15
Ashley John	Barnard, Sheffield, MA 56
Ashley John	Barnard, Sheffield, MA 56
Ashley John	Warrior Creek Bapt Ch Cem, Laurens Co, SC 70
Ashley Martin Dr	Cem, Walpole, NH 55
Ashley Martin Jr	Mt Holly Cem, Mt Holly, VT 55
Ashley Moses	Ashleyville Center, West Springfield, MA 15
Ashley Moses Lt	Stockbridge Cem, Stockbridge, MA 47
Ashley Oliver Capt	West Claremont Bur Gr, Claremont, NH 50
Ashley Percival	Fam Cem, Freetown, MA 45
Ashley Peter	Ref Ch Cem, Germantown, Columbia Co, NY 79
Ashley Samuel	Old Litchfield Yard, Hampton, CT 31
Ashley Samuel Sr	West part of Claremont, NH 48
Ashley Simeon	Mechanic St, Westfield, MA 56
Ashley Stephen	Long Plain Cem, Leverett, MA 47
Ashley William	Barnard, Sheffield, MA 56
Ashley William	Fam Cem, nr Barnwell, SC 51
Ashley William	Fam farm Cem, S of Ithaca, Darke Co, OH 78
Ashley William S	Bloomfield Cem, Marengo, Morrow Co, OH 34
Ashmead Jacob Capt	Hood's Cem, Germantown, PA 20
Ashmead Jacob Capt	[no cem named], PA 19
Ashmead James Capt	Hood's Cem, Germantown, PA 20
Ashmun John	Old Center Cem, Blandford, Hampden Co, MA 58
Ashmun Justus	Old Center Cem, Blandford, Hampden Co, MA 58
Ashton Isaac	Christ Ch Bur Gr, Philadelphia, PA 57
Ashton James	Old Turnpike Cem, Cambridge, Washington Co, NY 55
Ashton John	Collamer Cem, Malta, Saratoga Co, NY 76
Ashton John	Hall's Corner Cem, Malta, NY 39
Ashton John	Halls Corners Cem, Malta, Saratoga Co, NY 41
Ashton Joseph	Edinburg Christiana Ch Cem, Lawrence Co, PA 59
Ashurst William	Asher Cem, Farmersville Rd, Flat Rock, Caldwell Co, KY 73
Aske William	Hebron Ch Cem, Franklin Co, GA 42
Askey Thomas	Jacksonville Cem, Centre Co, PA 55
Askey Thomas Capt	Jacksonville, PA 15
Aspenwall Zalmon	School St Cem, Lebanon, NH 27
Aspinwall Caleb	Springfield Cem, Springfield, MA 47
Aspinwall Thomas	Walnut St Cem, Brookline, MA 55
Aspinwall William	Walnut St, Brookline, MA 56
Aspril Joseph	Old Drawyers Cem, New Castle Co, DE 46
Asters George	Old Cem, Washington Co, PA 38
At Peter	Mt Eaton Cem, Wayne Co, OH 56
Atchley Thomas	Alder Branch Cem, Sevier Co, TN 73
Ater George	Little Zion Bapt Cem, Deerfield Twp, Ross Co, OH 34

Atherton A	Killed in Wyoming Massacre, Wyoming, PA 52
Atherton Caleb	Old Cem, East Mansfield, MA 55
Atherton Consider	Pearl St Cem, Stoughton, MA 55
Atherton David	Old Center Cem, Harvard, MA 56
Atherton Eliakim	Old Cem, Bolton, MA 56
Atherton Jabez	Killed in Wyoming Massacre, Wyoming, PA 52
Atherton James	Cem, Forty Fort, PA 52
Atherton John Jr	Pearl St Cem, Stoughton, MA 55
Atherton Jonathan	Bilerica (now Harvard), Cavendish, VT 56
Atherton Joseph	Bernardston Rd Cem, Greenfield, MA 45
Atherton Joseph	Bilerica (now Harvard), Cavendish, VT 56
Atherton Joseph	Log Plain (Sage) Cem, Greenfield, MA 00
Atherton Joseph	Old Center Cem, Harvard, MA 56
Atherton Oliver	Bernardston Rd Cem, Greenfield, MA 45
Atherton Oliver	Log Plain (Sage) Cem, Greenfield, MA 00
Atherton Philip	Mansfield, MA 55
Atherton Samuel	Pearl St Cem, Stoughton, MA 55
Atherton Solomon	Whipple Hill Cem, Richmond, NH 36
Atherton Thomas	Turner, ME 18
Athey Thomas Sr	Indian Mound Cem, Romney, WV 45
Atkin Joseph Jr	West Hill Cem, Sherburne, Chenango Co, NY 72
Atkins Amos	Picket Cem, Portland (Charlotte), Chautauqua Co, NY 15
Atkins Benjamin	Old North Cem, Truro, MA 49
Atkins David	Old Center Cem, Blandford, Hampden Co, MA 58
Atkins David	Union Mills Cem, Broadalbin, NY 32
Atkins Henry	Copps Hill, Boston, MA 56
Atkins Hezekiah	West Hartland Cem, West Hartland, CT 60
Atkins Ica	Fam Cem, 10 mi fr Eastman, Pulaski Co, GA 24
Atkins Isaiah	North Truro, MA 55
Atkins Isaiah	Old North Cem, Truro, MA 49
Atkins Joseph	North Truro, MA 55
Atkins Josiah	Jefferson, Ashtabula Co, OH 18
Atkins Josiah	Oakdale Cem, Jefferson, Ashtabula Co, OH 34
Atkins Josiah Sgt	Jefferson, OH 15
Atkins Nathaniel	Truro Cem, Truro, MA 45
Atkins Samuel	Forest Lawn Cem, Buffalo, NY 33
Atkins Thomas	Adkins Fam Cem, nr Cane Creek, Whitley Co, KY 73
Atkinson Bezaleel	Old Cem, Leonard & Atkinson farm, Hilton, NY 21
Atkinson James	Rural Cem, Danby, NY 15
Atkinson James	Rural Cem, Danby, NY 34
Atkinson Joseph	Central South Water St Cem, Boscawen, NH 32
Atkinson Joseph	City Cem, Boscawen, NH 62
Atkinson Nathaniel	Central South Water St Cem, Boscawen, NH 32
Atkinson Samuel	Central South Water St Cem, Boscawen, NH 32
Atkinson Simeon Capt	Central South Water St Cem, Boscawen, NH 32
Atkinson Theodore	Town Cem, Sandwich Center, NH 29
Atkinson Thomas	Fam farm, S of Paoli, Orange Co, IN 72
Atlee Samuel John	Christ Ch Yard, Germantown, PA 47
Attwill Zachariah	Old Lynn Cem, end of common, Lynn, MA 46
Attwood Elizah	Riverview, East Haddam, CT 56
Atwater –	Coventry Twp, Summit Co, OH 15
Atwater –	Lockwood Coventry, Summit Co, OH 45
Atwater Abram	Cong Cem, Cheshire, New Haven Co, CT 24
Atwater Enos	Cong Cem, Cheshire, New Haven Co, CT 24
Atwater Ichabod	North Otis Cem, Otis, MA 56
Atwater Jeremiah	Grove Street Cem, New Haven, CT 56
Atwater John	West Genoa Cem, Genoa, NY 41
Atwater John	West Genoa Cem, Kings Ferry, NY 16
Atwater Reuben	Cheshire, CT 17
Atwater Reuben	Cong Cem, Cheshire, New Haven Co, CT 24
Atwater Samuel	Cheshire, CT 17

Atwater Samuel	Cong Cem, Cheshire, New Haven Co, CT 24
Atwell Benjamin	Old Cem, North Somers, Tolland Co, CT 78
Atwell John	Churchyard, Hollis, NH 39
Atwell John Cumings	Groton Cem, Groton, NH 46
Atwell Nathan	Old Western Cem, Lynn, MA 55
Atwell Paul	Old South Windsor Cem, Windsor, Broome Co, NY 78
Atwell Richard	Center Cem, Marlboro, NH 38
Atwell Zachariah	Old Western Cem, Lynn, MA 55
Atwood Abiel	Assonet Neck Rd Cem, Berkley, MA 55
Atwood Barnabas Capt	First Parish Unitarian Cem, Brewster, MA 46
Atwood Barnabus	Lakenham Cem, Carver, MA 59
Atwood David	Landaff, NH 26
Atwood David	Wellfleet Cem, Wellfleet, MA 46
Atwood Ebenezer	Jones Cem, East Rd, Orange, MA 31
Atwood Eleazer	Duck Creek Cem, Well Fleet, MA 49
Atwood Eleazer	Welfleet Cem, Welfleet, MA 59
Atwood Elisha	Duck Creek Cem, Well Fleet, MA 49
Atwood Ephraim	Duck Creek Cem, Well Fleet, MA 49
Atwood Freeman	Duck Creek Cem, Well Fleet, MA 49
Atwood Ichabod	Canfield Cem, Canfield, OH 56
Atwood Ichabod	Old Cem, The Green, Middleboro, MA 50
Atwood Isaac	Duck Creek Cem, Well Fleet, MA 49
Atwood Jedediah	Wysox Twp, PA 53
Atwood Jesse	Groveland Cem, Bradford, MA 55
Atwood John	Cem on Town Common, Nelson, NH 35
Atwood John	Lakenham Cem, Carver, MA 59
Atwood John	Town Cem, Atkinson, NH 28
Atwood John	Union Cem, Carver, MA 58
Atwood Jonathan Capt	Hillside Cem, South Weare, NH 32
Atwood Joseph	Berkley Common, Berkley, MA 55
Atwood Joseph	Carver, MA 30
Atwood Joseph	Cem nr old Emery house, Chatham, MA 49
Atwood Joseph	County Cem, Ontario, Can 58
Atwood Joseph	Fam Cem, Solon, Cortland Co, NY 36
Atwood Joseph	Pentucket, Haverhill, MA 27
Atwood Joshua	Duck Creek Cem, Well Fleet, MA 49
Atwood Joshua	Gumpus Cem, Pelham, NH 34
Atwood Moses	Center Sandwich Cem, Sandwich, NH 31
Atwood Moses	Town Cem, Alexandria, NH 28
Atwood Nathaniel	Union Cem, South Carver, MA 59
Atwood Philip	Cem on Town Common, Nelson, NH 35
Atwood Richard	Cem nr Cong Ch, Orleans, MA 49
Atwood Samuel	Duck Creek Cem, Well Fleet, MA 49
Atwood Samuel	Old Bennington Town Hill Cem, VT 41
Atwood Samuel	Old Bennington, VT 40
Atwood Stephen	Old Provincetown Cem, Provincetown, MA 55
Atwood Sylvester	Unitarian Ch Cem, Main St, Dighton, MA 55
Atwood Waite	Burial Hill Cem, Plymouth, MA 46
Atwood William	South Carver Cem, Carver, MA 34
Auger Felix	Greenwood Cem, Kendall Corners, NY 34
Aughe Harmon Capt	Frankfort, Clinton Co, IN 16
Aughe Harmon Capt	Old South Cem, IN 20
Augst Daniel	Jacob's Luth Ch, 2 mi W of Pine Grove, Schuylkill Co, PA 37
Augur Felix	Greenwood Cem, Kendall, NY 31
Augustine George	Forney Cem, Unity Twp, Columbiana Co, OH 55
Auld Hugh	Now Arlington National Cem, MD 52
Auld Hugh	Orig Claiborne MD, now Arlington Cem, Washington, DC 47
Auld William	Pleasant Valley Cem, Urbana, Steuben Co, NY 82
Aulenbach Daniel	St Johns Ch, Friedensburg, PA 49
Aulis William	Pleasant Valley Cem, Hammondport, Steuben Co, NY 69
Aull John	Pres Cem, New Castle, New Castle Co, DE 46

Ault Michael	Farm, W of Woodgrove, Manchester Twp, Morgan Co, OH	56
Aupamut Hendrick Capt	Indian Cem, Kaukauna, WI	29
Auryansen Garret	Closter, NJ	47
Auryansen John	Closter, NJ	47
Auryansen Resolvert	Closter, NJ	47
Austen Moses	Old Pres Ch Cem, Elizabeth, NJ	26
Austen Thomas	Pleasant Ridge Pres Cem, Hamilton Co, OH	41
Austin Aaron	Torrington Cem, Torrington, CT	55
Austin Andrew	Cem, Charlestown, Portage Co, OH	34
Austin Andrew	[no cem named], OH	26
Austin Appollas	Orwell (Shoreham), VT	15
Austin Arden	Austin Hill Cem, NY	33
Austin Augustine	Barnard Cem, Sheffield, MA	41
Austin Bailey	Plain Cem, Sheffield, MA	56
Austin Benjamin	Albany rural Cem, Albany, NY	31
Austin Benjamin	Pittstown, Rensselaer Co, NY	37
Austin Cyrenious	Torringford Cem, Torringford, CT	36
Austin David	Norton, MA	55
Austin Eliphalet	Cem, center of Austinburg, Ashtabula Co, OH	34
Austin George	First Cong Cem, Griswold, CT	62
Austin Isaac	Pres Ch Cem, Mahopac Falls, NY	35
Austin Joab	Hewins St Cem, Sheffield, MA	40
Austin Job	Pres Ch Cem, Mahopac Falls, NY	35
Austin John	Cave Hill Cem, Louisville, KY	55
Austin John	Cave Hill Cem, Louisville, KY	31
Austin John	North River Cem, Luzerne, Warren Co, NY	70
Austin John	Nr Cynthia Perry Bridge, Walton Co, GA	26
Austin Jonathan	Fam Cem, 9 mi NW of Lowville, NY	16
Austin Joseph	[no cem named], OH	45
Austin Joshua	Branch Ridge, New Salem, MA	30
Austin Joshua	Erving, MA	30
Austin Moses	Center Cem, Salem, NH	28
Austin Moses	First Pres Ch Cem, Elizabeth, NJ	52
Austin Nathaniel	Cem, center of Austinburg, Ashtabula Co, OH	34
Austin Nathaniel	Plain Cem, Sheffield, MA	56
Austin Philip	Old Cem, Jeffersonville, Clark Co, IN	72
Austin Phillip	Jeffersonville, Clark Co, OH	15
Austin Phineas	Wesley Denton Cem, Day, Saratoga Co, NY	78
Austin Richard	[no cem named], MD	19
Austin Seth	Unitarian Ch Cem, Main St, Dighton, MA	55
Austin Smith	Pres Ch Cem, Mahopac Falls, NY	35
Austin Stephen	Mountain View Cem, Auburn, ME	70
Austin Thomas	Suffield, CT	54
Austin William	Bethel Meth Ch Cem, Mauldin, SC	70
Austin William	Plain Cem, Sheffield, MA	56
Autisdel Simon	Middle Village Cem, Springfield, NY	33
Avara Alexander	Fam Cem, Averasboro Twp, Harnett Co, NC	60
Averell Nathaniel	Old Topsfield Cem, Pine Grove, MA	55
Averil Frederick	Pomfret Center Yard, Pomfret, CT	26
Averill Asa	Old Cem, Westminster, VT	46
Averill Daniel	Elmwood Cem, Barre, VT	48
Averill Isaac	Pine Grove Cem, Topsfield, Essex Co, MA	56
Averill John	Old Cem, Westminster, VT	42
Averill Jonathan	Jordanville Cem, Jordanville, NY	32
Averill Jonathan	Jordanville Cem, Warren, Herkimer Co, NY	41
Averill Joseph	Machias Cem, Machias, ME	56
Averill Perry	New Preston Cem, New Preston, CT	55
Averill Stephen	Pomfret Center Yard, Pomfret, CT	26
Averill Thomas Jr	Columbia Cem, Columbia Ave, Springfield, OH	58
Averill William	Warren Cem, Little Lakes, Warren, Herkimer Co, NY	41
Avery –	Town Yard, Hill Center, NH	29

Avery Abel	Briggs Cem, Malta, Saratoga Co, NY 76
Avery Abel	Southeast Cem, Cornwall, CT 22
Avery Benjamin	Ledyard Ch Cem, Ledyard, NY 56
Avery Benjamin	Lyons Rural Cem, Lyons, Wayne Co, NY 79
Avery Caleb	Avery-Morgan Cem, Poquonoc Bridge, CT 15
Avery Christopher	Killed in Wyoming Massacre, Wyoming, PA 52
Avery Christopher I	Gore Fam Cem, Sheshequin Twp, Bradford Co, PA 53
Avery Chrostopher	Cem, Gillett farm, Bradford Co, PA 53
Avery Daniel	Avery-Morgan Cem, Poquonoc Bridge, CT 15
Avery Daniel	Old Ground Cem, Poquonoc, Ft Griswold, CT 57
Avery Daniel Jr	Oak Glen, Aurora Village, Ledyard, NY 56
Avery David	Avery-Morgan Cem, Poquonoc Bridge, CT 15
Avery David	Center, Lebanon, CT 56
Avery Denison	Myrtle Hill Cem, Syracuse, NY 68
Avery Ebenezer	Avery-Morgan Cem, Poquonoc Bridge, CT 15
Avery Ebenezer Jr	Packer Rocks Cem, Groton, CT 51
Avery Ebenezer Lt	Groton Cem, Groton, CT 15
Avery Elisha	Avery-Morgan Cem, Poquonoc Bridge, CT 15
Avery Enos	Old Cem, Port Byron, Mentz, Cayuga Co, NY 41
Avery Ephraim	Montgomery Cem, Montgomery, MA 47
Avery Ephraim	Pitcher St Cem, Montgomery, MA 53
Avery George	Chandler Cem, Wilson Co, TN 24
Avery George	Gilkie Yard, Plainfield, NH 28
Avery George	Nr Leeville, TN 23
Avery George	Old Cem, Granville, OH 56
Avery George	Plainfield, NH 54
Avery Humphrey	Lakeview Cem, Patchogue, Suffolk Co, NY 77
Avery Jacob	[no cem named], CT 54
Avery Jasper	Avery-Morgan Cem, Poquonoc Bridge, CT 15
Avery John	Avery-Morgan Cem, Poquonoc Bridge, CT 15
Avery John	Howland Cem, Conway, MA 53
Avery Jonathan	East Charlmont Cem, Charlmont, MA 45
Avery Joseph	Old Center Cem, Monterey, MA 56
Avery Miles Capt	Blue Hill Cem, Great Barrington, MA 27
Avery Nathan	Chester Yard, East Haddam, CT 56
Avery Park	Avery-Morgan Cem, Poquonoc Bridge, CT 15
Avery Park Jr	Avery-Morgan Cem, Poquonoc Bridge, CT 15
Avery Peter	Avery-Morgan Cem, Poquonoc Bridge, CT 15
Avery Ransford	West part of Cem, Southampton, MA 49
Avery Richard	Priv plot, W of hwy betw Speigletown & Melrose, NY 38
Avery Samuel	North Whitefield, ME 39
Avery Samuel	Norwich Town Cem, Norwich, CT 18
Avery Solomon	Adams Corners Cem, Adams Corners, Putnam Co, NY 36
Avery Solomon	Avery-Morgan Cem, Poquonoc Bridge, CT 15
Avery Solomon	Tunkhannock Cem, Tunkhannock, Wyoming Co, PA 67
Avery Stephen	Old Plain Cem, North Stonington, CT 31
Avery Stephen	White Hall Cem, Mystic, CT 31
Avery Thatcher	Priv Cem, Avery, North Castine, Hancock Co, ME 56
Avery Thomas	Avery-Morgan Cem, Poquonoc Bridge, CT 15
Avery Waighstill	Fam Cem, NC 49
Avery William	Old Cem, nr Boston Post Rd, Groton, MA 45
Avery William	Pitcher St Cem, Montgomery, MA 53
Avey Joseph Sr	Tealtown Cem, Union Twp, Clermont Co, OH 56
Avis Joseph	Morav Cem, nr Swedesboro, NJ 47
Axford John	Mansfield Cem, nr Washington, NJ 35
Axford Samuel	Mansfield Cem, nr Washington, NJ 35
Axtel Luther	Prosperity Cem, Prosperity, Washington Co, PA 68
Axtell Daniel	Grafton Cem, Grafton, Windham Co, VT 74
Axtell Daniel	Priv Cem, New Vernon, Mercer Co, PA 70
Axtell Henry	Mendham, NJ 50
Axtell Moses	Fam farm, nr Deposit, Delaware Co, NY 71

Axtell Thomas	Meeting House Hill Cem, Grafton, MA 49
Ayde John	Bethel-Gilead Cem, Bethel, Windsor Co, VT 72
Ayer Ezekiel Jr	Hackettstown Cem, Hackettstown, Warren Co, NJ 73
Ayer James Maj	Walnut Cem, East Parish, Haverhill, MA 31
Ayer John	Pres Ch Cem, Basking Ridge, NJ 74
Ayer Jonathan Capt	North Parish Bur Gr, Haverhill, MA 31
Ayer Nathaniel	Pentucket Cem, Haverhill, MA 28
Ayer Obidiah	Samptown Cem, South Plainfield, Middlesex Co, NJ 79
Ayer Robert	First Pres Ch Cem, Cranbury, NJ 76
Ayer Samuel	Walnut Cem, East Parish, Haverhill, MA 31
Ayer Simon	Second West Parish Cem, Haverhill, MA 31
Ayer William	Cem nr church, Bradford Center, NH 29
Ayer William	Cem, nr Church, Bradford Center, NH 30
Ayer William	Center Cem, Salem, NH 28
Ayers Amos	West Cem, Amherst, MA 56
Ayers Christopher	Village Cem, Marlow, NH 35
Ayers Ellis	Colonial Cem, Metuchen, NJ 49
Ayers Ezekiel	Colonial Cem, Metuchen, NJ 49
Ayers Jacob	Colonial Cem, Metuchen, NJ 49
Ayers John	Old Pres Bur Gr, Dauphin, Dauphin Co, PA 62
Ayers John	Riverside Cem, Gouveneur, NY 15
Ayers Jonathan	Priv fam Cem, Northfield, NH 29
Ayers Jonathan	Priv bur gr, New Canaan, 8 mi fr Stamford, CT 16
Ayers Joseph	Priv fam Cem, Northfield, NH 29
Ayers Levi	Wantage Cem, Sussex Co, NJ 70
Ayers Mark	Barrington Cem, Barrington, NH 59
Ayers Moses	Embden, ME 15
Ayers Moses	Old Reed Creek Ch Cem, 5 mi fr Hartwell, Hart Co, GA 66
Ayers Nathan	Colonial Cem, Metuchen, NJ 49
Ayers Noah Rev	Pearl St Bapt Cem, Bridgeton, NJ 26
Ayers Thomas	Fam Cem, Jefferson Twp, Franklin Co, OH 53
Ayers Tuttle	Champlain Cem, Westfield, PA 52
Ayers William	Bradford, NY 15
Ayers William	Old Pres Bur Gr, Dauphin, Dauphin Co, PA 62
Ayers William Lt	North Brookfield, MA 15
Ayes Robert	Village Cem, Ballston, Saratoga Co, NY 39
Aylesworth David	Lucerne Cem, Lucerne, Indiana Co, PA 61
Aylsworth Abraham	Bapt Ch Cem, Burnt Hills, Saratoga Co, NY 78
Aylsworth Authur	Spence Cem, Rockdale, Otsego Co, NY 85
Ayrault Nicholas	West (New Boston) Cem, Sandisfield, MA 56
Ayres David	Mount Bethel, NJ 47
Ayres Eleazer	Granby, MA 55
Ayres Ezekial 1st	Old Cem, Hackettstown, NJ 47
Ayres Ezekiel	Union Cem, Hackettstown, NJ 56
Ayres Isaac	Morristown, NJ 32
Ayres John	Morristown, NJ 32
Ayres John	Pres Ch Cem, Morris Plains, NJ 62
Ayres John	Whitehead farm, Princeton Pike, Butler Co, OH 39
Ayres Nathaniel	Pres Ch Cem, Basking Ridge, NJ 47
Ayres Silas	Morristown, NJ 32
Ayres Silas	Pres Ch Cem, Morris Plains, NJ 62
Ayres William Lt	Maple St Cem, North Brookfield, MA 17
Azel Abel	Old Cem, Elizabethtown, NY 33

B

Baader Nicholas	Twin Churches, Colerain Twp, Rainsburg, Bedford Co, PA	77
Babb John	Farm at Green Hill, Barrington, NH	36
Babb John	Farm Cem, Paris, Henry Co, TN	75
Babb John	Nr Paris, TN	24
Babb Moses	Otis Yard, Otis farm, North Stratford, NH	28
Babb Peter	Sebago, ME	52
Babb Samson	Lewis Cem, Morris, Tioga Co, PA	77
Babb Seth Sr	Fam Cem, nr Greenville, Greene Co, TN	76
Babb Thomas	Newark Union Cem, Brandywine Hnd, New Castle Co, DE	42
Babb Thomas	Newark Union Cem, New Castle Co, DE	46
Babb William	Foss Cem, Strafford, Strafford Co, NH	62
Babbitt Asa	Rudsboro Cem, Hanover, NH	29
Babbitt Daniel	Mendham, NJ	50
Babbitt Ebenezer	Plain Cem, Taunton, MA	48
Babbitt Edward	Old Burrill Yard, Killingly, CT	29
Babbitt Elkanah	Old Cem, Fly Creek, Otsego, NY	71
Babbitt Gideon	Assonet Neck Rd, Berkley, MA	55
Babbitt Joel	Bethel-Gilead Cem, Bethel, Windsor Co, VT	72
Babbitt Nathan Dr	North Cem, Westmoreland, NH	25
Babbitt Seth	Covell Cem, Covell, CT	28
Babbitt Seth	Old Covell Yard, Killingly, CT	29
Babbitt Snellem	Fam Cem, Savoy, MA	53
Babbitt Ziba	Plain Cem, Taunton, MA	48
Babbs John	Booher Graveyard nr Napoleon, Ripley Co, IN	72
Babcock Amos	Meeting House Hill Cem, Grafton, MA	49
Babcock Benjamin	Potter Cem, S of East Galway, Saratoga Co, NY	76
Babcock David	Cleaver Cem, Marcy, Oneida Co, NY	82
Babcock David	Lower Cem, East Worcester, Otsego Co, NY	76
Babcock Ebenezer	West Cem, Sherborn, MA	74
Babcock Ethemer	Milton Cem, Milton, MA	46
Babcock George	Fairville, Arcadia, Wayne Co, NY	56
Babcock George	Green Cem, Hopewell, NY	57
Babcock Gershom	Mountain View Cem, New Concord, Columbia Co, NY	72
Babcock Gershom	New Concord, Columbia Co, NY	42
Babcock Henry	Fam Cem, rd to Watch Hill, Westerly, RI	35
Babcock Henry	Mastuxet Cem, Watch Hill Rd, Westerly, RI	48
Babcock Henry Col	Westerly, RI	15
Babcock Ichabod	Lebanon Spring Cem, New Lebanon, Columbia Co, NY	72
Babcock James	Mastuxet, Westerly, RI	35
Babcock James	Westerly, RI	15
Babcock James	Westerly, RI	48
Babcock Jeremiah	Fish farm, Riverside Drive, Augusta, ME	40
Babcock Jonas	New Cem, Northborough, MA	56
Babcock Jonas	Westford Ch Cem, Westford, Otsego Co, NY	74
Babcock Jonathan	Bemus Point Cem, Ellery, Chautauqua Co, NY	62
Babcock Jonathon	Grave obliterated, Cincinnatus, Cortland Co, NY	36
Babcock Joseph	Milton Cem, Milton, MA	46
Babcock Joshua	Westerly, RI	48
Babcock Joshua	Westerly, RI	15
Babcock Lemuel	Old Milton Cem, Milton, MA	47
Babcock Malachi	West Cem, Sherborn, MA	74
Babcock Nathan	Milton Cem, Milton, MA	46
Babcock Nathaniel	Farm Cem, nr Dublin, OH	56
Babcock Nathaniel Sgt	Miner Cem, North Stonington, CT	31

Babcock Oliver	Mastuxet, Westerly, RI	35
Babcock Oliver	Stonington Cem, Stonington, CT	56
Babcock Paul	Westerly, RI	15
Babcock Paul	Westerly, RI	48
Babcock Reuben	Brookside Cem, Barberville, Rensselaer, NY	41
Babcock Reuben	New Cem, Northborough, MA	56
Babcock Samuel	Groff Cem, Westford, Otsego Co, NY	71
Babcock Simon	Scoville, Lebanon, CT	56
Babcock William A	Goodrich farm, nr Red Rock, Columbia Co, NY	42
Baber James	Fam Cem, Edwardsville, AL	59
Babin Joseph	St Martin of Tours Cath Ch Cem, St Martinville, LA	74
Babit William	Monroe Center Bur Gr, Monroe, CT	34
Bachelder Jethro	Loudon, NH	56
Bacheller Theophilus	Old Western Cem, Lyon, MA	55
Bacheller Theophilus	Western Cem, West Lynn, MA	56
Bachellor Nathaniel	Old Cem, East Kingston, NH	56
Bachelor Enoch	North Main St Cem, Upton, MA	46
Bachelor James	Western Cem, West Lynn, MA	56
Bachert Jacob	Ben Salem, Mantz, PA	49
Bachert Jonathan	Ben Salem, Mantz, PA	49
Bachman Frederick	Zion's Stone Ch Cem, Kreidersville, Northampton Co, PA	40
Bachman George	Burgh Cem, Fayette, NY	15
Bachman Jacob Jr	Lowhill Ch Cem, Lowhill Twp, Lehigh Co, PA	40
Bachman Jacob Sr	Lowhill Ch Cem, Lowhill Twp, Lehigh Co, PA	40
Bachman Johannes	Old Cem, Freidensville, Lehigh Co, PA	40
Bachman Johannes	Saucon Mennonite Cem, Coopersburg, Lehigh Co, PA	40
Bachman Nicholas	Lowhill Ch Cem, Lowhill Twp, Lehigh Co, PA	40
Bachman Nicholas	Lowhill Ch Cem, Lowhill Twp, Lehigh Co, PA	40
Back John	Nr Simpson Chapel, Gosport, Monroe Co, IN	23
Back John	Old Stimson Chapel Cem, Monroe Co, IN	62
Backenstose Jacob	Shirks UMC Cem, East Hanover Twp, Lebanon Co, PA	83
Backus Andrew Maj	[no cem named]	15
Backus Ebenezer	Old Cem, Cazenovia, Madison, NY	56
Backus Elijah	Norwich Town Cem, Norwich, CT	18
Backus Ozias	[no cem named], CT	20
Backus Samuel	[no cem named], OH	26
Backus Timothy Capt	Cleveland Yard, Canterbury Twp, CT	22
Bacon Andrew	Bapt Cem, York St, Salem, NJ	26
Bacon Andrew	Salem Cem, Haddonfield, NJ	51
Bacon Asa	Peabody Cem, Adam's estate, Canaan, Columbia Co, NY	79
Bacon Benjamin	Ye Olde Bur Gr, Bedford, MA	55
Bacon Benjamin Col	Cleveland Yard, Canterbury Twp, CT	22
Bacon Darius	East Woodstock, CT	15
Bacon Darius	East Woodstock Cem, Woodstock, CT	55
Bacon Ebenezer	Attleboro, MA	55
Bacon Ebenezer	Bacon Hill Cem, Northumberland, Saratoga Co, NY	78
Bacon Ebenezer	Bacon Hill Cem, Saratoga, Saratoga Co, NY	76
Bacon Ebenezer	Mount Hope, North Attleboro, MA	56
Bacon Edward	Unit Cong Ch Cem, Barnstable, MA	55
Bacon Edward	Unit Cong Ch Cem, Barnstable, MA	55
Bacon Elias	Wrentham, MA	53
Bacon Ephriam	Pratt Dist Yard, Southbridge, MA	29
Bacon George	Brownhelm, OH	15
Bacon George	Brownhelm Cem, Lorain Co, OH	34
Bacon George	Brownhelm Cem, Lorain Cem, OH	56
Bacon Isaac	Unit Cong Ch Cem, Barnstable, MA	55
Bacon Jabez Jr	South Woodbury Cem, Woodbury, CT	55
Bacon James	Brimfield Center Cem, Brimfield, MA	55
Bacon Jeremiah	Dover Cem, Dover, MA	46
Bacon Jeremiah	Old Pine Ridge Cem, Hancock, NH	32
Bacon John	Arlington Cem, Arlington, MA	51

Bacon John	Needham, MA 50
Bacon John	Randolph Center Cem, Randolph, Orange Co, VT 72
Bacon John	St Paul's Ch Cem, Augusta, GA 16
Bacon John	Stockbridge Cem, Stockbridge, MA 47
Bacon Jonathan	Felchville, Natick, MA 56
Bacon Joseph	Center Cem, Peru, MA 52
Bacon Josiah	Anson, ME 15
Bacon Josiah	Groveland Cem, Bradford, MA 55
Bacon Josiah	Under Bunker Hill monument, Boston, MA 55
Bacon Josiah Sr	Bunker Hill monument, Charlestown, MA 55
Bacon Lemuel	Bemus Point Cem, Ellery, Chautauqua Co, NY 62
Bacon Nathaniel	Briggs Cem, Malta, Saratoga Co, NY 76
Bacon Nathaniel	Keeney Settlement Cem, Cuyler, Cortland Co, NY 36
Bacon Oliver	South Natick Ch, Natick, MA 56
Bacon Oliver Lt	Old Center Cem, Jaffrey, NH 37
Bacon Orris	Unit Cong Ch Cem, Barnstable, MA 55
Bacon Philo	East Cem, Whately, Hampshire Co, MA 55
Bacon Reuben	Ye Olde Bur Gr, Bedford, MA 55
Bacon Richard	Ferncliffe Cem, Springfield, OH 55
Bacon Richard Capt	Old Betts plantation, nr Madison, Madison Co, AL 15
Bacon Samuel	Groveland Cem, Bradford, MA 55
Bacon Samuel	Stillwater Union Cem, Stillwater, NY 41
Bacon Silas	Dover Cem, MA 48
Bacon Solomon	Waterville Cem, Waterville, Oneida Co, NY 55
Bacon Thomas	Bedford Cem, Bedford, MA 53
Bacon Thomas	Old Bedford Cem, MA 52
Bacon William	Ancient Cem, West Boxford, MA 29
Bacon William	Barnard, Sheffield, MA 56
Bacon William	Cedar Grove Cem, Patchogue, NY 34
Bacon William	Howlett Hill Cem, Onondaga, Onondaga Co, NY 75
Bacon William Jr	South Natick Ch, Natick, MA 56
Bacon William Lt	South Walpole Cem, Walpole, MA 45
Bacot Samuel	Fam Cem, McIver Rd, E of Darlington, SC 73
Badger Henry	Becket Center Cem, Becket, MA 56
Badger John Dr	Dell Park, Pond St, Natick, MA 56
Badger Joseph	Old Cem, Gilmanton, NH 56
Badger Joseph	Smith Mtg Hs Cem, Gilmanton, NH 32
Badger Joseph Rev	Perrysburg Cem, Maumee, Wood Co, OH 34
Badger Stephen	Kingston Plains Cem, Kingston, NH 30
Badgley Anthony	Pres Ch Cem, Westfield, NJ 76
Badgley James	Pres Ch Cem, Westfield, NJ 76
Badgley James	Westfield Cem, Westfield, NJ 24
Badlam Samuel	North Weymouth Cem, North Weymouth, MA 62
Badlam Samuel	Old North Cem, North Weymouth, MA 50
Badlam Stephen	North Dorchester Bur Gr, Boston, MA 55
Badlam William	Dedham, MA 56
Badley Anthony	Dewitt Cem, Dewitt, Onondaga Co, NY 63
Baer Adam	Muskingum Co, OH 29
Baer Henry	German Ref Ch Cem, Rt 40, Frederick, Frederick Co, MD 77
Bag Joseph	Cem betw Pittsfield & Williamstown, Lanesborough, MA 55
Bagby John	Fairview Pres Ch Cem, nr Lawrenceville, Gwinnett Co, GA 62
Bagby John Sgt	Barren Co, KY 45
Bagg Aaron	Ashleyville Center, West Springfield, MA 15
Bagg Aaron	Lanesboro Cem, MA 26
Bagg Daniel Jr	Mechanic St, Westfield, MA 56
Bagg John Dea	Ashleyville Center, West Springfield, MA 15
Bagg Oliver	Ashleyville Center, West Springfield, MA 15
Bagg Thomas	Ashleyville Center, West Springfield, MA 15
Baggerly David	Bailey Cem, nr Statesville, Iredell Co, NC 76
Baggerly Henry	Phelps, Ontario Co, NY 56
Baggley Anthony	Dewitt Cem, Dewitt, NY 32

Bagley Asher	Old Union Cem, Benton, Saline Co, AR 79
Bagley Enoch	Troy Memorial Cem, Troy, ME 31
Bagley Joshua	Town Cem, Newton, NH 32
Bagley Josiah	Green River Cem, Hillsdale, Columbia Co, NY 79
Bagley Josiah	Riverside Cem, Egremont, MA 56
Bagley Thomas	Amesbury, MA 56
Bagley Winthrop	Thornton Cem, Thornton, NH 36
Bagnell Richard	Burial Hill, Plymouth, MA 56
Bagwell John Daniel	Sweetwater Prim Bapt Ch Cem, 7 mi fr Lawrenceville, GA 34
Bailey Aaron	Pautipaug Cem, CT 18
Bailey Abijah	Old Parish Cem, MA 47
Bailey Adams	Forest Hills Cem, Boston, MA 46
Bailey Amherst	Old Cem, Berlin, MA 56
Bailey Amos	West Swanzey Cem, Swanzey, NH 35
Bailey Andrew	Churchyard, Hollis, NH 39
Bailey Ann Hennis T	Tu-Endie-Wei State Park, Point Pleasant, WV 50
Bailey Benjamin	Chesterfield, VA 56
Bailey Benjamin	Old Cem, Berlin, MA 56
Bailey Benjamin	West Parish Cem, West Haverhill, MA 52
Bailey Caleb	Central Bur Gr, Cohasset, MA 51
Bailey Caleb	Cromwell Upper House, CT 27
Bailey Callum	2 mi E of Oleoak, Depp farm, Barren Co, KY 45
Bailey Christopher	Lemington, VT 35
Bailey Daniel	Churchyard, Hollis, NH 39
Bailey Daniel Jr	Churchyard, Hollis, NH 39
Bailey David	Woodlawn Cem, Nashua, NH 45
Bailey David	Woodlawn Cem, Nashua, NH 40
Bailey Devoue	Fam bur gr, Mahopac, Westchester Co, NY 76
Bailey Dudley	West Dummerston, VT 17
Bailey Edmund	Poland, ME 18
Bailey Elijah	Dodd Mill Cem, Hague, Warren Co, NY 75
Bailey Elijah	Starr Cem, Stonington, CT 15
Bailey Elisha	Clear Springs Meth Ch, nr Hwy 80, Russell Springs Rd, KY 50
Bailey Enoch	Vesper Cem, Tully, Onondaga Co, NY 78
Bailey Ezakiel	Rowley Cem, Essex, MA 48
Bailey Henry	New Cem, Waterford, Saratoga Co, NY 76
Bailey Isaac	Old Center Cem, Jaffrey, NH 37
Bailey Jacob	Oxbow, VT 56
Bailey James	North East Cem, Wolcott, CT 57
Bailey James	North-East Cem, Wolcott, CT 56
Bailey James	Trumbull, Lebanon, CT 56
Bailey James B	Pres Ch Cem, Somers, NY 35
Bailey Jared	His farm, Center Twp, Guernsey Co, OH 34
Bailey Jeremiah	West Parish Cem, West Haverhill, MA 52
Bailey Jesse	Caroline Grove, Caroline, NY 31
Bailey Joel	Churchyard, Hollis, NH 39
Bailey John	Cong Ch Cem, Hanover Center, MA 53
Bailey John	Grammar School part, Pottsville, PA 49
Bailey John	Howes Corner, Turner, ME 29
Bailey John	Old Bapt Cem, Montgomery Co, OH 56
Bailey John	Rowley Cem, Essex, MA 48
Bailey John	Rural Cem, Poughkeepsie, Dutchess Co, NY 70
Bailey John	Rush Branch Ch Yard, moved to Buffalo Cem, Stanford, KY 33
Bailey John	South Bluefield, WV 30
Bailey John	South Bluefield, WV 29
Bailey John	Sterling Village, Sterling, NY 56
Bailey John	Turner, ME 18
Bailey John Capt	Bath, ME 39
Bailey John Capt	Old Bur Hill, Marblehead, MA 36
Bailey John Esq	St Paul's Ch Cem, New York City, New York Co, NY 78
Bailey Jonas	Old Cem, Sterling, MA 63

Abstract of Graves of Revolutionary Patriots

Bailey Jonathan	Old Cem, Sterling, MA 56
Bailey Jonathan	Second West Parish Cem, Haverhill, MA 31
Bailey Jonathan Jr	Groveland Cem, Bradford, MA 55
Bailey Joseph	Ellsworth Cem, Sharon, Litchfield Co, CT 66
Bailey Joseph	Grave obliterated, Virgil, Cortland Co, NY 36
Bailey Joseph	Pottsdum, St Lawrence Co, NY 56
Bailey Joseph	West Greenwich Cem, West Greenwich, RI 59
Bailey Joshua	Old Cem, Hopkinton, Merrimack Co, NH 27
Bailey Lewis	Riverview Cem, Aurora, Dearborn Co, IN 72
Bailey Luther	1st Cong Ch Cem, Hanover Center, MA 54
Bailey Moses Lt	West Parish Bur Gr, Andover, MA 26
Bailey Nathaniel	Minot, ME 18
Bailey Oliver	Granville Cem, PA 17
Bailey Oliver	Granville Center Cem, Rt 514, Bradford Co, PA 68
Bailey Peleg	Old Townsend Cem, Brewster Hill, SE Putnam Co, NY 57
Bailey Richard	At head of Beaver Pond Spring, Mercer Co, WV 73
Bailey Richard	Bailey Hill Cem, North Groton, NH 35
Bailey Richard	East Road Cem, VT 20
Bailey Richard	Glasgow Mem Cem, Glasgow, Barren Co, KY 73
Bailey Richard	South Bluefield, WV 30
Bailey Richard	South Bluefield, WV 29
Bailey Robert	Arnold farm, W of Spencer Corners, East Greenwich, RI 39
Bailey Robert	Fairview Cem, Adams Twp, Green Co, WI 29
Bailey Robert	Fam Cem, Bailey Brook, East Greenwich, RI 37
Bailey Robert	Middle Octoraro Pres Ch, Lancaster Co, PA 38
Bailey Samuel	Bunker Hill, Charlestown, MA 47
Bailey Samuel	Fam Cem, Greenfield, Saratoga Co, NY 78
Bailey Samuel	Old Pres Cem, Springfield, NJ 50
Bailey Samuel	Old Townsend Cem, Brewster Hill, SE Putnam Co, NY 57
Bailey Samuel	Pine Cem, West Lebanon, NH 27
Bailey Samuel	Village Cem, North Milford, ME 30
Bailey Seth	Cong Ch Cem, Hanover Center, MA 53
Bailey Shuball	Old Cem, Sterling, MA 56
Bailey Silas	New Cem, Northborough, MA 56
Bailey Silas	Old Cem, Berlin, MA 56
Bailey Silas Col	Cem, Perry, Lake Co, OH 34
Bailey Silas Col	Perry, OH 26
Bailey Solomon	Bartlett Bur Gr, Plymouth, NH 16
Bailey Solomon Lt	River Road Cem, Piermont, NH 32
Bailey Stephen	Old Cem, Berlin, MA 56
Bailey Thomas	Ebenezer Ch Cem, SC 17
Bailey Timothy	Newport Cem, Newport, RI 48
Bailey Timothy	Old Cem, Berlin, MA 56
Bailey Ward	Lemington, VT 35
Bailey William	Old Hill, Newburyport, MA 56
Bailey William	West Parish Cem, Andover, MA 55
Baily –	Massacred nr mouth of Lechry Creek, Dearborn Co, IN 24
Baily Cyrus Capt	Black Cem, VT 20
Baily Gilbert	Quaker Ch Cem, Peach Lake, N Salem, Westchester Co, NY 57
Baily Silas	Bolton Cem, MA 48
Bain Daniel	Franklin Co, IL 26
Bain James	Old Pioneer Cem, Bellbrook, OH 56
Baird Abijah	North Harpersfield, Schoharie Co, NY 71
Baird Absolom	Old Cem, Washington Co, PA 38
Baird Adam	Olney Cem, Gaston Co, NC 49
Baird Azariah	Old Kingsboro Cem (grave lost), nr Gloversville, NY 16
Baird David	Lebanon Cem, nr Indianola, Vermilion Co, IL 15
Baird David	Lebanon Cem, Indianapolis, IL 56
Baird David	Old Tennent Ch Cem, Tennent, NJ 47
Baird George	Springfield Cem, Albrecht Ave, Summit Co, OH 53
Baird George	Springfield Twp, Summit Co, OH 15

Baird George	White farm, Springfield Twp, Summit Co, OH 34
Baird George	White farm, Summit Co, OH 45
Baird James	Olney Cem, York Rd, Gaston Co, NC 56
Baird John	Bethel Cem, York Co, SC 56
Baird John	Guernsey Co, OH 53
Baird John	Muskingum Co, OH 56
Baird John	Old Neshanic Ref Cem, Frankfort, NJ 47
Baird John	Old Cem, sect E #190, Washington Co, PA 38
Baird John	Pres Ch Cem, Basking Ridge, NJ 47
Baird John	Pres Ch Cem, Basking Ridge, NJ 74
Baird Thomas	Upper Indiana Cem, Knox Co, IN 72
Baird William	Asbury Chapel, 8 mi NE of Springfield, Clark Co, OH 34
Baird William	Dixon-Wilson Cem, Mentz, Cayuga Co, NY 65
Baird William	Dunnston Cem, PA 21
Baird William	Fam Cem, 2 mi E of Russellville, Brown Co, OH 55
Baird William	Nr Russellville, OH 15
Baird William Jr	Dunnstown Meth Cem, Lock Haven, PA 56
Bake John	Bapt Cem, 2 mi W of Newton, Fountain Co, IN 25
Bake John	Bapt Cem, Richland Twp, Fountain Co, IN 72
Bakeman Daniel F	Olean, NY 15
Bakeman Daniel F	Sandusky Cem, Sandusky, NY 32
Bakeman Henry	Barnes Cem, Fulton, NY 30
Baker Abijah	Owasco Rural Cem, Owasco, NY 56
Baker Abner	Woodlawn Cem, Norwalk, OH 56
Baker Abner	Woodlawn Cem, Norwalk, OH 15
Baker Abraham	Hayground Cem, Bridgehampton, Long Island, NY 35
Baker Abraham	North End Cem, Easthampton, Long Island, NY 35
Baker Allen	County Road, Ipswich, MA 56
Baker Amos	Old Cem, Lincoln, MA 55
Baker Anthony	Queen Ann Rd Cem, Harwich, MA 49
Baker Asa	County Road, Ipswich, MA 56
Baker Beal	Nr Gainesville, Hall Co, GA 35
Baker Benjamin	Blairs Cem, Campton, NH 36
Baker Benjamin	[no cem named], NY 39
Baker Benjamin S	Market St Cem, Boston, MA 46
Baker Bradford	Cong Ch Cem, Marshfield, MA 50
Baker Charles	Fam Cem, nr Pine Log & Rydal, GA 72
Baker Charles	Marshfield, MA 53
Baker Cornelius	Old Cem, Wenham, MA 55
Baker Cornelius	Pres Ch Cem, Rahway, NJ 76
Baker Daniel	Ancient Bur Gr, Dedham, MA 48
Baker Daniel	Laurens Cem, Laurens, NY 34
Baker Daniel	Milford Cem, Milford, Otsego Co, NY 72
Baker Daniel	North End Cem, Easthampton, Long Island, NY 35
Baker Daniel	Old Pres, Westfield, NJ 47
Baker Daniel	Pembroke Centre Cem, Pembroke, MA 50
Baker Daniel	Stillwater Cem, Stillwater, NY 41
Baker Daniel	Westfield Cem, Westfield, NJ 24
Baker Daniel Jr	Connecticut Farms Pres Cem, Union, NJ 49
Baker Daniel Sr	Connecticut Farms Pres Cem, Union, NJ 49
Baker David	10 mi fr Lexington, Tates Creek Pike, Fayette Co, KY 46
Baker David	Baker Old Town Cem, Bakersville, NC 65
Baker David	Center Cem, (New Fairmont), Lee, MA 56
Baker David	Centerville Cem, Centerville, NY 32
Baker David	Lee Cem, Lee, MA 15
Baker Edey	Malt Ridge Cem, Malta, NY 41
Baker Edey	Malta Ridge Cem, Malta Ridge, Malta, Saratoga Co, NY 78
Baker Elias	Ten Mile Run Cem, NJ 32
Baker Elijah	Connecticut Farms Pres Cem, Union, NJ 49
Baker Elijah	Dingley Cem, North Duxbury, MA 50
Baker Enoch	Bakers Ground, Ft Ann, NY 56

Baker Ezekiel	Fam Cem, Van Hornesville, Herkimer Co, NY	41
Baker Ezekiel	First Pres Churchyard, Elizabeth, NJ	52
Baker Francis	Cem betw Pittsfield & Williamstown, Lanesborough, MA	55
Baker Frederick	Christ's Churchyard, Compass, PA	71
Baker George	Fam Cem, fam farm, Cheat Neck, WV	24
Baker George	North Cem, Dorchester, MA	46
Baker George F	Old Burns Cem, 6 mi fr Martinsville, Morgan Co, IN	72
Baker George F	Old Burns Cem, 6 mi fr Martinsville, IN	56
Baker Gideon	East Lebanon Cem, Mascoma, NH	27
Baker Henry	Millbrook Cem, Wayne Co, OH	57
Baker Henry	Pres Ch Cem, Westfield, Union Co, NJ	55
Baker Henry	Prospect Hill, Schuylerville, Saratoga Co, NY	78
Baker Herman Sgt	[no cem named], CT	19
Baker Herrington	Oakwood Cem, Baird & Whalen Rd, Penfield, Monroe Co, NY	77
Baker Hilary Jr	Schockoe Hill, Richmond, VA	54
Baker Hollister	Bridge St Cem, Northampton, MA	55
Baker Isaac	Fam Cem, Bristol-Abington Rd, VA	37
Baker Jabez	Dover Cem, Dedham, MA	55
Baker Jacob	Cem betw Pittsfield & Williamstown, Lanesborough, MA	55
Baker Jacob	Greenbush Pres Ch Cem, Blauvelt, Rockland Co, NY	78
Baker Jacob	Lawrenceville Cem, Lawrenceville, Clark Co, OH	58
Baker Jacob	Sipesville, Somerset Co, PA	55
Baker James	Cross Creek Cem, Fayetteville, Cumberland Co, NC	80
Baker James	Fam Cem, Edwardsville, AL	60
Baker James	Fam Cem, Stillwater, Sullivan Co, NY	42
Baker James	Fam Cem, Yellow Meeting House, Mechanicville, NY	41
Baker James	North Cem, Dorchester, MA	46
Baker James	North St Cem, Auburn, NY	41
Baker James	North St Cem, Auburn, NY	15
Baker James Jr	South Cem, Dorchester, MA	46
Baker Jeremiah	Cem, nr railroad, South Dennis, MA	50
Baker Jeremiah	Rockland Cem, Scituate, Providence Co, RI	31
Baker Jeremiah Sr	Canisteo Twp Cem, Steuben Co, NY	57
Baker Jethro	St Mary Anne's Cem, North East, MD	51
Baker Joel	Van Buren plot, Volney, NY	30
Baker John	Center Cem, Westhampton, MA	53
Baker John	County Road, Ipswich, MA	56
Baker John	Fam Cem, The Flats, Morgan Dist, Monongalia Co, WV	40
Baker John	Frisbie Cem, Yankeetown, Warrick Co, IN	58
Baker John	North Cem, Dorchester, MA	46
Baker John	West Hoosick, Rensselaer Co, NY	33
Baker John	Wilmington Cem, Hogan Twp, Dearborn Co, IN	78
Baker John Capt	Zion Cem, Bargaintown, NJ	23
Baker John Jr	Asbury Cem, Tompkins Co, NY	36
Baker John Samuel	Cem, fam farm, Day St, nr Keedysville, Washington Co, MD	51
Baker Johnathan	Pentucket Cem, Haverhill, MA	28
Baker Jonadab	Center Cem, Marlboro, NH	38
Baker Jonas	Great Neck Hill Cem, Killingly, Windham Co, CT	62
Baker Jonas	Old Village Cem, Lancaster, NH	37
Baker Jonathan	Four Corners Cem, Sullivan, NH	39
Baker Jonathan I	Pres Ch Cem, Westfield, NJ	76
Baker Jonathan I	Westfield Cem, Westfield, NJ	24
Baker Jonothan Sr	Cedar Grove Cem, Patchogue, NY	34
Baker Joseph	Gardner's Neck Rd, Swansea, MA	54
Baker Joseph	Mountain View Cem, Weld, Franklin Co, ME	83
Baker Joseph	River Road Cem, Bow, NH	32
Baker Joseph	South Yard, Brooklyn, CT	30
Baker Joshua	Colesville Cem, Colesville, Broome Co, NY	78
Baker Joshua	Rheuben Steven Cem, Greenville, NY	58
Baker Josiah	1st Parish Cem, Rochester, MA	58
Baker Josiah Jewett	Three Bridges, East Haddam, CT	56

Baker Judah	Christian Ch, Endfield Center, NY 31
Baker Jurdah Sr	Yarmouth Cem, MA 48
Baker Levi	Kirkland Avenue Cem, Clinton, Oneida Co, NY 79
Baker Lewis	Jackson farm Cem, Marcellus, Onondaga Co, NY 78
Baker Lewis	Parsippany Cem, Parsippany, NJ 30
Baker Lewis	Vail Cem, Parsippany, NJ 51
Baker Matthias	Pres Ch Cem, Rahway, NJ 76
Baker Melyn	Enon Cem, ¼ mi NE of Enon, Clark Co, OH 55
Baker Michael Capt	Brock's Gap, Rockingham Co, VA 34
Baker Michael Jr	Hood's Cem, Germantown, PA 20
Baker Michael Sr	Hood's Cem, Germantown, PA 20
Baker Milr Lt	Massacred nr mouth of Lechry Creek, Dearborn Co, IN 24
Baker Moses	Connecticut Farms Pres Cem, Union, NJ 49
Baker Moses Hon	Blairs Cem, Campton, NH 36
Baker Nathan	Newman place, 8 mi fr Nicholasville, Jessamine Co, KY 46
Baker Nathaniel	Unit Cong Ch Cem, Barnstable, MA 55
Baker Nathaniel	Village Cem, Walpole, NH 25
Baker Nathaniel	Walpole, NH 16
Baker Oliver	Essex, NY 15
Baker Osmond	Charlestown, NH 15
Baker Preserved	North Cem, Dorchester, MA 46
Baker Remember Jr	In wilderness nr St Johns, Can 56
Baker Reuben	Dennis, MA 55
Baker Reuben	Old Pine Grove Cem, Leominster, MA 47
Baker Reuben	South Dennis, MA 49
Baker Reynolds	Butternut Valley Cem, New Lisbon, Otsego Co, NY 72
Baker Robert	Mt Pleasant Cem, Geneseo, NY 59
Baker Samuel	Duck Creek Cem, Well Fleet, MA 49
Baker Samuel	North Cem, Dorchester, MA 46
Baker Samuel	Old Cem, Berlin, MA 56
Baker Samuel	Old Hixoff Rd, Brook St, Rehoboth, MA 54
Baker Samuel	Path Valley, Franklin Co, PA 56
Baker Samuel	Peak Cem, Westfield Twp, Morrow Co, OH 53
Baker Samuel	Pleasant Valley Cem, Urbana, Steuben Co, NY 73
Baker Samuel	Rockingham Cem, Newfields, NH 25
Baker Samuel	Town Line Cem, Cameron, Steuben Co, NY 57
Baker Samuel Sr	Tobias Cem, Springport, Cayuga Co, NY 57
Baker Sheribiah	North Orange, MA 30
Baker Silas	Mountain View Cem, Weld, Franklin Co, ME 83
Baker Silas	Old Cem, Phillipston, MA 55
Baker Simeon	Sandy Hill Cem, Taunton, MA 48
Baker Snow	Fern Hill Cem, #4-R, West Parish, Pembroke, MA 40
Baker Solomon	Freetown Corners Cem, Freetown, Cortland Co, NY 36
Baker Stephen	Wadsworth farm, Rt 9, New Lebanon, Columbia Co, NY 79
Baker Theophilus	Eden Valley Cem, Eden Valley, NY 33
Baker Thomas	Ash Swamp Cem, West Keene, Keene, NH 32
Baker Thomas	Cem on town common, Nelson, NH 35
Baker Thomas	Clifton Cem, Greene Co, OH 56
Baker Thomas	Fam Cem, Alton, NH 29
Baker Thomas	Groton Cem, Groton, MA 55
Baker Thomas	Keene, NH 56
Baker Thomas	North End Cem, Easthampton, Long Island, NY 35
Baker Thomas	Old South Cem, Ipswich, MA 48
Baker Thomas Capt	Grove St Cem, Upton, MA 46
Baker Thomas M	First Cem, Upton, Worcester Co, MA 68
Baker Timothy	Hawley Cem, Hawley, MA 46
Baker Timothy	Readington Cem, NJ 32
Baker Timothy	South Dennis, MA 49
Baker Timothy	Yarmouth Cem, MA 48
Baker Timothy Jr	Westwood, MA 55
Baker Timothy Sr	Westwood, MA 55

Baker Waterman	Brown Cem, Berkshire, NY 34
Baker William	1st Parish Cem, Rochester, MA 58
Baker William	Evergreen Cem, Marion, MA 59
Baker Ziba	Walpole Plain Cem, Walpole, MA 45
Bakersville William	Lombardy Grove Cem, Mecklenburg Co, VA 73
Balard Philip Sgt	North Cem, Gill, MA 34
Balch Amos	Bedford Co, TN 24
Balch Amos Sgt	[no cem named], TN 15
Balch Benjamin Rev	East Cem, Barrington, NH 31
Balch Caleb Maj	Cem on Hill, Range Rd, Windham, NH 26
Balch Caleb Maj	Hill Cem, Windham, NH 27
Balch Caleb Maj	Wind Haven, NH 26
Balch David	Old Topsfield (Pine Grove) Cem, Topsfield, MA 55
Balch David 3rd	Old Topsfield (Pine Grove) Cem, Topsfield, MA 55
Balch Hezekiah	Johnson Cem, Sullivan Co, IN 24
Balch Hezekiah James	Poplar Tent Pres Cem, Cabarrus Co, NC 72
Balch James	Mann Cem, Turman Twp, Sullivan Co, IN 72
Balch John	Amber Cem, Otisco, Onondaga Co, NY 75
Balch John	Old Bur Gr, Arlington, MA 56
Balch Jonathan	Second Cem, North Main St, West Hartford, CT 55
Balch Joseph	Johnstown Cem, Johnstown, NY 63
Balch Joseph Dea	West Hartford, CT 38
Balch Robert	New Boston Cem, New Boston, NH 48
Balch Roger	Old Topsfield (Pine Grove) Cem, Topsfield, MA 55
Balch Stephen Bloomer	Oak Hill Cem, Georgetown, DC 32
Balch Thomas	Hurricane Cem, Keene, NH 32
Balcolm Daniel	Briggs Corner Cem, MA 15
Balcom Asahel	Old Cem, Sudbury, MA 56
Balcom Bezaleel	Douglas Center, MA 16
Balcom David	Douglas Center, MA 16
Balcom David	Douglas Cem, MA 48
Balcom John	Douglas Center, MA 16
Balcom John	Douglass Center Cem, Douglass, MA 45
Balcom John	Old Douglass Cem, Douglass, MA 46
Balcom Jonas	Old Sudbury Center Cem, Sudbury, MA 55
Balcom Micah Jr	Hague Cem, Warren Co, NY 70
Balcom Samuel	Douglas Center, MA 16
Balcome Samuel	Douglass Center Cem, Douglass, MA 45
Baldridge Daniel	Parr Road Cem, Sharon, Weakley Co, TN 81
Baldridge John	Haynes Cem, nr Scribner Mill, Maury Co, TN 73
Baldridge William Rev	Cherry Fork Cem, Cherry Fork, Adams Co, OH 55
Baldwin Aaron	Pres Cem, Orange, NJ 32
Baldwin Aaron	Sibbes Hill, Branford, CT 56
Baldwin Aaron	Westford Cem, Westford, Otsego Co, NY 82
Baldwin Abel	Newtown Village, Newtown, CT 56
Baldwin Abiel	Hayward Rivenburgh Cem, Durham, Greene Co, NY 78
Baldwin Abner Jr	Old Chapel Bur Gr, Fly Creek, Otsego, Otsego Co, NY 81
Baldwin Abraham	Rock Creek Cem, Washington, DC 44
Baldwin Abraham	Washington, DC 43
Baldwin Amos	Schoharie Cem, Schoharie, Schoharie Co, NY 72
Baldwin Asa	Old Cem, Cong Ch, Spencer, MA 46
Baldwin Ashbel	Morris, CT 17
Baldwin Benjamin	Windham-Ashland Cem, Windham, Greene Co, NY 59
Baldwin Benjamin L	Oak Grove Cem, Morgantown, WV 41
Baldwin Caleb	Newtown Village, Newtown, CT 56
Baldwin Caleb	Oak Hill Cem, Youngstown, Mahoning Co, OH 55
Baldwin Caleb	Pres Cem, Orange, NJ 32
Baldwin Caleb	Youngstown, OH 15
Baldwin Caleb Capt	Old Village Cem, Claremont, NH 50
Baldwin Daniel	Newtown Village, Newtown, CT 56
Baldwin David	Atwater, OH 26

Baldwin David	Bloomfield, NJ	32
Baldwin David	Blue Hill Saddle River, Saddle River, NJ	55
Baldwin David	Carthage, IL	15
Baldwin David	Moss Ridge, Carthage, IL	56
Baldwin David	Newtown Village, Newtown, CT	56
Baldwin David	Old Southfield, New Marlborough, MA	56
Baldwin Eleazer	Pres Cem, Orange, NJ	32
Baldwin Elijah Dr	Elm St Cem, Ansonia, CT	15
Baldwin Elisha	Hughson farm, Lake Mahopac, NY	35
Baldwin Elisha	Royalton Cem, Royalton, Niagara Co, NY	65
Baldwin Ethan	Connecticut Farms Ch Cem, Union, NJ	47
Baldwin Ezekial	Parsippany Cem, Morris Co, NJ	32
Baldwin Henry	Cornwall Cem, Cornwall, CT	15
Baldwin Henry	In woods nr marker, General's Hwy, Anne Arundel Co, MD	52
Baldwin Isaac	Center Cem, New Milford, CT	55
Baldwin Isaac	Pompey Hill Cem, Pompey, Onondaga Co, NY	81
Baldwin Isaac Capt	Old Burying Ground, Medford, MA	46
Baldwin Isaac Dr	Water St Cem, Great Barrington, MA	41
Baldwin Isaac Jr	Riverside Cem, nr Elmira, NY	32
Baldwin Isaac Jr	The Knoll Cem, Lowman, Ashland, Chemung Co, NY	78
Baldwin Isaac Sr	Riverside Cem, nr Elmira, NY	32
Baldwin Isaac Sr	The Knoll Cem, Lowman, Ashland, Chemung Co, NY	78
Baldwin Israel	Center Cem, New Milford, CT	55
Baldwin Jabez	Canton, PA	15
Baldwin Jabez	Pres Cem, Newark, NJ	32
Baldwin Jabez	Sandy Creek Village, Oswego Co, NY	57
Baldwin Jacob	Old Center Cem, Jaffrey, NH	37
Baldwin James	Broad Street, Meriden, CT	56
Baldwin James	East Litchfield, CT	17
Baldwin James	Meth Cem, Seymour, CT	62
Baldwin James	Riverside Cem, Egremont, MA	56
Baldwin Jeduthan Col	Maple St Cem, North Brookfield, MA	17
Baldwin Jeduthan Col	North Brookfield Cem, North Brookfield, MA	45
Baldwin Jeremiah	Pres Cem, Orange, NJ	32
Baldwin Joel	Buckbee's Corners, Monroe Co, NY	33
Baldwin John	Adams Co, OH	56
Baldwin John	Kirker Cem, Liberty Twp, Adams Co, OH	55
Baldwin John	Land's End (Hawleyville), Newtown, CT	56
Baldwin John	Mount Pleasant Cem, Newark, NJ	32
Baldwin John	Old South Deerfield, MA	52
Baldwin John Capt	London, OH	17
Baldwin John N	Connecticut Farms Pres Cem, Union, NJ	49
Baldwin Jonathan	Milford, CT	36
Baldwin Jonathan	[no cem named], OH	26
Baldwin Jonathan	Old bur gr, Orange, NJ	26
Baldwin Jonathan	Riverside Cem, sect B, Waterbury, CT	55
Baldwin Jonathan	Riverside Cem, Waterbury, CT	57
Baldwin Joseph	Riverside Cem, Egremont, MA	56
Baldwin Joshua	Milford Center Cem, New Milford, CT	40
Baldwin Josiah	Mt Pleasant Cem, Port Byron, NY	58
Baldwin Juduthia	Old Cem, Washington Co, PA	38
Baldwin Levi	Old Cem, Spencer, MA	55
Baldwin Lewis	Connecticut Farms Pres Cem, Union, NJ	49
Baldwin Lewis	Pres Cem, Orange, NJ	32
Baldwin Loammi	North Woburn monument, North Brookfield, MA	49
Baldwin Miles	South Cem, Cornwall, VT	65
Baldwin Moses	First Pres Ch Cem, Newark, NJ	26
Baldwin Nahum	Village Cem, New Sharon, Franklin Co, ME	83
Baldwin Nahum Col	Chestnut Hill Cem, Amherst, NH	27
Baldwin Nathan	Baldwin-Hamilton Plot, nr Canaan, Columbia Co, NY	79
Baldwin Nathan	Hamilton-Carpenter Fam Plot, nr Canaan, Columbia Co, NY	48

Baldwin Nathan	Milford Cem, Milford, CT 56
Baldwin Nathaniel	Oakland Co, MI 15
Baldwin Reuben	Colonial Cem, Derby, CT 15
Baldwin Samuel	Back of First Cong Ch, Hanover Center, MA 52
Baldwin Samuel	Center Cem, New Milford, CT 55
Baldwin Samuel	Jewett Heights Cem, Greene Co, NY 68
Baldwin Samuel	[no cem named], OH 26
Baldwin Samuel M D	Oxford, NY 16
Baldwin Samuel W	Cleaver Cem, Marcy, Oneida Co, NY 82
Baldwin Seth C	Briggs Cem betw Middle Line Rd & Rt 20, Saratoga Co, NY 77
Baldwin Silas Dr	Colonial Cem, Derby, CT 15
Baldwin Stephen	Auburn North St Cem, Auburn, Essex Co, NY 69
Baldwin Stephen	Pres Cem, Newark, NJ 32
Baldwin Thaddeus	Colonial Cem, Derby, CT 15
Baldwin Theophelus	Center Cem, New Milford, CT 55
Baldwin Theophilus	Watertown, CT 15
Baldwin Thomas	Connecticut Farms Pres Cem, Union, NJ 49
Baldwin Thomas	Newtown Battlefield, PA 53
Baldwin Thomas	Riverside Cem, nr Elmira, NY 32
Baldwin Thomas	The Knoll Cem, Lowman, Ashland, Chemung Co, NY 78
Baldwin Timothy	Elm St Cem, Ansonia, CT 15
Baldwin Timothy	North Guilford Cem, North Guilford, CT 55
Baldwin Timothy	Old Colonial, Derby, CT 56
Baldwin Timothy Capt	Colonial Cem, Derby, CT 15
Baldwin Tyler	Anne Arundel Co, MD 52
Baldwin Waterman	Riverside Cem, nr Elmira, NY 32
Baldwin William	Billerica, MA 55
Baldwin William	Fam lot, South Canterbury, CT 21
Baldwin William	North Bur Gr, Wayland, MA 56
Baldwin William	Reave Twp, SE of Washington, Daviess Co, IN 72
Baldwin Woolsey	First Pres Ch Cem, Cranbury, NJ 76
Baldwyn Amos	Boardman Center Cem, Boardman Twp, Mahoning Co, OH 55
Baldy Christopher	Bridgeport Cem, Seneca Falls, NY 15
Baldy Paul	Lower Cem, Sunbury, PA 15
Balfour Andrew	Fam bur gr, Randolph Co, NC 49
Ball Abijah	Cem, Broadway, Rt 138, Taunton, MA 55
Ball Adonijah	Old Highland Cem, MA 29
Ball Benjamin	Old Yard, Pine Ridge, Hancock, NH 29
Ball Benjamin	Truxton Cem, Truxton, Cortland Co, NY 36
Ball Charles	Elmwood, Holyoke, MA 56
Ball David	Old bur gr, Orange, NJ 26
Ball Ebenezeer	Townsend, MA 29
Ball Ebenezer	Churchyard, Hollis, NH 39
Ball Ebenezer	Townsend, MA 30
Ball Ebenezer	Townsend Cem, Townsend, MA 47
Ball Ebenezer Jr	Old Bur Gr, Townsend, MA 48
Ball Eli	Whig Center Cem, 1 mi S of Herricksville, Branch Co, MI 19
Ball Eli	Whig Center Cem, Branch Co, MI 22
Ball Eli	Whig Center, Herricksville, Branch Co, MI 56
Ball Elijah	North Orange, MA 30
Ball Elijah	Old Cem, Boylston, MA 52
Ball Eliphalet	Briggs Cem betw Middle Line Rd & Rt 20, Saratoga Co, NY 77
Ball Jacob	Pres Cem, Morristown, NJ 32
Ball James	Newark Old Cem, Newark, VT 38
Ball James	Warwick Village, MA 31
Ball James Jr	St Mary's White Chapel Cem, Lively, Lancaster Co, VA 61
Ball Jeremiah Jr	Old Bur Gr, Townsend, MA 48
Ball John	Concord, ME 15
Ball John	Fam bur gr, Boonton, NJ 29
Ball John	Fam Cem, Arlington, VA 56
Ball John	Old Cem, Northborough, MA 56

Ball John	Old Village Cem, Temple, NH	28
Ball John Phillip	Freidensville Cem, Lehigh Co, PA	40
Ball Jonas	Old Cem, Southboro, MA	50
Ball Joseph	Bloomfield Cem, Bloomfield, Essex Co, NJ	55
Ball Joseph	Williamsburg Cem, Williamsburg, OH	52
Ball Josiah	Brown Cem, Berkshire, NY	34
Ball Josiah Jr	Vernon Grove Cem, Milford, MA	46
Ball Lebbeue	Sweet Rural Cem, N of Pompey Village, Onondaga Co, NY	52
Ball Lebbeus	Sweet Rural Cem, N of Pompey Village, NY	78
Ball Lebbins	Ballstown Springs Cem, Ballstown Springs, MA	56
Ball Lemuel	Maple Grove Cem, Hoosick Falls, Rensselaer Co, NY	36
Ball Moses	Old Highland Cem, MA	29
Ball Moses	Old Highland Cem, Athol, MA	46
Ball Nathan	Center Cem, (New Fairmont), Lee, MA	56
Ball Nathan	Lee Cem, Lee, MA	15
Ball Nathaniel	New Temple Cem, Temple, NH	45
Ball Samuel	Hanover, Morris Co, NJ	32
Ball Samuel	North Yard, Alstead, NH	43
Ball Samuel	Sempronius Cem, Sempronius, Cayuga Co, NY	57
Ball Silas	Center Cem, Leverett, MA	56
Ball Timothy	Connecticut Farms Pres Cem, Union, NJ	49
Ball William	Churchyard, Hollis, NH	39
Ball William	Fauquier Co, VA	56
Ballard Dane	Lebanon Rural Cem, Lebanon, Madison Co, NY	71
Ballard Dane	Lebanon, NY	15
Ballard Daniel	Wendell Cem, Wendell, MA	59
Ballard James	Pres Cem, Orange, NJ	32
Ballard Jeremiah Capt	[no cem named], NJ	24
Ballard John	Boston Common, Boston, MA	45
Ballard John	Glenwood Cem, Homer, Cortland Co, NY	36
Ballard John Murray	Corya farm, S of Vernon, Jennings Co, IN	72
Ballard John V	Old Meth Cem, West Burlington Twp, Bradford Co, PA	72
Ballard Joseph	Old Western Cem, Lynn, MA	55
Ballard Josiah	South Cem, Wendell, MA	30
Ballard Moses	West Cem, Smyrna, NY	16
Ballard Nathan Lt	Old North Bur Gr, Concord, NH	41
Ballard Rufus	Winney Cem, 1 mi E of Grangerville, Saratoga Co, NY	77
Ballard Thomas	Salem Cem, Hwy 521N, Heath Springs, Lancaster Co, SC	76
Ballard Timothy	South Parish Bur Gr, Andover, MA	26
Ballard Tracy	Cem back of fire house, Carmel, Putnam Co, NY	36
Ballard William	Press Peters farm Cem, Jackson Twp, Franklin Co, OH	56
Ballard Zaccheus	Bates Yard, East Thompson, Windham Co, CT	24
Ballentine Ebenezer	Marion Cem, Marion Co, OH	55
Balliet Jacob	Dryland Union Ch Cem, Hecktown, Northampton Co, PA	40
Balliet Stephen	Old Cem, Unionville, Neffs, Lehigh Co, PA	40
Ballou Abraham	Old Cem, Cherry Valley, NY	56
Ballou David	Old Cem, Kingston, RI	56
Ballou Edward	Cumberland, RI	52
Ballou Eleazer	Burrillville Cem, Burrillville, RI	46
Ballou Elias	Center Cem, Peru, MA	52
Ballou Eliel	Fam Cem, Cumberland, RI	56
Ballou James	Cass Cem, Richmond, NH	45
Ballou James	Cass Cem, Richmond, NH	51
Ballou Levi	Old bur gr, Cumberland, RI	45
Ballou Noah	Fam bur gr, East Woonsocket, RI	46
Ballou Samuel	North Monmouth, ME	29
Ballou Samuel	Nr North Monmouth, ME	20
Ballou Seth	Cass Cem, Richmond, NH	45
Balsgrof Heinrich	Swamp Ref Ch Cem, Montgomery Co, PA	59
Balsley Christian	Old Meth Epis Ch Cem, Back Creek, Augusta Co, VA	54
Balzius Gottleib	Old Cem, Tenth & Linden St, Allentown, Lehigh Co, PA	40

Bamford Jacob	Fam Cem, Tilton, NH 31
Bamper Jacob	Methodist Cem, Hohokus, NJ 54
Bancker Flores Maj	Oil Mill Hill, Brunswick, Rensselaer Co, NY 39
Bancker Flores Maj	Priv Cem, nr Miami Beach, Brunswick, Rensselaer Co, NY 41
Bancker James	Farmer's Creek Cem, Metamora, Lapeer Co, MI 79
Bancker James	Oakland Co, MI 15
Bancroft Abel	Groton, MA 55
Bancroft Caleb	Old Village Cem, Temple, NH 28
Bancroft Daniel	Warwick Village, MA 31
Bancroft Ebenezer Col	Old South Cem, Nashua, NH 40
Bancroft Edmund	North Otis Cem, Otis, MA 56
Bancroft Edmund	Pepperell Cem, Pepperell, MA 56
Bancroft Enoch	West Center Cem, Granville, Hampden Co, MA 63
Bancroft Ephraim	West Torrington Cem, Torrington, CT 55
Bancroft James	Central Bur Gr, Boston Common, MA 55
Bancroft James	Laurel Hill, Reading, MA 49
Bancroft James	Old Cem, Lynnfield Center, MA 55
Bancroft John	Columbia St Cem, W of Central Park, Springfield, OH 55
Bancroft Jonathan	Old South Cem, Nashua, NH 30
Bancroft Jonathan	The Old Cem, Gardner, MA 33
Bancroft Jonathan	The Old Cem, Gardner, MA 46
Bancroft Jonathan	Walton, Pepperell, MA 56
Bancroft Joseph	Dwinnelln Cem, Millbury, MA 48
Bancroft Joseph	Laurel Hill, Reading, MA 49
Bancroft Kendall	Old South Cem, Montague, MA 45
Bancroft Lemuel	West Center Cem, Granville, Hampden Co, MA 63
Bancroft Nathan	Center Cem, Phillipston, MA 55
Bancroft Noadiah	West Torrington Cem, Torrington, CT 55
Bancroft Oliver	Newtown Village, Newtown, CT 56
Bancroft Samuel	Laurel Hill, Reading, MA 49
Bancroft Samuel	Pond Cem, Granville, MA 53
Bancroft Samuel	West Center Cem, Granville, Hampden Co, MA 63
Bancroft Timothy	Cem on town common, Nelson, NH 35
Bancroft William	Groton, MA 55
Bandy Thomas	Fam Cem, La Guardo, Wilson Co, TN 67
Bane Ellis	Lazear Cem, Blair farm, Richhill Twp, Greene Co, PA 56
Banfield James	King's Cem, South Hill, NY 31
Banghart Andrew Sr	Cem, Columbia, Warren Co, NJ 30
Banghart Andrew Sr	Ramsaysburg, Warren Co, NJ 35
Banghart Andrew Sr	Ramsayburg, Warren Co, NJ 36
Bangs Allen	Cem, nr railroad, South Dennis, MA 50
Bangs Barnabas Sr	Gorham Cem, ME 48
Bangs Elkanah	Died on prison ship Jersey, MA 45
Bangs Isaac	First Parish Unitarian Cem, Brewster, MA 46
Bangs John	Old South Cem, Montague, MA 47
Bangs John	Old South Cem, Montague, MA 34
Bangs John	Old South Cem, Montague, MA 33
Bangs Jonathan	Cem, nr railroad, South Dennis, MA 50
Bangs Joshua	1st Parish Ch Cem, Brewster, MA 55
Bangs Nathan	Old South Cem, Montague, MA 34
Bangs Nathan	Old South Cem, Montague, MA 33
Bangs Nathan	Old South Cem, Mantague, MA 57
Bangs Solomon Capt	First Parish Unitarian Cem, Brewster, MA 46
Banister John	Fam Cem, Battersea Estate, Dinwiddie Co, VA 78
Banister Silas	Sheddesville Cem, Brownsville, Windsor Co, VT 55
Banker Abraham	Old Dutch Cem, Kingston, Ulster Co, NY 85
Banker Adolf	Millertown Cem, nr Johnsonville, Rensselaer Co, NY 36
Banker Evert	Old Dutch Cem, Kingston, Ulster Co, NY 85
Banker Frederick	St James, Staatsburgh, Hyde Park, NY 21
Bankes Andrew	Frieden's, New Ringold, PA 49
Banks Benjamin	Greenfield Hill Cem, Fairfield, CT 62

Banks Daniel	Greenfield Hill Cem, Fairfield, CT 62
Banks David	First Pres Ch Cem, Newark, NJ 26
Banks David	Greenfield Hill Cem, Fairfield, CT 62
Banks Ebenezer	Greenfield Hill Cem, Fairfield, CT 62
Banks Ebenezer Esq	Greenfield Hill Cem, Fairfield, CT 62
Banks Elijah	Greenfield Hill Cem, Fairfield, CT 62
Banks Eliphalet	Greenfield Hill Cem, Fairfield, CT 62
Banks Gershom	Greenfield Hill Cem, Fairfield, CT 62
Banks Gershom Jr	Greenfield Hill Cem, Fairfield, CT 62
Banks Hezekiah	West Side Cem, Easton, CT 33
Banks Hyatt	Greenfield Hill Cem, Fairfield, CT 62
Banks Isaac	Greenfield Hill Cem, Fairfield, CT 62
Banks James	Town Cem, Roxbury, NH 25
Banks Jesse	Greenfield Hill Cem, Fairfield, CT 62
Banks John	Center Cem, Alstead, NH 43
Banks John	Greenfield Hill Cem, Fairfield, CT 62
Banks John	North Cem, Hinsdale, NH 37
Banks Jonathan	Greenfield Hill Cem, Fairfield, CT 62
Banks Joseph	Greenfield Hill Cem, Fairfield, CT 62
Banks Joshua	Stuarts Corners Cem, NY 41
Banks Nathan	Greenfield Hill Cem, Fairfield, CT 62
Banks Nehemiah	Greenfield Hill Cem, Fairfield, CT 62
Banks Nehemiah Jr	Greenfield Hill Cem, Fairfield, CT 62
Banks Ralph	Coldwater Churchyard, Elbert Co, GA 69
Banks Samuel	St Peter's Cem, Bainbridge, NY 58
Banks Thomas	Daretown Cem, Daretown, NJ 28
Banks William	Putnam Co, IN 16
Bankston Abner	Moore home, southern Butts Co, GA 33
Bankston John	Dyson Fam Cem, nr Amite, Tangipahoa Parish, LA 57
Banning John	Christ Ch Cem, Dover, Kent Co, DE 46
Banta Abraham	South Ch Cem, Rahway, NJ 62
Banta Daniel	Prob farm, Warren Co, OH 55
Banta Dirck	Marcellus, NY 35
Banta Hendrick	South Ch Cem, Bergenfield, NJ 47
Banta Henry	Clark farm, Bourbon Co, KY 24
Banta Henry	Harrington, NJ 47
Banta Johannes	South Ch Cem, Bergenfield, NJ 54
Banta Samuel	South Ch Cem, Bergenfield, NJ 47
Banta Wiert	South Ch Cem, Bergenfield, NJ 47
Bar Jacob	Lowhill Ch Cem, Lowhill Twp, Lehigh Co, PA 40
Barbar John	Copps Hill Cem, Boston, MA 46
Barbar Nathaniel	Copps Hill Cem, Boston, MA 46
Barbau Jean Baptiste Sr	Randolph Co, IL 48
Barbee William	Aban graveyard, Troy, Miami Co, OH 49
Barber Bildad	Nr Syracuse, Onondaga Co, NY 35
Barber Daniel	Barbour Cem, Heddington, NH 63
Barber Daniel	Top Meadow Cem, Simsbury, CT 55
Barber Daniel Lt	New Hedding Camp Ground, Epping, NH 41
Barber David	Center Cem, Barkhamsted, CT 62
Barber David	Palisado Cem, Windsor, CT 55
Barber David Capt	Windsor, CT 15
Barber Elijah	Canton Center Cem, Canton, CT 55
Barber Elisha	Sherborn No 1, Sherborn, MA 56
Barber Ephraim	Center Cem, Barkhamsted, CT 62
Barber Ephraim Lt	Brigham Cem, Marlboro, MA 45
Barber George	Millis, Millis-Medway, MA 56
Barber James	Christ Churchyard, Cooperstown, NY 71
Barber James	Fam homestead, Glen Rock, South Kingston, RI 52
Barber Jared	Humphrey's Hollow Cem, Sheldon Twp, Wyoming Co, NY 64
Barber Jerijah	Palisado Cem, Windsor, CT 55
Barber Jerijah	Palisado Cem, Windsor, CT 55

Barber Jerijah	Windsor, CT	15
Barber Job	Lowly Mills, NY	35
Barber John	Bethel Cem, York Co, SC	56
Barber John	Goodwill Cem, Montgomery, Orange Co, NY	78
Barber John	North Canton Cem, West Simsbury, CT	71
Barber John	Oakwood Cem, Adrian, MI	58
Barber John	Oakwood, Adrian, MI	56
Barber John	Ticonderoga Cem, Ticonderoga, NY	56
Barber John	Warlick Fam Cem, Cleveland Co, NC	49
Barber John Capt	Center Cem, Lyman, NH	26
Barber Joseph	Goodwill Cem, Montgomery, Orange Co, NY	78
Barber Joseph	Pioneer Cem, Strykersville, Wyoming Co, NY	80
Barber Joseph	West Cem, Litchfield, CT	56
Barber Matthew	Brick Schoolhouse, Colrain, MA	55
Barber Nathan Capt	Westerly, RI	15
Barber Nathaniel	Gatch (now Greenlawn) Cem, Milford, Clermont Co, OH	55
Barber Nathaniel	Torringford Cem, Torringford, CT	36
Barber Nathaniel Jr	Copps Hill Bur Gr, Boston, MA	56
Barber Oliver	Sherborn No 1, Sherborn, MA	56
Barber Patrick	Goodwill Cem, Montgomery, Orange Co, NY	78
Barber Peter	Razor Hill Cem, Grafton, NH	38
Barber Reuben	Canton Center Cem, Canton, CT	55
Barber Reuben	Palisado Cem, Windsor, CT	55
Barber Reynolds	Orchard in rear of fam farm, Exeter, RI	47
Barber Rheuben	Fam Cem, Elmira, NY	33
Barber Samuel	Ancient Cem, West Parish, Haverhill, MA	31
Barber Samuel	Huxley Dist, New Marlborough, MA	56
Barber Simeon	Central Cem, Jay, Essex Co, NY	56
Barber Simeon	East Windsor Cem, East Windsor, CT	31
Barber Simeon	Jay Cem, Jay, NY	15
Barber Simeon	New Trenton Cem, Franklin Co, IN	70
Barber Simeon	New Trenton Cem, New Trenton, IN	71
Barber Simeon	Scantic Cem, East Windsor, CT	27
Barber Thomas	Harmony, Warren Co, NJ	39
Barber Thomas	Harmony Pres Cem, Warren Co, NJ	25
Barber Thomas	Palisado Cem, Windsor, CT	55
Barber Thomas	Williamsville Cem, Williamsville, NY	33
Barber Timothy	Grantville Cem, Norfolk, CT	62
Barber Uriah	Kinney Cem, Wallie St, Portsmouth, Scioto Co, OH	55
Barber William	Crandall Cem, East Hollow, NY	70
Barber William	Evergreen Cem, Ledyard, NY	69
Barber William	Evergreen Cem, Scipio, Cayuga Co, NY	57
Barber William Col	Priv Cem, Newbold estate, (no stones), Hyde Park, NY	21
Barbour Mordecai Maj	Beth Salem Cem, Boligee, Greene Co, AL	17
Barbour Solomon	Old Cem, Deer Isle, ME	58
Barbour Thomas	Barbourville, VA	54
Barbur David	Palisado Cem, Windsor, CT	55
Barclay Charles	First Pres Ch Cem, Cranbury, NJ	76
Barclay Hugh	Old Pres Ch Cem, Bedford Co, PA	80
Barclay John	Pres Ch Cem, Fannettsburg, Franklin Co, PA	78
Bard John M D	St James, Staatsburgh, Hyde Park, NY	21
Bard Richard	Church Hill Cem, nr Mercersburg, PA	21
Bard Samuel M D	St James, Staatsburgh, Hyde Park, NY	21
Bard William	Pres Ch Cem, Rocky Springs, PA	20
Bard William	Ricker-Berry Cem, Buckfield, ME	43
Bard William	Rocky Springs Pres Ch Cem, 6 mi fr Chambersburg, PA	19
Barden John	Old Cem, The Green, Middleboro, MA	50
Barden Lemuel Lt	Old Cem, Pawlet, VT	15
Barden Lemuel Lt	Old Mettowee Cem, Pawlet, VT	48
Barden Noah	Old Cem on hill, NH	29
Barden Stephen	Evergreen Cem, Marion, MA	59

Barden Thomas Capt	Bellona Cem, sect 3 lot 42, Bellona, Yates Co, NY 15
Barders Christopher	Spartanburg Cem, Greensfork Twp, Randolph Co, IN 60
Bardwell Ebenezer	Hill Cem, Shelburne, MA 56
Bardwell Giles	East Lawn Cem, Williamstown, MA 33
Bardwell Joseph Sr	South Main Cem, Belchertown, MA 47
Bardwell Noah	West Cem, Whately, Hampshire Co, MA 55
Bardwell Reuben	The Hill Cem, Old Village Rd, Shelburne Center, MA 74
Bardwell Samuel	Taylor Hill Cem, Montague, MA 58
Bardwell Silas	Fam Cem, Wysox, PA 53
Bardwell William	South Vienna Cem, sect B #51, Harmony Twp, Clark Co, OH 55
Barett John	Carmel, Barrett Hill Cem, Delhi, NY 35
Barge Lewis	Cross Creek Cem, Fayetteville, Cumberland Co, NC 80
Barger John	Adams Corners, Westchester Co, NY 41
Bargy Peter	Scripture Cem, Sandy Creek, Oswego Co, NY 76
Barkaloo Harmes	Priv Cem, Brooklyn, NY 38
Barkalow John	Brick Ch Cem, Monmouth Co, NJ 27
Barkalow Stephen	Bethesda Ch Cem, nr Blue Ball, Monmouth Co, NJ 27
Barkalow Stephen	Blue Ball Cem, Adelphia, NJ 30
Barkeloo Harms Lt	Fam Cem, Brooklyn, NY 35
Barkelow John	Kiser's Cem, Luzerne, PA 53
Barkely John	Goodwill Cem, Montgomery, Orange Co, NY 78
Barker Abijah	Antrim, NY 15
Barker Abijah	Gravesville Cem, Russia, NY 70
Barker Asa	Mt Vernon Cem, West Boxford, MA 56
Barker Asa	Stow Cem, MA 48
Barker Barnabas	Mount Pleasant Cem, St Johnsbury, VT 15
Barker Barnabas	Old Cem, Rindge, NH 36
Barker Benjamin	Gumpus Cem, Pelham, NH 34
Barker Benjamin Maj	Cong Ch Bur Gr, Stratham, NH 25
Barker Daniel	Exeter, Rockingham Co, NH 75
Barker David	Acton, MA 55
Barker David Jr	Pine Ridge (Old) Cem, Hancock, NH 36
Barker David Sr	Pine Ridge (Old) Cem, Hancock, NH 35
Barker Ebenezer	Center Cem, Pembroke, MA 58
Barker Ebenezer	Hancock, NH 15
Barker Ebenezer	Old Yard (Pine Ridge) Cem, Hancock, NH 30
Barker Ebenezer	Village Cem, Hancock, NH 29
Barker Eliphalet	Trumbull, Lebanon, CT 56
Barker Ethan	Palisado Cem, Windsor, CT 55
Barker Ethan	Windsor, CT 15
Barker Ezra	Old Cem, Cheshire, MA 45
Barker Francis	Acton, MA 55
Barker Francis	[no cem named], NJ 24
Barker Hezekiah	Old Fredonia Cem, Chautauqua Co, NY 15
Barker Hezekiah	Pioneer Cem, Pomfret, NY 62
Barker Isaac	Ancient Cem, West Boxford, MA 29
Barker Isaac	Old Cem, Middletown, RI 52
Barker Isaac B	Fern Hill Cem, #16-R, West Parish, Pembroke, MA 40
Barker Jairus	Clam River Cem, Sandisfield, MA 56
Barker James	Old Cem, Main Rd, Cheshire, MA 55
Barker Jared	Mamaroneck Cem, back of kindergarten, Mamaroneck, NY 35
Barker Jesse	Clark Bur Gr, Edinburg, NY 70
Barker John	Greenwich Pres Cem, Warren Co, NJ 40
Barker John	Old Bur Gr, Scituate, MA 50
Barker John	Pres Ch Cem, White Plains, NY 36
Barker John	Reed Cem, West Stoddard, NH 27
Barker John 3rd	Ancient Cem, West Boxford, MA 29
Barker John Capt	Mount Pleasant Cem, St Johnsbury, VT 15
Barker John Jr	Ancient Cem, West Boxford, MA 29
Barker John Lt	Old Cem, Rindge, NH 41
Barker John Sgt	Ancient Cem, West Boxford, MA 29

Barker Joseph	Chenoweth Cem, Pleasant Twp, Franklin Co, OH	53
Barker Joseph	Green St, Marblehead, MA	56
Barker Joseph	North Byron Cem, Byron, Genesee Co, NY	83
Barker Joseph	Old fam Cem, nr Georgetwon, Grant Dist, WV	41
Barker Joseph	Woodlawn Cem, Acton, MA	45
Barker Joseph Jr	Acton Cem, Acton, MA	59
Barker Joseph Jr	Augusta Cem, Augusta, Monongalia Co, WV	59
Barker Joseph Jr	Woodlawn Cem, Acton, MA	58
Barker Joshua	Old Plains Cem, Franklin, CT	18
Barker Nathan	Pleasant View Cem, nr Minquamicut, RI	48
Barker Noah	Old Cem, Newport, RI	52
Barker Oliver	Clam River Cem, Sandisfield, MA	56
Barker Peter	Antrim, NH	15
Barker Peter	Barker-Bentley Cem, New Lebanon Twp, Columbia Co, NY	79
Barker Petery	Forest Lawn Cem, Buffalo, NY	33
Barker Philip	Town Cem, Greenland, NH	28
Barker Phineas	First Cem, North Andover, MA	56
Barker Russell	Madison Center, NY	15
Barker Samuel	Christian Ch Cem, Saratoga, NY	32
Barker Samuel	Mamaroneck Cem, back of Kindergarten, Mamaroneck, NY	35
Barker Samuel	North Parish Bur Gr, Andover, MA	26
Barker Samuel Capt	Mount Pleasant Cem, St Johnsbury, VT	15
Barker Samuel Sgt	Ancient Cem, West Boxford, MA	29
Barker Stephen	Ancient Cem, West Boxford, MA	29
Barker Stephen	Village Cem, Methuen, MA	46
Barker Steven	Stowe, MA	56
Barker Thomas	Harmony Ch Cem, Harmony, Warren Co, NJ	40
Barker Thomas	Pres Ch Cem, White Plains, NY	36
Barker William	Acton, MA	55
Barker William	Amenia Bur Gr, 1 mi N of Amenia, Dutchess Co, NY	66
Barker William	Cem on town common, Nelson, NH	35
Barker William	Pres Ch Cem, White Plains, NY	36
Barker William	Quaker Cem, Union Spring, Springport, NY	56
Barker Zebediah	Barker-Tolin Cem, 1½ mi fr Burkesville, IL	59
Barker Zebediah	Randolph Co, IL	48
Barker Zenos	Forest Lawn Cem, Buffalo, NY	33
Barkley George	Calvary Cem, Washington Twp, Clermont, OH	56
Barkley Hugh	Lamington Pres Cem, Somerset Co, NJ	63
Barkley James	Pres Ch Cem, Fearisville, Lewis Co, KY	57
Barkley John	Lamington Pres Cem, Somerset Co, NJ	63
Barkley John	Waxhaw Pres Ch Cem, Lancaster Co, SC	57
Barkley Robert	Parker Hill Cem, Lyman, NH	26
Barkley Samuel	Goodwill Cem, Montgomery, Orange Co, NY	78
Barkley Thomas	Goodwill Cem, Montgomery, Orange Co, NY	78
Barkley William	Thompson farm, Winchester, Clark Co, KY	24
Barksdale Beverly	Cedar View Fam Cem, South Boston, Halifax Co, VA	76
Barksdale Joseph	Cem in Hancock Co, GA	67
Barksdale Peter	Cedar View Fam Cem, South Boston, Halifax Co, VA	76
Barley Thomas	Old Mulkey Mtg Hs Cem, Monroe Co, KY	39
Barley Timothy	Lisbon Cem, Harmony Twp, Clark Co, OH	55
Barlow Abner	Canandaigua Cem, Ontario Co, NY	33
Barlow Abner	Kenosha Cem, WI	29
Barlow Ambrose	Fountain Run, KY	31
Barlow David	Stratford Cem, Fairfield, CT	70
Barlow David Jr	Center Cem, Sherman, CT	68
Barlow Edmund Sr	West Center Cem, Granville, Hampden Co, MA	63
Barlow Jesse	Newport Cem, Rt 1, Philadelphia Co, PA	68
Barlow Jesse	Newport Cem, Newport, RI	59
Barlow John	Kent Hollow Cem, Kent, CT	40
Barlow John Capt	Cong Cem, Stratford, CT	31
Barlow Lemuel	Center Cem, (New Fairmont), Lee, MA	56

Barlow Lemuel	Lee Cem, Lee, MA	15
Barlow Micah	Bungay Cem, Woodstock, CT	55
Barlow Reuben	Center Cem, (New Fairmont), Lee, MA	56
Barlow Samuel	Cem, Sager farm, Virgil-Messengerville Rd, Virgil, NY	36
Barlow Thomas	Chenango Cem, Chenango, Broome Co, NY	78
Barnabe Francis	Zion Luth Ch Cem, Montgomery Co, PA	59
Barnaby Ambrose	Nr Mother's Brook, right hill, Freetown, MA	54
Barnard Benjamin	Harvard Common, Harvard, MA	54
Barnard Benjamin	New Cem, South Hampton, NH	30
Barnard Currier	[no cem named]	16
Barnard Currier	Bartlett Cem, Plymouth, NH	29
Barnard Currier	Cem, Plymouth, NH	49
Barnard David	East Weare Cem, East Weare, NH	33
Barnard David	Hill Cem, Shelburne, MA	56
Barnard David	Woodlawn (North), Acton, MA	56
Barnard Dorus	Old South Cem, Hartford, CT	19
Barnard Ebenezer Capt	Gold St Cem, Old Hartford, CT	19
Barnard Ebenezzer	St Andrews Cem, Bloomfield, CT	55
Barnard Elisha	Colrain Branch Cem, Shelburne, MA	46
Barnard Ephraim	New Cem, Northborough, MA	56
Barnard Grove	Old North Cem, Old Hartford, CT	19
Barnard Isaac	Union Cem, Amesbury, MA	46
Barnard Jacob	Old South Cem, Nashua, NH	30
Barnard Jesse	Windsor Cem, Windsor Twp, Ashtabula Co, OH	56
Barnard Joel	Spring Hill Cem, Marlboro, MA	45
Barnard John	West Parish Cem, Andover, MA	55
Barnard John Capt	Gold St Cem, Old Hartford, CT	19
Barnard John Capt	Union Cem, Amesbury, MA	46
Barnard Jotham	Harvard Cem, Harvard, MA	46
Barnard Jotham	Harvard Common, Harvard, MA	54
Barnard Moses	Windsor, Ashtabula Co, OH	18
Barnard Moses	Windsor, OH	15
Barnard Thomas	Copps Hill Bur Gr, Boston, MA	56
Barnard Thomas	Hillsboro, Fairfield Twp, OH	15
Barnard Thomas	Old Cem, South Hampton, NH	32
Barnard Timothy	Pittsford Cem, Monroe Co, NY	33
Barnard Timothy	Union Cem, Amesbury, MA	46
Barnard Tristram	East Weare Cem, East Weare, NH	33
Barnard William	Edson Corners, Milford, NY	34
Barnes Aaron	Pine Hill, Throop, NY	56
Barnes Abijah	Canaan Center Cem, Canaan, Columbia Co, NY	74
Barnes Abraham	Fam Cem, Chemung Co, NY	32
Barnes Abraham	South Cem, Easthampton, Long Island, NY	35
Barnes Abraham	Warwick Village, MA	31
Barnes Ambrose	Chenango Cem, Chenango, Broome Co, NY	78
Barnes Amos	North Conway Cem, Conway, Carroll Co, NH	77
Barnes Asa	Plantsville, CT	56
Barnes Chesley	Nr Buffalo Creek, NW sect of Rockingham Co, NC	74
Barnes Comfort	Barnes St Cem, Norway, Herkimer Co, NY	58
Barnes Daniel	Portland Cem, Portland, Chautauqua Co, NY	15
Barnes Dimon	Hillside Cem, Cheshire, CT	55
Barnes Dixon	Cong Cem, Cheshire, New Haven Co, CT	24
Barnes Ebenezer	Bloomington, IL	15
Barnes Edward Lt Col	Old Common Bur Gr, Marlboro, MA	45
Barnes Eli	Wilcox Cem, East Berlin, CT	56
Barnes Elisha	Canaan Center Cem, Canaan, Columbia Co, NY	74
Barnes Elisha	Mtg Hs Cem, Henniker, NH	30
Barnes Enoch	Fam bur gr, Wolf Hill Rd, Smithfield, RI	40
Barnes Enos	Marathon Cem, Marathon, Cortland Co, NY	36
Barnes Fortunatus	Old Cem, Berlin, MA	56
Barnes Gamaliel	Colosse Ch Cem, Mexico, Oswego Co, NY	64

Barnes George	St Andrew's Ch, Richmondtown, Staten Island, NY	72
Barnes Isaac	God's Acre Cem, Brutus, NY	69
Barnes Israel	Bristol, CT	54
Barnes Israel	Montville Center Cem, Geauga Co, OH	55
Barnes Israel	Southwest Cem, Canton, CT	15
Barnes Jacob	Bapt Cem, New Market, OH	15
Barnes Jacob	West St Cem, Fair Haven, VT	36
Barnes Jared	North Haven, CT	15
Barnes Jeremiah	West Granville, MA	54
Barnes John	Ramsaysburg, Warren Co, NJ	35
Barnes John	Rockdale, West Stockbridge, MA	56
Barnes John	West Farmington Cem, Trumbull Co, OH	55
Barnes John C	Caton-Meridian, Cato, NY	56
Barnes Jonathan	North Brookfield, MA	51
Barnes Jonathan	North Brookfield Cem, Brookfield, MA	46
Barnes Jonathan	North Haven, CT	56
Barnes Joseph	Derry Rd Cem, Litchfield, NH	26
Barnes Joseph	Village Cem, Orwell, VT	57
Barnes Joseph Dea	Hillcrest Cem, Litchfield, NH	31
Barnes Joseph Dr	Derry Rd Cem, Litchfield, NH	26
Barnes Joseph Dr	Hillcrest Cem, Litchfield, NH	31
Barnes Joshua	North Haven, CT	15
Barnes Josiah	Bristol Cem, Bristol, CT	55
Barnes Lemuel	North Hartford Cem, Hartford, Cortland Co, NY	36
Barnes Levi	Fam bur gr, Wolf Hill Rd, Smithfield, RI	40
Barnes Moses	Cong Cem, Brandon, VT	35
Barnes Moses Capt	Brigham Cem, Marlboro, MA	45
Barnes Orange	Footville, nr Litchfield, CT	17
Barnes Phineas	Oran Cem, Pompey, Onondaga Co, NY	78
Barnes Richard	Danville Cem, Hendricks Co, IN	25
Barnes Richard	East Cem, Danville, Hendricks Co, IN	72
Barnes Robert	Pres Cem, Abington, PA	33
Barnes Samuel	North Haven, CT	56
Barnes Samuel	Pres Ch Cem, Abington, Montgomery Co, PA	55
Barnes Silas	Center Cem, West Stockbridge, MA	49
Barnes Stephen	Center Cem, Sherman, CT	68
Barnes Stephen Jr	Old Plantsville Cem, Plantsville, CT	53
Barnes Theodore	Old Luth & Ref Cem, Martinsburg, WV	32
Barnes Thomas	Community, Weedsport, Throop, NY	56
Barnes Thomas	North Haven Cem, North Haven, CT	56
Barnes Thomas	Sharon Cem, Sharon, Litchfield Co, CT	67
Barnes Timothy	Kirkland Avenue Cem, Clinton, Oneida Co, NY	79
Barnes Timothy	Rockdale, West Stockbridge, MA	56
Barnes William	Main St Cem, Rutland, VT	23
Barnes William	Maple Grove Cem, Fairmont, WV	43
Barnes William	North Main St Cem, Rutland, VT	24
Barnes William	North Main St Cem, Rutland, VT	25
Barnes William	North East (Lindsey), Richmond, MA	56
Barnes William	Unity Pres, Unity Twp, nr Latrobe, Westmoreland Co, PA	56
Barnes William Dea	North End Cem, Easthampton, Long Island, NY	35
Barnet Hugh	Sugar Creek Pres Ch Cem #2, Mecklenburg Co, NC	49
Barnet Moses	Hoosick, nr VT, NY	34
Barnet Nathaniel	Priv Cem, nr Bennington Battlefield, NY	33
Barnet Oliver	Oldwick prop, Hunterdon Co, NJ	63
Barnett Alexander	Fam Cem, Hartford, KY	30
Barnett Joel	Noxubee Co, MS	44
Barnett John	Barnett Shoals, Clarke Co, GA	43
Barnett John	Barnett Shoals, Clarke Co, GA	42
Barnett John	Dayton, OH	26
Barnett John	Fam bur gr, Barnett Shoals, Oconee Co, GA	34
Barnett John	Freeman Cem, nr Edinburg, IN	16

Barnett Joseph	Bank of Rough Creek, Hardin Co, KY	45
Barnett Joseph	West Laurel Hill Cem, Montgomery Co, PA	59
Barnett Nathaniel	Nr Marks Place, Mount Meigs, AL	34
Barnett Robert	Nr Irwinton, Wilkinson Co, GA	24
Barnett William	First Pres Churchyard, Elizabeth, NJ	52
Barnett William	Green County Cem, Green Co, KY	61
Barnett William	Matthews place, Pike Rd, AL	34
Barnett William	Old Graveyard, South Bedford, NH	34
Barney Asa	Kingsbury Cem, Glens Falls, NY	49
Barney Christopher	Thomas Cem, North Swansea, MA	54
Barney Daniel	Summerhill, NY	56
Barney Edward	East Sandy Creek Cem, 1 mi fr Adams post office, NY	54
Barney Israel	Thomas Cem, North Swansea, MA	54
Barney Jabez	Razor Hill Cem, Grafton, NH	38
Barney Jacob	Plain Cem, Taunton, MA	48
Barney Jeffrey A	Laural Glen, Shrewsbury, VT	54
Barney John	Plain Cem, Taunton, MA	48
Barney Jonathan	Newport Cem, Herkimer Co, NY	55
Barney Jonathan	Old Rumford, Newman Ave, Rehoboth, MA	55
Barney Joseph	North Swansea, MA	54
Barney Joseph	Thomas Cem, North Swansea, MA	54
Barney Joseph Jr	Rutland, VT	56
Barney Joseph Sr	Taunton, MA	56
Barney Josiah Jr	Thomas Cem, North Swansea, MA	54
Barney Wheaton	Thomas Cem, North Swansea, MA	54
Barney William	Tylerville Cem, Rutland, Jefferson Co, NY	39
Barney William	Tylerville, NY	16
Barney William	Tylerville, Jefferson Co, NY	15
Barnhart Peter	Mayville Cem, Mayville, Chautauqua Co, NY	76
Barnhill Samuel	Home place, nr Muddy Ford, Scott Co, KY	20
Barnhiser John	Old Union Cem, Waynesboro, PA	21
Barns Asa	Oran Pioneer Cem, Fayetteville, NY	49
Barns Noah	North End Cem, Easthampton, Long Island, NY	35
Barns Seth	North End Cem, Easthampton, Long Island, NY	35
Barnum Azar Capt	South East Cem, South East Twp, Putnam Co, NY	35
Barnum Ezlon	Brookfield, CT	56
Barnum Jehial	Malone Cem, Malone, Franklin Co, NY	77
Barnum John	Ridgeville Center Cem, North Ridgeville, Lorain Co, OH	55
Barnum Joshua Capt	Cem, South East Twp, Putnam Co, NY	35
Barnum Joshua Jr Maj	Cem, South East Twp, Putnam Co, NY	35
Barnum Judge Stephen	Cem, South East Twp, Putnam Co, NY	35
Barnum Moses	Stockbridge Cem, Stockbridge, MA	47
Barnum Stephen	Center Cem, Alford, MA	56
Barnum Stephen	Shoreham, VT	15
Barnum Thomas	Shoreham, VT	15
Barr Adam	Union Star Cem, Breckenridge Co, KY	30
Barr David	Head of Christiana Cem, Newark, New Castle Co, DE	42
Barr David	Head of Christiana Cem, nr Newark, New Castle Co, DE	45
Barr Elisha	Upton Center Cem, fam lot, Upton, MA	45
Barr Hugh Rev	Barr-Johnson Cem, Edgar Co, IL	58
Barr James	Brannon's Cem, Hedgesville Dist, Berkeley Co, WV	42
Barr James	Brannum Cem, Back Creek Valley, Berkeley Co, WV	32
Barr Robert T	Old Cem, Washington Co, PA	38
Barr Samuel	Mt Carmel Cem nr Sardinia, Brown Co, OH	56
Barr Samuel Lt	Center Cem, Bedford, NH	34
Barratt Andrew	Barratt's Chapel, Kent Co, DE	46
Barratt Philip Col	Barratt's Chapel, Kent Co, DE	46
Barrell James	Assinippi Bur Gr, Scituate, MA	46
Barrell James	Scituate, MA	51
Barrell Joshua	Turner, ME	18
Barrell Joshua	Upper St Cem, Turner, ME	39

Abstract of Graves of Revolutionary Patriots

Barrell Noah	Assinippi Cem, Norwell-Hanover, MA 59
Barret Jonas	Unitarian Ch Cem, Ashby, MA 49
Barrett Abraham	Buxton Cem, Bedford, Westchester Co, NY 76
Barrett Arthur	Fam Cem on homestead, Cadiz, Harrison Co, OH 78
Barrett Arthur	Nr Cadiz, OH 54
Barrett Benjamin	Fosterville, Aurelius, NY 56
Barrett Benjamin	Kingsville, Ashtabula, OH 55
Barrett Benjamin	West Greece Corners, Monroe Co, NY 33
Barrett Charles Hon	Old Village Yard, New Ipswich, NH 29
Barrett Edward	Cabell Co, WV 56
Barrett Ezekiel	Norwich Town Cem, Norwich, CT 18
Barrett Francis	Priv Cem, fam plantation, Greensburg, KY 73
Barrett Humphrey	Main St Cem, Concord, MA 55
Barrett Humphrey Jr	Main St Cem, Concord, MA 55
Barrett Isaac	Carmel, Barrett Hill Cem, Delhi, NY 35
Barrett Isaac Lt	Center Cem, Hudson, NH 28
Barrett James Col	Old Concord battleground, Concord, MA 45
Barrett James Jr	Hill Bur Gr, Concord, Middlesex Co, MA 79
Barrett John	Main St Cem, Concord, MA 55
Barrett John	Van Cortlandville Cem, Peekskill, NY 41
Barrett John Lt Col	Springfield, VT 15
Barrett Jonas	Village Cem, Ashby, MA 55
Barrett Joseph	Pleasant View Cem, Mason, NH 71
Barrett Lemuel	Old Cem, Franconia, NH 32
Barrett Lemuel	Salmon Hole Cem, Lisbon, NH 26
Barrett Marcus	Carmel, Barrett Hill Cem, Delhi, NY 35
Barrett Nathan	Hill Cem, Concord, MA 55
Barrett Nathaniel	Cem on town common, Nelson, NH 35
Barrett Oliver	Bolton Cem, Bolton, MA 45
Barrett Oliver	Oak Hill Cem, Venice, Erie Co, OH 56
Barrett Oliver	Old Cem, Bolton, MA 56
Barrett Oliver	Sheddsville, West Windsor, VT 17
Barrett Peter	Hill Cem, Concord, MA 55
Barrett Samuel	Buxton Cem, Bedford, Westchester Co, NY 58
Barrett Samuel	Old Cem, Franconia, Grafton Co, NH 27
Barrett Simeon Capt	Center Cem, Hudson, NH 28
Barrett Stephen	Hill Cem, Concord, MA 55
Barrett Thomas	Hill Cem, Concord, MA 55
Barrett Thomas	Pratt Dist Yard, Southbridge, MA 29
Barrett William	South Yard, Brooklyn, CT 30
Barricklo Farrington	First Pres Ch Cem, Cranbury, NJ 76
Barricklo John	First Pres Ch Cem, Cranbury, NJ 76
Barrickman Jacob	Corey farm, Fairfield Twp, Franklin, IN 71
Barringer Henry	Wey's Crossing Cem, Old Rhinebeck, NY 70
Barringer John	Ref Ch Cem, Germantown, Columbia Co, NY 79
Barringer John Paul	St John's Evang Luth Ch Cem, Cabarrus Co, NC 49
Barron Benjamin	Village Cem, Woodstock, NH 36
Barron Ellis	Bur gr, First Pres Ch, Woodbridge, NJ 25
Barron John	Bur gr, First Pres Ch, Woodbridge, NJ 25
Barron Jonathon	Hillsdale, St Clair, MI 56
Barron Joshua	Humphrey Cem, Holland, NY 33
Barron Moses Corp	Hartland, VT 16
Barron Nicholas	Plainville, Shepardville Assoc, Wrentham, MA 55
Barron Samuel	Gray, GA 29
Barron Samuel	Old Cem, Merrimack, NH 52
Barron Timothy Capt	Horse Meadow Cem, Haverhill, NH 45
Barron William	Hammond Hollow or Vessel Rock Cem, Gilsum, NH 35
Barron William	Old fam place, 10 mi fr Waynesboro, Burke Co, GA 24
Barron William Col	Grasmere Cem, Goffstown, NH 28
Barron William Jr	Gilsom, NH 51
Barron William Sr	Vessel Rock Cem, Gilsum, NH 37

Barrow Andrew	South Carver Cem, Carver, MA 34
Barrow James	Oconee Cem, Athens, GA 32
Barrow William	Grasmere, Goffstown, NH 56
Barrows Aaron Lt	South Attleboro, MA 15
Barrows Abner	Old Cem, The Green, Middleboro, MA 50
Barrows Andrew	Carver, MA 30
Barrows Andrew	South Carver, MA 16
Barrows Benaiah	Old Bur Gr, Rockville, ME 56
Barrows Benjamin	South Attleboro, MA 15
Barrows Comfort	Tolman Cem, Rockland, ME 56
Barrows David	Bristol, RI 56
Barrows Ebenezer	Lakeville Cem, Rt 79, Middleboro, MA 55
Barrows George	Lakeville Cem, Rt 79, Middleboro, MA 55
Barrows Isaac	Hammond Cem, Mattapoisett, MA 59
Barrows Isaac	Hammond Cem, Mattapoisett, MA 56
Barrows James	Lakenham Cem, Carver, MA 59
Barrows John	Lakeville Cem, Rt 79, Middleboro, MA 55
Barrows Jonathan	Union Cem, Carver, MA 57
Barrows Joseph	Briggs Corner Cem, MA 15
Barrows Peleg	Carver, MA 30
Barrows Peleg	Union Cem, Carver, MA 57
Barrows Simon	South Attleboro, MA 15
Barrows Solomon	Africa Cem, Orange Twp, Delaware Co, OH 53
Barrows Thomas	Cushing Cem, Mattapoisett, MA 26
Barrows Thomas	Cushing Cem, Mattapoisett, MA 45
Barrows Thomas	School St Cem, Lebanon, NH 29
Barrows William	Old Burial Cem, Plympton, MA 57
Barrus Jeremiah	Whipple Hill Cem, Richmond, NH 36
Barrus Oliver	Whipple Hill Cem, Richmond, NH 36
Barry Andrew	Goshen Cem, Gaston Co, NC 49
Barry Hugh	Goshen Cem, Gaston Co, NC 49
Barry Hugh	Goshen Pres Ch Cem, Belmont, Gaston Co, NC 77
Barry John	Shrub Oak Cem, Meth Ch, Westchester Co, NY 41
Barry John	St Mary's Cem, Philadelphia, PA 52
Barry John	Tomb, Boston Common, Central Bur Gr, Boston, MA 56
Barry Richard	Hopewell Pres Ch Cem, Mecklenburg Co, NC 49
Barstow Benjamin	Highland Cem, Damariscotta Mills, Lincoln Co, ME 85
Barstow Gideon	Barlow Cem, Mattapoisett, MA 18
Barstow Jacob	Center Cem, Pembroke, MA 68
Barstow Jacob	Pembroke Centre Cem, Pembroke, MA 46
Barstow Joshua Capt	Old Town Cem, Exeter, NH 41
Barstow Samuel	Fern Hill Cem, #46-R, West Parish, Pembroke, MA 40
Barstow Samuel Jr	1st Cong Ch Cem, Hanover Center, MA 54
Barteau Francis	Cedar Grove Cem, Patchogue, Suffolk Co, NY 77
Bartee John	Putnam Co, IN 16
Barter Henry	Wilson farm, Gilmanton, NH 29
Bartholemew Abraham	Old North Cem, Bristol, CT 28
Bartholemew Oliver	Brownville Cem, Jefferson Co, NY 41
Bartholf John S	Fam farm, Oakland, NJ 54
Bartholmew Henry Jr	Zion's Stone Ch Cem, Kreidersville, Northampton Co, PA 40
Bartholmew Henry Sr	Zion's Stone Ch Cem, Kreidersville, Northampton Co, PA 40
Bartholmew Ira	Sangerfield Cem, Sangerfield, NY 32
Bartholmew Ludwig	Zion's Stone Ch Cem, Kreidersville, Northampton Co, PA 40
Bartholomew Andrew	Pitcher St Cem, Montgomery, MA 53
Bartholomew Benjamin	Great Valley Bapt Cem, Norristown, PA 15
Bartholomew Benjamin	Great Valley Bapt Ch, Tredyffrin Twp, Chester Co, PA 75
Bartholomew Benjamin	Woodstock Cem, Woodstock, CT 59
Bartholomew Daniel	Bradford Cem, Bradford, Steuben Co, NY 82
Bartholomew Gardner	West Thompson Cem, Thompson, CT 16
Bartholomew Gardner	West Thompson Cem, Thompson, MA 46
Bartholomew Henry	Zion Ch Cem, Kreidersville, PA 57

Bartholomew Henry	Zion Ch Cem, Kreidersville, PA	56
Bartholomew John Esq	Great Valley Bapt Ch, Tredyffrin Twp, Chester Co, PA	75
Bartholomew Joseph	Bloomington, IL	16
Bartholomew Joseph	Clarksville Cem, 3½ mi NW of Lexington, IL	41
Bartholomew Joseph Dea	Middlebury Cem, Middlebury, Medina Co, OH	55
Bartholomew Joseph Jr	Oran Cem, Pompey, Onondaga Co, NY	75
Bartholomew Luther	Christian St, White River Junction, VT	43
Bartholomew Reuben	Harwinton Cem, Harwinton, Litchfield Co, CT	78
Bartholomew Samuel	Old Brick Red Oak Cem, Union Twp, Brown Co, OH	55
Bartholomew Samuel	Unadilla Center Cem, Unadilla, NY	71
Bartle Philip Capt	Curtis farm, Harlemville, Columbia, NY	41
Bartlet Sylvanus	Burial Hill Cem, Plymouth, MA	62
Bartlett Aaron	[no cem named], MA	54
Bartlett Abiel	Old Town Cem, N of Old Center Harbor Rd, Meredith, NH	28
Bartlett Abner	White Horse Manomet Cem, Plymouth, MA	57
Bartlett Adam	Old Village Cem, Berlin, MA	46
Bartlett Andrew	Burial Hill, Plymouth, MA	56
Bartlett Andrew	White Horse Manomet Cem, Plymouth, MA	57
Bartlett Asa	Priv fam bur gr, Cumberland, RI	17
Bartlett Benjamin	Emerick Rd Cem, Ira, Cayuga Co, NY	69
Bartlett Cornelius	Center Cem, Westhampton, MA	53
Bartlett Daniel	North Cem, Hadley, MA	55
Bartlett David	Newton Center Cem, Newton, MA	45
Bartlett David	Old Town Cem, Campton, NH	36
Bartlett Ebenezer	Granby, MA	55
Bartlett Ebenezer	York Cem, York, Clark Co, IL	15
Bartlett Edward	Bryant Cem, Cummington, MA	56
Bartlett Elihu	Center Cem, Westhampton, MA	53
Bartlett Elisha	St Mary's Ch Cem, Newton Lower Falls, MA	45
Bartlett Evan	Town Cem, Hebron, NH	32
Bartlett Ezekial	Townsend, MA	50
Bartlett George	Town Cem, West Brentwood, NH	29
Bartlett Ichabod	Town Line Cem, Addison Co, VT	57
Bartlett Israel	Pentucket Cem, Haverhill, MA	29
Bartlett James	Eliot Cem, Eliot, ME	56
Bartlett Jeremiah	Pine Grove Cem, Gilford, NH	28
Bartlett Joel	Center Cem, Westhampton, MA	53
Bartlett John	Burial Hill, Plymouth, MA	56
Bartlett John	Hartford, ME	31
Bartlett John	Mercer Yard, Cornish, NH	29
Bartlett John	Old Burial Cem, Kingston, MA	57
Bartlett John	Salisbury Point Bur Gr, Salisbury, MA	33
Bartlett John	White Horse Manomet Cem, Plymouth, MA	57
Bartlett Joseph	Burial Hill, Plymouth, MA	56
Bartlett Joseph	Parade Cem, Lower Warner, Warner, NH	35
Bartlett Joseph	Town Cem, Newton, NH	32
Bartlett Joseph	Union Cem, Amesbury, MA	46
Bartlett Joshua Lt	East Unity Cem, Unity, NH	35
Bartlett Josiah	Goshen, Lebanon, CT	56
Bartlett Josiah	Phipps St Cem, Charlestown, MA	47
Bartlett Josiah	Village Cem, Kingston, NH	63
Bartlett Josiah	West Galway Cem, West Galway, Saratoga Co, NY	77
Bartlett Josiah H	In pine grove, Lee Hill, rd to Lee Depot, Lee, NH	39
Bartlett Levi	Bostwick Cem, nr DeLancy, Hamden, Delaware Co, NY	72
Bartlett Matthias	Town Cem, Newton, NH	32
Bartlett Moses	West Farms, Northampton, MA	56
Bartlett Moses Lt	North Parish Cem, Plaistow, NH	31
Bartlett Nathan	Swett Cem, Andover, NH	36
Bartlett Nathaniel	Alderbrook Cem, Guilford, CT	55
Bartlett Nathaniel	Mercer Yard, Cornish, NH	29
Bartlett Nathaniel	Mineville Cem, Mineville, NY	33

Bartlett Nathaniel	Sawyer Hill Cem, Canaan, NH 36
Bartlett Nicholas	Clark Cem, Pompey, Onondaga Co, NY 81
Bartlett Russell	Christ Ch Cem, Cooperstown, NY 59
Bartlett Samuel	Alderbrook Cem, Guilford, CT 55
Bartlett Samuel	At head of bay, Owl's Head, ME 55
Bartlett Samuel	Burial Hill, Plymouth, MA 56
Bartlett Samuel	Cem at head of bay, Owl's Head, ME 55
Bartlett Samuel	Old Village Yard, New Ipswich, NH 29
Bartlett Samuel	Sheshequin Cem, Sheshequin Twp, Bradford Co, PA 53
Bartlett Silas	Brandon, VT 15
Bartlett Simeon	Union Cem, Amesbury, MA 55
Bartlett Stephen Lt	Goshen Four Corners Cem, Goshen, NH 34
Bartlett Sylvanus	Old Bur Cem, Plympton, MA 58
Bartlett Thomas	Burial Hill, Plymouth, MA 56
Bartlett Thomas	Compton, NH 56
Bartlett Thomas	Old Cem, Lyndeboro, NH 53
Bartlett Thomas Gen	Cilley-Bartlett Cem, Nottingham Square, Nottingham, NH 27
Bartlett Thomas Gen	Nottingham Square, Nottingham, NH 17
Bartlett William	Burial Hill, Plymouth, MA 56
Bartlett William	Center Cem, Westhampton, MA 53
Bartlett William	Green St Cem, Marblehead, MA 47
Bartlett Wyman	Maple St Cem, North Brookfield, MA 17
Bartlett Zaccheus	White Horse Manomet Cem, Plymouth, MA 57
Bartley Samuel	Sheshequin Cem, Sheshequin Twp, Bradford Co, PA 72
Barto William	Texas Valley Cem, Marathon, Cortland Co, NY 36
Barton Benjamin	Croydon Cem, Croydon, NH 44
Barton Benjamin	Fam farm, Warwick, RI 52
Barton David	Granby, MA 55
Barton David	Nr St Clairsville & Baxtons Mills, Belmont Co, OH 55
Barton Elisha	Barton Fam Yard, Hunterdon, NJ 56
Barton Elisha	McManaway Fam Cem, Bedford Co, VA 47
Barton Elisha	Rosemont Cem, Bloomsburg, PA 15
Barton Elkanah	Chaplin, CT 15
Barton Isaac	Virgil Cem, Virgil, Cortland Co, NY 36
Barton Jedediah	Dwinnel Cem, West Millbury, Worcester Co, MA 77
Barton Johnathan	Old Cem, Windsor, Broome Co, NY 78
Barton Kimber	Franklin Furnace Cem, French Grant, Scioto Co, OH 43
Barton Lewis Sr	"Separate" Cem, Amenia, Dutchess Co, NY 68
Barton Phineas	Greenville Bapt Cem, Leicester, MA 55
Barton Seth	Fredericksburg, VA 29
Barton Seth	Fredericksburg, VA 30
Barton Stephen Dr	Well-marked grave in woods, Windsor, ME 42
Barton Stukey	Mt Vision, Blood Hill Farm, NY 34
Barton William	North Bur Gr, Providence, RI 51
Bartoo Silas	Eden, NY 33
Bartram Daniel	Unionville, OH 26
Bartram Ebenezer	Old Bur Gr, Fairfield, CT 62
Bartwell James Sr	Lyndborough, NH 56
Bascom Abiel	Exeter, Lebanon, CT 56
Bascom Elias	Shoreham, Orwell, VT 15
Bascom Elisha	Center Cem, Southampton, MA 49
Bascom Thomas	West Cem, Amherst, MA 56
Basford Ebenezer	Village Cem, Chester, NH 33
Bash Martin	Back (Summer) Cem, Pleasant Unity, Westmoreland Co, PA 56
Bashaw Peter	Priv fam Cem, Nashville, TN 56
Bashore Heinrich	Kline farm, North Lebanon Twp, Lebanon Co, PA 83
Bashore Johannes Sr	Old Reformed Ch Cem, Jonestown, Lebanon Co, PA 83
Basinger Sefrenes	Middle Village Cem, East Springfield, NY 33
Basinger Sefrenus	Town Ground, East Springfield, NY 15
Baskerville Samuel Lt	His farm, Paint Twp Cem, OH 17
Baskett Martin	Lea Place Cem, Shelby Co, KY 63

Bason Jacob	Hawfields Pres Ch Cem, Orange Co, NC	49
Bass Andrew	Turner, ME	18
Bass Benjamin	Back of First Cong Ch, Hanover Center, MA	52
Bass Benjamin	Cong Ch Cem, Hanover Center, MA	53
Bass Jonathan	Old North First Parish Cem, Braintree, MA	54
Bass Joseph	Rawson Brook, Leicester, Worcester Co, MA	56
Bass Samuel	Boston Commons Cem, Boston, MA	57
Bass Samuel	Boston Commons, MA	55
Bass Samuel	Boston Common Cem, Boston, MA	59
Bass Samuel	Union Cem, Holbrook, MA	55
Bass Samuel	Westford Cem, Ashford, CT	55
Basset Joseph	1st Parish Cem, Rochester, MA	58
Basset Jotham	Sempronius Cem, Sempronius, Cayuga Co, NY	57
Basset Samuel	West Barnstable, Barnstable, MA	55
Basset Thomas	1st Parish Cem, Rochester, MA	58
Basset William	1st Parish Cem, Rochester, MA	58
Basset William	Dennis Cem, Rt 6, Yarmouth, MA	55
Bassett Abraham	Old Cem, North Haven, CT	15
Bassett Abraham	Seymour Cem, Seymour, CT	15
Bassett Abraham	Trinity Cem, Seymour, CT	62
Bassett Abraham	Trinity Cem, Trinity, CT	37
Bassett Amos	Colonial Cem, Derby, CT	15
Bassett Benjamin	Colonial Cem, Derby, CT	15
Bassett Benjamin	Spring Grove Cem, Cincinnati, Hamilton Co, OH	76
Bassett Caleb	Thompson Hill Cem, Lakeville, MA	62
Bassett Cornelius	Center Cem (now Fairmont), Lee, MA	56
Bassett Cornelius	Lee Cem, Lee, MA	15
Bassett Daniel	Pine St Cong Ch Cem, Morton, MA	55
Bassett Daniel	Village Cem, Sandwich, MA	56
Bassett David	Colonial Cem, Derby, CT	15
Bassett Ebenezer	Easton Town Cem, Washington Co, NY	64
Bassett Edward	Riverside, Oxford, CT	56
Bassett Isaac	Cortland Cem, Cortlandville, Cortland Co, NY	36
Bassett Issac	Great Hill Cem, Seymour, CT	36
Bassett James	Great Hill Cem, Seymour, CT	35
Bassett James	Seymour Cem, Seymour, CT	15
Bassett Jatham	Kelloggsville Cem, Niles, NY	41
Bassett Jeremiah	Fam Cem, Taunton, MA	41
Bassett John	Ancient Cem, Yarmouth, Barnstable Co, MA	67
Bassett Jonathan	Kellogsville New Cem, Sempronius, NY	56
Bassett Joseph	Ancient Cem, Yarmouth, MA	63
Bassett Joseph	Barnstable Cem, Barnstable, MA	62
Bassett Joseph	Pleasant Twp Cem, Benington, IN	56
Bassett Joseph	Pleasant St Cem, Bridgewater, MA	55
Bassett Joshua	Cortland Cem, Cortlandville, Cortland Co, NY	36
Bassett Lot	Spruce Corners Cem, Ashfield, MA	54
Bassett Michael	Unitarian Cem, Marblehead, MA	55
Bassett Nathan	Evergreen Cem, South Amherst, Lorain Co, OH	55
Bassett Nathaniel	Kelloggsville, NY	15
Bassett Nathaniel	Lee Cem, Lee, MA	15
Bassett Nathaniel	Old Bur Gr, Mill Rd, Falmouth, MA	64
Bassett Nathaniel	Queen Ann Rd Cem, Harwich, MA	49
Bassett Richard	Wilmington & Brandywine Cem, Wilmington, DE	36
Bassett Richard Capt	Wilmington & Brandywine, New Castle Co, DE	46
Bassett Samuel	Keene, NH	16
Bassett Samuel Jr	Cem, Ansonia, CT	49
Bassett Thomas Dea	Village Cem, Sandwich, MA	56
Bassett William	Schuerman farm, Cross Plains, Ripley Co, IN	74
Bassett William	Village Cem, Sandwich, MA	56
Bassler Simon	Union Cem, Myerstown, Lebanon Co, PA	83
Bastedo William	Pres Ch Cem, Kingston, Somerset Co, NJ	74

Batchelder Asa	Beverly Cem, Beverly, MA 55
Batchelder Benjamin Lt	Old Cem, Andover, NH 43
Batchelder David	Northbridge, MA 53
Batchelder Davis	Old Cem in woods, Northwood, NH 45
Batchelder Henry	Old Cem in woods, Northwood, NH 45
Batchelder Isaiah	Springfield Cem, Springfield, PA 62
Batchelder Isaiah	Springfield Cem, Springfield, PA 46
Batchelder Jeremiah Col	Fam lot, his farm, Kimball Rd, Kensington, NH 47
Batchelder Jethro	Loudon Center Cem, Loudon, NH 32
Batchelder John	Beverly Cem, Beverly, MA 55
Batchelder John	East Cem, North Hampton, NH 31
Batchelder John	Laurel Hill, Reading, MA 49
Batchelder John	Little River Cem, New Hampton, NH 48
Batchelder John	Old Yard, Kensington, NH 47
Batchelder Jonathan	Beverly Cem, Beverly, MA 55
Batchelder Jonathan	Leavitt Hill (aban) Cem, Corbin Park, Grantham, NH 29
Batchelder Joseph	Center Cem, Plainfield, VT 48
Batchelder Josiah	Beverly Cem, Beverly, MA 55
Batchelder Josiah	Danville Cem, Danville, VT 32
Batchelder Josiah	Old Yard, Kensington, NH 47
Batchelder Josiah Capt	Taunton Hill Cem, Andover, NH 36
Batchelder Nathaniel	Old Cem, East Kingston, NH 28
Batchelder Reuben	Warren Cem, Warren, NH 36
Batchelder Samuel	Fam Cem, his farm, South Deerfield, NH 34
Batcheldor Elisha	Ye Olde Cem, Danville, NH 34
Batcheller Abraham	Dodge Cem, Sutton, MA 15
Batcheller Abraham	Stockton Cem, Stockton, Chautauqua Co, NY 15
Batcheller Benjamin	Dodge Cem, Sutton, MA 15
Batcheller David	Northbridge Center Cem, Northbridge Center, MA 47
Batcheller Jeremiah	Evergreen Cem, East Douglas, MA 16
Batchellor Amos	Main Rd, Wenham, MA 56
Batchellor Benjamin J	Bethel-Gilead Cem, Bethel, Windsor Co, VT 72
Batchellor Nehemiah	Boxboro Cem, Boxboro, MA 45
Batchellor Perley	Center Cem, Grafton, MA 49
Batchelor George	Miami Twp, OH 25
Batchelor Joseph	Earlville, NY 15
Bateman Joseph Corp	Old Center Cem, Rutland, VT 25
Bateman Joseph Corp	Old Center Rutland Cem, Rutland, VT 24
Bateman Joseph Corp	Old Cem, Center, Rutland, VT 23
Bateman Zadok	Stuarts Corners Cem, Venice, NY 41
Bates Aaron	Center Cem, Southampton, MA 49
Bates Aaron	Old Cem, Vernon, OH 56
Bates Abner	Center Cem, Chesterfield, MA 53
Bates Abraham	Weymouth, MA 53
Bates Adna	Central Cem, Cohasset, MA 60
Bates Alpheus	Tomb, Middle St, East Weymouth, MA 50
Bates Ambrose	Beechwood Cem, Cohasset, MA 55
Bates Barnabas	Agawam, Wareham, MA 56
Bates Barnabas	East Wareham, MA 16
Bates Barnabas	St Peter's Pres Ch Cem, Spencertown, Columbia Co, NY 74
Bates Barnabas Lt	East Wareham Cem, Wareham, MA 28
Bates Barnabas Lt	East Wareham (Agawam), Wareham, MA 34
Bates Bela	Center Cem, Southampton, MA 49
Bates Benjamin	Center Cem, Mansfield, MA 55
Bates Benjamin	Leroy, OH 26
Bates Benjamin	Mount Zion Cem, Abington, MA 45
Bates Benjamin Capt	Mount Zion Cem, Abington, MA 45
Bates Benjamin Jr	1st Cong Ch Cem, Hanover Center, MA 54
Bates Benjamin Lt	Bates Mills, NJ 47
Bates Caleb	Lake View Cem, Hillsdale, MI 15
Bates Caleb	Lakeview Cem, Hillsdale, Hillsdale Co, MI 46

Bates Carver	Elmwood Cem, Barre, VT	48
Bates Charles	Village Cem, Sharon, CT	68
Bates Christopher	Mount Zion Cem, Abington, MA	45
Bates Clement	Cong Ch Cem, Hanover Center, MA	53
Bates Comfort	Centre Cem, Pembroke, MA	50
Bates Comfort	Old farm, Savoy, MA	53
Bates Comfort Jr	Center, Pembroke, MA	56
Bates Cornelius	Mount Hope Cem, Scituate, MA	54
Bates Daniel	Bethel Cem, Hurffville, NJ	46
Bates Daniel	Sandusky Co, OH	25
Bates David	Whippany, Morris Co, NJ	32
Bates E	Nr Cooper's Fort, New Hope, MO	15
Bates Eleszer	Mount Zion Cem, Abington, MA	45
Bates Elias	Castle Dist Cem, Roxbury, CT	40
Bates Elias	West Settlement Cem, Ashland, Greene Co, NY	69
Bates Elijah	Rochester Cem, nr Church, Rochester, MA	55
Bates Elisha	Beechwood Cem, Cohasset, MA	60
Bates Elisha	Beechwood Cem, Cohasset, MA	51
Bates Elisha	Old Bedford Cem, Bedford, Westchester Co, NY	76
Bates Elisha Jr	Beechwood Cem, Cohasset, MA	60
Bates Elnathan	Old North Cem, North Weymouth, MA	50
Bates Ephraim	Fayette, MO	32
Bates Ephraim	Fielding Cem, 2 mi fr Fayette, MO	31
Bates Ephraim	McWilliams farm, nr Sarahsville, Noble Co, OH	55
Bates Ephriam	Leach Pasture, Howard Co, MO	15
Bates Francis	Oak Hill, Pownal, VT	56
Bates Gamaliel	Cong Ch Cem, Hanover Center, MA	53
Bates Hinsdale	Norton Center, Summit Co, OH	45
Bates Hinsdale	Norton Twp, Summit Co, OH	15
Bates Humphrey	Paint Lick, Garrard, KY	56
Bates Isaac	Spring Grove Cem, Cincinnati, Hamilton Co, OH	76
Bates Israel	Roy Mathe farm Cem, Barre, Orleans Co, NY	34
Bates Jabez	Greene, ME	18
Bates Jabez	Old Cem, Westminster, VT	46
Bates Jacob	Bridge St Cem, Northampton, MA	56
Bates Jacob	Hersey Cem, Minot, ME	43
Bates James	Chesterfield Cem, Chesterfield, MA	68
Bates James	Colebrook Cem, Whitman, MA	62
Bates James	Priv bur gr, 3 mi fr Palmyra, MO	15
Bates Jesse	Hingham, MA	54
Bates Jesse	Pleasant St, nr Pratt School, East Weymouth, MA	50
Bates John	Amenia Bur Gr, 1 mi N of Amenia, Dutchess Co, NY	66
Bates Jonathan	Central Cem, Cohasset, MA	53
Bates Jonathan	Gloucester Co, NJ	32
Bates Joseph	Center Cem, Bellingham, MA	55
Bates Joseph	Good Hill Cem, Kent, CT	40
Bates Joseph	Mendon Cem, Mendon, MA	60
Bates Joseph	Old Bur Gr, Cambridge, MA	56
Bates Josiah	Springfield, VT	15
Bates Josiah	Springfield Cem, Springfield, VT	60
Bates Laban	South Cem, Bellingham, MA	55
Bates Lemuel	Center Cem, Southampton, MA	49
Bates Lemuel	Cortland Rural Cem, Cortlandville, Cortland Co, NY	36
Bates Levi	Springfield Cem, Springfield, VT	60
Bates Lewis Lt	Springfield, VT	15
Bates Micah	Mendon Center Cem, Mendon, MA	46
Bates Michael	Fam Cem, Newberry, SC	70
Bates Moses	1st Parish Cem, Rochester, MA	58
Bates Moses	Dawes Cem, Cummington, Hampshire Co, MA	63
Bates Nathaniel	Beechwood, Cohasset, MA	54
Bates Nathaniel	West Center Cem, Granville, Hampden Co, MA	63

Bates Nehemiah	Center Cem, Chesterfield, MA 48
Bates Nehemiah Jr	Cummington Cem, Cummington, MA 60
Bates Oliver	Nuttings, Westford, MA 56
Bates Phineas	Canandaigua Cem, Ontario Co, NY 33
Bates Robert	Tomb, Middle St, East Weymouth, MA 50
Bates Samuel	Elmwood Cem, Union St, South Weymouth, MA 50
Bates Samuel	Kendall, NY 15
Bates Samuel	Morton Cem, Kendall, NY 34
Bates Samuel Jr	Cohasset, MA 51
Bates Stephen	Center Cem, Southampton, MA 49
Bates Stephen	Center Cem, Southampton, Hampshire Co, MA 60
Bates Sylvester	1st Parish Cem, Rochester, MA 58
Bates Theodore	Shaker's Cem, Watervliet, NY 66
Bates Urban	Old North Cem, North Weymouth, MA 50
Bates William	Mt Pleasant Cem, Benton, Yates Co, NY 69
Bates Zealous	Westboro, MA 51
Batey William Capt	[no cem named], TN 15
Bathrick Stephen Sr	Perry Center Cem, Perry, Wyoming Co, NY 64
Battelle Ebenezer	Newport Cem, Newport, Washington Co, OH 55
Batten Henry	Fam Cem nr Gossett Mill, Porter Co, IN 25
Batten James Jr	Hopewell M E Cem, nr Guthriesville, Chester Co, PA 55
Batten Richard	Town Cem, Francestown, NH 27
Batterman Christopher	Prospect Hill, Rt 20 & Vooheesville Rd, Albany Co, NY 66
Batterson Abijah	Hillman Cem, Chemung, Chemung Co, NY 78
Batterson Joseph	Unadilla Cem, Unadilla, Otsego Co, NY 71
Batterton Samuel	Farm nr county line, betw Millersburg & Cynthiana, KY 17
Battey Andrew	Mayfield Cem, Lawrence Co, IN 25
Battey William	Fam lot, Plainfield Pike, W of Kent Dam, Scituate, RI 35
Battie John	Sterling Village Cem, Sterling, NY 56
Battier Charles	Spring Grove Cem, sect 46 lot 61 #4, Cincinnati, OH 45
Battis Sampson	Canterbury Center Cem, Canterbury, NH 29
Battle Ebenezer	Dover Cem, Dedham, MA 55
Battle Ebenezer	Old Cem, Dedham, MA 56
Battle Ithiel	Tyringham, MA 15
Battle James	Tyringham, MA 15
Battles Asa	Turner, ME 18
Battles Jared	Scituate Harbor 1st Par Cem, Prospect St, Scituate, MA 60
Battles John	Old Cem, East Main St, Avon, MA 55
Battles Jonathan	Stoughton Cem, Stoughton, MA 46
Batts John	Old Western Cem, Lynn, MA 55
Bauer Christopher	Zion Luth Cem, Hummelstown, Dauphin Co, PA 61
Bauer Michael	Old Morav Cem, Emaus, Lehigh Co, PA 40
Baugh Henry Sr	Mt Zion Ch, Pulaski Co, KY 56
Baugh Joseph	Fam Cem, Callaway Twp, St Charles Co, MO 72
Baughman Anthony	Dague Cem, Jefferson Twp, Franklin Co, OH 53
Baughman George	Riverside Cem, OH 26
Baum Charles	Clermont Co, OH 56
Baum Daniel	Zion Luth Cem, Hummelstown, Dauphin Co, PA 61
Baum Frederick	Farm Cem, Oppenheim, Fulton Co, NY 39
Baum Jacob	St John's Luth Cem, E of Miamisburg, OH 56
Baum John	Fam Cem, Bloomberg farm, Patton, Cambria Co, PA 77
Bauman George	Mt Lebanon Cem, Lebanon, Lebanon Co, PA 83
Bausemann Philip	Frieden's, New Ringold, PA 49
Bausman John	Luth Cem, Reisterstown, MD 19
Baxter Aaron Jr	Baxter Rural Cem, Addison, Steuben Co, NY 73
Baxter Benjamin	Cem, nr railroad, South Dennis, MA 50
Baxter Benjamin	Thomas Cem, Pultney, Steuben Co, NY 80
Baxter Daniel	Rowesville, SC 16
Baxter Edward Willard	Hancock Cem, Quincy, MA 54
Baxter Edward Willard	North Cem, Dorchester, MA 46
Baxter James	Craig Cem, Jefferson Co, IN 52

Abstract of Graves of Revolutionary Patriots

Baxter John	Center, Perry Co, PA 16
Baxter John	Perch River Cem, Jefferson Co, NY 41
Baxter John	Porch River, NY 16
Baxter John	Vine Lake, Medfield, MA 56
Baxter John Corp	18 mi NE of Chatsworth, Murray Co, GA 32
Baxter Jonathan	Hancock Cem, Quincy, MA 54
Baxter Joseph	Hancock Cem, Quincy, MA 54
Baxter Pettit	June Cem, North Salem, Westchester Co, NY 76
Baxter Seth	Hancock Cem, Quincy, MA 54
Baxter Simon	Village Cem, Surry, NH 35
Baxter Thomas	June Cem, North Salem, Westchester Co, NY 76
Bay John	Claverack Ref Ch Cem, Columbia Co, NY 41
Bayard John Col	[no cem named], NJ 28
Bayard John Col	Van Liew Cem, New Brunswick, NJ 24
Bayard Stephen A	East Tower, Pres Ch Cem, 6th St, Philadelphia, PA 55
Bayer Jacob	Old Goshenhoppen Cem, Montgomery Co, PA 59
Bayer Peter	Old Pres Cem, Bound Brook, NJ 47
Bayles Augustin	Pres Cem, Morristown, NJ 32
Bayles William	Pres Cem, Morristown, NJ 32
Bayless Daniel	Cheesequake Bapt Ch Cem, Hwy 34, Madison Twp, NJ 76
Bayless Daniel	Prospect Cem, Jamaica, Queens Co, NY 78
Bayless Elias	Prospect Cem, Jamaica, Queens Co, NY 77
Bayless John	Cherokee Bapt Ch Cem, nr Jonesboro, Washington Co, TN 74
Bayless John	Corbettsville Cem, Corbettsville, Broome Co, NY 78
Bayless Thomas	Priv Cem, Brookhaven, Suffolk Co, NY 79
Bayley Abner Rev	Old Cem, Salem Center, NH 28
Bayley Edward	Minot, ME 18
Bayley Jacob	Oxbow Cem, Newbury, VT 51
Bayley James	Union Cem, Amesbury, MA 46
Bayley John	Dutch Ref Ch Cem, Belleville, NJ 27
Bayley Joshua	Derby, VT 35
Bayley Nathaniel	Highland Cem, South Weymouth, MA 50
Bayley Robert	Opposite church, Newbury, MA 56
Bayley Samuel	Highland Cem, South Weymouth, MA 50
Bayley Solomon	Bartlett Cem, Plymouth, NH 29
Baylies Hodijah	Unitarian Ch Cem, Main St, Dighton, MA 55
Baylies Nicholas	3½ mi S of Taunton Green, Dighton, MA 56
Baylies Thomas	Unitarian Ch Cem, Main St, Dighton, MA 55
Baylies William	Cem on hill, off Rt 138, Dighton, MA 55
Baylis William	Nr Calhoun, Henry Co, MO 23
Baylis William Lt	½ mi N of Calhoun, Henry Co, MO 15
Baylor George	St Michael's Cathedral, Bridgetown, Barbados, W Indies 78
Baylor Walker	Now in Kentucky State Cem, Frankfort, KY 62
Bayly Montjoy Gen	Congressional Cem, Washington, DC 26
Bayne Casparus	Lick Cem, nr South Argyle, Washington Co, NY 77
Beach Aaron	North Ridge Cem, Cambria, NY 33
Beach Abel	West Torrington Cem, Torrington, CT 55
Beach Abram	Common Grave, Milford, CT 56
Beach Adna	Jewett Heights Cem, Jewett, Greene Co, NY 69
Beach Ames	Kingsborough Colonial Cem, Gloversville, NY 32
Beach Amos	Plain City Cem, Plain City, OH 56
Beach Asa	South Milton Cem, South Milton, Ulster Co, NY 77
Beach Asa	Whitney Cem, Broome Co, NY 33
Beach Benjamin	North-West Bur Gr, Woodbridge, CT 56
Beach Benjamin	St Peter's Pres Ch Cem, Spencertown, Columbia Co, NY 74
Beach Daniel	Bur gr adjoining 1st Pres Ch, Caldwell, Essex Co, NJ 31
Beach David	Old Protestant Cem, Chateaugay, NY 62
Beach David	Rockaway, Morris Co, NJ 32
Beach David Jr	Center Cem, Bridgewater, CT 55
Beach Ebenezer	Monroe Center Bur Gr, Monroe, CT 34
Beach Edmund	Cornwell-Tilden Plot, New Lebanon, Columbia Co, NY 79

Beach Elihu	Old Cem, S of center of Vernon, OH 56
Beach Enoch	Hanover, Morris Co, NJ 32
Beach Ezekiel	Hartford Twp, Trumbull Co, OH 56
Beach Fisk	Old East Street, Goshen, Litchfield Co, CT 56
Beach George	Sunbury Cem, Berkshire Twp, Delaware Co, OH 53
Beach Jabez	Pres Cem, Morristown, NJ 32
Beach Jedediah	East Springfield, NY 15
Beach Jedidiah	Springfield Center Cem, Springfield, NY 33
Beach John	Monroe Center Bur Gr, Monroe, CT 34
Beach John	West Torrington Cem, Torrington, CT 55
Beach Jonathan	Mount Morris Cem, Pontiac, MI 18
Beach Joseph	Center, Wolcott, CT 56
Beach Joseph	Monroe Center, Monroe, CT 56
Beach Joseph Capt	Smith Cem, Charleston, NY 41
Beach Nathan	Beach Grove, Salem Twp, PA 52
Beach Nathaniel	Pres Cem, Newark, NJ 32
Beach Noah	West Litchfield, CT 17
Beach Obil	Plain City Cem, Plain City, Madison Co, OH 55
Beach Reuben	Akron, OH 15
Beach Reuben	Tallmadge Cem, Summit Co, OH 53
Beach Reuben	Talmadge, Summit Co, OH 45
Beach Samuel	Shoreham, VT 15
Beach Uriah	North Otis, Otis, MA 56
Beach Walt	West Torrington Cem, Torrington, CT 55
Beadle Joseph	Fam Cem, Fountain City, IN 69
Beal Abel	North Cohasset Cem, Cohasset, MA 55
Beal Andrew	Rocky Nook Cem, Cedar St, North Cohasset, MA 60
Beal Benjamin	Hingham Cem, Hingham, MA 70
Beal Benjamin	Old Cem, Liberty St, Rockland, MA 54
Beal Daniel	Cohasset, MA 55
Beal David	Ancient Bur Gr, Kingston, MA 50
Beal Jacob	Plainfield Cem, Plainfield, VT 60
Beal Jonathan	Rocky Nook Cem, Cedar St, North Cohasset, MA 60
Beal Joshua	Central Cem, Cohasset, MA 54
Beal Lazarus	Rocky Nook Cem, Cedar St, North Cohasset, MA 60
Beal Lazarus A	Rocky Nook Cem, Cedar St, North Cohasset, MA 60
Beal Manwarren	Beals Cem, Jonesport, Washington Co, ME 78
Beal Noah	Fam Cem, Webster St, Rockland, MA 54
Beal Obediah	Rocky Nook Cem, Cedar St, North Cohasset, MA 60
Beal Samuel	Kings Chapel Cem, Boston, MA 60
Beal Thomas	River St Cem, West Newton, MA 56
Beale Benjamin	North Auburn, ME 29
Beale Joseph	Hancock Cem, Quincy, MA 54
Beale Joshua	Central Cem, Cohasset, MA 53
Beale Matthew	Spencertown Ch Cem, Austerlitz, Columbia Co, NY 41
Beale Zephaniah Capt	Christ's Epis Ch, Bunker Hill, Berkeley Co, WV 18
Beall Josiah	Boxwood Lodge, Urbana Rd, Frederick, MD 52
Beall Ninian	Washington Cem, nr Versailles, Ripley Co, IN 72
Beall Seth Jr	Hicksite Cem, Hicksite, Farmington, Wayne Co, NY 79
Beall Thomas	Cumberland, MD 56
Beall Zachariah	Mt Bethel Ch Cem, nr Statesville, Iradell Co, NC 72
Beall Zachary	Pace farm, nr Kiddville, Clark Co, KY 55
Beall Zephaniah	Beallsville, PA 56
Beall Zephaniah	Christ Epis Ch Cem, Bunker Hill, Berkeley Co, WV 42
Beals Adams	St Albans Cem, St Albans, VT 46
Beals Benjamin	Auburn, ME 18
Beals David	Fern Hill Cem, #17-R, West Parish, Pembroke, MA 40
Beals David	Fern Hill Cem, Hanson, MA 59
Beals Jeremiah	Melrose Cem, Brockton, MA 15
Beals Joshua	Shaw, Windsor, MA 56
Beals Samuel	King's Chapel Cem, Boston, MA 46

Abstract of Graves of Revolutionary Patriots

Beam Christain	Steelstown Evang Ch, North Annville Twp, Lebanon Co, PA	83
Beam Christian	Palmyra area, South Londonderry Twp, Lebanon Co, PA	83
Beam Jacob	Maple Grove Cem, Findlay, OH	15
Beam John	New Prospect Bapt Ch, Cleveland Co, NC	49
Beam Michael	Universalist Cem, Jersey Twp, Licking Co, OH	55
Beam Peter	Malloy Farm Cem, Starkey, Yates Co, NY	69
Beam Rudolph	Annville area farm plot, Annville Twp, Lebanon Co, PA	83
Beaman Ezra Maj	Fam bur gr, West Boylston, MA	45
Beaman Gideon	Old Cem, Sterling, MA	56
Beaman Joseph	Old Bennington Cem, Bennington, VT	46
Beaman Joseph	Old Bennington Cem, Bennington, VT	30
Beamen Josiah	Pres Cem, Rockaway, NJ	50
Beamesderfer Johannes	Luth Ref Ch Cem, Schaefferstown, Lebanon Co, PA	83
Bean Benjamin	River Road Cem, Piermont, NH	32
Bean Daniel	Burlington, IA	56
Bean David	Union Cem, Laconia, NH	29
Bean Ebenezer	West Side, Bean or Dearing Cem, Conway, NH	32
Bean Henry	Lower Mennonite Ch Cem, Montgomery Co, PA	59
Bean James	St James Cem, above Norristown, PA	52
Bean James Alexander	Cem nr Edgefield, SC	66
Bean Jeremiah	Bunker Hill Cem, Wilmot, NH	34
Bean John	Clark, KY	56
Bean John Capt	Epis Cem, Evansburg, PA	17
Bean John Jr	New Sharon, ME	52
Bean Joseph	South Rd Cem, Salisbury Heights, Salisbury, NH	29
Bean Josiah Capt	Weed Cem, North Sandwich, NH	31
Bean Moody	Bean Yard, Center Harbor, NH	29
Bean Nathan	First Cem, Candia, NH	29
Bean Nicholas	Fam Cem, nr Cleone, Clark Co, IL	15
Bean Samuel	North Bur Gr, Sutton, NH	37
Bean Thomas	Asbury Cem, 4 mi SW of Inkerman, WV	52
Bean William A	Old Salem Cem, Hempfield, Mercer Co, PA	15
Beane Joshua	Readfield Corner, Readfield, ME	29
Beanes William	Knoll above School House Pond, Upper Marlboro, MD	75
Bear John P	Old Cem, Unionville, Neffs, Lehigh Co, PA	40
Bearce Isaiah	Fern Hill Cem, #18-R, West Parish, Pembroke, MA	40
Bearce Samuel	Phinney's Lane Cem, Centerville, Barnstable Co, MA	61
Beard Amos	Lower Cem, Burton, Geauga Co, OH	55
Beard Andrew	Gold Hill Cem, Corner Cabarrus & Rowan Co, NC	49
Beard Andrew	Milford Cem, Milford, CT	56
Beard Andrew	The Old Cem, Gardner, MA	46
Beard Andrew	The Old Cem, Gardner, MA	33
Beard David	Pompey Hill Cem, Pompey Hill, Onondaga Co, NY	78
Beard Ithamar	Gumpus Cem, Pelham, MA	50
Beard James Sr	Pres Cem, Martin Creek, Mt Bethel Twp, Northampton Co, PA	30
Beard John	Beard's Ch, Chewsville Dist, Washington Co, MD	51
Beard John	Nr Lewisburg, Greenbriar, VA	58
Beard Joseph	Blandford, MA	56
Beard Josiah	Venice Center Cem, Venice, Cayuga Co, NY	57
Beard William	New Boston, NH	16
Beard William	New Boston Cem, New Boston, NH	28
Beard William Sr	Mt Union Cem, Union Twp, Ross Co, OH	55
Beardley William	Clark Cem, Providence Twp, NY	41
Beardsby Salmon W	Eden Center Cem, Eden, NY	33
Beardslee Abraham	Epis Bur Gr, Stratford, CT	31
Beardslee Charles	North Ch Cem, Hardyston Twp, Sussex Co, NJ	79
Beardslee Curtis	Epis Bur Gr, Stratford, CT	31
Beardslee Henry	Epis Bur Gr, Stratford, CT	31
Beardslee John	Old bur place, Nichols Farms, Nichols, CT	33
Beardsley Abijah	Stratfield Old Bur Gr, Bridgeport, CT	16
Beardsley Benjamin	East Venice Cem, Genoa, NY	56

Beardsley Elijah	Old Columbia St Cem, Springfield, Clark Co, OH 55
Beardsley John	Stratford, CT 56
Beardsley Joseph	Wilcox Cem, Locke, Cayuga Co, NY 57
Beardsley Josiah	Prentiss Cem, Butternuts, Gilbertsville, Otsego Co, NY 77
Beardsley Nehemiah	Cong Cem, New Fairfield, CT 31
Beardsley Philo	Newtown Village, Newtown, CT 56
Beardsley Phineas	Cem, New Fairfield, CT 49
Beardsley Phineas Capt	New Fairfield, CT 31
Beardsley Robert C	Old bur place, Nichols Farms, Nichols, CT 33
Beardsley Salmon	Eden Cem, Eden, NY 54
Beardsley Thomas	Roxbury Center Cem, Roxbury, CT 40
Beardsley Wells	Long Mountain Cem, New Milford, CT 40
Bears Joseph	Fairfield Co, CT 56
Bearse Isaac	Phinney's Lane Cem, Centerville, Barnstable, MA 58
Bearse Samuel	Phinney's Lane Centerville Cem, Barnstable Co, MA 60
Beasley Cornelius	Bowling Green, MO 15
Beasley Leonard	Duncan Creek Pres Ch Cem, Laurens Co, SC 70
Beath John	Boothbay Cem, Boothbay, ME 56
Beath Joseph	Boothbay Cem, Boothbay, ME 56
Beath Joseph	Copps Hill Cem, Boston, MA 46
Beatman William	North Afton Cem, Afton, Chenango Co, NY 73
Beattie Francis	Deer Creek Cem, Harmarville, PA 56
Beatty Andrew Capt	Kelly farm, Hillsboro, OH 15
Beatty Archibald	Goodwill Cem, Montgomery, Orange Co, NY 78
Beatty Benjamin	Unity Cem, Latrobe, PA 15
Beatty Erkuries	Princeton Cem, Princeton, NJ 26
Beatty Henry	Mt Hebron Cem, Winchester, VA 60
Beatty Hugh	Cave Creek Cem, Roane Co, TN 24
Beatty Hugh	Cave Creek Cem, TN 23
Beatty Isaac	Oakwood Cem, Monroe Co, NY 33
Beatty John	Battle of Kings Mountain, SC 52
Beatty John	First Pres Ch Cem, Trenton, NJ 28
Beatty John	Little Brittain Ch Cem, Pine Bush, NY 48
Beatty Joseph	Goodwill Cem, Montgomery, Orange Co, NY 78
Beatty Thomas	Frederick Cath Cem, Frederick Co, MD 55
Beatty Thomas	Goodwill Cem, Montgomery, Orange Co, NY 78
Beatty Thomas	Mount Olivet Cem, Frederick, MD 30
Beatty Thomas Jr	Goodwill Cem, Montgomery, Orange Co, NY 78
Beatty William	Fam Cem, W of Murfreesboro, Rutherford Co, TN 74
Beatty William	Glade Springs Cem, Abbington Washington, VA 82
Beatty William	Goodwill Cem, Montgomery, Orange Co, NY 78
Beatty William	Old Salem Cem, Hempfield, Mercer Co, PA 15
Beatty William	Tuscarawas Co, OH 45
Beatty William Capt	Fam Cem, Rutherford Co, TN 24
Beatty William Capt	Fam Cem, TN 23
Beaty John	Old Bur Gr Cem, Salem, Washington Co, NY 70
Beaty John	Pres Ch Cem, Conway, SC 70
Beaty Robert	Providence Bapt Ch Cem, Otterville, Pettis Co, MO 58
Beauford James	[no cem named], VA 55
Beauman Sebastian	Dutch Ch Cem, Nassau & Liberty St, Winchester, NY 58
Beaumont Samuel III	Huntington, WV 31
Beaumont William	Scoville, Lebanon, CT 56
Beaver Anthony	Schultz Cem, Huntingdon Co, PA 56
Beaver Barnaby	St Peter's Luth Ch, Gwynedd, Montgomery Co, PA 82
Beaver Jacob	Old Cem, Jerusalem Ch, West Salisbury, Lehigh Co, PA 68
Beaver Martin	Priv Cem, 3 mi S of Westminster, Carroll Co, MD 41
Beavers George	Bethlehem Pres Cem, Grandin, NJ 35
Beavers Joseph	Greenwich Pres Cem, Warren Co, NJ 40
Beavers Joseph	Greenwich Cem, Warren Co, NJ 32
Beavers Robert	Mansfield Cem, nr Washington, NJ 35
Beavers William	Old Providence Bapt Ch, Coweta Co, GA 27

Bebout Daniel	Aban Cem, Rushville Twp, Rush Co, IN 72
Bebout John Jr	Neshannock Pres Ch, W of New Wilmington, Lawrence Co, PA 57
Bebout Peter Jr	Pres Cem, New Providence, NJ 63
Bebout William	Pres Cem, New Providence, NJ 63
Bechet Humphrey	Mound Cem, E of Covington, IN 25
Bechtel George	Zion & Emmanuel Ref Ch Cem, Montgomery Co, PA 59
Bechtel Heinrich	Zoar Cem, Mt Zion, Lebanon Co, PA 83
Bechtel Philip	Mahantongo Twp, PA 49
Beck George	Fam Cem, Howard Twp, Washington Co, IN 72
Beck George Sr	Beck's Mill, Washington Co, IN 23
Beck Jeffrey	Stamp Creek Bapt Ch Cem, Salem, Oconee Co, SC 70
Beck Johan Henrich	Dryland Union Ch Cem, Hecktown, Northampton Co, PA 40
Beck Johan Phillip	Bethel Morav Ch Cem, Swatara Twp, Lebanon Co, PA 83
Beck John	Nr Gainesville, Hall Co, GA 35
Beck John	Old Wansley fam bur plot, Elbert Co, GA 68
Beck John Heinrich	Dryland Ch Cem, Hecktown, Northampton Co, PA 22
Beck Thomas	Fam Cem, Tays farm, nr Princeton, Caldwell Co, KY 73
Becker Albert	Van Schoonhoven Cem, Waterford, Saratoga Co, NY 77
Becker Jacob	Ellerton Cem, Ellerton, OH 56
Becker Jacob	Old Cem, lot A-115, Sunbury, PA 56
Becker John	Minnich Cem, Randolph, Montgomery Co, OH 56
Becker John Mathias	Canadochly Ch Cem, Windsor Twp, York Co, PA 52
Becker John P	Bottskill Cem, Greenwich, NY 32
Becker Lawrence	Krum Cem, Harlemville, Columbia Co, NY 71
Becker Lodowick	South Worcester Cem, Worcester, Otsego Co, NY 76
Becker Peter	Krum Cem, Harlemville, Hillsdale, Columbia Co, NY 74
Becker Philip	South Worcester Cem, Worcester, Otsego Co, NY 71
Becket Humphrey	Dublin, Franklin Co, OH 18
Beckett Humphrey	Mound Cem, Warren Co, IN 72
Beckett James	Greenwood Cem, Hamilton, OH 56
Beckett John	Round Hill Cem, Monongahela, Washington Co, PA 75
Beckett John C	Brookside Cem, US 25, West Chester, Butler Co, OH 55
Beckett Joseph	Round Hill Cem, Monongahela, Washington Co, PA 75
Beckham Abner	Bank of Bogue Chito River, 2 mi N of Franklinton, LA 68
Beckham Sherwood	Fam prop, 3 mi fr Zebulon, Pike Co, GA 60
Beckham Solomon	Gwynne prop, Pike Co, GA 64
Beckley Daniel	Little Bethel Ch, Utica, NY 56
Beckley Jacob	Luth Cem, Reisterstown, MD 19
Beckley John	Luth Cem, Reisterstown, MD 19
Beckley John 2nd	Luth Cem, Reisterstown, MD 19
Beckley Zebadee	Maplewood Cem, Barre, VT 48
Beckman John R	Smithtown Cem, Seabrook, NH 32
Beckwith –	Weathersfield, VT 16
Beckwith Andrew	Center Cem, Alstead, NH 43
Beckwith Baraillat	Three Bridges, East Haddam, CT 56
Beckwith Benjamin	Wiseman Cem, Malta Twp, Morgan Co, OH 55
Beckwith Ira	West Yard Cem, Marlow, NH 25
Beckwith Jabez Col	East Lempster Cem, Lempster, NH 34
Beckwith Jason	Cedar Grove Cem, New London, CT 70
Beckwith Jason	West Yard Cem, Marlow, NH 25
Beckwith John	Hebron Cem, Bullitt Co, KY 60
Beckwith Nahemiah Jr	Fam bur gr, Cedar farm, Cornersville, Dorchester Co, MD 55
Beckwith Niles	East Lempster Cem, Lempster, NH 34
Beckwith Samuel	Braceville Cem, Braceville, OH 56
Beckwith Silas	Kitchell Cem, Crawford Co, IL 15
Beckwith Sylvanus	Bapt Ground, lot #1, Stanford, Dutchess Co, NY 21
Beddle Joel	Pintard Cem, Curtis farm, nr Keyport, NJ 32
Beddle Thomas	Pintard Cem, Curtis farm, nr Keyport, NJ 32
Beddow Thomas	Berlin Twp, OH 18
Bedel John	East Sweden Cem, Sweden, NY 31
Bedel Timothy Col	Ladd St Cem, Haverhill, NH 15

Bedell Abraham — Vaughan's Cem, Sparta, Sussex Co, NJ 79
Bedell Daniel — Village Cem, Bath, Grafton Co, NH 27
Bedell David — Old Salem Cem, 12 mi NE of Springfield, Greene Co, MO 15
Bedell David — Salem Cem, 10 mi N of Springfield, MO 23
Bedell Moody — Village Cem, Bath, Grafton Co, NH 27
Bedell Samuel — White Cem, Yorktown, NY 34
Bedell Timothy Col — Ladd St Cem, Haverhill, NH 30
Bedford Gunning — Epis Cem, New Castle, New Castle Co, DE 46
Bedford Gunning Jr — Lawn of Masonic Home, New Castle Co, DE 46
Bedford Gunning Jr — Orig 1st Pres Cem, now Wilmington & Brandywine Cem, DE 36
Bedford Thomas — Charlotte Cem, Charlotte, VA 61
Bedinger Daniel — Old Epis Cem, Shepherdstown, WV 24
Bedinger Daniel Lt — Old Epis Cem, Shepherdstown, Jefferson Co, WV 27
Bedinger Daniel Lt — Old Epis Cem, Shepherdstown, WV 26
Bedinger Henry Capt — Old Epis Cem, Shepherdstown, Jefferson Co, WV 27
Bedinger Henry Capt — Old Epis Cem, Shepherdstown, WV 26
Bedinger Henry Maj — Old Epis Cem, Shepherdstown, WV 24
Bedlow William — Champlain Cem, Champlain, NY 45
Bedwell Robert — Moody Cem, nr Pleasantville, Sullivan Co, IN 72
Beebe Alexander — Primitive Cem, Mexico, NY 15
Beebe Asa — West Greece Corners, Monroe Co, NY 33
Beebe Asahel — Maplewood (Dimmick) Cem, Malone, Franklin Co, NY 15
Beebe Ashahen — Grassy Hill Cem, Falls Village, CT 65
Beebe Bezaleel — West Litchfield, CT 17
Beebe Constant — New Concord Cem, Chatham, Columbia Co, NY 74
Beebe Daniel — Good Hill Cem, Kent, CT 40
Beebe Daniel — Grassy Hill Cem, Falls Village, CT 65
Beebe Daniel — Meth Epis Cem, Pleasant Mills, NJ 25
Beebe David — North Ridgeville Cem, Lorain Co, OH 55
Beebe Ezekial — Seneca, NY 54
Beebe Ezekiel — Old South Cem, Seneca Falls, NY 15
Beebe Ezra — Perry, OH 26
Beebe Ezra — South Lawn Cem, Williamstown, MA 33
Beebe Ezra — South Williamstown, MA 15
Beebe Hopson — [no cem named], OH 26
Beebe Hosea — Brown farm, New Concord, Columbia Co, NY 41
Beebe James Capt — Walnut Grove Cem, Onondaga Hill, Syracuse, NY 31
Beebe Jeduthan — Rogers Fam Cem, Great Neck Rd, Waterford, CT 56
Beebe John — New Concord Cem, Chatham, Columbia Co, NY 74
Beebe Joseph Sgt — Riches, Columbus, Chenango Co, NY 48
Beebe Martin — Brown farm, New Concord, Columbia Co, NY 41
Beebe Martin — Riverside Cem, Oxford, CT 56
Beebe Nathaniel — Grassy Hill Cem, Falls Village, CT 65
Beebe Peter — Perry Center Cem, Perry Center, Wyoming Co, NY 80
Beebe Philo — New Concord Cem, toward East Chatham, Columbia Co, NY 48
Beebe Roderick — Old Chatham Cem, Columbia Co, NY 42
Beebe Samuel — Canaan Twp, Madison Co, OH 17
Beebe Thomas — Fam Cem, Battle Creek Rd, New Scotland, Albany Co, NY 66
Beebe Thomas — Ohio Twp, Clermont Co, OH 74
Beebe Zerah — Pritchard farm, Solon, NY 36
Beebee Amon — Clymer Cem, Chautauqua Co, NY 63
Beecher Abraham — Sharon, CT 55
Beecher Amos — Hill Cem, Barkhamsted, CT 35
Beecher Amos — Willard Cem, Chenango Forks, Broome Co, NY 78
Beecher Burr — Northfield, CT 17
Beecher Eli — City Bur Gr, New Haven, New Haven Co, CT 24
Beecher Hezekiah — Fam plot, Union Cem, Lovonia, Livingston Co, NY 56
Beecher Hezekiah — Sperry Cem, Bethany, New Haven Co, CT 24
Beecher Jonathan — Sheshequin Cem, Sheshequin Twp, Bradford Co, PA 53
Beecher Joseph — North-East, Wolcott, CT 56
Beecher Linus — Milford Bur Gr, Woodbridge, CT 56

Beede Aaron	Fam Cem, West Sandwich, NH 31
Beede John	Fam Cem, West Sandwich, NH 31
Beede Phineas	Fam lot, Beede Hill, Fremont, NH 37
Beede Thomas	Fam Cem, West Sandwich, NH 31
Beegle Karl	Twin Ch Cem, Colerain Twp, Bedford Co, PA 80
Beekman Geraurd	Van Cortlandville Cem, Peekskill, NY 41
Beekman Tjerck	Old Dutch Cem, Kingston, Ulster Co, NY 85
Beeler Joseph	Nr Beeler Ch, Liberty Hill, Grainger Co, TN 63
Beeler Samuel	Bloomington, IL 15
Beeman Ebenezer	Merryall Cem, Wyalusing, PA 53
Beeman John	Hallowell Cem, Hallowell, ME 17
Beeman Jonas	Meeting House Hill Cem, Princeton, MA 49
Beeman Lemuel	Kent Hollow Cem, Kent, CT 40
Beeman Nathaniel	Old West St Cem, Rutland, VT 51
Beeman Tracey	Kent Hollow Cem, Kent, CT 40
Beemer Adam	Dutch Ref Brick Ch Cem, Montgomery, Orange Co, NY 76
Beemer John	St James Luth Cem, nr Phillipsburg, NJ 25
Beer Robert	Country Cem, nr Fairview, Fulton Co, IL 17
Beer Robert	Fulton Co, IL 16
Beermer John	St James Luth Ch Cem, E of Phillipsburg, NJ 35
Beers Abner	Fam Cem, Danbury, NY 15
Beers Abner	Fam Cem, Danby, NY 32
Beers Barnabus	Ithaca City Cem, Ithaca, NY 15
Beers Daniel	Curtis Cem, Danby, NY 32
Beers Daniel	Danby, NY 15
Beers David	Beaver Bogs, New Fairfield, CT 55
Beers David	Danby Cem, Danby, NY 32
Beers David	Ithaca City Cem, Ithaca, NY 15
Beers David	Old Bur Gr, Fairfield, CT 62
Beers Henry	Barbours Corners Cem, Barbours Corners, NY 32
Beers Isaac	Oak Ridge Cem, Springport, NY 41
Beers Jabez	Fam Cem, Danby, NY 34
Beers Jabez	Fam Cem, Danbury, NY 15
Beers Jabez	Killed in Wyoming Massacre, Wyoming, PA 52
Beers John	Cedar Grove Cem, Patchogue, NY 34
Beers John	Elm St Cem, Ansonia, CT 15
Beers John	Maple Grove Cem, Horseheads, NY 32
Beers Nathan	Old Bur Gr, Fairfield, CT 62
Beers Richard	Old Cem, Spencer, MA 55
Beeson Edward	Milledgeville, GA 29
Beeson Mercer	Old Bapt Ch Cem, New Jasper Park, E of New Jasper, OH 56
Beeston Jeremiah	St Ann's Cem, Middletown, New Castle Co, DE 46
Beetle Thomas	Edgartown, MA 15
Beiber Michael	Christ Union Ch Cem, Shoenersville, Lehigh Co, PA 40
Beidelman Samuel	Riverside Cem, Chemung, Chemung Co, NY 78
Beidelman Valentine	St James Luth Ch Cem, Phillipsburg, Warren Co, NJ 40
Beinhower Peter	Zion Luth Cem, Hummelstown, Dauphin Co, PA 61
Beisecker Johann	Drybands Ch Cem, Hecktown, Lehigh Co, PA 55
Beisel Jacob	Howerter's Ch, Pitman, PA 49
Beisel John P	Christ Union Ch Cem, Shoenersville, Lehigh Co, PA 40
Beisel John P	Christ Union Ch, Schoenersville, Northampton Co, PA 22
Beitelman Lenhart	Old Cem, Hecktown, Northampton Co, PA 21
Beiterman Johann G	Swamp Luth (Falkner) Cem, Montgomery Co, PA 59
Beitleman Lenhart	Dryland Union Ch Cem, Hecktown, Northampton Co, PA 40
Belch Hezekiah	Poplar Tent Pres Ch Cem, Cabarrus Co, NC 49
Belcher Daniel 3rd	Romney March Bur Gr, Revere, MA 31
Belcher Elijah	Hancock Cem, Quincy, MA 54
Belcher Elisha	Next to 2nd Cong Ch, Greenwich, CT 57
Belcher John	Gerold, Wrenthan, MA 54
Belcher Jonathan	First Cong Cem, Griswold, CT 62
Belcher Jonathan	Old Cem, Canton St, Sharon, MA 56

Belcher Joseph	Union Cem, Holbrook, MA	55
Belcher Michael	Fam Cem, nr Aberdeen, MD	51
Belcher Nathaniel	Union Cem, Holbrook, MA	55
Belcher Nathaniel	Union Cem, Holbrook, MA	55
Belcher Nathaniel Jr	Romney Marsh Bur Gr, Revere, MA	47
Belcher Samuel	North Cem, Dorchester, MA	46
Belden Azor	Sharp Hill Cem, Wilton, CT	55
Belden Ezekiel	Old Cem, Wethersfield, CT	56
Belden James	Clam River Cem, Sandisfield, MA	56
Belden Othniel	Chester Hill Cem, Chester, MA	53
Belden Thomas	Old Cem, Wethersfield, CT	56
Belden William	Widown Wholey's Bur Gr, Castile, NY	56
Belding Elijah	Mount Caesar Cem, Swanzey, NH	35
Belding Hezekiah	Hatfield Cem, Hatfield, MA	56
Belding Jonathan	Grassy Hill Cem, Falls Village, CT	65
Belding Jonathan	Pekin Cem, Pekin, NY	33
Belding Joshua	Whatley, MA	51
Belding Moses	Meth Cem, Barnard, VT	45
Belding Moses	Mount Caesar Cem, Swanzey, NH	35
Belding Selah Corp	Darrow Cem, W of Geneva, NY	15
Belding Silas	Valley View Cem, Dutchess Co, NY	58
Belding William	Shiley's Bur Gr, Castile, NY	51
Beldon Bildad	Old Cem, Rt 2, nr Brownheim, OH	56
Belk Brittan	Antioch Cem, Trinity Rd, Union Co, NC	58
Belk John Sr	Shiloh Assoc Ref Pres Cem, 5 mi N of Lancaster, SC	70
Belknap Abel	Middlefield Cem, Middlefield, Otsego Co, NY	72
Belknap Abel	North Chili Cem, Monroe Co, NY	33
Belknap Calvin	Hickok Cem, Austinburg, Ashtabula, OH	55
Belknap David	Farm 6 mi fr Smithville, Harrison Co, OH	51
Belknap David	Goodwill Cem, Montgomery, Orange Co, NY	78
Belknap Ezekiel Lt	Town Cem, Atkinson, NH	28
Belknap Francis	Central Bur Gr, Ellington, CT	56
Belknap Isaac	Old Town Bur Gr, Newburgh, Orange Co, NY	61
Belknap Josiah	Springfield, VT	16
Belknap Nathaniel	Old Cem, Salem Center, NH	28
Belknap Nathaniel	Town Cem, Dublin, NH	34
Belknap Samuel	West section, Old Town Bur Gr, Newburgh, NY	57
Belknap Simeon	Randolph Center Cem, Randolph, Orange Co, VT	72
Belknap William	Old Town Bur Gr, Newburgh, Orange Co, NY	77
Bell Abraham	Noroton River Cem, Darien, CT	68
Bell Andrew	Mount Olivet Cem, Newstead, NY	33
Bell Archibald	North Middletown Cem, KY	17
Bell Arthur	East Ripley Cem, Ripley, Chautauqua Co, NY	76
Bell Arthur	McClure Cem, Pike Twp, Clearfield Co, PA	56
Bell Arthur Sr	McClure Cem, nr Curvensville, PA	59
Bell Benjamin	Okalla Cem, Putnam Co, IN	70
Bell Benjamin	Viggera Cem, Hamilton Co, IA	42
Bell Daniel	Mayslick Cem, Mayslick, Mason Co, KY	62
Bell David	Old Augusta Stone Ch Cem, Ft Defiance, VA	62
Bell Elijah	Fleming Hill, Fleming, NY	56
Bell Francis	First Cong Ch Cem, Stamford, CT	68
Bell Francis	Old Liberty Meth Cem, Jackson, GA	57
Bell George	Camp Creek UMC Cem, Lancaster, SC	75
Bell Hendrick	Tappan Ref Ch Cem, Rockland Co, NY	78
Bell Hugh	Burks Cem, Jennings Twp, Alquina, Fayette Co, IN	79
Bell Isaac	Noroton River Cem, Darien, CT	55
Bell James	Fort Republic, NJ	36
Bell James	Houck Cem, Hilliar Twp, Knox Co, OH	53
Bell James	New Scotland Ch Cem, Albany Co, NY	66
Bell James	Valley Graveyard, Graham Twp, Jefferson Co, IN	72
Bell James Capt	Botetourt Co Cem, Botetourt Co, VA	35

Bell Jason	Dimick Cem, Malone, NY 62
Bell Johanns	Tappan Ref Ch Cem, Rockland Co, NY 78
Bell John	Mossy Creek Cem, Augusta Co, VA 55
Bell John	Old Cem, Bedford, NH 47
Bell John	Skipley Graveyard, Londonbury, NH 52
Bell John Sr	Bethel Pres Cem, Harford Co, MD 30
Bell Jonathan	Grasmere Cem, Goffstown, NH 28
Bell Jonathan	Mather Cem, West Norwalk, CT 68
Bell Jonathan	Milford, NH 15
Bell Joseph	Fairview Cem, nr Vincennes, Knox Co, IN 60
Bell Joseph Capt	Old Stone Ch, N of Staunton, Augusta Co, VA 36
Bell Kitchell Jr	Cornwall Cem, Cornwall, CT 15
Bell Martha McFarlane	Martha Bell Cem, Randolph Co, NC 49
Bell Matthew	George Bell Estate, Newcastle, NH 49
Bell Meshach Capt	Frost Cem, Newcastle, NH 28
Bell Nathaniel	Lowes's Bur Gr, Johnson Co, IN 60
Bell Robert	Friendsville, 9 mi S of Mount Carmel, IL 26
Bell Robert	Oakdale Cem, Wilmington, NC 49
Bell Robert	Silver Springs, NY 34
Bell Samuel	Morganville, NY 15
Bell Thaddeus	Darien, CT 48
Bell Thaddeus Jr	Slason Cem, Darien, CT 68
Bell Thomas	Broyles Cem, Washington Co, TN 24
Bell Thomas	Broyles Cem, TN 23
Bell Thomas	Kilpatrick Cem, Gibson Co, IN 66
Bell Thomas	Kilpatrick Cem, East Barton Twp, Gibson, IN 60
Bell William	Greenfield Cem, OH 15
Bell William	Greenfield Cem, Greenfield, Highland Co, OH 25
Bell William	Rev War Cem, Salem, Washington Co, NY 78
Bell William	Washington Court House Cem, Washington Court House, OH 18
Bellach James	Pres Cem, Dover, Kent Co, DE 46
Bellard John	Old Market St Cem, moved, Youngstown, OH 56
Bellesfelt John	Old Richard Cem, Mahoning Co, OH 45
Bellesfelt Peter	Old Richard Cem, Mahoning Co, OH 45
Belleville Nicholas Dr	First Pres Ch Cem, Trenton, NJ 28
Bellew Jacob	Mt Airy, GA 32
Bellew Stephen	Priv Cem, Union Co, NC 49
Belli John	Greentown Cem, Portsmouth, Scioto Co, OH 55
Bellinger Frederick P	Bellinger, E of Fort Herkimer, Herkimer Co, NY 70
Bellinger Peter	Nr Stone Ch, Fall Hill, NY 57
Bellis Adam	Knowlton Frame, Warren Co, NJ 38
Bellows Benjamin	Walpole, NH 16
Bellows Benjamin Gen	Village Cem, Walpole, NH 25
Bellows Isaac	Old Cem, Hubbardston, MA 50
Bellows John	Village Cem, Walpole, NH 25
Bellows John	Walpole, NH 16
Bellows Joseph	Village Cem, Walpole, NH 25
Bellows Joseph	Walpole, NH 16
Bellows Peter	Charlestown, NH 15
Bellows Simeon	Midland Cem, Westboro, MA 50
Bellows Theodore	Cem, Charleston, NH 49
Bellows Theodore	Charlestown, NH 15
Bellows Thomas	Old South Cem, Seneca Falls, NY 15
Belmear Francis	Fam plot nr Great Fork of Patuxent, nr Myers Station, MD 52
Belnap Jesse	Philips Cem, main road E of North East, PA 57
Belnap Joseph	Old Bur Gr, Arlington, MA 56
Belsher Michael	Fam Cem, White House Farm, Aberdeen, MD 52
Belt Middleton	On priv farm, Prince Georges Co, MD 52
Belton Abraham	Waxhaws, SC 56
Bemaine George	Antrim, NH 15
Beman Daniel	East Hartland Cem, East Hartland, CT 60

Beman Nathan	Evergreen Cem, Chateaugay, NY 53
Beman Samuel	Riverside Cem, old part W of Bailey lot, Plattsburg, NY 15
Beman Thomas	East Hartland Cem, East Hartland, CT 60
Beman Thomas	Old Cem, Gustavus Center, Trumbull Co, OH 56
Bement Asa	Stockbridge Cem, Stockbridge, MA 47
Bement Benjamin	Woodtick Cem, Wolcott, CT 55
Bemis Amasa	Old Cem, Spencer, MA 55
Bemis David	Old Cem, Spencer, MA 55
Bemis Edmund Capt	Westminster Cem, MA 44
Bemis Henry	North Littleton Cem, Littleton, NH 32
Bemis Isaac	Grove Hill Cem, Waltham, MA 45
Bemis James	Old North Cem, Marlboro, NH 39
Bemis Jesse	Old Cem, Spencer, MA 55
Bemis Jonas Jr	Old Cem, Spencer, MA 56
Bemis Jotham	Duell's Corners Cem, Orchard Park, NY 33
Bemis Nathaniel	Cem, Weston, MA 49
Bemis Sylvester	North Chester Cem, Chester, MA 62
Bemis William	Bemus Point Cem, Ellery, Chautauqua Co, NY 62
Bemiss Jonas	Huron Co, OH 15
Benbow Edward	West Grove Graveyard, Wayne Co, IN 72
Benchler Peter	Jacob's Luth Ch, 2 mi W of Pine Grove, Schuylkill Co, PA 37
Bender David	Heller Ch Cem, Leola, Lancaster Co, PA 80
Bender David	Hellers Ch Cem, Lancaster Co, PA 22
Bender Jacob	Salem Union Ch, Moore Twp, Northampton Co, PA 55
Bender Sebastion	Brunswick Twp, PA 49
Benedict A	Killed in Wyoming Massacre, Wyoming, PA 52
Benedict Aaron Dea	Cem, Leet farm, Marathon, NY 36
Benedict Aaron Sr	Alum Creek Friends Ch Cem, Peru Twp, Morrow Co, OH 53
Benedict Abner	Old Meth Epis Ch Cem, Grand Gorge, NY 32
Benedict Abraham	Elba, NY 15
Benedict Amos	Fabius Cem, Fabius, NY 56
Benedict Daniel	Milford, CT 56
Benedict Elisha Jr	Italy Hill Cem, Benton, Yates Co, NY 80
Benedict Felix	Farm nr Rutland, Meigs Co, OH 56
Benedict Hezekiah	Braceville, OH 24
Benedict Isaac	Parade Gr Cem, New Canaan, CT 21
Benedict Isaac	Ridgefield Cem, Gilbertsville, Otsego Co, NY 71
Benedict Joseph	Salem Cem, Salem, Westchester Co, NY 76
Benedict Joseph Col	Unionville Cem, Unionville, Westchester Co, NY 35
Benedict Lemuel	Spring Arbor Cem, Jackson Co, MI 25
Benedict Levi	Briggs Cem betw Middle Line Rd & Rt 20, Saratoga Co, NY 77
Benedict Peter	Priv Cem, nr Old Pigeon Hill School, Franklin Co, PA 56
Benedict Thaddeus	Unionville Cem, Unionville, Westchester Co, NY 35
Benedict Thomas	Rockdale, West Stockbridge, MA 56
Benedict Thomas Jr	McLean Cem, Groton, Tompkins, NY 36
Benedict Timothy	Danbury Quarter Cem, Winchester, CT 59
Benedict Uriah	Armstrong Cem, Malta, Saratoga Co, NY 76
Benedict Uriah	East line Union Cem, Malta, NY 41
Benefiel George	Jefferson Churchyard, Jefferson Co, IN 72
Benefiel John	Johnson Cem, Sullivan Co, IN 72
Benfer John George	New Berlin Cem, New Berlin, Union Co, PA 71
Benham Isaac	East Farms Cem, Waterbury, CT 55
Benham Jared	Broad St Cem, Meriden, CT 71
Benham John	"Separate" Cem, Amenia, Dutchess Co, NY 68
Benham John	Cong Cem, Cheshire, New Haven Co, CT 24
Benham Robert	Cincinnati, Hamilton Co, OH 55
Benham Thomas	Ashtabula, OH 18
Benham Thomas	Ashtabula, OH 15
Benjamin Aaron Col	New Fairfield, CT 31
Benjamin Amaziah	Mt Pleasant Cem, East Moriches, Suffolk Co, NY 79
Benjamin Asa	Old Bur Gr, lot 16, Pierpont, OH 56

Abstract of Graves of Revolutionary Patriots

Benjamin Barzilla	Milford Cem, Milford, CT 56
Benjamin Darius	Cem on Cuyler Hill, Cuyler, Cortland Co, NY 36
Benjamin Ebenezer Capt	Farm nr Red Rock, SE Chatham, Columbia Co, NY 48
Benjamin Ezra	Rixton Cem, Griswold, CT 57
Benjamin George	Old Epis Cem, Stratford, CT 56
Benjamin James	Scotch Cem, West Charlton, Saratoga Co, NY 77
Benjamin James Jr	Leonard-Curtis Cem, Worthington, Hampshire Co, MA 75
Benjamin John	Robinson Run Unit Pres Cem, nr Mcdonald, PA 21
Benjamin John Col	Epis Bur Gr, Stratford, CT 31
Benjamin John Jr	First Cong Cem, Griswold, CT 62
Benjamin Jonas	Muscalonge Cem, Hounsfield, Jefferson Co, NY 41
Benjamin Jonathan	Coram Cem, Brookhaven, Suffolk Co, NY 79
Benjamin Jonathan	Old Cem, Granville, Licking Co, OH 55
Benjamin Joseph	Meth Cem, North East, MD 51
Benjamin Nathan	Baiting Hollow, Suffolk Co, NY 56
Benjamin Nathan	Baiting Hollow, Suffolk Co, NY 56
Benjamin Nathan Capt	Bow Wow Cem, Sheffield, MA 40
Benjamin Phinehas	Ellsworth Cem, Sharon, Litchfield Co, CT 66
Benjamin Richard	Aquebogue Cem, Aquebogue, Suffolk Co, NY 79
Benjamin Richard	Storr's Farm Cem, Bradford, PA 53
Benjamin Samuel	East Hartland Cem, East Hartland, CT 60
Benjamin Samuel Lt	Livermore, ME 18
Benner Hendrick Esq	Dutch Ch Cem, Upper Red Hook, NY 21
Benner Henry Jr	East Coventry Mennonite Ch Cem, Chester Co, PA 75
Benner John Felton	St Paul's Luth Ch Cem, Red Hook Village, NY 21
Benner Johnnes	Franconia Mennonite Cem, Montgomery Co, PA 59
Benner Peter	Pittston Cem, Pittston, ME 47
Benner Peter Jr	St Paul's Luth Ch Cem, Red Hook Village, NY 21
Benner Sebastian	Franconia Mennonite Cem, Montgomery Co, PA 59
Bennet Asahel P	Sand Beach Cem, Fleming, NY 41
Bennet John	Old Pine Grove Cem, Leominster, MA 47
Bennet John	Plain Cem, Weathersfield, VT 36
Bennet John L	Old Bur Gr, Reade farm, nr Vanderburg, NJ 48
Bennet Miles	Warren Cem, Van Buren, NY 35
Bennet Samuel	Fam Cem, his farm, Brookline, VT 53
Bennet Thomas	Old Groton Cem, Groton, MA 46
Bennet Timothy	Old Cem, Huntington, NY 15
Bennett Aaron	Old Mettowee Cem, Pawlet, VT 48
Bennett Abraham	First Ref Ch Cem, New Brunswick, NJ 28
Bennett Abraham	First Dutch Ref Ch Cem, New Brunswick, NJ 24
Bennett Amos	Sennett Old Cem, Sennett, NY 56
Bennett Andrew	Cem, Forty Fort, PA 52
Bennett Asahel P	Sand Beach Cem, Fleming, NY 15
Bennett Asher	Line Cem, Foster, RI 55
Bennett Batchelder	Winthrop Village, Winthrop, ME 29
Bennett Benjamin	East Ripley Cem, Ripley, Chautauqua Co, NY 76
Bennett Benjamin	Liberty Hill, Lebanon, CT 56
Bennett Benjamin	Lower Ripley Cem, Ripley, NY 15
Bennett Caleb	Bennettsville Cem, Bainbridge, Chenango Co, NY 51
Bennett Caleb	Center Cem, New Milford, CT 55
Bennett Caleb	Stockbridge Cem, Stockbridge, MA 47
Bennett Caleb Prew	Friends Cem, Wilmington, New Castle Co, DE 36
Bennett Daniel	Cem, Judson farm, Foster Twp, RI 55
Bennett Daniel	Johnson Cem, Moosup Valley Rd, Foster, RI 55
Bennett David	Old Cem, Hubbardston, MA 50
Bennett David Dea	Dummerston, VT 17
Bennett Ebenezer	Fam farm, Northwood, NH 27
Bennett Ebenezer	Old Parish Cem, North Rochester, MA 59
Bennett Ebenezer	Old Cem, The Green, Middleboro, MA 50
Bennett Edmund	Sharon Cem, Sharon, Litchfield Co, CT 66
Bennett Eleazer Capt	Fam lot on farm, Durham, NH 50

Bennett	Elisha	Redbank Cem, Genoa Twp, Delaware Co, OH 46
Bennett	Ephrahim	Shoreham, VT 15
Bennett	Ephraim	New Haven, CT 56
Bennett	Ephraim Jr	Dix Twp Cem, Montour Falls, Schuyler Co, NY 71
Bennett	Ephraim Sr	Howard, Steuben Co, NY 57
Bennett	Ephraim Sr	Montour Falls Cem, Montour, Chemung Co, NY 84
Bennett	Ezekiel	Weatherly Cem, nr West Laurens, Otsego Co, NY 71
Bennett	H Pressel	Cem, Claysburg, PA 52
Bennett	Henry	Elmwood Cem, Pike, Wyoming Co, NY 64
Bennett	Isaac	Baldwin-Hamilton plot, New Lebanon, Columbia Co, NY 79
Bennett	Isaac	Main St Cem, Northville, Fulton Co, NY 39
Bennett	Isaac	Prospect Cem, Jamaica, Queens Co, NY 78
Bennett	Isaac	South Yard, Hampton, CT 31
Bennett	Isaiah	Union Chapel Cem, Warren Co, NJ 35
Bennett	Jabez	Woodstock Cem, Woodstock, Windsor Co, VT 74
Bennett	Jacob	Cem, Marion Rd, betw Long Point & Middleboro, MA 55
Bennett	Jacob	Old Cem, The Green, Middleboro, MA 50
Bennett	James	Newtown Village, Newtown, CT 56
Bennett	James	Nr Little Canada, Bethany, Genesee Co, NY 65
Bennett	James Col	Cortland Cem, Cortlandville, Cortland Co, NY 36
Bennett	Jared	East Cem, Smyrna, NY 16
Bennett	Jeames	Mt Moriah Cem, Rt 125, Union nr Tabasco, OH 56
Bennett	Jesse Dr	His farm, Ohio River 8 mi above Pt Pleasant, WV 19
Bennett	John	Durham, NH 58
Bennett	John	Hawkins Cem, lot 6, Genoa, NY 56
Bennett	John	Old Cem, The Green, Middleboro, MA 50
Bennett	John	Old North Cem, Old Hartford, CT 19
Bennett	John	Old Parish Cem, North Rochester, MA 59
Bennett	Jordan	Fam Cem, Mecklenburg Co, VA 63
Bennett	Joseph	Framingham, MA 55
Bennett	Joshua	Rehoboth Boone Twp, Harrison Co, IN 72
Bennett	Josiah	Bennett Yard, Piscassic Dist, Newfields, NH 35
Bennett	Jotham	Pine Grove Cem, Leominster, MA 49
Bennett	Micajah	West Burlington Cem, Burlington, NY 58
Bennett	Miles	Warners Cem, Warners, NY 56
Bennett	Nathan	Elbridge Cem, Elbridge, Onondaga Co, NY 78
Bennett	Nathan	Lower Page Brook Cem, Chenango Forks, Chenango Co, NY 82
Bennett	Nathan	Union Cem, Easton, CT 33
Bennett	Nathan	Yonst Hickory Cem, Steuben Co, Nr Knoxville, PA 69
Bennett	Nathaniel Lt	Cem, lower Main St, Sanford, ME 40
Bennett	Nathaniel Lt	Old Cem, Sanford, ME 45
Bennett	Nehemiah	Old Cem, The Green, Middleboro, MA 50
Bennett	Oliver	Orange Twp, OH 18
Bennett	Oliver	Redbank Cem, Genoa Twp, Delaware Co, OH 46
Bennett	Oliver	Redbank Cem, Genoa Twp nr Westerville, Delaware Co, OH 72
Bennett	Oliver C	West Hill Cem, Rushford, NY 31
Bennett	Reuben	Forest Home Cem, Waverly, NY 15
Bennett	Reuben	New Hope Bapt Ch Cem, Lancaster Co, SC 70
Bennett	Richard	Fam Cem, 7 mi W of Jesup, Wayne Co, GA 59
Bennett	Richard	Head of Christiana, New Castle Co, DE 46
Bennett	Rufus	Hanover Green, Hanover Twp, PA 52
Bennett	Samuel	Brookline, VT 17
Bennett	Samuel	Old Meth Cem, Manahawkin, NJ 47
Bennett	Solomen	Old Settlers Cem, Willowbend Farm, Canisteo Twp, NY 57
Bennett	Stephen	Froze on Lake Winnepesaukee and left there, MA 49
Bennett	Stephen	Paupeck Cem, E of Scranton, Palmyra Twp, Pike Co, PA 78
Bennett	Sylvanus	Old Cem, The Green, Middleboro, MA 50
Bennett	Thaddeus	His farm, nr Minford, Scioto Co, OH 55
Bennett	Thomas	Cem, Forty Fort, PA 52
Bennett	Thomas	Claverack Ref Ch Cem, Claverack, Columbia Co, NY 74
Bennett	Timothy	Old Huntington Cem, Huntington, Suffolk Co, NY 36

Bennett Walcott — Lincklaen, NY 16
Bennett Wilbur — Wysox Cem, PA 53
Bennett Wilbur — Wysox Cem, Wysox Twp, Bradford Co, PA 72
Bennett William — Aurora, IL 15
Bennett William — Farm nr Plato Center, IL 40
Bennett William — Handy Cem, West Woodstock, Windsor Co, VT 75
Bennett William — North Cem, Westmoreland, NH 25
Bennett William — Old Cem, The Green, Middleboro, MA 50
Bennett William — Pres Cem, Flemington, NJ 32
Bennett William Lt — Maple Shade, WV 42
Bennett Wolcott — Lincklaen Cem, Lincklaen, Chenango Co, NY 72
Bensinger Daniel — Zions Red Ch, Orwigsburg, PA 49
Bensinger Frederick — Frieden's, New Ringold, PA 49
Bensinger George — Steigerwalt's Ch, Brunswick Twp, PA 49
Bensinger Jacob — Steigerwalt's Ch, Brunswick Twp, PA 49
Benson Aaron — Douglas Center, MA 16
Benson Aaron Capt — Douglass Center Cem, Douglass, MA 45
Benson Abel — Church Hill Cem, Framingham, MA 56
Benson Asa — Old Cem, South Middleboro, MA 56
Benson Benoni Jr — Chestnut Hill Cem, Millville, MA 46
Benson Benoni Lt — Chestnut Hill Cem, Millville, MA 46
Benson Consider — Old Cem, South Middleboro, MA 56
Benson Egbert — Prospect Cem, Jamaica, Long Island, Queens Co, NY 77
Benson Elkanah — Owasco Rural Cem, Owasco, NY 56
Benson Henry — Chestnut Hill Cem, Millville, MA 46
Benson Henry — Fam Cem, New Hebron, MS 79
Benson Henry W — Fam Cem, Grange, MS 57
Benson Isaac Capt — Benson Yard, Richmond, NH 36
Benson Jacob — Lawrenceville Cem, Lawrenceville, NJ 26
Benson Joel — Pendergast farm, E of Ripley, Chautauqua Co, NY 77
Benson John — Chestnut Hill Cem, Millville, MA 46
Benson John — Rutland, Tioga Co, PA 53
Benson John Capt — Cedar Hill Cem, Paterson, NJ 24
Benson Jonah — Summer St Cem, Bridgewater, MA 55
Benson Jonathan — South Parish, Bridgewater, MA 56
Benson Jonathan — Summer St Cem, Bridgewater, MA 55
Benson Joshua — Union Cem, Springport, NY 41
Benson Joshua Maj — First Pres Ch, Columbia, SC 44
Benson Matthew — Mt Repose Cem, Haverstraw, Rockland Co, NY 78
Benson Peter — Central Cem, Brookline, VT 34
Benson Stephen — Owasco Rural Cem, Owasco, Cayuga Co, NY 57
Benson Stutson — Delphi Cem, Pompey, Onondaga Co, NY 75
Benson William — Owasco Rural Cem, Owasco, Cayuga Co, NY 57
Bent David — Cem, Uxbridge, MA 49
Bent Ebenezer — Old Cem, Milton, MA 56
Bent Francis — Center Cem, Wareham, MA 55
Bent Jabez — Old Common Bur Gr, Marlboro, MA 45
Bent Jason — Old Wayland Cem, Wayland, MA 46
Bent John — Old Milton Cem, Milton, MA 46
Bent Jonathan — Old Cem, Sudbury, MA 46
Bent Mathias — Church Hill Cem, Framingham, MA 56
Bent Peter — Old Common Bur Gr, Marlboro, MA 45
Bent Samuel — Town Cem, Fitzwilliam, NH 32
Bent Silas — Cedarville Cem, nr Belpre, Washington Co, OH 55
Bent Stephen — Sterling Valley Cem, Sterling, NY 41
Bent Thomas — Church Hill Cem, Framingham, MA 56
Bentalon Paul — Gloucester Co, NJ 32
Bentalon Paul Col — West Pres Ch Cem, Baltimore, MD 19
Bentalou Paul Col — Westminster Pres Cem, lot 6, Baltimore, MD 15
Bentley Benjamin — Sharon (Wadsworth) Cem, Sharon Center, Medina Co, OH 55
Bentley Caleb — Center Berlin Cem, Berlin, Rensselaer, NY 60

Bentley Charles	Cem N of Caleshire (now Monterey), Monterey, MA 56
Bentley Elisha	Greenwich, NY 34
Bentley Elisha Sr	Corashire, Monterey, MA 56
Bentley George	Wheeler Bur Gr, Stonington, CT 27
Bentley Gideon	Episcopal Cem, Constantia, Oswego Co, NY 72
Bentley Green	Greene Cem, Millport Veteran, Chemung Co, NY 78
Bentley John	Boyce Cem, Milton, Ulster Co, NY 77
Bentley Joseph	Kellogsville, Sempronius, NY 56
Bentley Joshua	Center Cem, Groton, MA 55
Bentley Tillinghast	Moe Cem, South Victory Mills, Saratoga Co, NY 76
Bentley Tillinghast	Moe Cem, South Victory Mills, Saratoga Twp, NY 41
Bentley William	Fam Cem, Great Bend & Champion Rd, Jefferson Co, NY 41
Bentley William	Priv bur plot, 1 mi fr Great Bend, Jefferson Co, NY 16
Bentley William Sgt	Huntington, WV 31
Benton Abijah	Village Cem, Surry, NH 35
Benton Adoniram	Village Cem, Surry, NH 35
Benton Amos	Lenox, MA 55
Benton Bethel	At or nr Seneca Falls, NY 52
Benton Bethel	Gates Cem, Seneca Twp, Sutton Rd, Ontario Co, NY 57
Benton Caleb	Clam River Cem, Sandisfield, Berkshire Co, MA 79
Benton David	Cande Fam (Sage) Cem, Sheffield, MA 41
Benton Elihu	North Guilford Cem, North Guilford, CT 55
Benton Elihu S	Windsor, CT 15
Benton John	Old South Cem, Hartford, CT 19
Benton Jonathan	Eaton Cem, Marshfield, VT 55
Benton Lemuel	Pres Cem, Darlington, SC 60
Benton Nathaniel	West Litchfield, CT 17
Benton Nathaniel	West Cem, Litchfield, CT 18
Benton Noah	West Side, North Madison, CT 54
Benton Stephen	Cone Hill Cem, Richmond, MA 55
Benton Zadock	Chardon, OH 26
Benton Zadock Sr	Chardon, OH 15
Benton Zebulon	West Cem, Rowe, Franklin Co, MA 54
Berard Jean	St Martin of Tours Cath Ch Cem, St Martinville, LA 74
Berdan Henry	Hudson St Cem, Hudson, NJ 47
Berdan Isaac	Hackensack Green Cem, Hackensack, NJ 47
Berdsley Wells	Long Mountain Cem, New Milford, CT 55
Berean Peter	Dry Creek Cem, Moravia, Niles, NY 56
Berean Thomas	Old Dresserville, Sempronius, NY 56
Berge Johannes	Franconia Mennonite Cem, Montgomery Co, PA 59
Bergen Jacob C	Old Neshanic Ref Cem, Frankfort, NJ 47
Bergen Jacob G	Old Neshanic Ref Ch Cem, Somerset Co, NJ 48
Bergen John	Old Town Cem, Lancaster, NH 36
Bergen John B	First Pres Ch Cem, Cranbury, NJ 76
Bergen P John	First Pres Ch Cem, Cranbury, NJ 76
Berger Casper	Readington Cem, Hunterdon, NJ 60
Berger John	Holmes Co, OH 44
Bergey Isaac	Franconia Mennonite Cem, Montgomery Co, PA 59
Bergher Jacob	St Paul's Ch Cem, Upper Saucon Twp, Northampton Co, PA 56
Berkeley Michael	Fairview Luth Ch, 16 mi fr Dunnsville, Albany Co, NY 75
Berlin Isaac	Peiffertown Cem, Saegertown, Crawford Co, PA 72
Berlin Isaac	Peiffertown Cem, Saegertown, Crawford Co, PA 69
Bernard David	The Hill Cem, Old Village Rd, Shelburne Center, MA 74
Bernard Elisha	The Hill Cem, Old Village Rd, Shelburne Center, MA 74
Bernard Michael	St Martin of Tours Cath Ch Cem, St Martinville, LA 74
Bernard Nathan	Common Cem, Union, Knox Co, ME 79
Bernard Walter	Tanyard-Bernard-Hill Cem, Rocky Mount, Franklin Co, VA 75
Bernhardt John Mathias	Bear Creek Ref Ch, Cabarrus Co, NC 59
Bernhart Arndt	Dryland Union Ch Cem, Hecktown, Northampton Co, PA 40
Bernheisel Johannes	St Paul's Ch, Summer Hill, PA 49
Berray Seth	Randolph Cem, Randolph, NY 71

Abstract of Graves of Revolutionary Patriots

Berry Andrew	Goshen Cem, Belmont, Gaston Co, NC 56
Berry Barnabas	Briggs St Cem, Westville, Franklin Co, NY 77
Berry Benjamin	Embden, ME 15
Berry Benjamin Capt	First Parish Cem, Brewster, MA 46
Berry George	Fam Cem, Strafford Corner Strafford, NH 38
Berry George	Greene, ME 18
Berry George	Nr Corydon, Henderson Co, KY 34
Berry George Capt	Fam bur gr, Cincinnati Pike, 10 mi fr Georgetown, KY 20
Berry Hugh Jr	Goshen Cem, Belmont, Gaston Co, NC 56
Berry Hugh Sr	Goshen Cem, Belmont, Gaston Co, NC 56
Berry Isaac	West Yarmouth Cem, Yarmouth, MA 46
Berry John	Ebenezer Cem, Effingham Co, GA 27
Berry John	Meth Ch Cem, Shrub Oak, Westchester Co, NY 36
Berry John	Olney Pres Ch Cem, Gaston Co, NC 52
Berry John	Passaic, NJ 32
Berry John	Second Cem, North Andover, MA 26
Berry John Jr	Machias, ME 18
Berry John Sr	Machias, ME 18
Berry Joseph	In woods on farm, New Durham Corner, New Durham, NH 39
Berry Joshua Capt	Small Cem, his farm, nr Berry Pond Rd, Pittsfield, NH 29
Berry Judah	Brewster, MA 55
Berry Nathaniel	Good Hill Cem, Kent, CT 55
Berry Richard	Goshen Cem, Gaston Co, NC 49
Berry Samuel	Auburn, ME 18
Berry Samuel	Briggs Cem, Auburn, ME 39
Berry Samuel	Fam Cem, Barrington, NH 41
Berry Scotto	1st Parish Ch, Brewster, MA 55
Berry Sidney Col	Nevins Cem, Northumberland, NY 41
Berry Thomas	Achorn Cem, Rockland, ME 55
Berry Thomas	Achorn Cem, Rockland, MA 55
Berry Thomas	Meth Cem, Strafford Corner, Strafford, NH 38
Berry Thomas	Miltonville Cem, Madison Twp, Butler Co, OH 55
Berry William	Bean Cem, Center Harbor, NH 29
Berry William Capt	First Parish Cem, Brewster, MA 47
Berryhill Alexander	Pioneer Cem, Bellbrook, OH 25
Berryhill William	Steele Creek Pres Ch Cem, Mecklenburg Co, NC 72
Berryman William	Luth Cem, Reisterstown, MD 19
Bert Thomas	[no cem named], OH 26
Bertholf James	Bartholf Fam Cem, Stafford, Genesee Co, NY 65
Bertolet Samuel	Bertolet's Mennonite Cem, Montgomery Co, PA 59
Bertsch Christian	St Paul's Churchyard, Indianland, Northampton Co, PA 59
Besanson Pierre	Elmwood Cem, Pike, Wyoming Co, NY 64
Bescherer Abraham	Union Brick Cem, Warren Co, NJ 38
Besore Daniel	Salem Ref Ch Cem, Rt 3, Waynesboro, Franklin Co, PA 56
Besore David	Salem Ref Ch Cem, Rt 3, Waynesboro, Franklin Co, PA 56
Bess Isaac	Fam Cem, Halifax Co, NC 60
Besse Jabez Jr	Evergreen Cem, Wayne, ME 30
Besse Nathaniel	Hammond Cem, Mattapoisett, MA 18
Besson Richard	Old Burial Hill, Marblehead, MA 55
Best Henry	Fam bur gr nr Shine, Greene Co, NC 49
Best Johannes Jr	Livingston, NY 15
Best John	Ch Cem, Livingston, Columbia Co, NY 41
Best John J	Ch Cem, Livingston, Columbia Co, NY 42
Best Nicholas	Williams Twp, Northampton Co, PA 59
Best Thomas	Deerfield, OH 53
Best William Jr	St Paul's Union Cem, Beaver Twp, Clarion Co, PA 68
Bester Job	Cartwright Cem, Sharon, Litchfield Co, CT 66
Betchel Martin	Mennonite Cem, Borough of Bally, Berks Co, PA 70
Bethea John	Dillon, SC 30
Bethnal Norris	Pisgah Cem, Sycamore Twp, Hamilton Co, OH 55
Betterley Thomas	West Dummerston, VT 17

Betterly William C	Cem, St Johns, PA 52
Bettersmith Richard	Old Cem, Bowling Green, KY 26
Bettes Jeremiah	Woodlawn Cem, Biddeford, ME 29
Bettes Leonard	Rose Road Cem, Sandsfield, MA 53
Bettes Nathaniel	Akron, OH 15
Bettes Nathaniel	Bettes Corners, Summit Co, OH 45
Bettes Silas W	Fam Cem, lot 30 #5, Akron, OH 53
Bettin Adam Capt	Jockey Hollow Rd, 1 mi N of Morristown, NJ 24
Bettisworth Charles	Carthage, IL 53
Betton James	Cem on the Plains, Windham, NH 28
Betton Richard	Francestown Cem, Francestown, NH 28
Betts –	Washington St Cem, Geneva, NY 15
Betts Hezekiah	Prob Norwalk, CT 34
Betts Isaac	Old Town Cem, Norwalk, CT 34
Betts Isaiah	West Galway Cem, Galway, Saratoga Co, NY 78
Betts James Jr	Old Jordan Cem, Elbridge, Jordan, Onondaga Co, NY 75
Betts Jeremiah	Dunning Street Cem, Malta, Saratoga Co, NY 78
Betts Jeremiah	Pres Cem, Morristown, NJ 32
Betts John	Elm St Cem, Ansonia, CT 15
Betts Justus	East Chatham Cem, NY 48
Betts Moses	Greenfield Hill Cem, Fairfield, CT 62
Betts Selah	Mount View Cem, West Pawlet, VT 48
Betts Selah	West Pawlet Cem,, VT 15
Betts Silas	Union Cem, Norwalk, CT 34
Betts Spencer	Plantation Cem, Halifax Co, VA 63
Betts Stephen	Church Hill, New Canaan, CT 56
Betts Thaddeus	Cem Norwalk, CT 49
Betts Uriah	Old Town Bur Gr, Newburgh, Orange Co, NY 69
Betts William	Nr Denmark, Madison Co, TN 24
Betts William	Nr Denmark, TN 23
Betts William	Old homestead, 13 mi fr Jackson, Madison Co, TN 15
Betts Zopher	Sharon Cem, Sharon, Litchfield Co, CT 66
Betts Zopher	Ten Broeck Cem, Oxford, NY 16
Betzer Wilhelm	Salem Ref Cem, Green Twp, Ross Co, OH 53
Beuchle Conrad	Long Run, North Huntington Twp, Westmoreland Co, PA 56
Beuchler John	Jacob's Ch, Pine Grove Twp, PA 49
Beuchler Peter	Jacob's Ch, Pine Grove Twp, PA 49
Bevan Isaac	St Vincent #1, Minersville, PA 49
Bevans Evan	Mettler Cem, Sandyston Twp, Sussex Co, NJ 79
Bevans Evan	Mettler Cem, Sussex Co, NJ 29
Bevans Jacob	Thomas Cem, West Woodstock, VT 65
Bevans John	Marietta, IL 53
Bevier Elias	Kirkwood Cem, Kirkwood, Broome Co, NY 78
Bevier Jacob I	Owasco Rural Cem, Owasco, NY 56
Bevier Samuel	Owasco Rural Cem, Owasco, NY 56
Bevier Solomon	Fitzsimmons Cem, Southport, Chemung Co, NY 78
Bevis Issachur	Johnson's Cem, nr Venice, Hamilton Co, OH 55
Beyden Daniel	Old bur gr, Holden, MA 45
Bibbins Israel	Old Bur Gr, Fairfield, CT 62
Bickel Christian	Fam Cem, Traquar farm, Mt Carmel Rd, Ancor, OH 56
Bickel Jacob	Kratzerville Cem, PA 15
Bickel Jacob	Luth Swamp Ch, Montgomery Co, PA 21
Bickel John	Old Reformed Ch Cem, Jonestown, Lebanon Co, PA 83
Bickford Benjamin	Dearborn Cem, Dearborn, ME 45
Bickford Henry	Cotton Cem, Portsmouth, NH 34
Bickford John	Old fam farm, Ten Rod Rd, Rochester, NH 39
Bickford Micajah	Old Town Cem, Mast Rd, Lee, NH 41
Bickford William	Old Gardner Cem, Gardner, MA 46
Bickford William	The Old Cem, Gardner, MA 33
Bickings Richard	Fam Cem, Montgomery Co, PA 59
Bickley Charles	Fam Cem, Bickley Mills, Russell Co, VA 63

Bicknell Bennett	Morrisville, NY	15
Bicknell Jacob	Mt Vernon, Abington, MA	54
Bicknell John	Mount Zion Cem, Whitman, MA	56
Bicknell Joseph	Mt Vernon Cem, Abington, MA	62
Bicknell Joshua	Princes Hill Cem, Barrington, RI	46
Bicknell Josiah	Enfield Cem, Enfield, CT	59
Bicknell Luke Capt	Mount Zion Cem, Abington, MA	45
Bicknell Nathaniel	Old Cem, Milton, MA	56
Bicksler Joseph	Wolf Union Cem, Bethel Twp, Lebanon Co, PA	83
Biddis Samuel	Hood's Cem, Germantown, PA	20
Biddis Samuel	[no cem named], PA	19
Biddle John	Milford Cem, Milford, CT	56
Biddlecome Richard	Warren Co, IN	15
Bidlack James Jr	Killed in Wyoming Massacre, Wyoming, PA	52
Bidlack Philemon	Sunbury, OH	18
Bidwell Adonijah	Old Center Cem, Monterey, MA	56
Bidwell Allen	West Cem, Langdon, NH	35
Bidwell Ashbel	Old Farm Hill Cem, Middletown, CT	57
Bidwell Daniel Jr	Center Cem, East Hartford, CT	19
Bidwell David Jr	Salisbury Cem, Crow Hill, Maltaville, NY	41
Bidwell Eleazer	Colebrook Cem, Colebrook, CT	56
Bidwell Ephriam	His farm, Bidwell Hill, PA	48
Bidwell John	Kinderhook Cem, Columbia Co, NY	42
Bidwell Jonathan	Old Bloomfield Cem, Bloomfield, CT	55
Bidwell Joseph	Griegsville Cem, Livingston Co, NY	33
Bidwell Rev	Cem on the hill, Monterey, MA	41
Bidwell Thomas	Dyer Cem, Canton, CT	55
Bidwell Thomas	Dyer Cem, Canton, CT	15
Bidwell William Sr	Middle Ridge Cem, Madison, OH	26
Bieber John	Western Salisburg Old Cem, Lehigh Co, PA	40
Bieber Michael	Christ Union Ch, Schoenersville, Northampton Co, PA	22
Bieber Nicholas	Grindstone Hill Union Ch Cem, nr Chambersburg, PA	60
Bierbauer Casper	Hancock Cem, Hancock, Washington, MD	71
Bierce James	Cornwall Cem, Cornwall, CT	15
Bierce Joseph	Cornwall Cem, Cornwall, CT	15
Bierce William	Nelson, OH	26
Biery Henry	Western Salisburg Old Cem, Lehigh Co, PA	40
Biery Michael	Western Salisburg Old Cem, Lehigh Co, PA	40
Biesecker Johan Jacob	Dryland Union Ch Cem, Hecktown, Northampton Co, PA	40
Biesecker Johan Jacob	Old Cem, Hecktown, Northampton Co, PA	21
Bievenu Antoine Sr	Randolph Co, IL	48
Biffle Jacob	Pisgah Cem, Pisgah Hill, W of Mt Pleasant, Maury Co, TN	73
Bigelar Nicholas	Napoli, Cattauragus Co, NY	71
Bigelow Abijah	Greenwood Cem, Michigan City, IN	24
Bigelow Alpheus	Old Yard Cem, Weston, MA	55
Bigelow Asa	Old Center Cem, Monterey, MA	56
Bigelow Asa G	Old Cem, Brookfield, MA	45
Bigelow Converse	Old Yard Cem, Weston, MA	55
Bigelow Daniel	Old Highland Cem, MA	29
Bigelow David	Highland Cem, Athol, MA	55
Bigelow Eli	Mt Parnassus, East Haddam, CT	56
Bigelow Elisha	Woodside Cem, Westminster, MA	53
Bigelow Elisha Jr	Old South Cem, Hartford, CT	19
Bigelow Ivory Lt	Spring Hill Cem, Marlboro, MA	45
Bigelow Jabez	Woodside Cem, Westminster, MA	52
Bigelow Jabez Jr	Fam Cem, New Lebanon, Columbia Co, NY	79
Bigelow James	South Side Cem, Skowhegan, ME	45
Bigelow John	Old Cem, nr Cong Ch, Spencer, MA	54
Bigelow John Maj	Gold St Cem, Old Hartford, CT	19
Bigelow Jonas	Maple St Cem, North Brookfield, MA	17
Bigelow Josiah	Old Yard Cem, Weston, MA	55

Bigelow Josiah	Pompey Hill Cem, Pompey, Onondaga Co, NY 75
Bigelow Otis	Goshen, Lebanon, CT 56
Bigelow Russel Sr	Galena Cem, Berkshire Twp, Delaware Co, OH 53
Bigelow Thomas	Douglass Center Cem, Douglass, MA 45
Bigelow Timothy	Bloomfield Cem, Bloomfield, Trumbull Co, OH 55
Bigelow Timothy	Spring Hill Cem, Marlborough, MA 56
Bigelow Timothy Col	Worcester Common, under shaft, Worcester, MA 46
Bigelow William	Bonnyvale Cem, West Brattleboro, VT 46
Bigelow William	South Natick Ch Cem, Natick, MA 56
Bigelow William	West Cem, Bolton, MA 56
Bigford Jeremiah	Killed in Wyoming Massacre, Wyoming, PA 52
Bigford Samuel	Killed in Wyoming Massacre, Wyoming, PA 52
Bigger John	Pioneer Cem, Village of Bellbrook, Greene Co, OH 56
Bigger Joseph	Beavertown Cem, Beavertown, OH 56
Biggs Elijah	Old Wade Bur Gr, IL 26
Biggs John	Fam farm, Wyandot Co, OH 46
Biggs William	Belle Fontaine, now Waterloo, IL 16
Biggs William	Old Sewell Cem, nr Cuba, Clinton Co, OH 46
Bigham William	Hamilton, OH 51
Bignal Abner	Bald Hill Cove, Winterport, Waldo Co, ME 57
Bigoney Francis	Zion Ref Ch Cem, Montgomery Co, PA 62
Bilbory Isham	Polk Bilbrey Cem, Oak Hill, Overton Co, TN 82
Bilgear Frederick	Washingtonville Cem, Columbiana Co, OH 55
Bilisoly Antonio S	Slab moved to Cedar Grove Cem, Portsmouth, VA 34
Bill Daniel	East Hartland Cem, East Hartland, CT 60
Bill David	Centennial Cem, Gilsum, NH 32
Bill Ebenezer	Amherst Cem, Amherst, NH 56
Bill Ebenezer	Centennial Cem, Gilsum, NH 32
Bill Eleazer	Exeter Cem, Lebanon, CT 26
Bill Elisha	Old Hartwick Cem, Hartwick, Otsego Co, NY 78
Bill Ephraim	City Cem, Oak St, Norwich, CT 18
Bill Jonathan	Exeter Cem, Lebanon, CT 26
Bill Oliver	Exeter Cem, Lebanon, CT 26
Billheimer Conrad	Beach Haven Cem, Salem Twp, PA 52
Billing Elkanah Dr	Howard (rural) Cem, Lyn, Ontario, Can 56
Billings Abel	Settlers Rest Cem, South Brooksville, ME 58
Billings Benager	East Avon Cem, Livingston Co, NY 33
Billings Benjamin	Factory Village Cem, Milton, Saratoga Co, NY 78
Billings Benjamin	Mansfield, MA 53
Billings Benjamin	Palmyra Village Cem, Palmyra, Wayne Co, NY 79
Billings Benjamin MD	Town Yard, Mansfield, MA 56
Billings Ephrain	Acton, MA 55
Billings Ezekial	Hope Cem, Perry, Wyoming Co, NY 64
Billings James	Clarkson, NY 15
Billings James	Knapp Cem, Parma, Monroe Co, NY 79
Billings Jasper	Fam Cem, fam farm, Dockery, Wilkes Co, NC 77
Billings Jess	Bapt Ch Cem, Wilton, Saratoga Co, NY 78
Billings Jesse Capt	Moe Cem, South Victory Mills, Saratoga Twp, NY 41
Billings Joel	North Cem, Amherst, MA 56
Billings John	North Cem, Amherst, MA 56
Billings John Jr	First Cong Cem, Griswold, CT 62
Billings Jonathan	North Cem, Acton, MA 56
Billings Jonathan Jr	Acton, MA 55
Billings Joseph	Center Bur Gr, Lincoln, MA 55
Billings Joseph	Mottsville Cem, Skaneateles, Onondaga Co, NY 75
Billings Lemuel	In tomb, Westerly Cem, West Roxbury, MA 46
Billings Oliver Capt	North Cem, Dorchester, MA 46
Billings Peleg	First Cong Cem, Griswold, CT 62
Billings Roger	First Cong Cem, Griswold, CT 62
Billings Samuel	Old Common Cem, Newport, RI 35
Billings Sanford Capt	North Stonington, CT 31

Billings Silas	Amherst Cem, Amherst, MA 56
Billings Solomon	Roberts Cem, Walker Pond, Brooksville, ME 54
Billings Timothy	Old Cem, Lincoln, MA 55
Billings Timothy Jr	Center Bur Gr, Lincoln, MA 55
Billingsly John	Old Union Ch, 12 mi SE of Bowling Green, Warren Co, KY 77
Billington John	Clarkson Cem, Monroe Co, NY 58
Billows Isaac Rev	McGraw Cem, Cortland, Cortland Co, NY 36
Bills Daniel	Houston Graveyard, Marshall Co, TN 67
Bills Elijah	Hope Cem, Wyoming Co, NY 55
Bills Hosea	Lower Plain Cem, Sheffield, MA 41
Billups Joseph Jr	Old Billups Cem, Moon, Mathews Co, VA 57
Binder Anthony	Swamp Luth (Falkner) Cem, Montgomery Co, PA 59
Binder Jacob	Palmer Street Cem, Philadelphia, PA 52
Binder Jacob	Swamp Luth (Falkner) Cem, Montgomery Co, PA 59
Binegar George	Greene Co, OH 55
Bingaman Frederick	Troxelville Cem, PA 15
Bingham Abel	Cong Cem, East Haddam, CT 56
Bingham Abner	West Yard Cem, Marlow, NH 25
Bingham Alvan	[no cem named], OH 26
Bingham Calvin	Old Bennington, VT 40
Bingham Calvin	Old Bennington Town Hill Cem, VT 41
Bingham Daniel	Chapinville Cem, Taconic, nr Salisbury, CT 64
Bingham Elias	Chase (orig Mercer) Cem, Cornish, Sullivan Co, NH 75
Bingham Elijah	East Lempster Cem, East Lempster, NH 35
Bingham Elisha	Belcoda Cem, Wheatland, Monroe Co, NY 79
Bingham Jeremiah	Cong Ch, Cornwall, VT 56
Bingham John C	[no cem named] 15
Bingham Johnson	Old Bapt Ch Cem, nr Solon, Cortland Co, NY 36
Bingham Nathaniel	Chesterfield Center Cem, Chesterfield, NH 36
Bingham Ozias	Riverside Cem, Towanda Borough, Bradford Co, PA 72
Bingham Ripley	West Yard Cem, Marlow, NH 25
Bingham Samuel	Kirkland Avenue Cem, Clinton, Oneida Co, NY 79
Bingham Silas Sr	Athens, OH 26
Bingham Thomas Lt	Haven Cem, Royalton, VT 45
Binkley Adam	Fam Cem, Cheatham Co, TN 42
Binkley John	Fam Cem, nr Hermitage, Davidson Co, TN 41
Binkley John	Fam Cem, Davidson Co, TN 42
Binkly Johannes	Fam Cem, Reading Twp, Perry Co, OH 53
Binney Benjamin	Hull Cem, Hull, MA 60
Binninger Isaac	Camden Valley Cem, Salem, NY 63
Birch Thomas	Fam Cem, Fountain Co, IN 72
Birch William	Newtown Village, Newtown, CT 56
Birchard David	Old Mill River Rd, New Marlborough, MA 56
Bird Aaron	West Auburn, ME 29
Bird Benjamin	Pearl St Cem, Stoughton, MA 55
Bird Ebenezer	Bethlehem Cem, left of entrance, Bethlehem, CT 55
Bird Edward	Antioch Bapt Ch Cem, York, NC 49
Bird Edward	North Cem, Dorchester, MA 46
Bird Elisha	First Pres Ch Cem, Hackettstown, NJ 47
Bird Ezekial	North Cem, Dorchester, MA 46
Bird George	Old Stone Ch Cem, Ruraldale, Muskingum, OH 55
Bird Henry	Fam Cem, Poor House Fork, Little Caney Cr, Morgan Co, KY 72
Bird Henry	North Cem, Dorchester, MA 46
Bird Henry	South Cem, Dorchester, MA 46
Bird Isaac	Old Town Hall Cem, Salisbury, CT 64
Bird Isaac	Pearl St Cem, Stoughton, MA 55
Bird Jacob	North Cem, Dorchester, MA 46
Bird John	Cem, Forty Fort, PA 52
Bird John	Hermon Ch Cem or Tusculum Cem, Greene Co, TN 57
Bird John	Needham, MA 50
Bird Jonathan	Hop Meadow Cem, Simsbury, CT 55

Bird Jonathan	North Cem, Dorchester, MA 46
Bird Joseph	North Cem, Dorchester, MA 46
Bird Joseph	North Cem, Dorchester, MA 46
Bird Joseph	Old Center Cem, Monterey, MA 41
Bird Lemuel	Pearl St Cem, Stoughton, MA 55
Bird Nathaniel	Westfield Cem, Westfield, Chautauqua Co, NY 77
Bird Samuel	Broadway Cem (McCollough Park), Ft Wayne, Allen Co, IN 72
Bird Samuel	North Cem, Dorchester, MA 46
Bird Thomas	North Cem, Dorchester, MA 46
Birdsall Benjamin Col	Jones plot, Massapequa, Long Island, NY 34
Birdsall Benjamin Col	Old Cem, Greene, NY 16
Birdsall Daniel	Van Cortlandville Cem, Peekskill, NY 41
Birdsall Daniel William	Van Cortlandville Cem, Peekskill, NY 41
Birdsall John	Otego, NY 34
Birdsall John	Unadilla Cem, Unadilla, Otsego Co, NY 72
Birdsall Lemuel	Quaker Hill Cem, Harpersfield, NY 58
Birdsall Nathan IV	Quaker Cem, Haviland Hollow, Dutchess Co, NY 57
Birdseye Nathan	Cong Cem, Stratford, CT 31
Birdseye Thaddeus	Cong Cem, Stratford, CT 31
Birge Asahel	Center Cem, Southampton, MA 49
Birge Benjamin	Headquarters, CT 17
Birge Hosea	Chatham Rural Cem, Chatham, Columbia Co, NY 41
Birge James	Headquarters, CT 17
Birge John	Torrington Cem, Torrington, CT 55
Birge Roswell	Torrington Cem, Torrington, CT 55
Birge Simeon	Torrington Cem, Torrington, CT 55
Birsall Squire	Fam Cem, Otsego, NY 58
Birt George	Hosensack, Salem Evangelical Cem, Lehigh Co, PA 40
Bisbe Gamaliel	Fern Hill Cem, Hanson, MA 59
Bisbee Abner	Old Cem, Plympton, MA 56
Bisbee Abner Capt	[no cem named] 15
Bisbee Benjamin	Pearl St Cem, Stoughton, MA 55
Bisbee Charles	Sumner Cem, Sumner, ME 47
Bisbee Elijah Jr	Old Cem, Plympton, MA 50
Bisbee Gamaliel	Mt Zion Cem, Whitman, MA 62
Bisbee George	Old Bur Cem, Plympton, MA 58
Bisbee Hopestill	North Ave, North Rochester, MA 56
Bisbee Hopestill	Old Burial Cem, Plympton, MA 57
Bisbee Issachar	Old Burial Cem, Plympton, MA 57
Bisbee John	Old Cem, Plympton, MA 50
Bisbee John Lt	Springfield, VT 15
Bisbee Noah	Old Burial Cem, Plympton, MA 57
Bisbee Samuel	Pearl St Cem, Stoughton, MA 55
Bisbing Bernard	St Thomas Epis Ch Cem, Montgomery Co, PA 59
Bishop Abraham	Dale Cem, Middlebury, Wyoming Co, NY 64
Bishop Bela	Center Cem, Norfolk, CT 62
Bishop Daniel	Meth Epis Ch Cem, Clarksfield, OH 56
Bishop David	Town Green (grave), Riverside Cem (stone), Guilford, CT 55
Bishop Ebenezer	Fam bur plot, Camp Hill, Rockland Co, NY 78
Bishop Ezekiel	Miller Cem, Mamaroneck, NY 34
Bishop Ezekiel	Scituate, MA 52
Bishop Hezekiah	Second Cong Ch Cem, Attleboro, MA 56
Bishop Hezekiah	Simsbury Cem, High Ridge & Cross Rd, Stamford, CT 68
Bishop Hooper	Novi Cem, Novi Twp, Oakland Co, MI 57
Bishop Hooper	Novi, MI 15
Bishop Isaac	Jug City Cem, Leroy, NY 31
Bishop Isaac	North Haven, CT 56
Bishop James	North Guilford Cem, North Guilford, CT 55
Bishop James	Old Cem, Plympton, MA 50
Bishop Jared	Cheshire, CT 17
Bishop Jared	Cong Cem, Cheshire, New Haven Co, CT 24

Abstract of Graves of Revolutionary Patriots

Bishop Jared	Riverside Cem, Guilford, CT 55
Bishop Jeremiah	Stillwater Bur Gr, Stillwater, NY 41
Bishop Job	Meth Cem, Canaan, Jefferson Co, IN 72
Bishop Joel	Norwich Cem, 2½ mi S of Havana, OH 56
Bishop John	Old Rumford Cem, Rehoboth, MA 55
Bishop John Sr	Monkton Cem, Monkton, Addison Co, VT 61
Bishop Jonathan	Noroton River Cem, Darien, CT 55
Bishop Joseph	Marcellus, NY 35
Bishop Josiah	Salmon Hole Cem, Lisbon, NH 28
Bishop Joy	Old Cem, North Haven, CT 15
Bishop Levi	Manlius, NY 35
Bishop Nathanial Jr	Maple Grove Cem, Hoosick Falls, NY 34
Bishop Nathaniel	Maple Grove, Hoosick Falls, NY 33
Bishop Newman Sr	Hazard Pond, Russell, MA 56
Bishop Noah	Wolf Creek Cem, Saline Co, IL 30
Bishop Phanuel	Newman Ch Cem, Rumford, RI 55
Bishop Phanuel	Old Rumford Cem, Rehoboth, MA 55
Bishop Richard	Hope Cem, Perry, NY 59
Bishop Samuel	Mt Hope Cem, Rochester, Monroe Co, NY 79
Bishop Samuel	North Guilford Cem, North Guilford, CT 55
Bishop Shotwell	Rowley farm, Union Co, NJ 32
Bishop Squier	Stanley Ground, Winthrop, ME 20
Bishop Stephen	North Stamford Cong Ch Cem, Stamford, CT 68
Bishop Sylvanus	Rural Cem, Oswego, NY 30
Bishop Thomas	Gider Brook Cem, Avon, CT 56
Bishop William	Pres Cem, Morristown, NJ 32
Bishop Zadock	Leeds, ME 20
Bishop Zadok	Leeds, ME 18
Bishop Zephamiah Capt	Old Kirk Yard, Attleboro, MA 15
Bispham Eleazer	North Cem, Dorchester, MA 47
Bissel Benjamin	Torrington Cem, Torrington, CT 55
Bissel Ebenezer F Jr	Palisado Cem, Windsor, CT 55
Bissel Ebenezer Fitch	Palisado Cem, Windsor, CT 55
Bissel Elijah	Torrington Cem, Torrington, CT 55
Bissel Elipha	Torrington Cem, Torrington, CT 55
Bissel Elisha	Torrington Cem, Torrington, CT 55
Bissel Elisha	West Torrington Cem, Torrington, CT 55
Bissel Ezekiel	Torringford Cem, Torringford, CT 36
Bissel Hezekiah	Torrington Cem, Torrington, CT 55
Bissel John P	Youngstown, OH 15
Bissel John Partridge	Oak Hill Cem, Youngstown, Mahoning Co, OH 55
Bissel Josiah	Palisado Cem, Windsor, CT 55
Bissel Oliver	Torrington Cem, Torrington, CT 55
Bissel Return	Torrington Cem, Torrington, CT 55
Bissell Archelaus	West Litchfield, CT 17
Bissell Benjamin	Evergreen Cem, Painesville, OH 26
Bissell Benjamin	Goshen, Lebanon, CT 56
Bissell Benjamin	West Litchfield, CT 17
Bissell Calvin	West Litchfield, CT 17
Bissell Daniel	Allen's Hill Cem, nr Honeoye, Ontario Co, NY 74
Bissell Elias	Rural Cem, Lancaster, NY 33
Bissell George	Sharon Cem, Sharon, Litchfield Co, CT 66
Bissell Hezekiah Capt	North Stonington, CT 31
Bissell Hezekiah Capt	Scantic Cem, East Windsor, CT 27
Bissell Isaac	Hartwig, NY 56
Bissell Isaac	Old Bur Gr, Suffield, Hartford Co, CT 24
Bissell John	Milton, CT 17
Bissell John	Town Hill Cem, Lakeville, CT 64
Bissell Ozias	Manchester Cem, Manchester, CT 56
Bissell Ozias Capt	Village Cem, Colebrook, NH 36
Bissell Russell	Ft Bellefontaine, St Louis, MO 56

Bissell Samuel	Chase Cem, Hartwick, Otsego Co, NY 71
Bissell Samuel	Flat Rock Dist, Plainfield, CT 26
Bissell Samuel	Town Hill Cem, Lakeville, CT 64
Bissell Thomas	Rye St Cem, East Windsor, CT 27
Bissell William Joseph	Evergreen Cem, South St, Lairdsville, NY 36
Bissell Zebulon	West Cem, Litchfield, CT 18
Bissell Zebulon	West Litchfield, CT 17
Bissom Jonathan	Bur on hill toward Boston in Roxbury, MA 49
Bisson Charles	Bethel Meth Epis Cem, Montgomery Co, PA 59
Bisson Charles	Worcester Bethel Meeting, PA 15
Bisson Joshua	Central Cem, Beverly, MA 31
Biteley John	Bitley Cem, Moreau, Saratoga Co, NY 78
Bittenbender Conrad	LaWall plot, N 7th St, Easton, PA 48
Bittenbender Jacob	Briar Creek, St Peters Cem, nr Berwick, Columbia Co, PA 58
Bitting Anthony	Nazareth Luth Ch Cem, NC 49
Bitting Joseph	White Deer Luth Ch Cem, White Deer Twp, Union Co, PA 64
Bitting Yost	Lower Salford Mennonite Cem, Montgomery Co, PA 59
Bittinger Nicholas	Luth Ch Cem, nr Abbottstown & Hanover, York Co, PA 56
Bittler John	Old Cem, Ringtown, PA 49
Bittner Andreas	Weisenburg Old and New Cem, Lehigh Co, PA 40
Bitzell Henry	Balsar Homestead Cem, Reading, Hamilton Co, OH 71
Bivins David	West of Columbus, IN 48
Bivins John	Marietta, Fulton Co, IL 17
Bixbee Jacob	Cem, East Thompson, Windham Co, CT 24
Bixby Acy	Number Two Cem, Francestown, NH 34
Bixby Adonijah	Springfield, VT 15
Bixby Adonijah	Sumner Hill Cem, Springfield, VT 23
Bixby Daniel Capt	Pine Crest Cem, Litchfield, NH 31
Bixby David	Killed in Wyoming Massacre, Wyoming, PA 52
Bixby Edward	Francestown Cem, Francestown, NH 28
Bixby Edward	Town Cem, Francestown, NH 27
Bixby Elias	Killed in Wyoming Massacre, Wyoming, PA 52
Bixby Jonathan	Krum Ch Cem, Hillsdale, Columbia Co, NY 41
Bixby Jonathan	Lyme Plain Cem, Lyme, NH 30
Bixby Jonathan	South Bur Gr, Newton Highlands, MA 30
Bixby Jonathan	South Bur Gr, Newton Highlands, MA 47
Bixby Jonathan	South Bur Gr, Newton Highlands, MA 29
Bixby Nathaniel	West Dummerston, VT 19
Bixby Sampson	East Campbell Cem, Campbell, Steuben Co, NY 80
Bixby Samuel	Lyme Plain Cem, Lyme, NH 30
Bixby Thomas	Francestown Cem, Francestown, NH 28
Bixby Thomas	Town Cem, Francestown, NH 27
Bixby Thomas Jr	Hopkinton Cem, Hopkinton, MA 45
Blachley Daniel	Comac, Long Island, NY 16
Blachly Benjamin	Commack Meth Ch Cem, Huntington, Suffolk Co, NY 72
Blachly Ebenezer Dr	Cem, Pennington, NJ 26
Black Alexander	Ebenezer Ch Cem, SC 17
Black Col	Pres Ch Cem, Columbia, SC 30
Black Daniel	Old Bur Gr, Holden, MA 15
Black David	Old Cem, now park, Hamilton, St Clair Twp, Butler Co, OH 55
Black George	Farm, grave obliterated, Scott, NY 36
Black George	Pres Cem, Blaine, PA 16
Black Henry	Sandy Point Cem, Stockton, ME 27
Black Hugh	Seneca #9 Cem, Stanley, Ontario Co, NY 86
Black Isaac	Africa Cem, Delaware Co, OH 18
Black Jacob	Black Cem, VT 20
Black James	His land, Lancaster Rd, nr Richmond, KY 39
Black James	St Helene Epis Ch Cem, Beaufort, Beaufort Co, SC 78
Black James Jr	Beech Spring Ch Cem, Green Twp, Harrison Co, OH 56
Black James Maj	Head of Christiana Cem, nr Newark, New Castle Co, DE 45
Black John	Alexander prop, nr Blacksburg, Montgomery Co, VA 73

Black John	Massacred nr mouth of Lechry Creek, Dearborn Co, IN	24
Black Joseph	Ebenezer Ch Cem, SC	17
Black Joseph Col	First Pres Ch Cem, Columbia, SC	41
Black Joseph Sr	Eusebia Pres Ch, 12 mi NE of Maryville, Blount Co, TN	76
Black Nicholas	Killinstown, OH	56
Black Richard	Mount Pleasant Cem, Kingston Twp, Ross Co, OH	53
Black Robert	Ebenezer, Jessamine Co, KY	56
Black Thomas	Bethesda Pres Ch Cem, nr McConnellsville, York Co, SC	56
Black Thomas	Deer Creek, Pulaski, PA	56
Black William	Millcreek Cem, Delaware Co, OH	18
Blackbourne Moses	Petersburg Center Cem, Mahoning Co, OH	55
Blackbreen Sam	Filson Cem, Fleming Co, KY	45
Blackburn Ambrose Capt	Old fam bur gr, Swans Creek, Maury Co, TN	41
Blackburn John	Rev Bur Gr, nr courthouse, Dandridge, Jefferson Co, TN	74
Blackburn Moses	Columbiana Cem, Unity Twp, Columbiana Co, OH	61
Blackburn Moses	First Bur Gr, Dorchester, MA	45
Blackburn Thomas	Rippon Lodge priv Cem, Woodbridge, Prince William Co, VA	73
Blackburn William	Battle of Kings Mountain, SC	52
Blackburn William	Donaldson Bapt Ch Cem, nr Princeton, Caldwell Co, KY	73
Blackesley David	Spartansville Cem, Sparta Twp, PA	21
Blackford David	Samptown Cem, South Plainfield, Middlesex Co, NJ	79
Blackford Nathan	Middlesex Hillside Cem, Middlesex, NJ	24
Blackford Nathan	Samptown Cem, South Plainfield, Middlesex Co, NJ	80
Blackington Benjamin	Tolman Cem, Rockland, ME	56
Blackington James	Thomaston, ME	56
Blackington James	Thomaston, ME	16
Blackington James Capt	Thomaston, ME	30
Blackington William	Plainville, Norfolk Co, MA	31
Blackinton George	North Attleboro, MA	56
Blackinton Othniel	Old bur gr, North Attleboro, MA	39
Blackinton Samuel	Plainville Cem, Wrentham, MA	55
Blackler William	Waterside Cem, Marblehead, MA	48
Blackman David	New Andover Cem, Andover, CT	55
Blackman David	Zion Cem, Bargaintown, NJ	23
Blackman Eleazer	Hollenbeck Cem, Wilkes-Barre, PA	52
Blackman Elijah	[no cem named], OH	26
Blackman Elisha I	Hanover Green, Hanover Twp, PA	52
Blackman Elisha II	Hanover Green, Hanover Twp, PA	52
Blackman Elisha Jr	The Green Cem, Wilkes-Barre, Luzerne Co, PA	78
Blackman Ichabod	Rutland, Tioga Co, PA	53
Blackman John Jr	Lands End (Hawleyville), Newtown, CT	56
Blackman Josiah	Dry Pond Cem, Stoughton, MA	55
Blackman Lemuel	North Dorchester, Dorchester, MA	56
Blackman Moses	North Cem, Dorchester, MA	46
Blackman Samuel	North Cem, Dorchester, MA	47
Blackman Samuel	Union Cem, Norwalk, CT	34
Blackman Samuel Jr	Liverpool Cem, Salina, Onondaga Co, NY	75
Blackman Trueman	Johnstown, Rock Co, WI	29
Blackman Truman	Johnstown, WI	37
Blackmar John	Fabyan Yard, Thompson, CT	29
Blackmer Jacob	Munyan Yard, East Putnam, CT	26
Blackmon Zachariah	Farmersville Center Cem, Farmersville, NY	65
Blackmore Samuel Capt	Farm, #1, nr Christian Ch, Peter Twp, Washington Co, PA	38
Blackshear David Gen	Springfield, his home, Laurens Co, GA	15
Blackshere Ebenezer	Snider Cem, Lincoln Dist, WV	40
Blackstone John	Branford, CT	52
Blackwell Andrew	Drake Cem, nr Centreville School, 2 mi fr Pennington, NJ	45
Blackwell Benjamin	Old School Bapt Cem, Hopewell, NJ	45
Blackwell Jesse	Nr Kingston, TN	23
Blackwell Jesse	Nr Kingston, Roane Co, TN	24
Blackwell John	His farm, Muhlenburg Twp, nr Darbyville, Pickaway Co, OH	18

Blackwell John	Old fam Cem nr Darbyville, Pickaway Co, OH	55
Blackwell Joseph Rev	Jones Cem, Upward, Henderson Co, NC	43
Blackwell Micah	Village Cem, Sandwich, MA	56
Blackwell Micha	Howard Cem, Winslow, ME	29
Blackwell Stephen	Bapt Cem, Hopewell, NJ	32
Blackwood James	Cem, Pembroke, ME	49
Blain Alan	Genoa Twp, OH	18
Blain James	Walker farm nr Stinesville, Monroe Co, IN	72
Blain Thomas	Old Blain farm, Orange Co, NY	57
Blair Abraham	His farm, Franklin Twp, Knox Co, OH	55
Blair Absolom Capt	Westlawn Cem, Williamstown, MA	15
Blair Absolom Capt	West Lawn Cem, Williamstown, MA	33
Blair Alexander	Edgefield, SC	16
Blair Asa	Old Center Cem, Blandford, Hampden Co, MA	58
Blair David	Madison Center, NY	15
Blair Jacob	Old Center Cem, Blandford, Hampden Co, MA	58
Blair James	Brown Cem, nr Dale, Spencer Co, IN	72
Blair James	Erie Co, PA	55
Blair James	Woolwich, ME	21
Blair John	Cedar Valley Meth Ch Cem, Caldwell Co, NC	56
Blair John	Fam Cem, N of West Galway, Galway, Saratoga Co, NY	78
Blair John	Old Cem, Peterborough, NH	29
Blair John	Old Salem Cem, Washington Co, TN	31
Blair John	Oxford, Warren Co, NJ	35
Blair John	Peterborough, NH	15
Blair John Sr	Pine Corners Cem, Rushville, NY	29
Blair Matthew	Old Center Cem, Blandford, Hampden Co, MA	58
Blair Reuben	Old Cem, West Brookfield, MA	29
Blair Reuben	Old Center Cem, Blandford, Hampden Co, MA	58
Blair Robert	Old Center Cem, Blandford, Hampden Co, MA	58
Blair Rufus	Old Center Cem, Blandford, Hampden Co, MA	58
Blair Samuel	Brick Ch Cem, Sodus, Wayne Co, NY	79
Blair Samuel	Fam Cem, Davidson Co, TN	42
Blair Seth	Madison Center, NY	15
Blair Seth	Madison Center Cem, Madison, Madison Co, NY	82
Blair Thomas	Salem Pres Ch Cem, Salem Cross Rds, Fairfield Co, SC	60
Blair William	Nr Kossuth, Des Moines Co, IA	42
Blair William	Old Cem, Peterborough, NH	29
Blair William	Old Waxhaw Pres Ch Cem, SC	17
Blair William	Peterborough, NH	15
Blaire Absolom Capt	Westlawn Cem, Williamstown, MA	46
Blaisdell Abner	Knowlton Cem, Chocorua, NH	29
Blaisdell Daniel	Town Cem, Canaan, NH	29
Blaisdell Ephreman	Bartlett Cem, Amesbury, MA	49
Blaisdell Henry	Grasmere Cem, Goffstown, NH	28
Blaisdell Henry	Knowlton Cem, Chocorua, NH	29
Blaisdell Hezekiah	South Sutton Cem, Sutton, NH	37
Blaisdell Isaac	Village Cem, Chester, NH	25
Blaisdell Jacob	Georgetown (Cambridge) Cem, Dearborn Co, IN	78
Blaisdell Jacob	McCoy Cem, Old Gilmanton, Gilford, NH	28
Blaisdell Jedediah	Allen farm, South Berwick, ME	39
Blaisdell John	East Kingston Cem, Kingston, NH	46
Blaisdell John	First Yard, Meredith, NH	29
Blaisdell John	Old Cem, East Kingston, NH	43
Blaisdell John	Union Cem, Amesbury, MA	33
Blaisdell John Rev	Lebanon Cem, Lebanon, ME	45
Blaisdell Levi	Grove Cem, Coeymans, NY	30
Blaisdell Samuel	McCoy Cem, Old Gilmanton, Gilford, NH	28
Blaisdell Samuel	Union Cem, Amesbury, MA	33
Blaisdell Thomas	First Yard, Meredith, NH	29
Blake Aaron	Old Blake Cem, Walpole, MA	45

Blake Aaron Jr	Old Blake Cem, Walpole, MA 45
Blake Amariah	Old Milton Cem, Milton, MA 46
Blake Ariel	Bradford St Cem, Keene, NH 25
Blake Asa	North Bellingham Cem, Bellingham, MA 46
Blake Benjamin	Lake View Cem, Wolfeboro, NH 26
Blake Ebenezer	McGraw Cem, Cortland, Cortland Co, NY 36
Blake Ebenezer	Plainville Cem, Wrentham, MA 55
Blake Ebenezer	Plainville Cem, Wrentham, MA 55
Blake Edward	Central Bur Gr, Boston Common, MA 15
Blake Edward	Central Cem, Boston, MA 46
Blake Edward	Old Granary Bur Gr, Boston, MA 55
Blake Edward	Old Granary Bur Gr, Boston, MA 55
Blake Edward	Walker-Blake Cem, Taunton, MA 41
Blake Eleazer	Old Cem, Rindge, NH 36
Blake Elijah	Center Cem, Winchester, CT 59
Blake Elisha	Blake Cem, Stark, Coos Co, NH 76
Blake Elisha	Fam Cem, Stark, NH 32
Blake Elisha	Old Yard, Kensington, NH 47
Blake Elisha Jr	Old Yard, Kensington, NH 47
Blake Enoch Lt	Town Cem, Pittsfield, NH 28
Blake Enos	Old Cem, Milton, MA 56
Blake Ezra	Wrentham Cem, Wrentham, MA 46
Blake Freelove	Dewitt Cem, Dewitt, NY 32
Blake George	Springfield Cem, Springfield, MA 46
Blake George Kennett	Pisgah Cem, Jefferson Co, IN 72
Blake Grenfill	Walker-Blake Cem, Taunton, MA 41
Blake Henry	Copps Hill Bur Gr, Boston, MA 55
Blake Henry	Peacham, VT 56
Blake Hezekiah	New Cem, Kensington, NH 25
Blake Isham	Cross Creek Cem, Fayetteville, Cumberland Co, NC 80
Blake James	Old Milton Cem, Milton, MA 46
Blake Jason	Town Yard, Mansfield, MA 56
Blake Jeremiah	Park Ave Cem, Holden, MA 15
Blake Jeremiah Ens	Old Cem, Crossroad, Hampton Falls, NH 30
Blake John	Gardiner, ME 20
Blake John E	Ira Union Cem, Ira, Cayuga Co, NY 57
Blake Josiah	Old Yard, Kensington, NH 47
Blake Moses	Town Cem, Sutton, NH 37
Blake Moses Jr	Old Yard, Kensington, NH 47
Blake Paul Dearborn	West Mount Vernon, ME 52
Blake Philemon	Old Cem, Kensington, NH 29
Blake Philemon	Old Yard, Kensington, NH 47
Blake Richard	Union Cem, Livonia, NY 16
Blake Robert	Plainville Cem, Wrentham, MA 55
Blake Royal	Keene, NH 16
Blake Samuel	Roxbury Cem, Roxbury, MA 46
Blake Samuel	Turner, ME 18
Blake Sherburne Maj	Town Cem, Epping, NH 28
Blake Simeon	Chestnut Hill Cem, Millville, MA 46
Blake Solomon	Franklin, MA 56
Blake Thomas	Central Cem, Boston, MA 46
Blake Willing	Old Blake Cem, Warren, ME 56
Blake Ziba	Old Milton Cem, Milton, MA 46
Blakely David	Old Mettowee Cem, Pawlet, VT 48
Blakely Davis	Old Cem, Pawlet, VT 15
Blakely Gabriel	Old Cem, triangle grave #30, Washington Co, PA 38
Blakely James	Fam farm, 1½ mi S of Wilksville, OH 56
Blakeman James	Putney & Oronoque, Stratford, CT 56
Blakeman Trueman	Johnston Cem, Rock Co, WI 56
Blakeman Zachariah	Putney Cem, Stratford, CT 70
Blakeney John	Fam Cem, Chesterfield, SC 56

Blakeney John	Fam Cem, Pageland, SC 70
Blakeney John Sr	Fam Cem, Pageland, Chesterfield Co, SC 78
Blakeslee Asa	Cong Cem, Cheshire, New Haven Co, CT 24
Blakeslee Caleb	North Haven Cem, North Haven, CT 56
Blakeslee Caleb	North Cem, Rowe, Franklin Co, MA 54
Blakeslee David	Old Cem, Plymouth Hollow, CT 57
Blakeslee Lealans	Center Cem, Wolcott, CT 56
Blakeslee Samuel	Avon Cem, Avon, Livingston Co, NY 79
Blakeslee Samuel	Avon Cem, Livingston Co, NY 33
Blakeslee Samuel	Northfield, CT 17
Blakeslee Zealous	North Haven Cem, North Haven, CT 56
Blakesley Samuel	East Hartland Cem, East Hartland, CT 60
Blakesley Samuel Col	Avon Cem, Avon, Livingston Co, NY 22
Blakey George	Cem at Russellville, Logan Co, KY 59
Blakey George	Russellville Cem, Russellville, KY 50
Blanch Thomas	Tappan Ref Ch Cem, Rockland Co, NY 78
Blanchard Aaron	Bailey Cem, Dracut, MA 55
Blanchard Abner	Highland Cem, South Weymouth, MA 50
Blanchard Adam	Mt Vernon, Abington, MA 54
Blanchard Amos	Old Western Cem, Lynn, MA 55
Blanchard Augustus Capt	Milford, NH 15
Blanchard Azariel	Keeney Settlement Cem, Cuyler, NY 36
Blanchard Benjamin	South Yard, Wilton, NH 34
Blanchard Daniel	Highland Cem, South Weymouth, MA 50
Blanchard Daniel	North Weymouth Cem, North Weymouth, MA 56
Blanchard Daniel Jr	Highland Cem, South Weymouth, MA 50
Blanchard David	Old North Cem, North Weymouth, MA 50
Blanchard David	Williams Cem, Northfield, NH 34
Blanchard David Sr	Old North Cem, North Weymouth, MA 50
Blanchard Edward	Hodgdon Cem, Northfield, NH 31
Blanchard Elias	Grave obliterated, Cincinnatus, Cortland Co, NY 36
Blanchard Elias	South Yard, Brooklyn, CT 30
Blanchard Ephraim	Dyer Hill, Braintree, MA 55
Blanchard George	Milford, NY 15
Blanchard Isaac	Milford, NY 15
Blanchard Isaac	On Rt 106, East Mansfield, MA 56
Blanchard Jacob	First Cong Ch Cem, Stamford, CT 68
Blanchard Jedediah	Itaska Cem, Whitney Point, Broome Co, NY 81
Blanchard John	Lakeview Cem, South Weymouth, MA 50
Blanchard John 2nd	Grave obliterated, Cincinnatus, Cortland Co, NY 36
Blanchard Jonathan	Pearl St Cem, Stoughton, MA 55
Blanchard Jonathan Hon	Old South Cem, Nashua, NH 30
Blanchard Joseph	East Montpelier Cem, Montpelier, VT 46
Blanchard Joseph	Long Meadow Cem, Chester, NH 33
Blanchard Joseph	Old Cem, Acworth, NH 34
Blanchard Joseph	On Rt 106, East Mansfield, MA 56
Blanchard Joshua	South Yard, Wilton, NH 34
Blanchard Josiah	Highland Cem, South Weymouth, MA 50
Blanchard Josiah	South Parish Cem, Andover, MA 55
Blanchard Jotham	Perham Corner Cem, Lyndeboro, NH 54
Blanchard Justus	Palenville farm, (priv), Palenville, NY 56
Blanchard Lemuel	Worcester Cem, Washington Co, VT 59
Blanchard Samuel	Lakeview Cem, South Weymouth, MA 50
Blanchard Samuel	Worcester Cem, Worcester, VT 15
Blanchard Simeon	Milford, NH 15
Blanchard Simon	Cherry Hill Cem, Bethel, Windsor Co, VT 72
Blanchard Soleman	Priv Cem, Dresden, Lincoln Co, ME 74
Blanchard Thomas	Carpenter's Bur Gr, Henderson, Jefferson Co, NY 79
Blanchard Thomas	Lakeview Cem, South Weymouth, MA 50
Blanchard Thomas	Lakeview Cem, South Weymouth, MA 62
Blanchard Timothy	East Wilton, ME 15

Abstract of Graves of Revolutionary Patriots

Blanchard William	First Cong Ch Cem, Stamford, CT 68
Blanchard William	Old Cem, East Main St, East Stoughton, now Avon, MA 55
Blanchard William	South Cem, Wilmington, MA 56
Bland Richard	Fam Cem, Jordan's Point, Prince George Co, VA 37
Bland Richard	Jordan's Point Cem, Prince George Co, VA 49
Bland Theodrick Col	Trinity Ch Cem, City, NC 37
Blandford Richard	St John's Cath Ch, Bardstown, Nelson & Bullitt Co, KY 77
Blandin Benjamin Capt	Old Cem, Norton, MA 45
Blandin Jonathan	Bethlehem St Cem, Bethlehem, NH 32
Blanding Christopher	Rehoboth Village Cem, Rehoboth, MA 54
Blanding Daniel	Old Kirk Yard, Attleboro, MA 15
Blanding Elisha	West Sutton Cem, Sutton, Worcester Co, MA 78
Blanding Noah	Old Kirkyard Cem, Attleboro, MA 47
Blanding Noah Lt	Old Kirk Yard, Attleboro, MA 15
Blaney Daniel	Pres Cem, New Castle, New Castle Co, DE 46
Blank George	Blue Church, old Cem, nr Coopersburg, Lehigh Co, PA 40
Blank Peter	Western Salisburg Old Cem, Lehigh Co, PA 40
Blankenbaker Nicholas	Shelby Co, KY 39
Blankinship Charles	Evergreen Cem, Marion], MA 59
Blankinship George	Evergreen Cem, Marion, MA 59
Blankinship Job	Evergreen Cem, Marion, MA 59
Blankinship Paul	Fam Cem, Marion, MA 59
Blankinship William	1st Parish Cem, Rochester, MA 58
Blanton Burwell	5 mi S of Shelby, NC 40
Blanton Burwell	Fam Cem, NC 49
Blarcom Jon	Union Cem, Ramsey, NJ 47
Blasdel Jacob	Cambridge Cem, nr Guilford, Dearborn Co, IN 72
Blaso John	McLary Cem, Epsom Center, NH 29
Blass Peter	Ref Ch Cem, Germantown, Columbia Co, NY 41
Blassingame –	Nr Greenville, SC 51
Blassingame John W A	Fam Cem, Greenville Co, SC 70
Blatchely Seely	Jordanville Cem, Log Cabin, Herkimer Co, NY 41
Blatchford John	Old Cem, Rockport, MA 56
Blatchley Ebenezer	Pres Ch Cem, Pennington, NJ 46
Blatchley Joel	West Side, North Madison, CT 54
Blatchley Joshua	West Side Cem, Madison, CT 38
Blatchley Seely	Jordanville Cem, Jordanville, NY 32
Blattenberger John	Middletown, PA 56
Blatzly John I	The Old Cem, New Philadelphia, OH 58
Blauvelt Abraham	Harrington Park Cem, Harrington Park, NJ 47
Blauvelt Abraham	Martinus-Hogencamp Cem, New City, Rockland Co, NY 78
Blauvelt Abraham David	Middletown Bur Plot, Pearl River, Rockland Co, NY 78
Blauvelt Auri (Aaron)	Brick Ch Cem, Monsey, Rockland Co, NY 78
Blauvelt Cornelius A	Brick Ch Cem, Monsey, Rockland Co, NY 78
Blauvelt Cornelius A	Scotland Hill Cem, Nanuet, Rockland Co, NY 78
Blauvelt Cornelius J	True Ref Ch Cem, Nanuet, Rockland Co, NY 78
Blauvelt Frederick	Harrington Park Cem, Harrington Park, NJ 47
Blauvelt Frederikus	Tappan Ref Ch Cem, Rockland Co, NY 78
Blauvelt Garret Isaac	Tallman Bur Gr, Blauvelt, NY 53
Blauvelt Garret J	Sickletown Cem, Nauraushaun, Orangetown, Rockland Co, NY 78
Blauvelt Garret Joseph	Greenbush Pres Ch Cem, Blauvelt, Rockland Co, NY 78
Blauvelt Harman	Harrington Park, NJ 54
Blauvelt Harmanus	Scotland Hill Cem, Nanuet, Rockland Co, NY 78
Blauvelt Hendrick A	Orangeburg-Clausland Cem, Orangeburg, Rockland Co, NY 78
Blauvelt Isaac A	Martinus-Hogencamp Cem, New City, Rockland Co, NY 78
Blauvelt Isaac I	Harrington Park Cem, Harrington Park, NJ 47
Blauvelt Issac	Paramus Ch Cem, Paramus, NJ 51
Blauvelt Jacob	Harrington Park Cem, Harrington Park, NJ 47
Blauvelt Jacobus J	Tappan Ref Ch Cem, Rockland Co, NY 78
Blauvelt James J	Valleau Cem, Paramus, NJ 51
Blauvelt Johannes	Martinus-Hogencamp Cem, New City, Rockland Co, NY 78

Blauvelt Johannes	Orangeburg-Clausland Cem, Orangeburg, Rockland Co, NY 78
Blauvelt Johannes J	Orangeburg-Clausland Cem, Orangeburg, Rockland Co, NY 78
Blauvelt Johannes J	Orangeburg-Clausland Cem, Orangeburg, Rockland Co, NY 78
Blauvelt Johannes J	Orangeburg-Clausland Cem, Orangeburg, Rockland Co, NY 78
Blauvelt John	Harrington Park Cem, Harrington Park, NJ 47
Blauvelt John	Orangeburg-Clausland Cem, Orangeburg, Rockland Co, NY 78
Blauvelt Joseph J	Sickletown Cem, Nauraushaun, Orangetown, Rockland Co, NY 78
Blauvelt Richard	Orangeburg-Clausland Cem, Orangeburg, Rockland Co, NY 78
Blazer Peter	Nr Bloserville, Lancaster Co, PA 56
Blean David	Church Cem, Newville, PA 58
Bledsoe Anthony	Bledsoe's Lick, Sumner, TN 56
Bledsoe Anthony	Cactillian Springs Cem, (marker) Cactillian Springs, TN 55
Bleekman Daniel	Round Top Cem, Stratford, Fulton Co, NY 39
Blethen Increase	Androscoggin Co, ME 18
Blethen Increase	Byron Yard, 4 mi N of Phillips, ME 48
Blevins Dillon	Fam Cem, Pleasant Valley, Dallas Co, AL 64
Blevins James	Scotland Cem, Greene Co, IN 24
Blevins John	Shipley Cem, nr Morell's Creek, Sullivan Co, TN 73
Blevins William Jr	Shipley Cem, nr Morell's Creek, Sullivan Co, TN 73
Blewer Jacob	Old Swedes Ch Cem, Philadelphia, PA 52
Blewer Joseph	Gloria Dei (Old Swedes) Ch, Philadelphia, PA 53
Bleyler Michael	Ziegel's Ch Cem, Breinigsville, Lehigh, PA 40
Blickensderfer Christ'n	Sharen Morav Cem, Warwick Twp, Tuscarawas Co, OH 55
Blinn Elisha	Red Rock Rural Cem, Canaan, Columbia Co, NY 79
Blish Benjamin	Lake Co, OH 26
Bliss Abdiel	Cong Ch Cem, West Dighton, MA 55
Bliss Abel	Homestead, Reynolds Ave, Rehoboth, MA 54
Bliss Abiah	Rehoboth Village Cem, Rehoboth, MA 54
Bliss Abraham	Mtg Hs Gr, Schodack, Rensselaer Co, NY 41
Bliss Azariah	Pine Cem, West Lebanon, NH 27
Bliss Beriah	Village Cem, Union Springs, Springport, NY 41
Bliss Calvin	Springfield Cem, Springfield, MA 45
Bliss Darius	Rehoboth Village Cem, Rehoboth, MA 54
Bliss Elisha	Reed St nr Aldrich farm, Rehoboth, MA 55
Bliss Ephraim 3rd	Rehoboth Village, MA 55
Bliss Isaac	Old North Cem, Old Hartford, CT 19
Bliss Jacob	Rehoboth Village Cem, Rehoboth, MA 54
Bliss James	Rehoboth Village, MA 55
Bliss James Dr	Rehoboth Village, MA 55
Bliss John	Portageville Cem, Genessee Falls, Wyoming Co, NY 80
Bliss John Col	Wilbraham Cem, Wilbraham, MA 45
Bliss Jonathan Jr Capt	Rehoboth Cem, Rehoboth, MA 47
Bliss Joseph	West Barnstable, MA 55
Bliss Levi	Salisbury Cem, Herkimer Co, NY 61
Bliss Matthew	Cem on hill off Rt 138 S, Dighton, MA 55
Bliss Nathan	Rehoboth Cem, Rehoboth, MA 47
Bliss Nathaniel	Rehoboth Village Cem, Rehoboth, MA 54
Bliss Reuben	Kirkland Avenue Cem, Clinton, Oneida Co, NY 79
Bliss Samuel Jr	Rehoboth Village Cem, Rehoboth, MA 54
Bliss William Sr Rev	Newport, RI 52
Bliss Zenus	North St Cem, Auburn, Cayuga Co, NY 57
Bliss Zephaniah	Norwich Town Cem, Norwich, CT 18
Bliven Arnold Capt	Putnam Center, Saratoga Springs, NY 41
Bliven William Maj	Fam bur gr, Bradford, RI 48
Bliven William Maj	Westerly, RI 15
Blodgett Admantha	Groton rural Cem, Groton, NY 31
Blodgett Amos	Colby Cem, Sanbornton, NH 35
Blodgett Asa	Cornwall, VT 52
Blodgett Asa	Cornwall Cem, Cornwall, VT 51
Blodgett Benjamin	Randolph Center Cem, Randolph, Orange Co, VT 72
Blodgett David	West Cem, Amherst, MA 16

Blodgett Henry	Randolph Center Cem, Randolph, Orange Co, VT	72
Blodgett James	Randolph Center Cem, Randolph, Orange Co, VT	72
Blodgett James	Randolph Center, VT	23
Blodgett John	Old Village Cem, NH	17
Blodgett Jonas	Fairview Cem, Swansey, NH	56
Blodgett Jonathan	Cem across Baker River fr Swainsboro Station, Rumney, NH	36
Blodgett Jonathan	Fam Cem, Hudson, NH	28
Blodgett Joseph	Fam Cem, Hudson, NH	28
Blodgett Josiah	East Windsor Cem, East Windsor, CT	31
Blodgett Luden	Baldwin Corners Cem, Rushville, Yates Co, NY	80
Blodgett Nathan	Cortland Cem, Cortlandville, Cortland Co, NY	36
Blodgett Phineas	East Windsor Cem, East Windsor, CT	31
Blodgett Phineas	Scantic Cem, East Windsor, CT	27
Blodgett Roswell	East Windsor Cem, East Windsor, CT	31
Blodgett Roswell	Scantic Cem, East Windsor, CT	27
Blodgett Rufus	Prattsburg Cem, Prattsburg, NY	70
Blodgett Samuel	Cem, Cornwall, VT	49
Blodgett Samuel	Valley Cem, Manchester, NH	32
Blodgett Solomon	Baldwin Corners Cem, Rushville, Yates Co, NY	80
Blodgett William	Dunstable Cem, Dunstable, MA	56
Blood Abel	Goshen, NH	22
Blood Abel	North Goshen Cem, Goshen, NH	34
Blood Amos	Tarbell (Pole) Cem, Mason, Hillsborough Co, NH	70
Blood Asa Capt	Orford St Cem, Orford, NH	31
Blood Caleb Jr	Groton, MA	55
Blood David	Pres Ch Cem, Stillwater, NY	41
Blood David	Walton, Pepperell, MA	56
Blood Francis	Temple, NH	15
Blood Francis Gen	Old Village Cem, Temple, NH	28
Blood Israel	Victor Cem, Ontario Co, NY	33
Blood John	Marlette farm nr Bloods Mills, Laurens, Otsego Co, NY	72
Blood Jonas	Churchyard, Hollis, NH	39
Blood Joseph	Prob Bunker Hill, NH	39
Blood Josiah Jr	Churchyard, Hollis, NH	39
Blood Jothan	Hill Cem, Concord, MA	55
Blood Lemuel	On his farm, now Newton prop, Acworth, NH	55
Blood Nathan	Killed at Bunker Hill, marker in Charleston, MA	45
Blood Samuel	Bailey Hill Cem, Groton, NH	36
Blood Samuel	Bolton Pan Cem, Bolton, MA	56
Blood Sewall	[no cem named], MA	17
Blood Stephen	Central Bur Gr, Carlisle, MA	55
Blood Stephen Jr	Old Cem, Carlisle, MA	55
Bloom Ephraim	Gloucester Co, NJ	32
Bloom Ephraim	Lansing Cem, NY	15
Bloom Ephraim	Lansing Cem, Chemung Co, NY	32
Bloom William	McClure Cem, Curwensville, Clearfield Co, PA	61
Bloomer Gilbert	New Rochelle Cem, New Rochelle, NY	56
Bloomfield Benjamin	Pres Ch Cem, Rahway, NJ	76
Bloomfield John	Colonial Cem, Metuchen, NJ	49
Bloomfield Jonathan	Bur gr, First Pres Ch, Woodbridge, NJ	25
Bloomfield Jonathan	Bloomfield Cem, Bloomfield, NY	34
Bloomfield Jonathan	Fam Cem, Warren, Herkimer Co, NY	41
Bloomfield Moses Dr	Bur gr, First Pres Ch, Woodbridge, NJ	25
Bloomfield Robert	Pres Ch Cem, Rahway, NJ	76
Bloomfield Thomas	Bur gr, First Pres Ch, Woodbridge, NJ	25
Bloomhart Daniel	Orange Twp Cem, Connersville, IN	15
Bloss John George	Heidelberg Ch Cem, Lehigh Co, PA	40
Bloss Joseph	Brighton Cem, Brighton, Monroe Co, NY	79
Bloss Joseph	Brighton Cem, Monroe Co, NY	33
Bloss Valentine	Buford Ch, nr Dickson, Wayne Co, WV	29
Bloss Valentine	Nr Dickson, Wayne Co, WV	30

Blosser Jacob	Blasser Graveyard, York Co, PA 62
Blossom Barnabas	Stark Cem, Conway, NH 32
Blossom Benjamin	Acushnet Cem, Fairhaven, MA 55
Blossom Churchhill	West Barnstable, MA 55
Blossom Ezra	Brighton Cem, Monroe Co, NY 33
Blossom Joseph	West Barnstable, MA 55
Blossom Peter	Farm of his son, Clarkson, NY 15
Blottenberger John	St Peter's Luth Ch Cem, Union & High St, Uniontown, PA 21
Blough Christian	Quemahoning Dam, Somerset Co, PA 15
Blough Jacob	Quemahoning Dam, Somerset Co, PA 15
Blouin Daniel	Randolph Co, IL 48
Blount Andrew	Blunt Cem, Webster Twp, Harrison Co, IN 72
Blount Charles Worth	Bapt Ch Cem, Bethel, Perquimans Co, NC 76
Blount Jacob	Blount Hall Cem, Pitt Co, NC 60
Blount John Gray	Washington, NC 15
Blount Jonathan	Fillmore Cem, Clarence, NY 33
Blount Reading Maj	Washington, NC 15
Blount Walter	Troy, MI 52
Blount William	First Pres Ch Cem, Knoxville, TN 24
Blount William	Muncie, Delaware Co, IN 72
Blout Reading	Old Home Bellefonte, Pitt Co, NC 59
Blue Frederick	Meth Cem, E of Rd 89, Jeromesville, Ashland Co, OH 55
Blue Michael	Bloomingburg Cem, Paint Twp, Fayette Co, OH 55
Blue Peter	Fayette Co, OH 46
Blue Stephen	[no cem named], NC 17
Blue Uriah	His farm, nr Troy, Miami Co, OH 55
Blumer Abraham	Jordan Ref Old Cem, Walberts, Lehigh Co, PA 40
Blun Peter	Old Cem, Wethersfield, CT 56
Blunt John	Frost Cem, Newcastle, NH 28
Blunt John Gray	St Peter's Ch Cem, NC 49
Blunt Reading	Fam Cem, 10 mi NW of Washington, NC 49
Blunt Walter	Union Cem, Troy Twp, Oakland Co, MI 44
Bly John	Boehm Cem, nr Clary, Shenandoah Co, VA 83
Bly John	Pond Cem, Lakeville, MA 57
Bly Moses	North Parish Cem, Plaistow, NH 31
Bly Rouse	First Cong Cem, Griswold, CT 62
Blye John	Pond Cem, Lakeville, MA 58
Blythe Samuel	Cem, Mecklenburg Co, NC 60
Boal Robert	Dicks Creek Pres Ch Cem, E of Blue Ball, Warren Co, OH 56
Board David	Fam plot, Boardville, Passaic Co, NJ 85
Board Phillip S	Old fam graveyard, Nevada, KY 52
Boardman Aaron	Old Cem, Monument Square, Saugus, MA 45
Boardman Amos Col	Old Cem, Wakefield, MA 27
Boardman Benjamin Capt	Winter St Cem, Exeter, NH 15
Boardman Benjamin Rev	Old North Cem, Old Hartford, CT 19
Boardman Caleb	Chippenhook Cem, Clarendon, VT 25
Boardman Caleb	Chippenhook Cem, Clarendon, VT 24
Boardman Daniel	Barnard Cem, Sheffield, MA 56
Boardman Elias	Old Bur Cem, Wakefield, MA 45
Boardman Elias	Wakefield Cem, Wakefield, MA 29
Boardman Elijah	Fam farm, OH 45
Boardman Elijah	Fam plot, Boardman, OH 43
Boardman Elijah	Small Cem, Junius, Seneca Co, NY 57
Boardman Elisha	East Clarendon Cem, Clarendon, VT 25
Boardman Elisha	East Clarendon Cem, Clarendon, VT 24
Boardman Elizur	Clam River Cem, Sandisfield, MA 56
Boardman Ephraim	Westford Cem, 20 mi E of Cobleskill, Otsego Co, NY 74
Boardman Jehiel	Mt View Cem, Cattaraugus Co, NY 71
Boardman Jonathan	Highland-New Hill, Newburyport, MA 56
Boardman Moses	East Hartland Cem, East Hartland, CT 62
Boardman Offin	Old Cem, Newburyport, MA 55

Boardman Oliver	Old North Cem, Old Hartford, CT	19
Boardman Samuel	Old Cem, Wethersfield, CT	56
Boardman Sherman	Milford Center Cem, New Milford, CT	40
Boardman Theodore	West Lawn Cem, Williamstown, MA	33
Boardman Timothy	Mt Pleasant Cem, West Rutland, VT	55
Boardman William	Old North Cem, Old Hartford, CT	19
Boas Henry	Ridge Cem, nr Medora, Jackson Co, IN	72
Boatman Barnard	Quaker Cem, East Palestine, OH	56
Bobenmeir Gabriel	St Peters Luth Ch Cem, Amanda Twp, Fairfield Co, OH	55
Bock Balthaser	McKeansburg, PA	49
Bock Johannes	Zions Red Ch, Orwigsburg, PA	49
Bock Michael	Blackwell farm, 2 mi fr Homer, Banks Co, GA	69
Bock Michael	Fam Cem, nr Farmington, WV	41
Bockover George	Pres Ch Cem, Basking Ridge, NJ	47
Boden James	Lamberton, NJ	32
Boden William	Boden, Natick, MA	56
Bodfish Benjamin	West Barnstable, MA	55
Bodfish Jonathan	West Barnstable, MA	55
Bodfish William	Village Cem, Sandwich, MA	56
Bodine Jacob	Dutch Ref Brick Ch Cem, Montgomery, Orange Co, NY	76
Bodine James	First Pres Ch Cem, Cranbury, NJ	76
Bodine John Capt	Lower Bank, NJ	47
Bodine William	Dutch Ref Brick Ch Cem, Montgomery, Orange Co, NY	76
Bodley William	Adams Cem, New State Rd, nr London, OH	26
Bodley William Maj	Lower Providence Pres, PA	15
Bodman Scamen	Springfield Chapel, Springfield Twp, Muskingum Co, OH	55
Bodourtha Joseph	Agawam Center Cem, Agawam, MA	17
Bodurtha Stephen	Agawam Center, Agawam, MA	46
Bodurtha Stephen	Agawam Center Cem, Agawam, MA	17
Bodwell Benjamin	Hop Meadow Cem, Simsbury, CT	55
Bodwell Daniel	Meeting House Hill Cem, Methuen, MA	45
Bodwell Daniel 3rd	Village Cem, Methuen, MA	45
Bodwell Henry	Frye Hill, Methuen, MA	56
Bodwell John Capt	Acton, ME	26
Bodwell William	Meeting House Hill, Methuen, MA	56
Bogan Isaac	Fam Cem, 10 mi fr Union, Union Co, SC	39
Bogardus Benjamin	Old Dutch Cem, Kingston, Ulster Co, NY	85
Bogardus Henry	Dewitt Cem, Dewitt, NY	32
Bogardus Jacob	Fam Cem, Greenville, Greene Co, NY	59
Bogardus Nicholas	Old Dutch Cem, Kingston, Ulster Co, NY	85
Bogardus Peter	Dewitt Cem, Dewitt, NY	32
Bogart Cornelius	On the Green, Hackensack, NJ	54
Bogart David A	Fam bur gr, Pearl River, NY	53
Bogart Gilliam	South Ch Cem, Bergenfield, NJ	47
Bogart Gysbert	Pine Bank, Myer farm, South Branch, NJ	47
Bogart Jacob	Sand Beach Cem, Fleming, NY	56
Boger Adam	Ziegel's Ch Cem, Breinigsville, Lehigh, PA	40
Boger Peter	Zions Red Ch, Orwigsburg, PA	49
Boger Valentine	Hill Luth Ch Cem, North Annville Twp, Lebanon Co, PA	83
Bogert Cornelius	French Cem, River Edge, NJ	47
Bogert Cornelius C	Hackensack Green Cem, Hackensack, NJ	47
Bogert Cornelius C	Hackensack Green Cem, Hackensack, NJ	47
Bogert Jacob	Western Salisburg Old Cem, Lehigh Co, PA	40
Bogert James	French Cem, River Edge, NJ	47
Bogert James L Col	Pine Grove Cem, Charleston, NY	41
Bogert Peter Matthew	South Ch Cem, Bergenfield, NJ	54
Boggan Patrick	Marker on Hwy 74, 3 mi fr Wadesboro, NC	49
Boggan Patrick Capt	Hwy 74, 2 mi NW of Wadesboro, NC	43
Boggs James Capt	Fam Cem, nr Athens, Fayette Co, KY	45
Boggs John	Hill nr Logan Elm Park, nr Circleville, Pickaway Co, OH	55
Boggs John Rev	Welsh Tract Cem, New Castle Co, DE	46

Boggs Robert	Pres Cem, White Clay Creek, New Castle Co, DE 46
Bogle Andrew	Eusebia Ch Cem, TN 23
Bogle Andrew	Eusebia Ch Cem, Blount Co, TN 24
Bogle Andrew	Eusebia Pres Ch, 12 mi NE of Maryville, Blount Co, TN 76
Bogle Joseph	Eusebia Pres Ch, 12 mi NE of Maryville, Blount Co, TN 76
Bogle Joseph Sr	Eusebia Cem, Blount Co, TN 72
Bogle Thomas	Wardsboro, VT 18
Bogler –	Hickory Grove Cem, Menard Co, IL 26
Bogue Daniel	Brunswick Cem, Medina Co, OH 40
Bogue Publius Virgilius	Kirkland Avenue Cem, Clinton, Oneida Co, NY 79
Bohannan John	Calais Cem, Calais, ME 59
Bohny Melchior	St John's Ch Cem, Fredericksburg, Lebanon Co, PA 83
Bohon John	Deshazer farm, Warwick Rd, Mercer Co, KY 52
Bohr Burkhart	Jacob's Luth Ch, 2 mi W of Pine Grove, Schuylkill Co, PA 37
Bohr Burkhart	Jacob's Ch, Pine Grove Twp, PA 49
Boies David	New Center Cem, Blandford, MA 58
Boies Samuel	Old Center Cem, Blandford, Hampden Co, MA 58
Boies William	Old Center Cem, Blandford, Hampden Co, MA 58
Boies William	Old Center Cem, Blandford, Hampden Co, MA 58
Boland David	Sharon Cem, Sharon, Litchfield Co, CT 66
Boland David Jr	Fam Cem, Sharon, CT 65
Boland W Capt	Pleasant St Cem, West Rutland, VT 24
Boland W Capt	Pleasant St Cem, West Rutland, VT 25
Boland William Capt	West Rutland Cem, Rutland, VT 23
Bolcom Elijah	Town Yard, Mansfield, MA 56
Bolding Elisha	Priv Cem, Lake Mahopac, Putnam Co, NY 36
Boldrey John	Pilgrim's Home Ch, Old Regular Bapt Cem, Ripley Co, IN 74
Bolendar Stephen	Franklin, nr Felicity, OH 56
Boler Simon	Union Cem, Stillwater, NY 41
Boles Samuel	Fam farm, Callaway Co, MO 23
Boleyn David	King St Cem, Enfield, CT 23
Bolich Andrew	Frieden's, New Ringold, PA 49
Bolin Thomas	Fam Cem, Cannelton, Perry Co, IN 75
Bolkcom Jacob	Old Kirk Yard, Attleboro, MA 15
Bolkcom William Lt	Old Kirk Yard, Attleboro, MA 15
Bolkeom Jacob	Second Cong Ch Cem, Attleboro, MA 56
Bolles Asa	Goshen, Lebanon, CT 56
Bolles Ebenezer	Evergreen Cem, Marion, MA 59
Bolling Robert	Blanford Cem, Petersburg, VA 37
Bollman Abraham	Defiance Cem, Defiance, Defiance Co, OH 61
Bolls John	Jefferson Co, MS 44
Bolstar Nathan	Four Corners Cem, Sullivan, NH 38
Bolster Baruch	South Londonderry, VT 18
Bolster Joel	Guilford, VT 18
Bolt William	Parade Grounds, New Canaan, CT 56
Bolter Lemuel R	Shavehead Cem, Porter Twp, Cass Co, MI 31
Bolton Aaron	Woodside Cem, Westminster, MA 53
Bolton David	Eddy Cem, Scipio, NY 41
Bolton Ebenezer	Old Cem, Gardner, MA 46
Bolton Ebenezer	The Old Cem, Gardner, MA 33
Bolton Thomas	Eddy Cem, Scipio, Cayuga Co, NY 59
Bolton William Jr	Shirley Cem, Shirley, MA 47
Boltwood Ebenezer	West Cem, Amherst, MA 16
Boltwood John	Cem, Windsor, VT 56
Boltwood Solomon	West Cem, Amherst, MA 16
Boltwood Solomon	West Cem, Amherst, MA 60
Boltz John Jacob Sr	English Luth Cem, Middleway, Jefferson Co, WV 42
Boltz John Michael	Union Ch Cem, Middleway, Jefferson Co, WV 42
Boltz Michael	Wurtemburg, Rhinebeck, NY 21
Boltz Michael Sr	English Luth Cem, Middleway, Jefferson Co, WV 42
Boman John	Stockton's Valley, Roane Co, TN 24

Bond Bethuel	Mayville Cem, Mayville, Chautauqua Co, NY	76
Bond Daniel	Old Village Cem, Claremont, NH	50
Bond David	Centennial Cem, Gilsum, NH	32
Bond Gilbert	Forest Hill Cem, East Derry, NH	38
Bond Henry	Livermore, ME	18
Bond Henry	Madison Center, NY	15
Bond Israel	Madison Center, NY	15
Bond John	Conway, MA	17
Bond John	Howland Cem, Conway, MA	53
Bond John	Stone Co, MS	44
Bond John (Job) Lt	Old Village Cem, Claremont, NH	50
Bond Jonas	Westminister Ch Cem, Canterbury Twp, CT	21
Bond Joseph	Wildwood, Wilmington, MA	56
Bond Josiah	Howland Cem, Conway, MA	53
Bond Phineas	Wardsboro, VT	18
Bond Solomon	West Cem, Amherst, MA	41
Bond Stephen	Centennial Cem, Gilsum, NH	32
Bond Thomas Capt	Maple St Cem, North Brookfield, MA	17
Bond Thomas Lt	North Brookfield, MA	15
Bond William	Charlestown, NH	15
Bond William	Old Granary Bur Gr, Boston, MA	56
Boneaux Piere	Cathedral Cem, Vincennes, IN	64
Bones William	Snow Creek Meth Ch, betw Statesville & N Wilkesboro, NC	77
Bonesteel Nicholas	Stone Ch, Rhinebeck, Dutchess Co, NY	21
Bonfoy Henry	East Winfield, Herkimer Co, NY	71
Bonin Jean Louis	St Martins of Tours Cath Ch Cem, St Martinville, LA	73
Bonin Michael	St Martin of Tours Cath Ch Cem, St Martinville, LA	74
Bonine Thomas	Woodward Hill Cem, Lancaster, PA	46
Bonnel Aaron	Park, Harrison, Hamilton Co, OH	55
Bonnel Joseph	Connecticut Farms Pres Cem, Union, NJ	49
Bonnell Abram	Bethlehem, NJ	32
Bonnell Isaac	Winterset, OH	53
Bonnell John	Bethany Cem, Honesdale, Wayne Co, PA	71
Bonnell John	Fairmount Cem, Chatham, NJ	24
Bonnell John	Hillside Cem, Madison, NJ	30
Bonnell Nathaniel	Hillside Cem, Madison, NJ	30
Bonnell Samuel	Pleasant Ridge Pres Cem, Hamilton Co, OH	41
Bonner Frederick	Otsquago Cem, nr Van Hornesville, NY	30
Bonner Henry	St Peter's Epis Ch Cem, Washington, NC	49
Bonner James	Hamburg Cem, Oak Hill, Wilcox Co, AL	76
Bonner James	St Peter's Epis Ch Cem, Washington, NC	49
Bonner James Col	Epis Ch Cem, Washington, NC	15
Bonner John	Cedar Springs Cem, Cedar Springs, PA	47
Bonner John	St Peter's Epis Ch Cem, Washington, NC	49
Bonner William	Fam Cem, Calloway Co, KY	60
Bonnett Lewis	Fam Cem, Elm Grove area, Wheeling, Ohio Co, WV	77
Bonnett Lewis	Smith Cem, Birmingham, Van Buren Co, IA	76
Bonnett Lewis Sr	Fam Cem, RFD 3, 4 mi fr Elm Grove, nr Wheeling, WV	56
Bonney A	Old Pres Cem, Bound Brook, NJ	47
Bonney Ebenezer	Fern Hill Cem, #19-R, West Parish, Pembroke, MA	40
Bonney Ebenezer	Old Cem, Plympton, MA	50
Bonney Ezekiel	Fern Hill Cem, #8-R, West Parish, Pembroke, MA	40
Bonney James	Centre Cem, Pembroke, MA	50
Bonney Joseph	Fern Hill Cem, #45-R, West Parish, Pembroke, MA	40
Bonney Joseph	Old Bur Cem, Plympton, MA	58
Bonney Lemuel	Fern Hill Cem, #20-R, West Parish, Pembroke, MA	40
Bonney Nathaniel	Old Burial Cem, Plympton, MA	57
Bonney Nathaniel	Old Cem, Plympton, MA	50
Bonney Noah	Fern Hill Cem, #21-R, West Parish, Pembroke, MA	40
Bonney Perez	Cornwall, CT	53
Bonney Perry	Cornwall Cem, Cornwall, CT	15

Bonney Samuel	Old Burial Cem, Plympton, MA 57
Bonney Samuel	Rochester Cem, 4 Corners nr Church, Rochester, MA 55
Bonney Simeon	Winthrop Cem, ME 48
Bonny James	Pres Ch Cem, Rahway, NJ 76
Bonny James Dea	Rahway Cem, Rahway, NJ 26
Bonny Lemuel	Fern Hill Cem, Hanson, MA 59
Bonny Samuel	Fern Hill Cem, Hanson, MA 59
Boodey Joseph	Fam Cem, Bow Lake, Strafford, NH 71
Booge Aaron Jordon	Cem of Evergreens, New Lebanon, Columbia Co, NY 42
Booker Daniel	Woodlawn Cem, West Bowdoin, ME 40
Booker Lewis	Essex County Cem, Essex Co, VA 55
Booker Richard Marot	Shelby Co, KY 56
Bookhout James	Clark Cem, Pompey, Onondaga Co, NY 81
Bookman Jacob	Lexington Co, SC 41
Bookstaver Jacob F Jr	Dutch Ref Brick Ch Cem, Montgomery, Orange Co, NY 76
Bookstaver William	Dutch Ref Brick Ch Cem, Montgomery, Orange Co, NY 76
Bookter Jacob	Upper Richland Co, SC 41
Boone Daniel Col	St Charles Co, MO 15
Boone Jeremiah	Fam Cem, on Indian Creek, Lawrence Co, IN 72
Boone Richard	Fam lot, Downes prop, off rd by Boone Pond, Exeter, RI 39
Boone Squire Jr	In natural cave nr Buck Creek, Harrison Co, IN 72
Boone Thomas	Oxford, OH 45
Boone William	Snow Creek Cem, Iredell Co, NC 49
Boone William	Snow Creek Cem, off Hwy 115, 10 mi N of Statesville, NC 40
Booraem Jacob	Van Liew Cem, New Brunswick, NJ 24
Boorse Arnold	Mennonite Mtg Cem, Towamencin Twp, Philadelphia, PA 56
Boorse Peter	Towamencin Mennonite Cem, Montgomery Co, PA 59
Boosinger Conrad	Tallmadge, OH 15
Booth Abel	Newtown Village, Newtown, CT 56
Booth Agur Capt	Cong Cem, Stratford, CT 31
Booth Andrew	Eddytown Cem, Starkey, Yates Co, NY 80
Booth Bartholomew	Delamere Cem, Tilghmanton, Washington Co, MD 77
Booth Caleb	Scantic Cem, East Windsor, CT 27
Booth Caleb Col	East Windsor Cem, East Windsor, CT 31
Booth Daniel	Phillipi, WV 51
Booth Daniel	Phillipi Cem, Phillipi, WV 60
Booth Daniel	Stratford, CT 53
Booth David	Briggs Cem, Malta, Saratoga Co, NY 78
Booth Ebenezer	Welsh Tract, ½ mi S of Newark, New Castle Co, DE 45
Booth Elisha	East Hartland Cem, East Hartland, CT 62
Booth Epaphras	East Lempster Cem, Lempster, NH 34
Booth Ephraim	Old bur place, Nichols Farms, Nichols, CT 33
Booth Fregrace	East Lempster Cem, Lempster, NH 34
Booth James	Boothville Cem, Marion Co, WV 60
Booth James Capt	Cong Cem, Stratford, CT 31
Booth James Capt	Nr Booth's Schoolhouse, on Booths Creek, WV 27
Booth James Wheelock	Old Pres Ch Cem, Southold, Suffolk Co, NY 79
Booth John	Blown up at Hudson's Ferry, SC 42
Booth John	Dry Forks Cem, Jefferson Co, IN 25
Booth John	Fam Cem, nr Smith Mt Lake, Franklin Co, VA 73
Booth John	Race Course Cem, Lakeville, MA 57
Booth John Sr	McCaleb Cem, nr Hermanville, Claiborne Co, MS 65
Booth Joshua	East Lempster Cem, East Lempster, NH 35
Booth Nathaniel	Briggs Cem betw Middle Line Rd & Rt 20, Saratoga Co, NY 77
Booth Oliver	East Lempster Cem, Lempster, NH 34
Booth Reuben	Center Cem, New Milford, CT 55
Booth Samuel	Island Hill Cem, Buskirk, NY 34
Booth Thomas	St Georges, New Castle Co, DE 46
Booth Walter	Milford Cem, Milford, CT 56
Boothby Ebenezer	Boothby Yard, Maplewood Rd, West Newfield, York Co, ME 74
Boothe George	Fam Cem, Little River, Christiansburg, VA 56

Abstract of Graves of Revolutionary Patriots

Bope Abraham	Zeigler Cem, Pleasant Twp, Rt 37, 6 mi fr Lancaster, OH 57
Boraem Jacob	Willow Grove Cem, New Brunswick, NJ 28
Borah Jacob	Sunbury, PA 56
Borden Elijah	Fam Cem, Pompey, Onondaga Co, NY 78
Borden Elijah	Westport, MA 53
Borden Jonathan	Ledyard Ch Cem, Ledyard, Cayuga Co, NY 57
Borden Nathan	Jacksonville Cem, Lysander, Onondaga Co, NY 78
Borden Richard	North Bur Gr, Fall River, MA 54
Borden Thomas	North Bur Gr, Fall River, MA 54
Borders Christopher	Greensfork Cem, Spartansburg, Randolph Co, IN 72
Borders Christopher	Prob Old Water St Cem, Greenville, OH 55
Borders Peter	Irish Grove Cem, nr Greenview, IL 26
Borders Peter	Menard Co, IL 30
Bordin John	East Hartland Cem, East Hartland, CT 60
Boren Nicholas	New Mt Moriah Cem, nr Cynthiana, Gibson Co, IN 78
Borgardus Everadus	Dutch Ch, Rhinebeck Village, Dutchess Co, NY 21
Borin Aron	Manheim Twp, PA 49
Boring Isaac	Ebenezer Ch Cem, Jackson Co, GA 22
Boring Isaac	Hancock Cem, fam prop, Jackson Co, GA 34
Bork George C F Rev	Franklin St Ch (Cypress Hills) Cem, New York City, NY 48
Bornler Charles	Guilford, CT 56
Borough John	Upper Alloways, NJ 32
Borrall John	Hood's Cem, Germantown, PA 20
Borst Joseph	Cold Springs, small bur gr, Benson, NY 55
Bortle John	West Ghent Ref Ch Cem, Ghent, Columbia Co, NY 74
Bortle Philip	Woodlawn Cem, Valatie, Columbia Co, NY 79
Bortle Philip H	St Thomas Luth Ch Cem, Claverack, Columbia Co, NY 48
Bortner Phillip	Jacob's Ch, Pine Grove Twp, PA 49
Bortz Jacob	St Peter's Cem, nr Shimersville, Lehigh Co, PA 40
Boshart John	Gross Cem, 2 mi W of Johnstown, NY 63
Bosler John	Silver Springs, Carlisle, PA 56
Boss Benjamin	Fam farm, North Scituate, RI 55
Boss Elias	St John's Luth Ch Cem, off Hwy 73, nr Concord, NC 74
Boss George	St John's Evang Luth Ch, nr Concord, Cabarrus Co, NC 75
Boss John	Organ Luth Ch Cem, Rockwell, Rowan Co, NC 77
Boss William	Old St Paul's Luth Ch Cem, Hickory, Catawba Co, NC 76
Boss William	West Milton Cem, West Milton, Ulster Co, NY 77
Bossart Melchoir	Christ Ch Cem, Hamilton Twp, Monroe Co, PA 68
Bossert Henry	Brunswick Twp, PA 49
Bossinger Conrad	Talmadge, Summit Co, OH 45
Bossworth Ichabod	Cem, shore of Monponsett, Halifax, MA 50
Bossworth John	Thompson St Cem, Halifax, MA 50
Bossworth Richard	Thompson St Cem, Halifax, MA 50
Bost Jacob Sr	St John's Luth Churchyard, nr Concord, Cabarrus Co, NC 59
Boston John	Priv fam Cem, Guilford Co, NC 55
Bostwick Ames	St Matthew's Cem, Unadilla, NY 32
Bostwick Arthur	Jerico Cem, Jerico, Chittenden Co, VT 61
Bostwick Benjamin Jr	Center Cem, New Milford, CT 55
Bostwick David	Gallows Hill Cem, New Milford, CT 55
Bostwick David	Old Cem, nr Treadwell, Franklin, Delaware Co, NY 71
Bostwick Doctor	[no cem named], OH 26
Bostwick Ebenezer	Cem, Rt 44 & Rt 18, Rootstown, OH 36
Bostwick Ebenezer	[no cem named], OH 26
Bostwick Eleazer	Edinburg, OH 26
Bostwick Elijah	Canaan Cem, Columbia Co, NY 38
Bostwick Elijah	Canaan Center Cem, Columbia Co, NY 42
Bostwick Elisha	Center Cem, New Milford, CT 55
Bostwick Elizor	Edinburg Twp, OH 53
Bostwick Joel	Upper Merryall, New Milford, CT 55
Bostwick John	Elmwood Cem, Pike, Wyoming Co, NY 52
Bostwick Jonathan	Center Cem, Bridgewater, CT 55

Bostwick Littleberry	Old Walker Dist, 85th Dist, Jefferson Co, GA 32
Bostwick Littleberry Sr	Louisville Cem, Jefferson Co, GA 40
Bostwick Nathan	Becker farm, Pike Twp, Bradford Co, PA 53
Bostwick Nathan	Walker Cem, Jefferson Co, GA 40
Bostwick Reuben	Durham Cem, Durham, Greene Co, NY 75
Bostwick Reuben Capt	Newton Falls, OH 24
Bostwick William	St Peters Ch Cem, Auburn, NY 58
Bostworth Peter	Brownville, OH 24
Boswell Reuben	[no cem named], NC 17
Boswell Reuben	Weddington Cem, Union Co, NC 49
Boswell William	Line Cem, Foster, RI 48
Boswell William	Line Cem, North Rd, nr Connecticut Line, Foster, RI 75
Bosworth Allen	Eastford Cem, CT 16
Bosworth Allen	Old Eastford Yard, Eastford, CT 29
Bosworth Amos	Clam River Cem, Sandisfield, MA 56
Bosworth Benjamin	Coles Cem, Towanda Twp, Bradford Co, PA 72
Bosworth Benjamin	North Cem, Bristol, RI 55
Bosworth Ichabod	Moores, Clinton Co, NY 53
Bosworth Ichabod	South Cem, Bellingham, MA 55
Bosworth Ichabod	West Otis Cem, Otis, MA 56
Bosworth Jabez	Clam River Cem, Sandisfield, MA 56
Bosworth Jabin	Old Cem, Fair Haven, VT 59
Bosworth John	Bapt Ch Cem, Strongsville, Cuyahoga Co, OH 55
Bosworth John	Old Rottstown Cem, Rootstown, OH 53
Bosworth John	Rushford Cem, Rushford, Alleghany Co, NY 62
Bosworth Jonathan	Pierce Cem, Solon, ME 15
Bosworth Nathaniel	Berlin Cem, nr Montpelier, VT 15
Bosworth Nathaniel	Berlin Corner Cem, Berlin Corner, VT 20
Bosworth Nathaniel	Clam River Cem, Sandisfield, MA 56
Bosworth Nathaniel	Four Corners Cem, Berlin, VT 45
Bosworth Nathaniel	Pittstown Cem, Pittstown, NY 34
Bosworth Nathaniel	Town Hill Cem, Lakeville, CT 64
Bosworth Sala	Mound Cem, Marietta, Washington Co, OH 55
Bosworth Zadoo	Pitcher St Cem, Montgomery, MA 53
Botsford Abel	Newtown Village, Newtown, CT 56
Botsford Clement	Newtown Village, Newtown, CT 56
Botsford David	Milford Cem, Milford, CT 56
Botsford Edmund	Georgetown, SC 56
Botsford Eli	Milford Cem, Milford, CT 56
Botsford Jabez	Newtown Village, Newtown, CT 56
Bottum Jabez L	Dry Creek Cem, Moravia, NY 16
Bottum Jabez L	Dry Creek Cem, Moravia, NY 41
Boude Thomas	Mt Bethel Cem, Columbia, Lancaster Co, PA 77
Bouden Twisden	Old Burial Hill, Marblehead, MA 47
Boudinot Elisha	Pres Cem, Newark, NJ 32
Bougher John	Old Four Mile Run Cem, Austintown Twp, Mahoning Co, OH 55
Boughner Martin	Nr Woodsfield, Monroe Co, OH 55
Boughten John	Evergreen Cem, Scipioville, Scipio, NY 56
Boughton Enos	Boughton Hill Cem, Ontario Co, NY 33
Boughton Hezekiah	Boughton Hill Cem, Ontario Co, NY 33
Boughton Hezekiah Jr	Boughton Hill Cem, Ontario Co, NY 33
Boughton Selleck	Stockbridge Cem, Stockbridge, MA 47
Boulden Nathan	Welsh Tract Bapt Cem, nr Newark, DE 52
Boulden Thomas	His estate, Back Creek Neck, Cecil Co, MD 51
Bouldin Thomas	Plantation, Charlotte Co, VA 56
Boulding Thomas	Fam plantation, Bristol, Back Creek Neck, Cecil Co, MD 52
Boulogne Charles Felix	Meth Ch Cem, Hills Grove, PA 53
Boulter Lemuel R	Shavehead Cem, Cass Co, MI 20
Boulware Mark	Greenlawn Cem, Bowling Green, VA 70
Boulware Muscoe	Boulware Walls Cem, Fairfield Co, SC 70
Boundy George Jr	Unitarian Cem, Marblehead, MA 55

Abstract of Graves of Revolutionary Patriots

Boundy Jonathan	Unitarian Cem, Marblehead, MA 55
Bouner Thomas Col	St Peter's Ch Cem, Warrenton, NC 37
Bourdett Peter	[no cem named], NJ 32
Bourn Benjamin	Agawam Cem, Wareham, MA 56
Bourn Lemuel	Old Cem, The Green, Middleboro, MA 50
Bourn Melitiah	Village Cem, Sandwich, MA 56
Bourn Samuel	Old Bur Gr, Mill Rd, Falmouth, MA 64
Bourn Silas	Village Cem, Sandwich, MA 56
Bourn Stephen	Hillside Cem, Dodgeville, Attleboro, MA 47
Bourne Abner	Nemasket Hill Cem, Middleboro, MA 46
Bourne Amos	Manchester Cem, Manchester, Bennington Co, VT 61
Bourne Andreas	Old Kirk Yard, Attleboro, MA 15
Bourne Andrew	Woodlawn Cem, Attleboro, MA 15
Bourne Ebenezer Capt	East Wareham (Agawam), Wareham, MA 34
Bourne Ebenezer Capt	East Wareham Cem, Wareham, MA 28
Bourne Ebenezer Capt	East Wareham, MA 16
Bourne John	East Wareham (Agawam), Wareham, MA 34
Bourne John	Hope Cem, Kennebunk, York Co, ME 78
Bourne John	[no cem named], MA 17
Bourne Lemuel	Cong Ch Cem on Green, Middleboro, MA 55
Bourne Stephen	Dodgeville, MA 15
Bourne Thomas	Hingham Cem, Hingham, MA 60
Bourne Thomas	Old Bur Gr, Mill Rd, Falmouth, MA 64
Bourns John	Willow Glen Farm, nr Waynesboro, PA 20
Boush William	Fam Cem, Lynhaven house, Virginia Beach, VA 77
Boutell James	Old Pine Grove Cem, Leominster, MA 47
Boutell John	Old Pine Grove Cem, Leominster, MA 47
Boutell Timothy Col	Old Pine Grove Cem, Leominster, MA 47
Boutell William Jr	Old Pine Grove Cem, Leominster, MA 47
Boutelle Jacob	Ashford Cem, Ashford, CT 55
Boutelle Joseph	Chestnut Hill Cem, Amherst, NH 27
Boutelle Kendall	Laurel Hill Cem, Fitchburg, MA 55
Boutelle William	Old Yard, Pine Ridge, Hancock, NH 29
Bouton Daniel	Ponua Ridge, Fairfield, CT 56
Bouton Jeriel Sr	Knox Co, OH 45
Bouton Noah	Cem, South East Twp, Putnam Co, NY 35
Bouton Seth	Grave obliterated, Virgil, Cortland Co, NY 36
Bouton William	Pine Island, CT 34
Boutte Francois Cesar	St Martin of Tours Cath Ch Cem, St Martinville, LA 74
Boutte Phillippe	St Martin of Tours Cath Ch Cem, St Martinville, LA 74
Boutwell Ebenezer	Chenango Cem, Truxton, Cortland Co, NY 36
Boutwell Joseph	Laurel Hill, Reading, MA 49
Boutwell Reuben	Antrim, NH 15
Bovee Nicholas	Pomfret Cem, Pomfret, Chautauqua Co, NY 65
Bovie Jacob	Hoosick Rural Cem, Hoosick, NY 33
Bovier Solomon	Fitzsimmons Cem, nr Elmira, NY 32
Bow Edward	Cem, Scott farm, nr Arnolds Lake, NY 32
Bowden Matthew	Caldwell Pres Cem, Caldwell, NJ 32
Bowden William	Howard St Cem, Salem, MA 55
Bowdish Abraham	Old Cem, nr Vision Village, Laurens, Otsego Co, NY 71
Bowdoin Elias	Cottage Grove Cem, Cottage Grove, Henry Co, TN 79
Bowdoin Elias	Fam Cem, Harding farm, Lampkins Rd, Paris Henry Co, TN 77
Bowdoin James	Old Granary Bur Gr, Boston, MA 55
Bowdoin James Jr	Old Granary Bur Gr, Boston, MA 55
Bowe Thaddeus	[no cem named] 17
Bowel John	Town Cem, Andover, NH 29
Bowen Aaron	Galpin Hill Cem, Fleming, NY 41
Bowen Aaron	Galpin Hill, Fleming, NY 15
Bowen Aaron Col	Fam lot, Bowens Hill, Coventry, RI 30
Bowen Abel	Elm Row Cem, Laurens, NY 32
Bowen Arthur Capt	Aspenvale, Smyth Co, VA 50

Bowen Barzillai	Old Rumford Cem, Rehoboth, MA	55
Bowen Charles	Putnam Co, IN	16
Bowen Daniel	Weathersfield, VT	16
Bowen David	Northbridge Cem, Northbridge, MA	47
Bowen Eleazer	Old Quadric Cem, Thompson, Windham Co, CT	24
Bowen Elijah	Thorn Hill Cem, Marcellus, Onondaga Co, NY	75
Bowen Henry Dea	Old Eastford Yard, Eastford, CT	29
Bowen Ichabod	Fam Cem, Summit, RI	30
Bowen Israel Capt	Fam lot, Bowens Hill, Coventry, RI	30
Bowen Jabesh	Corson's Cem, Norridgewock, ME	17
Bowen James	Farm nr end of Ponegansett Trail, West Gloucester, RI	55
Bowen Jeremiah	Landaff (no stone), NH	26
Bowen Joel	Old Rumford Cem, Rehoboth, MA	55
Bowen Joseph	Barnard Cem, Sheffield, Berkshire Co, MA	77
Bowen Micajah	His prop, nr Red Hill, Albemarle Co, VA	48
Bowen Moses	Lippitt Cem, Hartwick, Otsego Co, NY	71
Bowen Nathan	Bowen Bliss Cem, Cheshire, MA	53
Bowen Nathan	Oak Grove Cem, Fall River, MA	51
Bowen Nathan	Rehoboth, MA	55
Bowen Oliver	Edgefield, SC	16
Bowen Oliver Commodore	St Paul's Ch Cem, Augusta, GA	15
Bowen Rees	Battle of Kings Mountain, SC	52
Bowen Ries Lt	Kings Mountain, NC	50
Bowen Seth	Broad St Pres Ch Cem, Bridgeton, NJ	47
Bowen Simeon Sr	Rehoboth Cem, Rehoboth, MA	46
Bowen Stephen	Stevens Cem, Annawan St, Rehoboth, MA	54
Bowen Stoddard	Killed in Wyoming Massacre, Wyoming, PA	52
Bowen Stoddard	Pres Ch Cem, Cooperstown, Otsego Co, NY	74
Bowen Thomas	Greene Co, PA	55
Bowen Thomas	Old Rumford Cem, Rehoboth, MA	55
Bowen Valentine	Bowen Bliss Cem, Cheshire, MA	53
Bowen William	Davidson-Selover Cem, Niles, NY	56
Bowen William Capt	12 mi fr Nashville, Sumner Co, TN	50
Bower George	Stone Ch Cem, Brady Twp, Lycoming Co, PA	56
Bower George Michael	St Peters Union Ch Cem, Briar Creek, Columbia Co, PA	56
Bower Jacob	Uniontown, Summit Co, OH	15
Bower John	Redmount or Bowers Cem, York Springs, York Co, PA	50
Bower Voluntine	Cook Cem, Haymaker, nr Eldred, PA	52
Bowers Benjamin	Priv Cem, Lowell, ME	56
Bowers David Capt	Died at sea, MA	47
Bowers Henry	Priv fam Cem, Riverside Ave & South St, Somerset, MA	55
Bowers Isaac	Hillside Cem, Nashua, NH	30
Bowers James	Fam Cem, nr Fairlee, Chestertown, Kent Co, MD	71
Bowers Jerahmiel	Pine Grove Cem, Leominster, MA	50
Bowers John	Lower Cem, Sunbury, PA	15
Bowers John	Old Yard, Pine Ridge, Hancock, NH	29
Bowers John	Pine Ridge Cem, Hancock Village, NH	55
Bowers Jonathan	South Cem, Billerica, MA	55
Bowers Jonathan Jr	Priv fam Cem, Riverside Ave & South St, Somerset, MA	55
Bowers Philip	Priv fam Cem, Riverside Ave & South St, Somerset, MA	55
Bowers Samuel	Old Pine Grove Cem, Leominster, MA	47
Bowers William	South Cem, Billerica, MA	55
Bowie Allen	Rockville Cem, Rockville, MD	15
Bowie William 3rd	Thorpland, nr Upper Marlboro, Prince Georges Co, MD	51
Bowker Daniel	Old Sudbury Center, Sudbury, MA	55
Bowker Isaiah	Madison Twp, Columbiana Co, OH	56
Bowker Jonathan	Old Cem, Phillipston, MA	55
Bowker Joseph	Old Center Rutland Cem, Rutland, VT	59
Bowker Josiah	Old Cem, Northborough, MA	56
Bowker Lazarus Jr	Norwell Central Cem, Norwell, MA	46
Bowker Silas	Cem, Greenleaf farm, S of Locke Village, NY	16

Abstract of Graves of Revolutionary Patriots

Bowker Silas	Green Leaf Farm Cem, Locke, NY 41	
Bowles Isaac	Cushing Cem, Mattapoisett, MA 58	
Bowles Samuel	North Cem, Portsmouth, NH 34	
Bowles Thomas Philip	Fam Cem, Hanover Co, VA 55	
Bowles William	Cole farm, 3 mi fr Harrodsburg, Mercer Co, KY 31	
Bowley Daniel	St Paul's Cem, Freemont St & Lombard St, Baltimore, MD 15	
Bowman Abraham Corp	Cem, sect H, Lexington, KY 45	
Bowman Benjamin Sr	Harris Hill Cem, Clarence, NY 70	
Bowman Christian	Bachman bur plot, South Annville Twp, Lebanon Co, PA 83	
Bowman David	Trissel Cem, Jackson Twp, Montgomery Co, OH 56	
Bowman Francis	Depot Hill Cem, Henniker, NH 32	
Bowman James	Midland Cem, Westboro, MA 50	
Bowman Johannes	Bachman bur plot, South Annville Twp, Lebanon Co, PA 83	
Bowman John	Bellevue, Mercer Co, KY 52	
Bowman John	Clarendon Cem, Clarendon, VT 24	
Bowman John	Clarendon Cem, Clarendon, VT 25	
Bowman John	Fooshee Cem, Loudon, Loudon Co, TN 77	
Bowman John	Nr Salem, Montgomery Co, OH 55	
Bowman John	Stockton's Valley Cem, TN 23	
Bowman Jonas Capt	Depot Hill Cem, Henniker, NH 32	
Bowman Nicholas	Weisenberg Cem, Weisenberg Twp, PA 73	
Bowman Peter	Belle Isle Cem, Camillus, NY 56	
Bowman Philip Casper	Grandview Cem, Salem, Perry Twp, Columbiana Co, OH 55	
Bowman Samuel	Hollenbeck Cem, Wilkes-Barre, PA 52	
Bowman Samuel	Hollenback Cem, Wilkes-Barre, PA 53	
Bowman Samuel	Warwick Village, MA 31	
Bowman Sparling	Zion Unit Pres Ch Cem, Greeneville, Greene Co, TN 73	
Bowman William	West Cem, Amherst, MA 41	
Bowne Cornelis	Old Neshanic Ref Ch Cem, Somerset Co, NJ 48	
Bowne Henry	Sweetman Cem, Ballston, Saratoga Co, NY 78	
Bowne John	Provost fam lot, Morgan, NJ 56	
Bowne Joseph	Old Tennent Ch Cem, Tennent, NJ 47	
Bowne Samuel	Schanck-Conover Bur Gr, Holmdel, Monmouth Co, NJ 78	
Bowsher Anthony	Old Bowsher Cem, Island Rd, Circleville, OH 56	
Bowyer John Col	Lexington, VA 36	
Bowyer Peter	Mays Cem, Tipton Twp, Case Co, IN 72	
Bowyer Peter	West end, Ulay Cem, Cass Co, IN 25	
Boy Jacob	Nr Bluff City, Sullivan Co, TN 37	
Boyce John	Boice Cem, Wilton, Saratoga Co, NY 78	
Boyd –	Newton Co, MS 44	
Boyd Adams	First Dutch Ref Ch Cem, Hackensack, NJ 30	
Boyd Alex Lt	Valley Cem, Londonderry, NH 35	
Boyd Andrew	Columbia, Maury Co, TN 24	
Boyd Andrew Capt	[no cem named], TN 15	
Boyd Colonel	Mennonite Ch Cem, Toyemencin, PA 52	
Boyd David	Fishing Creek Ch Cem, Chester Co, SC 73	
Boyd David	Pres Ch Cem, Buffalo, Hopewell Twp, Washington Co, PA 15	
Boyd Ebenezer	Pres Ch Cem, Mahopac Falls, NY 35	
Boyd Francis	Farm nr Washington Court House, Fayette Co, OH 55	
Boyd George	Middlefield Cem, Otsego Co, NY 33	
Boyd James	Albany Rural Cem, Albany, NY 30	
Boyd James Esq	Faggs Manor Pres Ch, Londonderry Twp, Chester Co, PA 75	
Boyd John	Bull Creek Pres Cem, Culmerville, Allegheny Co, PA 68	
Boyd John	Cem of Brick Ch, Princeton Rd, 6 mi fr Hopkinsville, KY 50	
Boyd John	Chestnut Level Pres Ch, Drumore Twp, Lancaster Co, PA 78	
Boyd John	City Mills Cem, Franklin, MA 55	
Boyd John	Clayton Cem, Clayton, Hendricks Co, IN 72	
Boyd John	Faggs Manor Pres Ch, Londonderry Twp, Chester Co, PA 75	
Boyd John	Killed in Wyoming Massacre, Wyoming, PA 52	
Boyd John	Kings Mountain, NC 49	
Boyd John	Old Shiloh Ch Cem, nr Bedford, Lawrence Co, IN 72	

Boyd John	South Amenia Cem, Dutchess Co, NY 66
Boyd John	Unit Pres Ch Cem, West Newton, PA 55
Boyd John Dr	Westminster Pres Cem, lot 29, Baltimore, MD 15
Boyd John F	Revolutionary War Cem, Salem, Washington Co, NY 78
Boyd John Sr	Eusebia Pres Ch, 12 mi NE of Maryville, Blount Co, TN 76
Boyd Joseph	Antrim, NH 15
Boyd Joseph	Lewis Cem, Ellery, Chautauqua Co, NY 62
Boyd Patrick	Pickaway Cem, Pickaway, Greenbrier Co, WV 55
Boyd Robert	Hill Cem, Londonderry, NH 35
Boyd Samuel	Jacksonburg Cem, Jacksonburg, Wayne Co, IN 72
Boyd Thomas	Boothbay Cem, Boothbay, ME 55
Boyd Thomas	Carrington, MO 23
Boyd Thomas	Fam Cem, 4 mi fr Pinetown, NC 49
Boyd Thomas	Hiatte farm, New Bloomfield, Callaway Co, MO 76
Boyd Thomas	Salem, Washington Co, NY 70
Boyd Thomas Lt	Mount Hope Cem, Rochester, Monroe Co, NY 33
Boyd William	Frazure Cem, Burnt Hills, Ballston, Saratoga Co, NY 77
Boyd William	Hill Cem, Londonderry, NH 35
Boyd William Capt	Spring Hill Cem, Marlboro, MA 45
Boyd William Capt	Valley Cem, Londonderry, NH 35
Boyd William T	Londonderry, NH 56
Boyden Amos	North Orange, MA 30
Boyden Isaac	Dummerston, VT 18
Boyden James	Blanchard Cem, Guilford, VT 25
Boyden James	Blanchard Cem, Guilford, VT 24
Boyden John	Howland Cem, Conway, MA 53
Boyden Josiah	Howland Cem, Conway, MA 53
Boyden Josiah Maj	Dummerston, VT 18
Boyden Phineas	South Walpole Cem, Walpole, MA 45
Boyden William Col	Dummerston, VT 18
Boydston William	Faubeau Cem, Clay Co, MO 65
Boyer Assamus Jr	Pine Grove Twp, PA 49
Boyer Assamus Sr	Pine Grove Twp, PA 49
Boyer Christian	Freeburg Cem, Freeburg, PA 15
Boyer Christopher	Zions Red Ch, Orwigsburg, PA 49
Boyer Christopher	Zions Red Ch, Orwigsburg, PA 49
Boyer Frederick	Old Luth Cem, Orwigsburg, PA 49
Boyer George	St John's Luth Ch Cem, Montgomery Co, PA 59
Boyer Jacob	Ridge Lawn Cem, Newstead, NY 33
Boyer Johannes	Flowery Field, nr Pottsville, PA 49
Boyer John	Big Flats Cem, NY 32
Boyer John Jr	Fam Cem, 4 mi fr Greensburg, Decatur Co, IN 78
Boyer Jonathan	Miller Cem, Big Flats, Chemung Co, NY 78
Boyer Lewis	Wesley Chapel Cem, Shelby Co, OH 53
Boyer Michael	Dryland Union Ch Cem, Hecktown, Northampton Co, PA 40
Boyer Michael	Dryland Ch Cem, Hecktown, Northampton Co, PA 22
Boyer Peter	Old Pres Ch Cem, Bound Brook, NJ 48
Boyer Samuel	Luth Cem, Port Carbon, PA 49
Boyer Thomas	Fincastle Pres Churchyard, Fincastle, Botetourt Co, VA 73
Boyes James	Forest Hill Cem, East Derry, NH 38
Boyes James	Valley Cem, Londonderry, NH 35
Boyes Thomas	North Hillsdale Meth Ch Cem, Hillsdale, Columbia Co, NY 77
Boykin Burwell	Fam Cem, Tomb Field, 6 mi S of Camden, Kershaw Co, SC 71
Boykin Byers	Fam Cem, 12 mi fr Clinton, Sampson Co, NC 51
Boykin Francis	Fam Cem, fam plantation, Baldwin Co, GA 25
Boykin Francis	Shinholzer farm, 10 mi fr Milledgeville, GA 27
Boylan Benjamin D	Lebanon, Active Lebanon, Warren Co, OH 55
Boylan John	Baskingridge, NJ 32
Boyle George	Revolutionary Cem, Deposit, NY 55
Boyle Patrick	Salem Ch Cem, Campbelltown, Lebanon Co, PA 83
Boyles John	Bellwood Cem, Blair Co, PA 21

Boyles John	Logan Valley Cem, Bellwood, PA 52
Boyles Timothy	Scioto Co, OH 55
Boyles William	Bellwood Cem, Blair Co, PA 21
Boyles William	Logan Valley Cem, Bellwood, PA 52
Boylston Joshua	Walnut Street Cem, Brookline, MA 56
Boynton Aaron	Bapt Ch Cem, Barnwell, SC 51
Boynton Asa	Scioto Co, OH 55
Boynton Caleb	Vernon Grove Cem, Milford, MA 46
Boynton David	Boynton Yard, Meredith & New Hampton Line, NH 29
Boynton David	Cem nr Columbia Bridge, Columbia, NH 36
Boynton David Emery	Four Corners Cem, Sullivan, NH 38
Boynton Elias	New Cem, Temple, NH 29
Boynton Elias	Temple, NH 15
Boynton Elias	Temple Center Cem, Temple, NH 46
Boynton Ephraim	Four Corners Cem, Sullivan, NH 39
Boynton Jewett	Grout Cem, Weathersfield, VT 36
Boynton John	Cem on town common, Nelson, NH 35
Boynton John	Churchyard, Hollis, NH 39
Boynton John	Grout Cem, Weathersfield, VT 36
Boynton John	High St Cem, Greenfield, MA 34
Boynton John	High St Cem, Greenfield, MA 33
Boynton Joseph	North Cem, Westmoreland, NH 25
Boynton Joseph	Walton, Pepperell, MA 56
Boynton Joshua	Grave in field E of Bapt Ch, Canterbury, NH 35
Boynton Moses	Rowley Cem, Essex, MA 48
Boynton Moses Ens	East Weare Cem, East Weare, NH 33
Boynton Nathaniel	West Cem, Westford, MA 48
Boynton Richard	Old Town Cem, opposite Pound, Old Meredith, Laconia, NH 28
Boynton Samuel	Cornish Cem, Cornish, ME 45
Boynton Samuel	Groveland Cem, Groveland, MA 56
Boynton Samuel	Rockdale, West Stockbridge, MA 56
Boynton Samuel T	Warren Cem, Pittstown, Rensselaer Co, NY 37
Boynton Thomas	West Parish Bur Gr, Andover, MA 26
Boys M	Calvary Cem, Washington Twp, OH 56
Boyton Gershom	Beechwood Cem, Cohasset, MA 53
Bozeman John	Holaday's Creek Cem, Marion Co, MS 57
Bozworth Nathaniel	Unitarian Ch Cem, Dighton, MA 55
Brabham Joseph	Mizpsah Ch Cem, Barnwell, SC 51
Brabrook Benjamin	Acton, MA 55
Brace Henry	Ancient Bur Gr, Hartford, Hartford Co, CT 86
Brace Henry	Old Cem, North Main St, West Hartford, CT 31
Brace Henry	West Hartford Cem, Hartford, CT 19
Brace Henry	West Hartford, CT 38
Brace Joseph	Orange, PA 56
Brack Benjamin	Fam plantation, 3 mi fr Midville, Burke Co, GA 25
Brackenberry Sam	Sugar Hill Cem, East Weare, NH 33
Bracket Ebenezer	Old Yard Cem, Weston, MA 55
Brackett Benning	Brackett-Treadwell Cem, Ashwamp Dist, Newmarket, NH 31
Brackett Daniel	Pettengill Cem, Clarendon, NY 34
Brackett Ebenezer	Hancock Cem, Quincy, MA 54
Brackett James	Brackett Yard, North Berwick, ME 56
Brackett James	Fam Cem, fam farm, Greenland, NH 30
Brackett James	Terrace Cem, East Madrid, Franklin Co, ME 83
Brackett James Dr	Fam farm, right of Creek Bridge, Lee, NH 36
Brackett James Jr	Hancock Cem, Quincy, MA 54
Brackett Jeremiah	Meth Ch Cem, Cumberland, ME 45
Brackett Joseph	Hancock Cem, Quincy, MA 54
Brackett Joseph	Old Lancaster Cem, Lancaster, NH 37
Brackett Joshua	Fam Cem, fam farm, Greenland, NH 30
Brackett Joshua	North Cem, Portsmouth, NH 34
Brackett Moses	Hancock Cem, Quincy, MA 54

Brackett Moses Jr	Hancock Cem, Quincy, MA 54
Brackett Nathan	Brackett Yard, Winchell Rd, Action, York Co, ME 74
Brackett Nathaniel	Syman, ME 56
Brackett Thomas Lt	Fam bur gr, his farm, now Hatch prop, Greenland, NH 38
Bradbury Amirhuhama	Old Smith Bur Gr, Marlboro, Ulster Co, NY 61
Bradbury David	Jacksonburg Cem, Jacksonburg, Wayne Co, IN 72
Bradbury Samuel	Island of Santa Domingo, W Indies 45
Bradbury William	Sawyer Hill Cem, Canaan, NH 36
Bradford Andrew	North Springfield, VT 15
Bradford Calvin	Old Burial Cem, Plympton, MA 57
Bradford Carpenter	Marcy Cem, Bradford, CT 55
Bradford David	Ancient Bur Gr, Kingston, MA 50
Bradford Dea Samuel	Old Burial Cem, Plympton, MA 57
Bradford Elisha	Cheshire Cem, West Mountain Rd, Cheshire, MA 55
Bradford Ezekial	Woodlawn Cem, West Bowdoin, ME 40
Bradford Gamaliel	Center St Cem, South Duxbury, MA 50
Bradford Gamaliel Sr	Mayflower Cem, Duxbury, Plymouth Co, MA 78
Bradford Gideon	Old Burial Cem, Plympton, MA 57
Bradford Gideon Jr	Old Cem, Plympton, MA 50
Bradford Henry	Fam Cem, GE prop, Hendersonville, Somerset Co, TN 74
Bradford Israel	Plymton Green Cem, MA 47
Bradford James	Bradford, Whitely Twp, Greene Co, PA 56
Bradford James	Oak St City Cem, Norwich, CT 18
Bradford James	Poplar Tent Cem, Pres Ch Cem, Mecklenburg Co, NC 61
Bradford Jesse	Turner, ME 18
Bradford Jesse	Turner Corner, Turner, ME 29
Bradford Jesse	Turner Center, ME 30
Bradford John	Beaverton Cem, Beaverton, OH 56
Bradford John	Beaverton Cem, Montgomery Co, OH 57
Bradford John	Braceville, OH 24
Bradford John	Old Cem, Plympton, MA 50
Bradford John	St Paul's Parish Cem, Hanover Co, VA 57
Bradford John Capt	Old Yard, Pine Ridge, Hancock, NH 29
Bradford John Capt	Pine Ridge Cem, Hancock, NH 46
Bradford John Lt	Atwood Cem, Pelham, NH 34
Bradford Joseph	Old Burial Cem, Plympton, MA 57
Bradford Joshua	Braceville Cem, Trumbull Co, OH 55
Bradford Lemuel	Burial Hill, Plymouth, MA 56
Bradford Lt	Nr Ocilla, GA 39
Bradford Nathaniel	Burial Hill, Plymouth, MA 56
Bradford Oliver	Old Burial Cem, Plympton, MA 57
Bradford Peabody	Ancient Bur Gr, Kingston, MA 50
Bradford Peabody	West Auburn, ME 29
Bradford Perez	Mayflower Cem, Duxbury, MA 58
Bradford Perez	Old Cem, Plympton, MA 50
Bradford Robert	Ancient Bur Gr, Kingston, MA 50
Bradford Robert	Francestown Cem, Francestown, NH 28
Bradford Robert	Ohio Company Bur Gr, Belpre, Washington Co, OH 55
Bradford Robert	Town Cem, Francestown, NH 27
Bradford Samuel	Center St Cem, South Duxbury, MA 50
Bradford Samuel	East Woodstock Yard, Woodstock, CT 26
Bradford Samuel	Miles Standish Cem, Duxbury, MA 46
Bradford Samuel	Old Cem, Plympton, MA 50
Bradford Samuel	Old Drawyers, New Castle Co, DE 46
Bradford Samuel	Old Cem, Acworth, NH 34
Bradford Seth	Mayflower Cem, Duxbury, MA 50
Bradford Seth	Mayflower Cem, Duxbury, MA 58
Bradford Shubel	Poland Dist Cem, Conway, MA 53
Bradford Thomas	Cem on Old Line Rd, Clarke Co, AL 60
Bradford Wait	Center Cem, Pembroke, MA 57
Bradford Walt	Turner, ME 18

Bradford William	Burial Hill, Plymouth, MA	56
Bradford William	Old Cem, Plympton, MA	50
Bradford William	Spear Hill Cem, Salem, NH	36
Bradford William Maj	Elmwood Cem, Barre, VT	48
Bradford Winslow	Old Burial Cem, Plympton, MA	57
Bradish David	Eastern Promanade Cem, Portland, ME	49
Bradish Elisha	Second Cem, Worcester, MA	68
Bradish James	Townsend Cem, Stittville, Oneida Co, NY	82
Bradish James Dea	North Upton Cem, Upton, MA	46
Bradish John	Palmyra Village Cem, Palmyra, Wayne Co, NY	79
Bradlee David Capt	Central Bur Gr, Dorchester, MA	45
Bradley Aaron	Bantam, CT	17
Bradley Abijah	Old Colonial Cem, Derby, CT	56
Bradley Amos Dea	Hildreth Bur Gr, Dracut, MA	58
Bradley Amos Dr	Hildreth Bur Gr, Dracut, MA	58
Bradley Amos Lt	Mount Carmel Bur Gr, Hamden, CT	31
Bradley Aner Col	Watertown, CT	15
Bradley Ariel	Akron, OH	15
Bradley Ariel	Waterville, OH	53
Bradley Ariel	Wood Co, OH	45
Bradley Ashabel	West Cem, Madison, New Haven Co, CT	24
Bradley Azariah	Old Hartwick Village Cem, Hartwick, Otsego Co, NY	72
Bradley Benjamin	Center Cem, Canterbury, NH	29
Bradley Cornelius	Bellefontaine Cem, Mt Vernon, Posey Co, IN	69
Bradley Cornelius	Exact site not known, IN	25
Bradley Daniel	East Litchfield, CT	17
Bradley Daniel	Lime Rock Cem, Salisbury Twp, CT	64
Bradley Daniel	Pentucket Cem, Haverhill, MA	28
Bradley David	Pentucket Cem, Haverhill, MA	28
Bradley David	Rockdale, West Stockbridge, MA	56
Bradley Diman	Water St Cem, Great Barrington, MA	41
Bradley Dimon	North Haven Cem, North Haven, CT	56
Bradley Eli	Lee Cem, Lee, MA	15
Bradley Eli	West Genoa Cem, Genoa, Cayuga Co, NY	57
Bradley Elihu	Plot 2 mi E of Fulton, NY	30
Bradley Elisha	Greenfield Hill Cem, Fairfield, CT	62
Bradley Elisha	Stockbridge Cem, Stockbridge, MA	47
Bradley Elnathan	Greenfield Hill Cem, Fairfield, CT	62
Bradley Enoch	Second West Parish Cem, Haverhill, MA	31
Bradley Enos	Colonial Cem, Derby City, CT	15
Bradley Enos	West Side Cem, Easton, CT	33
Bradley Francis	Hopewell Pres Ch Cem, Mecklenburg Co, NC	49
Bradley Francis	Hopewell Pres Ch Cem, Charlotte, Mecklenburg Co, NC	80
Bradley Francis	West Side Cem, Easton, CT	33
Bradley Hezekiah	Greenfield Hill Cem, Fairfield, CT	62
Bradley Hezekiah Jr	Greenfield Hill Cem, Fairfield, CT	62
Bradley James	Canfield Cem, Mahoning Co, OH	55
Bradley James	Fam Cem, Dixon Springs, Smith Co, TN	79
Bradley James	[no cem named], NC	17
Bradley James	Sweetman Cem, Ballston, Saratoga Co, NY	77
Bradley James Corp	Johnstown, OH	24
Bradley Jared	Lee Cem, Lee, MA	15
Bradley Jesse Capt	Lee Cem, Lee, MA	15
Bradley John	Grantville Cem, Norfolk, CT	62
Bradley John	Greenfield Hill Cem, Fairfield, CT	62
Bradley John	Old City Cem, Murfreesboro, TN	60
Bradley John	Old Milton Cem, Milton, MA	46
Bradley John	Old North Bur Gr, Concord, NH	41
Bradley John	Sinking Spring Cem, Abingdon, VA	30
Bradley John	Sinking Spring Cem, Abingdon, VA	29
Bradley Johnathan	Second Cem, North Andover, MA	26

Bradley Joseph	Greenfield Hill Cem, Fairfield, CT 62
Bradley Joseph	North Parish Bur Gr, Andover, MA 26
Bradley Josiah	Stockbridge Cem, Stockbridge, MA 47
Bradley Josiah	Village Cem, Chester, NH 33
Bradley Lemuel	Ira Allen Cem, Sunderland, Bennington Co, VT 61
Bradley Levi	Village Cem, West Charleston, ME 54
Bradley Levi	West Side Cem, Easton, CT 33
Bradley Lyman	West Side Cem, Easton, CT 33
Bradley Moses	Cong Cem, Cheshire, New Haven Co, CT 24
Bradley Moses	Handy Cem, West Woodstock, Windsor Co, VT 75
Bradley Nathan	Greenfield Hill Cem, Fairfield, CT 62
Bradley Nathaniel	Pentucket, Haverhill, MA 27
Bradley Nathaniel	Pentucket Cem, Haverhill, MA 28
Bradley Oliver	Cong Cem, Cheshire, New Haven Co, CT 24
Bradley Roger	Fam bur gr, Black River Crossing, Upper Salem, SC 51
Bradley Samuel	Boyce Cem, Milton, Ulster Co, NY 78
Bradley Samuel	Greenfield Hill Cem, Fairfield, CT 62
Bradley Samuel Capt	[no cem named], NY 41
Bradley Seely	Warren Cem, Warren, NY 41
Bradley Seth	Greenfield Hill Cem, Fairfield, CT 62
Bradley Stephen Rowe	Old Cem, Westminster, VT 42
Bradley Sturgis	Grove Cem, Bath, Steuben Co, NY 73
Bradley Thomas	Head of Christiana Cem, nr Newark, New Castle Co, DE 45
Bradley Zalmon	Greenfield Hill Cem, Fairfield, CT 62
Bradshaw Henry	Old Bur Gr, Arlington, MA 56
Bradshaw James	Sweetman Cem, Ballston, Saratoga Co, NY 77
Bradshaw John	Stevensville Cem, Stevens Twp, PA 53
Bradshaw Joseph	Rose Hill Cem, Hagerstown, MD 51
Bradshaw Joseph	Rose Hill Cem, Hagerstown, Washington Co, MD 77
Bradshaw Nathaniel	North Dorchester Cem, Boston, MA 55
Bradshaw Thomas	Old bur gr, Medford, MA 45
Bradstreet Henry	Pres Ch Cem, Hancock, Delaware Co, NY 56
Bradstreet John	Palermo, ME 29
Bradstreet Moses	Rowley Cem, Essex, MA 48
Bradstreet Nathaniel	Old Cem, Rowley Center, MA 55
Bradstreet Pearson	Rowley Cem, Essex, MA 48
Bradstreet Samuel	Old Topsfield Cem, Pine Grove, Topsfield, MA 55
Brady Benjamin	Allegany Co, MD 54
Brady Francis	Hopewell Pres Ch Cem, Mecklenburg Co, NC 49
Brady Hugh	Elmwood, Detroit, MI 56
Brady Hugh	Middle Spring Pres Ch Cem, Shippensburg, PA 56
Brady James Capt	Gilgal Ch Cem, Indiana Co, PA 22
Brady John	Monument, Muncy, PA 55
Brady John Jr	Lewisburg Cem, Lewisburg, PA 15
Brady Samuel	Gilgal Cem, nr Marion Center, PA 55
Brady Samuel Capt	Gilgal Ch Cem, Indiana Co, PA 22
Brady Samuel Capt	Liberty Cem, WV 24
Brady William	Fam Cem, fam farm, nr Harrisonville, Cass Co, MO 70
Bragdon Arthur	Bragdo Yard, Rt 11, Shapleigh Corner, York Co, ME 74
Bragdon Samuel	Pulaski, NY 15
Bragdon Samuel	Pulaski Old Cem, Pulaski, NY 30
Bragg Moses	Pleasant View Cem, Randolph, Orange Co, VT 74
Bragg Nicholas	Cem, shore of Connecticut River, Dalton, NH 37
Bragg Nicholas	Springfield, VT 15
Bragg William	Springfield, VT 15
Braidfoot John	Trinity Ch Cem, under Old Cath Ch, Portsmouth, VA 34
Brailey Gideon	Milan Cem, Erie Co, OH 55
Brainard Abner	Moodus, East Haddam, CT 56
Brainard Amasa	Riverview, East Haddam, CT 56
Brainard Ames	Brookmere Cem, Cleveland, OH 15
Brainard Amos	Brookmere Cem, Brooklyn Heights, OH 56

Abstract of Graves of Revolutionary Patriots

Brainard Ansel	Friendsville Cem, Westfield Twp, Medina, OH 58
Brainard Asahel	Jerusalem Hills Cem, Litchfield, Herkimer Co, NY 81
Brainard Asahel	Village Cem, Rumney, NH 37
Brainard Berziahrel	Cong Cem, East Haddam, CT 56
Brainard Daniel	Fremont Cem, Fremont, OH 57
Brainard Daniel	Glastenburg Cem, Glastenburg, CT 55
Brainard Daniel	Riverview, East Haddam, CT 56
Brainard Daniel Dr	Oak Harbor Cem, Sandusky Co, OH 51
Brainard Eliakim	Haddam Cem, Haddam, CT 61
Brainard Jabez	Lake View Cem, Euclid Ave, Cleveland, Cuyahoga Co, OH 55
Brainard Jeptha	Valley Home Cem, Bradford Co, PA 53
Brainard Joshua	Warner, East Haddam, CT 56
Brainerd David	Old Fort Cem, nr Ironton, Lawrence Co, OH 79
Brainerd James Dea	Cleveland, OH 45
Brainerd Josiah	Rock Landing Cem, Haddam Neck, Haddam, CT 55
Brainerd Josiah Jr	Rock Landing Cem, Haddam Neck, Haddam, CT 55
Brainerd Reuben	East Winthrop, ME 29
Brakebill Peter Sr	Farm, Nail's Creek Rd, Maryville, Blount Co, TN 76
Braley Nathaniel	Palmyra Village Cem, Palmyra, Wayne Co, NY 79
Bralton James Capt	Montgomery Co, VA 35
Braman James	Berlin Cem, nr Montpelier, VT 15
Braman James	Berlin Corner Cem, Berlin Corner, VT 20
Braman Sylvanus	Cem on West Main St, Norton, MA 55
Bramble William Capt	Quechee Cem, VT 41
Bramble William Capt	Queechee Cem, VT 40
Bramhall Capt	Rahway Cem, Rahway, NJ 26
Bramhall Joseph III	Burial Hill, Plymouth, MA 56
Branch Daniel	Old Cem, Pawlet, VT 15
Branch Daniel	Old Mettowee Cem, Pawlet, VT 48
Branch Samuel	Old Village Cem, Locke, NY 41
Branch Vine	Lindsey, Richmond, MA 56
Branch William	Middle Ridge Cem, Madison, OH 26
Brand John	Tarlton Cem, Salt Creek Twp, Pickaway Co, OH 53
Brand Philip	Swamp Ref Ch Cem, Montgomery Co, PA 59
Brandegee Etishima	Maple Cem, Berlin, CT 52
Brandenburg Samuel	Ref Ch Cem, Middletown, Frederick Co, MD 77
Brandhoefer Adam	Hill's Emanuel Cem, Franklin Twp, Westmoreland Co, PA 71
Brandon Christopher	Union Cem, SC 17
Brandon Gerard	[no cem named], MS 44
Brandon James	Thyatira Pres Ch Cem, Rowan Co, NC 49
Brandon John	Mt Moriah Cem, Pulaski, Giles Co, TN 73
Brandon John	Thyatira Pres Ch Cem, Rowan Co, NC 49
Brandon Matthew	Thyatira Pres Ch Cem, Rowan Co, NC 49
Brandon Matthew	Thyatira Pres Ch Cem, Rowan Co, NC 72
Brandon Patrick	Stewart's Corner Cem, Venice, Cayuga Co, NY 65
Brandon Richard	Thyatira Pres Ch Cem, Rowan Co, NC 49
Brandon Thomas Col	Davidson Fam Cem, Jasper Co, GA 22
Brandon Thomas Col	Union Cem, SC 17
Brandon William	Lower Lott's Creek Prim Bapt Ch Cem, Bulloch Co, GA 63
Brandon William	Mt Nebo Cem, Connoquenissing Twp, Butler Co, PA 57
Brandow Godfrey	Coxsackie Cem, Coxsackie, Greene Co, NY 72
Brandt Adam	[no cem named], PA 55
Brandt David	Pres Ch Cem, Rahway, NJ 76
Brandt John	Dicks Creek Pres Ch Cem, E of Blue Ball, Warren Co, OH 56
Brandt Lewis	Pres Ch Cem, Rahway, NJ 76
Brandt Reuben	Crowder Cem, Illini Country Club Grounds, IL 30
Branham John Sr	His land, Iron Works Pike, nr Midway Pike, Scott Co, KY 20
Brank Robert	Paint Lick, Garrard, KY 56
Brann Jeremiah	Layhigh Cem, Kirchling Rd, Ross, OH 56
Brannon John	Old Cem, Cadiz, OH 56
Branson Joseph	Newton Union Sloan Cem, West Collingswood, NJ 50

Brant John	St Thomas Epis Ch Cem, Montgomery Co, PA 59
Brant Lewis Capt	Rahway Cem, Rahway, NJ 26
Brant Matthias	Connecticut Farms Pres Cem, Union, NJ 49
Brant Samuel	Hillside Cem, Madison, NJ 30
Brant William	Connecticut Farms Cem, Union Co, NJ 32
Brant William Capt	Connecticut Farms Ch, Union, NJ 26
Brantley Amos	Sparta, GA 36
Brantly William Sr	Mays Chapel Cem, Brunswick Co, NC 60
Braselton Jacob	Walnut Ch Cem, nr Braselton, Jackson Co, GA 42
Braselton Jacob	Walnut Ch Graveyard, E of Braselton, GA 78
Braselton Jacob Sr	Walnut Cem, nr Braselton, Jackson Co, GA 43
Brashear Ignacious	Old Crow Brashear Cem, nr Shepherdsville, Bullitt Co, KY 46
Brasher Abraham	Pres Cem, Morristown, NJ 32
Brass Garrit	Mentor, Lake Co, OH 26
Brass Garrit	Mentor, Lake Co, OH 55
Brassee Andreas	Old Orchard Cem, Hillsdale, Columbia Co, NY 42
Brastow Beriah	Vine Lake, Medfield, MA 56
Braswell William	Three Mile Creek, Avery Co, NC 49
Bratney Robert	Randolph Co, IL 48
Bratt Garret Capt	Hoosick rural Cem, Hoosick, NY 34
Bratt John	Island Hill Cem, Buskirk, NY 34
Bratt Peter A	Jerusalem Cem, Albany Co, NY 66
Brattle William	Pittsfield Cem, Pittsfield, ME 26
Bratton James	Guernsey Co, OH 53
Bratton James	Pleasant Hill Cem, Center Twp, Guernsey Co, OH 55
Bratton Robert	Fam Cem, nr Goshen, Augusta Co, VA 59
Bratton William	Brattonville Cem, York Co, SC 60
Braucher Christian	Laurelton Cem, Laurelton, PA 15
Braun Christian	Dryland Union Ch Cem, Hecktown, Northampton Co, PA 40
Braun Johan Adam	Dryland Union Ch Cem, Hecktown, Northampton Co, PA 40
Braun John Adam	St Paul's Ch, Summer Hill, PA 49
Brawley Neil	Center Pres Ch Cem, Iredell Co, NC 49
Braxton Carter	His estate, Chericoke, King, VA 74
Bray Aaron	Old Town Cem, Newbury, MA 36
Bray Daniel	Canaan Cem, Columbia Co, NY 38
Bray Daniel	Charter St, Salem, MA 56
Bray Daniel	Rittenhouse Cem, Rosemont, Hunterdon Co, NJ 31
Bray Daniel	Rosemont, Kingwood Township, NJ 51
Bray David	Ancient Cem, Yarmouth, MA 63
Bray Edmund	Ancient Cem, Yarmouth, Barnstable Co, MA 67
Bray John	McKay Cem, Craig Twp, Switzerland Co, IN 72
Bray John	Rosemont Cem, Hunterdon Co, NJ 54
Bray Joseph	Nr Pelton Brook, Starks, ME 17
Bray William	Ancient Cem, Yarmouth, MA 63
Brayton Borden	Adamsville Stone Ch Cem, Adamsville, RI 54
Brayton David	Adamsville Stone Ch Cem, Adamsville, RI 54
Brayton James W Capt	North Cem, Warren, RI 38
Brayton John	Fam Cem, back of theater, B Point Rd, Somerset, MA 55
Brazee Andrews F	Copake Meth Ch Cem, Copake, Columbia Co, NY 79
Brazelton John	Springfield Friends Ch Cem, Guilford Co, NC 49
Brazer Christopher	Central Cem, Boston, MA 56
Breadsley William	Clark Cem, Providence, Saratoga Co, NY 78
Breakbill Peter Sr	Priv Cem, Bay's Mtn, nr Cedar Grove Bapt Ch, Blount, TN 60
Breakenridge James Lt	Old Bennington, VT 40
Breakenridge James Lt	Old Bennington Town Hill Cem, VT 41
Brearley David	St Michael's Ch Cem, Trenton, NJ 28
Brearley David	St Michael's Ch Cem, Warren St, Trenton, NJ 26
Brearley Isaac	Cem, Lawrenceville, NJ 26
Breast John	Back of old log house, betw Paris & Little Rock, KY 17
Breaux Firmin	Old Churchyard Cem, St Martinville, LA 71
Brechbill Johannes	Walmer's Cem, Indiantown Gap, Lebanon Co, PA 83

Abstract of Graves of Revolutionary Patriots

Brecht Christian	Hite farm Cem, Snake Spring Twp, Bedford Co, PA 80
Breck John	Old Cem, Sterling, MA 46
Breck Samuel	Copps Hill Cem, Boston, MA 46
Breckenbridge James	Pres Ch Cem, Rocky Springs, PA 20
Breckenridge Alexander	Clay farm, Bourbon Co, KY 24
Breckenridge James	Fam Cem, Grove Hill, Fincastle, VA 59
Breckenridge James	Rocky Springs Pres Ch Cem, 6 mi fr Chambersburg, PA 19
Breckenridge Robert Lt	Fam Cem, Jefferson Co, KY 31
Brecount Daniel	Pres Ch Cem, Rahway, NJ 76
Bredwell Yelventon	Priv Cem, fam farm, Donald Rd, Tate Twp, OH 56
Breece Timothy	Lost Creek Cem, nr Green Bay, 7 mi N of Ft Madison, IA 42
Breece Timothy	Lost Creek Cem, Lee Co, IA 15
Breed Allen	South Cem, Spafford, NY 35
Breed Ephraim	Old Western Cem, Lynn, MA 55
Breed Gershom Elder	Fam Cem, Fayetteville, NY 53
Breed Joel	Old Western Cem, Lynn, MA 55
Breed John Capt	Fam Cem, Anguilla, CT 31
Breed Joseph	Western Cem, West Lynn, MA 56
Breed Josiah	Old Western Cem, Lynn, MA 55
Breed Nathan	Fam Cem, Anguilla, CT 31
Breed Nathan	Old Mulky Mtg Hs, State Park, Barren Co, KY 33
Breed Nathaniel	Henderson, Jefferson Co, NY 16
Breed Nathaniel Dr	Cem on town common, Nelson, NH 35
Breed Thomas	Antrim, NH 15
Breed Thomas	Meech Cem, Brutus, NY 41
Breeder Lt	Greene Co, VA 37
Breedon Enoch	Lipscomb Fam Cem, nr Winchester, Franklin Co, TN 78
Brees John	Cem, Horseheads, Chemung Co, NY 55
Breese Garret	Ten Mile Run Cem, NJ 32
Breese Garret T V	Cupperly farm, Breese Hollow, Hoosick, Rensselaer Co, NY 36
Breese Henry	Barbours Corners Cem, Chemung, Chemung Co, NY 78
Breese Henry	Hoosick Rural Cem, Hoosick, NY 34
Breese Henry	Hossick Rural Cem, Hossick Falls, NY 49
Breese John	Maple Grove Cem, Horseheads, Chemung Co, NY 78
Breese John Jr	Pres Ch Cem, Basking Ridge, NJ 74
Breese Samuel	Cem, Forty Fort, PA 52
Breese Stephen	Pres Ch Cem, Basking Ridge, NJ 74
Breese Timothy	Lost Creek Cem, Augusta Rd, Lee Co, IA 68
Breevoort Elias	First Dutch Ref Ch Cem, Hackensack, NJ 30
Breitenstein John P	Fam plot, South Lebanon Twp, Lebanon Co, PA 83
Brelsfoard John	Priv Cem, Pelfrey farm, Wayne Twp, E of Jacksonburg, OH 69
Bremer Conrad	Morav Cem, Gnadenhutten, Tuscarawas Co, OH 55
Bremner John	Prospect Cem, Jamaica, Long Island, Queens Co, NY 77
Brendlinger Frederick	Blackbird Cem, Harmony Twp, OH 56
Brendlinger Henry	Harmony Chapel Cem, Morrow Co, OH 53
Brendlinger Joseph	Swamp Luth (Falkner) Cem, Montgomery Co, PA 59
Breneman Christian	Liberty Cem, W of Brownstown, Jackson Co, IN 72
Brengman Martin	Middletown Cem, Middletown, Jefferson Co, KY 83
Brenig George Col	Lehigh Ch Cem, Albertus, PA 17
Breninig George Ludwig	Lehigh Ch Cem, nr Alburtis, Lehigh Co, PA 40
Brenner John	Jacob's Ch, Pine Grove Twp, PA 49
Brenner John	Jacob's Luth Ch, 2 mi W of Pine Grove, Schuylkill Co, PA 37
Brent John Sr	Fam Cem, Holmesville, Pike Co, MS 85
Brenton James	Indian Mound Graveyard, Washington Twp, Pike Co, IN 72
Brenton John	Old Antioch Cem, Clark Co, IN 15
Brenton John	Old Antioch Graveyard, Clark Co, IN 72
Brenton Robert	Old Antioch Graveyard, Clark Co, IN 72
Brenton Robert	Old Antioch Cem, Clark Co, IN 15
Brenton Samuel	The Platform, Kingstown, RI 35
Brenton William	Old Antioch Cem, Clark Co, IN 15
Brenton William	Old Antioch Graveyard, Clark Co, IN 72

Bressler George Simon	Hetzel's Church, Pine Grove Twp, PA 49
Bressler Nicholas	Pine Grove Twp, PA 49
Bressler Peter	Jacob's Luth Ch, 2 mi W of Pine Grove, Schuylkill Co, PA 37
Bressler Peter	Jacob's Ch, Pine Grove Twp, PA 49
Brett Peter	Saile-Abeel Cem, Rt 32, far south Greene Co, NY 58
Brett Simeon	South Main St Cem, Brockton, MA 15
Brett William	Ashland St Cem, Brockton, MA 55
Bretton Ebenezer Sr	Westmoreland Cem, Westmoreland, NH 56
Bretz Ludwig	Middletown Cem, Middletown, PA 21
Bretz Michael	Hetzel's Church, Pine Grove Twp, PA 49
Bretz Michael Jr	Hetzel's Church, Pine Grove Twp, PA 49
Brevard Ephriam	First Pres Ch Cem, Charlotte, NC 72
Brevard Ephriam M D	County courthouse prop, Charlotte, NC 18
Brevard John	His farm, nr Whaleyville, Worcester Co, MD 51
Brevard Joseph	Old Quaker Cem, Camdon, SC 50
Brevard Joseph Judge	Quaker Cem, Camden, SC 45
Brevard Robert	Jackson City Cem, Jackson, Cape Girardeau Co, MO 78
Brewer Abraham	Brower fam plot, New City, Rockland Co, NY 78
Brewer Abraham	Riverside Cem, nr Elmira, NY 32
Brewer Abraham	Riverside Cem, Chemung, Chemung Co, NY 78
Brewer Ambrose	Fam Cem, Sneedville, Hancock Co, TN 85
Brewer Archibald	Orwell, Shoreham, VT 15
Brewer Benjamin	Cooly Cem, Washington Co, IN 61
Brewer Daniel	Spencer Hill Cem, Manchester, CT 19
Brewer David	Church Hill Cem, Framingham, MA 56
Brewer David	Old Center Cem, Monterey, MA 41
Brewer David B	Tappan Ref Ch Cem, Rockland Co, NY 78
Brewer Elias	Riverside, Oneonta, NY 34
Brewer Gaius	Adams Cem, Wilbraham, MA 56
Brewer Isaac	Lee Cem, Lee, MA 15
Brewer James	Central Yard, Boston Common, Tomb 39, Boston, MA 54
Brewer James	West Swanzey Cem, Swanzey, NH 35
Brewer James Jr	Old Pres Cem, Yorktown, NY 34
Brewer John	Oak Hill Cem, Brewer, ME 51
Brewer John	Old Center Cem, Monterey, MA 41
Brewer John	Riverside Cem, nr Elmira, NY 32
Brewer Jonas	Brookfield, Worcester Co, MA 56
Brewer Joseph	Old Center Cem, Monterey, MA 41
Brewer Joseph	Old Cem, Monterey, MA 56
Brewer Josiah	Dean Hill Cem, Orrington Center, Penobscot Co, ME 75
Brewer Josiah	Orrington Cem, Orrington, Penobscot Co, ME 27
Brewer Lewis	Rudy Cem, Hwy 660, Independence, Grayson Co, VA 77
Brewer Nathaniel	Tyringham, MA 15
Brewer Peter	St Paul Ch, Clear Spring Luth Parish, Washington Co, MD 72
Brewer Peter W	Riverside Cem, Oneonta, NY 31
Brewer Samuel	Old Mud Meeting House, Mercer Co, KY 45
Brewer Samuel	Orwell, Shoreham, VT 15
Brewer Uldreck	Brower fam plot, New City, Rockland Co, NY 78
Brewester Jonathan	Middletown, VT 56
Brewster Aaron	Leeds, ME 18
Brewster Agnes	Campus, Indiana Univ, Monroe, IN 55
Brewster Benjamin	Roarke farm, Brunswick, Rensselaer Co, NY 39
Brewster Caleb	Old Bur Gr, Fairfield, CT 62
Brewster Charles	Cong Cem, Tinmouth, VT 57
Brewster Daniel	South Williamstown, MA 15
Brewster Darius	Tolman Cem, Rockland, ME 55
Brewster David	South Lawn Cem, Williamstown, MA 33
Brewster Ebenezer	Hanover Cem, Hanover, NH 31
Brewster Elias	Fam Cem, Preston, CT 68
Brewster Elijah	Brewster's Neck Cem, Norwich, CT 18
Brewster Elijah	Old Plain Cem, North Stonington, CT 31

Abstract of Graves of Revolutionary Patriots

Brewster Ephraim	Smith Cem, South Rd, Woodstock, Windsor Co, VT 75
Brewster Isaac	Francestown Cem, Francestown, NH 28
Brewster Isaac	Town Cem, Francestown, NH 27
Brewster James	Sharon Cem, Sharon, Litchfield Co, CT 66
Brewster John	Fam Cem, Rt 202, Rochester, NH 71
Brewster John	Joseph Brewster Cem, Setauket, Suffolk Co, NY 79
Brewster Jonah	Cambridge, VT 54
Brewster Jonathan	Cem off Kinney Brook Rd, Worthington, MA 68
Brewster Joseph	Fam Cem, Setauket, Suffolk Co, NY 77
Brewster Joseph	Galway Village Cem, Galway Twp, Saratoga Co, NY 78
Brewster Joseph	Jonesville Cem, Clifton Park Twp, Saratoga Co, NY 77
Brewster Joseph W	Onondaga Hill Cem, Onondaga, Onondaga Co, NY 78
Brewster Joshua	Mayflower Cem, Duxbury, MA 50
Brewster Joshua	Mayflower Cem, Duxbury, Plymouth Co, MA 78
Brewster Martin	Ancient Bur Gr, Kingston, MA 50
Brewster Ozem	[no cem named], OH 46
Brewster Paul	Fam farm, nr Parker Mountain, Strafford, NH 28
Brewster Samuel	Jonesville Cem, Jonesville, Saratoga Co, NY 78
Brewster Samuel	Waldron Cem, Grassy Point, Rockland Co, NY 78
Brewster Samuel	Waldron Cem, Stony Point, NY 58
Brewster Samuel Sr	Goodwill Cem, Montgomery, Orange Co, NY 78
Brewster Seabury	Oak St City Cem, Norwich, CT 18
Brewster Surion	Fam Cem, Griswold, CT 55
Brewster Timothy	Bur gr, First Pres Ch, Woodbridge, NJ 25
Brewster Timothy	Fam Cem, Ellisburgh, NY 15
Brewster Timothy	Woodbridge Pres Ch Cem, Woodbridge, NJ 76
Brewster William	Fern Hill Cem, #7-R, West Parish, Pembroke, MA 40
Brewster William Col	North Cem, Portsmouth, NH 34
Brewster Wrestling	Ancient Bur Gr, Kingston, MA 50
Brewster Zadoc	Tolman Cem, Rockland, ME 55
Bria Peter	Christ Luth Ch Cem, Stroudsburg, PA 56
Briant Benjamin	Beverly, MA 55
Briant Edmund Capt	Old Village Yard, New Ipswich, NH 29
Briant John	North Yard, Alstead, NH 43
Briant John	Old Center Cem, Jaffrey, NH 37
Briant Joseph	Milford Cem, Milford, CT 56
Brice James	West St Cem, Athens, Athens Co, OH 55
Brice James Jr	Athens, OH 15
Brick Daniel	Sherborn No 1, Sherborn, MA 56
Brick Elijah	Sherborn No 1, Sherborn, MA 56
Brick John	Cem, Haddonfield, NJ 44
Brick Thomas	Sherborn No 1, Sherborn, MA 56
Bricker Adam	Williamsburg Cem, Williamsburg, OH 52
Brickett James	Pentucket Cem, Haverhill, MA 28
Brickett James	Town Cem, Hampstead, NH 28
Brickett Nathaniel	Hampstead Cem, Hampstead, NH 56
Brickey Jared	Fam Cem, Crawford Co, MO 23
Brickle Matthias	Old Indian Bur Gr, nr Winton, Hertford Co, NC 49
Brickley Jacob	Manheim Twp, PA 49
Brickley Peter	Manheim Twp, PA 49
Brickman Godfrey	Goat Hill Cem, Minden, Hallsville, Montgomery Co, NY 65
Brickman Peter	Massacred nr mouth of Lechry Creek, Dearborn Co, IN 24
Bridge Benjamin	Knob Prairie Cem, Enon, Clark Co, OH 55
Bridge Benjamin	Knob Prairie Cem, Enon, Clark Co, OH 86
Bridge Benjamin	Long Run Cem, Eastwood, Jefferson Co, KY 83
Bridge Benjamin	West Cem, Holliston, MA 74
Bridge Ebenezer	Jacquith Cem, South Woodstock, VT 65
Bridge Edmund	Dresden Mills, ME 29
Bridges Edmund	Castine Cem, Castine, ME 31
Bridges Isaac	Deerfield Cem, Deerfield, MA 45
Bridges James	North Parish Bur Gr, Andover, MA 26

Bridges James	Second Cem, North Andover, MA 56
Bridges James Jr	North Parish Bur Gr, Andover, MA 26
Bridges John	Fam Cem, Anderson Twp, OH 56
Bridges Martin	Elm Row Cem, Laurens, NY 32
Bridges Mathias	Church Hill Cem, Framingham, MA 56
Bridges Nathan	Old Cem, Bakersfield, MA 50
Bridges Philip	Old Bur Hill, Marblehead, MA 30
Bridges Stephen	Village Cem, York, ME 30
Bridgewater Samuel	Fam Cem, Scottsburg, Scott Co, IN 76
Bridgham John	West Minot Cem, West Minot, ME 45
Bridgham John Capt	Minot, ME 18
Bridgham Joseph Dr	Old Bur Gr, Seekonk Common, now East Providence, RI 55
Bridghan Abel	Center Cem, Hanover, NH 27
Bridgman Isaac	Center Cem, Hanover, NH 27
Bridgman John	Center Cem, Hanover, NH 27
Bridgwater Levi	Prob Mounts Cem, Washington Co, IN 25
Brier Samuel	Boothbay, ME 31
Briesler John	Tomb, Hancock Cem, Quincy, MA 54
Brigdon Michael	Old Cem, Wethersfield, CT 56
Briggs Abiel	Assonet Neck Rd, Berkley, MA 55
Briggs Abiezer	Wellington St Cem, Dighton, MA 55
Briggs Abner	Wellington St Cem, Dighton, MA 55
Briggs Abraham	Berkley Common Cem, Berkley, MA 55
Briggs Arnold	Briggs Lane Cem, Rochester, MA 58
Briggs Asa	Gourdneck Prairie Cem, Kalamazoo Co, MI 30
Briggs Asa	Gourdneck Prairie Cem, Kalamazoo Co, MI 20
Briggs Benjamin	Center Cem, Wareham, MA 55
Briggs Benjamin	South Lawn Cem, Williamstown, MA 33
Briggs Benjamin Gen	Liberty Cem, WV 24
Briggs Benjamin Jr	Center Cem, Wareham, MA 55
Briggs Caleb	Fam Cem, Stanford, NH 21
Briggs Caleb	Meth Epis Ch Cem, Armonk, NY 35
Briggs Danius	Old Kirk Yard, Attleboro, MA 15
Briggs Ebenezer	Center Cem, Wareham, MA 55
Briggs Ebenezer	Old Cem, Lakeville, MA 56
Briggs Ebenezer	Old Cem, The Green, Middleboro, MA 50
Briggs Elihu	Old Parish Cem, North Rochester, MA 59
Briggs Elijah	Assonet Neck Rd, Berkley, MA 55
Briggs Eliphalet Capt	Washington St Cem, Keene, NH 32
Briggs Elisha	Fam bur gr, Pembroke, MA 50
Briggs Elisha	Old Parish Cem, North Rochester, MA 59
Briggs Elisha	Old Parish Cem, North Rochester, MA 59
Briggs Elisha	Old Parish Cem, North Rochester, MA 59
Briggs Elkanah	Chatham Center Cem, Chatham, Columbia Co, NY 79
Briggs Ephraim	Cem, shore of Monponsett, Halifax, MA 50
Briggs Ephraim	Sardinia Cem, Sardinia, NY 31
Briggs Ezra Sr	1st Cong Ch Cem, Hanover Center, MA 54
Briggs Gideon	Fort Bridgman Cem, Vernon, VT 15
Briggs Hallett	Quaker Cem, Marion, MA 59
Briggs Henry	West Constable, NYC, NY 56
Briggs Isaac	Van Cortlandville Cem, Peekskill, NY 41
Briggs Jacob	Mansfield Cem, Mansfield, MA 47
Briggs James	Unitarian Ch Cem, Dighton, MA 55
Briggs James	Unitarian Ch Cem, Dighton, MA 55
Briggs Jedediah	Berkley Common Cem, Berkley, MA 55
Briggs Jesse	Center Cem, Wareham, MA 55
Briggs Job	Glebe St, Taunton, MA 56
Briggs Joel	Oakland Cem, Randolph, MA 54
Briggs John	Berkley Common Cem, Berkley, MA 55
Briggs John	Berkley Common Cem, Berkley, MA 55
Briggs John	Little Neck Cem, Marion, MA 59

Abstract of Graves of Revolutionary Patriots

Briggs Joseph	Dover Center, VT 17	
Briggs Joseph	Hingham Cem, Hingham, MA 60	
Briggs Joseph	Old Cem, Newport, RI 52	
Briggs Joshua	Center Cem, Wareham, MA 16	
Briggs Lemuel	Old Cem, Lakeville, MA 56	
Briggs Nathan	Hammond Cem, Mattapoisett, MA 18	
Briggs Nathaniel	Little Neck Cem, Marion, MA 59	
Briggs Peleg Sr	City Hill Cem, Torrey, Yates Co, NY 70	
Briggs Perez	Wareham Centre, MA 34	
Briggs Philip	1st Parish Cem, Rochester, MA 58	
Briggs Phillip Capt	Cavanaugh Cem, Clarendon, VT 24	
Briggs Phillip Capt	Cavanaugh Cem, Clarendon, VT 25	
Briggs Richard	Plymouth St Cem, Halifax, MA 58	
Briggs Samuel	Carratunk, ME 17	
Briggs Samuel	Old Burial Cem, Plympton, MA 57	
Briggs Samuel	Pleasant Ridge, ME 15	
Briggs Samuel	Wellington St Cem, Dighton, MA 55	
Briggs Seth	Fam Cem, Pembroke, MA 56	
Briggs Seth	Fam Cem, Pembroke, MA 53	
Briggs Seth	First Parish Cem, Rochester, MA 57	
Briggs Silas	1st Parish Cem, Rochester, MA 58	
Briggs Silas	Evergreen Cem, Marion, MA 59	
Briggs Silas Dea	Elmwood Cem, Barre, VT 48	
Briggs Thomas	Assonet Neck Rd, Berkley, MA 55	
Briggs Thomas	Fam Cem, Stanford, NH 21	
Briggs Thomas 3rd	Assonet Neck Rd, Berkley, MA 55	
Briggs Timothy	Pine St Cong Ch Cem, Norton, MA 55	
Briggs W Capt	Cavanaugh Cem, Clarendon, VT 25	
Briggs W Capt	Cavanaugh Cem, Clarendon, VT 24	
Briggs William	Quidnessett, North Kingston, RI 52	
Briggs Zephaniah	Gaylordsville Cem, Gaylordsville, CT 55	
Brigham Aaron	Fam Cem, Marlborough, MA 56	
Brigham Abijah	Old Sudbury Center, Sudbury, MA 55	
Brigham Abner	Cushing Cem, Woodstock, VT 65	
Brigham Asa Maj	Town Cem, Fitzwilliam, NH 32	
Brigham Benajah	Old Granary Bur Gr, Boston, MA 56	
Brigham Daniel	Old Common Bur Gr, Marlboro, MA 46	
Brigham Edmund Capt	Old Cem, Westboro, MA 45	
Brigham Elijah	Old Cem, Southboro, MA 50	
Brigham Gershom	Waite Cem, Fayston, Washington Co, VT 30	
Brigham Ithaniel Capt	Old Common Bur Gr, Marlboro, MA 45	
Brigham Joel	Madison Cem, Madison, NY 58	
Brigham Joel	Old Pine Grove Cem, Leominster, MA 47	
Brigham John	Fredonia Cem, Pomfret, Chautauqua Co, NY 15	
Brigham John C	Sumner Hill Cem, Springfield, VT 23	
Brigham Jonas	Old Cem, Bakersfield, MA 50	
Brigham Jonas	Town Cem, Dublin, NH 34	
Brigham Jonathan	Mayville Cem, Chautauqua Co, NY 62	
Brigham Joseph	Old Common, Marlborough, MA 56	
Brigham Josiah	Old Vars Cem, Hartwick, Otsego Co, NY 75	
Brigham Levi	Old Cem, Northborough, MA 56	
Brigham Paul	Norwich Cem, Norwich, VT 72	
Brigham Paul	Old Common, Marlborough, MA 56	
Brigham Roger	Old Center Cem, Jaffrey, NH 37	
Brigham Samuel	Augusta Cem, Augusta, Oneida Co, NY 58	
Brigham Stephen	North Yard, Alstead, NH 43	
Brigham Timothy	Old Cem, Northborough, MA 56	
Brigham Timothy Col	Old Cem, Southboro, MA 50	
Brigham Uriah	Fam Cem, Marlborough, MA 56	
Brigham William Capt	Fam Cem, Marlboro, MA 45	
Brigham Winslow	New Cem, Northborough, MA 56	

Brigham Winslow	Old Common Bur Gr, Marlboro, MA 45
Bright John	[no cem named], VA 15
Bright Joseph	Acton, MA 55
Bright Michael	Needham, MA 50
Bright Michael Jr	Evans Cem, Reading, PA 53
Brillhart Christian	Cem nr Codorus by school, Coldspring, York Co, PA 58
Brimblecom Samuel	Burial Hill, Pond St, Marblehead, MA 56
Brimfield Humphrey	Lawrence Co, OH 45
Brimhall Sylvanus	Gilman Cem, Sanbornton, NH 35
Brinard Moses	Brookmere Cem, Brooklyn Heights, Cuyahoga Co, OH 55
Brinckerhoff Abraham I	Dutch Ref Cem, Hopewell Junction, NY 85
Brindley James	Pres Cem, Red Clay Creek, New Castle Co, DE 46
Briney Mark	Brush Creek Cem, North Huntington, Westmoreland Co, PA 76
Bringhurst Samuel	Germantown, PA 52
Bringhurst Samuel	Hood's Cem, Germantown, PA 20
Bringhurst Samuel	[no cem named], PA 19
Brink Benjamin	Sheshequin Cem, Sheshequin Twp, Bradford Co, PA 53
Brink John C	Plattekill Cem, NY 15
Brink John Jr	Main St Cem, Saugerties, NY 15
Brink Moses	Candor, NY 51
Brink Moses	Maple Grove Cem, Hoosick Falls, NY 34
Brink Peter	Plattekill Cem, NY 15
Brink Petrus	Old Hurley Bur Gr, Ulster Co, NY 36
Brink Thomas	Le Raysville Cem,, PA 53
Brink Thomas	LeRaysville Cem, Pike Twp, PA 72
Brink William	Riverside Cem, Union, Broome Co, NY 38
Brinker Andrew	St Jacobs Ch Cem, Salem Twp, OH 56
Brinkerhoff Garret	Hudson St Cem, Hackensack, NJ 47
Brinkerhoff George G	Selover Cem, Niles, Cayuga Co, NY 69
Brinkerhoff George R	Parsell Cem, Owasco, NY 56
Brinkerhoff Henry J	Hackensack Green Cem, Hackensack, NJ 47
Brinkerhoff Jacob	Hackensack Green Cem, Hackensack, NJ 47
Brinkerhoff Jacob	Parsell Cem, Owasco, NY 56
Brinkerhoff Jacob	Parsell Cem, Owasco, NY 41
Brinkerhoff Jacobus	Hudson St Cem, Hackensack, NJ 47
Brinkerhoff James	Parsell Cem, Owasco, NY 56
Brinkerhoff Roelef	Parsell Cem, Owasco, NY 41
Brinsmade Daniel N	Judea Cem, Washington, CT 55
Brintnall Thomas	Maplewood Cem, Clarendon, Orleans Co, NY 75
Brintnell Job	Williams St Cem, Mansfield, MA 55
Brinton Moses	Sadsbury, PA 56
Brion Daniel	Zions Red Ch, Orwigsburg, PA 49
Brisban John	Old Paxtan Cem, Harrisburg, PA 59
Brisbane James	Fam Cem, Schuylerville, Saratoga Co, NY 77
Brisbane James I	Fam Cem, Schuylerville, Saratoga Co, NY 77
Brisbane William	Schuylerville Cem, Schuylerville, Saratoga Co, NY 78
Brisbin James	State Rd & Bemis Heights Cem, NY 41
Briscoe Henry	Fam Cem, Westfield, Clark Co, IL 15
Briscoe William	Wallace Cem, Madison Co, KY 27
Bristol Benjamin Jr	Maple Lawn Cem, Gainesville, Wyoming Co, NY 64
Bristol Bezaleel	Chestnut Hill Cem, North Killingsworth, CT 55
Bristol Bezaleel	Pine Orchard Cem, Killingworth, Middlesex Co, CT 24
Bristol Daniel	[no cem named], OH 26
Bristol Gideon	Cong Cem, Cheshire, New Haven Co, CT 24
Bristol Moses	Kirkland Avenue Cem, Clinton, Oneida Co, NY 79
Bristol Nathan	Milford Cem, Milford, CT 56
Bristol Thomas	Cong Cem, Cheshire, New Haven Co, CT 24
Brittain James	Nr Mills Academy, Henderson Co, NC 49
Brittain Samuel	Sand Bay Cem, Cape Vincent, NY 41
Brittain Zebeoth	Riverview Cem, Easton, PA 57
Brittan Nathaniel	First Pres Ch Cem, Cranbury, NJ 76

Brittin Elihu	[no cem named], NJ 24
Brittin William	[no cem named], NJ 24
Britton Claudius	Pinckney Cem, Pinckney, MI 51
Britton James	Riverside Cem, Union, Broome Co, NY 78
Britton John	Easton Cem, Easton, MA 47
Britton John	Horton Cem, Atlas, MI 17
Britton John C	Ionia Cem, VanBuren, Onondaga Co, NY 75
Britton Joseph	Grubbs Ch, Snyder Co, PA 15
Britton William	Britton's Cove, nr Dula Springs, NC 49
Britton William	Fam Cem, Britton's Cove, Buncombe Co, NC 74
Britton William	Horton Bur Gr, Atlas Twp, Genesee Co, NY 21
Britton William	Horton Cem, nr Atlas, Genesee Co, MI 40
Britton William	Meth Epis Cem, Pleasant Mills, NJ 25
Britton William	Pleasant Hill Cem, Center Twp, Guernsey Co, OH 55
Brizendine William Sr	Priv Cem, nr Glade Hill, Franklin Co, VA 71
Broad Hezekiah	South Natick, Natick, MA 56
Broad Thomas	Dell Park, Pond St, Natick, MA 56
Broad Timothy	Needham, MA 50
Broadback Henry	Broadback Ch Cem, Chester, PA 52
Broadbrooks Ebenezer	Center Cem, Harwich, MA 49
Broaddus John Col	Crew farm, Howard Co, MO 16
Broaddus William	Cem, Harpers Ferry, WV 24
Broaddus William Lt	Harpers Ferry Cem, Harpers, WV 26
Broaddus William Lt	Harpers Ferry, WV 27
Broadhead Daniel Gen	Orig Kittaning Ch, now New Cem, Armstrong Co, PA 15
Broadhurst Joseph	First Pres Ch Cem, Trenton, NJ 28
Broadus William Maj	Old Harper Cem, Harpers Ferry, WV 30
Broadwater Charles B	Nr Vienna, VA 17
Broadwater Charles Gray	Nr Vienna, VA 17
Broadwater Charles Guy	Fam Cem, Falls Church, VA 56
Broadwater Charles L	Fairfax Co, VA 54
Broadwater Charles L	Nr Vienna, VA 17
Broadwater Lewis Lt	Nr Vienna, VA 48
Brobst Michael	Jerusalem Luth Ch Cem, Albany Twp, Berks Co, PA 58
Brock George	Reyman farm, Salem, Washington Co, IN 76
Brock Nathaniel	Fam Cem, Trenton, GA 51
Brock Uriah	Old City Cem, Cape Girardeau, MO 23
Brockelbank Job	Rowley Cem, Essex, MA 48
Brockett Enos	Old Cem, North Haven, CT 56
Brockett Hezekiah	Riverview Cem, Oxford, NY 16
Brockett Hezekiah	Wallingford, CT 48
Brockett Isaiah	Montowese Cem, North Haven, CT 15
Brockett Jacob	North Haven, CT 56
Brockett Joel	Montowese Cem, North Haven, CT 16
Brockett Joel	North Haven, CT 56
Brockett John	Montowese Cem, North Haven, CT 15
Brocklebank Joseph	Upper Cem, Bridgeton, ME 45
Brocklebank Samuel	Old West Part Cem, New London, NH 41
Brockman John	Clear Springs Cem, Simpsonville, SC 63
Brockway Consider	Hydes, Elk Co, PA 15
Brockway Isaiah	Old Cem, Southampton, MA 16
Brockway Martin	Bethel Cem, Cardington Twp, OH 56
Brod Paul	Lower Saucon Twp, Northampton Co, PA 50
Broderick William	Crabapple Cem, Wheeling Twp, nr Athens, Belmont Co, OH 56
Brodhead Garret	Dansbury Cem, Lower Main St, Stroudsburg, Monroe Co, PA 68
Brodhead Garret	Delaware Cem, Dingman's Ferry, Delaware Twp, Pike Co, PA 68
Brodrick William	Prob Old Friendship Cem, W of New Madison, Darke Co, OH 55
Brohawn John	Christ P E Ch Cem, Cambridge, MD 51
Brokaw Abraham	Gospel Lot Cem, Ovid, Seneca Co, NY 65
Brokaw Bergun	Old Pres Cem, Bound Brook, NJ 47
Brokaw George	Crabapple Cem, Wheeling Twp, nr Athens, Belmont Co, OH 56

Brokaw Isaac	Bound Brook, NJ	47
Brokaw Isaac	Fam Cem, Zarepath, NJ	47
Brokaw John	Pine Bank, Myer farm, South Branch, NJ	47
Brokaw John L	Fam Cem, Zarepath, NJ	48
Brokow Caleb	West Genoa Cem, Genoa, Cayuga Co, NY	59
Brondson Benjamin	Old Cem, Milton, MA	56
Bronner Christian	Otsquago Cem, nr Van Hornesville, NY	30
Bronner Jacob	Otsquago Cem, nr Van Hornesville, NY	30
Bronsdon John B	Old Milton Cem, Milton, MA	46
Bronson Abel	Watertown, CT	15
Bronson Benjamin	Center Cem, New Milford, Litchfield Co, CT	68
Bronson Elijah	Tully Cem, Tully, Onondaga Co, NY	78
Bronson Isaac	Babcock Hill Cem, Winham Twp, Bradford Co, PA	53
Bronson Isaac	Wolcott Center Cem, Wolcott, CT	28
Bronson James	Clinton Cem, Oneida Co, NY	56
Bronson Joel	Orwell Cem, Orwell Twp, Bradford Co, PA	72
Bronson Joel	Orwell Cem, Bradford Co, PA	53
Bronson John	Center Cem, Wolcott, CT	56
Bronson John	Center Cem, Wolcott, CT	57
Bronson Josiah	Walnut Grove Cem, Onondaga Hill, NY	32
Bronson Luke	Rock Ledge, Berlin, CT	56
Bronson Michael	Fam Cem, Library Park, Waterbury, CT	55
Bronson Ozais	Winchester Center Cem, Winchester, CT	59
Bronson Phineas	Princeville Cem, Princeville, IL	72
Bronson Roswell	Kirkland Ave Cem, Clinton, Oneida Co, NY	79
Brook Cornelius	Oak Lawn Cem, Orlean, Cattaraugus Co, NY	71
Brook William	St David's Cem, Radnor, PA	52
Brooke Isaac	On his farm, Prince Georges Co, MD	52
Brooke John	St James Luth & Ref Ch Cem, Montgomery Co, PA	59
Brooke John Capt	Limerick Square, PA	17
Brooke Matthew	Norristown, PA	16
Brooke Matthew	St David's Cem, Radnor, VA	17
Brooke Richard	Fam plot, Kirk farm, nr Olney, MD	15
Brooke William	Brooks fam Cem, Lexington, GA	52
Brookes David	Cheshire, CT	17
Brookes Enos	Cheshire, CT	17
Brookes John	St Paul's Evan Luth Cem, Montgomery Co, PA	59
Brookfield Brown	Meth Cem, New Providence, NJ	50
Brookfield Jacob	Springfield, Union Co, NJ	33
Brookhouse Robert	Broad St, Salem, MA	56
Brookins Col	Melrose Hwy, Perry farm, nr Troy, NY	16
Brookins Col	Priv plot, W of hwy betw Speigletown & Melrose, NY	38
Brookins Reuben	North Bush Cem, Caroga, Fulton Co, NY	39
Brookins Silas	Shoreham, VT	15
Brooks Abijah	Strode Station, Clark, KY	56
Brooks Abijah	Union Cem, Stratford, CT	31
Brooks Ahira	Oak Hill Cem, Sturgis, MI	59
Brooks Ahira	Sturgis, MI	15
Brooks Almarine Maj	Broad St Cem, Bridgeton, NJ	26
Brooks Amasa	Hillside Cem, Cheshire, CT	55
Brooks Asa	Hill Cem, Concord, MA	55
Brooks Benjamin	Cem on the Plain, Brookline, NH	36
Brooks Benjamin	Cem, shore of Connecticut River, Dalton, NH	37
Brooks Benjamin	Old Bur Gr, Townsend, MA	56
Brooks Benjamin	Pine St Cem, Cameron Co, PA	51
Brooks Charles	Meeting House Hill Cem, Princeton, MA	49
Brooks Daniel	Acton, MA	55
Brooks Daniel	Evergreen Cem, Spencer, NY	56
Brooks David	Acton, MA	55
Brooks David	Braceville, OH	24
Brooks David	Cong Cem, Cheshire, New Haven Co, CT	24

Brooks David	Lower Cem, Burton, Geauga Co, OH 55
Brooks Dudley	Springfield, TN 29
Brooks Elijah	Center Cem, Grafton, MA 49
Brooks Enoch	Meeting House Cem, Princeton, MA 49
Brooks Ephraim Jr	Lincoln Cem, Lincoln, MA 46
Brooks Ephraim Sr	Lincoln Cem, Lincoln, MA 46
Brooks Ethurel	Cong Cem, Cheshire, New Haven Co, CT 24
Brooks Francis Soucee	Fowler Cem, Unity, ME 45
Brooks Hananiah	Riverview Cem, Martins Ferry, Belmont Co, OH 56
Brooks Isaac	Columbiana Co, OH 56
Brooks Isaac	Evergreen Cem, South St, Lairdsville, NY 36
Brooks James	Acton, MA 55
Brooks James	Huron Co, OH 15
Brooks James	La Porte Cem, La Porte, Lorain Co, OH 55
Brooks James	Pioneer Cem, Wellington, OH 22
Brooks James	Schoonover Bur Gr, nr Smithboro, Tioga Co, NY 57
Brooks Jerre	Cong Cem, Cheshire, New Haven Co, CT 24
Brooks Jesse	Hillside Cem, Cheshire, CT 55
Brooks Job	Hill Cem, Concord, MA 55
Brooks Job F	North Cem, Westmoreland, NH 25
Brooks Joel	Center Cem, Grafton, MA 49
Brooks John	Cem, Medford, MA 49
Brooks John	Cong Ch Cem, Worcester, Otsego Co, NY 74
Brooks John	Field nr Wakeman, OH 15
Brooks John	Nr Sprague Corner, Florence, Erie Co, OH 26
Brooks John D	Village Cem, Langdon, NH 35
Brooks John Dr	Florence, PA 55
Brooks John Hanna Jr	Nr Clinton, Jones Co, GA 34
Brooks John Jr	Old Cem, Sterling, MA 63
Brooks John Lt	Old Yard, Pine Ridge, Hancock, NH 29
Brooks John Maj	Cable Cem, Florence, Erie Co, OH 43
Brooks John Sr	Nr Spragues Corners, Florence, OH 15
Brooks Jonas	Massacred nr mouth of Lechry Creek, Dearborn Co, IN 24
Brooks Joseph	1st Cong Ch Cem, Hanover Center, MA 54
Brooks Joseph	Dekalb, St Lawrence Co, NY 56
Brooks Joseph	Knox County Cem, Knox Co, TN 60
Brooks Josiah	Fairview Cem, Westford, MA 56
Brooks Lemuel	Steuben Cem, Steuben, OH 56
Brooks Levi	Center Bur Gr, Lincoln, MA 55
Brooks Levi	Norwich, NY 16
Brooks Micajah	Hubbard Cem, Rockmart, Polk Co, GA 70
Brooks Moses	Fam farm, nr Boyd's Bridge, Knoxville, TN 29
Brooks Moses	McDonald farm, TN 23
Brooks Nathaniel	Westford Yard, Ashford, CT 31
Brooks Nathaniel	Westford Yard, Ashford, CT 29
Brooks Noah	Center Bur Gr, Lincoln, MA 55
Brooks Noah	Center Cem, Grafton, MA 49
Brooks Oliver	Mahoning Ave, Warren, OH 24
Brooks Reuben	Cherry Hill Cem, Bethel, Windsor Co, VT 72
Brooks Samuel	Greenwood Cem, Bristol, Addison Co, VT 79
Brooks Samuel Lewis	Oakwood Cem, Baird & Whalen Rd, Penfield, Monroe Co, NY 77
Brooks Seth	Acton, MA 55
Brooks Seth	Old Cem, Sterling, MA 63
Brooks Silas	Meredith, Delaware Co, NY 71
Brooks Simeon	Cedar Lake Cem, Chester, Middlesex Co, CT 78
Brooks Simeon	Fairview Cem, Bethel, Windsor Co, VT 72
Brooks Simon	Center Cem, Alstead, NH 37
Brooks Simon	Center Cem, Alstead, NH 43
Brooks Simon	Center Cem, Alstead, NH 37
Brooks Theophilis	Elm St Cem, VT 20
Brooks Thomas	Oakwood Cem, Baird & Whalen Rd, Penfield, Monroe Co, NY 77

Brooks Thomas Maj — Stewarts Corners Cem, Plymouth, NY 16
Brooks Timothy — Old Center Bur Gr, Lincoln, MA 55
Brooks William — Cong Cem, Stratford, CT 31
Brooks William — Farm Cem, Thompson Valley, Tazewell, Tazewell Co, VA 77
Brooks William — Sandy Run Bapt Ch Cem, Mooresboro, Cleveland Co, NC 76
Brooks William Col — Fam Cem, Elbert Co, GA 35
Brooks William Maj — Old Yard, Pine Ridge, Hancock, NH 29
Brooks Wilson — Fam Cem, Lexington, GA 52
Brooks Zacharia Smith — [no cem named], SC 15
Brookshire Mannering — Fam Cem, home place, Randolph Co, NC 60
Brothers Matthias — Stark Co, OH 44
Brotherton Samuel — Pres Ch Cem, Rocky Springs, PA 20
Brotherton Samuel — Rocky Springs Pres Ch Cem, 6 mi fr Chambersburg, PA 19
Brothwell Joseph — Old Stratford, Bridgeport, CT 56
Brothwell Joseph Lt — Stratfield Old Bur Gr, Bridgeport, CT 15
Brothwell Thomas — Stratfield Old Bur Gr, Bridgeport, CT 15
Brotzman Nicholas — Farm, Bradford Co, PA 53
Brough Daniel — W side of Rt 11, 9 mi S of Buchanan, Botetourt Co, VA 73
Broughton Michael — City Cem, Pawlet, VT 58
Broughton Nicholson — Harris St Cem, Marblehead, MA 45
Broughton Noah — Cotton Cem, Portsmouth, NH 34
Brouillette Mitchell — Old Cathedral Cem, Vincennes, Knox Co, IN 72
Brouse M — Wadsworth, Medina Co, OH 22
Brouse M — Woodlawn Cem, Summit Co, OH 53
Brouse Michael — Woodlawn Cem, Wadsworth, Medina Co, OH 55
Broussard Armand — St Martins of Tours Cath Ch Cem, St Martinville, LA 73
Broussard Claude — St Martin of Tours Cath Ch Cem, St Martinville, LA 74
Broussard Francois — St Martin of Tours Cath Ch Cem, St Martinville, LA 74
Broussard Jean Baptiste — Cathedral of St John the Evangelist Cem, Lafayette, LA 73
Broussard Joseph — St Martin of Tours Cath Ch Cem, St Martinville, LA 76
Broussard Pierre — St Martin of Tours Cath Ch Cem, St Martinville, LA 74
Broussard Silvain — St Martin of Tours Cath Ch Cem, St Martinville, LA 74
Browe Abraham — First Dutch Ref Ch Cem, Hackensack, NJ 30
Brower Abraham I — Hackensack Green Cem, Hackensack, NJ 47
Brower David — Old Tappan Cem, Tappan, NJ 28
Brower Jacob — Fishkill, NY 54
Brower John — Old Tappan, NY 29
Brown Aaron — Austerlitz Cem, Columbia Co, NY 42
Brown Aaron — Fiske farm, Ashland, MA 56
Brown Aaron Corp — First Cem, Candia, NH 29
Brown Abel — Churchyard, Hollis, NH 39
Brown Abel — Old Cem, South Hampton, NH 30
Brown Abial — North Burial Ground, Providence, RI 55
Brown Abishai Maj — Old Concord Cem, Concord, MA 46
Brown Abner — County Rd, Ipswich, MA 56
Brown Abraham — County Cem, Northfield, NH 29
Brown Abraham — East Alstead, (Old) Cem, Alstead, NH 36
Brown Abraham — Somers Pres Ch Cem, Somers, NY 35
Brown Abraham Lt — North Yard, Alstead, NH 43
Brown Adam — Fayette Co, PA 56
Brown Adam — Jake's Run, nr Pirce, WV 24
Brown Allen — Church Hill Cem, Mercersburg, PA 21
Brown Amos — Fam Cem, Notley River section, Clay Co, NC 73
Brown Amos — Rixtown Cem, Groswold, CT 52
Brown Amos — Stonington, CT 32
Brown Andrew — Church Hill Cem, Framingham, MA 56
Brown Andrew — North Woodstock, CT 29
Brown Andrew — Nr Elberton, GA 35
Brown Andrew — Old Cem, Knox, NY 32
Brown Andrew — Park Ave Cem, Holden, MA 15
Brown Asa Capt — Old Beverly Cem, Beverly, MA 47

Abstract of Graves of Revolutionary Patriots

Brown Asher	Connecticut Farms Pres Cem, Union, NJ 49
Brown Austin	Lima Cem, Lima, Livingston Co, NY 79
Brown Barnabas	St Andrews Cem, New Berlin, NY 15
Brown Bartholomew	Old Brimfield (Palmer) Cem, Brimfield, MA 74
Brown Ben	North Woodstock Cem, Woodstock, CT 55
Brown Benjamin	Fam Cem, 11 mi fr Fayetteville, Fayette Co, GA 34
Brown Benjamin	Old Bur Gr, East Hartford, now Manchester, CT 51
Brown Benjamin	Old Cem, Kensington, NH 28
Brown Benjamin	Old Cem, Kensington, NH 28
Brown Benjamin	Old Cem, Hamilton, MA 56
Brown Benjamin	Old Yard, Kensington, NH 47
Brown Benjamin	Physics Springs, Buckingham, VA 56
Brown Benjamin	Ruckersville Dist, Elbert Co, GA 34
Brown Benjamin	Unionville Cem, Unionville, Westchester Co, NY 35
Brown Benjamin	West State St Cem, Athens, Athens Co, OH 55
Brown Benjamin A	Bur gr, First Pres Ch, Woodbridge, NJ 25
Brown Benjamin A	Pres Ch Cem, Woodbridge, Middlesex Co, NJ 75
Brown Benjamin Dr	Sproul Cem, Waldoboro, ME 30
Brown Benjamin Gen	Old Cem, Wakefield, MA 27
Brown Benjamin Sr	Old Cem, Winchenden, Worcester Co, MA 57
Brown Bernis	Fam Cem, Browns Cove, Albemarle Co, VA 55
Brown Caleb	Town Cem, Hill Center, Hill, NH 29
Brown Chad	Fam Cem, Winsor farm, off Putnam Ave, Harmony, RI 55
Brown Chaddus	Harmony Cem, Union, RI 56
Brown Charles	East Greenwich Cem, Shippeetown Rd, East Greenwich, RI 75
Brown Charles	White Schoolhouse Cem, Cato, Cayuga, NY 65
Brown Charles J	Boiling Springs, nr Barnwell, SC 51
Brown Christian	Old Cem, Hecktown, Northampton Co, PA 21
Brown Christopher	North Stonington, CT 31
Brown Christopher	Oak Grove Cem, Ashaway, RI 48
Brown Christopher	Pres Ch Cem, Somers, NY 35
Brown Christopher	Westerly, RI 15
Brown Cyrus	Maryland Cem, Maryland, Otsego Co, NY 74
Brown Daniel	Bapt Cem, Stephentown, NY 56
Brown Daniel	Benton Rural Cem, Benton, Yates Co, NY 70
Brown Daniel	Center Cem, Goshen, MA 51
Brown Daniel	Fairfield Cem, Ogden, Monroe Co, NY 79
Brown Daniel	Grover Cem, Bradford Co, PA 53
Brown Daniel	Hillside Cem, Madison, NJ 30
Brown Daniel	Ogden, NY 56
Brown Daniel	Old Bur Gr, Arlington, MA 56
Brown Daniel	Old Cem, Hamilton, MA 56
Brown Daniel	Old bur gr, Newark, NJ 26
Brown Daniel	St Peter's Epis Ch Cem, Spotswood, NJ 56
Brown Daniel	Union Brick Cem, Warren Co, NJ 38
Brown Daniel	West Mountain Rd Cem, Cheshire, MA 55
Brown Daniel Gen	Glenwood Cem, Homer, Cortland Co, NY 36
Brown David	Cem on Old Warren Rd, Swansea, MA 54
Brown David	Cem, Upper Cincinnatus, Cincinnatus, Cortland Co, NY 36
Brown David	Duck Creek Cem, Wellfleet, MA 49
Brown David	Eastham Cem, # 2, Rt 6, Truro, MA 55
Brown David	Hill Cem, Concord, MA 55
Brown David	Old Cem, Downey Street, Rising Sun, Ohio Co, IN 78
Brown David	Old Yard, Kensington, NH 47
Brown David	Spear Cem, Bradford Co, PA 53
Brown Ebenezer	Hubbardston Cem, Hubbardston, MA 45
Brown Ebenezer	Lansing, NY 15
Brown Ebenezer	Lansing Cem, Lansing, NY 32
Brown Edward	Broad St, Salem, MA 56
Brown Eliada	Greenwood Cem, Jefferson Co, WI 56
Brown Elias	Center Cem, Alstead, NH 43

Brown Elias	Old Bloomfield Cem, Bloomfield, CT	55
Brown Elias Jr	Center Cem, Alstead, NH	43
Brown Elida	[no cem named], WI	29
Brown Elihu	Uxbridge Cem, Uxbridge, MA	47
Brown Elijah	Mount View Cem, West Pawlet, VT	48
Brown Elijah	Stockbridge Cem, Stockbridge, MA	47
Brown Elijah	Town Farm Cem, Mendon Rd, Cumberland, RI	47
Brown Elijah	West Dummerston, VT	19
Brown Elijah	West Pawlet Cem, VT	15
Brown Eliphalet	Churchyard, Hollis, NH	39
Brown Elisha	Cem on Old Warren Rd, Swansea, MA	54
Brown Elisha	Priv Cem, Guilford, VT	47
Brown Elisha	Priv Cem, fam lot, Guilford, VT	45
Brown Elisha	Racine, WI	29
Brown Elisha	Springfield, VT	15
Brown Elisha	Tomb, Old South Cem, Ipswich, MA	48
Brown Elisha Esq	Line Cem, Seabrook, NH	29
Brown Enoch	Sebec, ME	39
Brown Ezekial	Sunbury, Delaware Co, OH	18
Brown Ezekiel	Nr Shiloh, Harris Co, GA	56
Brown Ezekiel	St John's Ch Cem, Greenfield, Saratoga Co, NY	78
Brown Ezeliel Dr	Ames Cem, Benton, ME	42
Brown Ezra	Holliston Center Cem, Holliston, MA	56
Brown Ezra	Old Cem, Monument Square, Saugus, MA	45
Brown Francis	Cornwall Cem, Cornwall, CT	15
Brown Francis	Old Cem, Hamilton, MA	56
Brown Francis	Old Lexington Cem, Lexington, MA	55
Brown Francis	Old Town Bur Gr, Newburgh, Orange Co, NY	69
Brown Frederick	Green Lawn Cem, South Charleston, Clark Co, OH	55
Brown George	Brownville, Jefferson Co, NY	41
Brown George	Fisher farm, Richland Twp, Milroy, Rush Co, IN	64
Brown George	Milroy Cem, Milroy, Rush Co, IN	78
Brown George	Rouchy Cem, nr Elmira, NY	32
Brown George	Woodbridge Pres Ch Cem, Woodbridge, Middlesex Co, NJ	78
Brown Gershom	Middle Island Pres Ch Cem, Brookhaven, Suffolk Co, NY	79
Brown Greenwood	Center Cem, Goshen, MA	51
Brown Greer	Abbott Cem, OH	15
Brown Heman	Bethany, NY	15
Brown Heman Sr	Bethany Center Cem, Bethany, Genesee Co, NY	65
Brown Henry	Boston Twp, OH	45
Brown Henry	Boston Twp, Summit Co, OH	15
Brown Henry	Dutch Ref Ch Cem, Belleville, NJ	27
Brown Henry	Fam Cem, Otter River, SE Bedford Co, VA	47
Brown Henry	New Lyme, Ashtabula Co, OH	18
Brown Henry	Phipps St Cem, Boston, MA	47
Brown Henry	Phipps St Cem, Brighton, MA	46
Brown Hope	Old Cem, Sudbury, MA	56
Brown Hopestill	Old Cem, Sudbury, MA	56
Brown Ichabod Capt	Cedar Swamp Bur Gr, S of Milltown, North Stonington, CT	16
Brown Isaac	Dutch Ref Ch Cem, Belleville, NJ	27
Brown Isaac	Fairmont, Camillus, NY	56
Brown Isaac	Glenwood Cem, Homer, Cortland Co, NY	36
Brown Isaac Capt	Pleasant View Cem, Mason, NH	39
Brown Isaiah	Benton, ME	30
Brown Jacob	Bur gr nr Amesbury Depot, Amesbury, MA	46
Brown Jacob	East Readfield, ME	29
Brown Jacob	Flatrock Cem, Henry Co, IN	45
Brown Jacob	Hill Cem, Concord, MA	55
Brown Jacob Jr	Cem, North Yarmouth, ME	51
Brown Jacob Jr	Hill Cem, Concord, MA	55
Brown Jacob Jr	Old Cem, Hamilton, MA	56

Abstract of Graves of Revolutionary Patriots

Brown James	Ames Cem, Scott, Cortland Co, NY	36
Brown James	Fam bur gr, Gilman farm, Porter, ME	45
Brown James	Greeley's Corners Cem, Palermo, ME	53
Brown James	New London Cem, New London, CT	55
Brown James	Pleasant Ridge Cem, Borden, Clark Co, IN	72
Brown James	Pleasant Ridge Cem, 3 mi S of Borden, IN	25
Brown James	Village Cem, Stratford, NH	36
Brown James	Woodbridge Pres Ch Cem, Woodbridge, Middlesex Co, NJ	78
Brown James Daniel	Mountain View (Lester) Cem, Lester, Broome Co, NY	78
Brown James II	Oak Hill Cem, Maine, Broome Co, NY	71
Brown James Jr	Old Cem, Hamilton, MA	56
Brown James Sr	Old Cem, Kittanning, PA	56
Brown James Sr	Ramsaysburg, Warren Co, NJ	35
Brown Jeremiah	East Cem, North Hampton, NH	51
Brown Jeremiah	First Pres Ch Cem, Cranbury, NJ	76
Brown Jeremiah	Old Cem, Wakefield, MA	55
Brown Jesse	Cedar Springs Cem, Blakely, Early Co, GA	59
Brown Job	Old bur gr, Orange, NJ	26
Brown Joel Dr	Center Cem, Hanover, NH	27
Brown John	Antrim, NH	15
Brown John	Bapt Cem, York St, Salem, NJ	26
Brown John	Bur gr, First Pres Ch, Woodbridge, NJ	25
Brown John	Canton Center Cem, Canton, CT	55
Brown John	Cem, Beverly, MA	49
Brown John	Cem, Schantz farm, 3 mi N of Lowell, Washington Co, OH	55
Brown John	Center Cem, Douglas, MA	53
Brown John	Central Cem, Cohasset, MA	60
Brown John	Dansbury Cem, lower Main St, Stroudsburg, Monroe Co, PA	68
Brown John	Dover, MA	55
Brown John	Dreisbach's Cem, Union Co, PA	15
Brown John	Dutch Ref Ch Cem, Belleville, NJ	27
Brown John	East Belfast Cem, East Belfast, ME	31
Brown John	East Cem, Granby, MA	58
Brown John	Fam Cem, Rye, NY	35
Brown John	Fam Cem, Mifflinville, PA	15
Brown John	Fam Cem, Swansea, Touisset, MA	54
Brown John	Fam Cem, nr Wilkesboro, Wilkes Co, NC	49
Brown John	First Bapt Cem, York St, Salem, NJ	27
Brown John	Hainesburg Cem, Warren Co, NJ	38
Brown John	Killed in Wyoming Massacre, Wyoming, PA	52
Brown John	Madison Center, NY	15
Brown John	Mifflinville, McKean Co, PA	57
Brown John	Monegan, Locke, NY	56
Brown John	Mount Zion Cem, East Bridgewater, MA	45
Brown John	Nauset, Mount Desert, ME	56
Brown John	Noroton River Cem, Bloomfield, CT	55
Brown John	Oktibbeha, MS	56
Brown John	Old Burial Hill, Pond St, Marblehead, MA	56
Brown John	Old Cem, Wakefield, MA	27
Brown John	Old Cem, Hamilton, MA	56
Brown John	Old McLean Cem, Ithaca, NY	31
Brown John	Old Rumford Cem, Rehoboth, MA	55
Brown John	Old Sudbury Cem, Sudbury, MA	47
Brown John	Palermo, ME	29
Brown John	Potter Co, PA	52
Brown John	Pres Ch Cem, Woodbridge, Middlesex Co, NJ	75
Brown John	Rehoboth Cem, Rehoboth, MA	62
Brown John	Sugar Grove, Boone Co, KY	30
Brown John	West Alexander, PA	38
Brown John	Windsor, OH	15
Brown John	Windsor, Ashtabula Co, OH	18

Brown John 3rd	Canton Center Cem, Canton Center, NY 55
Brown John 4th	Opposite First Cong Ch, Hamilton, MA 56
Brown John 5th	Opposite First Cong Ch, Hamilton, MA 56
Brown John Adam	Shirk's Cem, Brownstown, PA 56
Brown John Adams	Hecktown Cem, Hecktown, Northampton Co, PA 21
Brown John Capt	Douglass Center Cem, Douglass, MA 45
Brown John David	Zoar Cem, Mt Zion, Lebanon Co, PA 83
Brown John Dea	Center Cem, Heath, Franklin Co, MA 55
Brown John H	Cowansque, PA 52
Brown John Hon	State Cem, Frankfort, KY 15
Brown John Mathias	Carlisle Cem, Carlisle, NY 70
Brown John R	Nr Barnesville, GA 35
Brown John Rev	[no cem named] 15
Brown Johnston	Farm, Milton Twp, Jefferson Co, IN 72
Brown Jonas Ens	New Cem, Temple, NH 28
Brown Jonathan	Old Brimfield Cem, Brimfield, MA 73
Brown Jonathan	Old Yard, Kensington, NH 47
Brown Jonathan	Otselic, NY 16
Brown Jonathan	Raymerstown, Rensselaer Co, NY 35
Brown Jonathan Col	South Tewksbury Cem, Tewksbury, MA 46
Brown Jonathan Jr	Noroton River Cem, Darien, CT 68
Brown Jonathan Jr	Old Brimfield (Palmer) Cem, Brimfield, MA 74
Brown Joseph	Acton, MA 55
Brown Joseph	Connecticut Farms Pres Cem, Union, NJ 49
Brown Joseph	Kingsborough Colonial Cem, Gloversville, NY 32
Brown Joseph	Knox Co, NJ 32
Brown Joseph	Northampton, Fulton Co, NY 15
Brown Joseph	Old Cem, Waretown, NJ 53
Brown Joseph	Old Yard Cem, Weston, MA 55
Brown Joseph	Pittstown Cem, Rensselaer Co, NY 37
Brown Joseph	Rowley Cem, Essex, MA 48
Brown Joseph	Sweetman Cem, Ballston, Saratoga Co, NY 77
Brown Joseph	Tennent, Monmouth Co, NJ 50
Brown Joseph	Tomb, Old South Cem, Ipswich, MA 48
Brown Joseph Capt	Old Cem, Kensington, NH 29
Brown Joshua	Mystic Cem, Stonington, New London Co, CT 64
Brown Josiah	Beaches Corners Cem, Jewett, Greene Co, NY 75
Brown Josiah	Monmouth, NH 20
Brown Josiah	New Ipswich Cem, Ipswich, NH 46
Brown Josiah	Old Yard, Kensington, NH 47
Brown Lemuel	Old Cem, Hamilton, MA 56
Brown Levi	Berrien Springs, MI 33
Brown Lewis	Plot on fam farm, Cheesequakes, NJ 56
Brown Martin	Oak Ridge Church, NJ 45
Brown Mathew	Field N of Meek house, Gregg Twp, Union Co, PA 15
Brown Mathias Capt	Carlisle, NY 34
Brown Matthew	Federal Prison Camp Gr, White Deer Valley, PA 72
Brown Matthew	Little Blue River Cem, Shelby Co, IN 72
Brown Matthew Sr Lt	Mount Hope Cem, Rochester, Monroe Co, NY 33
Brown Michael	Bindnagle Ch Cem, N of Palmyra, Lebanon Co, PA 83
Brown Moses	Buried at sea, nr coast, NJ 48
Brown Moses	Haven Hill Cem, Rochester, NH 36
Brown Moses Capt	Died at sea, MA 46
Brown Nathan	Old Cem, South Hampton, NH 30
Brown Nathan	Somers Pres Ch Cem, Somers, NY 35
Brown Nathan	Springville, IA 42
Brown Nathaniel	Nr Goss Hollow, St Johnsbury, VT 15
Brown Nathaniel	Old Cem, Hamilton, MA 56
Brown Nathaniel	Old Rumford Cem, Rehoboth, MA 55
Brown Nathaniel	Old White Plains Rd, Rye, NY 35
Brown Nathaniel	Potter Hill Cem, Hoosick, NY 34

Brown Nathaniel	West Bethany Cem, Bethany, Genesee Co, NY	65
Brown Nathaniel	West Yard, Alstead, NH	43
Brown Nicholas	Fam Cem, Center Strafford, Strafford, NH	38
Brown Nicholas	Fletchers Chapel Cem, 2½ mi S of Kirkersville, OH	51
Brown Oliver	Concord, Lake Co, OH	26
Brown Oliver	Sheshequin Cem, Sheshequin Twp, Bradford Co, PA	53
Brown Othniel	Union Cem, Union, CT	46
Brown Owen	Old Cem, Hudson, Summit Co, OH	56
Brown Paul	Town Cem, Epping, NH	28
Brown Pelatiah	Old Cem, Rt 1A, Wenham, MA	55
Brown Peleg	Tennessee Gas prop, S of West Winfield, Herkimer Co, NY	77
Brown Peter	Fam Cem, 7 mi N of Knoxville, TN	56
Brown Peter	Old Burial Hill, Pond St, Marblehead, MA	56
Brown Peter	Plot on fam farm, Cheesequakes, NJ	56
Brown Peter	Riverside Cem, Apalachin, NY	35
Brown Peter Capt	White Hall Cem, Mystic, CT	31
Brown Philip	Bindnagle Ch Cem, N of Palmyra, Lebanon Co, PA	83
Brown Philip	Salem Ch Cem, Campbelltown, Lebanon Co, PA	83
Brown Phineas	1st Cem, Vergennes, VT	56
Brown Phineas	Jordan Cem, Royalston Twp, Fulton Co, OH	25
Brown Rans	Farm nr Ohio River below Aberdeen, Brown Co, OH	56
Brown Rebecca	Noroton River Cem, Bloomfield, CT	55
Brown Reuben	Hill Cem, Concord, MA	55
Brown Reuben	Preston Plains, CT	56
Brown Richard	Bur gr nr Amesbury Depot, Amesbury, MA	46
Brown Richard	East Unity Cem, Unity, NH	30
Brown Richard	St John's Epis, Brooke Co, WV	56
Brown Robert	Fam farm, Belchertown, MA	46
Brown Robert	Habersham Co, GA	40
Brown Robert	Stowe Cem, Stowe, RI	57
Brown Roger	Old Cem, Downey Street Rising Cem, Ohio Co, IN	78
Brown Rufus	Center, New Marlborough, MA	56
Brown Ruhamah	St Johns, Greenfield Center, NY	41
Brown Samuel	Bern Twp, Athens, Athens Co, OH	26
Brown Samuel	Broad St Cem, Salem, MA	56
Brown Samuel	Fam Cem, Rye, NY	35
Brown Samuel	Fam farm, Sanbornton, NH	35
Brown Samuel	Heart Pond Cem, Chelmsford, MA	57
Brown Samuel	Hill Cem, Concord, MA	55
Brown Samuel	Old Cem, Sterling, MA	56
Brown Samuel	Rockdale, West Stockbridge, MA	56
Brown Samuel	Seekonk, Seekonk, MA	56
Brown Samuel	Springfield Center, OH	45
Brown Samuel	Springfield Center, Summit Co, OH	15
Brown Samuel	Union Cem, Acton, OH	56
Brown Samuel Capt	Small Cem, Shaw Field, Lily Lake Rd, Pittsfield, NH	28
Brown Samuel Jr	Old Bloomfield Cem, Bloomfield, CT	55
Brown Sanford	Clam River Cem, Sandisfield, MA	56
Brown Seth	Fam Cem, Swansea, Touisset, MA	54
Brown Sewell	First Cem, Candia, NH	29
Brown Shubael	Brooklyn Cem, Canterbury, Windham Co, CT	78
Brown Silas Sgt	Townsend, VT	18
Brown Simon Capt	Town Cem, North Hampton, NH	33
Brown Solomon	Belcoda Cem, Monroe Co, NY	33
Brown Solomon	East Venice Cem, Venice, NY	41
Brown Solomon	Potter Cem, S of East Galway, Saratoga Co, NY	77
Brown Stephen	Connecticut Farms Pres Cem, Union, NJ	49
Brown Stephen	First Cong Ch Cem, Stamford, CT	68
Brown Stephen	Milford, CT	56
Brown Stephen	Old Cem, Hamilton, MA	56
Brown Stephen	Old Cem, Kensington, NH	25

Brown Stephen	Old Yard, Kensington, NH 47
Brown Stephen	Rockdale, West Stockbridge, MA 56
Brown Sylvanus	Jamesport Cem, Jamesport, Suffolk Co, NY 79
Brown Sylvanus	Priv Cem, nr East Chatham, Columbia Co, NY 42
Brown Tarleton	Boiling Springs Bapt Ch, nr Barnwell, SC 51
Brown Thaddeus	Grave obliterated, farm, Solon, Cortland Co, NY 36
Brown Thomas	Antrim, NH 15
Brown Thomas	Brownesville, PA 46
Brown Thomas	Bur gr, First Pres Ch, Woodbridge, NJ 25
Brown Thomas	Carver's Creek Ch Cem, Bladen Co, NC 72
Brown Thomas	Hannah farm, Bethel, Clermont Co, OH 55
Brown Thomas	Killed in Wyoming Massacre, Wyoming, PA 52
Brown Thomas	New Cem, Charlton, Saratoga Co, NY 77
Brown Thomas	Old Mtg Hs Cem, Webster, NH 34
Brown Thomas	Old Mulkey Mtg Hs Cem, Monroe Co, KY 39
Brown Thomas	On Collins River, nr McMinnville, TN 40
Brown Thomas	Pres Ch Cem, Woodbridge, Middlesex Co, NJ 75
Brown Thomas	Randall Cem, South Woodstock, VT 65
Brown Thomas	Reedsville, Preston Co, WV 15
Brown Thomas	Sterling Valley, Sterling, NY 56
Brown Thomas	Wyalusing Cem, Wyoming, PA 47
Brown Thomas Jr	Christ Epis Ch Cem, Brownsville, Fayette Co, PA 80
Brown Thomas Sr	Lebanon, OH 56
Brown Timithy	Yellow Frame Cem, Warren Co, NJ 38
Brown Timothy	Elm Grove, Washington, IA 42
Brown Timothy	West of Columbus, IN 48
Brown Titus	Center Cem, Norfolk, CT 45
Brown Titus	Old Norfolk Bur Gr, Norfolk, Litchfield, CT 51
Brown Titus Jr	Center Cem, Norfolk, CT 62
Brown Walter	Union Brick Cem, Warren Co, NJ 38
Brown White	Browns Chapel Cem, Deerfield Twp, Ross Co, OH 55
Brown William	Bur gr nr Amesbury Depot, Amesbury, MA 46
Brown William	Bur gr, First Pres Ch, Woodbridge, NJ 25
Brown William	Eagle Hills, Scott Co, VA 56
Brown William	Fam Cem, Rt 1318, S of Red Springs, Robeson Co, NC 75
Brown William	First Pres Churchyard, Elizabeth, NJ 52
Brown William	Lee Cem, Amanda Twp, Hancock Co, OH 53
Brown William	Lee Cem, Amanda Twp, Hancock Co, OH 15
Brown William	Liberty Cem, WV 24
Brown William	North Springfield, VT 15
Brown William	Old Bur Hill, Marblehead, MA 30
Brown William	Priv bur gr, W of Troy-Bennington Hwy, Pittstown, NY 37
Brown William	Pumpkin Hook Cem, Springfield, NY 33
Brown William	Pumpkin Hook Cem, Springfield, Otsego Co, NY 72
Brown William	Pumpkin Hook Cem, Van Hornesville, NY 15
Brown William	Putnam Co, IN 16
Brown William	Rear of Page farm, Dover, NH 50
Brown William	Unity Pres Ch Cem, Greensburg, Westmoreland Co, PA 79
Brown William	Water St Cem, Greenville, Darke Co, OH 55
Brown William	West Laurel Hill Cem, Montgomery Co, PA 59
Brown William	Whitehall Cem, Owen Co, IN 25
Brown William Jr	Old Cem, Hamilton, MA 56
Brown William P	Spotswood Ref Ch Cem, Spotswood, NJ 75
Brown William Sanford	Thomas Cem, North Swansea, MA 54
Brown Woodbridge	Mt Zion Cem, Whitman, MA 62
Brown Woodbridge Jr	Abington Cem, Abington, MA 45
Brown Wright Sr	City Hill Cem, Torrey, Yates Co, NY 70
Brown Zaccheus Corp	Chestnut Hill, Putnam Heights, Killingly, CT 15
Brown Zacheus	Chestnut Hill Cem, CT 28
Brown Zacheus	Ring Swamp Cem, Hampton, NH 31
Browne Henry Capt	Sweetman Cem, Charleton, NY 41

Browne John Lt	Fam vault, Laurel Hill Cem, MA 44
Brownell Abner	Fam lot, Palmer farm, Westport, Central Village, MA 54
Brownell Benjamin	Central Village Cem, Westport, MA 46
Brownell Daniel	Main St Cem, Northville, Fulton Co, NY 39
Brownell George	Pleasant View Cem, Adamsville, RI 46
Brownell Jonathan	Fam Cem, Ledyard, Cayuga Co, NY 65
Brownell Jonathan	North Cem, Fall River, MA 46
Brownell William Lt	Fam Cem, Rocky Hill Rd, Steere farm, North Scituate, RI 29
Brownfield Robert	Reinholdt Cem, nr Yearsley Cem, Urbana, Champaign Co, IL 58
Brownfield Robert Sr	Fam Cem, Smithfield, PA 56
Browning Basil Sr	Myers Cem, OH 53
Browning Jacob Capt	Colestown, NJ 47
Browning John	Fam prop, nr Salem Bapt Ch, Rappahannock Co, VA 59
Browning John	Old Cem, Hubbardston, MA 50
Browning Robert	Browning Hill, Hope Valley, RI 48
Browning Robert	Fam lot, nr Hope Valley, RI 35
Brownlee George	Old Greenville Ch, nr Ware Shoals, SC 53
Brownlee James	Flat Rock Cem, Rush Co, IN 72
Brownlee James	Flat Rock Cem, Rush Co, IN 24
Brownlee Lee	Bentonville Cem, Bentonville, Fayette Co, IN 79
Brownlee Robert Jr	East Windsor Cem, East Windsor, CT 31
Brownlee Robert Jr	Scantic Cem, East Windsor, CT 27
Brownlee William	East Windsor Cem, East Windsor, CT 31
Brownlee William	Scantic Cem, East Windsor, CT 27
Brownson Benjamin Capt	Center Cem, New Milford, CT 55
Brownson Eli	Ira Allen Cem, Sunderland, Bennington Co, VT 61
Broyles Michael	Broyles Cem, Washington Co, TN 24
Broyles Michael	Fam Cem, TN 23
Brua John Peter	Christ Luth Ch Cem, Stroudsburg, PA 56
Brubacher Conrad	Lower Cordorus Ref Ch Cem, Windsor Twp, PA 71
Bruce Benjamin	Jay Cem, Jay, NY 15
Bruce Charles	Fam Cem, Summerfield, NC 58
Bruce Charles	Greer, SC 41
Bruce George	Rawson Brook Cem, Leicester, MA 58
Bruce Isaiah	Springhill Cem, Marlboro, MA 50
Bruce Jesse	Cushing Cem, Woodstock, VT 65
Bruce John	Berlin, MA 50
Bruce John	Grantsburg, Lewis Co, KY 52
Bruce Jonathan	Old Cem, Northborough, MA 56
Bruce Joseph	North Thetford, VT 17
Bruce Lewis	Old Western Cem, Lynn, MA 55
Bruce Nathaniel	Main St Cem, Hudson, MA 50
Bruce Phillip	Fam Cem, Fayetteville, Lincoln Co, TN 75
Bruce Simon	Center Cem, Grafton, MA 49
Bruce Timothy	North Yard, Alstead, NH 43
Bruce William	Hubble Cem, Hubble, KY 68
Bruen Caleb	Pres Cem, Newark, NJ 32
Bruen Eleazer	Pres Cem, Newark, NJ 32
Bruen Jabez	[no cem named], OH 17
Bruen Jeremiah	First Pres Ch Cem, Newark, NJ 26
Bruen Joseph	Connecticut Farms Pres Cem, Union, NJ 49
Bruere James Capt	Pres Churchyard, Allentown, NJ 49
Bruin Peter B	[no cem named], MS 44
Brumer Christian	Otsquago Cem, North Van Hornesville, Herkimer Co, NY 41
Brumley John	1 mi W of Latham, Pike Co, OH 43
Brumley William	Union Springs Village Cem, Springport, Cayuga Co, NY 57
Brundage David	Friends Cem, Armonk, Westchester Co, NY 36
Brundage Israel	Old bur gr, Orange, NJ 26
Brundage Jesse	Fam farm, Pittstown-Tomhannock Hwy, Rensselaer Co, NY 37
Brundate Nathaniel	Old Town Bur Gr, Newburgh, Orange Co, NY 69
Bruner Adam	Bruner, Knox Co, IL 56

Bruner	Elias Sr	Ref Memorial Park Cem, Frederick, Frederick Co, MD 77
Bruner	George	Fritz Cem, Little Oley, Berks Co, PA 78
Bruner	Heinrich	Walmer's Cem, Indiantown Gap, Lebanon Co, PA 83
Bruner	John	German Ref Ch Cem, Rt 40, Frederick, Frederick Co, MD 77
Bruner	John	Mount Olivet Cem, Frederick, Frederick Co, MD 77
Bruner	Peter	Bethel Morav Ch Cem, Lebanon Co, PA 83
Bruner	Peter	German Ref Ch Cem, Rt 40, Frederick, Frederick Co, MD 77
Bruner	Valentine	Mount Olivet Cem, Frederick, Frederick Co, MD 77
Brunn	Johannes	Hill Luth Ch Cem, North Annville Twp, Lebanon Co, PA 83
Brunner	Frederick	Wentz's Ref Cem, Montgomery Co, PA 59
Brunson	Elisha	Milford, CT 56
Brunson	William	Bradford Cem, Williamsburg Co, SC 55
Brunson	William	West Cem, Alford, MA 56
Brush	Alexander	Bayside Cem, Potsdam, NY 30
Brush	Benjamin	[no cem named], CT 27
Brush	Benjamin Capt	New Bur Gr, no state 31
Brush	Gilbert	Brush Corners, Danbury-Brewster Rd, Putnam Co, NY 36
Brush	Jacob	Brush Corners, Danbury-Brewster Rd, Putnam Co, NY 36
Brush	John	Brush Corners, Danbury-Brewster Rd, Putnam Co, NY 36
Brush	Nehemiah	Comac, Long Island, NY 16
Brush	Nehemiah Jr	Commack Meth Ch Cem, Huntington, Suffolk Co, NY 72
Brush	William	Mount Hope Cem, Norwich, NY 16
Brusie	Andrews C	Copake Meth Ch Cem, Copake, Columbia Co, NY 79
Brusstar	Samuel	Ashtabula Co, OH 45
Brust	Jacob	Brunswick, Rensselaer Co, NY 39
Brust	John	Luth Ch, Brunswick, Haynerville, Rensselaer Co, NY 39
Brust	Matthias	Brunswick, Rensselaer Co, NY 39
Bruyn	Jacobus Severyn	Old Dutch Cem, Kingston, Ulster Co, NY 85
Bryan	Alexander	Green Ridge Cem, Saratoga, Saratoga Co, NY 77
Bryan	Benajah	Watertown, CT 15
Bryan	Cornelius	Watson Cem, nr Summerfield, OH 56
Bryan	Daniel Boone	Lexington Cem, Lexington, KY 60
Bryan	Elijah	Granville, OH 15
Bryan	Elijah	Licking Co, OH 45
Bryan	Hardy	Evergreen Cem, East Feliciana Parish, LA 63
Bryan	James	Mill Creek Cem, York Co, SC 70
Bryan	James	St Charles Co, MO 15
Bryan	Jeheil Jr	Milford Cem, Milford, CT 56
Bryan	Jeheil Sr	Milford Cem, Milford, CT 56
Bryan	John	Bryan-Parks Fam Cem, Antioch Twp, Wilkes Co, NC 60
Bryan	John	Garrard Co, KY 27
Bryan	John	Orange, CT 56
Bryan	Joseph	Caldwell Cem, Essex Co, NJ 67
Bryan	Lewis	Plot on N side of Valley Falls-Schaghticoke Hwy, NY 38
Bryan	Richard	Center Cem, New Marlborough, MA 56
Bryan	Samuel	Bapt Ch Cem, Perry Twp, Marion Co, IN 72
Bryan	Samuel	West Bloodville Cem, Milton, Ulster Co, NY 77
Bryan	Samuel Jr	Fam Cem, Saratoga, Saratoga Co, NY 77
Bryan	William	Beaver Twp, Noble Co, OH 56
Bryan	William	Wardsworth prop, Core Creek, Craven Co, PA 57
Bryan	William After	Stevensville Cem, Kent Island, Queen Annes Co, MD 52
Bryan	William Jr	West Hill Cem, Salem, Pittsylvania Co, VA 73
Bryan	William Sr	Cem nr Bryan Station, Fayette, KY 64
Bryan	Zephania	Plum Twp, Allegheny Co, PA 56
Bryans	Alexander	Greenridge Cem, Saratoga Springs, NY 41
Bryant	–	Orchard next to Hopkins farm, Plainfield, CT 51
Bryant	Alexander	Church Cem, Butternuts, nr Gilbertsville, Otsego Co, NY 77
Bryant	Amos	Cem on town common, Nelson, NH 35
Bryant	Andrew	Lyme Plain Cem, Lyme, NH 36
Bryant	Benjamin	Center Cem, Chesterfield, Hampshire Co, MA 75
Bryant	Benjamin	Old Cem, Plympton, MA 50

Abstract of Graves of Revolutionary Patriots

Bryant Boss	Nr Greenfield, OH 18
Bryant Caleb	Old Burial Cem, Plympton, MA 57
Bryant Daniel	North Thetford, VT 17
Bryant Daniel	Old Cem, Stoneham, MA 55
Bryant David	Country Cem, 17 mi NW of Ft Wayne, IN 55
Bryant David	Pine Grove Cem, Leicester, MA 55
Bryant Ebenezer Jr	Manchester Center Cem, Manchester, CT 19
Bryant Ephraim	Old Cem, Plympton, MA 50
Bryant Jacob	Old Burial Cem, Plympton, MA 57
Bryant James	Spencer Cem, Owen Co, IN 72
Bryant Jeremiah	Old Cem, Wakefield, MA 27
Bryant Jeremiah	Wakefield Cem, Wakefield, MA 29
Bryant Jesse	Nemasket Cem, Middleboro, MA 50
Bryant Jonathan	St Michael's Ch Cem, Trenton, NJ 28
Bryant Joseph	Old Cem, Wakefield, MA 27
Bryant Joseph	Old Plympton Cem, Plympton, MA 57
Bryant Joshua	Old Cem, Plympton, MA 50
Bryant Luther	Old Bur Cem, Kingston, MA 62
Bryant Micah	Nemasket Cem, Middleboro, MA 50
Bryant Nicholas	Westfield Pres Ch Cem, Mt Jackson, Lawrence Co, PA 59
Bryant Robert Ens	Old Cem, Meredith Neck, Meredith, NH 28
Bryant Stephen	Upper St Cem, Turner, ME 40
Bryant Thomas	Best Cem, (now a field), nr Trenton, MO 15
Bryant Timothy	Manchester Center Cem, Manchester, CT 19
Bryant William	Cem, Marion Rd, Middleboro, MA 55
Bryant William	Claysville, MO 32
Bryant William	Newton Union Sloan Cem, West Collingswood, NJ 50
Bryant William	Old Cem, Wakefield, MA 27
Bryant Zenas	Plympton, MA 31
Bryer John	Cem betw Allen's Mills & Loudon Ridge, NH 40
Brynberg John	Old Swede's Cem, New Castle Co, DE 46
Brynberg Peter	Old Swede's Cem, New Castle Co, DE 46
Bryson Alexander	Mount Nebo Pres Ch Cem, nr Whitetown, Butler Co, PA 15
Bryson James	Military Cem, Ft Newport, KY 56
Bryson Samuel	Academia Pres Cem, Mifflintown, PA 15
Bubier Christopher	Old Burial Hill, Pond St, Marblehead, MA 56
Bubier John Horton	Drowned off Grand Banks, MA 49
Bubies Joseph Capt	Old Bur Hill, Marblehead, MA 29
Buchanan Alexander	Calvary Cem, Washington Twp, Clermont Co, OH 55
Buchanan Andrew	Druid Hill Park Cem, Park Heights Ave, Baltimore, MD 77
Buchanan Andrew	Fam Cem, Augusta, VA 56
Buchanan George	Fam farm, nr Barbersville, Jefferson Co, IN 25
Buchanan George	Nr Madison, IN 56
Buchanan Gilbert	Edinburg, PA 56
Buchanan John	Fam Cem, Buchanan Station, SC 60
Buchanan John	Fam Cem, Locust Cove, 4 mi W of Chatham Hill, VA 56
Buchanan John	Meth Ch Cem, Winnsboro, SC 70
Buchanan Robert	Mt Pleasant Cem, Charleston, SC 70
Buchanan William Col	Westminster Cem, Baltimore, MD 20
Buchanan William Gen	Westminster Pres Cem, lot 18, Baltimore, MD 15
Bucher John Conrad	Tabor Reformed Cem, PA 37
Bucherber Phillip	Old Cem, Freidensville, Lehigh Co, PA 40
Buchingham Ebenezer	Carthage Twp, OH 26
Buchlin John	Fam farm Cem, betw Little Falls & Herkimer, NY 58
Buchman Andrew	Weisenburg Old and New Cem, Lehigh Co, PA 40
Buchman Martin	Weisenburg Old and New Cem, Lehigh Co, PA 40
Buchtel John	Sherman Ch Cem, Stark Co, OH 54
Buchwalter Daniel	Pine Grover Cem, Berks Co, PA 54
Buck Aaron	Westfield Cem, Westfield, CT 28
Buck Aboliab	Killed in Wyoming Massacre, Wyoming, PA 52
Buck Amasa	Town Cem, West Bath, NH 27

Buck Asaph	Fam Cem, New Lisbon Twp, Otsego Co, NY 71
Buck Christian	Sprint Mt (Nearhoof), Warriors Mark, Montgomery Co, PA 66
Buck Daniel	Old Buck, Bucksport, ME 56
Buck Daniel	Old Cem, Wethersfield, CT 56
Buck Daniel	Old Epis Cem, Great Bend, PA 21
Buck David	Aspinwall Cem, Putnam, CT 46
Buck David	North St Cem, Auburn, NY 15
Buck Ebenezer	Cem, betw Pittsfield & Williamstown, Lanesborough, MA 55
Buck Ebenezer	City Cem, Conneaut, OH 56
Buck Ebenezer	Fam Cem, Bucksport, ME 31
Buck Ebenezer	North Upton Cem, Upton, MA 46
Buck Edmund	Fam Cem, Lincoln Twp, OH 56
Buck Elijah	Chemung Cem, Chemung Co, NY 32
Buck Francis	Old Cem, Monroe Co, NY 33
Buck Henry	Killed in Wyoming Massacre, Wyoming, PA 52
Buck Isaac	Erie Co, NY 55
Buck Isaac	Leg Cem, Stirling, MA 45
Buck Israel	Alum Creek Friends Cem, Peru Twp, Monroe Twp, OH 53
Buck James	Center Cem, New Milford, Litchfield Co, CT 68
Buck James	New Milford, CT 53
Buck John	Center Cem, Shaftsbury, Bennington Co, VT 74
Buck John	Putnam Co, IN 16
Buck Jonathan	Bucksport Cem, ME 48
Buck Jonathan Col	Fam Cem, Bucksport, ME 31
Buck Jonathan Jr	Fam Cem, Bucksport, ME 31
Buck Josiah	Center Cem, Sherman, CT 68
Buck Josiah	Union (Myer) Cem, Springport, Cayuga Co, NY 69
Buck Nathan	Wildwood Cem, Wilmington, MA 56
Buck Reuben	New Cem, Wilmington, MA 58
Buck Samuel	New Cem, Wilmington, MA 58
Buck Thomas	Brockport, NY 15
Buck Thomas	Worthington, MA 56
Buck William	Center Cem, Heath, Franklin Co, MA 55
Buck William	Chemung Cem, Chemung Co, NY 78
Buck William	Chemung Cem, Elmira, NY 33
Buck William	Killed in Wyoming Massacre, Wyoming, PA 52
Buck William	St Mary's Cem, St Mary's, OH 56
Buck William Jr	Poland Cem, Poland, OH 56
Buck William Sr	Poland Cem, Poland, OH 56
Buck Zebediah	Oldest Killingly, Putnam, CT 56
Buckbee Edward	Adams Corners Cem, Adams Corners, Putnam Co, NY 36
Buckbee Ezekiel	Holmes farm, Gotham, Bedford, NY 35
Buckbee John	Holmes farm, Gotham, Bedford, NY 35
Buckelew Fred	Old Homestead, George's Rd, New Brunswick, NJ 47
Buckerlew Peter	Van Liew Cem, New Brunswick, NJ 75
Bucket James	Pentucket, Haverhill, MA 27
Buckholte Jacob	Amite Co, MS 44
Buckingham David	Watertown, CT 15
Buckingham Ebenezer	Cooley Bur Gr, Carthage Twp, Athens Co, OH 55
Buckingham Enoch	Evergreen Cem, Miamiville, OH 52
Buckingham John	Cem, Milford, CT 56
Buckingham John	Franklin Cem, West Bethlehem Twp, Lancaster Co, PA 38
Buckingham Lloyd	Luth Cem, Reisterstown, MD 19
Buckland George	Fam Cem, Manchester, CT 19
Buckley Daniel	Greenfield Hill Cem, Fairfield, CT 62
Buckley Gershom	Greenfield Hill Cem, Fairfield, CT 62
Buckley Israel	Quaker Cem, Academy Corners, PA 53
Buckley John	Copps Hill Cem, Boston, MA 46
Buckley Nathan	Old Bur Gr, Fairfield, CT 70
Buckley Nicholas	Mahaiwe, Great Barrington, MA 56
Bucklin Benjamin	Old Cem, W of Camillus, Camillus, NY 56

Abstract of Graves of Revolutionary Patriots

Bucklin John	Gravestone Cheshire Cem, Cheshire, MA 58
Bucklin John	Old Rumford Cem, Rehoboth, MA 55
Bucklin Nehemiah	Old Rumford Cem, Rehoboth, MA 55
Bucklin Squire Jr	Foster Cem, Foster, RI 47
Buckman Benjamin	Fairview Cem, New Albany, Floyd Co, IN 71
Buckman John	Old Lexington Cem, Lexington, MA 55
Buckman Nathan	Millis, Millis-Medway, MA 56
Buckman Stephen	East Woodstock, CT 15
Buckmaster Thomas	Union Protestant Epis Cem, Burrsville, Kent Co, DE 46
Buckminster Lawson	Church Hill Cem, Framingham, MA 56
Buckminster Solomon	Town Cem, Roxbury, NH 25
Buckminster Thomas	Church Hill, Framingham, MA 30
Buckminster William	Church Hill, Framingham, MA 30
Bucknam Daniel	Poland, ME 18
Bucknam Edwards	Field, old home, nr Beaverbrook, Lancaster, NH 37
Bucknam John	Old Cem, Stoneham, MA 51
Bucknam Nathan	Old Town Cem, Eastport, ME 59
Buckner Daniel	Nr Medora, Jackson Co, IN 23
Buckner Francis	Hwy 68, Todd Co, KY 45
Buckner Philip	Nr Brooksville, Bracken Co, KY 26
Buckout Jacob	Scipioville (Evergreen) Cem, Scipio, NY 56
Buckwalter Daniel	Pine Grove Cem, nr Morgantown, Berks Co, PA 63
Budd Bern	Pres Cem, Morristown, NJ 32
Budd Daniel Capt	Mount Olive Bur Gr, Mount Olive, NJ 24
Budd George	Newton Union Sloan Cem, West Collingswood, NJ 50
Budd Gilbert Col	Mamaroneck Cem, back of Kindergarten, Mamaroneck, NY 35
Budd James	Killed in Wyoming Massacre, Wyoming, PA 52
Budd John	Budd Lake Cem, Chester, NY 70
Budd John	Harlem Cem, Harlem Twp, Delaware Co, OH 46
Budd John	Mahaiwe, Great Barrington, MA 56
Budd John 1st	Austinville Cem, PA 53
Budd John Col	Mount Olive Bur Gr, Mount Olive, NJ 24
Budington Walter	Milford Center Cem, New Milford, CT 40
Buehler Henry	Hebron Morav Cem, Lebanon, Lebanon Co, PA 83
Buehler Henry	Morav Cem, Lebanon, Lebanon Co, PA 77
Buel Cyrus	Benton Rural Cem, Benton, NY 70
Buel Elias	Albany rural Cem, Albany, NY 31
Buel Jesse	Town Hill Cem, Lakeville, CT 64
Buel John	Townsend Cem, Andover, CT 55
Buel Levi	Townsend Cem, Andover, CT 55
Buel Nathaniel	Old Town Hall Cem, Salisbury, CT 64
Buel Oliver	Flat Brook Cem, Canaan, Columbia Co, NY 42
Buel Peter Jr	East Litchfield, CT 17
Buel Salmon	West Litchfield, CT 17
Buel Samuel	Benton Rural Cem, Benton, NY 70
Buel Samuel	Middle Farms, Westfield, MA 56
Buel Samuel	Middle Farms, Westfield, MA 56
Buel Samuel Rev	South Cem, Easthampton, Long Island, NY 35
Buel Solomon Jr	Hop Meadow Cem, Simsbury, CT 55
Buell Abraham	Groton Village Cem, Groton, NH 35
Buell Asa	Fam Cem, Rt 5, E of LeRoy, Genesee Co, NY 65
Buell Benjamin	Hebron, CT 56
Buell David	Center Cem, New Milford, CT 55
Buell Eliphalet	Sharon Cem, Sharon, Litchfield Co, CT 66
Buell Ezra	Union Cem, Stillwater, NY 41
Buell Jedediah	Indian River Cem, Clinton, CT 55
Buell Jeremiah	Chestnut Hill Cem, North Killingsworth, CT 55
Buell Job	Indian River Cem, Clinton, CT 55
Buell Jonathan	Oran Cem, Pompey, Onondaga Co, NY 75
Buell Joseph	Chatham, now East Haddam, CT 56
Buell Josiah	Trumbull,Lebanon, CT 56

Buell Orange	Ouleout Cem, Franklin, Delaware Co, NY 71
Buell Reuben	Green Ridge Cem, Saratoga, Saratoga Co, NY 77
Buell Reuben	Greenridge Cem, Saratoga Springs, NY 41
Buell Samuel	Middle Farms, Westfield, MA 56
Buell Solomon	Hop Meadow Cem, Simsbury, CT 55
Buell Solomon	West Bur Gr, Litchfield, CT 45
Buell Timothy	Rice Cem, East Bloomfield, Ontario Co, NY 77
Buffington David	New Salem Cem, New Salem, OH 56
Buffington Ebenezer	Meth Ch Cem, St Clairsville, OH 56
Buffington Preserved	Numan farm, Bradford, PA 53
Buford Abram Col	Cem, Georgetown, Scott Co, KY 20
Buford Henry	Fam Cem, Locust Level, nr Montvale, Bedford Co, VA 47
Buford John Abraham	Rockingham Co, VA 15
Bugbee Amasa	Lyme Plain Cem, Lyme, NH 30
Bugbee Elijah	Grove St Cem, Putnam, CT 30
Bugbee Elisha	Grove St, Putnam, CT 56
Bugbee Hezekiah	Woodstock Hill Cem, CT 16
Bugbee Jonathan	Bungay Cem, Woodstock, CT 55
Bugbee Samuel	Bungay Cem, Woodstock, CT 55
Bugbee Samuel	[no cem named], CT 19
Bugbee Samuel	Wrentham Cem, Wrentham, MA 46
Bugbee William	Bungay Cem, Woodstock, CT 55
Bugbee William Corp	[no cem named], CT 19
Bugh Peter	New Reading Cem, Perry Co, OH 55
Buirne –	Mount Evergreen, Jackson, MI 45
Buker Israel	Town Cem, Otsego, Musk, OH 55
Bulkeley Eliphalet	Hallenback Cem, Wilkes-Barre, PA 56
Bulkley Charles	Old Cem, Wethersfield, CT 56
Bulkley Francis	Old Cem, Wethersfield, CT 56
Bulkley James	Old Bur Gr, Fairfield, CT 62
Bulkley John	Old Cem, Wethersfield, CT 56
Bulkley Joseph	Greenfield Hill Cem, Fairfield, CT 62
Bulkley Joseph	Old Bur Gr, Fairfield, CT 62
Bulkley Nathan	Old Bur Gr, Fairfield, CT 62
Bulkley Turney	Greenfield Hill Cem, Fairfield, CT 62
Bull Asa	West Litchfield, CT 17
Bull Asher	Pioneer Cem, Prattsburg, Steuben Co, NY 72
Bull Caleb Capt	Gold St Cem, Old Hartford, CT 19
Bull Henry	Donallys Mills, PA 16
Bull Isaac	Fam Cem, Hamptonbourgh, Orange Co, NY 56
Bull John	Cem, Philadelphia, PA 56
Bull John Capt	Lebanon Springs, NY 35
Bull John D	Union Cem, Stillwater, Saratoga Co, NY 77
Bull John Serior	Evergreen Cem, New Lebanon, Columbia Co, NY 42
Bull Jonathan	Town Hall Cem, Salisbury, CT 68
Bull Richard	Donallys Mills, PA 16
Bull Richard	Kings Station Cem, Woodvale St, Gallatin, Sumner Co, TN 77
Bull Thomas	South Woodbury Cem, Woodbury, CT 55
Bull Thomas	St Mary's Epis Ch Cem, Warwick Twp, Chester Co, PA 75
Bull Thomas Jr	Union Cem, Clintonville, OH 26
Bull William	Donallys Mills, PA 16
Bull William Sr	Massie's Creek Cem, nr Xenia, OH 25
Bullard Adam	Millis, Millis-Medway, MA 56
Bullard Asa	Sherborn No 2, Sherborn, MA 56
Bullard Asa	South Cem, Holliston, MA 74
Bullard Baruch	Prospect Hill Cem, Uxbridge, MA 57
Bullard Benjamin	Old Cem, Canton St, Sharon, MA 56
Bullard David	Gaines Cem, Gaines, NY 34
Bullard David	Gaines Cem, Gaines, Orleans Co, NY 80
Bullard Ephraim	Wellesley Village Cem, Wellesley, MA 40
Bullard Henry	Millis, Millis-Medway, MA 56

Abstract of Graves of Revolutionary Patriots

Bullard Henry Jr	Millis, Millis-Medway, MA 56
Bullard Isaac	Holliston Center, Holliston, MA 56
Bullard Isaac	Millis, Millis-Medway, MA 56
Bullard Isaac	Village, Dedham, MA 56
Bullard James	Sherborn No 2, Sherborn, MA 56
Bullard Jonathan	Old Yard, Pine Ridge, Hancock, NH 29
Bullard Lemuel	Epis Cem, Cheshire, New Haven Co, CT 24
Bullard Nathan	South Cem, Holliston, MA 74
Bullard Royal	Millis, Millis-Medway, MA 56
Bullard Samuel	Central Bur Gr, Holliston, Middlesex Co, MA 73
Bullard Samuel	Plain Cem, Sherborn, MA 48
Bullard Samuel Col	Plain Cem, Sherborn, MA 46
Bullard Seth Col	Old Town Cem, Walpole, MA 45
Bullard Timothy	Millis, Millis-Medway, MA 56
Bullen Daniel	Millis, Millis-Medway, MA 56
Bullen Jeduthan	Millis, Millis-Medway, MA 56
Bullen John	Cem Behind City Hall, Paris Hills nr Clinton, NY 78
Bullen Jonathan	Millis, Millis-Medway, MA 56
Bullen Moses	Vine Lake, Medfield, MA 56
Bullen Samuel Jr	Center Mtg Hs Cem, Farmington, Franklin Co, ME 83
Bullington Robert	Nr Sandy River, Pittsylvania Co, VA 55
Bullitt Alexander Scott	Bullitt Cem, Jefferson Co, KY 31
Bullock Amos	Killed in Wyoming Massacre, Wyoming, PA 52
Bullock Barnard	Stevens Cem, Annawan St, Rehoboth, MA 54
Bullock Calvin	Burial Place Hill, Rehoboth, MA 54
Bullock Comfort	North Hillsdale Cem, Columbia Co, NY 42
Bullock Darius	Halifax, VT 17
Bullock David	Razor Hill Cem, Grafton, NH 38
Bullock Ebenezer	Stevens Cem, Annawan St, Rehoboth, MA 54
Bullock Hawkins	Fam Cem, nr Hull, Madison Co, GA 25
Bullock Hezekiah	Razor Hill Cem, Grafton, NH 38
Bullock James	6 mi fr Lexington, Denton farm, Fayette Co, KY 39
Bullock Jeremiah	Village Cem, Winchester, NH 36
Bullock Joseph	Old Hix Cem, nr Brooks St, Rehoboth, MA 54
Bullock Micajah	Fleming Bur Gr, Granville Co, NC 49
Bullock Nathan	Old Cem, Sennett, NY 41
Bullock Richard	Old North Chatham Cem, North Chatham, Columbia Co, NY 79
Bullock Samuel	Burial Place Hill, Rehoboth, MA 54
Bullock Sawyer	Razor Hill Cem, Grafton, NH 38
Bullock Stephen Capt	Rehoboth Cem, Rehoboth, MA 47
Bullock William	Burial Place Hill, Rehoboth, MA 54
Bullock William Col	Guilford, VT 18
Bulsen John	Waldron Cem, Grassy Point, Rockland Co, NY 78
Bump Aaron	North Galway Cem, North Galway, Saratoga Co, NY 77
Bump Joseph	Day Fam Cem, Greenfield, Saratoga Co, NY 77
Bump Joseph	Nemasket Cem, Middleboro, MA 50
Bumpus Asa	Center Cem, Wareham, MA 55
Bumpus Jeremiah	Center Cem, Wareham, MA 16
Bumpus Jeremiah	Center Cem, Wareham, MA 55
Bumpus Joseph	East Wareham, MA 16
Bumpus Joseph	East Wareham Cem, Wareham, MA 28
Bumpus Lemuel	Center Cem, Wareham, MA 55
Bumpus Lot	DeRuyter, NY 56
Bumpus Rueben	South Litchfield Cem, PA 53
Bumpus Sylvester	Bur gr, Stillwater, NY 41
Bumstead Thomas	Granary Cem, Boston, MA 46
Bunce Isaiah	New Preston Cem, New Preston, CT 55
Bunce Timothy Sgt	Old North Cem, Old Hartford, CT 19
Bundy Asahel	Village Cem, Walpole, NH 25
Bundy Asahel	Walpole, NH 16
Bundy Elias	Walpole, NH 16

Bundy Elias Capt	North Stratford Cem, Stratford, NH 36
Bundy Elias Lt	Village Cem, Walpole, NH 25
Bundy Elijah	Main Cem, Salisbury, CT 64
Bundy Isaac	Village Cem, Walpole, NH 25
Bundy Isaac	Walpole, NH 16
Bundy Peter	Fam Cem, Otsego, Otsego Co, NY 71
Bunker Eli	Barnstead Parade Cem, Barnstead, NH 45
Bunker Isaac	Priv fam Cem, S of Gouldsboro, Hancock Co, ME 79
Bunker Jonathan	Barnstead Parade Cem, Barnstead, NH 45
Bunker Jonathan	Parade Cem, Barnstead, NH 33
Bunker Richard	Edgartown, MA 15
Bunker Richard	Edgartown Cem, Edgartown, MA 45
Bunn Jonathan	Cem 1 mi W of Pennington, NJ 32
Bunnel John	Cong Cem, Cheshire, New Haven Co, CT 24
Bunnell Benjamin	Middle Smithfield Pres Ch Cem, Northampton Co, PA 68
Bunnell Joseph	Cornwall Cem, Cornwall, CT 22
Bunnell Nathaniel	Cong Cem, Cheshire, New Haven Co, CT 24
Bunnell Noah	Dutch Reform Ch Cem, Hyde Park, NY 65
Bunnell Samuel	Hillside Cem, Cheshire, CT 55
Bunner John Lt	Malone Cem, Clinton Dist, Monongalia Co, WV 40
Bunner Joseph	Malone Cem, Clinton Dist, Monongalia Co, WV 40
Buntain William	Fall Creek Cem, OH 15
Bunten John	Center Cem, Dunbarton, NH 31
Buntin Robert	Greenlawn Cem, Vincennes, Knox Co, IN 72
Bunting Joshua	Orthodox Cem, Crosswicks, NJ 51
Bunting Ramoth	Williamsburg Twp, Clermont Co, OH 55
Burbank Caleb	Old Cem, West Millbury, MA 56
Burbank Daniel Lt	South Williamstown, MA 15
Burbank David	Boothby Yard, Maplewood Rd, West Newfield, York Co, ME 74
Burbank Ebenezer	Mtg Hs Hill Cem, Redstone, Carroll Co, NH 77
Burbank Ebenezer	Old Bur Gr, Suffield, Hartford Co, CT 24
Burbank Eleazer	Cherry Hill Cem, Bethel, Windsor Co, VT 72
Burbank Gersham Capt	Campton Cem, Campton, NH 29
Burbank Isaac	Assonet, MA 30
Burbank Isaac	Assouet Cem, Assouet, MA 45
Burbank Joel	Handy Cem, West Woodstock, Windsor Co, VT 75
Burbank John	Alfred Road, ME 29
Burbank John	Central Cem, Cohasset, MA 60
Burbank John	Groveland Cem, Bradford, MA 55
Burbank John	Tuttle Corner Cem, Freeman, Franklin Co, ME 83
Burbank Jonathan	Blodgett Cem, Hudson, NH 28
Burbank Moses Sr	Boscawen Cem, Boscawen, NH 57
Burbank Nathan	Groveland Cem, Bradford, MA 55
Burbank Samuel	Cavendish Cem, Cavendish, VT 45
Burbank Samuel	Chester, VT 16
Burbank Samuel	Metcalf Rock Pasture Bur Gr, Rowley, MA 48
Burbank Samuel	Smokeshire Cem, Chester, VT 36
Burbank Samuel Lt	South Lawn Cem, Williamstown, MA 33
Burbank Timothy	Hope Cem, Newark Valley, NY 34
Burbeck James	Blairs Cem, Campton, NH 36
Burbeck William	Copps Hill Cem, Boston, MA 46
Burbride Roland	Buffalo Cem, nr Louisiana, Pike Co, MO 15
Burbridge George	Old home place, nr Stamping Ground, Scott Co, KY 20
Burch Daniel	Franklin, IN 71
Burch David	Fam Cem, Wyckoff Rd, Scipio, Cayuga Co, NY 69
Burch Eddy	Liberty Hill, Aurelius Twp, Washington Co, OH 56
Burch George	Rodes & Burch Bur Gr, Long Lick Pike, KY 20
Burch Increase	Plot on fam farm, W of Johnsville, Schaghticoke, NY 38
Burch James	Old Stone Ch Cem, Fairton, NJ 47
Burch John	Bales Cem, Barren Co, KY 45
Burch Jonathan	Prob The Boulder, VT 48

Abstract of Graves of Revolutionary Patriots

Burch William	Fam Cem, Indian Creek Twp, Monroe Co, IN 72
Burchard Jabez	Hamilton, NY 15
Burchard Joseph	Brookside Cem, Preston Hollow, NY 32
Burchard Samuel	Westlawn Cem, Williamstown, MA 15
Burche Benjamin	Mt Olivet Cem, sect 2, lot 4, Washington, DC 57
Burchfield Robert	Whitham Cem, Brum Twp, Wabash Co, IN 72
Burcholder Christian	Geeseman farm plot, South Annville Twp, Lebanon Co, PA 83
Burchsted Benjamin B	Western Cem, West Lynn, MA 56
Burchsted Henry	Western Cem, West Lynn, MA 56
Burd James Col	Middletown Cem, Middletown, PA 21
Burd James Col	Norristown, PA 15
Burden Abraham	East Ripley Cem, East Ripley, Chautauqua Co, NY 77
Burden Nathan	North Bur Gr, Freetown, Fall River, MA 54
Burden Thomas II	Bellona Cem, Benton, Yates Co, NY 78
Burden Thomas III	Bellona Cem, Benton, Yates Co, NY 78
Burdett John	Old Pine Grove Cem, Leominster, MA 47
Burdge Samuel	Fam Cem, nr Roann, Wabash Co, IN 72
Burdick Caleb	Greene, Chenango Co, NY 35
Burdick Ichabod	Charleston Cem, Charleston, RI 47
Burdick Isaih	Charlestown Cem, RI 48
Burdick James Capt	Old bur gr, Newport, RI 39
Burdick Oliver	Westerly, RI 48
Burdick Perry	Scott Cem, Scott, Cortland Co, NY 36
Burdick Peter Jr	Fam lot, Lower Paucatuck, Stonington, CT 51
Burdick Thompson	Spafford Fam Cem, Spafford, Onondaga Co, NY 76
Burdick Thompson	Spafford, NY 35
Burditt Joseph	Old Cem, Wakefield, MA 55
Burdon John	Lackey Cem, Whitinsville, MA 53
Burdon Jonathan Lt	Pigeon Hill Cem, Putnam Hill, Sutton, MA 46
Burdue Nathaniel	Bapt Cem, Berlin Heights, Erie Co, OH 56
Burford Philip	Fam Cem, Covington Rd, De Kalb Co, GA 50
Burford Philip	McCurdy Fam Cem, on Indian Creek, nr Stone Mountain, GA 27
Burford Thomas	Prop nr Flowery Branch, Yagles Dist, Hall Co, GA 64
Burford William	Old Bethel Cem, nr Jackson, Butts Co, GA 39
Burford William	Old Bethel Ch Cem, 3 mi N of Jackson, Butts Co, GA 33
Burge Benjamin	Old Cem, Wayne, ME 45
Burge Ephraim	Churchyard, Hollis, NH 39
Burge Nathaniel	Summer Hill Cem, Springfield, VT 38
Burger George	Wurtemburg, Rhinebeck, NY 21
Burger Jacob	5 mi W of Gretna, Pittsylvania Co, VA 73
Burger Martinus	Ref Dutch Rhinebeck Cem, Rhinebeck, Dutchess Co, NY 55
Burger Nicholas	St Jacob Cem, N of Lisbon, Columbiana Co, OH 55
Burgert Lambert	Stuyvesant Falls Cem, Columbia Co, NY 42
Burges Jedediah	Ch Cem, South Dennis, MA 49
Burges Phillip	Center Cem, Harwich, MA 49
Burgess Covill	Harwich, MA 53
Burgess Ichabod	Betw Wayne & Stricklands Ferry, ME 20
Burgess Isaac	Brick Ch Cem, Niagara Co, NY 33
Burgess Isaac	North Ridge Cem, Niagara Co, NY 57
Burgess Jacob	Mayflower Cem, Duxbury, MA 50
Burgess Jeremiah	Ridge Cem, Malta, Saratoga Co, NY 41
Burgess John	Ithaca City Cem, Ithaca, NY 15
Burgess John	Ithaca City Cem, Ithaca, NY 32
Burgess John	Mt Tabor, Champaign, OH 56
Burgess Jonathan	Center Cem, Harwich, MA 49
Burgess Joseph Capt	Westminster Ch Cem, Canterbury Twp, CT 21
Burgess Michael	Ithaca City Cem, Ithaca, NY 32
Burgess Michael	Ithaca City Cem, Ithaca, NY 15
Burgess Nathaniel	Duxbury Cem, Duxbury, MA 56
Burgess Prince	East Wareham, MA 16
Burgess Prince Lt	East Wareham (Agawam), Wareham, MA 34

Burgess Prince Lt	East Wareham Cem, Wareham, MA	28
Burgess Samuel	Stockdale Cem, Roann, Wabash Co, IN	77
Burgess Seth	Kelloggsville Cem, Sempronius, Cayuga Co, NY	57
Burgess Thomas	Center Cem, Harwich, MA	49
Burgess Thomas	Mayflower Cem, Duxbury, MA	58
Burgess William	Ch Cem, Butternuts, nr Gilbertsville, Otsego Co, NY	77
Burget Christopher	Stark Co, OH	44
Burgett Lambert	Erwin-Townsend Cem, Erwin, Steuben Co, NY	82
Burghert Christian	Peter Rothermal's priv Cem, Walnut Town, PA	59
Burgie Thomas	Pres Ch Cem, Basking Ridge, NJ	47
Burgin Mark	Concord Bapt Ch Cem, Forest City, Rutherford Co, NC	76
Burgis John	1st Parish Cem, Rochester, MA	58
Burham John Sr	Saile-Abeel Cem, Rt 32, far south Greene Co, NY	58
Burham Thomas	Pratt Corner Cem, Shutesbury, MA	53
Burhans Abraham	Burhans Ground, Flatbush, NY	36
Burhans Abraham Jr	Burhans Ground, Flatbush, NY	36
Burhans Benjamin	Burhans Ground, Flatbush, NY	36
Burhans Cornelius	Old Dutch Cem, Kingston, Ulster Co, NY	85
Burhans Cornelius	Potter Hollow, Rensselaerville, NY	32
Burhans Edward	Roxbury Cem, Delaware Co, NY	63
Burhans Henry	Dewitt Cem, Dewitt, NY	32
Burhans Ljerick	Finger Bur Gr, Mt Marian, NY	56
Burhans Petrus	Flatbush Cem, Kingston, Ulster Co, NY	73
Burhans Tjerck	Plattekill Cem, NY	15
Burk Edward	St Thomas Epis Ch Cem, Montgomery Co, PA	59
Burk Jesse	Old Cem, Westminster, VT	42
Burk John	Elkhorn Cem, Wayne Co, IN	72
Burk Jonathan	Hartland, VT	16
Burk Joseph	Columbia Twp Cem, Lorain Co, OH	53
Burk Silas	Dewitt Cem, Dewitt, NY	32
Burk Silas	Old Cem, Westminster, VT	42
Burke Henry	Vanderburg Cem, Decatur Co, IN	72
Burke Isaiah	Hartland, VT	16
Burke J	Fayette, MS	44
Burke John Maj	Old Cem, Bernardston, MA	46
Burke Joseph	Harvard Grove Cem, Lansing Ave & E 57th, Cleveland, OH	55
Burke Simeon	Old Cem, Westminster, VT	46
Burke Solomon	[no cem named], VT	17
Burke Thomas	Horseshoe Cem, Horseshoe Farm, Giles Co, VA	73
Burke William	Copps Hill Cem, Boston, MA	46
Burke William Jr	Burke Homestead Cem, Italy Valley, Yates Co, NY	69
Burkehalter John	[no cem named]	17
Burkhalter Joshua	Fam Cem, nr Buena Vista, Marion Co, GA	24
Burkhalter Peter	Egypt Churchyard, Lehigh Co, PA	50
Burkhalter Peter	Old Cem part, Egypt, Lehigh Co, PA	40
Burkhalter Peter Col	Egypt Cem, Egypt, PA	16
Burkhard Jehu	Ft McKinley on fam farm, Stringtown, OH	56
Burkhardt John	[no cem named], OH	25
Burks John	Spain Cem, nr Fayette, Franklin Co, MS	84
Burks Samuel	Matthew's Cem, St Francois Twp, Madison Co, MO	23
Burleigh Joseph	Union Bridge Cem, Lochmere, NH	29
Burleigh Samuel	Burleigh-Bartlett, NH	39
Burleigh Samuel	Sandwich Center Cem, Sandwich, NH	29
Burleigh Stevens	South Road Cem, Belmont, NH	36
Burleigh Thomas	Epping Cem, Epping, MA	45
Burleigh William	Burleigh Yard, Calef Hill, Sanbornton, NH	29
Burler Samuel	Old Cem, South Berwick, ME	55
Burley Ebenezer	Mansfield, PA	52
Burley Ebenezer	Prospect Cem, Mansfield, Tioga Co, PA	15
Burley Gordon	King Cem, Dorchester, NH	37
Burley Jacob	Fam Cem, Newmarket, NH	41

Abstract of Graves of Revolutionary Patriots 135

Burley John Lt	Old Cem at the Junction, Newmarket, NH 28
Burley Josiah	Fam Cem, Newmarket, NH 41
Burley Josiah Jr	Fam Cem, Newmarket, NH 41
Burley Nathaniel	D A R Cem, Sanbornton, NH 31
Burley William	Beverly, MA 55
Burlingame Christopher	Harmar Cem, across Muskingum River, Washington Co, OH 55
Burlingame Clark	Door Village Cem, La Porte, La Porte Co, IN 64
Burlingame David	Priv Cem, Kent farm, North Scituate, Providence Co, RI 31
Burlingame Eseck	Harrisville Cem, Harrisville, RI 51
Burlingame Jeremiah	Petersburg, NY 56
Burlingame Nathan	Mountain View (Lester) Cem, Lester, Broome Co, NY 78
Burlingame Nathan	Oneco Cem, Rt 14A, Sterling, CT 74
Burlingame Philip	Castleton Cem, Elmont, Queens Co, NY 80
Burlingame Stephen	East Greenwich Cem, Greenwich, RI 46
Burlingame Wanton	Attica Center Cem, Attica, Wyoming Co, NY 54
Burlingham Hopkins	Old Maples farm, Burke Hill Rd, Hartwick, NY 58
Burlingham Jeremiah	White Store (Evergreen) Cem, Norwich, Chenango Co, NY 71
Burlison David	Fam Cem, Nashville Rd, Rutherford Co, TN 33
Burman Wesley Jr	Old Cem, Essex, MA 45
Burnam John	6 mi N of Bowling Green, KY 26
Burnam John	McGinnis farm, 5 mi N of Bowling Green, Warren Co, KY 57
Burnap Abraham	Old Cem, Andover, CT 55
Burnap Daniel	New Andover Cem, Andover, CT 55
Burnap John	Cem on town common, Nelson, NH 35
Burnap Samuel	Old Village Cem, Temple, NH 28
Burnap Timothy	County Bridge Cem, Millbury, MA 56
Burnapp Isaac	Hopkinton Cem, Hopkinton, MA 60
Burne Alexander	West Alexander, PA 38
Burnell Ephraim	Harlow Cem, Cummington, Hampshire Co, MA 63
Burnell Joseph	Center Cem, Chesterfield, MA 53
Burnes Edmond	Cem, MacRansdell farm, Mercer Co, KY 45
Burnet Andrew	Pres Cem, Morristown, NJ 32
Burnet Daniel	Hillside Cem, Madison, NJ 30
Burnet David	Old First Pres Ch Cem, Newark, NJ 26
Burnet Matthias	Pres Cem, Morristown, NJ 32
Burnet Robert	Bush farm, nr Jasper, OH 56
Burnett Edmund	Old Cem, Hubbard, Trumbull, OH 55
Burnett Henry	Warwick Village, MA 31
Burnett James	Little Britain, NY 56
Burnett James	South Yard, Hampton, CT 31
Burnett Jonathan	West Cem, Granby, MA 58
Burnett Mathias	Whippany Cem, Whippany, Morris Co, NJ 81
Burnett Matthias	Connecticut Farms Pres Cem, Union, NJ 49
Burnett Robert	Bush Cem, Washington Court House, OH 57
Burnett Robert	Little Britain Cem, Little Britain, NJ 58
Burnett Samuel	Concord Cem, Williamsburg Twp, Clermont Co, OH 57
Burnett William	Old City Cem, Murfreesboro, TN 60
Burnett William	Warwick Village, MA 31
Burnham Abraham	Village Cem, Dunbarton, NH 45
Burnham Andrew	Milford, NH 15
Burnham Asa	Center Cem, Dunbarton, NH 31
Burnham Asa	Wellsburg Cem, Elmira, NY 33
Burnham Asa Maj	Aurora Village Cem, NY 15
Burnham Asa Maj	Aurora Village Cem, Ledyard, NY 41
Burnham Asahel	Wells (Hilltop) Cem, Chemung, Chemung Co, NY 78
Burnham Augustus	Laona, NY 15
Burnham Daniel	South Yard, Hampton, CT 31
Burnham Ebenezer	Old Essex Cem, Essex, MA 48
Burnham Elisha Capt	Beaver Meadow, Leyden, MA 00
Burnham Francis	Old Essex Cem, Essex, MA 48
Burnham Isaac	County Rd, Ipswich, MA 56

Burnham Isaac	East Hartland Cem, East Hartland, CT 60
Burnham Jacob	Priv Cem, Dame farm, North Nottingham, NH 27
Burnham James	Granby, MA 55
Burnham James	Hanson's Corners Cem, Somersworth, NH 31
Burnham James	South Yard, Hampton, CT 31
Burnham Jedediah	South Yard, Hampton, CT 31
Burnham Jedediah Dr	Old Cem, Kinsman, Trumbull Co, OH 55
Burnham John	Hampton Cem, Hampton, Windham Co, CT 62
Burnham John	South Yard, Hampton, CT 31
Burnham John Maj	Forest Hill Cem, East Derry, NH 38
Burnham Jonathan	Foster Cem, Wentworth, NH 36
Burnham Jonathan	Old Essex Cem, Essex, MA 48
Burnham Joseph	South Yard, Hampton, CT 31
Burnham Joshua Col	Milford, NH 15
Burnham Josiah	Clark's Corner, Hampton, CT 31
Burnham Nathan	Ackley, East Haddam, CT 56
Burnham Offen	North Cem, Hinsdale, NH 37
Burnham Petrus	Priv Cem, fam estate, Ulster Sanding, NY 45
Burnham Phineas	Center Cem, East Hartford, CT 19
Burnham Reuben	West Hartland Cem, West Hartland, CT 60
Burnham Roger	Center Cem, East Hartford, CT 19
Burnham Samuel	Center Cem, East Hartford, CT 19
Burnham Samuel	High Street Cem, Ipswich, MA 48
Burnham Thomas	High Street Cem, Ipswich, MA 48
Burnham Thomas	High St Cem, Ipswich, MA 56
Burnham Thomas	Putney Hill Cem, Hopkinton, NH 32
Burnham Thomas M	Essex, MA 55
Burnham Thomas Sr	High Street Cem, Ipswich, MA 48
Burnham Wesley Jr	Old Cem, Essex, MA 46
Burnham William	Schenectady Cem, Schenectady, NY 41
Burns Alexander	Massacred nr mouth of Lechry Creek, Dearborn Co, IN 24
Burns Alexander	Montour Cem, Allegheny Co, PA 57
Burns Ebenezer	Massacred nr mouth of Lechry Creek, Dearborn Co, IN 24
Burns George	Cem across Baker River fr Swainsboro Station, Rumney, NH 36
Burns John	Chestnut Ridge Bapt Ch Cem, Laurens Co, SC 70
Burns John	Massacred nr mouth of Lechry Creek, Dearborn Co, IN 24
Burns John	Milford, NH 15
Burns John Maj	Cem overlooking Burns Pond, Whitefield, NH 32
Burns John Maj	Whitefield, NH 48
Burns Walter	Old Cem, Newport, Newport Co, RI 31
Burns William	Fam Cem, nr Maysville, Jackson Co, GA 43
Burns William Capt	Blodgett Cem, Hudson, NH 28
Burnside Daniel	Seceder Ch (Portland Mills), Greene Twp, Parke Co, IN 71
Burnside Thomas	Cooperstown Junction, NY 31
Burnside Thomas	Old Bur Gr, Northumberland, NH 36
Burnside Thomas	Oneonta Cem, Oneonta, NY 34
Burnside Walter	Paint Lick Cem, Paint Lick, KY 58
Burpe Elijah	Old Cem, Sterling, MA 56
Burpee Elijah	Old Cem, Sterling, MA 63
Burpee Moses	Old Cem, Sterling, MA 49
Burpee Moses	Old Center Cem, Jaffrey, NH 37
Burpee Nathan	MacFarlan Cem, Grand Blanc, MI 38
Burpee Nathan	McFarlam Cem, Perry Rd, Genesee Co, MI 33
Burpee Nathan	Old Mtg Hs Cem, Webster, NH 34
Burpee Nathaniel Jr	First Cem, Candia, NH 29
Burr Aaron	Princeton Cem, Princeton, NJ 26
Burr Asa	Center Cem, Bellingham, MA 55
Burr Asa	River View Cem, Henrietta, Monroe Co, NY 79
Burr Charles	Old Bur Gr, Fairfield, CT 62
Burr Charles Capt	Oak Hill Cem, Brewer, ME 31
Burr Daniel	Mercer Village Cem, Mercer, ME 39

Burr David	Hingham Centre Cem, Hingham, MA	70
Burr David	Hingham, MA	52
Burr David	Old Bur Gr, Fairfield, CT	62
Burr Ebenezer	Greenfield Hill Cem, Fairfield, CT	62
Burr Ebenezer 3d	Greenfield Hill Cem, Fairfield, CT	62
Burr Elisha	Center Cem, Billingham, MA	51
Burr Elisha	Thomas Cem, North Swansea, MA	54
Burr Hezekiah	Fairfield East Bur Gr, Fairfield, CT	31
Burr Ichabod	Greenfield Hill Cem, Fairfield, CT	62
Burr Isaac	Hingham Cem, Hingham, MA	60
Burr Isaac	Rehoboth Village Cem, Rehoboth, MA	54
Burr Jesse	Greenfield Hill Cem, Fairfield, CT	62
Burr Joel	Village Cem, Galway, Saratoga Co, NY	77
Burr Joel	Village Cem, Galway, NY	41
Burr John	Armstrong Bur Gr, Malton, Saratoga Co, NY	77
Burr John	Torringford Cem, Torringford, CT	36
Burr John	Torrington Cem, Torrington, CT	31
Burr John	Van Cortlandville Cem, Peekskill, NY	41
Burr Jonathan	Village Cem, Sandwich, MA	56
Burr Joseph	Greenfield Hill Cem, Fairfield, CT	62
Burr Nathaniel	Thomas Cem, North Swansea, MA	54
Burr Ozias	Pease Cem, Pompey, Onondaga Co, NY	81
Burr Reuben	Torrington Cem, Torrington, CT	55
Burr Rufus	North Cem, Warren, RI	54
Burr Russell	Torrington Cem, Torrington, CT	55
Burr Samuel	Old Bloomfield Cem, Bloomfield, CT	55
Burr Thaddeus	Old Bur Gr, Fairfield, CT	62
Burr Thomas	Hingham Centre Cem, Hingham, MA	70
Burr Thomas Lt	Hingham Center Cem, Hingham, MA	46
Burr Timothy	Gold St Cem, Old Hartford, CT	19
Burr Timothy	Greenfield Hill Cem, Fairfield, CT	62
Burr Wakeman	Old Bur Gr, Fairfield, CT	62
Burr William	North Easton Cem, corner Elm St, Easton, MA	55
Burr William	Southford, East Haddam, CT	56
Burr William	Southford Cem, Southford, CT	37
Burrage John	Western Cem, West Lynn, MA	56
Burrage Thomas	Dover, MA	55
Burrage William	Pine Grove Cem, Leominster, MA	50
Burrall Charles	Grassy Hill Cem, Falls Village, CT	65
Burrall Charles	Protestant, Canaan, CT	56
Burrell Abraham	Hewins St Cem, Sheffield, MA	40
Burrell Andrew	North Weymouth Cem, North Weymouth, MA	62
Burrell Benjamin	Reed Cem, South Weymouth, MA	62
Burrell David	Hewins St, Sheffield, MA	56
Burrell Ebenezer	Western Cem, West Lynn, MA	56
Burrell Ephraim	North Weymouth Cem, North Weymouth, MA	62
Burrell James	Reed Cem, South Weymouth, MA	62
Burrell John	[no cem named], PA	19
Burrell Micajah	Western Cem, West Lynn, MA	56
Burrell Nathaniel	West State St Cem, Athens, Athens Co, OH	55
Burrell Reuben	Highland Cem, South Weymouth, MA	50
Burrell Samuel	Elmwood Cem, South Weymouth, MA	50
Burres Ebenezzer	Old Bloomfield Cem, Bloomfield, CT	55
Burrett Peleg	Hanover Green, Hanover Twp, PA	52
Burrill Abraham	Hewins St Cem, Sheffield, Berkshire Co, MA	80
Burrill David	Hewins St Cem, Sheffield, MA	41
Burrill Ebenezer	Howard St, Salem, MA	56
Burrill Ebenezer	Old Cem, Newport, RI	52
Burrill Ebenezer	Western Cem, West Lynn, MA	56
Burrill John	Foxcraft Cem, Sangerville, Piscataquis Co, ME	61
Burrill John	Western Cem, West Lynn, MA	56

Burrill John	Western Cem, West Lynn, MA 56
Burrill Samuel	Western Bur Gr, West Lynn, MA 46
Burris Soloman	Pleasant Grove Ch Cem, Stanly Co, NC 49
Burris William	Bethesda Cem, York Co, SC 70
Burritt Anthony Dr	Southbury Cem, Southbury, CT 46
Burritt Charles Sgt	Stratfield Old Bur Gr, Bridgeport, CT 15
Burritt Hezekiah	Cong Cem, Stratford, CT 31
Burritt Joseph	Union Cem, Stratford, CT 31
Burritt Nathan	Union Cem, Stratford, CT 31
Burritt Zolman	Old Cem, Jeffersonville, IN 15
Burrough Benjamin	Haddonfield Friends Cem, Haddonfield, NJ 47
Burrough Ed Lt	Stratfield Old Bur Gr, Bridgeport, CT 15
Burrough George Capt	Greenwood Cem, East Parish, New Haverhill, MA 31
Burrough Gideon	Haddonfield Friends Cem, Haddonfield, NJ 47
Burrough Joseph	Haddonfield Friends Cem, Haddonfield, NJ 47
Burrough Thomas	Haddonfield Friends Cem, Haddonfield, NJ 47
Burroughs Benjamin	East Kay Cem, Pike, Wyoming Co, NY 64
Burroughs Benjamin	Hillside Cem, Madison, NJ 46
Burroughs Benjamin	Pittsgrove Pres Cem, Pittsgrove, NJ 47
Burroughs Benjamin	Pres Cem, Daretown, NJ 47
Burroughs Benjamin	Quaker Cem, Clinton, Dutchess Co, NY 56
Burroughs Boaz	Old Zoar Cem, Dents Run, WV 41
Burroughs Cornelius	Pittsgrove Pres Cem, Pittsgrove, NJ 47
Burroughs Daniel	Griswold Cem, Plano, Kendall Co, IL 73
Burroughs David	Pine Grove Cem, Warren, MA 46
Burroughs Edward	Old Stratfield, Bridgeport, CT 56
Burroughs Elijah	Hillside Cem, Shalersville, OH 53
Burroughs Ezekial	Old fam Cem, nr Brown's Chapel, Monongalia Co, WV 40
Burroughs Greene	Old Newport Cem, Newport, RI 65
Burroughs James	Pittsgrove Pres Cem, Pittsgrove, NJ 47
Burroughs Jeremiah	Skenesborough, NY 52
Burroughs Joel	Ye Old Trail Cem, Alstead, NH 43
Burroughs John	Pittsgrove Pres Cem, Pittsgrove, NJ 47
Burroughs John	Shepard Settlement, Onondaga Co, NY 52
Burroughs John	Ye Old Trail Cem, Alstead, NH 43
Burroughs Phillip	Warwick, NY 32
Burroughs Steven Capt	Stratfield Old Bur Gr, Bridgeport, CT 15
Burroughs William	Old bur gr, Newport, RI 39
Burrowes Stephen	Pres Ch Cem, Pennington, NJ 46
Burrowes Stephen	Pres Cem, Pennington, NJ 32
Burrows Elisha	Fam Cem, East Hartford, NY 57
Burrows Hubbard	Burnet's Corners Cem, Groton, New London Co, CT 61
Burrows John	Cem, Mystic, CT 51
Burrows John	Mystic Cem, Mystic, CT 46
Bursley John	West Barnstable, MA 55
Bursley Joseph Jr	West Barnstable, MA 55
Burt Abel	Glebe St, Taunton, MA 56
Burt Abner Jr	Berkley Common Cem, Berkley, MA 55
Burt Alvin	East End Cem, East Aurora, NY 33
Burt Benjamin	Immanuel Ch Cem, Bellows Falls, VT 48
Burt Benjamin	Wellsburg Cem, Wellsburg, NY 32
Burt Caleb	West (New Boston) Cem, Sandisfield, MA 56
Burt Daniel	Riverside, NY 30
Burt Daniel	Walker Bur Gr, Taunton, Bristol Co, MA 86
Burt David	Wellsburg Cem, Wellsburg, NY 32
Burt Deen	Berkley Common Cem, Berkley, MA 55
Burt Ebenezer	Old Pine Ridge Cem, Hancock, NH 32
Burt Ebenezer	West Brattleboro Cem, Brattleboro, VT 25
Burt Enos	Common, Berkley, MA 52
Burt George	Cem, Broadway, Rt 138, Taunton, MA 55
Burt Henry	Oakland Cem, Taunton, Bristol Co, MA 86

Abstract of Graves of Revolutionary Patriots

Burt James	Cem, Broadway, Rt 138, Taunton, MA	55
Burt Joel	Center Cem, Westhampton, MA	53
Burt John	Plain Cem, Taunton, Bristol Co, MA	86
Burt John Jr	Chatham Co Cem, nr Pittsboro, Chatham Co, NC	58
Burt Joseph	West Parish Bur Gr, Andover, MA	26
Burt Martin	West Part Cem, Southamptom, MA	37
Burt Moses	Village Cem, Walpole, NH	25
Burt Moses	Walpole, NH	16
Burt Samuel Jr	Cem, West Part, Southampton, MA	49
Burt Samuel Sr	Cem, West Part, Southampton, MA	49
Burt Simeon	Berkley Commons, Berkley, MA	55
Burt Simeon	Bethlehem St Cem, Bethlehem, NH	32
Burt Stephen	Berkley Commons, Berkley, MA	55
Burt Thomas	Drake Cem, Chemung Co, NY	32
Burt Thomas	Oakland Cem, Taunton, Bristol Co, MA	86
Burt Thomas	Upper Lisle Cem, Upper Lisle, Broome Co, NY	78
Burt Williams	White Fam Cem, Taunton, MA	48
Burtis James	Elmont Cem, Elmont, Queens Co, NY	80
Burtis John	Elmont Cem, Elmont, Queens Co, NY	80
Burton – Col	Nr Lebanon, Wilson Co, TN	24
Burton Abraham	Vale End Cem, Wilton, NH	34
Burton Alazor	Bapt Ch Cem, Wilton, Saratoga Co, NY	78
Burton Benjamin	Baker Cem, 9 mi NE of Millsboro, Sussex Co, DE	46
Burton Benjamin	Newcomb Cem, Warren, ME	55
Burton Benjamin Capt	Woolsey Cem, 10 mi NE of Millsboro, Sussex Co, DE	46
Burton Col	Nr Lebanon, TN	23
Burton George	Halls Ridge, Jefferson Co, IN	25
Burton Jacob	Hedges Cem, 3½ mi W of Lancaster, OH	56
Burton Joab	First Cong Cem, Griswold, CT	62
Burton John	Fam Cem, 4 mi E of Harbeson, Sussex Co, DE	46
Burton John	St Georges Cem, New Castle Co, DE	46
Burton John Pleasant	Burton, Mitchell, Lawrence Co, IN	56
Burton John Pleasant	Fam Cem, nr Mitchell, Lawrence Co, IN	72
Burton Josiah	Pres Cem, Albany, NY	30
Burton Robert	Judge Williams Cem, Vance Co, NC	49
Burton Rufus	Pomfret, Windham Co, CT	24
Burton William	Crew farm, Fayette, Howard Co, MO	15
Burton William	Wallace Cem, Prairie Twp, Howard Co, MO	85
Burton William M	Nr Cooper's Fort, New Hope, MO	15
Burwell Lewis	Fam Cem, his mansion, Stoneland, VA	57
Burwell Lewis	Stoneland, Mecklenburg Co, VA	56
Burwell Nathaniel	Vermont Place Cem, King William Co, VA	55
Busbee Samuel	Schuylerville Cem, Schuylerville, Saratoga Co, NY	77
Bush Aaron	Mechanic St Cem, Westfield, MA	56
Bush Amos	Mechanic St Cem, Westfield, MA	56
Bush Benjamin	Shepard Settlement Cem, Skaneateles, Onondaga Co, NY	78
Bush Caleb	Clam River Cem, Sandisfield, MA	56
Bush Conradt	Fam Cem, N of Pompey Hill, Pompey, Onondaga Co, NY	78
Bush Conradt	Parma Center Cem, Parma, NY	41
Bush Conradt	Sand Knoll, his farm, Pompey, NY	52
Bush Daniel	Barnard, Sheffield, MA	56
Bush Daniel	Fam plantation, Franklin Co, GA	54
Bush Daniel	Harrold Cem, Hempfield Twp, Westmoreland Co, PA	56
Bush David	Congruity, Westmoreland Co, PA	56
Bush David	Epis Cem, New Castle, New Castle Co, DE	46
Bush David Capt	Pittsfield Cem, South Border, Pittsfield, MA	40
Bush David Jr	Barnard Cem, Sheffield, MA	41
Bush Ebenezer	Fairhaven Cem, Fairhaven, VT	47
Bush Ebenezer	Shoreham, VT	15
Bush Francis	Farm, Clark Co, KY	56
Bush George	Minden Cem, Minden, Montgomery Co, NY	72

Bush George	Shawnee Cem, PA 38
Bush Henry	Dutch Ch Cem, Hyde Park, NY 21
Bush Henry	Hawley Cem (field stone marker), Taylor, Cortland Co, NY 36
Bush Henry	Peruville Cem, Peruville, NY 31
Bush Henry Sr	Pres Cem, Middle Smithfield, Monroe Co, PA 55
Bush Jacobus	Hawley Cem, Taylor, Cortland Co, NY 36
Bush John	Beers Cem, Danby, NY 32
Bush John	Clark, KY 56
Bush John	Epis Ch Cem, Clarenceville, Ontario, Can 64
Bush John	St Andrew's Ch Cem, Staten Island, Richmond Co, NY 74
Bush John Capt	Beers Cem, Danbury, NY 15
Bush Jonathan	Turin, NY 15
Bush Joseph Lt	Maple St Cem, North Brookfield, MA 17
Bush Leonard	Fam Cem, Fayette Co, OH 18
Bush Leonard Sr	Fam Cem, Sugar Creek, Union Twp, Fayette Co, OH 56
Bush Michael	Nr Austin, Concord Twp, Ross Co, OH 55
Bush Obidiah	Barnard, Sheffield, MA 56
Bush Peter	Zion's Stone Ch Cem, Kreidersville, Northampton Co, PA 40
Bush Prescott	Poplar Springs Cem, Preston, Webster Co, GA 40
Bush Richard	Common Bur Gr, Newport, RI 56
Bush Richard	Rehobeth Village Cem, Rehobeth, MA 38
Bush Richard Maj	Beers Cem, Danbury, NY 15
Bush Rufus	Enfield St Cem, Enfield, CT 24
Bush Samuel	Barnard Cem, Sheffield, MA 41
Bush Samuel Dr	Barnard Cem, Sheffield, MA 41
Bush Silas	Mechanic St Cem, Westfield, MA 56
Bush Stephen	Sheridan Center Cem, Sheridan, Chautauqua Co, NY 71
Bush Stephen	Sheridan, NY 15
Bush William	Cem, 7 mi S of Winchester, Boonesboro Pike, Clark Co, KY 51
Bush William	Clark, KY 56
Bush Zacheus	Houseville, NY 16
Bushanan Archibald	Fam Cem, 9 mi NE of Nashville, TN 57
Bushee Consider	Surles Fam Cem, nr Hanna's Pond, Dunn, Harnett Co, NC 67
Bushee Consider Corp	Nr Dunn, NC 48
Bushes Samuel	Aban Cem, Broad St, Schuylerville, Saratoga Twp, NY 41
Bushey Henry	Luth Cem, Reisterstown, MD 19
Bushnell Alexander	Hartford, Trumbull Co, OH 55
Bushnell Daniel	Center of Hartford, Trumbull, OH 55
Bushnell Dowd	Waitsfield Cem, Waitsfield, VT 47
Bushnell Elijah	Bushnell Cem, Lexington, Greene Co, NY 75
Bushnell Gideon	Town Hill Cem, Lakeville, CT 64
Bushnell Jabez	Christ Ch Yard, Norwich, CT 18
Bushnell Jason	Spring Grove Cem, Cincinnati, Hamilton Co, OH 76
Bushnell Jeremiah	Old Town Hall Cem, Salisbury, CT 64
Bushnell John	Antrim, NH 15
Bushnell John	Norwich, CT 30
Bushnell John Handley	Garland Cem, Clarkson, Monroe Co, NY 79
Bushnell Samuel Jr	Old Town Hall Cem, Salisbury, CT 64
Buss Ebenezer	Old Cem, Sterling, MA 63
Buss John	Old Pine Grove Cem, Leominster, MA 47
Buss Samuel Lt	Old Center Cem, Jaffrey, NH 37
Buss Silas	South Yard, Wilton, NH 34
Buss Stephen	Pine Grove Cem, Leominster, MA 50
Bussard Andrew	Stumpf Ch Cem, Salt Creek Twp, Pickaway Co, OH 53
Bussee John	South Cem, Dorchester, MA 46
Bussell William	Tunells Hill, nr Rogersville, Hawkins Co, TN 71
Busseron Francois Riday	St Francis Xavier Cem, Vincennes, Knox Co, IN 72
Bussey Benjamin	Old Parish (Tomb), Jamaica Plain, Boston, MA 56
Bussey John	North Dorchester Cem, Boston, MA 55
Bussing Harman	Florida Cem, Ref Ch, Minaville, Montgomery Co, NY 36
Buswell Daniel	Ancient Bur Gr, Bradford, MA 28

Buswell Daniel	Garland, NY 15
Buswell Elias	Old Town Farm Cem, Sanbornton, NH 34
Buswell John	Cem betw Allen's Mills & Loudon Ridge, NH 40
Buswell John	Grasmere Cem, Goffstown, NH 28
Buswell John	Old Cem, Rindge, NH 36
Buswell Moses	First Cem, Candia, NH 29
Buswell Noah	Tin Corner Cem, Tilton, NH 35
Buswell Samuel Ens	First Cem, Candia, NH 29
Buswell Thomas Capt	Cleveland Yard, Canterbury Twp, CT 22
Butcher George	Massacred nr mouth of Lechry Creek, Dearborn Co, IN 24
Butcher Samuel	Kincheloe Cem, Staunton Pike, nr Parkersburg, WV 20
Butler Abijah	Old Pine Grove Cem, Leominster, MA 47
Butler Beethland Foot	[no cem named], SC 15
Butler Benjamin	Parade Cem, Deerfield, NH 28
Butler Comfort	Broad Street Cem, Meriden, CT 56
Butler Daniel	Old Bur Gr, Mill Rd, Falmouth, MA 64
Butler Daniel	Pelham, NH 54
Butler Daniel Dr	Old North Cem, Old Hartford, CT 19
Butler David	Old Bur Gr, Mill Rd, Falmouth, MA 64
Butler David	Old Bur Gr, NW Corner, Granville, OH 56
Butler David Lt	Gumpus Cem, Pelham, NH 34
Butler Ebenezer Jr	West of Columbus, OH 56
Butler Ebenezer Sr	Pompey Hill Cem, Pompey Hill, Pompey, Onondaga Co, NY 78
Butler Eli Capt	Utica, NY 16
Butler Elijah	Edgartown, MA 55
Butler Enoch	Town Hall Cem, Pittsfield, NH 28
Butler Ephraim	Riverside Cem, Farmington, ME 55
Butler Ezekial	Farm Cem, Branford, CT 41
Butler Ezekiel 2nd	City Cem, sect B, Hudson, Columbia Co, NY 41
Butler Ezra	Seymour Cem, Seymour, CT 15
Butler Ezra	Trinity, CT 37
Butler Gideon	West Hartford, CT 38
Butler Henry Gen	Fam Cem, Nottingham Square, Nottingham, NH 27
Butler Henry Gen	Nottingham Square, Nottingham, NH 17
Butler Hezekiah	Old Cem, Wethersfield, CT 56
Butler Jacob	Gumpus Cem, Pelham, NH 34
Butler James	Aban Cem, Cass Co, IN 24
Butler James	Church Cem, Buckland, MA 56
Butler James	Torey Massacre site, Clouds Creek, Edgefield Co, SC 52
Butler Jethro	Hebron Cem, Summmerfield, Claiborne Co, LA 78
Butler John	Cherry Valley Cem, East Springfield, NY 33
Butler John	Mt Pleasant Christian Ch Cem, Adair Co, KY 49
Butler John	Old Cem, Wethersfield, CT 56
Butler John	Old Essex Cem, Essex, MA 48
Butler John	Town Cem, Sandown, NH 33
Butler John George	Rose Hill Cem, Cumberland, Allegany Co, MD 80
Butler John Jr	Edgartown, MA 15
Butler Jonathan Corp	Lyndboro Cem, Lyndboro, NH 31
Butler Joseph	Fam Cem, 3 mi fr Henderson, KY 31
Butler Joseph	Old fam Cem, Tapp farm, Henderson, Henderson Co, KY 74
Butler Medad	Butler-Bailey Cem, Stuyvesant, Columbia Co, NY 41
Butler Moses	Gold St Cem, Old Hartford, CT 19
Butler Nathan	Gumpus Cem, Pelham, NH 34
Butler Nathaniel	Kirkland Avenue Cem, Clinton, Oneida Co, NY 79
Butler Nathaniel	Mount Hope Cem, nr old schoolhouse, Sanford, ME 40
Butler Patrick	Nr Elberton, GA 35
Butler Percival	Old Cem, W side of Lock Rd, Butler Park, Carroll Co, KY 51
Butler Phineas	Framingham Cem, Framingham, MA 47
Butler Phineas	Old Butler Cem, Thomaston, ME 55
Butler Richard	In St Clair's defeat in Northwest Territory, OH 55
Butler Rufus	Old Bur Gr, Mill Rd, Falmouth, MA 64

Butler Salmon — Kirkland Avenue Cem, Clinton, Oneida Co, NY 79
Butler Silas — Edgartown Cem, Edgartown, MA 45
Butler Silas — Edgartown, MA 15
Butler Stephen — Paradise Park, Stow, OH 45
Butler Stephen — Stow Corners, Summit Co, OH 15
Butler Thomas — Cem, Stanford, ME 51
Butler Thomas — Phippsburg, ME 53
Butler Thomas Sr — Springs Cem, Roaring Springs, Blair Co, PA 56
Butler Tobias — Antrim, NH 15
Butler William — Cincinnati, OH 44
Butler William — Huntington, OH 56
Butler William Maj Gen — [no cem named], SC 15
Butler Zachariah — Nr Elberton, GA 35
Butler Zebulon — Hollenbeck Cem, Wilkes-Barre, PA 52
Butler Zebulon — Hollenback Cem, Wilkes-Barre, PA 53
Butler Zebulon — Prob Hamilton Co or Butler Co, OH 55
Butler Zephaniah — Fam Cem, Bood farm, Deerfield Rd, NH 27
Butler Zephaniah — Old Edgartown Cem, Edgartown, MA 47
Butman Benjamin — Dixmont Corner Cem, Dixmont, ME 31
Butt Epaphroditus — Old Brooks farm, St Julian Creek, Norfolk, VA 34
Butterfield Ebenezer — Dunstable Cem, Dunstable, MA 45
Butterfield Isaac — Caledonia, NY 15
Butterfield Isaac — East Wilton, ME 15
Butterfield Isaac — North Cem, Westmoreland, NH 25
Butterfield James — Cooperstown, Otsego Co, NY 56
Butterfield John Maj — Grasmere Cem, Goffstown, NH 28
Butterfield Jonathan — Old Bur Gr, Arlington, MA 56
Butterfield Jones — North Cem, Westmoreland, NH 25
Butterfield Leonard — Old Mtg Hs, Dunstable, MA 56
Butterfield Peter — Old Bur Gr, Townsend, MA 48
Butterfield Peter Capt — Grasmere Cem, Goffstown, NH 28
Butterfield Samuel — Cem back of courthouse, Farmington, ME 45
Butterfield Samuel — Fam Cem, Farmington, ME 53
Butterfield Samuel — West Cambridge Cem, Cambridge, MA 45
Butterfield Timothy — North Cem, Westmoreland, NH 25
Butterfield Timothy — Old Cem, Westmoreland, NH 60
Butters James — New Cem, Wilmington, MA 56
Butters James — Wildwood Cem, Wilmington, MA 56
Butters Jesse — New Cem, Wilmington, MA 56
Butters Joseph — New Cem, Wilmington, MA 56
Butters Reuben — New Cem, Wilmington, MA 56
Butters Reuben — New Cem, Wilmington, MA 56
Butters Samuel — New Cem, Wilmington, MA 56
Butters Samuel — Old North Bur Gr, Concord, NH 41
Butters Samuel — Old North Cem, Concord, NH 56
Butters Simeon — Exeter Cem, Exeter, ME 56
Butters William — New Cem, Wilmington, MA 56
Butters William — Wildwood Cem, Wilmington, MA 56
Butterworth Hezekiah — Fam farm, East Warren, RI 51
Button Asa — Rural Cem, Danby, NY 15
Button Charles — Fam Cem, Clarendon, VT 38
Button Charles — Smith Cem, Clarendon, VT 24
Button Charles — Smith Cem, Clarendon, VT 25
Button Edward — Westerly, RI 15
Button Matthias Capt — Wells Cem, VT 15
Button Matthias Capt — Wells Village Cem, VT 48
Button Newberry — New Haven, CT 17
Button Samuel — River Bend Cem, Westerly, RI 48
Button Samuel — Westerly, RI 15
Buttrick John Maj — Hill Cem, Concord, MA 46
Buttrick Oliver — Pioneer Cem, Gainesville, Wyoming Co, NY 80

Buttrick Samuel Jr — Old Bur Gr, Concord, MA 47
Buttrill William — Bethel Cem, Jackson, Butts Co, GA 78
Buttrill William — Old Bethel Bur Gr, 2 mi fr Jackson, Butts Co, GA 15
Buttrill William — Old Bethel Cem, Butts Co, GA 24
Butts James Lt — Fam Cem, Hancock Co, GA 31
Butts Josiah — Old Cem, Dalton, MA 29
Butts Samuel — South Yard, Brooklyn, CT 30
Butts Sherebiah Capt — Westminster Ch Cem, Canterbury Twp, CT 21
Butts William — Mount Albion Cem, Albion, NY 34
Butts William — Mount Albion Cem, Albion, NY 31
Buxton Benjamin — New Boston Cem, New Boston, NH 28
Buxton Benjamin — New Boston, NH 16
Buxton James Capt — Fam Cem, Smithfield, RI 45
Buxton James Capt — Fam bur gr, Rt 146, Slatersville, North Smithfield, RI 40
Buxton John — Burdette Loomis Cem, nr Danby line, VT 48
Buxton John — Danby, VT 15
Buxton Stephen — Park St Cem, North Reading, MA 42
Buys Simon — Rumbout Precinct, Dutchess Co, NY 56
Buzzell Jonathan Ens — Jenness farm, Middleton Ridge, Middleton, NH 39
Buzzell Solomon — Priv Cem, Northwood, NH 37
Byam Samuel — Templeton Cem, Templeton, MA 47
Byer Frederick — Hoke Cem, nr Greencastle, Franklin Co, PA 56
Byerly Jacob — Brush Creek Ch Cem, nr Manor, Westmoreland Co, PA 56
Byers David — Priv Cem on hilltop, fam prop, 4 mi SW of Gettysburg, PA 56
Byers James — Kirkwood Cem, London, OH 43
Byers Nathan — Fam bur gr, betw Gaffney & Chesnee, Spartanburg Co, SC 71
Byers Robert — Center Cem, Iredell Co, NC 49
Byers Thomas — Claysville, priv plot, Washington Co, PA 56
Byers William — Darke Co, OH 55
Byers William — Nr Franklin, Howard Co, MO 34
Byington Daniel — Center Cem, Wolcott, CT 57
Byington Daniel — Center, Wolcott, CT 56
Byington Samuel — Center Cem, Southwick, MA 56
Byram Edward — Rocky Spring Cem, nr New Petersburg, OH 15
Byram Joseph — Caldwell Pres Cem, Caldwell, NJ 32
Byrd Jonathan — Putnam Co, IN 16
Byrns Larry — Point Pleasant Cem, Clermont Co, OH 55
Byrum Benjamin — Randolph Co, IL 48
Byxbe Moses — Oak Grove Cem, Delaware Co, OH 18

Abstract of Graves of Revolutionary Patriots

C

Cabbage Adam	Fam Cem, Washburn, Grainger Co, TN 80
Cabbage John	Fam Cem, Washburn, Grainger Co, TN 80
Cabel Joseph	Bruton Parish Ch Cem, Williamsburg, VA 52
Cabell William Sr	Union Hall, VA 52
Cable Philip	Union Cem, Steubenville, Jefferson Co, OH 78
Cable Philip Capt	Union Cem, Steubenville, OH 25
Cable Wheeler	Stratfield Old Bur Gr, Bridgeport, CT 15
Cabot Stephen	Broad St, Salem, MA 56
Cackler Christian	Fam Cem, Streetsboro, OH 53
Cadmus Andries	Dundee Lake, Alyeas farm, Bergen Co, NJ 54
Cadmus Henry	Belleville Ref Ch Cem, NJ 26
Cadmus Henry	Dutch Ref Ch Cem, Belleville, NJ 27
Cadmus Henry	Dutch Ref Ch Cem, Belleville, NJ 27
Cadmus Isaac	Dutch Ref Ch Cem, Belleville, NJ 27
Cadmus John	Belleville Ref Ch Cem, NJ 26
Cadmus John H	Dutch Ref Ch Cem, Belleville, NJ 27
Cadmus John P	Dutch Ref Ch Cem, Belleville, NJ 27
Cadmus Peter	Belleville Ref Ch Cem, NJ 26
Cadmus Peter	Dutch Ref Ch Cem, Belleville, NJ 27
Cadmus Peter	Second River Dutch Ref Ch Cem, Belleville, NJ 73
Cadmus Thomas	Bur gr adjoining 1st Pres Ch, Caldwell, Essex Co, NJ 31
Cadmus Thomas	Dutch Ref Ch Cem, Belleville, NJ 27
Cadwallader John	Shrewsbury Ch Cem, Kennedyville, Kent, MD 74
Cadwell –	West Hartford Cem, Hartford, CT 19
Cadwell Aaron	Old Cem, North Main St, West Hartford, CT 31
Cadwell Aaron	West Hartford, CT 38
Cadwell Joseph	West Hartford, CT 38
Cadwell Mathew Jr	Stockbridge Cem, Stockbridge, MA 47
Cadwell Mathew Sr	Stockbridge Cem, Stockbridge, MA 47
Cadwell Matthew	Spencer Hill Cem, Manchester, CT 19
Cadwell Phineas	Brookfield, WI 29
Cadwell Reuben	Old Cem, Fabius, Onondaga Co, NY 75
Cadwell Theodore	Cadwell's Corners, Cattaraugus Co, NY 35
Cady Benjamin	Oldest Killingly, Putnam, CT 56
Cady David	Ayvault Rd Cem, Monroe Co, NY 33
Cady David	Florida Cem, Ref Ch, Minaville, Montgomery Co, NY 36
Cady David	South Killingly Cem, South Killingly, CT 28
Cady David Capt	Old Yard, South Killingly, CT 29
Cady Ebenezer	Babcock plot, Surowiec farm, Red Rock, Columbia Co, NY 79
Cady Ebenezer	New Concord Cem, Columbia Co, NY 42
Cady Eleazer	Maple St, Hinsdale, MA 54
Cady Eleazer	New Canaan Cem, Columbia Co, NY 42
Cady Elias	Nr Holly, MI 15
Cady Elias Lt	Trinity Ch Cem, Cornish, NH 29
Cady Elijah	East Chatham Cem, Columbia Co, NY 42
Cady Elisha	Florida Cem, Ref Ch, Minaville, Montgomery Co, NY 36
Cady Jeremiah	Sempronius, NY 56
Cady Ladol	Dry Creek, Moravia, NY 15
Cady Manasseh	[no cem named] 17
Cady Oliver	Canaan, Columbia Co, NY 56
Cady Rufus	Garbutts, Monroe Co, NY 33
Cady Solomon	Oldest Killingly, Putnam, CT 56
Cady Squire	Old Town Cem, Plainfield, CT 15
Cady Zadoc	Dry Creek Cem, Moravia, NY 41

Cage William	Cage's Bend, Sumner Co, TN	29
Cahall James	Shinkle Ridge Cem, Lewis Twp, Brown Co, OH	55
Cahel – Ens	Massacred nr mouth of Lechry Creek, Dearborn Co, IN	24
Cahill James	Nr Higginsport, OH	15
Cahoon William	Kirtland, Lake Co, OH	26
Cahoone John	Old Cem, Farewell St, Newport, RI	35
Cahoone John Jr	Old Cem, Farewell St, Newport, RI	35
Cain Daniel	Fort Hill Cem, Hingham, MA	53
Cain Dennis	St Michael's Ch Cem, Trenton, NJ	28
Cain James	Massacred nr mouth of Lechry Creek, Dearborn Co, IN	24
Cain James Jr	Williamsburg Cem, Williamsburg, Clermont Co, OH	74
Cain Jonathan	Ft Hill, Hingham, MA	56
Cain Richard	Forks of Cheat Bapt Cem, nr Stewarttown, WV	41
Cain William	Massacred nr mouth of Lechry Creek, Dearborn Co, IN	24
Caison John G	Britton Pres Ch Cem, Cleveland Co, NC	49
Caldcleugh Andrew	Lexington City Cem, Davidson Co, NC	72
Calder George Beston	Phipps St Cem, Boston, MA	47
Calder John	Nr Darien, McIntosh Co, GA	39
Calder Robert	Nantucket, MA	52
Calder William	Phipps St Cem, Brighton, MA	46
Caldwell Aaron	Green Mount Cem, VT	20
Caldwell Daniel	Sugar Creek Pres Cem, Mecklenburg Co, NC	72
Caldwell David Rev	Buffalo Pres Ch Cem, Guilford Co, NC	49
Caldwell Ebenezer	South Side Cem, Ipswich, MA	48
Caldwell Hugh Jr	Center Cem, Lawrence Twp, Hyde, Clearfield Co, PA	75
Caldwell James	Blodgett Cem, Hudson, NH	28
Caldwell James	Cem, Old Davisville, S of Iron City, Calhoun Co, AL	15
Caldwell James	Fam Cem, Westport, PA	56
Caldwell James	Greenwood Cem, WV	24
Caldwell James	New Boston Cem, New Boston, NH	28
Caldwell James	New Boston, NH	16
Caldwell James	Trenton Cem, Condit, Trenton Twp, Delaware Co, OH	53
Caldwell James Rev	Elizabethtown Point, NJ	24
Caldwell James S	Nr Farmington, MO	16
Caldwell John	Caldwell Cem, Vigo Co, IN	72
Caldwell John	Fam Cem, Adair Co, KY	49
Caldwell John	Killed in Wyoming Massacre, Wyoming, PA	52
Caldwell John	Old North Cem, Ipswich, MA	55
Caldwell John	State Cem, Frankfort, KY	15
Caldwell John	Sugar Hill Cem, East Weare, NH	33
Caldwell John	West Northfield, Northfield, MA	55
Caldwell Joseph	Old Cem, East Buckland, MA	51
Caldwell Joseph Jr	Old Cem, East Buckland, MA	51
Caldwell Perrin	Washington Pike Ch Cem, Knoxville, TN	29
Caldwell Philip	Honeoye Falls Cem, Mendon, Monroe Co, NY	34
Caldwell Phineas	Union Grove, Racine Co, WI	56
Caldwell Robert	Concord Cem, Rushville Twp, Rush Co, IN	72
Caldwell Robert	Fam Cem, W of Carthage, Hamilton Co, OH	55
Caldwell Robert	Perkins Fam Cem, Burke Co, NC	49
Caldwell Robert	Pricetown Cem, Newton Twp, Trumbull Co, OH	55
Caldwell Samuel	Antrim, NH	15
Caldwell Samuel	Carthage, IL	15
Caldwell Samuel	Goshen Cem, Gaston Co, NC	49
Caldwell Samuel Lt	Sugar Hill Cem, East Weare, NH	33
Caldwell Thomas	Center Cem, Dunbarton, NH	31
Caldwell Thomas	Old North Cem, Ipswich, MA	55
Caldwell Thomas Capt	Dunbarton, NH	15
Caldwell William	Lamington, Somerset Co, NJ	48
Caldwell William	Lee Hill Cem, Lee, NH	50
Caldwell William	Oxford Cem, Oxford, Butler, OH	55
Caldwell William	Westfield Cem, Columbiana Co, OH	55

Abstract of Graves of Revolutionary Patriots

Calef James	Webster, ME 18
Calef John Col	Kingston Plains Cem, Kingston, NH 30
Calef Joseph	Kingston Plains Cem, Kingston, NH 30
Calfe John Capt	Town Cem, Hampstead, NH 28
Calfin Ebenezer	Eustis St Cem, Boston, MA 46
Calhohn Thomas	Aban Cem, East Springfield, Jefferson Co, OH 41
Calhoon James Jr	Lebanon Cem, Mifflin Twp, Allegheny Co, PA 71
Calhoon James Sr	Lebanon Cem, Mifflin Twp, Allegheny Co, PA 71
Calhoun George	Jones Cem, 1 mi S of Sorgho, Daviess Co, KY 31
Calhoun George	Jones Cem, Daviess Co, KY 30
Calhoun George	Ruby farm, 1 mi SW of Sorgho, Daviess Co, KY 27
Calhoun James	Palmyra, NY 44
Calhoun James	Westminster Pres Cem, lot 24, Baltimore, MD 15
Calhoun Patrick	Old fam Cem, Arlington, Calhoun Co, GA 58
Calhoun Rev	Mount Hope Cem, Rochester, Monroe Co, NY 33
Calhoun Samuel	Nr Vinton, OH 56
Calhoun Thomas	Aban Cem, East Springfield, Jefferson Co, OH 55
Calhoun Thomas	Steubenville, Jefferson Co, OH 40
Calingham Robert	Cem, Milford, CT 56
Calkins Elijah	Sharon, NY 56
Calkins John	Earlville, NY 15
Calkins John	Galpin Hill Cem, Fleming, Cayuga Co, NY 57
Calkins John Jr	Bapt Ch Cem, Wilton, Saratoga Co, NY 77
Calkins John Prentiss	Avon Cem, Avon, OH 56
Calkins Moses	Hilton Cem, West Burlington Twp, Bradford Co, PA 72
Calkins Moses	Hilton Cem, West Burlington, PA 16
Calkins Moses	Hilton Cem, West Burlington, PA 53
Calkins Seth	Cornell Cem, Wilton, Saratoga Co, NY 77
Calkins Stephen Jr	Sharon Cem, Sharon, Litchfield Co, CT 66
Call James	Quenchy Village Cem, Hartford, CT 54
Call Joseph	Tisdel Cem, sect 4 lot 34 #2, Madison Twp, Lake Co, OH 55
Call Joseph	West Madison, OH 26
Call Moses	Schoodic Cem, Warner, NH 34
Call Moses Lt	Old Mtg Hs Cem, Webster, NH 34
Callaham William	On farm, sect 28, Beaver Creek Rd, Green Twp, OH 56
Callahan Daniel	Fam Cem, Jersey Mills, PA 16
Callahan James	Snow Creek Cem, off Hwy 115, 10 mi N of Statesville, NC 40
Callahan Jeremiah	Greenford Cem, Greenford, Mahoning Co, OH 55
Callahan Patrick	Mt Pleasant Cem, South Bethlehem, Albany Co, NY 75
Callaway Charles	Altavista, VA 30
Callaway Charles	Bedford Cem, Pittsylvania Co, VA 61
Callaway Charles Capt	Fam Cem, Pittsylvania Co, VA 37
Callaway James	Callaway-Steptoe Cem, New London, VA 52
Callaway James Col	Fam Cem, New London, VA 37
Callaway John	Otter Oaks, nr Evington, VA 52
Callaway John Col	Otter Oaks, nr Evington, VA 37
Callaway Micajah	Peugh Cem, Washington Twp, Washington Co, IN 72
Callaway Micajah	Peugh Cem, Washington Co, IN 23
Callaway William Col	Fam Cem, New London, VA 37
Callaway Willis Jr	Callaway-Steptoe Cem, New London, VA 52
Callendar Aaron	Plain Cem, Sheffield, MA 56
Callendar Abner	Plain Cem, Sheffield, MA 56
Callendar John	East Cem, Spear Cem, Shelburne, VT 70
Callendar Joseph	Plain Cem, Sheffield, MA 56
Callendar Thomas	St James Cem, Wilmington, NC 49
Callender Amos	Shoreham, VT 15
Callender Benjamin	Old Granary Bur Gr, Boston, MA 56
Callender Samuel	Green Grove, Lackawanna Co, PA 15
Callender Samuel	Montdale Cem, Scott Twp, PA 56
Callender Thomas	Smithville, NH 32
Calley Jonathan	Fam Cem, Sanbornton, NH 29

Callhan James	Snow Creek Cem, 10 mi N of Statesville, NC 49
Calloway Charles	Altavista, VA 29
Calloway Elijah	Fam Cem, Rt 163, 9 mi fr West Jefferson, Ashe Co, NC 75
Calloway James	Crew farm, Howard Co, MO 15
Calloway James	Nr Cooper's Fort, New Hope, MO 15
Calloway James Col	Priv walled Cem, nr New London, VA 31
Calloway John Lt Col	His home, Otter Oaks, nr Evington, VA 31
Calloway Peter	Springfield, Laurens Co, GA 16
Calloway Richard	Nr Boonesboro, Clark Co, KY 56
Calloway Thomas Sr	Fam Cem, off Hwy 163, nr West Jefferson, Ashe Co, NC 77
Calvert John	First Pres Ch Cem, Columbia, SC 42
Calvert John	Sweetman Cem, Ballston, Saratoga Co, NY 77
Calvert Spencer	Calvert Cem, nr Princeton, Caldwell Co, KY 73
Cambridge John	East Lempster Cem, Lempster, NH 34
Camburn Joseph	Old Cem, Waretown, NJ 53
Camerer Henry	Christian Ch Cem, Old Salem, OH 56
Camerer John	Calvary Cem, Washington Co, OH 56
Cameron James	Bapt Ch Cem, Delphi Falls, Pompey, Onondaga Co, NY 81
Cameron Josiah	Killed in Wyoming Massacre, Wyoming, PA 52
Cameron Lewis	Hickman farm, on ridge, nr Calcutta, Columbiana Co, OH 55
Camery P H	Calvary Cem, Washington Co, OH 56
Camfield Abiel	First Pres Ch Cem, Newark, NJ 26
Camfield Elijah	Copley, OH 56
Camp Abel	Elmwood Cem, Barre, VT 48
Camp Abel	Morris, CT 17
Camp Asa	Riverside Cem, Owego, NY 34
Camp Benjamin	West Creek Rd, nr Hartwick, NY 71
Camp Eldad	Clam River Cem, Sandisfield, MA 56
Camp Ezra	Morris, CT 17
Camp Israel	Center Cem, Hanover, NH 27
Camp Israel	Gallows Hill Cem, New Milford, CT 55
Camp Jesse	Orchard on fam farm, nr Albany, OH 56
Camp Job	Merryall Cem, Wyalusing, PA 53
Camp John	Center Cem, New Milford, CT 55
Camp John	Lebanon Ch Cem, Greenville District, SC 62
Camp John	Nr Smith place, 3 mi fr Winder, GA 26
Camp John	Old Town Hall Cem, Salisbury, CT 64
Camp Joseph	Old bur gr, Newark, NJ 26
Camp Joseph	Pres Cem, Newark, NJ 32
Camp Luke	Old Town Hall Cem, Salisbury, CT 64
Camp Moses	Norfolk, CT 56
Camp Samuel	Old fam Cem, nr Jewell, Warren Co, GA 24
Camp Samuel	Port Carbon, PA 49
Camp Samuel	Pres Cem, Orange, NJ 32
Camp Thomas	Homestead Bur Gr, nr Kings Mountain, NC 57
Campbell Capt	Massacred nr mouth of Lechry Creek, Dearborn Co, IN 24
Campbell Aeneas	Campbell-Belt Estate, Rock Hill, nr Leesburg, VA 42
Campbell Aeneas Jr	New Hope Bapt Ch Cem, Iredell Co, NC 56
Campbell Alexander	Conquest, NY 56
Campbell Alexander Rev	Bethany, WV 56
Campbell Archibald	Church on the Green, Hackensack, NJ 55
Campbell Archibald	Fam Cem, Harnett Co, NC 48
Campbell Archibald	Friendship Meth Epis Cem, nr Buena, NJ 25
Campbell Archibald	Friendship Meth Epis Cem, NJ 23
Campbell Archibald	Grave obliterated, Willett, Cortland Co, NY 36
Campbell Archibald	Priv Cem, Albany, NY 56
Campbell Charles	Hinds Co, MS 44
Campbell Charles Capt	Bethel Ch Cem, Indiana Co, PA 22
Campbell Colin	Old Bull Ch, Cumberland Co, NC 48
Campbell Daniel	Old Cem, Acworth, NH 34
Campbell David	Fam farm, nr Luthers Mills, PA 53

Campbell David	Old Rockingham Cem, VT 48
Campbell David	Old South Ch, Bergenfield, NJ 31
Campbell David	Old Washington Cem, Washington Ferry, Rhea Co, TN 73
Campbell David	Old Cem on the Plains, Windham, NH 26
Campbell David	Sopertown Cem, Sopertown, PA 52
Campbell David Col	Leeville, TN 23
Campbell David Col	Leeville, Wilson Co, TN 24
Campbell David Maj	Depot Hill Cem, Henniker, NH 32
Campbell David Maj	Washington, TN 23
Campbell David Maj	Washington, Rhea Co, TN 24
Campbell Dougall	Colonial Cem, Metuchen, NJ 49
Campbell Edward	Christ Epis Ch Cem, Brownsville, Fayette Co, PA 80
Campbell Farquhard	Cumberland Co, NC 48
Campbell Francis L Capt	Great Bridge, VA 36
Campbell Francis Lee	Clover Hill Cem, S Anna River, Hwy 647, Louisa Co, VA 77
Campbell George	Church on the Green, Hackensack, NJ 55
Campbell Henry	Cem on the Plains, Windham, NH 28
Campbell Henry	Old Cem on the Plains, Windham, NH 26
Campbell Henry	Old Cem on the Plains, Windham, NH 26
Campbell Hugh	Tuppers Corners Cem, Venice, NY 41
Campbell Isaac	Killed in Wyoming Massacre, Wyoming, PA 52
Campbell Isaac	Pine Hill Cem, Rush, Monroe Co, NY 79
Campbell James	Cem on the Plain, Brookline, NH 36
Campbell James	Dutch Ref Ch Cem, Belleville, NJ 27
Campbell James	Hamonton, NJ 15
Campbell James	Ingell Cem, Chester, MA 62
Campbell James	Maple Grove Cem, nr Sweetser, Grant Co, IN 72
Campbell James	Meth Epis Cem, Pleasant Mills, NJ 25
Campbell James	New Cem, Acworth, NH 34
Campbell James	Old Brown Marsh Ch Cem, nr Clarkton, Bladen Co, NC 75
Campbell James	Old Rockingham Cem, VT 48
Campbell James	Paint Rock Cem, Roane Co, TN 24
Campbell James	Pentucket Cem, Haverhill, MA 28
Campbell James	Point Rock Cem, TN 23
Campbell James	Sutton Village, Sutton, VT 38
Campbell James	Tuscarora Ch Cem, Berkeley Co, WV 42
Campbell James	Village Cem, Walpole, NH 25
Campbell James	West Galway Cem, West Galway, Saratoga Co, NY 77
Campbell James Capt	Cem adj old Tuscarora Pres Ch, Berkeley Co, WV 18
Campbell James Capt	Old Meth Cem, Alexandria, VA 35
Campbell James Capt	Tuscarora Pres Cem, nr Martinsburg, WV 24
Campbell James Col	Nr Old Bluff Ch, Cumberland Co, NC 48
Campbell James Jr Col	Cape Fear River bank, Cumberland Co, NC 43
Campbell James Sr	Fam farm, nr Luthers Mills, PA 53
Campbell James Sr	Wilmington & Brandywine, New Castle Co, DE 46
Campbell Jane	Cherry Valley Cem, East Springfield, NY 33
Campbell Jeremiah	Hampton, TN 24
Campbell Jeremiah	Hampton Cem, Carter Co, TN 33
Campbell Jesse Capt	Old Village Cem, Claremont, NH 50
Campbell John	Buffalo Cross Roads Pres Ch Cem, Union Co, PA 17
Campbell John	Cem on The Plains, Windham, NH 32
Campbell John	Center Cem, Henniker, NH 32
Campbell John	Clymer Cem, Chautauqua Co, NY 62
Campbell John	Hampshire Co, WV 56
Campbell John	Kesslers Cross Lanes, Nicholas Co, WV 56
Campbell John	Milford Cem, Milford, NY 31
Campbell John	Mount Holly Cem, Warren Co, OH 29
Campbell John	NY or Willoughby, OH 26
Campbell John	Old Village Cem, Claremont, NH 50
Campbell John	Orangeville Cem, Orangeville, Wyoming Co, NY 64
Campbell John	Pyrmont Cem, Pyrmont, OH 56

Campbell John — Rich Valley Pres Ch Cem, Saltville, Smyth Co, VA 77
Campbell John — Rosehill Cem, Bloomington, Monroe Co, IN 72
Campbell John B — Nr Brownsville, TN 23
Campbell John B — Nr Brownsville, TN 24
Campbell John Capt — Cem on the Plains, Windham, NH 28
Campbell John Capt — Sauger Cem, Elk Creek, Grayson Co, VA 36
Campbell John Jr — Cherry Valley Cem, East Springfield, NY 33
Campbell John Jr — Salem-Lloyd, 6 mi fr Washington Court House, Marion, OH 56
Campbell Jonas — Old Bur Gr, Townsend, MA 56
Campbell Joseph — Old Cem, nr Chattanooga, TN 29
Campbell Matthew — Aberdeen's 1st Cem, upper river bank, Brown Co, OH 55
Campbell Matthew — Ingell Cem, Chester, MA 62
Campbell Matthew — Ohio River bank, Mason, KY 56
Campbell McDonald — Mt Tabor Cem, Morrow Co, OH 56
Campbell Moses — Stafford, NY 15
Campbell Nathan — Conquest, NY 56
Campbell Nicholas — Bristol, NJ 32
Campbell Phineas — Old bur gr, Orange, NJ 26
Campbell Robert — Campbell Hill Cem, Pike, Wyoming Co, NY 64
Campbell Robert — New Boston Cem, New Boston, NH 28
Campbell Robert — New Boston, NH 16
Campbell Robert — Old Bur Gr, Townsend, MA 48
Campbell Robert — Old Cem, Salem Center, NH 28
Campbell Robert — Pigeons Creek Cem, Washington, PA 51
Campbell Robert — Slate Run, Lycoming Co, PA 15
Campbell Robert — Yellow Mtg Hs Cem, Stillwater, Saratoga Co, NY 78
Campbell Sam Col — Cherry Valley Cem, East Springfield, NY 33
Campbell Samuel — Conquest Village, Conquest, NY 56
Campbell Samuel — Hulse Cem, Rockford, IL 73
Campbell Samuel — Perry Twp, Gallia Co, OH 56
Campbell Samuel — South Hero Cem, Grand Isle, VT 56
Campbell Samuel Dea — Old Cem on the Plains, Windham, NH 26
Campbell Samuel Lt — West Rutland Cem, Rutland, VT 23
Campbell Solomon — Hillside Cem, Campbell, Steuben Co, NY 80
Campbell Stephen — Greensburgh Pres Ch Cem, Westchester Co, NY 34
Campbell Thomas — Bur gr, Stillwater, NY 41
Campbell Thomas — Church Cem, Anchor, OH 56
Campbell Thomas — Fam Cem, nr Irving, Bedford Co, VA 47
Campbell Thomas — Goshen Cem, Gaston Co, NC 49
Campbell Thomas — Hart Cem, Stillwater, Saratoga Co, NY 77
Campbell William — Cem on the Plains, Windham, NH 28
Campbell William — Columbus Twp, IN 48
Campbell William — Lafayette, NY 35
Campbell William — Law farm, nr Deputy, Jefferson Co, IN 72
Campbell William — Martinus-Hogencamp New City, Rockland Co, NY 78
Campbell William — New Boston Cem, New Boston, NH 28
Campbell William — New Boston, NH 16
Campbell William — Old Cem, Reagen farm, Berry Hollow, Willett, NY 36
Campbell William — Old Tennent Ch Cem, Tennent, NJ 47
Campbell William — Old Valley Bapt Cem, Philadelphia, PA 56
Campbell William — Pine Grove Cem, Lafayette, Onondaga Co, NY 55
Campbell William — Pres Ch Cem, Poland, OH 56
Campbell William — Railroad ground. Dalton Cem, 1 mi SW of Orville, OH 56
Campfield John — Morristown, NJ 49
Campfield William — Old Whippany Cem, Hanover, Morris Co, NJ 70
Campston Edward Maj — North St Cem, Auburn, NY 41
Canada David — Chewink Cem, Chaplain, CT 55
Canary Charles — Shinkle Ridge Cem, nr Higginsport, OH 15
Canby Samuel — Friends Mtg Yard, Wilmington, New Castle Co, DE 41
Canby William — Friends Mtg Yard, Wilmington, New Castle Co, DE 41
Canda David — Oran Pioneer Cem, Fayetteville, NY 49

Cande Zaccheus	Fam Cem, Sheffield, MA 40
Candee Caleb	Jacks Hill Cem, Oxford, CT 23
Candee Daniel	Oran Cem, Oran, Onondaga Co, NY 71
Candee Job	Cong Cem, Oxford, CT 37
Candee Medah	Bur Gr, Stillwater, NY 41
Candee Samuel	Southford Cem, Southford, CT 37
Cane Daniel	Allen farm, Sugar Creek Twp, Greene Co, OH 55
Cane Daniel	[no cem named], OH 26
Canedy William	Lakeview Cem, Rt 179, Middleboro, MA 55
Caner George	Hoover Hill Cem, Warren, Herkimer Co, NY 36
Canfield Abiel	Seymour Cem, Seymour, CT 15
Canfield Daniel	Great Hill Cem, Seymour, CT 35
Canfield Daniel	Seymour Cem, Seymour, CT 15
Canfield David	Bloomfield Cem, Essex Co, NJ 33
Canfield Ebenezer	Old bur gr, Orange, NJ 26
Canfield Elijah	Palmyra, OH 26
Canfield Elijah	Palmyra Cem, Palmyra, OH 56
Canfield Gideon	Old Southfield, New Marlborough, MA 56
Canfield Israel	Pres Cem, Morristown, NJ 32
Canfield James	Ref Ch Cem, Rhinebeck, NY 54
Canfield John	Center Cem, Bridgewater, CT 55
Canfield John	Pres Cem, Morristown, NJ 32
Canfield John	Sharon Cem, Sharon, Litchfield Co, CT 66
Canfield Joseph	Clam River Cem, Sandisfield, MA 56
Canfield Joseph Dr	Old Colonial Cem, Derby, CT 56
Canfield Judson	Fam Cem, Canfield, Mahoning Co, OH 55
Canfield Levi	Copley, OH 45
Canfield Levi	Copley Twp, Summit Co, OH 15
Canfield Nathan Dea	Bapt Ground, lot #1, Stanford, Dutchess Co, NY 21
Canfield Oliver	Besley Cem, Columbia Twp, Bradford Co, PA 53
Canfield Oliver	Besley Cem, Columbia Twp, Bradford Co, PA 72
Canfield Samuel	Sharon Cem, Sharon, Litchfield Co, CT 66
Canfield Samuel	West Yard Cem, Marlow, NH 25
Canfield Samuel Col	Center Cem, New Milford, CT 55
Canfield Thomas	First Pres Ch Cem, Newark, NJ 26
Canfield William	Hanover, Morris Co, NJ 32
Canfield William Capt	Hanover Pres Ch Cem, NJ 48
Canning William	Champoeg, OR 53
Cannon Andrew	Cherry Valley Cem, Cherry Valley, NY 71
Cannon Cornelius	West Cem, Amherst, MA 16
Cannon Eleanor	Cherry Valley Cem, East Springfield, NY 33
Cannon Isaac	Aurora, IN 54
Cannon Isaac	Holman Hill Cem, Dearborn Co, IN 72
Cannon Isaac	New Center Cem, Blandford, MA 58
Cannon James	Cherry Valley Cem, East Springfield, NY 33
Cannon James	Shelby Co, OH 55
Cannon Maulien	Cherry Valley Cem, East Springfield, NY 33
Cannon Minos	Old Cannon Place, College Grove, Williamson Co, TN 74
Cannon Thomas	Saxton farm, Venice, NY 56
Cannon William	Old Cem, St Paul, OR 50
Cannon William	St Paul Ch Cem, Marion Co, OR 21
Canon Daniel	Paul (Laurel Hill) Cem, nr Dunbar, Fayette Co, PA 79
Cantelou Louis Capt	Fam plot, 12 mi fr Edgefield toward Modoc, SC 41
Canter Daniel	Carter's Station Cem, Greeneville, Greene Co, TN 75
Canterbury Jacob	Front St Cem, South Weymouth, MA 50
Cantey James Capt	East Baldwin Co, GA 36
Cantine John Col	Brookton Cem, Brookton, NY 15
Cantine William	Claverack Ref Ch Cem, Claverack, Columbia Co, NY 74
Cantrel Thomas	Williamsburg Cem, Etowah, TN 31
Cantrell Stephen	Nr Goodlettville, Long Hollow Pike, TN 29
Cantrell Thomas	Williamsburg, TN 23

Cantrell Thomas	Williamsburg Cem, McMinn, TN 24
Cantrelle Jacques	Cabahanose, St James Parish, LA 57
Cantrelle Miguel	St James Cem, Donaldsonville, St James Parish, LA 77
Capelle Philippe Eugene	Old Swede's Cem, Wilmington, New Castle Co, DE 46
Capelle Philippe Eugene	Old Swedes Ch Cem, Wilmington, New Castle Co, DE 36
Capen Bernard	North Cem, Dorchester, MA 46
Capen Ebenezer	Old Cem, Canton St, Sharon, MA 56
Capen Elijah	Old Cem, Canton St, Sharon, MA 56
Capen James	Old Cem, Spencer, MA 55
Capen James	Pearl St Cem, Stoughton, MA 55
Capen John	Pearl St Cem, Stoughton, MA 55
Capen John Jr	North Cem, Dorchester, MA 46
Capen Jonathan Jr	Stoughton, MA 52
Capen Lemuel	Old Cem, Canton St, Sharon, MA 56
Capen Nathaniel	Elm St, Braintree, MA 54
Capen Robert	Pearl St Cem, Stoughton, MA 55
Capen Samuel	Pearl St Cem, Stoughton, MA 55
Capen Timothy	Old Cem, Spencer, MA 55
Capers William Capt	Woodland, 10 mi fr Sumter, SC 44
Capes Solomon	McKinley Ave Park Cem, Canton, OH 44
Capp Andreas	Luth Ref Ch Cem, Schaefferstown, Lebanon Co, PA 83
Capp Anthony	Luth Ref Ch Cem, Schaefferstown, Lebanon Co, PA 83
Capp Christopher	Bethel Morav Cem, Swatara Twp, Lebanon Co, PA 83
Capps William Jr	Fortune Fam Cem, nr Green River, Henderson Co, NC 43
Capron Benjamin	North Main St Cem, Rutland, VT 24
Capron Benjamin	North Main St Cem, Rutland, VT 25
Capron Benjamin	Old Kirk Yard, Attleboro, MA 15
Capron Comfort Dr	Harford, PA 16
Capron Elijah	Attleboro Cem, Attleboro, MA 46
Capron Elijah	Old Kirk Yard, Attleboro, MA 15
Capron Elisha	Ford Cem, Canadice Rd, Springwater, Livingston Co, NY 74
Capron Ephraim	West Hill Cem, Williamstown, VT 40
Capron John	Prospect Hill Cem, Uxbridge, MA 46
Capron Joseph	Fam Cem, Woonsocket, RI 31
Capron Joseph	Old Kirk Yard, Attleboro, MA 15
Capron Joseph Jr	Old Kirkyard Cem, Attleboro, MA 47
Capron Oliver	Mount Caesar Cem, Swanzey, NH 35
Capron Phillip	Cook Cem, Mendon & Cumberland Rds, Woonsocket, RI 75
Caption James	North St Cem, Auburn, NY 41
Capwell Stephen	Bethel Cem, Factoryville, Wyoming Co, PA 37
Capwell William	West Middlebury, Wyoming, RI 56
Capwell William R	West Middlebury, Genesee, NY 56
Caraway Henry	Fam Cem, Jefferson Twp, Adams Co, OH 55
Card Bowen	The Platform, Kingstown, RI 35
Card William	Willoughby, OH 26
Carder Sanford	His farm, Union Twp, Fayette Co, OH 55
Cardinal Nicholas	St Francis Xavier Cem, Vincennes, Knox Co, IN 72
Cardozo David Nunez	Coming St Cem, Charleston, SC 43
Carew Eliphalet	Norwich Town Cem, Norwich, CT 18
Carew Joseph	Norwich Town Cem, Norwich, CT 18
Carey Benjamin	Hanover Green, Hanover Twp, PA 52
Carey Ezra Dea	Upper St Cem, Turner, ME 39
Carey Henry Rev	Pleasant St Cem, West Rutland, VT 55
Carey John	Wilkes-Barre, PA 52
Carey Jonathan	Copps Hill Cem, Boston, MA 46
Carey Joseph	Killed in Wyoming Massacre, Wyoming, PA 52
Carey Joseph	Ontario Cem, Ontario, Wayne Co, NY 62
Carey Levi	Union Square Cem, NY 15
Carey Luther Dr	Upper St Cem, Turner, ME 39
Carey Nathan	Arkport, NY 56
Carey Nathan	Hanover Green, Hanover Twp, PA 52

Abstract of Graves of Revolutionary Patriots

Carey Samuel	City Cem, Wilkes-Barre, PA 52
Carey Seth	Putney Cem, Putney, VT 58
Cargill Hugh	Hill Cem, Concord, MA 55
Cargill James	Sheepscot, New Castle, ME 56
Carhart Cornelius	Mansfield Wood Hs Pres, Washington Twp, Warren Co, NJ 33
Carhart Cornelius	Mansfield Cem, nr Washington, NJ 35
Carhart Samuel S	Mount Pleasant Cem, Matawan, NJ 51
Carhart Thomas	Cedarwood Cem, Keyport, NJ 50
Carkin John	South Cem, Lyndeborough, NH 47
Carl Daniel	Old Cem, grave #3, Washington Co, PA 38
Carl George	Zionsville Luth Cem, Shimersville, Lehigh Co, PA 40
Carl Isaiah	Little Germany Cem, nr Elliottsburg, PA 16
Carl Robert	Mt Abram Cem, Salem, Franklin Co, ME 83
Carle Israel	Ewing Ch Cem, nr Trenton, NJ 28
Carle John Esq	Pres Ch Cem, Basking Ridge, NJ 47
Carle Jonas	Pres Ch Cem, Basking Ridge, NJ 47
Carleton Aaron Sr	North Parish Bur Gr, Haverhill, MA 31
Carleton Eben	Murray Hill Cem, Bristol, NH 39
Carleton Israel	Second West Parish Cem, Haverhill, MA 31
Carleton Jesse	Bath Village Cem, Bath, NH 31
Carleton John	North Cem, Lowell, MA 46
Carleton John	Town Cem, Mount Vernon, NH 27
Carleton Joseph	Attalla Cem, Sheppard plot, Attalla, AL 82
Carleton Nehemiah	Bradford Cem, Bradford, MA 46
Carleton Peter	Landaff, NH 26
Carley Ebenezer Capt	Marathon Cem, Marathon, Cortland Co, NY 36
Carley Jonathan	East Sidney Cem, Sidney, Delaware Co, NY 75
Carley Jonathan	Whitingham Cem, nr Newell Place, Whitingham, MA 45
Carley Jonathan	Whitingham, VT 18
Carlisle Basil	Fam bur gr, nr Farmdale, Franklin Co, KY 16
Carlisle Daniel	North Cem, Westmoreland, NH 25
Carlisle David Capt	Village Cem, Walpole, NH 42
Carlisle James	Clover Creek Cem, Clover Creek, Highland Co, VA 86
Carlock Hanchrist	Fam Cem, Lick Run, VA 58
Carlton Ambrose	Carlton Cem, Buddha, Lawrence Co, IN 72
Carlton Ambrose	Nr Buddha, Lawrence Co, IN 24
Carlton Amos	Ancient Bur Gr, Bradford, MA 28
Carlton Amos	Ancient Bur Gr, Bradford, MA 27
Carlton Amos	Merrimack Cem, West Newbury, MA 50
Carlton Caleb	Mantua, OH 26
Carlton Daniel	Ancient Bur Gr, Bradford, MA 28
Carlton Daniel	Ancient Bur Gr, Bradford, MA 27
Carlton Daniel	North Parish Bur Gr, Andover, MA 26
Carlton Darius	Fam Cem, now USS cinder dump, McDonald, OH 56
Carlton David	Rural Cem, Sedwick, Hancock Co, ME 55
Carlton Dudley	Ancient Bur Gr, Bradford, MA 27
Carlton Dudley	Ancient Bur Gr, Bradford, MA 28
Carlton Ebenezer	Frye Hill, Methuen, MA 56
Carlton Elijah	Frye Hill, Methuen, MA 56
Carlton Ezekiel	Second Cem, North Andover, MA 26
Carlton Francis	Old Youngstown, OH 56
Carlton Isaac	North Parish Bur Gr, Andover, MA 26
Carlton John	[no cem named], MA 26
Carlton Joseph	Ancient Cem, West Boxford, MA 29
Carlton Michael	Second Cem, North Andover, MA 26
Carlton Michail	Pentucket Cem, Haverhill, MA 28
Carlton Peter	North Parish Bur Gr, Andover, MA 26
Carlton Phineas	Groveland Cem, Haverhill, MA 55
Carlton Phineas	Second Cem, North Andover, MA 26
Carlton Reuben	Ancient Bur Gr, Bradford, MA 27
Carlton Reuben	Ancient Bur Gr, Bradford, MA 28

Carlton Samuel	Ancient Cem, West Boxford, MA	29
Carlton Samuel	Howard St, Salem, MA	56
Carlton Samuel	Mt Vernon Cem, Roxford, MA	55
Carlton Stephen	Pentucket Cem, Haverhill, MA	28
Carlton Thomas	Pentucket Cem, Haverhill, MA	28
Carlton Timothy	Cem back of church, Merrimac, NH	40
Carly Abraham	Old Cem, nr 1st Bapt Ch, N Hillsdale, Columbia Co, NY	42
Carmack John	Nr Bristol, Washington Co, VA	37
Carmack William	Nr Bristol, Washington Co, VA	37
Carman Henry	Meth Cem, Shrub Oak, Westchester Co, NY	41
Carman Henry	Meth Ch Cem, Shrub Oak, Westchester Co, NY	36
Carman Samuel Capt	St George Cem, Hempstead, Long Island, NY	31
Carmany Johannes	Ref Ch Cem, Campbellstown, PA	17
Carmer Abraham	Clarence Center Cem, Clarence, Erie Co, NY	67
Carmichael John Dr	Adams Co, MS	44
Carmichael John Flavel	Elgin prop, nr Surgeon, Natchez, Adams Co, MS	74
Carmod Godfrey	Oakwood Cem, PA	15
Carnaghey William	Nr Ohio River, Georgetown, PA	56
Carnaham James	Drowned in Allegheny River, Philadelphia, PA	56
Carnahan John	Old Center Cem, Blandford, Hampden Co, MA	58
Carnes Edward	Copps Hill Bur Gr, Boston, MA	56
Carnes John	Western Cem, West Lynn, MA	56
Carnes Rufus	Troy Cem, Troy, WI	56
Carney Edward	Liberty Cem, WV	24
Carney John	Carney Flats Cem, Tunkhannock, Wyoming Co, PA	67
Carney John	Ruggles Twp Cem, Ashland Co, OH	55
Carney John	South of Columbus, IN	48
Carney Mark	Fam Cem, Dresden, ME	31
Carnham John	Deer Creek, nr Cochranton, Crawford Co, PA	56
Carothers James	Ebenezer Ch Cem, SC	17
Carothers John	Steele Creek Pres Ch Cem, Charlotte, Mecklenburg Co, NC	75
Carothers John Sr	Steele Creek Pres Ch Cem, Mecklenburg Co, NC	49
Carothers Robert Sr	[no cem named], TN	15
Carpenter –	Charlotte Cem, Chautauqua Co, NY	15
Carpenter Abel	Rehoboth Village Cem, Rehoboth, MA	54
Carpenter Abner	Stockbridge Cem, Stockbridge, MA	47
Carpenter Adam	4 mi fr Hustonville, Casey Co, KY	56
Carpenter Adam	Major Russell farm, Casey Co, KY	72
Carpenter Allen	Grave obliterated, Homer, Cortland Co, NY	36
Carpenter Amasa	East Woodstock Cem, Woodstock, CT	55
Carpenter Asahel	Old Rumford Cem, Rehoboth, MA	55
Carpenter Baker	St James Luth Ch Cem, Phillipsburg, Warren Co, NJ	40
Carpenter Barlow	Mendon Center Cem, Mendon, MA	46
Carpenter Benjamin	Carpenter Hill, Stanford, NY	21
Carpenter Benjamin	Fam bur gr, Surrey, NH	29
Carpenter Benjamin	Fam lot, nr House farm, Cowesett Rd, Warwick, RI	35
Carpenter Benjamin	Fam Cem, Guildford, VT	45
Carpenter Benjamin	Galena, OH	18
Carpenter Benjamin Jr	Fam bur gr, Surrey, NH	29
Carpenter Caleb	Old Rumford Cem, Rehoboth, MA	55
Carpenter Caleb	Old Rumford Cem, Rehoboth, MA	55
Carpenter Caleb	Rehoboth Village Cem, Rehoboth, MA	54
Carpenter Caleb 2nd	Old Rumford Cem, Rehoboth, MA	55
Carpenter Cephas	West St Cem, Fair Haven, VT	36
Carpenter Conrad	Carpenter Cem, Hustonville, Lincoln Co, KY	72
Carpenter Conrad	Carpenter Station Cem, Hustonville, KY	68
Carpenter Cyrel Dea	Woodlawn Cem, Attleboro, MA	15
Carpenter Daniel	Erie Co, OH	15
Carpenter Daniel	Houfstatter Cem, Ripley Twp, OH	56
Carpenter Daniel	North St, Auburn, NY	56
Carpenter Daniel	Old Rumford Cem, Rehoboth, MA	55

Carpenter Daniel	Own farm, road fr Goshen to Florida, Orange Co, NY	49
Carpenter Daniel Capt	Old Kirk Yard, Attleboro, MA	15
Carpenter David	Fam Cem, Kilmer farm, 3 mi N of La Fayette, Milan, NY	21
Carpenter David	Randolph Cem, Randolph, Orange Co, VT	74
Carpenter Ebenezer	Rehoboth Village Cem, Rehoboth, MA	54
Carpenter Elihu	Old Rumford Cem, Rehoboth, MA	55
Carpenter Elijah	Town Cem, Old Sturbridge, MA	48
Carpenter Elijah Corp	West Thompson Cem, CT	16
Carpenter Elisha	Nettleton, Genoa, NY	56
Carpenter Elisha Rev	Barkerville Cem, Providence Twp, Saratoga Co, NY	41
Carpenter Emanuel I	Fam Cem, Earlville, OH	56
Carpenter Emanuel Jr	Fam bur gr, S of Lancaster, Fairfield Co, OH	55
Carpenter Emanuel Sr	Fam bur gr, S of Lancaster, Fairfield Co, OH	55
Carpenter Ephraim	Charlestown, NY	15
Carpenter Exekial	Old Rumford Cem, Rehoboth, MA	55
Carpenter Ezra	Kirtland, Lake Co, OH	26
Carpenter Gabriel	Hoke Cem, nr Greencastle, PA	56
Carpenter Gardner	Norwich Town Cem, Norwich, CT	18
Carpenter George	Fam farm graveyard, Hyndman, Bedford Co, PA	80
Carpenter George	Goodrich Cem, Atlas Twp, Genesee Co, MI	33
Carpenter George	Goodrich Village Cem, Genesee Co, MI	35
Carpenter Gilbert Rev	Galena, OH	18
Carpenter Hiram	Liberty Twp, OH	18
Carpenter Hope	Connecticut Farms Pres Cem, Union, NJ	49
Carpenter Hope	Hillside Cem, Dundee, Yates Co, NY	69
Carpenter Increase	Prospect Cem, Jamaica, Queens Co, NY	71
Carpenter Jabes	Moriah, Essex Co, NY	33
Carpenter Jacob	Randolph Center Cem, Randolph, Orange Co, VT	72
Carpenter Jacob	St James Luth Ch Cem, Phillipsburg, Warren Co, NJ	40
Carpenter James	Connecticut Farms Pres Cem, Union, NJ	49
Carpenter Jesse	Lyme Plain Cem, Lyme, NH	29
Carpenter Job	Fam lot, nr House farm, Cowesett Rd, Warwick, RI	35
Carpenter John	Carpenter Station Cem, Hustonville, KY	68
Carpenter John	Carpenter Cem, Hustonville, Lincoln Co, KY	72
Carpenter John	Mount Hope Cem, nr Forest Hills, MA	51
Carpenter John	Newtown Cem, Hector, Schuyler, NY	36
Carpenter John	Old Koontz Cem, S of Lancaster, Fairfield Co, OH	55
Carpenter John	Randolph Center Cem, Randolph, Orange Co, VT	72
Carpenter John	Rehoboth Village Cem, Rehoboth, MA	54
Carpenter John	Tarbox Cem, Moose Horn Rd, East Greenwich, RI	35
Carpenter John	Tomhannock Village Cem, Pittstown, Rensselaer Co, NY	36
Carpenter John	Tomhannock Cem, nr Pillstown, NY	50
Carpenter Jonah	Lyon Yard, Eastford, CT	31
Carpenter Jonathan	Old Rumford Cem, Rehoboth, MA	55
Carpenter Jonathan	Randolph Center Cem, Randolph, VT	23
Carpenter Jonathan	Randolph Center Cem, Randolph, Orange Co, VT	72
Carpenter Joseph	Baldwin-Hamilton Plot, nr Canaan, Columbia Co, NY	79
Carpenter Joseph	Buffalo, NY	15
Carpenter Joseph	Prospect Hill Cem, Uxbridge, MA	46
Carpenter Joseph	Prospect Hill Cem, Uxbridge, MA	57
Carpenter Josiah	Edmunds Cem, Chichester, NH	31
Carpenter Josiah	Old Kirk Yard, Attleboro, MA	15
Carpenter Lewis	Ashley Cem, Springwater, Livingston Co, NY	74
Carpenter Matthew	Woodlawn Cem, Elmira, Chemung Co, NY	78
Carpenter Matthew Gen	Wisner Park Cem, Elmira, NY	33
Carpenter Nathan	Fam Cem, South Corinth, Saratoga Co, NY	77
Carpenter Nathan	Fam farm, Liberty Twp, Delaware Co, OH	39
Carpenter Nathan	Foot St Cem, Middlebury, VT	30
Carpenter Nathan	Liberty Twp, OH	18
Carpenter Nathaniel	Rehoboth Cem, Rehoboth, MA	59
Carpenter Nathaniel	South Cem. Leyden, MA	55

Carpenter Nehemiah	Dewitt, NY 35
Carpenter Penuel	Old Rumford Cem, Rehoboth, MA 55
Carpenter Peter	Pine St Cong Ch Cem, Norton, MA 55
Carpenter Peter	Rehoboth Village Cem, Rehoboth, MA 54
Carpenter Reuben C	Jamison Cem, Blendon Twp, Franklin Co, OH 53
Carpenter Rufus	Cheshire Cem, W Mount Rd, Cheshire, MA 55
Carpenter Rufus	Cushing Cem, Woodstock, VT 15
Carpenter Samuel	Baldwin-Hamilton Plot, nr Canaan, Columbia Co, NY 79
Carpenter Samuel	Rehoboth Village Cem, Rehoboth, MA 54
Carpenter Simon	Baldwin-Hamilton Plot, nr Canaan, Columbia Co, NY 79
Carpenter Stephen	Old Bapt Cem, Jenks Rd, Cheshire, MA 55
Carpenter Thomas	Baldwin-Hamilton Plot, nr Canaan, Columbia Co, NY 79
Carpenter Thomas	Columbia Ave, off Fair St, Pawtuxet, RI 35
Carpenter Thomas	Old Kirk Yard, Attleboro, MA 15
Carpenter Thomas	Rehoboth Village Cem, Rehoboth, MA 54
Carpenter Thomas Col	Rehobeth Village Cem, Rehobeth, MA 38
Carpenter Thomas Jr	Rehoboth Cem, Rehoboth, MA 47
Carpenter Walter	Meth Cem, Shrub Oak, Westchester Co, NY 41
Carpenter Walter	Meth Ch Cem, Shrub Oak, Westchester Co, NY 36
Carpenter Walter	South Schodack Cem, Schodack, Rensselaer Co, NY 80
Carpenter Wilbor	Fam lot, nr House farm, Cowesett Rd, Warwick, RI 35
Carpenter William	East Clarendon Cem, Clarendon, VT 24
Carpenter William	East Clarendon Cem, Clarendon, VT 25
Carpenter William	Garland, PA 52
Carpenter William	Norton Common Cem, Norton, MA 46
Carpenter William Jr	Carpenter Cem, Boone, KY 70
Carr Andrew	Center Pres Ch Cem, Iredell Co, NC 49
Carr Aquilla	Beersheba Cem, SW of Gnadenhutten, Tuscarawas Co, OH 55
Carr Benjamin	Plainfield Cem, Plainfield, Hampshire Co, MA 78
Carr Benjamin	Plainfield Cem, Plainfield, Hampshire Co, MA 77
Carr Benjamin	Salisbury Point Cem, Amesbury, MA 55
Carr Caleb	Novi, MI 15
Carr Caleb	Novi, MI 15
Carr Caleb Jr	Watervale Cem, Watervale Pompey, Onondaga Co, NY 81
Carr Christopher	Ivy Hill Cem, Easton Rd, Philadelphia, PA 65
Carr Clement	Torrington Cem, Torrington, CT 55
Carr Conrad	Peck Cem, nr Williamsport, Pickaway Co, OH 53
Carr Conrad	Peck's Cem, S of Williamsport, Pickaway Co, OH 55
Carr Dabney	Monticello Cem, Albemarle Co, VA 55
Carr David	Mill Creek Cem, Hookstown, Beaver Co, PA 65
Carr Elliot	Cem, Sanborn farm, Gilmanton, NH 29
Carr Isaac	Fam Cem, nr Toddsville, Otsego Co, NY 71
Carr Jacob	River Road or Oil Mills Cem, Weare, NH 33
Carr James	3 mi E of Magnolia, Duplin, NC 56
Carr James	Fam bur gr, nr Rollinsford Railroad Station, NH 30
Carr James	Fam Cem, Rollinsford, NH 31
Carr James	Luyster farm, nr Franklin, Johnson Co, IN 72
Carr James	Quaker Cem, Union Springs, Springport Twp, NY 41
Carr James	Union Springs Quaker Cem, NY 15
Carr Jesse	Carr or Webber Cem, Northfield, NH 36
Carr John	Carr Cem, Speedwell, Claiborne Co, TN 72
Carr John	Cem on The Plains, Windham, NH 32
Carr John	Chase-Leavitt Cem, Fremont, NH 31
Carr John	Fam Cem, Jamestown, RI 51
Carr John	Old Cem, Newport, RI 52
Carr John	Stony Point Rd, 5 mi fr Charlottesville, Albemarle Co, VA 40
Carr John Capt	Fam lot, Jamestown, Conanicut Island, RI 47
Carr John Col	First Cem, Candia, NH 29
Carr John Jr	Chase-Leavitt Cem, Fremont, NH 31
Carr Joseph	Cem on Turkey Hill, Freeburg Twp, St Clair Co, IL 56
Carr Joseph	Village Cem, Chester, NH 33

Carr Pelig	Elm Row Cem, Laurens, NY 32
Carr Robert	New Bethel Cem, Marion Co, IN 72
Carr Robert	Old Warren Cem, Warren, RI 51
Carr Robert	Todd-Carr Cem, nr Toddsville, NY 71
Carr Samuel	First Pres Ch Cem, Cranbury, NJ 76
Carr Samuel	First Yard, Meredith, NH 32
Carr Thomas	Oxford Cem, Butler Co, OH 55
Carr Thomas	Silver Creek Cem, nr Sellersburg, Clark Co, IN 72
Carr Thomas Jr	Old Town Cem, Sudbury, MA 56
Carr William	Antrim, NH 15
Carr William	Temple Hill Cem, Geneseo, Livingston Co, NY 22
Carr William	Woodlawn Cem, Elmira, Chemung Co, NY 78
Carrico Alexander	Beverly, MA 55
Carriel Nathanial	Sutton Center Cem, Sutton, MA 15
Carrier David	Howland Cem, Conway, MA 53
Carrier Timothy	Boland Cem, Sharon, Litchfield Co, CT 66
Carrier Titus	Old East Hampton Cem, East Hampton, CT 56
Carrigan William	Coddle Creek Cem, 7 mi fr Mooresville, Iredell Co, NC 77
Carriger Godfrey Jr	Nr Elizabethton, Carter Co, TN 24
Carriger Godfrey Sr	Nr Elizabethton, Carter Co, TN 24
Carril Joseph Jr	South Walpole Cem, Walpole, MA 47
Carringer Martin	Kelso Cem, Sheakleyville, Mercer Co, PA 83
Carringer Martin	Kelso Cem, nr Sheakleyville, PA 82
Carrington Elias Dr	Cem, Milford, CT 56
Carrington Jesse	Colebrook Center, Colebrook, CT 59
Carrington Paul	Fam Cem, Berry Hill, nr South Boston, Halifax Co, VA 77
Carrington Paul	Fam Cem, Mulberry Hill, Charlotte Co, VA 37
Carrington Riverius	North-West Bur Gr, Woodbridge, CT 56
Carroll Amos	Cem, Thompson, CT 49
Carroll Amos	Thompson, CT 48
Carroll Charles	Dunhard Cem, nr Pleasant Hill, W of Troy, Miami Co, OH 55
Carroll Charles	In the chapel of Doughoregan Manor, nr Ellicott City, MD 74
Carroll Daniel	Forest Glen Cem, Montgomery Co, MD 16
Carroll Daniel II	St John's Ch Cem, Forest Glen, MD 76
Carroll Joseph Jr	South Walpole Cem, Walpole, MA 45
Carroll William	Cem, fam farm, Mercer Co, PA 53
Carroll William	Hancock Co, OH 55
Carroll William	McCook, NE 15
Carruth James	Center Bur Gr, Phillipston, MA 45
Carruth James	[no cem named], MA 26
Carruth John	Buffalo Pres Ch Cem, Guilford Co, NC 49
Carruth John	Old part, Northboro, MA 49
Carson Andrew	Snow Creek Cem, 10 mi N of Statesville, NC 49
Carson Andrew	Young's Cem, Hwy 21, 20 mi N of Statesville, NC 40
Carson Charles	Coleman farm, Grave Plowed Over, Saluda, SC 15
Carson Charles	West Franklin Cem, Posey Co, IN 72
Carson John	Alger Cem, Rush Co, IN 53
Carson L	Cooper's Fort, New Hope, MO 15
Carson Lindsy	Nr Estill, MO 15
Carson Robert	Old Swamp, New Washington, OH 56
Carson Robert	Swamp Cem, Venice Twp, OH 26
Carson Thomas	Old Carson Place Place, Butler Co, KY 59
Carson Walter	Graham Ch Cem, nr Vernon, Jennings Co, IN 72
Carson Walter	Old Bur Gr, Fairfield, CT 62
Carson William	Grandview Cem, Chillicothe, Ross Co, OH 55
Carswell Abner	Revolutionary War Cem, Salem, Washington Co, NY 78
Carswell David	Oakland Cem, Sandusky, OH 26
Carswell David	Oakland Cem, Sandusky, OH 15
Carswell Joseph	Cem nr Bow Pond, Strafford, NH 34
Carswell Nathaniel	Revolutionary War Cem, Salem, Washington Co, NY 78
Cartee C M	Killed in Wyoming Massacre, Wyoming, PA 52

Carter Andon Capt	Elizabethton, Carter Co, TN	24
Carter Asaph	Old Pine Grove Cem, Leominster, MA	47
Carter Benjamin	North Cem, Wayland, MA	48
Carter Benjamin Capt	Quaker Cem, Camden, SC	45
Carter Benoni	Dutcher Bridge Cem, Salisbury, CT	64
Carter Charles	Stillwagon farm, Butler Co, PA	15
Carter Daniel Lt	Plains Cem, Boscawen, NH	28
Carter David	Mount Zion Ch Cem, nr Hartwell, Hart Co, GA	34
Carter David	Mt Zion Cem, 6 mi E of Hartwell, GA	32
Carter David	Pres Ch Cem, Manorville, Suffolk Co, NY	79
Carter Edward	Fam bur gr, nr Middleburg, VA	56
Carter Edward	Priv Cem, Dillard, Rabun Co, GA	55
Carter Edward	Shirley plantation, James River, James City Co, VA	63
Carter Elias	Charlotte Center, NY	15
Carter Elias	Newfane Hill Cem, Newfane, VT	47
Carter Elijah	Charlotte Center, NY	15
Carter Ephraim	Old Pine Grove Cem, Leominster, MA	47
Carter Ezekiel	Dresden Cem, Jefferson Twp, Muskingum Co, OH	55
Carter Ezra	New Cem, Wilmington, MA	58
Carter Heman	Geneganslet Cem, Greene, NY	16
Carter Isaac	Carter-McSwain Cem, Old Augusta, Perry Co, MS	72
Carter Isaac	Rock Creek Cem, Pike Co, MS	57
Carter Isaac Lt	Kent Cem, Kent, CT	46
Carter Jabez	Kirtland, Lake Co, OH	26
Carter Jabez	Old South Cem, Seneca Falls, NY	15
Carter Jacob	Old North Bur Gr, Concord, NH	41
Carter James	Old Sudbury Center, Sudbury, MA	55
Carter James Maj	Bugg Cem, Kissing Bower Rd, nr Augusta, Richmond Co, GA	34
Carter John	Bennington Center Cem, Bennington, NY	53
Carter John	Carter Street, New Canaan, CT	56
Carter John	Carter's Station Cem, Greeneville, Greene Co, TN	74
Carter John	Fam Cem, Monongalia, WV	55
Carter John Col	Elizabethton, Carter Co, TN	24
Carter John Col	Old North Bur Gr, Concord, NH	41
Carter John Jr	Carter's Station Cem, Greeneville, Greene Co, TN	75
Carter Jonas	Mumford Cem, Troy Twp, Geauga Co, OH	55
Carter Jonathan	New Cem, Wilmington, MA	58
Carter Jonathan	Old Pine Grove Cem, Leominster, MA	47
Carter Joseph	Goodwin Chapel Bur Gr, Grocery Creek, Morgan Co, KY	51
Carter Joseph	Indian River Cem, Clinton, CT	55
Carter Josiah Jr	Old Pine Grove Cem, Leominster, MA	47
Carter Josiah Maj	Old Pine Grove Cem, Leominster, MA	47
Carter Moses	Town Cem, New Hampton, NH	36
Carter Nathan	Wildwood Cem, Wilmington, MA	56
Carter Nathaniel	Pine Grove Cem, Leominster, MA	50
Carter Nathaniel Capt	Old Pine Grove Cem, Leominster, MA	47
Carter Phineas Jr	Old Pine Grove Cem, Leominster, MA	47
Carter Phineas Sr	Pine Grove, Leominster, MA	49
Carter Robert William	Carter Cem, betw Rosehill & Gantt, Covington Co, AL	66
Carter Samuel	Beach Plain, Sandisfield, MA	56
Carter Samuel	Cem, Keene, NH	55
Carter Silas	Leominster, MA	49
Carter Spencer	Greenwich Cem, Warren Co, NJ	32
Carter Stephen	Northeast Beecher Rd, Wolcott, CT	55
Carter Thomas	Dempseytown, nr Franklin, PA	56
Carter Thomas	Fam bur gr, nr Middleburg, VA	56
Carter Thomas	Fam Cem, nr fam home, Elbert Co, GA	34
Carter Thomas	Glenrock, Pittsylvania Co, VA	35
Carter Thomas	Off Hartwell Rd, 3 mi fr Elberton, GA	32
Carter Thomas A	Nr electric light plant, Elbert Co, GA	25
Carter Thomas M	Bapt Ch, Barnwell, SC	51

Abstract of Graves of Revolutionary Patriots

Carter William	Bunnell Cem, IN 20
Cartright Robert	Nr Dickson Pike, Davidson Co, TN 29
Cartwell Thomas	Newark Union Cem, New Castle Co, DE 46
Cartwright John	Old Four Mile Run Cem, Austintown Twp, Mahoning Co, OH 55
Cartwright Reuben	Cartwright Cem, Sharon, Litchfield Co, CT 66
Cartwright Robert	Fam Cem, Solitude farm, Goodlettsville, Davidson Co, TN 73
Cartwright Samuel	Cartwright Cem, Sharon, Litchfield Co, CT 67
Caruthers Andrew Capt	Coldwater Creek, Lincoln Co, TN 15
Caruthers Samuel	On farm, east fork of Goose Creek, Trousdale Co, TN 40
Carvell Henry	Gracelon Cem, Lewiston, ME 29
Carver Aldric	Old Cem, Hebron, CT 52
Carver Barnabas	Raymond Cem, Carmel, Putnam Co, NY 35
Carver David	Summer St Cem, Taunton, MA 41
Carver Edward	Copps Hill Bur Gr, Boston, MA 55
Carver Eleazer	In his field, Bridgewater, MA 55
Carver Eleazer Dr	Summer St Cem, Bridgewater, MA 55
Carver Jabez	West Elm St, Raynham, MA 56
Carver John	Community Ch Cem, Rock Village, Middleboro, MA 55
Carver John	Old Bridgewater Cem, Bridgewater, MA 47
Carver John	Pleasant St Cem, Raynham, MA 55
Carver Nathan	Galpin Hill Cem, Fleming, NY 41
Carver Nathan	Galpin Hill, Fleming, NY 56
Carver Nathaniel	Burial Hill, Plymouth, MA 56
Carver Nathaniel	Mount View Cem, West Pawlet, VT 48
Carver Nathaniel	West Pawlet Cem, VT 15
Carver Rufus	Mound Cem, Racine, WI 37
Carver Samuel	Machias, Cattaraugus Co, NY 35
Carville Henry	Lewiston, ME 18
Carwile Zachariah	Newberry District, SC 70
Cary Anson	Riverview Cem, Oxford, NY 16
Cary Barnabas	Old Cem, Rindge, NH 41
Cary Caleb	Old Graveyard, Bridgewater, MA 59
Cary Caleb	Summer St Cem, Bridgewater, MA 55
Cary Calvin	Stevenson Cem, now Massie Creek, nr Xenia, OH 53
Cary Christopher	Spring Grove Cem, Cincinnati, Hamilton Co, OH 76
Cary Eliphalet	Summer St Cem, Bridgewater, MA 55
Cary Ephraim	Densmore Hill Bur Gr, Hartland, VT 85
Cary Ephriam	First Unitarian Parish, East Bridgewater, MA 56
Cary Ezra	Old Cary Cem, Hardin, OH 53
Cary Howard	Ashland St Cem, Brockton, MA 15
Cary Isaac	North Ch Cem, Hardyston Twp, Sussex Co, NJ 79
Cary Jabez	Carr Cem, Marcy, Oneida Co, NY 85
Cary Jonathan	Copps Hill Bur Gr, Boston, MA 56
Cary Jonathan	Summer St Cem, Bridgewater, MA 55
Cary Jonathan Capt	Copp's Hill Bur Gr, Boston, MA 45
Cary Jonithan	Ashland St Cem, Brockton, MA 15
Cary Levy	Mapleview Cem, Mexico, Oswego Co, NY 64
Cary Luther	[no cem named], OH 17
Cary Phineas	Olden (Wolcotte) Cem, Barneveld, Oneida Co, NY 80
Cary Richard	Patchin Cem, Buffalo, NY 33
Cary Richard	Peartree Hall Site Cem, Newport News, VA 75
Cary Richard Col	Christ Ch Cem, Cooperstown, NY 33
Cary Samuel	Hightop Cem, Samantha nr Hillsboro, Highland Co, OH 78
Cary Simeon	Ashland St Cem, Brockton, MA 15
Cary William Capt	East Lempster Cem, Lempster, NH 34
Caryell George	Pres Churchyard, Lambertsville, NJ 52
Casbott Robert	Lawrence Cem, Francisco, Gibson Co, IN 78
Case Aaron	Glenwood Cem, Troy Twp, PA 53
Case Abel	Dyer Cem, Canton, CT 15
Case Adam	Turin, Lewis Co, NY 52
Case Amos	Center Cem, Barkhamsted, CT 62

Case Asa	Dyer Cem, Canton, CT 55
Case Augustus Sr	Maple Grove Cem, Plain Township, Wayne Co, OH 55
Case Benjamin	Evergreen Cem, Owego, NY 35
Case Benjamin	Manchester farm, Warren Twp, Bradford Co, PA 72
Case Benoni	Windsor, CT 15
Case Daniel	Dyer Cem, Canton, CT 15
Case Daniel Jr	Dyer Cem, Canton, CT 55
Case Dudley	Dyer Cem, Canton, CT 55
Case Ebenezer	Phinney's Lane Cem, Centerville, Barnstable, MA 58
Case Edward	Dyer Cem, Canton, CT 15
Case Elias	Dyer Cem, Canton, CT 15
Case Elias	Dyer Cem, Canton, CT 15
Case Elijah Sr	Cem, Woodland, OH 25
Case Elisha	Canton St Cem, Canton, CT 55
Case Elisha	Canton Street Cem, Canton, CT 62
Case Ephriam	Barnard, Sheffield, MA 56
Case Fithian	Canton Center Cem, Canton, CT 55
Case George	Fam Cem (priv), Baker St, Swansea, MA 56
Case George	Fam farm, E of Powell, Delaware Co, OH 39
Case Gideon	Old Bur Gr, Poquonock, CT 55
Case Giles Sr	Howlett Hill Cem, Onondaga, Onondaga Co, NY 75
Case Humphrey	Center Cem, Barkhamsted, CT 62
Case Isaac	Fam Cem (priv), Baker St, Swansea, MA 56
Case Isaac	Little Valley Cem, Little Valley, NY 58
Case Isaac	Monks Hill, Manchester, MI 20
Case Isaac Rev	Baptist Cem, East Readfield, ME 29
Case Jacob	Hop Meadow Cem, Simsbury, CT 55
Case James	Salem Cem, Washington Twp, Harrison Co, IN 72
Case Jedediah	Hop Meadow Cem, Simsbury, CT 55
Case Jedediah	Hop Meadow Cem, Simsbury, CT 55
Case Jesse	Hop Meadow Cem, Simsbury, CT 55
Case Job	Hop Meadow Cem, Simsbury, CT 55
Case John	Antrim, NH 15
Case John	Braysville nr Harrison, Dearborn Co, IN 78
Case John	Braysville Cem, Dearborn Co, IN 72
Case John	Hebron Village Cem, Hebron, NH 35
Case John	Old Cem, West Millbury, MA 56
Case John	West Hartland Cem, West Hartland, CT 60
Case Joseph	Hoosick Falls Cem, Hoosick, NY 34
Case Joshua	Succasunna, NJ 24
Case Joshua	Succasunna Pres Ch Cem, Succasunna, NJ 75
Case Meshel	Oake Grove Cem, Warren, Trumbull Co, OH 55
Case Meshel	Oak Grove, Warren, OH 24
Case Moses	Hop Meadow Cem, Simsbury, CT 55
Case Nathan	Case St Cem, Middlebury, VT 29
Case Oliver	Center Cem, Barkhamsted, CT 62
Case Philip	Candor, NY 56
Case Phineas	North Canton Cem, Canton, CT 55
Case Seth	1st farm N of Case farm, Liberty Twp, Delaware, OH 53
Case Seth	Farm, W of Olentangy River, N of Powell Rd, Liberty, OH 56
Case Silas	Dyer Cem, Canton, CT 55
Case Solomon	Hop Meadow Cem, Simsbury, CT 55
Case Tunis	Bapt Cem, Sandy Ridge, NJ 33
Case Uriah	Canton St Cem, Canton, CT 55
Case William	Trimble Cem, Northeast Twp, Orange Co, IN 72
Case William	Trimble Cem, Orange Co, IN 25
Case Zenas	River Road Cem, Piermont, NH 32
Casey Christopher	Cem, Jefferson City, MO 23
Casey John	Fam farm, Lexington-Covington Pike, KY 30
Casey Nicholas	Indian Mound Cem, Romney, WV 30
Casey Randolph	Smith Co, TN 56

Cash Daniel	Queen Ann Reservation Cem, Wawayanada, Orange Co, NY 51
Cash George	Old Burial Hill, Marblehead, MA 55
Cash John	Priv Cem, nr Piney Woods Ch, Fairburn, Fulton Co, GA 66
Cash Jonathan	Tomhannock Village Cem, Pittstown, Rensselaer Co, NY 36
Cash Samuel	Center Cem, Harwich, MA 49
Cash Warren	Gilead Ch Cem, Hardin Co, KY 49
Cash William	Bapt Ground, lot #1, Stanford, Dutchess Co, NY 21
Cash William	Doydsville, Belmont Co, OH 44
Casho Jacob	Head of Christiana Cem, nr Newark, DE 51
Cashon Thomas	Old Rocky River Bapt Ch, Hwy 73, 5 mi E of Davidson, NC 77
Casky Joseph	Nr Casky, KY 15
Casper Peter	Old Cem, Unionville, Neffs, Lehigh Co, PA 40
Cass Benjamin Lt	First Cem, Candia, NH 29
Cass Daniel	Priv Cem, Richmond, Cheshire Co, NH 57
Cass John	Village Cem, Hill, NH 29
Cass Jonathan	Dresden Cem, Jefferson Twp, Muskingum Co, OH 55
Cass Jonathan	South Yard, Richmond, NH 36
Cass Luke Lt	Benson Yard, Richmond, NH 36
Cass Moses	Fam Cem, Tilton, NH 31
Cass Nasson Capt	Rhoades Cem, Alexandria, NH 36
Cassady Thomas	Kelly Cem, Rush Co, IN 72
Cassedy William	St Paul's Evan Luth Cem, Montgomery Co, PA 59
Cassel Johannes	St Peter's Luth Ch Cem, Union & High St, Uniontown, PA 21
Cassell Abraham	Cem, sect G 1, Lexington, KY 45
Cassell Jacob	Fam Cem, nr Westminster, MD 52
Cassell Jacob	Jessamine Co, KY 45
Cassidy William	Copiah Co, MS 44
Casteel William	Price home, Kimberlin Heights Rd, Knox Co, TN 72
Casterline Jacob	Pres Cem, Morristown, NJ 32
Castille Joseph	St Martin of Tours Cath Ch Cem, St Martinville, LA 74
Castle Amasa	Ashtabula, OH 15
Castle Amasa	Ashtabula Co, OH 18
Castle Gideon	Schodack, Dutchess Co, NY 56
Castle Phineas	East Farms Cem, Waterbury, CT 55
Castle Seely	Pompey Hill Cem, Pompey, Onondaga Co, NY 81
Castle Thomas	Stanly Co, NC 56
Castleman Benjamin	Fam Cem, Wilson Co, TN 42
Castleman Jacob	Fam Cem, nr Hermitage, Davidson Co, TN 41
Castleman Jacob	Fam Cem, nr Hermitage, Davidson Co, TN 41
Castleman Jacob	Fam Cem, Davidson Co, TN 42
Castleman Jacob Jr	Fam Cem, Davidson Co, TN 42
Castleman John	Fam Cem, Davidson Co, TN 42
Castlio John	Fam bur gr, ½ mi W of Wentzville, MO 15
Castner James	Compton-Castner Cem, Foothill Rd, Somerville, NJ 47
Caston Bishop	Yorkshire Corners Cem, Cattaraugus Co, NY 32
Caston Bishop	Yorkshire Cem, Yorkshire Corners, NY 31
Caston Glass	Flat Creek Bapt Cem, Lancaster Co, SC 70
Castor John	Elbridge Cem, Elbridge, Onondaga Co, NY 75
Castor Noah	Old Perrysville Cem, Perrysville, Ashland Co, OH 55
Caswell Abner	Berkley Common Cem, Berkley, MA 55
Caswell Abraham	Pine Hill Cem, Taunton, MA 41
Caswell David	Lakeville Cem, Rt 179, Middleboro, MA 55
Caswell Elijah	Quaker Cem, Rochester, MA 59
Caswell Richard	10 mi W of Kinston, NC 73
Caswell Samuel	Beverly, MA 49
Caswell Simeon	Turner, ME 18
Caswell Timothy	Cem on Boody Hill, Strafford, NH 41
Caswell William	Green St Cem, Marblehead, MA 47
Catchings Joseph Maj	Pike Co, MS 44
Cate Andrew	Fam lot, nr Old Bayside Cem, Greenland, NH 45
Cate Enoch	Fam Cem, nr North Village, VT 20

Cate Enoch	Nr Montpelier, VT 15
Cate James Sr	Sanborn Rd Cem, Tilton, NH 31
Cate John	Old Yard, nr Province Rd, Meredith, NH 29
Cate Neal	Fam Cem, Brookfield, NH 25
Cate Simeon	Old Yard, Roller Coaster Rd, nr State Rd, Laconia, NH 29
Cater J R	Nr LaGrange, GA 35
Cater John Jr	Old fam Cem, Barring, NH 53
Cathcart James Leander	Rock Creek Cem, Washington, DC 56
Cathcart John	Cem back of Washington Twp School, Elkhart Co, IN 72
Cathcart Thomas	Corfu, NY 15
Cather Jasper	Gainesboro Cem, Frederick, VA 61
Cathey George	Goshen Cem, Gaston Co, NC 49
Catlett Jonas	East Fairfield Cem, Columbiana Co, OH 56
Catlin Benjamin	Torrington Cem, Torrington, CT 55
Catlin David A	Houghtaling Cem, Kingston, Ulster Co, NY 70
Catlin Joel	Harwinton, CT 56
Catlin Samuel	Center, New Marlborough, MA 56
Catlin Theodore	Highland (Mitchell) Cem, Odessa, NY 70
Catlin Thomas Jr	East Litchfield, CT 17
Catlin Thomas Jr Lt	East Cem, Litchfield, CT 18
Catlin Uriah	Northfield, CT 17
Catlin Uriah	Northfield Cem, Litchfield, CT 18
Cato Prince	Parting Ways Cem, Plymouth, MA 57
Catt John	Massacred nr mouth of Lechry Creek, Dearborn Co, IN 24
Catt Philip	West Salem Ch Cem, Johnson Twp, Knox Co, IN 72
Caudill James	Fam Cem, 3 mi above Blackey, Letcher Co, KY 50
Caufield Dennis J	Hamburgh, NY 33
Caughran Joseph	Prob old aban Cem, Danville, IL 15
Caulkins Roswell	Blockhouse Cem, Berlin Twp, OH 18
Caulkins Roswell	Blockhouse, Berlin, OH 56
Caulkins William	White House Cem, Otsego, Otsego Co, NY 71
Causey Ezekial	Fam Cem, 5 mi E of Louisville, Jefferson Co, GA 66
Causey William Capt	Nr Liberty, MS 44
Causten Isaac	Westminster Pres Cem, lot 84, Baltimore, MD 15
Cauthorn James	Salem Cem, Hwy 521N, Heath Springs, Lancaster Co, SC 76
Cauthorn Thomas	Salem Cem, Hwy 521N, Heath Springs, Lancaster Co, SC 76
Cauthorn William	Salem Cem, Hwy 521N, Heath Springs, Lancaster Co, SC 76
Cavanaugh Patrick	Old Cem, Washington Co, PA 38
Cave Benjamin	Stanhope Cem, Ross Co, OH 55
Cave John	Bapt Ch, Barnwell, SC 51
Cave William	Hon-Cave Cem, Powell Co, KY 61
Caverly Charles	Newport, ME 51
Caverly John	Fam Cem, Strafford, NH 27
Caverly John	Hall Bur Gr, Colchester, CT 75
Caverly Nathaniel	Chapel Cem, Sanbornton, NH 34
Caverly Philip	Town Cem, Strafford, NY 27
Caverly Phillip	Town Cem, Strafford, NH 45
Cavett Alexander	Cavett Station, TN 23
Cavett Alexander	Cavett Station, Knox Co, TN 24
Cavileer John	Farm, Green Bank, Burlington Co, NJ 23
Cawood Berry	Harlan, Harlan Co, KY 33
Cecil Samuel Sr	Fam plot nr Radford, Pulaski Co, VA 55
Cecil Zachariah	Hardin Cem, OH 53
Cecil Zachariah	Hart Cem, nr Grayson Station, E of Troy, Shelby Co, OH 55
Cessna John	Wertz farm Cem, Bedford Valley, Bedford Co, PA 80
Chace Enoch	Sharp's Lot Rd, Chace Ave, Swansea, MA 54
Chace Ezra	Priv Cem, Pratt St nr Weir Bridge, Taunton, MA 57
Chadbourne Silas	Old Cem, Gorham Village, ME 48
Chadbourne Silas Lt	Old Cem, Gorham, ME 45
Chadbourne Simeon	Fam Cem, Lyman, ME 55
Chadbourne Thomas	North Cem, Portsmouth, NH 34

Chaddock Thomas	Stafford, NY 15
Chadsey Benjamin	Jonesville Cem, Jonesville, Clifton Park Twp, NY 77
Chadsey Jabez	North Kingston Cem,, RI 47
Chadwell David	Breastwork Hill Cem, Tazewell, Claiborne Co, TN 79
Chadwell Moses	Copps Hill Bur Gr, Boston, MA 56
Chadwick Abiather	Lee Cem, Lee, MA 15
Chadwick David	Old Center Cem, Jaffrey, NH 37
Chadwick Ebenezer	Old Center Cem, Monterey, MA 41
Chadwick Edmund	Central South Water St Cem, Boscawen, NH 32
Chadwick Edmund Dr	Old Center Cem, Deerfield, NH 34
Chadwick Elihu	Cem, Old Smethport, PA 52
Chadwick Ephraim	Ancient Cem, West Boxford, MA 29
Chadwick Isaac	Ancient Cem, West Boxford, MA 29
Chadwick James Sr	Fam Cem, South China, ME 58
Chadwick John	Ancient Cem, West Boxford, MA 29
Chadwick Peter	Ancient Cem, West Boxford, MA 29
Chadwick Samuel	Ancient Cem, West Boxford, MA 29
Chadwick Samuel	Lee Cem, Lee, MA 15
Chadwick Samuel	Pentucket Cem, Haverhill, MA 28
Chadwick Thomas	Ancient Cem, West Boxford, MA 29
Chadwick Thomas	Ancient, West Boxford, MA 56
Chafe John	Acushnet Cem, Fairhaven, MA 55
Chafee Nathaniel	Old Rumford Cem, Rehoboth, MA 55
Chaffee Amos	North Hollow Cem, Rochester, VT 59
Chaffee Amos	North Hollow Cem, Rochester, Windsor Co, VT 76
Chaffee Atherton	Old Cem, Westminster, VT 46
Chaffee Chester	East Woodstock Cem, Woodstock, CT 55
Chaffee Comfort	Cem nr West Berkshire, VT 45
Chaffee David	West Hill Cem, Ashford, CT 55
Chaffee Joel	Ellsworth Cem, Sharon, Litchfield Co, CT 66
Chaffee Joshua	Ellsworth Cem, Sharon, Litchfield Co, CT 66
Chaffee Samuel B	Old Rumford Cem, Rehoboth, MA 55
Chaffee Stephen	Maple Grove Cem, Springville, NY 33
Chaffee Stephen	Springville, Buffalo, NY 15
Chaffee Thomas	North Becket, Becket, MA 56
Chaffin David	Old Village Cem, Claremont, NH 50
Chaffin David	Seeley Dist Cem, Middlebury, VT 30
Chaffin Elias	Acton, MA 55
Chaffin Isham	Wilkes Co, GA 55
Chaffin John	Acton, MA 55
Chaffin Joseph	Acton, MA 55
Chaffin Robert	Acton, MA 55
Chaffin Samuel	Holden Cem, Holden, MA 45
Chaffin Simon	East Union Twp, OH 45
Chaffin Tilla	Park Ave Cem, Holden, MA 15
Chaison Jean Baptiste	Now in Pipkin Park, Beaumont, Jefferson Co, TX 75
Chaison Jonas	Jirou Cem, Beaumont, TX 44
Chalfant Soloman	Nr Pentress, Clay dist, Monongalia Co, WV 21
Chalfaut Mordecai	Fam Cem, nr Augusta, KY 31
Challis Enos	Humphrey Cem, Holland, NY 33
Challis Nathaniel	Charlestown, NH 15
Challis Thomas	Old Mill Cem, Meriden, NH 46
Challis Timothy	Town Cem, Newton, NH 32
Chalmette Ignace	St Louis Cem #1, New Orleans, LA 58
Chamberlain Aaron	Blue Ball Cem, Adelphia, NJ 32
Chamberlain Aaron	Old Village Yard, New Ipswich, NH 29
Chamberlain Aaron	Sheridan, Calhoun Co, MI 22
Chamberlain Benjamin	Chelmsford Center Cem, Chelmsford, MA 55
Chamberlain Benjamin	Dummerston, VT 18
Chamberlain Benjamin	First Unitarian Parish, East Bridgewater, MA 56
Chamberlain Benjamin	Humphrey Center, Cattaraugus Co, NY 35

Chamberlain Benjamin	Pres Ch Cem, Sparta, Morris Co, NJ	75
Chamberlain Benjamin	Turner, ME	18
Chamberlain Benjamin	Walton, Pepperell, MA	56
Chamberlain Colbe	Amenia Union Cem, Amenia, Dutchess Co, NY	66
Chamberlain Daniel	Midland Cem, MA	50
Chamberlain Ebeneezer	Memorial Cem, Westborough, MA	60
Chamberlain Eleuzer	Good Hill Cem, Kent, CT	40
Chamberlain Elias	Union Cem, Livonia, NY	16
Chamberlain Eliphalet	Evergreen Cem, Springwater, Livingston Co, NY	74
Chamberlain Ephraim	Spencer Cem, Plymouth, NH	29
Chamberlain Ephraim Lt	Plymouth, NH	16
Chamberlain Freedom	Center Cem, Pembroke, MA	58
Chamberlain Isaac	Forefathers Bur Gr, Chelmsford, MA	57
Chamberlain Isaac	Sharon Cem, Sharon, Litchfield Co, CT	66
Chamberlain James	Town Cem, Dublin, NH	34
Chamberlain James	West Cem, Amherst, MA	60
Chamberlain James Maj	West Cem, Amherst, MA	16
Chamberlain Jason	Fam lot, Neck Rd Cem, Tuftonboro, NH	26
Chamberlain Jason	Holliston, MA	53
Chamberlain Job	First Unitarian Parish, East Bridgewater, MA	56
Chamberlain John	Bapt Cem, Cranbury, NJ	32
Chamberlain John	Mt Hope Cem, Rochester, Monroe Co, NY	79
Chamberlain John	North Cem, Westmoreland, NH	25
Chamberlain John	Old Cem, West Point Pleasant, NJ	26
Chamberlain John	Pres Cem, Kingwood, NJ	35
Chamberlain John	West Point Pleasant, NJ	35
Chamberlain Jonathan	Austerlitz Cem, Columbia Co, NY	42
Chamberlain Jonathan	East Hill Rd Cem, Austerlitz, Columbia Co, NY	79
Chamberlain Joseph	First Unitarian Parish, East Bridgewater, MA	56
Chamberlain Joseph	Newbury, VT	56
Chamberlain Lemuel	Old Cem, Southboro, MA	50
Chamberlain Lewis	Bapt Cem, Flemington, NJ	32
Chamberlain Lewis	First Unitarian Parish, East Bridgewater, MA	56
Chamberlain Moses	Bingham, ME	17
Chamberlain Nathan	Old Bur Gr, Arlington, MA	56
Chamberlain Nathaniel	First Unitarian Parish, East Bridgewater, MA	56
Chamberlain Nathaniel	Needham, MA	50
Chamberlain Nathaniel	Wardsboro, VT	18
Chamberlain Ninian	Owasco Rural Cem, Owasco, NY	56
Chamberlain Peleg	Good Hill Cem, Kent, CT	40
Chamberlain Remembrance	Old Cem, Harvard, MA	48
Chamberlain Richard	Oxbow Cem, Newbury, VT	48
Chamberlain Samuel	Good Hill Cem, Kent, CT	40
Chamberlain Thomas	Brookfield, NH	31
Chamberlain Thomas	Fam Cem, Dick Rd, Brookfield, NH	31
Chamberlain Thomas	First Unitarian Parish, East Bridgewater, MA	56
Chamberlain Wilder	Churchyard, Hollis, NH	39
Chamberlain William	Amenia Union Cem, Amenia, Dutchess Co, NY	66
Chamberlain Wilson	Pentucket, Haverhill, MA	27
Chamberland Joseph	Tater Hill, East Haddam, CT	56
Chamberlin Aaron	Ouleout Cem, Franklin, Delaware Co, NY	71
Chamberlin Freegift	Mt Pleasant Cem, South Bend, IN	58
Chamberlin John	Quasset Yard, Woodstock, CT	29
Chamberlin Joshua	Pontiac, MI	15
Chamberlin Nilson	Pentucket Cem, Haverhill, MA	28
Chamberlin William	Haven Hill Cem, Rochester, NH	36
Chamberlin William	Lewisburg Cem, Lewisburg, PA	15
Chambers Alexander	Chambers Cem, nr Edwardsport, Knox Co, IN	72
Chambers Alexander	First Pres Ch Cem, Trenton, NJ	28
Chambers Alexander	White River Cem, nr Kent, Jefferson Co, IN	72
Chambers Benjamin	Chester Cem, Chestertown, Kent Co, MD	71

Chambers Benjamin Jr	Falling Spring Pres Ch Cem, Franklin Co, PA	19
Chambers Benjamin Jr	Falling Spring Pres Ch Cem, Chambersburg, PA	20
Chambers Cuff	Leeds, ME	18
Chambers David	First Pres Ch Cem, Trenton, NJ	28
Chambers James	Falling Spring Pres Ch Cem, Chambersburg, PA	20
Chambers James	First Pres Ch Cem, Cranbury, NJ	76
Chambers James	Lewis Cem, Union Co, PA	15
Chambers John	First Pres Ch Cem, Trenton, NJ	28
Chambers John	Friends Cem, New Garden, PA	42
Chambers John	Hornbrook farm, nr Union, Pike Co, IN	72
Chambers John	Kennedy Cem, nr Wright City, MO	23
Chambers John	Lebanon Cem, Mifflin Twp, Allegheny Co, PA	71
Chambers Matthew Capt	Old South Cem, Nashua, NH	40
Chambers Nathaniel	Monroe Cem, Washington Co, IN	72
Chambers Robert	First Pres Ch Cem, Trenton, NJ	28
Chambers Robert	Old Founders Cem, Cambridge, OH	53
Chambers William	First Pres Ch Cem, Trenton, NJ	28
Chambers William	Sweetman Cem, Ballston, Saratoga Co, NY	77
Chambers William Capt	Falling Spring Ch Cem, Chambersburg, PA	21
Champe John	Lane, Onondaga Twp, Ingham Co, MI	56
Champion Daniel	Fam Cem, Mays Landing, NJ	23
Champion Epaphriditus	Riverview, East Haddam, CT	56
Champion Job Elder	Peck Cem, Clifton Park Center, Clifton Twp, NY	41
Champion Joel	Old North Chatham Cem, North Chatham, Columbia Co, NY	79
Champion John	Aetna Cem, nr Tuckahoe, NJ	23
Champion John	East Worcester Cem, East Worcester, Otsego Co, NY	75
Champion Judah	East Litchfield, CT	17
Champion Judah	East Cem, Litchfield, CT	18
Champion Lynde	Green River Cem, Austerlitz, Columbia Co, NY	48
Champion Medes	Ashleyville Center, West Springfield, MA	15
Champion Reuben Dr	Ticonderoga Battlefield Cem, NY	46
Champion Reuben Jr	Meeting House Hill Cem, West Springfield, MA	46
Champlin Adam	River Bend Cem, Westerly, RI	48
Champlin Adam	Westerly, RI	15
Champlin Christopher	Old Cem, Newport, Newport Co, RI	31
Champlin George	Old Cem, Newport, Newport Co, RI	31
Champlin Joseph	Kenyon Grounds, Richmond, RI	51
Champlin Joseph	Old Bur Gr, Stonington, CT	56
Champlin Stephen	Liberty Hill, Lebanon, CT	56
Champney Caleb	North Cem, Dorchester, MA	46
Champney John	North Cem, Dorchester, MA	46
Champney Jonathan	Old Cem, Southboro, MA	50
Champney Richard	North Cem, Portsmouth, NH	34
Chancellor David	Chancellor Graveyard, Hammond Twp, Spencer Co, IN	72
Chancellor Thomas	Pioneer Cem, nr Harrisville, Ritchie Co, WV	50
Chandler Aaron	Old Cem, Westmoreland, NH	60
Chandler Abiel	West Parish, Andover, MA	56
Chandler Asa	Mayflower Cem, Duxbury, MA	50
Chandler David	Center Cem, Hanover, NH	27
Chandler David Lt	Enfield, CT	15
Chandler Ebenezer	Cem 1 mi N of Chandler's Pond, Canterbury, NH	66
Chandler Enos	North Yarmouth, ME	53
Chandler Ichabod	First Pres Churchyard, Elizabeth, NJ	52
Chandler Isaac	Duell's Corners Cem, Hamburgh, NY	33
Chandler Isaac	Duels Corners Cem, Orchard Park, Erie Co, NY	15
Chandler Isaac	Plains Cem, Boscawen, NH	29
Chandler Isaac	South Parish, Andover, MA	56
Chandler Isaac	Windsor, CT	15
Chandler Isaac Maj	Old Cem, Hopkinton, NH	29
Chandler James	First Parish Cem, Andover, MA	46
Chandler James	West Parish Bur Gr, Andover, MA	26

Chandler James Jr	First Pres Churchyard, Elizabeth, NJ	52
Chandler Joel	Center Cem, Alstead, NH	37
Chandler John	Androscoggin Co, ME	18
Chandler John	Chandlersville Cem, OH	55
Chandler John	Durham, ME	29
Chandler John	Marcy Cem, Bradford, CT	55
Chandler John	Mayflower Cem, Duxbury, MA	62
Chandler John	Meeting House Hill Cem, East Princeton, MA	49
Chandler John	Old Lexington Cem, Lexington, MA	55
Chandler John Jr	Old Lexington Cem, Lexington, MA	55
Chandler John Lt	Maple Cem, Winthrop, ME	45
Chandler Jonathan	First Pres Churchyard, Elizabeth, NJ	52
Chandler Jonathan Capt	River Road Cem, Piermont, NH	32
Chandler Joseph	Copps Hill Bur Gr, Boston, MA	55
Chandler Joseph	Hill Cem, Concord, MA	55
Chandler Joseph	Noble Cem, Otterville, Jersey Co, IL	73
Chandler Joshua	Cem of Brick Ch nr Centerville, New Castle Co, DE	46
Chandler Joshua	Hammond Cem, Mattapoisett, MA	18
Chandler Joshua	Mayflower Cem, Duxbury, MA	62
Chandler Joshua	South Parish Bur Gr, Andover, MA	26
Chandler Josiah	Cem, Chandlers Valley, PA	52
Chandler Josiah	South of Rochester Village, Windsor Co, VT	29
Chandler Lewis	Old Bennington, VT	40
Chandler Lewis	Old Bennington Town Hill Cem, VT	41
Chandler Mordecai	Spartanburg Co, SC	17
Chandler Moses	Cem in Jay, across Wilton line, ME	45
Chandler Nathan	Cem nr RR station, Norwood, Potsdam, St Lawrence Co, NY	29
Chandler Nathan	Old North Cem, Concord, NH	33
Chandler Nathan	Old North Bur Gr, Concord, NH	41
Chandler Peter	Cem on town common, Nelson, NH	35
Chandler Philip	Mayflower Cem, Duxbury, MA	58
Chandler Samuel	Center Cem, Alstead, NH	37
Chandler Samuel	East Woodstock, CT	15
Chandler Samuel	First Pres Churchyard, Elizabeth, NJ	52
Chandler Samuel	Mayflower Cem, Duxbury, MA	50
Chandler Samuel	Woodstock Hill Cem, Woodstock, CT	55
Chandler Seth	East Woodstock Cem, Woodstock, CT	55
Chandler Silas	Fairview Cem, Westford, MA	55
Chandler Stephen	Union Grave Yard, Potsdam, NY	29
Chandler Thomas	Mayflower Cem, Duxbury, MA	50
Chandler Thomas	[no cem named], WV	29
Chandler William	Center Cem, Hanover, NH	27
Chandler William	[no cem named], MA	26
Chandler William	North Cem, Westford, MA	48
Chandler Zebedee	Priv Cem, Plympton, MA	56
Chandler Zebulon	Cady Fam Cem, nr Archers Fork, Washington Co, OH	56
Chaney John	Nr Ooley's Mill & Worthington, Greene Co, IN	72
Chaney John Capt	East Wilton, ME	15
Chapel Amos	Chestnut Ridge, Monterey, MA	56
Chapel Isaac	LeRoy Cem, LeRoy Twp, PA	53
Chapel Samuel	Chestnut Ridge, Monterey, MA	56
Chapin Abel	Chicopee St Cem, Chicopee, MA	54
Chapin Able Col	Chicopee St Cem, Chicopee, MA	46
Chapin Amariah	Prospect Hill Cem, Uxbridge, MA	57
Chapin Amos	Crossroads Cem on Brush Hill, Sheffield, MA	41
Chapin Asahel	Elmwood Cem, Holyoke, MA	57
Chapin Benoni	Fam Cem, Chicopee, MA	57
Chapin Caleb Capt	Old Cem, Burks Flat, Bernardston, MA	00
Chapin Calvin	Shedsville, VT	30
Chapin Charles	Chapinville Cem, Taconic, nr Salisbury, CT	64
Chapin David	Fam Cem, Chicopee, MA	57

Chapin Ebenezer	Cem, Ensfield, MA 49
Chapin Elijah	Fam Cem, Chicopee, MA 57
Chapin Elijah	Venice Center Cem, Venice, NY 56
Chapin Elisha Capt	Elmwood Cem, Holyoke, MA 17
Chapin Ephraim Capt	Chicopee St Cem, Chicopee, MA 46
Chapin Ezekial	Fam Cem, Chicopee, MA 57
Chapin Gideon	North Cem, Rowe, Franklin Co, MA 54
Chapin Henry	Fam Cem, Chicopee, MA 57
Chapin Hiram	Village Cem, Surry, NH 35
Chapin Israel	Canandaigua Cem, Ontario Co, NY 33
Chapin Japhet	Taylor Cem, Buckland, MA 56
Chapin Japheth	Fam Cem, Chicopee, MA 57
Chapin Joel Lt	Old Cem, Burks Flat, Bernardston, MA 00
Chapin John	Granby Cem, Granby, MA 55
Chapin Joseph	Cem on The Hill, Monterey, MA 41
Chapin Joseph	Center Cem, Middlesex, VT 33
Chapin Joseph	Old Center Cem, Monterey, MA 41
Chapin Joseph	Prospect Hill Cem, Uxbridge, MA 57
Chapin Joseph	Vernon Grove Cem, Milford, MA 46
Chapin Josiah	Skinner Cem, Vernon Center, Oneida Co, NY 83
Chapin Josiah	Skinner Cem, Vernon Center, Oneida Co, NY 84
Chapin Lucius	Spring Grove Cem, Cincinnati, Hamilton Co, OH 76
Chapin Martin	Elmwood Cem, Holyoke, MA 57
Chapin Mirick	Sykes priv Cem, Ludlow, MA 30
Chapin Moses	Vernon Grove Cem, Milford, MA 46
Chapin Moses Col	East Clarendon Cem, Clarendon, VT 25
Chapin Moses Col	East Clarendon Cem, Clarendon, VT 24
Chapin Phineas	Chapinville Cem, Taconic, nr Salisbury, CT 64
Chapin Phineas	Old Cong Ch Cem, Chicopee, MA 53
Chapin Phineas Jr	Chicopee, MA 54
Chapin Samuel	Oquawka Cem, Oquawka, GA 29
Chapin Seth	Chapin Cem, Chicopee, MA 57
Chapin Seth Dea	Mendon Center Cem, Mendon, MA 46
Chapin Silas	Fam Cem, Chicopee, MA 57
Chapin Simeon	Fam Cem, Chicopee, MA 57
Chapin Stephen	Vernon Grove Cem, Milford, MA 46
Chapin William	Fam Cem, Chicopee, MA 57
Chaplain M	Stone Church Cem, WV 24
Chaplin Asa	Rowley Cem, Rowley, MA 45
Chaplin Ebenezer	Old Bur Gr, Suffield, Hartford Co, CT 24
Chaplin John	Nr Stiles Pond, Waterford, VT 15
Chaplin John	South Bridgeton, ME 50
Chaplin John	South Bridgton Cem, South Bridgton, Cumberland Co, ME 57
Chaplin Micah	Town Cem, Fitzwilliam, NH 32
Chaplin Moses	Rowley Cem, Essex, MA 48
Chaplin Moses Caton	Stone Ch Cem, Elm Grove, Ohio Co, WV 81
Chaplin Moses Caton	Stone Ch Cem, Elm Grove, Ohio Co, WV 78
Chapline Isaac Sr	Fam Cem, nr Shepherd Grade, WV 42
Chapman Benjamin	Westford Hill Cem, Ashford, CT 55
Chapman Benjamin Capt	Gilkie Yard, Plainfield, NH 28
Chapman Caleb	Moodus, East Haddam, CT 56
Chapman Caleb	Stockbridge Cem, Stockbridge, MA 47
Chapman Constant	Brimfield, OH 26
Chapman Daniel	Chapman Cem, nr Vienna, Tunnell Hill Twp, IL 72
Chapman Daniel	Harmony Grove, Boxford, MA 55
Chapman Daniel	Harmony Cem, East Boxford, MA 29
Chapman David	Center Cem, Westhampton, MA 54
Chapman David	Dennis Cem, Rt 6, Yarmouth, MA 55
Chapman David	Old Town Cem, Newmarket, NH 32
Chapman Ebenezer	Medway, MA 56
Chapman Ebenezer	Salem (Belcher) Cem, Salem, NY 65

Chapman Elijah	First or Sadler Cem, Greenfield, Saratoga Co, NY 77
Chapman Elisha	Fam Cem, corner nr Winnisquam Bridge, Sanbornton, NH 29
Chapman Elisha	Oyster River, Saybrook, CT 56
Chapman Elisha Dr	Nr Syracuse, Onondaga Co, NY 35
Chapman Frederick	Windsor, CT 15
Chapman Giles	Fam bur gr, 4 mi fr Chappells Depot, Saluda Co, SC 15
Chapman Herman	Hoagland Cem, Barlow Twp, Washington Twp, OH 55
Chapman Isaac	Beverly, MA 55
Chapman Isaac	Chapman Cem, Mt Prospect, Ripplemeade, Giles Co, VA 73
Chapman Jabez	East Haadam, CT 54
Chapman James	Kings Station Cem, Woodvale St, Gallatin, Sumner Co, TN 77
Chapman Jedediah	Saybrook Cem, Saybrook, Middlesex Co, CT 61
Chapman John	Dennis Cem, Dennis, MA 33
Chapman John	Fam bur gr, mouth of Walker's Creek, VA 50
Chapman John	Mount Hope Cem, Rochester, Monroe Co, NY 33
Chapman John	Three Bridges, East Haddam, CT 56
Chapman John	West Hoosick, Hoosick Twp, Rensselaer Co, NY 37
Chapman John Jr	Dennis Cem, Dennis, MA 33
Chapman John Sr	Mt Zion Bapt Ch Cem, Spartanburg Co, SC 70
Chapman Jonathan	Sutherland Cem, Thomas farm, nr Chatham, Columbia Co, NY 42
Chapman Joseph	Fam lot, Windsor Cem, Windsor, NH 45
Chapman Joseph	Old Linebrook Cem, Newbury Rd, Ipswich, MA 55
Chapman Joshua	Becket Center, Becket, MA 56
Chapman Lemuel	Brandon Cem, Knox Co, OH 55
Chapman Levi Capt	Fam Cem, Bartlett farm, North Nottingham, NH 27
Chapman Micah Capt	Dennis Cem, Dennis, MA 33
Chapman Michael	Huron, OH 26
Chapman Michael	Huron Cem, Erie Co, OH 55
Chapman Michael	Sandusky, OH 15
Chapman Nathan	Fam Cem, Bedford Co, VA 73
Chapman Nathaniel	Kingfield, ME 22
Chapman Nathaniel	Old Jointer Ch Cem, VA 35
Chapman Nathaniel	Riverside Cem, Kingfield, ME 30
Chapman Nehemiah	Cartwright Cem, Sharon, Litchfield Co, CT 67
Chapman Reuben Rowley	Town Hill Cem, Lakeville, CT 64
Chapman Robert	Boland Cem, Sharon, Litchfield Co, CT 66
Chapman Robert	Boland District Cem, Sharon, CT 45
Chapman Samuel	Old Bur Hill, Marblehead, MA 56
Chapman Smith	Old Cem, nr West Parish Ch, Newmarket, NH 41
Chapman Stephen	Lyme Plain Cem, Lyme, NH 29
Chapman Sumner	Lone grave by RR tracks, nr Bradford, Westerly, RI 35
Chapman Sumner	Nr railroad, Westerly, RI 48
Chapman Sumner	Westerly, RI 15
Chapman Thomas	Westford Cem, Ashford, CT 55
Chapman Titus	Akron, OH 15
Chapman Titus	Old Middlebury, OH 45
Chapman Valentine	Town Cem, Barnstead Center, NH 28
Chapman William	Boland Cem, Sharon, Litchfield Co, CT 66
Chapman William	Reeves Twp, Jo Daviess Co, IN 56
Chapman William Dea	Saybrook Cem, Middlesex, CT 57
Chappel John	Hackensack Green Cem, Hackensack, NJ 47
Chappel John	Townsend Cem, Andover, CT 55
Chappel Nathan Jr	Norwich Town Cem, Norwich, CT 18
Chappel Noah	Farmington Twp, PA 52
Chappell Abner	Fayette, Howard Co, MO 15
Chappell Curtis	Old Cem, Elbridge, Onondaga Co, NY 75
Chappell Hicks Maj	Plain St Bapt Ch, Columbia, SC 42
Chappell Isaac	LeRoy Cem, Rt 414, E of LeRoy, Bradford Co, PA 68
Chappell Laban	His prop (grave), Brick Ch (marker), Fairfield Co, SC 40
Chappell Robert	Cabin Branch (grave), Brick Ch (marker), Richland Co, SC 40
Chappell William	Old Hartwick Cem, Hartwick, NY 58

Chapple James	Church on the Green, Hackensack, NJ	55
Chapple Thomas	Church on the Green, Hackensack, NJ	55
Chard Consider	Briggs Cem betw Middle Line Rd & Rt 20, Saratoga Co, NY	77
Charles Aaron	Brimfield Cem, Brimfield, MA	58
Charles Elijah	[no cem named], IL	26
Charles Elijah	Moore Cem, Belleville, St Clair Co, IL	77
Charles Pierre L'E	Arlington Natl Cem, Arlington, Arlington Co, VA	77
Charleville Francis	Randolph Co, IL	48
Charleville Jean B	Randolph Co, IL	48
Charley George	Fam farm, Indian Creek nr Corydon, Harrison Co, IN	72
Charlick Henry	Green farm, Bedford, NY	35
Charlick John	Green farm, Bedford, NY	35
Charlock Henry	Hopewell, East Fishkill, NY	56
Charlton John	Meth Epis Cem, Newtown, Anderson Twp, Hamilton Co, OH	55
Chase Abner	Old aban Cem, Unity, NH	35
Chase Abner	Yarmouth, MA	48
Chase Abraham	Downing-Winn Richmond Plot, Hillsdale, Columbia Co, NY	42
Chase Abraham	Schoolhouse Rd Cem, Austerlitz, Columbia Co, NY	79
Chase Abraham	Spring Grove Cem, Cincinnati, OH	72
Chase Amos Lt	County Farm Cem, Unity, NH	34
Chase Asa	Douglass Center Cem, Douglass, MA	45
Chase Augustus	Across fr Freetown Ch, Assonet, MA	54
Chase Benjamin	Fam Cem, Cooperstown Rd, Hartwick, Otsego Co, NY	72
Chase Benjamin	Hartwick, NY	52
Chase Beverly	Fam Cem, South Bloomfield, OH	56
Chase Caleb	Mad River Cem, Thornton, NH	36
Chase Consider	Carver, MA	30
Chase Consider	South Carver Cem, Carver, MA	34
Chase Consider	South Carver, MA	16
Chase Daniel	Flat Cem, Cornish, NH	29
Chase David	Island Hill Cem, Buskirk, Hoosick, NY	36
Chase Enoch	West Parish Bur Gr, Andover, MA	26
Chase Ephraim	Walnut Cem, East Parish, Haverhill, MA	31
Chase Ezekiel	Chase Cem, Sebec, ME	29
Chase Ezekiel	Dartmouth, MA	52
Chase Ezra	Cooper Cem, Taunton, MA	58
Chase Ezra	Greenwood Cem, East Parish, New Haverhill, MA	31
Chase Greenfield	Across fr Freetown Ch, Assonet, MA	54
Chase Holder	Portsmouth Cem, Portsmouth, RI	55
Chase Jacob	Lee, Oneida Co, NY	71
Chase James	West Dummerston, VT	17
Chase Jeremiah	Old Cem, Virgil, Cortland Co, NY	36
Chase Jeremiah	Town Cem, Bristol, NH	29
Chase Job	North Harwich, MA	50
Chase John	Flat Cem, Cornish, NH	29
Chase John	North Parish Cem, Plaistow, NH	31
Chase John	Old Cem, Main Rd, Cheshire, MA	55
Chase John	Sharp's Lot Rd nr end, Swansea, MA	54
Chase John	Town Hall Cem, Pittsfield, NH	28
Chase John Capt	Hill Cem, Conway, NH	32
Chase John Ens	Blodgett Cem, Hudson, NH	28
Chase Jonathan	Fitz Cem, Auburn, ME	70
Chase Jonathan	Site of orig First Bapt Ch, Sanbornton, NH	33
Chase Jonathan Col	Cornish Cem, Cornish, MA	45
Chase Jonathan Col	Trinity Ch Cem, Cornish, NH	29
Chase Jonathan Jr	Durgin Cem, Tilton, NH	31
Chase Jonathan Sgt	South Wolfeboro Cem, Wolfeboro, NH	26
Chase Joseph	Hill Top Cem, Deerfield, NH	28
Chase Joseph	Pulaski Town Cem, Pulaski, Oswego Co, NY	66
Chase Joshua	Blodgett Cem, Hudson, NH	28
Chase Joshua	South Cem, Hudson, NH	46

Chase Josiah — Old Center Cem, Deerfield, NH 34
Chase Josiah — Schenevus Cem, Maryland, Otsego Co, NY 75
Chase Josiah — Walnut Cem, East Parish, Haverhill, MA 31
Chase Levi — Lakenham Cem, Carver, MA 59
Chase Lot — West Litchfield, CT 17
Chase Metaphor Maj — Old Pine Grove Cem, Leominster, MA 47
Chase Moody — Long Meadow Cem, Chester, NH 33
Chase Moody — Shirley, now Ayer, MA 56
Chase Moses — Center Cem, Alstead, NH 43
Chase Moses — Mercer Cem, Cornish, NH 30
Chase Moses — Springfield, VT 15
Chase Moses — Union Cem, Amesbury, MA 46
Chase Nathaniel — Litchfield, ME 20
Chase Nathaniel — Town Hall Cem, Pittsfield, NH 29
Chase Obadiah — Cem back of fire house, Carmel, Putnam Co, NY 36
Chase Oliver — Chase #2 Cem, CT 28
Chase Parker — Campton, Grafton Co, NH 51
Chase Parker — [no cem named], IL 19
Chase Parker — Village Cem, Campton, NH 36
Chase Perley — Village Cem, Chester, NH 33
Chase Philip — Cem, Assonet, MA 26
Chase Reuben Capt — Old North Bur Gr, Nantucket, MA 45
Chase Richard — Center Cem, Tyringham, MA 57
Chase Richard — North Harwich, MA 50
Chase Roger — [no cem named] 17
Chase Samuel — Church Cem, South Dennis, MA 49
Chase Samuel — Old St Paul's Cem, Baltimore, MD 20
Chase Samuel — Pine Crest Cem, Litchfield, NH 49
Chase Samuel — St Paul's Cem, Freemont St & Lombard St, Baltimore, MD 15
Chase Samuel — Trinity Ch Cem, Cornish, NH 29
Chase Samuel 3rd — Trinity Ch Cem, Cornish, NH 29
Chase Samuel Col — Pine Crest Cem, Litchfield, NH 31
Chase Samuel Jr — Trinity Ch Cem, Cornish, NH 36
Chase Solomon Capt — Fam Cem, north part of Cornish, NH 45
Chase Solomon Dr — Trinity Ch Cem, Cornish, NH 29
Chase Somerby — Old Hill Cem, Newburyport, MA 56
Chase Stephen — North Cem, Portsmouth, NH 34
Chase Steven — Old Pine Grove Cem, Leominster, MA 47
Chase Thomas — Chase-Leavitt Cem, Fremont, NH 31
Chase Thomas — Livermore, ME 18
Chase Thomas — Warwick Cem, Warwick, MA 30
Chase Timothy — Causeway Cem, Tisbury, Martha's Vineyard, MA 46
Chase Wells — Long Meadow Cem, Chester, NH 33
Chase William — Greenwood Cem, East Parish, New Haverhill, MA 31
Chase William — Site of orig First Bapt Ch, Sanbornton, NH 33
Chase Zephaniah — Fam Cem (aban), Jewett Center, Greene Co, NY 69
Chatfield Isaac — Hawkins Cem, Quaker Farms, Oxford, New Haven Co, CT 39
Chatfield Joel — Fleming Hill Cem, Fleming, NY 41
Chatfield John — Hayground Cem, Bridgehampton, NY 35
Chatfield Josiah — Fleming Hill Cem, Fleming, NY 56
Chatfield Thomas — Hawkins, Oxford, CT 56
Chatham William — Bridgeport, Seneca Falls, NY 15
Chatterton Joseph — Old Cem, Acworth, NH 34
Cheadle Asa — Nr Big Bottom, Windsor Twp, Morgan Co, OH 55
Cheesebrough James — Alden Cem, Alden, NY 33
Cheesebrough Perez — Leffingwell Town Cem, Leffingwell, CT 18
Cheesman Elijah — St John's Cem, Chew's Landing, NJ 44
Cheesman Ephraim — St John's Cem, Chews Landing, NJ 32
Cheesman Richard — Chews Landing, NJ 32
Cheesman Richard Sr — St John's Cem, Chews Landing, NJ 32
Cheesman Samuel — Chew-Powell Cem, Blackwood, NJ 47

Cheesman Ziba	Dyer Hill Cem, Braintree, MA	55
Cheever Bartholomew	Mtg Hs Hill Cem, Princeton, MA	49
Cheever Daniel	Mtg Hs Hill Cem, Princeton, MA	49
Cheever Ebenezer	Cornwell farm Cem, Scipio, Cayuga Co, NY	69
Cheever Samuel	Walnut Grove Cem, Danvers, MA	55
Cheever Thomas	Western Cem, West Lynn, MA	56
Cheever Thomas	Western Cem, West Lynn, MA	56
Chellis Nathaniel	Charlestown, NH	16
Chellis Thomas Ens	Town Cem, Newton, NH	32
Chenery Elihu	Vine Lake, Medfield, MA	56
Chenery Ephraim	Vine Lake, Medfield, MA	56
Chenery Isaac	Old Bur Gr, Holden, MA	15
Chenery Isaac Dr	Old Cem, Holden, MA	45
Chenery Jesse	Old Cem, Weston, MA	56
Chenery Simeon	Vine Lake, Medfield, MA	56
Chenery Timothy	Vine Lake, Medfield, MA	56
Cheney Abram	Fam Cem, nr Keeling, Pittsylvania Co, VA	59
Cheney Ebenezer	Kiantone Cem, Kiantone, Chautauqua Co, NY	62
Cheney Ebenezer	North Orange, MA	30
Cheney Ebenezer	North Orange Cem, Orange, MA	31
Cheney Ebenezer	Old Cem, Fly Creek, Otsego Co, NY	71
Cheney Ebenezer	South Bur Gr, Newton Highlands, MA	30
Cheney Ebenezer	South Bur Gr, Newton Highlands, MA	29
Cheney Francis	Philpott farm, 1 mi S of Newark, Greene Co, IN	24
Cheney Johnson	Perry Center Cem, Perry, Wyoming Co, NY	64
Cheney Joseph	Old Cem, Bradford, MA	50
Cheney Levi	North Orange Cem, Orange, MA	31
Cheney Moses	North Orange, MA	30
Cheney Nathaniel	Armsby Cem, MA	15
Cheney Nathaniel	Jamaica Cem, Jamaica, Windham Co, VT	61
Cheney Nathaniel	South Sutton Cem, Sutton, NH	37
Cheney Samuel	Dover Cem, Walpole, MA	55
Cheney Solomon	Old Bur Gr, Holden, MA	15
Cheney Thomas	Forest Hill Cem, East Derry, NH	38
Cheney Thomas	Small farm Cem, Union Twp, Champaign Co, OH	55
Cheney William	Center Cem, Alstead, NH	37
Cheney William	Colebrook, Ashtabula Co, OH	18
Chenoweth Arthur	Fam estate, betw Darksville & Arden, Berkeley Co, WV	42
Chenoweth Arthur Jr	South of Columbus, IN	48
Chenoweth Elijah Sr	Farm, Pleasant, SW part of Franklin Co, OH	56
Chenoweth John	Elkins, WV	42
Chenoweth John	Rockhill, Darkvil, New Castle, Berkeley Co, WV	55
Chenoweth Richard	Long Run Cem, Eastwood, Jefferson Co, KY	78
Chenoweth Richard	Salem Cem, Sheffield Twp, Tippecanoe Co, IN	69
Chenoweth Thomas Jr	Fam Cem, fam farm, Pleasant Twp, OH	56
Chenoweth William	Elizabethtown, Hardin Co, KY	56
Chenowith John	Chenowith Cem, nr Elkins, WV	30
Cherry Aaron	Georgetown (Cambridge) Cem, nr Guilford, Dearborn Co, IN	78
Cherry Henry	Huron, Erie Co, OH	15
Cherry Henry	Milan Cem, fam lot, Milan, OH	56
Cherry John	Miles, Trumbull Co, OH	56
Cherry Samuel	New Haven Cem, Oswego Co, NY	65
Cherry Thomas P	Walnut Twp, Fairfield Co, OH	53
Cheseborough Charles	Died on English prison ship, NY	46
Chesebrough Perez	Bozrah Cem, New London, CT	55
Chesebrough Thomas	Factory Village Cem, Milton, Ulster Co, NY	77
Chesley Phillip Corp	Daley farm, Madbury, NH	50
Chesley Jonathan	His farm, Barnstead, NH	28
Chesley Philip Corp	Bur gr on rd fr Mast Rd to railroad, NH	35
Chesley Samuel Lt	Fam farm, Durham, NH	50
Chesley Simeon	Windfall Cem, Granville Twp, Bradford Co, PA	53

Chesley Simeon	Windfall Cem, N of E Canton, Bradford Co, PA 68
Chesrow Peter	Dutch Luth Ch Cem, Fallowfield Twp, Washington Co, PA 83
Chester Christopher	Westerly, RI 15
Chester Daniel	Groton Cem, Groton, CT 15
Chester Eldredge	Groton Cem, Groton, CT 15
Chester John	Old Cem, Wethersfield, CT 56
Chestnut Daniel	His farm, Huntington Twp, Ross Co, OH 55
Cheswell Wentworth	Fam Cem, Newmarket, NH 28
Cheuvront Joseph	Fam Cem, VanScoy Land, Goodhope, Harrison Co, WV 72
Chew Aaron	St John's Protestant Epis Cem, Chew's Landing, NJ 47
Chew David	Old fam Cem, Mantua, NJ 47
Chew John	Fredericksburg, VA 30
Chew John	Fredericksburg, VA 29
Chew John	Ketoctin (Short Hill) Cem, Purcellville, Loudoun Co, VA 77
Chew Robert	Chew-Powell Cem, Blackwood, NJ 47
Chewning Samuel	Caroline Co, VA 55
Cheyney Thomas	Cheyney, Delaware Co, PA 52
Chickering Nathaniel	Dover Cem, Dover, MA 55
Chickering Oliver	Old Cem, Rutland, MA 49
Chickering Samuel Jr	North Parish Bur Gr, Andover, MA 26
Chickering Timothy	North Cem, Westmoreland, NH 36
Chidester Daniel	Manchester Cem, Scipio, Cayuga Co, NY 69
Chidester Phineas	Pres Cem, Succasunna, Morris Co, NJ 30
Chidester William	Canfield, OH 17
Chidester William	Canfield, OH 18
Chidester William	Village Cem, Canfield, Mahoning Co, OH 55
Chidsey Joseph	North Guilford Cem, North Guilford, CT 55
Child Abel	East Woodstock Cem, Woodstock, CT 55
Child Abijah	Waltham, MA 49
Child Abijah Jr	Village Cem, Constable, NY 15
Child Abram	Groton, MA 55
Child Alpha	East Woodstock, CT 15
Child Amasa	East Woodstock Cem, Woodstock, CT 55
Child Asa	East Woodstock, CT 15
Child Charles	East Woodstock, CT 15
Child Chester	East Woodstock Cem, Woodstock, CT 55
Child Cromwell	Union Cem, Smithfield Twp, Bradford Co, PA 53
Child Elias	[no cem named], CT 19
Child Elias	East Woodstock Cem, Woodstock, CT 55
Child Elisha	East Woodstock, CT 15
Child Henry	East Woodstock Cem, Woodstock, CT 55
Child Increase Capt	Greenfield Cem, Saratoga, NY 47
Child Increase Capt	North Milton Cem, Milton, Saratoga Co, NY 41
Child Jacob	[no cem named], CT 19
Child John	Bungay Cem, Woodstock, CT 55
Child Jonathan	[no cem named], CT 19
Child Jonathan	North Thetford, VT 17
Child Jonathan	Old Yard Cem, Weston, MA 55
Child Levi	East Woodstock Cem, Woodstock, CT 55
Child Moses	Old Village Cem, Temple, NH 28
Child Nathaniel	East Woodstock, CT 15
Child Nehemiah	East Woodstock Cem, Woodstock, CT 55
Child Obadiah	East Woodstock Cem, Woodstock, CT 55
Child Pennel	Pittsfield, VT 56
Child Peter	East Woodstock Cem, Woodstock, CT 55
Child Phineas	Eliot St Cem, Boston, MA 46
Child Phineas	Eliot St Cem, Jamaica Plain, Boston, MA 56
Child Phineas Jr	Eliot St Cem, Jamaica Plain, Boston, MA 56
Child Salmon	Honey Creek Cem, Rochester Twp, Racine, WI 56
Child Samuel	Addison Co, VT 56
Child Samuel	[no cem named], CT 19

Child Shubael	Bungay Yard Cem, W Woodstock, Windham Co, CT 69
Child Shubael	[no cem named], CT 19
Child Stephen	Cornish Flat Cem, Cornish, NH 30
Child Thomas Sgt	[no cem named], CT 19
Child Timothy	Walnut Street Cem, Brookline, MA 56
Child Willard	East Woodstock Cem, Woodstock, CT 55
Child Zachariah	Old Cem, West Boylston, MA 55
Childers Pleasant	Pikeville Cem, Pike Co, KY 71
Childers William	Mount Zion Bapt Ch Cem, Cherryville, NC 49
Childress John	Mt Harmony Cem, Knoxville, Knox Co, TN 77
Childress John	Old Graveyard, Carmi, White Co, IL 65
Childress Thomas	Nr Fayetteville, TN 29
Childs Elijah	Barnstable Cem, Rt 6, Barnstable, MA 55
Childs Jonas	Becket Center, Becket, MA 56
Childs Jonas	Hallowell Cem, Augusta, ME 15
Childs Jonas	Hallowell Cem, Hallowell, ME 17
Childs Jonathan	Wilmington, VT 17
Childs Josiah	United Cong Ch Cem, Barnstable, MA 55
Childs Lemuel	Deerfield, MA 55
Childs Reuben	Howland Cem, Conway, MA 53
Childs Salmon P	Honey Creek Cem, Waukesha, WI 37
Chiles William	Fam Cem, Abbeville, SC 56
Chilson Ezra	Silver Brook Cem, Niles, MI 15
Chilson Levi	Rawson Brook Cem, Leicester, MA 55
Chilton John	Rockspring, Fauquier Co, VA 56
Chin Samuel	Old Burial Hill, Marblehead, MA 56
Chinn Samuel	Old Bur Hill, Marblehead, MA 29
Chipman Amos	Ira Allen Cem, Sunderland, Bennington Co, VT 36
Chipman Daniel	West Cem, Middlebury, VT 29
Chipman Jacob	Stetson Cem, #47-R, Monponsett, MA 40
Chipman Jesse	Dimmick Cem, 2 mi NW of Malone, NY 15
Chipman John	North Beverly Cem, Beverly, MA 46
Chipman John	Village Cem, Sandwich, MA 56
Chipman John Col	Seeley Dist Cem, Middlebury, VT 29
Chipman Joseph Dea	United Cong Ch Cem, Barnstable, MA 55
Chipman Lemuel	Sheldon Cem, Sheldon Twp, Wyoming Co, NY 64
Chipman Thomas	Chipmans Corners Cem, Locke Twp, NY 41
Chipman Timothy	Shoreham, VT 15
Chipman William	Duck Fleet Cem, Wellfleet, MA 46
Chipman William	Poland, ME 18
Chipp John	Old Dutch Cem, Kingston, Ulster Co, NY 85
Chipp Joseph	Old Dutch Cem, Kingston, Ulster Co, NY 85
Chirst Michael	Palmer St Cem, Philadelphia, PA 52
Chishelum Elijah	Cem 20 mi fr Sparta, White Co, TN 58
Chism James	Old Mulky Mtg Hs, State Park, Barren Co, KY 33
Chittenden Abraham	Alderbrook Cem, Guilford, CT 55
Chittenden Benjamin	Alderbrook Cem, Guilford, CT 55
Chittenden Cornelius	Westbrook Cem, Westbrook, Middlesex Co, CT 61
Chittenden James	Town Ground, East Springfield, NY 15
Chittenden Jared	Evergreen Cem, South St, Lairdsville, NY 36
Chittenden Jared	North Guilford, CT 54
Chittenden Josiah	North Guilford Cem, North Guilford, CT 55
Chittenden Levi	North Guilford Cem, North Guilford, CT 55
Chittenden Nathan	Riverside Cem, Guilford, CT 55
Chittenden Nathaniel	First Parish Cem, Norwell, MA 39
Chittenden Reuben	Ridgefield Cem, Gilbertsville, NY 71
Chittenden Shem	North Guilford Cem, North Guilford, CT 55
Chittenden Simeon	North Guilford Cem, North Guilford, CT 55
Chittenden Solomon	Hopkinton Cem, Hopkinton, NY 56
Chittenden Thomas	Arlington Cem, Arlington, VT 46
Chittenden Timothy	Old Town Hall Cem, Salisbury, CT 64

Chittenden Timothy Jr	Old Town Hall Cem, Salisbury, CT 64
Chittenden William	Leets Island Cem, Guilford, CT 55
Chittim John	Bethel Cem, York Co, SC 56
Chiver Ebenezer	Scipio Cem, Scipio, NY 41
Choat James	Forest Hill Cem, East Derry, NH 38
Choate David	Old Cem, Wrentham, MA 55
Choate Humphrey	Forest Hill Cem, East Derry, NH 38
Choate Humphrey	Old Cem, Essex, MA 45
Choate Jeremiah	Essex, MA 55
Choate John	Old Essex Cem, Essex, MA 48
Choate Nehemiah	Old Essex Cem, Essex, MA 48
Choate William	Old Essex Cem, Essex, MA 48
Choice Tully	Fam Cem, Hancock Co, GA 31
Choice Tully	Nr Oconee River, 17 mi fr Sparta, Hancock Co, GA 34
Choice William	Nr Simpsonville, Greenville Co, SC 51
Chowning William	Lancaster Co, VA 56
Choyce James	Pres Ch Cem, east side, Flemington, NJ 26
Chrichlow John	Oxbow Cem, Cath Ch, Ritchie Co, WV 50
Chrisler Sylvester	Farm Cem, Matlock prop, Albany Co, NY 66
Christ George	Old Morav Cem, Emaus, Lehigh Co, PA 40
Christian Daniel Sr	Oak Hill Cem, Mt Carroll, IL 38
Christian Gilbert	Knoxville, TN 24
Christian Gilbert Maj	[no cem named], TN 15
Christian John	Fam farm Cem, Mentz, NY 41
Christian Turner	Fam Cem, nr Dewey Rose, Elbert Co, GA 34
Christian Turner	Stinchcomb Cem, off Bowman Rd, Elbert Co, GA 32
Christian William Col	Bullitt Cem, Jefferson Co, KY 31
Christie George Capt	New Boston Cem, New Boston, NH 47
Christie James	Bergenfield, NJ 31
Christie Jesse	Columbia St Cem, Springfield, Clark Co, OH 55
Christie John	Old Cem, back of Mahwah Ch, Mahwah, Bergen Co, NJ 26
Christie John F	Old South Ch, Bergenfield, NJ 31
Christie John W	South Ch Cem, Hackensack, NJ 56
Christie Peter	Middle Village Cem, East Springfield, NY 33
Christie Peter	Town Ground, East Springfield, NY 15
Christie William	Old South Ch, Bergenfield, NJ 31
Christman George	St Peter's Luth Cem, Montgomery Co, PA 59
Christman Jacob	Argusville Cem, Schoharie Co, NY 35
Christmas George	Luth Cem, Barren Hill, PA 52
Christmas Richard	Columbus, GA 29
Christmas Richard	Muscogee Co, GA 27
Christmen Henry	Zion's Luth Ch Cem, Chester, PA 52
Christopher Chester	Nr railroad, Westerly, RI 48
Christopher Walter	Hawthorne farm, Guernsey Co, OH 55
Christy Andrew	Pine Corners Cem, Middlesex, Yates Co, NY 80
Christy George Capt	New Boston Cem, New Boston, NH 28
Christy John	Washington Court House, sect 6 lot 195, Fayette Co, OH 55
Christy John Rev	Washington Court House, OH 18
Christy Peter	Fam Cem, nr Grenwich, NY 55
Christy Robert	Washington Court House, sect 6 lot 195, Fayette Co, OH 55
Christy Thomas	Copps Hill, Boston, MA 56
Chronicle William	Kings Mountain, NC 49
Chubb Gideon	North Hillsdale Cem, Columbia Co, NY 42
Chubbuck Ebenezer	Orwell Cem, Orwell Twp, PA 53
Chullis Ezekiel	Goshen, NH 50
Church Amasa	Otsego County Cem, Burlington, Otsego Co, NY 71
Church Benjamin	1st Parish Cem, Rochester, MA 58
Church Benjamin	Center Cem, Hubbardston, MA 26
Church Constant	Plainville Cem, Marshfield, MA 50
Church Daniel Jr	Center (now Fairmont), Lee, MA 56
Church David	Granby, MA 55

Abstract of Graves of Revolutionary Patriots 175

Church Earl	1st Parish Cem, Rochester, MA	58
Church Jabez	Blake Cem, West Thornton, Thornton, NH	36
Church James	Cem on Rt 8, across fr South Edmeston, Otsego Co, NY	71
Church James	Cherry Valley Cem, Otsego Co, NY	34
Church Joel	Killed in Wyoming Massacre, Wyoming, PA	52
Church Joel	South Hadley, MA	15
Church John	Center Cem, Dunbarton, NH	31
Church John	Central Cem, Winchester, CT	56
Church John	Court House Cem, Farmington, ME	39
Church John	Erie Co, OH	15
Church John	Mount Hope Cem, Norwich, NY	16
Church Jonathan	Huron Cem, Huron, OH	56
Church Jonathan	Rochester Cem, 4 Corners nr Church, Rochester, MA	55
Church Jonathan	Rossie, NY	15
Church Jonathan	Wethersfield Cem, Wethersfield, CT	47
Church Joseph	Old Hadley Cem, Hadley, MA	56
Church Joshua	Brookside Cem, Chester, VT	38
Church Josiah	South Hadley, MA	15
Church Moses	Pine St Cem, Springfield, MA	47
Church Moses Jr	Mahaiwe, Great Barrington, MA	56
Church Moses Sr	Mahaiwe, Great Barrington, MA	56
Church Nathaniel	Main Cem, Salisbury, CT	64
Church Paul	Old Highland Cem, MA	29
Church Peter	North Cem, Bristol, RI	78
Church Samuel	Holland Patent Cem, Holland Patent, Oneida Co, NY	80
Church Thomas	North Cem, Bristol, RI	51
Church Thomas	St James Epis Cem, Montgomery Co, PA	59
Church Uriah	Old North Granby Cem, Granby, CT	26
Church Uriah Sr	East Hartland Cem, East Hartland, CT	59
Church Willard	Hodge Cem, Hartland Twp, Livingston Co, MI	22
Church William	Hodge Cem, Hartland Twp, Livingston Co, MI	21
Church William G	Brick Ch Cem, Ira, Cayuga Co, NY	57
Church William H Jr	Pine Ridge Cem, Navarino, Onondaga Co, NY	78
Churchill Benjamin	Old Town Hall Cem, Salisbury, CT	64
Churchill Daniel	Schuyler Lake Cem, Exeter, Otsego Co, NY	71
Churchill Daniel	Stockbridge Cem, Stockbridge, MA	47
Churchill David	Old Cem, Plympton, MA	50
Churchill David Jr	Old Burial Cem, Plympton, MA	59
Churchill Ebenezer	Old Bur Cem, Plympton, MA	57
Churchill Elijah	Bell Cem, Middlefield, Hampshire Co, MA	82
Churchill Ichabod	Old Bur Cem, Plympton, MA	58
Churchill Ichabod	Shaw Cem, West Woodstock, Windsor Co, VT	75
Churchill Ichabod II	Cushing Cem, Woodstock, Windsor Co, VT	75
Churchill Isaac	Burial Hill, Plymouth, MA	56
Churchill Isaac	Old Bur Cem, Plympton, MA	57
Churchill Jabez	Cox Cem, Hartford, ME	31
Churchill James	Cold Brook (Spafford) Cem, Spafford, Onondaga Co, NY	75
Churchill James	Old Cem, Plympton, MA	50
Churchill Janna	Georgia, VT	56
Churchill Jesse	Old Cem, Wethersfield, CT	56
Churchill John	Burial Hill, Plymouth, MA	56
Churchill John	Chittenden Cem, Chittenden, VT	57
Churchill John	Cold Brook (Spafford) Cem, Spafford, Onondaga Co, NY	75
Churchill John	Scott Cem, Scott, Cortland Co, NY	62
Churchill John	Terrace Grove Cem, Pittsfield, MA	46
Churchill Joseph	New Portland Cem, Somerset Co, ME	54
Churchill Josiah	Old Bur Cem, Plympton, MA	57
Churchill Nathaniel	Old Cem, Plympton, MA	50
Churchill Perez	Lakenham Cem, Carver, MA	57
Churchill Samuel	Burial Hill, Plymouth, MA	56
Churchill Samuel	Old Cem, Sterling, MA	63

Churchill Samuel	Old Cem, Plympton, MA 50
Churchill Samuel	Old Cem, Wethersfield, CT 56
Churchill Samuel	Reynolds Corners Cem, Moreau, Saratoga Co, NY 77
Churchill Seth	Burial Hill, Plymouth, MA 56
Churchill Seth	Old Bur Cem, Plympton, MA 57
Churchill Stephen	Plymouth Cem, Plymouth, MA 47
Churchill Stephen Capt	Old North Bur Gr, Kingston, MA 45
Churchill Thomas	Fam Cem, N of his home, The Plains, Newmarket, NH 41
Churchill William	Old Cem, Plympton, MA 57
Chute Daniel	Byfield Cem, Byfield, MA 60
Chute James	Old Cem (now a park), Madison, Jefferson Co, IN 72
Chute Thomas	Windham Cem, Windham, ME 46
Cilley Cutting Col	Cilley Cem, Northfield, NH 35
Cilley John	Fam Cem, Bean Hill, Northfield, NH 36
Cilley Jonathan	Dunlap Cem, Colerain Twp, Hamilton Co, OH 55
Cilley Joseph Gen	Fam Cem, Nottingham Square, Nottingham, NH 27
Cilley Joseph Gen	Nottingham Square, Nottingham, NH 17
Cilley Samuel	Fam Cem, on Morey Hill, Andover, NH 36
Cisna Stephen	Old Pres Cem, moved to Greenlawn, Chillicothe, OH 56
Clack John Maj	Pulaski Cem, Giles Co, TN 42
Clack Spencer	Fam farm, Sevier Co, TN 29
Clack Spencer	Nr Harriman, TN 23
Clack Spencer	Nr Harriman, Roane Co, TN 24
Clader Jacob	Old part Cem, Tenth & Linden, Allentown, Lehigh Co, PA 40
Clafin John	South Cem, Holliston, MA 74
Clafin John	Tomlinson Corners Cem, Mendon, Monroe Co, NY 79
Claflin Daniel	Old Kirk Yard, Attleboro, MA 15
Claflin Ebenezer	Eustis St Cem, Roxbury, MA 55
Claflin John	Church Hill, Framingham, MA 56
Claflin Nehemiah	Dodgeville, MA 15
Claflin Phineas	Dodgeville, MA 15
Claflin Phineas	Hillside Cem, Dodgeville, Attleboro, MA 47
Claggett Samuel	[no cem named], WV 42
Claggett Wyzeman	Church Yard, Litchfield, NH 31
Claghorn George	[no cem named] 15
Claghorn John	West St Cem, Fair Haven, VT 36
Claghorn William	1st Parish Cem, Rochester, MA 58
Claiborne Augustine Col	Fam Cem, Sussex Co, VA 37
Claiborne William	Fam Cem, Sweet Hall, Rocky Mt, King William Co, VA 71
Clap Abiel	Center Cem, Mansfield, MA 55
Clap Abner	North Cem, Dorchester, MA 46
Clap David	North Dorchester Cem, Boston, MA 55
Clap David Jr	North Dorchester, Dorchester, MA 56
Clap Ebenezer	North Cem, Dorchester, MA 46
Clap Eleazer	Walpole Plain Cem, Walpole, MA 45
Clap Elisha	North Cem, Dorchester, MA 46
Clap Elkanah	East Mansfield Cem, Mansfield, MA 55
Clap Ezekiah	North Cem, Dorchester, MA 46
Clap Ichabod Corp	Rural Cem, East Walpole, MA 45
Clap Jacob	Rural Cem, East Walpole, MA 45
Clap Joel	Center Cem, Southampton, MA 37
Clap John	1st Parish Cem, Rochester, MA 58
Clap John	Pearl St Cem, Stoughton, MA 55
Clap Jonathan	North Cem, Dorchester, MA 46
Clap Jonathan Jr	North Cem, Dorchester, MA 46
Clap Joseph Jr	North Cem, Dorchester, MA 46
Clap Joshua Capt	Main St Cem, Walpole, MA 45
Clap Moses	Center Cem, Southampton, MA 37
Clap Nathaniel	North Cem, Dorchester, MA 46
Clap Oliver Capt	Old Town Cem, Walpole, MA 45
Clap Roger	Center Cem, Southampton, MA 37

Abstract of Graves of Revolutionary Patriots

Clap Roger	Dorchester North, Boston, MA	56
Clap Samuel	North Dorchester Cem, Boston, MA	55
Clap Thaddeus	Rural Cem, East Walpole, MA	45
Clap Thomas	Dorchester North, Boston, MA	56
Clap Thomas	Rock Hill Cem, Foxboro, MA	45
Clapp Adam	St John's Luth Ch Cem, Mill Creek, Union Co, IL	75
Clapp Asabel	Northampton, MA	56
Clapp Asahel	Bridge St Cem, Northampton, MA	55
Clapp Azariah	Bridge St Cem, Northampton, MA	55
Clapp Barney	Brick Ch, Guilford Co, NC	43
Clapp Bela Capt	West Claremont Cem, Claremont, NH	50
Clapp Benjamin	Church Hill, Framingham, MA	56
Clapp Caleb	Dudley Cem, Dudley, MA	55
Clapp Caleb Capt	Federal St Cem, Greenfield, MA	00
Clapp Daniel	Taylor Hill Cem, Montague, MA	58
Clapp David	Old North Cem, Dorchester, MA	45
Clapp David	Scituate, MA	54
Clapp Earl	East Woodstock, CT	15
Clapp Earl B	Sinking Spring Cem, Abingdon, VA	29
Clapp Earl B	Sinking Spring Cem, Abingdon, VA	30
Clapp Ebenezer	1st Parish Cem, Rochester, MA	58
Clapp Eliakim	Littleville Cem, Huntington, MA	46
Clapp Elijah	Southampton, MA	54
Clapp Elijah Jr	Center Cem, Southampton, MA	49
Clapp Galen	Scituate, MA	55
Clapp Israel	Throopville Cem, Throop, Cayuga Co, NY	69
Clapp John	Cem nr Jacobs Pond, Assinippi, MA	51
Clapp John	Easthampton, MA	53
Clapp John	Rochester Cem, 4 Corners nr Church, Rochester, MA	55
Clapp John	Taylor Hill Cem, Montague, MA	58
Clapp John Capt	North Yard Hollis, NH	39
Clapp Joseph	North Dorchester Cem, Boston, MA	55
Clapp Joseph Capt	East Hampton Cem, VA	50
Clapp Joseph Jr	North Dorchester Cem, Boston, MA	55
Clapp Joshua	Old Cem, Westminster, VT	46
Clapp Lemuel	North Dorchester Cem, Boston, MA	55
Clapp Nathaniel	1st Parish Cem, Rochester, MA	58
Clapp Oliver	Old North Cem, Old Hartford, CT	19
Clapp Oliver	West Cem, Amherst, MA	60
Clapp Paul	Manlius Cem, Manlius, Onondaga Co, NY	75
Clapp Perez	Center Cem, Southampton, MA	49
Clapp Phineas	Center Cem, Southampton, MA	37
Clapp Preserved Dr	Old Village Cem, Claremont, NH	50
Clapp Roswell	Old Village Cem, Claremont, NH	50
Clapp Samuel	Briggs Cem betw Middle Line Rd & Rt 20, Saratoga Co, NY	77
Clapp Selah	West Part Cem, Southampton, MA	37
Clapp Seth	Church Hill, Framingham, MA	56
Clapp Stephen	Revolutionary Cem, Salem, NY	56
Clapp Supply	North Cem, Portsmouth, NH	34
Clappe John	Log Cabin Mtg Hs Gr, Schodack, Rensselaer Co, NY	41
Clapper George	Salt Creek Bapt Ch Cem, 6 mi E of Zanesville, OH	55
Clapper John	Nichols Cem, betw Niverville & North Chatham, NY	48
Clapsaddle Daniel	Jordanville Cem, Centre Twp, Lisbon, Columbiana Co, OH	77
Clapsaddle Daniel	Rose Hill Cem, Hagerstown, Washington Co, MD	77
Clark –	Hamonton, NJ	15
Clark Aaron	Orange, CT	56
Clark Abel	Morris, CT	17
Clark Abijah	South Parish Bur Gr, Andover, MA	26
Clark Abner	Center Cem, Southampton, MA	37
Clark Abner	Oak Mound Cem, Young America, Cass Co, IN	76
Clark Abraham	Rahway Pres Ch Graveyard, Rahway, Union Co, NJ	74

Clark Abraham	Rahway Cem, Rahway, NJ	26
Clark Abraham Capt	Old Pres Cem, Rahway, NJ	48
Clark Abram	Rural Cem, Oswego, NY	30
Clark Abram	Wollens Cem, Pleasant Ridge Twp nr W Point, Lee Co, IA	74
Clark Adrial	Clarks Mill Bur Gr, nr Port Republic, NJ	23
Clark Adriel	Clark's Mill, NJ	36
Clark Amasa	Cong Cem, Cheshire, New Haven Co, CT	24
Clark Amos	West Center Cem, Granville, Hampden Co, MA	63
Clark Anciel	Central Cem, North Rochester, MA	58
Clark Andrew	Exeter, Lebanon, CT	56
Clark Andrew	Harwich Center Cem, Harwich, MA	55
Clark Andrew	Mt Olivet Cem, Harrison Twp, Bedford Co, PA	80
Clark Andrew	Sheridan, NY	52
Clark Andrew	Wells Cem, VT	15
Clark Andrew	Wells Village Cem, VT	48
Clark Andrew	Ye Old Trail Cem, Alstead, NH	43
Clark Anthony	Pine Grove Cem, Warner, NH	47
Clark Asa	Farm road Cem, Sherborn, MA	74
Clark Asa	Murray Cem, Orleans Co, NY	34
Clark Asa	Vine Lake, Medfield, MA	56
Clark Asahel	Marcy Cem, Bradford, CT	55
Clark Atkins	Oakland, Randolph, MA	54
Clark Augustus	Newman Hill Cem, West Galway, Saratoga Co, NY	77
Clark Azariah	Westfield Cem, Westfield, NJ	24
Clark Barnabas	Union Cem, Holbrook, MA	55
Clark Barnabus	1st Parish Cem, Rochester, MA	58
Clark Benjamin	Cem nr railroad station, Eastham, MA	49
Clark Benjamin	Church Hill, Framingham, MA	56
Clark Benjamin	Orange, CT	56
Clark Benjamin	Rural Cem, Lancaster, NY	33
Clark Benjamin	Ulster Cem, Ulster Twp, Bradford Co, PA	53
Clark Benjamin Maj	Fairview Cem, Naples, NY	35
Clark Benoni	Rural Cem, Throopsville, Throop, NY	41
Clark Caleb	Lakevale Cem, Belchertown, MA	30
Clark Caleb	Pickett Cem, Portland, Charlotte, NY	15
Clark Caleb	South Yard, Brooklyn, CT	30
Clark Charles	Pres Ch Cem, Westfield, NJ	76
Clark Charles	Westfield Cem, Westfield, NJ	24
Clark Christopher	Old fam bur gr, nr Elberton, Elbert Co, GA	34
Clark Cornelius	Buxton Cem, Bedford, Westchester Co, NY	76
Clark Cornelius	West Hill Cem, Sherburne, NY	16
Clark Cyrus	Orwell, Shoreham, VT	15
Clark Daniel	Aban Cem, Parkman farm, Stratham, NH	33
Clark Daniel	Exeter Cem, Lebanon, CT	26
Clark Daniel	Old Temple Village Yard, Temple, NH	29
Clark Daniel	Sharon Cem, Sharon, Litchfield Co, CT	66
Clark Daniel	Sharon, CT	56
Clark David	Acushnet Cem, Fairhaven, MA	55
Clark David	Bethel Meth Epis Cem, Kent Co, DE	46
Clark David	Center Cem, Harwich, MA	49
Clark David	Connecticut Farms Pres Cem, Union, NJ	49
Clark David	Cornwall Cem, Cornwall, VT	15
Clark David	Fam bur gr, Elbert Co, GA	34
Clark David	Lyons farm Cem, Windsor, Broome Co, NY	78
Clark David	Marcy Cem, Bradford, CT	55
Clark David	Millis, Millis-Medway, MA	56
Clark David	North Side Cem, Sandown, NH	35
Clark David	Pres Ch Cem, Rahway, NJ	76
Clark David	Vine Lake, Medfield, MA	54
Clark David	Wilmington & Brandywine, New Castle Co, DE	46
Clark David E	Cem, Milford, CT	56

Clark	Ebenezer	Clark's Yard, Moultonborough, NH 29
Clark	Ebenezer	Judea Cem, Washington, CT 55
Clark	Ebenezer	Pumpkin Hollow Cem, Conway, MA 53
Clark	Ebenezer	Vine Lake, Medfield, MA 56
Clark	Edmond Capt	Cave Hill Cem, Louisville, KY 31
Clark	Edmund	Colonial Cem, Derby, CT 15
Clark	Edward	Old Colonial Cem, Derby, CT 56
Clark	Edward	Westfield Cem, Westfield, NJ 24
Clark	Eleazer Ens	West Claremont Cem, Claremont, NH 50
Clark	Eli	Center Cem, Hubbardston, MA 26
Clark	Eli	Lakeview Cem, Skaneateles, Onondaga Co, NY 75
Clark	Eli	Old Cem, Hubbardston, MA 50
Clark	Eliakim	Otisco Otisco, Onondaga Co, NY 78
Clark	Elijah	Canton St Cem, Canton, CT 55
Clark	Elijah	Millis, Millis-Medway, MA 56
Clark	Elijah Lt	Worthington Cem, Worthington, MA 46
Clark	Eliphalet	Ogden, NY 56
Clark	Eliphalet	Old Jefferson Cem, Jefferson, Schoharie Co, NY 76
Clark	Elisha	Cem, Milford, CT 56
Clark	Elisha	Cricket Hill Cem, Conway, MA 53
Clark	Elisha Dea	Rock Cem, Middleboro, MA 59
Clark	Enoch Capt	First Parish Unitarian Cem, Brewster, MA 46
Clark	Ephraim	In field, Old Laird, N of Maine, OH 24
Clark	Ephriam	Mesopotamia, OH 15
Clark	Ezra	Pond Cem, Lakeville, MA 57
Clark	Francis	Center Cem, Tyringham, MA 57
Clark	Friend	Center of Cem, Bethlehem, CT 55
Clark	Gad	Center Cem, Southampton, MA 49
Clark	George	Hudson City Cem, Hudson, Columbia Co, NY 74
Clark	George	Milton Cem, Litchfield, CT 22
Clark	George Rogers Gen	Cave Hill Cem, Louisville, KY 31
Clark	Gersham	Ascutney Cem, Weathersfield, VT 36
Clark	Gershom	Guilford Center, NY 49
Clark	Gideon	Fam farm, Petersburgh, NY 46
Clark	Giles	Center Cem, Westhampton, MA 53
Clark	Greenleaf	Newburyport, MA 56
Clark	Gregory	Nazareth Luth Ch Cem, Red Bank Lexington, SC 77
Clark	Henry	Fam bur gr, Beaverkill farm, Brookfield, Madison Co, NY 82
Clark	Henry	Hilltop Cem, Mendham, NJ 24
Clark	Henry	Lost in privateer brig, MA 45
Clark	Henry A	Fam Cem, adj Old White Mill, Chatham, Columbia Co, NY 54
Clark	Henry Jr	First Cem, Candia, NH 29
Clark	Hezekiah	Pompey Hill Cem, Pompey, Onondaga Co, NY 81
Clark	Heziakiah	Bethany, CT 54
Clark	Ichabod	Oakridge Cem, Union Springs, Springport, NY 56
Clark	Ichabod	Pres Ch Cem, Westfield, NJ 76
Clark	Ira	Exeter, Lebanon, CT 56
Clark	Isaac	Barlow Cem, Mattapoisett, MA 58
Clark	Isaac	Church Hill, Framingham, MA 56
Clark	Isaac	Hallowell Cem, Hallowell, ME 17
Clark	Isaac	Milford Center Cem, New Milford, CT 40
Clark	Isaac	Old Cem, Hubbardston, MA 50
Clark	Isaac	Old Laird Cem, OH 25
Clark	Isaac	Orange, CT 56
Clark	Isaac	Spencertown Cem, Austerlitz, Columbia Co, NY 48
Clark	Isaack	Becket Center, Becket, MA 58
Clark	Israel	Evergreen Cem, South Hadley, Hampshire Co, MA 80
Clark	Israel	Granby Cem, Granby, MA 56
Clark	Israel	Marion Twp, Marion Co, OH 15
Clark	Israel	Smith Twp, Marion Co, OH 44
Clark	Isrial	Smith Cem, Marion Twp, Marion Co, OH 55

Clark Jacob	Buried in small Cem, Plainfield, MA	46
Clark Jacob	Emery prop, Blackbury Hill Rd, Berwick, York Co, ME	78
Clark Jacob	Fam Cem, Pond Hill Rd, Barrington, NH	75
Clark Jacob	Fam Cem, Pittsburgh, PA	56
Clark Jacob	Old Pres Cem, Westfield, NJ	47
Clark Jacob	Rockland, Rockland Co, NY	56
Clark Jacob	Vine Lake, Medfield, MA	56
Clark Jacob Rev	Exeter, Lebanon, CT	56
Clark James	1st Parish Cem, Rochester, MA	58
Clark James	Beech Spring Ch Cem, Green Twp, OH	56
Clark James	Clark's Grove Pres Ch Cem, Maryville, Blount Co, TN	76
Clark James	Clough Bapt Cem, Clough Rd, nr Bogart Rd, nr Newton, OH	56
Clark James	Pine Island, CT	34
Clark James	Pres Cem, Dover, Kent Co, DE	46
Clark James	Pres Cem, Rahway, NJ	55
Clark James	Pres Cem, Williamsburg, PA	52
Clark James	Trinity Ch Cem, Staunton, VA	36
Clark James	Trumbull, Lebanon, CT	56
Clark James Jr	Hancock Cem, Quincy, MA	54
Clark James M	Rahway, Union Co, NJ	33
Clark Jehiel	North St, Auburn, NY	56
Clark Jephtha	Southbridge Cem, Southbridge, MA	26
Clark Jeremiah	Clarkston, MI	15
Clark Jeremiah	Pres Cem, Rahway, NJ	55
Clark Jeremiah	Shaftsbury, VT	56
Clark Jeremiah Jr	Randolph Center Cem, Randolph, Orange Co, VT	72
Clark Jerome	Cherry Valley Cem, East Springfield, NY	33
Clark Jesse	Pres Ch Cem, Westfield, NJ	76
Clark Jesse Capt	Groton, Tompkins Co, NY	34
Clark Job	East St Cem, Easthampton, MA	46
Clark Job	Stannard Cem, Blandford, MA	58
Clark Joel	Mount Hope Cem, Rochester, Monroe Co, NY	33
Clark John	1st Parish Cem, Rochester, MA	58
Clark John	1st Parish Cem, Rochester, MA	58
Clark John	Belle Isle, Camillus, NY	56
Clark John	Blairs Cem, Campton, NH	36
Clark John	Bradford-Marcy Yard, Woodstock, CT	26
Clark John	Chester, VT	52
Clark John	Clark's Grove Pres Ch Cem, Maryville, Blount Co, TN	76
Clark John	Clarktown Cem, East Barnstead, NH	28
Clark John	Connecticut Farms Pres Cem, Union, NJ	49
Clark John	Dudley, MA	55
Clark John	Ebenezer Cem, Lewis Twp, OH	56
Clark John	Fam Cem, Hawkins Co, TN	40
Clark John	Forest Hill Cem, East Derry, NH	38
Clark John	Jewel farm Cem, Westville, NY	31
Clark John	Log Plain Cem, Bernardston Rd, Greenfield, MA	57
Clark John	Meth Epis Cem, Newport, New Castle Co, DE	46
Clark John	Mountain View Cem, New Concord, Columbia Co, NY	72
Clark John	Mountain View Cem, Chatham, Columbia Co, NY	73
Clark John	Old Bur Hill, Marblehead, MA	30
Clark John	Plymouth, MA	54
Clark John	Rear of fam home, 2 houses fr South Barnstead Cem, NH	48
Clark John	Rochester Cem, 4 Corners nr Church, Rochester, MA	55
Clark John	Schoharie Cem, Schoharie, NY	71
Clark John	Site of fam home, Bannister Lodge, Halifax Co, VA	73
Clark John	Town Cem, Sanbornton, NH	29
Clark John	West Claremont Bur Gr, Claremont, NH	50
Clark John C	Ulster Cem, Ulster Twp, Bradford Co, PA	53
Clark John Capt	Amsterdam, NY	29
Clark John Capt	Amsterdam, NH	15

Abstract of Graves of Revolutionary Patriots

Clark John Capt	Log Plain (Sage) Cem, Greenfield, MA 00
Clark John Capt	Old part, Pres Cem, St Georges, DE 42
Clark John Corp	First Cem, Candia, NH 29
Clark John Jr	Old Bur Hill, Marblehead, MA 30
Clark John Lt	King Cem, Dorchester, NH 37
Clark John M	Pres Ch Cem, Rahway, NJ 76
Clark John M	Wheatsheaf, Rahway, Union Co, NJ 33
Clark John Scott	Town Cem, Copenhagen, Lewis Co, NY 73
Clark John Shadrock	Lunenburg Cem, Lunenburg Co, VA 60
Clark Jonas	Copps Hill Cem, Boston, MA 46
Clark Jonas	Cotton Grove, Madison Co, TN 24
Clark Jonathan	1st Parish Cem, Rochester, MA 58
Clark Jonathan	Berwick, ME 54
Clark Jonathan	Cave Hill Cem, Louisville, KY 31
Clark Jonathan	Center Cem, Westhampton, MA 53
Clark Jonathan	East Otis, Otis, MA 56
Clark Jonathan	Eastern Cem, Danbury, NH 36
Clark Jonathan	Fam Cem, Northwood Ridge, Northwood, NH 38
Clark Jonathan	His old home, nr Crofton, KY 15
Clark Jonathan	Old Cem, Washington Center, Washington, NH 33
Clark Joseph	Copps Hill Cem, Boston, MA 46
Clark Joseph	Nr Town Hall, Chester, CT 56
Clark Joseph	Old Cem, The Green, Middleboro, MA 50
Clark Joseph	Old Cem, Gardner, MA 46
Clark Joseph	Old fam Cem, Leist farm, Washington Twp, OH 56
Clark Joseph	The Old Cem, Gardner, MA 33
Clark Joseph	Vine Lake, Medfield, MA 56
Clark Joseph Jr	Old Bedford Cem, Bedford, Westchester Co, NY 76
Clark Joshua	Beech St, Rockport, MA 56
Clark Joshua	Genoa New Cem, Genoa, NY 56
Clark Josiah	United Cong Ch Cem, Barnstable, MA 55
Clark Josiah	Wells Cem, Canaan, NH 36
Clark Judah	Cricket Hill Cem, Conway, MA 53
Clark Larkin	Bethlehem Cem, Elbert Co, GA 25
Clark Lemuel	Center Cem, Winstead, CT 59
Clark Lemuel	Elmwood Cem, Barre, VT 48
Clark Lemuel	Orwell, Shoreham, VT 15
Clark Lemuel	Rochester Cem, 4 Corners nr Church, Rochester, MA 55
Clark Lemuel	Woodbridge Cem, Catatonk, NY 35
Clark Levi	Elm Grove Cem, Poquonock, CT 55
Clark Martin	Center Cem, Westhampton, MA 53
Clark Mathias	Westfield Cem, Westfield, NJ 24
Clark Matthew	Brick Ch Cem, Sodus, Wayne Co, NY 79
Clark Matthew	Center Cem, Westhampton, MA 53
Clark Matthew	Forest Hill Cem, East Derry, NH 38
Clark Matthias	Pres Ch Cem, Rahway, NJ 76
Clark McGie	Damson Homestead, S of Russellville, KY 50
Clark Melatiah	1st Parish Cem, Rochester, MA 58
Clark Mitchell	Christian St Cem, Hartford, VT 40
Clark Moses	Walker, Kent Co, MI 56
Clark Nathan	Cem, Milford, CT 56
Clark Nathan	Center Cem, Westhampton, MA 53
Clark Nathan Jr	Bedford Union Cem, Bedford, Westchester Co, NY 76
Clark Nathaniel	East Hartland Cem, East Hartland, CT 60
Clark Nathaniel	Exeter Cem, Lebanon, CT 26
Clark Nathaniel	Fam Cem, VT 20
Clark Nathaniel	Fork Hill Bapt Ch Cem, Lancaster Co, SC 70
Clark Nathaniel	North Parish Cem, Plaistow, NH 31
Clark Nathaniel	Rochester Cem, 4 Corners nr Church, Rochester, MA 55
Clark Nathaniel	Second West Parish Cem, Haverhill, MA 31
Clark Nathaniel	Springfield Cem, Springfield, NH 40

Clark Nathaniel	Village Cem, Langdon, NH 35
Clark Nathaniel S	Gore Bur Gr, Morgan, Orleans Co, VT 30
Clark Nathaniel Sr	Second Bur Gr, West Parish, Haverhill, MA 50
Clark Nehemiah	Howard Cem, Sutton, Worcester Co, MA 78
Clark Noah	Fam Cem, Lakeville, MA 62
Clark Noah	Kirkland & Clark Mills, Oneida Co, NY 56
Clark Noah	Roxbury, Somerset Co, PA 52
Clark Noah	Scotch Plains Bapt Cem, NJ 47
Clark Noah	West Cem, Granby, MA 55
Clark Noah	West part of Southampton, MA 49
Clark Oliver	Center Cem, Southampton, MA 49
Clark Parker	Clark's Mill, NJ 36
Clark Parker	Clarks Mill Bur Gr, nr Port Republic, NJ 23
Clark Paul	Center Cem, Westhampton, MA 53
Clark Paul	River Dale Cem, Webster, NH 34
Clark Peter	Beverly, MA 55
Clark Reuben	Chestnut Ridge Cem, Lockport, NY 33
Clark Reuben	Nr Town Hall, Chester, CT 56
Clark Reuben	Royalton Cem, nr Lockport, NY 57
Clark Reuben Capt	First Parish Unitarian Cem, Brewster, MA 46
Clark Richard	Hillside Cem, Samptown, S Plainfield, Middlesex Co, NJ 77
Clark Richard	Sawyer Hill Cem, Canaan, NH 36
Clark Robert	Clark, KY 56
Clark Robert	Copps Hill Cem, Boston, MA 46
Clark Robert	Rock Landing, Haddam Neck, CT 56
Clark Robert Capt	Old Cem, Rockingham Junction, Newmarket, NH 35
Clark Robert Jr	Pres Ch Cem, Rahway, NJ 76
Clark Roger	Pond Cem, Lakeville, MA 57
Clark Roswell	White Store (Evergreen) Cem, Norwich, Chenango Co, NY 71
Clark Samuel	Cem, Milford, CT 56
Clark Samuel	Center Cem, Hubbardston, MA 26
Clark Samuel	Conewango Twp, PA 52
Clark Samuel	Forest Hill Cem, East Derry, NH 38
Clark Samuel	Highland Cem, Belmont, NH 36
Clark Samuel	Raynesford Cem, Meriden, NH 35
Clark Samuel	St Johnsbury Cem, St Johnsbury, VT 46
Clark Samuel	Stockbridge Cem, Stockbridge, MA 47
Clark Samuel	Tupper Corner, Genoa, NY 56
Clark Samuel	Walnut St, Brookline, MA 56
Clark Samuel	West Cem, Granby, MA 58
Clark Samuel B	Cem, Milford, CT 56
Clark Samuel Corp	Old South Cem, Old Hartford, CT 19
Clark Samuel Gen	East line Union Cem, Malta, NY 41
Clark Sarah	Fam Cem, adj Old White Mill, Chatham, Columbia Co, NY 54
Clark Satchwell	Town Cem, Sanbornton, NH 29
Clark Saul	Center Cem, Southampton, MA 37
Clark Scotto	1st Parish Ch Cem, Brewster, MA 55
Clark Selah	Center Cem, Southampton, MA 37
Clark Selvanus	Hillside Cem, Cheshire, CT 55
Clark Seth	[no cem named] 15
Clark Seth	1st Parish Ch Cem, Brewster, MA 55
Clark Seth	Vine Lake, Medfield, MA 56
Clark Simeon	Center Cem, Paxton, MA 49
Clark Simeon	Second Bur Gr, Keene, NH 32
Clark Simeon	West Cem, Amherst, MA 41
Clark Stephen	1½ mi N of Leonardsville, Brookfield, NY 56
Clark Stephen	Cem, London Center, NH 49
Clark Stephen	Cong Cem, Cheshire, New Haven Co, CT 24
Clark Stephen	Millis, Millis-Medway, MA 56
Clark Steven	Church Hill, Framingham, MA 56
Clark Sylvanus	Cheshire, CT 17

Clark Sylvanus	Riverside Cem, Guilford, CT	55
Clark Theodore	Millis, Millis-Medway, MA	56
Clark Theophilus	Fam Cem, VT	20
Clark Theophilus	Priv Cem, East Montpelier, VT	33
Clark Thomas	1st Parish Cem, Rochester, MA	58
Clark Thomas	Asbury Meth Epis Cem, New Castle Co, DE	46
Clark Thomas	Clark's Mill, NJ	36
Clark Thomas	Clarks Mill Bur Gr, nr Port Republic, NJ	23
Clark Thomas	Cong Cem, Oxford, CT	37
Clark Thomas	Cotton Grove Cem, TN	23
Clark Thomas	Dummerston Center, VT	17
Clark Thomas	Hartland, VT	16
Clark Thomas	Leyden Center Cem, Leyden, MA	34
Clark Thomas	Old Mill River, New Marlboro, MA	56
Clark Thomas	Plantation, Strawberry Branch, N Halifax Co, VA	73
Clark Thomas	Pleasant Ridge Pres Cem, Hamilton Co, OH	43
Clark Thomas	Pres Ch Cem, Charters Twp, Cannonsburg, PA	78
Clark Thomas	Pres Ch Cem, Rahway, NJ	76
Clark Thomas	Scotch Cem, West Charlton, Saratoga Co, NY	77
Clark Thomas Capt	Rahway Cem, Rahway, NJ	26
Clark Thomas H	Bonecamp Cem, Northport, Tuscaloosa Co, AL	67
Clark Thomas Sr	Fam Cem, Walnut Twp, Gallia Co, OH	55
Clark Timothy	Center Cem, Southampton, MA	49
Clark Timothy	Millis, Millis-Medway, MA	56
Clark Timothy	West Swanzey Cem, Swanzey, NH	35
Clark Timothy Jr	Center Cem, Southampton, MA	37
Clark Tolles	Plain Cem, Weathersfield, VT	42
Clark Walter	Geneseo, Livingston Co, NY	33
Clark Walter	Mount Jackson, PA	15
Clark Watrous	Mann Cem, Butternuts, nr Gilbertsville, Otsego Co, NY	77
Clark Wells	Avon Cem, Avon, NY	33
Clark Willard	Old Parish Cem, North Rochester, MA	59
Clark William	Church Hill, Framingham, MA	56
Clark William	Copake Meth Ch Cem, Copake, Columbia Co, NY	79
Clark William	Fabius, NY	35
Clark William	Fam Cem, nr Chatham, Pineville, VA	73
Clark William	Massacred nr mouth of Lechry Creek, Dearborn Co, IN	24
Clark William	Mt Pleasant Cem, Geneseo, NY	59
Clark William	Old Bur Gr, Townsend, MA	48
Clark William	Old Cem, West Charlton, Saratoga Co, NY	77
Clark William	Old Drawyers Ch Cem, DE	36
Clark William	Pleasant Ridge Pres Cem, Hamilton Co, OH	43
Clark William	Preston, NY	16
Clark William	Sherborn No 2, Sherborn, MA	56
Clark William	Vine Lake, Medfield, MA	56
Clark William	Westfield Cem, Westfield, NJ	24
Clark William	Wilmington & Brandywine, New Castle Co, DE	46
Clark William Capt	Old Drawyers, New Castle Co, DE	46
Clark William Col	Fairview Cem, Naples, NY	35
Clark William Col	Old Cowan Cem, 5 mi fr Gainesville, Hall Co, GA	25
Clark William Col	Orig Old Cowan Cem, now Alta Vista Cem, Gainesville, GA	27
Clark Zelotus	Twinsburg, OH	15
Clark Zelotus	Twinsburg, OH	45
Clarke Abraham	Woolen's Cem, Lowell, IA	42
Clarke Atkins	Oakland Cem, Randolph, MA	45
Clarke Christopher	Clarke Cem, Elbert Co, GA	32
Clarke Christopher	Fam home, nr Woodbridge Post Office, Woodbridge, VA	35
Clarke Elijah Gen	On banks of Savannah River, Lincoln Co, GA	24
Clarke George	Windham Cem, NH	52
Clarke James	Marlboro Twp, OH	18
Clarke John	Lewis Cem, Union Co, PA	15

Clarke John	Pioneer Cem, Utica, NY 56
Clarke Johnathan	Norton Lot, Otis Cem, Otis, MA 28
Clarke Joseph	Otis Cem, Otis, MA 29
Clarke Joseph	Westerly, RI 15
Clarke Joshua	Hopkinton, RI 35
Clarke Joshua Rev	Hopkinton Cem, Hopkinton, RI 48
Clarke Josiah	Old Hopkinton Cem, Hopkinton, RI 48
Clarke Larkin	Nr Elberton, GA 35
Clarke Paul Capt	Old Hopkinton Cem, Hopkinton, RI 48
Clarke Peter Lynsen	Montezuma Old Cem, Montezuma, NY 56
Clarke Seth	Salisbury Plains Bur Gr, Amesbury, MA 46
Clarke Thomas	Clarke's Yard, Clarksboro, NJ 50
Clarke Thomas	Millis, Millis-Medway, MA 56
Clarke Thomas	Sandfork Cem, Gallia Co, OH 55
Clarke William	Nr Gainesville, Hall Co, GA 35
Clarkson James	Pres Ch Cem, Woodbridge, Middlesex Co, NJ 75
Clarkson Jeremiah	Bur gr, First Pres Ch, Woodbridge, NJ 25
Clarkson John	Pres Ch Cem, MI 29
Clarkson John	Woodbridge, NJ 29
Clarkson Randolph	Bur gr, First Pres Ch, Woodbridge, NJ 25
Clason Isaac	Roxbury Cem, Stamford, CT 68
Clason Jacob	Lakeview Cem, Penn Yan, Yates Co, NY 80
Clason James	New Market Bapt Ch Cem, New Market, NJ 76
Clason Nathaniel	Small Cem, W of Hunting Ridge Rd, Stamford, CT 68
Clason Stephen Jr	Roxbury Cem, Stamford, CT 68
Class Vincent	Rock Hill Cem, Flushing Twp, Belmont Co, OH 44
Clay Charles V	Clay Cem, Galbraith farm, nr Corydon, Henderson Co, KY 74
Clay James Capt	Putney North Cem, Putney, VT 19
Clay John	First Cem, Candia, NH 29
Clay Samuel	Farm betw his house and Stoner Creek, nr Paris, KY 17
Clay Samuel	Old Cem on The Meadow, Littleton, NH 32
Clay Thomas	Epis Cem, New Castle, New Castle Co, DE 46
Clay Thomas	Nr Yelvington, Daviess Co, KY 26
Clay Thomas	Nr Yelvington, KY 25
Clay Thomas	Yelvington, KY 30
Clay Timothy	Simsbury Cem, Galesburg, IL 58
Clay Timothy	Simsbury, VT 56
Clay Walter	First Cem (no stone), Candia, NH 29
Clay William	Epis Cem, New Castle, New Castle Co, DE 46
Clay William	Old Stewart Cem, ½ mi fr Boyd Co line, Lawrence Co, KY 45
Clay William M Sr	Priv grave, nr Celanese, Pearisburg, Giles Co, VA 55
Claypoole Elizabeth G	Flag House Cem, Philadelphia, PA 78
Clayton David	Beavertown Cem, Beavertown, OH 56
Clayton Elisha	Cunningham Cem, Baxter, WV 42
Clayton Elisha	Cunningham Cem, nr Baxter, Marion Co, WV 27
Clayton Joshua	Bethel, nr Elkton, MD 42
Clayton Lambert	Davidson River Cem, Buncombe Co, NC 59
Clayton Lambert	Davidson River Cem, Pisgah Forest, Buncombe Co, NC 49
Clayton Richard Capt	Old Bethel, New Castle Co, DE 46
Clayton Thomas	Quaker Cem, Catawissa, PA 15
Claywell Peter	Snow Creek Cem, off Hwy 115, 10 mi N of Statesville, NC 40
Claywell Peter	Snow Creek Cem, 10 mi N of Statesville, NC 49
Clearman John	Evergreen Cem, Morristown, NJ 29
Cleaveland David	West Dedham Cem, Dedham, MA 48
Cleaveland Ebenezer	Beach St, Rockport, MA 56
Cleaveland Ebenezer Rev	Old Parish Cem, Beach St, Rockport, MA 45
Cleaveland Edward	West Dedham Cem, Dedham, MA 48
Cleaveland Frederick	Brick Chapel Cem, Canton, NY 55
Cleaveland Jedediah	Oran Pioneer Cem, Fayetteville, NY 49
Cleaveland John	Old Essex Cem, Essex, MA 48
Cleaveland Nehemiah	Skaneateles, NY 35

Abstract of Graves of Revolutionary Patriots

Cleaves Nathaniel	Opposite 1st Cong Ch, Hamilton, MA 56
Cleeves Joshua	Second Street Cem, Elmira, Chemung Co, NY 78
Clegg Alexander	Mt Olive Ch, nr Pentress, Clay Dist, Monongalia Co, WV 41
Cleland John	Pickett Cem, Portland, Charlotte, NY 15
Cleland Samuel	Jordanville Cem, Log Cabin, Herkimer Co, NY 41
Clelland James	Forks of Cheat Bapt Cem, nr Stewarttown, WV 41
Clemens Abraham	Lower Salford Mennonite Cem, Montgomery Co, PA 59
Clemens Gerhart	Lower Salford Mennonite Cem, Montgomery Co, PA 59
Clement Benjamin Moody	New London Cem, New London, NH 37
Clement Christopher	North Parish Cem, Plaistow, NH 31
Clement Ezra	River Road or Oil Mills Cem, Weare, NH 33
Clement James	First or Sadler Cem, Greenfield, Saratoga Co, NY 77
Clement John	Village Cem, Bath Grafton Co, NH 27
Clement John Capt	Old Cem, Warner Village, NH 35
Clement Lambert	Middlebury Cem, Akron, OH 15
Clement Lambert	Old Middlebury, OH 45
Clement Philip	Old Village Cem, Claremont, NH 50
Clement Philip	Old Village Cem, NH 17
Clement Phillip	Old Village Cem, Claremont, NH 45
Clement Richard	Landaff, NH 26
Clement Tobias	Service Cem, Calendar, Saratoga Co, NY 77
Clements Aaron	Old Bapt Cem, Yorktown, NY 34
Clements David	White Hall Cem, nr Bloomington, Owen Co, IN 72
Clements Isaac	Holland, VT 35
Clements James	Old Perrysville Cem, Ashland, OH 55
Clements John	Cem, Milford, CT 56
Clements John	Old Bapt Cem, Yorktown, NY 34
Clements Peter	Taylor Cem, Bemis Heights Crossing, Stillwater, NY 41
Clements William	Old Bapt Cem, Yorktown, NY 34
Clemes William	Rosemont, Newberry, SC 56
Clemments Benaiah	North Parish Bur Gr, Haverhill, MA 31
Clemmer Johann	Lower Salford Mennonite Cem, Montgomery Co, PA 59
Clemons John	Farm, Hiram, Oxford Co, ME 61
Clemons Jonathan	Ontario Center Cem, Ontario, Wayne Co, NY 79
Clency George	Old Cem, Sunbury, Montgomery, OH 55
Clendenin John	Randolph Co, IL 48
Clendinen William Lt	Steenbergen Cem, Gallipolis Ferry, VA 19
Clenney William	Bloomfield Cem, Greene Co, IN 24
Cleveland Benjamin Col	Oconee Co, SC 43
Cleveland Chester	West Webster, Monroe Co, NY 33
Cleveland Ebenezer	Gloucester, MA 55
Cleveland Edward	Fairview Cem, Bethel, Windsor Co, VT 72
Cleveland Elijah	Orr Land, nr site of old Bapt Ch, NY 48
Cleveland Elijah P	Cem, Coventry, VT 46
Cleveland Ezra	Edgarton, Dukes Co, MA 56
Cleveland Ezra	Edgartown, MA 15
Cleveland Gardner	Clymer Cem, Clymer, Chautauqua Co, NY 62
Cleveland Ichabod	Hackensack Green Cem, Hackensack, NJ 47
Cleveland Isaac	Arsenal St Cem, Watertown, NY 41
Cleveland Jacob	Cleveland Cem, CT 28
Cleveland Jacob	Nr Elberton, GA 35
Cleveland John	Lercester Cem, Livingston Co, NY 33
Cleveland John	Old fam Cem, nr Madison, SC 27
Cleveland John	Stone Bridge Cem, Durham, Greene Co, NY 65
Cleveland Joseph	Riverside Cem, Union, Broome Co, NY 78
Cleveland Josiah Capt	Cleveland Yard, Canterbury Twp, CT 22
Cleveland Larkin Col	Buford Station, Giles Co, TN 24
Cleveland Moses Lt	Cleveland Yard, Canterbury Twp, CT 22
Cleveland Nehemiah Jr	Lakeview Cem, Skaneateles, Onondaga Co, NY 75
Cleveland Robert	Fam Cem, Purlear nr North Wilkesboro, Wilkes Co, NC 81
Cleveland Robert	Purlear Cem, nr Rendezvous Mountain, Catawba Co, NC 55

Cleveland Roswell	Cazenovia Cem, Manlius, Onondaga Co, NY 75
Cleveland Samuel	Chardon, OH 26
Cleveland Solomon	Grove St Cem, Putnam, CT 30
Cleveland Solomon	Sand Hill Cem, Wilna, Jefferson Co, NY 41
Cleveland Squire	East Bethel Cem, Bethel, Windsor Co, VT 72
Cleveland Stephen Esq	East Bethel Cem, Bethel, Windsor Co, VT 72
Cleveland Timothy	Cleveland Yard, Canterbury Twp, CT 22
Cleveland Tracy	Harman farm, Kirtland, Lake Co, OH 26
Cleveland William Sr	Dalton, MA 54
Cleveland Zimri	Vine Lake, Medfield, MA 56
Clevenger Abraham	Sideling Hill, Fulton Co, PA 56
Clevenger Eben	Salem-Lloyd Cem, Marion Twp, Fayette Co, OH 55
Clever Peter	St Thomas Epis Ch Cem, Montgomery Co, PA 59
Clewell Joseph	Old Morav Cem, Emaus, Lehigh Co, PA 40
Clewley Isaac	Brewer, ME 52
Clewley Isaac	Mt Recluse Cem, Stockton Springs, ME 59
Clifford Anthony	Langford Rd Cem, Candia, NH 29
Clifford Charles	Fort Palmer, Rt 711, nr Ligonier, Westmoreland Co, PA 56
Clifford Ebenezer	Rhoades Cem, Alexandria, NH 36
Clifford Ebenezer	Winter St Cem, Exeter, NH 27
Clifford Isaac	Edgecomb, Boothbay, ME 56
Clifford Israel	North Cem, Dunbarton, NH 31
Clifford Jacob	Langford Rd Cem, Candia, NH 29
Clifford James	Wadsworth, Medina Co, OH 22
Clifford Joseph Capt	Old Yard, Kensington, NH 47
Clifford Nathan	West Tisbury Cem, Vineyard Haven, MA 55
Clifford Samuel	Old Yard, Kensington, NH 47
Clifford Samuel	Old Yard, Kensington, NH 47
Clifford William	Rand Cem, Northfield, NH 35
Clift Adney	Old Cem, East Bridgewater, MA 56
Clift Adney Winslow	First Unitarian Parish, East Bridgewater, MA 56
Clift Joseph	Two Mile Cem, North Marshfield, MA 50
Clift Joseph Capt	Two Mile Cem, MA 17
Clift William	Marshfield Hill Cem, Marshfield, MA 50
Clift Wills Capt	Back of Unit Ch, Marshfield Hills, MA 17
Clifton Nathan	Fam Cem, 6 mi S of Marshfield, Webster Co, MO 63
Cline Conrad	Salt Creek Twp, Pickaway Co, OH 56
Cline George	Mouth of Mill Creek, Grandview Twp, Washington Co, OH 56
Cline John	Center Cem, Mt Washington, MA 56
Cline John	Cline farm, Harrison Co, IN 72
Cline Jonas	Fulton Co, IL 17
Cline William	Pleasant Hill Cem, Randolph Co, IN 72
Cline William	Pleasant Hill Cem, Portland, IN 17
Cline William	Portland, ME 16
Clingan William Jr	Lewisburg Cem, Lewisburg, PA 15
Clinger Phillip	West Alexandria, OH 56
Clingman John Michael	Kinney Cem, Waller St, Portsmouth, Scioto Co, OH 55
Clinton George	Old Dutch Cem, Kingston, Ulster Co, NY 85
Clinton James	Crittenden, KY 56
Clinton James	Fam Cem, Little Britain, Orange Co, NY 56
Clinton John	Old Cem, Fly Creek, Otsego Co, NY 71
Clinton Thomas	Hooks Cem, Cumberland, MD 56
Clisby Joseph	Park Cem, Tilton, NH 31
Clizbe James	Jersey Hill Cem, S of Galway Village, Saratoga Co, NY 77
Clizbe Joseph	Green Hill Cem, Silver Creek, NY 70
Clizbie Joseph	Green Hill Cem Amsterdam, NY 35
Clock John A	Spring Grove Cem, Darien, CT 55
Clock Jonas	Noroton River Cem, Darien, CT 55
Clock Jonathan	Noroton River Cem, Darien, CT 68
Clodfelter George	Fam plot, Rowan Co, NC 59
Cloes Charles	Webster, NY 33

Abstract of Graves of Revolutionary Patriots

Clontz Corporal	1 mi fr Brief, Union Co, NC 49
Clontz Jeremiah	[no cem named], NC 17
Clopton John	Fam bur gr, St Peter's Parish, VA 56
Close Abraham	Now Christ Ch, Greenwich, CT 56
Close Benjamin	June Cem, North Salem, Westchester Co, NY 76
Close Benjamin	Northville Cem, Genoa Twp, NY 41
Close Christian	Elias Luth Ch Cem, Emmitsburg, Frederick Co, MD 77
Close Jabez	Stewarts Corner Cem, Venice, Cayuga Co, NY 57
Close Joseph	Christ Epis Ch, Greenwich, CT 56
Close Mical	East Oak Grove, Morgantown, WV 40
Close Odle	Close, Greenwich, CT 56
Close Solomon	Christ Epis Ch, Greenwich, CT 56
Closson Ichabod	Parker Hill Cem, Rockingham, VT 48
Closson Ichabod	Springfield, MA 15
Closson Ichobod	Parker Hill Cem, Springfield, VT 23
Closson Nehemiah	Hornellsville, NY 57
Closson Richard	Delaware Co, OH 45
Closson Timothy	Old Town Cem, Rockingham, VT 46
Cloud A S	Friend's Meeting, Hockessin, New Castle Co, DE 46
Cloud Jeremiah	Bradford, PA 56
Cloud John	Fam prop, Winn Parish, Natchitoches, LA 63
Clough Benjamin	Glenwood Cem, Homer, Cortland Co, NY 36
Clough Benjamin	Kingston Plains Cem, Kingston, NH 30
Clough Benjamin	Monmouth, ME 20
Clough Benjamin Col	Old aban Cem, Unity, NH 35
Clough Caleb	Jenness Pond Cem, Northwood, NH 32
Clough David	Center Cem, Henniker, NH 32
Clough Ithamer	Hartford Cem, Washington Co, NY 58
Clough Jeremiah Capt	Priv Cem, nr site of Old Fort Canterbury, NH 29
Clough John Capt	South Road Cem, Belmont, NH 36
Clough Jonathan	Arch Hill Cem, Northfield, NH 36
Clough Jonathan	Loudon Center Cem, Loudon, NH 32
Clough Jonathan	Town Cem, Sandown, NH 33
Clough Joseph	Pine Grove Cem, Springfield, MA 56
Clough Nehemiah	Center Cem, Canterbury, NH 28
Clough Obadiah	Center Cem, Canterbury, NH 29
Clough Oliver	Village Cem, Meredith, NH 29
Clough Reuben	Schoodic Cem, Warner, NH 34
Clough Samuel	Old Burial Hill, Marblehead, MA 56
Clough Theophilus	Lockhaven Cem, Enfield, NH 38
Clough Thomas	Gorrell Cem, Northfield, NH 35
Clough Thomas Capt	Hodgdon Cem, Northfield, NH 34
Clough William Jr	Old Cem, Salem, Rockingham Co, NH 61
Clough William Sgt	Parker Hill Cem, Lyman, NH 26
Clouse John	Smith Cem, Plain Twp, nr New Albany, OH 26
Clow John	Wolfeboro Center Cem, College Rd, Carroll Co, NH 27
Clower Daniel	Bethesda Meth Ch, W of Lawrenceville, Gwinnett Co, GA 34
Clower John	Pikeland Pres Ch Cem, Pikeland, PA 57
Clowes John	Cem on dirt rd, Milton to Boulevard, Sussex Co, DE 46
Clowes John	Dirt rd fr Milton to Boulevard, DE 36
Clowney Samuel	Fair Forest Cem, SC 17
Cluff Isaac	Old Bur Gr, Salem Center, NH 46
Cluggston Robert	Cross Roads Cem, nr Monroeville, Allegheny Co, PA 16
Clum Adam	Cheviot Cem, Germantown, Columbia Co, NY 75
Clum Philip	S of road, 2 mi E of Pine Plains, NY 21
Clum Philip H	Ref Ch Cem, Germantown, Columbia Co, NY 79
Clunn John	St Michael's Ch Cem, Trenton, NJ 28
Clunn Joseph	St James Epis Ch Cem, Bristol, Bucks Co, PA 76
Clute Geradus	Old Cem, SW of Glenwood Cem, rear of Homer Churches, NY 36
Clute Geradus	Van Schoonhoven Cem, Waterford, Saratoga Co, NY 78
Clute Isaac	Oswego Bitter Cem, Camillus, NY 56

Clute	Jacob	Old Village Cem of Fultonville, Glen, Montgomery Co, NY 65
Clute	Jacob N	Albany rural Cem, Albany, NY 31
Clyd	John	Old Cem on the Plains, Windham, NH 26
Clyd	John	Old Cem on Plains, Windham, NH 70
Clyd	Joseph	Old Cem on Plains, Windham, NH 70
Clyd	Joseph Col	Old Cem on the Plains, Windham, NH 26
Clyde	Samuel Col	Cherry Valley Cem, East Springfield, NY 33
Clymer	George	Mtg Hs Yard, W Hanover & W Montgomery, Trenton, NJ 46
Coan	John	North Guilford Cem, North Guilford, CT 55
Coates	John Capt	Springfield Center, NY 15
Coats	Benjamin	Bapt Ch Cem, Delphi Falls, Onondaga Co, NY 81
Coats	Joseph	Monticello Hilltop Cem, Richfield Springs, NY 53
Coats	William	Dublin, GA 29
Coats	Zebulon	Olcott, NY 33
Cobb	Andrew	Old Cem, The Green, Middleboro, MA 50
Cobb	Asa	Fam Cem, Mt Cobb, Jefferson Twp, Lackawanna Co, PA 61
Cobb	Benjamin	Carver, MA 30
Cobb	Benjamin	South Carver, MA 16
Cobb	Benjamin	South Carver Cem, Carver, MA 34
Cobb	Binney	Handy Cem, West Woodstock, Windsor Co, VT 75
Cobb	Cornelius	Burial Hill, Plymouth, MA 56
Cobb	Daniel	United Cong Ch Cem, Barnstable, MA 55
Cobb	David	Cem, Taunton, MA 34
Cobb	Ebenezer	Ancient Bur Gr, Kingston, MA 50
Cobb	Ebenezer	Ancient Bur Gr, Kingston, MA 50
Cobb	Ebenezer	Lakenham Cem, Carver, MA 59
Cobb	Ebenezer	Plainville Cem, Wrentham, MA 55
Cobb	Ebenezer	Putnam, Middleboro, MA 56
Cobb	Edward	Knapp Cem, Taunton, MA 48
Cobb	Edward	Midland Cem, Westboro, MA 50
Cobb	Edward	West Abington Cem, Abington, MA 54
Cobb	Eleazer	Old Bur Gr, Brewster, MA 71
Cobb	Eleazer	United Cong Ch Cem, Barnstable, MA 55
Cobb	Elisha	South Eastham Cem, Bridge Rd, Eastham, MA 55
Cobb	Fleming	Fam Cem, Kanawha, Charleston, WV 55
Cobb	James	Rockdale, West Stockbridge, MA 56
Cobb	Job	Burial Hill, Plymouth, MA 56
Cobb	John	Old Bur Cem, Kingston, MA 62
Cobb	John	Old Cem, The Green, Middleboro, MA 50
Cobb	John	Orwell, Shoreham, VT 15
Cobb	John	Plainville Cem, Wrentham, MA 55
Cobb	John	United Cong Ch Cem, Barnstable, MA 55
Cobb	John	United Cong Ch Cem, Barnstable, MA 55
Cobb	John	West Abington Cem, West Abington, MA 62
Cobb	Jonathan	Blain Cem, Taunton, MA 41
Cobb	Joseph	Lakenham Cem, Carver, MA 59
Cobb	Joseph	United Cong Ch Cem, Barnstable, MA 55
Cobb	Malatiah	Londonderry Cem, Londonderry, NH 46
Cobb	Mason	Town Yard, Mansfield, MA 56
Cobb	Nathan	Cem, Hartford, VT 40
Cobb	Nathan	Hartford Cem, VT 41
Cobb	Nathan	Lakenham Cem, Carver, MA 58
Cobb	Nathan	Old Bur Cem, Plympton, MA 58
Cobb	Nathan	Westville Cem, Taunton, MA 41
Cobb	Nehemiah	South Carver Cem, Carver, MA 34
Cobb	Nehemiah Dea	South Carver, MA 16
Cobb	Nehimiah	Carver, MA 30
Cobb	Pharoah	Nr Three Springs, TN 23
Cobb	Pharoah	Nr Three Springs, Hawkins Co, TN 24
Cobb	Salmon	Canaan St Cem, Canaan, NH 36
Cobb	Samuel	Community Ch Cem, Rock Village, Middleboro, MA 55

Abstract of Graves of Revolutionary Patriots

Cobb Samuel	Fam bur gr, nr Union City, Madison Co, KY 39
Cobb Samuel Capt	North Bellingham Cem, Bellingham, MA 46
Cobb Seth	Old Bur Cem, Kingston, MA 62
Cobb Seth	Old Cem, The Green, Middleboro, MA 50
Cobb Seth	Town Cem, Dublin, NH 34
Cobb Simeon	St Johnsbury Center, VT 16
Cobb Simeon Capt	North Cem, Westmoreland, NH 36
Cobb Sylvanus	Hardwick, MA 54
Cobb Thomas	Parsippany Cem, Morris Co, NJ 32
Cobb Thomas	Parsippany, NJ 16
Cobb Thomas	Pres Ch Cem, Parsippany, NJ 29
Cobb Timothy	Lakenham Cem, Carver, MA 57
Cobb William	Holland, VT 35
Cobb William	Lakenham Cem, Carver, MA 57
Cobb William	Nr Syracuse, Onondaga Co, NY 35
Cobbs Charles	Fam Cem, nr Hot Creek Ch Cem, Campbell Co, VA 59
Cobbs Fleming	Fam Cem, nr Charleston, Kanawha Co, WV 54
Cobbs John	Hot Creek Ch Cem, Campbell Co, VA 59
Coble George	Coble's Luth Ch Cem, Greensboro, Guilford Co, NC 76
Coble Nicholas	Luth Ch Cem, nr Spanker, OH 56
Cobler Michael	Fam Cem, 2 mi W of Shreve, OH 25
Coburn Alpheus	Cabot, VT 56
Coburn Asa	Nr Wolf Creek Mills, Waterford, Washington Co, OH 55
Coburn Benjamin	Old West (Goodrich) Cem, Chesterfield, NH 36
Coburn Daniel	Mount Auburn Cem, MA 50
Coburn Ebenezer	Coburn-Dewing Cem, Warren Twp, PA 72
Coburn Ebenezer	Joppa Cem, Bedford, NH 34
Coburn Ebenezer	North Warren Pres Cem, Warren Twp, Bradford Co, PA 53
Coburn Henry	School St Cem, Lowell, MA 46
Coburn Hezekiah	Dracut Cem, Dracut, MA 46
Coburn Lemuel	North Thetford, VT 17
Coburn Morrill	Flat Cem, Cornish, NH 29
Coburn Nathaniel	New Brighton, PA 15
Coburn Saul	New Boston Cem, Dracut, MA 51
Coburn Zebediah	Grave obliterated, Homer, NY 36
Cochran Charles	Cochranton, PA 56
Cochran Cornelius	Old Center Cem, Blandford, Hampden Co, MA 58
Cochran Elijah	New Boston Cem, New Boston, NH 28
Cochran Isaac	Windham, NH 15
Cochran James	Forest Hill Cem, East Derry, NH 38
Cochran James	New Boston Cem, New Boston, NH 28
Cochran James	New Boston, NH 16
Cochran James Henry	Ref Ch Cem, Middletown, Frederick Co, MD 77
Cochran James Maj	Pembroke Cem, Pembroke, NH 45
Cochran John	Cem on Hill, Windham Twp, NH 58
Cochran John	Chambersburg, PA 56
Cochran John	Forest Hill Cem, East Derry, NH 38
Cochran John	Hagerstown, MD 56
Cochran John	New Boston, NH 16
Cochran John	New Boston Cem, New Boston, NH 28
Cochran Joseph Lt	Goshen Four Corners Cem, Goshen, NH 34
Cochran Nathaniel	Willow Tree Cem, Thoburn, WV 42
Cochran Nathaniel Capt	Willow Tree Cem, nr Monongah, WV 27
Cochran Robert	Spears Cem, 3 mi fr Rocky River Ch, Cabarrus Co, NC 49
Cochran Samuel	Fam Cem, Tryon Twp, Fayette Co, PA 56
Cochran Samuel	Lebanon Cem, Mifflin Twp, Allegheny Co, PA 71
Cochran Samuel	Old Pres Bur Gr, Dauphin, Dauphin Co, PA 62
Cochran William	Ebenezer Cem, OH 15
Cochran William	Ebenezer, Bradysville, OH 56
Cochran William	Fam farm, nr Fitch Bridge, Eagle Creek, Brown Co, OH 56
Cochran William	Rushings Creek Bapt Ch Cem, Camden, Benton Co, TN 73

Cochrane Jacob	George Hill Cem, Enfield, NH 36
Cochrane John Dr	Utica, NY 16
Cochrane Samuel Capt	Hill Crest Cem, Litchfield, NH 31
Cochren Elijah	New Boston, NH 16
Cochrun Simon	Ash Grove Cem, Allen Co, OH 55
Cocke William	Friendship Cem, MS 44
Cockerill Thomas	Quaker Cem, Walnut Creek, Fayette Co, OH 18
Cockley John	Rich's, Pleasant City, OH 56
Cockran James	Cem nr center of Windham, NH 45
Cockrell Peter	Lebanon Cem, Lebanon, MO 56
Cockrell Robert	Canaan Bend Cem, Canaan Twp, OH 56
Cockrem Daniel	Hillside Cem, Madison, NJ 48
Codding James	Attleboro, MA 53
Codding James	Stevens Cem, Annawan St, Rehoboth, MA 54
Coddington Enoch	Woodbridge Pres Ch Cem, Woodbridge, NJ 76
Coddington James	Bur gr, First Pres Ch, Woodbridge, NJ 25
Coddington James	Pres Ch Cem, Woodbridge, Middlesex Co, NJ 75
Coddington John	Old Mount Horeb, NJ 47
Coddington John	Pres Ch Cem, Woodbridge, Middlesex Co, NJ 75
Coddington Joseph	Bur gr, First Pres Ch, Woodbridge, NJ 25
Coddington Joseph	Pres Ch Cem, Woodbridge, Middlesex Co, NJ 75
Coddington Robert	1st Pres Ch Cem, Woodbridge, NJ 58
Coddington Robert	Bur gr, First Pres Ch, Woodbridge, NJ 25
Coddington William	Goodwill Cem, Montgomery, Orange Co, NY 78
Codill Stephen	Watly Caudill Cem, nr Whitesburg, Letcher Co, KY 79
Cody Isaac	Oneida, NY 56
Coe Aaron	West Granville, lot 6, Hampden, MA 56
Coe Asa	Mahaiwe, Great Barrington, MA 56
Coe Benjamin	Brick Ch Cem, Monsey, Rockland Co, NY 78
Coe Benjamin	Old bur gr, Newark, NJ 26
Coe Benjamin	Springdale, PA 30
Coe Daniel Jr	Fam bur gr, Pomona, Rockland Co, NY 78
Coe David	Charlestown, OH 53
Coe David Sr	Old North Cem, Middletown, Middlesex Co, CT 61
Coe Ebenezer	Cong Cem, Stratford, CT 31
Coe Ebenezer	Dalton Cem, Dalton, OH 56
Coe Halstead	Newark, NJ 48
Coe Isaac	Fam bur gr, Pomona, Rockland Co, NY 78
Coe Israel	Rootstown Cem, Rootstown, OH 53
Coe James	Cong Bur Gr, Stratford, CT 52
Coe James	Cong Ch Cem, Stratford, CT 78
Coe James	West Center Cem, Granville, Hampden Co, MA 63
Coe Joel	Scipio Cem, Scipio, NY 41
Coe John	Colonial Cem, Derby, CT 15
Coe John	New Lakemont Cem, Starkey, Yates Co, NY 69
Coe John	Old Colonial Cem, Derby, CT 56
Coe John	Red Bird Cem, Ellery, Chautauqua Co, NY 62
Coe John D Sr	Fam Cem, Hempstead, NY 53
Coe John Dea	Fam Cem, Hempstead, NY 53
Coe John Sr	Cem, West Torrington, CT 56
Coe John Sr	Fam bur gr, Pomona, Rockland Co, NY 78
Coe Jonas Rev Dr	Troy, NY 15
Coe Levi	West Litchfield, CT 17
Coe Matthew	Fam bur gr, Pomona, Rockland Co, NY 78
Coe Matthew Jr	Mt Pleasant Cem, Benton, Yates Co, NY 70
Coe Milburn	Old Cem nr farm, survey 799, Eagle Creek, Brown Co, OH 56
Coe Moses	Morristown, NJ 56
Coe Oliver	Winchester Cem, Winchester, CT 46
Coe Phinias	East Hartland Cem, East Hartland, CT 60
Coe Samuel	Cong Ch Cem, Granville, MA 54
Coe Samuel	State Bridge Cem, State Bridge, Chenango Co, NY 78

Abstract of Graves of Revolutionary Patriots

Coe Samuel Jr	Fam bur gr, Pomona, Rockland Co, NY 78
Coe Samuel W	Fam bur gr, Pomona, Rockland Co, NY 78
Coe Seth	Torrington Cem, Torrington, CT 55
Coe Thomas	East Hammonassett Cem, Madison, CT 23
Coe Timothy	West Hartland Cem, West Hartland, CT 60
Coe Uzal	Pres Cem, Morristown, NJ 32
Coe William	North Yard, Pomfret, CT 26
Coe Zachariah	Cong Cem, Stratford, CT 31
Coenradt Plass	Fam Cem, Greenport, Suffolk Co, NY 83
Cofer Jesse	Fam Homestead Cem, Harrisburg, Boone Co, MO 77
Coffer Thomas	Harper Chapel Cem, Caldwell Co, NC 49
Coffien John Capt	Cavendish, VT 16
Coffin Alexander	Hudson City Cem, Columbia Co, NY 41
Coffin Enoch 3rd	Buried at sea, MA 45
Coffin Enoch Capt	Old North Bur Gr, Concord, NH 41
Coffin Enoch Jr	Ship foundered at sea, MA 45
Coffin Henry	Ship foundered at sea, MA 45
Coffin Josiah 3rd	Died on prison ship Jersey, MA 45
Coffin Lemuel	Old Hill, Newburyport, MA 56
Coffin Matthew	Columbia Cem, Columbia, ME 45
Coffin Nathaniel Lt	Fam prop, North Lebanon, ME 46
Coffin Nicholas	First Settlers Cem, Lee, ME 30
Coffin Nicholas	Lee Cem, Lee, ME 31
Coffin Peter	Old Cem, Gloucester, MA 53
Coffin Peter Capt	Central South Water St Cem, Boscawen, NH 32
Coffin Ruth	Cushing Cem, Mattapoisett, MA 52
Coffin Thomas	Edgartown, MA 15
Coffin Tristram	Old Cem, Gloucester, MA 53
Coffin William	Guilford, NC 56
Coffinberry George	Springmill Cem, Springmill, OH 26
Coffren Robert	Vienna, ME 30
Coffrin James	Killed in Wyoming Massacre, Wyoming, PA 52
Coffrin William	Killed in Wyoming Massacre, Wyoming, PA 52
Coggeshall John May	Oak Grove Cem, New Bedford, MA 45
Coggeshall Joseph	Middletown Hist Cem, Main Rd, Middletown, RI 75
Coggeshall Thomas	Fam Cem, Middletown, RI 51
Coggeshall William	Cem, Milford, CT 56
Coggeshall William	Old North Cem, Bristol, RI 46
Coggswell James	Randolph Center Cem, Randolph, Orange Co, VT 72
Coggswell John	Pentucket Cem, Haverhill, MA 29
Coggswell Mason F Dr	Old North Cem, Old Hartford, CT 19
Coggswell Noah	Southington, CT 29
Cogswell Amos Maj	Pine Hill Cem, Dover, NH 31
Cogswell Daniel	Becket Center, Becket, MA 56
Cogswell Ferris	Fosterville, NY 56
Cogswell Nathaniel	Town Cem, Atkinson, NH 28
Cogswell Reuben	Galway Village Cem, Galway, Saratoga Co, NY 77
Cogswell Samuel	South Parish Bur Gr, Andover, MA 26
Cogswell Samuel	Village Cem, Lansingburgh, Troy, Rensselaer Co, NY 77
Cogswell Thomas	Essex, MA 48
Cogswell Thomas	Smith Mtg Hs Cem, Gilmanton, NH 32
Cogswell William	Old Cem, Essex, MA 55
Cogswell William	Old Atkinson, NH 52
Cogswell William Dr	Town Cem, Atkinson, NH 28
Coiner Conrad	Mount Zion Cem, Montebello, Rockbridge Co, VA 36
Coit Daniel	Maple Hill Cem, Rouses Point, NY 15
Coit Samuel	Fam Cem, Griswald Ch, Preston, Norwich, CT 60
Coit Solomon	First Cong Cem, Griswold, CT 62
Colbath George	Harmony Grove Cem, Portsmouth, NH 34
Colbaugh William	Nr Elizabethton, Carter Co, TN 24
Colbdourn Samuel Sr	Milford, MA 50

Colbert James	Big Indian Creek, Godfrey, GA 32
Colburn Ebenezer	Grove Cem, Belfast, Waldo Co, ME 76
Colburn Ebenezer	Pine Grove Cem, Leominster, MA 50
Colburn Elias	Old Village Cem, Temple, NH 28
Colburn Isaac	Ford Cem, Hudson, NH 34
Colburn Issac Capt	Old Bur Gr, Westford, MA 47
Colburn James	Churchyard, Hollis, NH 39
Colburn John	Old Pine Grove Cem, Leominster, MA 47
Colburn Jonathan	Leominster, MA 54
Colburn Jonathan	Pine Grove Cem, Leominster, MA 50
Colburn Joseph	1st Parish Ch, Needham, MA 54
Colburn Nathan	Churchyard, Hollis, NH 39
Colburn Nathan	Pine Grove Cem, Leominster, MA 50
Colburn Oliver	Cem, Pittstown, ME 55
Colburn Robert	Churchyard, Hollis, NH 39
Colburn Samuel Jr	Third Parish Cem, West Dedham, MA 50
Colburn Selvanus	Old Cem, Springfield, MA 47
Colburn Stephen	School St Cem, Lebanon, NH 27
Colburn Thomas Capt	East Dixfield, ME 31
Colby Benjamin	Sandown Center CeM, Sandown, NH 36
Colby David	Old (Center) Cem, Henniker, NH 34
Colby Ebenezer	His farm, Sanbornton, NH 35
Colby Ebenezer Jr	His farm, Sanbornton, NH 35
Colby Eli	Bennington, NH 32
Colby Elliot	Parade Cem, Lower Warner, Warner, NH 35
Colby Elliott	Warner, NH 15
Colby Enoch	First Cem, Candia, NH 29
Colby Ephraim	Colby Cem, Colby Rd, Ogden, NY 70
Colby Ezekial	Holland Cem, Holland, NY 32
Colby Ichabod	Lake View Cem, Wolfeboro, NH 26
Colby Isaac	Town Cem, Springfield, NH 38
Colby Jethro	Village Cem, Chester, NH 33
Colby John	Evergreen Cem, Bennington, NH 26
Colby John	Evergreen Cem, Bennington, NH 56
Colby John	Jotham Rollins Cem, Sanbornton, NH 36
Colby Levi	Center Cem, Henniker, NH 32
Colby Moses	Canaan St Cem, Canaan, NH 37
Colby Moses	Ye Old Cem, Danville, NH 30
Colby Nicholas	Colby Cem, Henniker, NH 32
Colby Rowel	George Hill Cem, Enfield, NH 36
Colby Thomas	Litchfield Plains, ME 42
Colby Thomas	Litchfield, ME 20
Colby Thomas	North (Evans) Cem, Bow, NH 32
Colby Timothy	Union Cem, Amesbury, MA 46
Colby William	Lewis Corners, NY 30
Colcord John	George Hill Cem, Enfield, NH 36
Colcord Joseph Corp	Hixon farm, Newmarket, NH 29
Colcord Samuel	Kingston Plains Cem, Kingston, NH 30
Colcord Samuel	Winter St Cem, Exeter, NH 40
Colcord Thomas	Town Cem, Springfield, NH 38
Coldcleugh Andrew	Lexington City Cem, Davidson Co, NC 49
Coldsberry Henry	Asbury Meth Epis Cem, New Castle Co, DE 46
Cole Abial	Cem nr Cong Ch, Orleans, MA 49
Cole Abiel	Shutesbury, MA 15
Cole Abijah	Village Cem, Prospect Harbor, Hancock Co, ME 56
Cole Abraham	Black Rock Bapt Ch Cem, Baltimore, Baltimore Co, MD 77
Cole Abraham	Woodrow Meth Churchyard, Staten Island, NY 72
Cole Allen	North Cem, Warren, RI 54
Cole Ambrose	Ormsbee Cem, Moolyville, Greenfield Twp, NY 41
Cole Amos	Stevens Cem, Annawan St, Rehoboth, MA 54
Cole Amos	West Hill Cem, Sherburne, NY 16

Abstract of Graves of Revolutionary Patriots

Cole Andrew	Kickemuit, Warren, RI	54
Cole Andrew	Old Lakeville, Lakeville, MA	56
Cole Azor	Green Gull Cem, Springwater, Livingston Co, NY	74
Cole Benjamin	Cole Cem, Humphrey, Cattaraugus Co, NY	71
Cole Benjamin	Farm Cem, Hebron, NY	66
Cole Benjamin	Hanover Cem, Shelby Co, IN	63
Cole Benjamin	Old Hill River, New Marlborough, MA	56
Cole Benjamin	Potter Cem, S of East Galway, Saratoga Co, NY	77
Cole Benjamin	Varysburg, NY	35
Cole Bethuel	Lakeview Cem, Skaneateles, Onondaga Co, NY	75
Cole Consider	Fern Hill Cem, #15-R, West Parish, Pembroke, MA	40
Cole Constant	Off Old Warren Rd, Sherman land, Swansea, MA	54
Cole Cornelius	Old Hurley Bur Gr, Ulster Co, NY	36
Cole Curtis	Aban Cem, Battonville & Cambridge Rds, Jackson, NY	64
Cole Daniel	Duck Creek Cem, Wellfleet, MA	49
Cole Daniel	Old Bapt Cem, Carmel, Putnam Co, NY	57
Cole Daniel	Plainfield Plains Cem, Plainfield, NH	28
Cole Daniel Jr	LaFayette Cem, LaFayette, Onondaga Co, NY	78
Cole Daniel Sr	Old Cole Cem, Asylum Lane, Warren, RI	54
Cole David	Cem back of fire house, Carmel, Putnam Co, NY	36
Cole David	Clark Schoolhouse Rd Cem, Edinburgh, Saratoga Co, NY	77
Cole David	Duck Creek Cem, Wellfleet, MA	49
Cole David	Sharon Cem, Sharon, Litchfield Co, CT	66
Cole David	Wellfleet Cem, Wellfleet, MA	46
Cole David Sr	Grove Cem, Trumansburg, NY	31
Cole Ebenezer	Highland Cem, Chesterfield, MA	53
Cole Ebenezer	Lakenham Cem, Carver, MA	59
Cole Ebenezer	Old Hurley Bur Gr, Ulster Co, NY	36
Cole Eleazer	Woodstock, ME	56
Cole Elisha Jr	Fam farm, nr Long Pond, Putnam Co, NY	56
Cole Ephraim	Collins Cem, S of West Union, Adams Co, OH	55
Cole Ephraim	Melrose Cem, Brockton, MA	15
Cole Ephraim	Melrose Cem, Brockton, MA	46
Cole Ezra	Benton Rural Cem, Benton, Yates Co, NY	70
Cole Francis	Old Cem, Medfield, MA	46
Cole Gideon	Old Bur Gr Cem, Prattsburg, Steuben Co, NY	70
Cole Hezekiah	Lakenham Cem, Carver, MA	58
Cole Hugh Col	Hopkins Mills Cem, Foster, Providence Co, RI	31
Cole Isaac	Broadalbin Cem, Broadalbin, Fulton Co, NY	78
Cole Isaac	Cem, Oakvale, WV	52
Cole Jacob	New Albany Cem (aban), Floyd Co, IN	72
Cole Jacob	South Ch Cem, Bergenfield, NJ	55
Cole James	Old Fowler Cem, Fowler, St Lawrence Co, NY	56
Cole Jesse	Center Cem, New Milford, CT	55
Cole Job	Lewiston, ME	18
Cole John	Canoe Brook Cem, Westmoreland, NH	25
Cole John	Cornwall Cem, Cornwall, Litchfield Co, CT	24
Cole John	Cross Roads Cem, nr Monroeville, Allegheny Co, PA	16
Cole John	Lakenham Cem, Carver, MA	59
Cole John	Sutton Center Cem, Sutton, MA	15
Cole John	Wales Center, NY	33
Cole John Esq	Odd Fellows Cem, Dover, Kent Co, DE	46
Cole Jonathan	Canoe Brook Cem, Westmoreland, NH	25
Cole Jonathan	Cem nr railroad station, Eastham, MA	49
Cole Joseph	Acton, MA	55
Cole Joseph	Carmel Cem, Putnam Co, NY	61
Cole Joseph	Old Rumford Cem, Rehoboth, MA	55
Cole Joseph Jr	Sinclair Botom Ch Cem, Chilhowie, VA	59
Cole Joshua	Carver Cem, Rt 44, Carver, MA	55
Cole Justin	Madison Village Cem, OH	26
Cole Lemuel	Old Cem, Plympton, MA	57

Cole Mathew	Sharon, CT 56
Cole Matthew	South Bur Gr (Blur Hills), CT 56
Cole Micah	Old Parish Cem, North Rochester, MA 59
Cole Nathan	Eastern Cem, Danbury, NH 36
Cole Nathaniel	Akeley Cem, Guilford, VT 22
Cole Nathaniel	Colesville Cem, nr Harpursville, Broome Co, NY 78
Cole Parker	East Plainfield Cem, Plainfield, NH 30
Cole Parker Capt	Center Shaftsbury Cem, Center Shaftsbury, VT 45
Cole Richard Sr	Midway Cem, Midway, Woodford Co, KY 55
Cole Richard Sr	St Peter's Cath Ch Cem, Libertytown, Frederick Co, MD 77
Cole Samuel	Barkers Mills, Lewiston, ME 20
Cole Samuel	Bentonville Cem, Bentonville, Fayette Co, IN 79
Cole Samuel	Beverly, MA 55
Cole Samuel	Hale St Cem, Beverly, MA 45
Cole Samuel	Killed in Wyoming Massacre, Wyoming, PA 52
Cole Samuel	Lewiston, ME 18
Cole Samuel	Old Union Cem, Johnston, PA 17
Cole Samuel	Old Union Cem, Johnstown, PA 15
Cole Samuel	Willett Cem, Cortland Co, NY 64
Cole Seth	Fredonia Cem, Pomfret, Chautauqua Co, NY 15
Cole Simeon	Stevens Cem, Annawan St, Rehoboth, MA 54
Cole Sisson	Meth Cem, Richfield, Otsego Co, NY 70
Cole Solomon	Ashtabula Co, OH 55
Cole Solomon	Sugar Hill Cem, Lisbon, NH 27
Cole Thomas	Watertown, CT 15
Cole Thomas Herrick	Old Cem, Beverly, MA 45
Cole Timothy	Cornwall, Litchfield, CT 56
Cole Timothy	Long Mountain Cem, New Milford, CT 40
Cole William	Fam Cem, Ashbury Community nr Halifax, Halifax Co, VA 78
Cole William	Fam Cem, Asbury, Halifax Co, VA 76
Cole William	Mann Cem, Butternuts, nr Gilbertsville, Otsego Co, NY 77
Cole William	Old Rumford Cem, Rehoboth, MA 55
Cole William	Wellfleet Cem, Wellfleet, MA 46
Colegrove Jonathon	Whitestone, Norwich Twp, Chenango Co, NY 56
Colehamer Andrew	Middletown Cem, Half Moon, Saratoga Co, NY 77
Coleman Charles	Eutaw, Greene Co, AL 56
Coleman Christopher	McMillan Ch Cem, Canonsburg, PA 61
Coleman Daniel	Culpeper Cem, Culpeper, VA 34
Coleman Daniel	Nr Clarys Mineral Spring, SC 15
Coleman Dudley	Cem nr Brookfield Corner, NH 26
Coleman Enos	West Cem, Amherst, MA 60
Coleman Jacob	Township Cem, Euclid, Cuyahoga Co, OH 55
Coleman James	Providence Cem, Mercer Co, KY 52
Coleman Jesse	Fairview Cem, Rodman, Jefferson Co, NY 41
Coleman John	Fam prop, nr Saluda River, SC 15
Coleman John	West Laurel Hill Cem, Montgomery Co, PA 59
Coleman Jonathan	Bark Camp Cem, 5 mi fr Midville, Burke Co, GA 78
Coleman Jonathan	Bark Camp Cem, 5 mi fr Midville, Burke Co, GA 34
Coleman Joseph	Meeting House Cem, Newington, NH 25
Coleman Josiah	Cartwright Cem, Sharon, Litchfield Co, CT 67
Coleman Lemuel	Center Cem, Southampton, MA 49
Coleman Nathaniel	Wayne, Ashtabula Co, OH 18
Coleman Neniad	Pleasant Ridge Pres Cem, Hamilton Co, OH 41
Coleman Noah	Old Chapel Bur Gr, Fly Creek, Otsego Co, NY 81
Coleman Phineas	Meeting House Cem, Newington, NH 25
Coleman Robert	Nr Feasterville, Fairfield Co, SC 42
Coleman Samuel	Center Cem, Southampton, MA 49
Coleman Thomas	Grandview Cem, Altoona, PA 52
Coleman Thomas	Grand View Cem, Juniata, Blair Co, PA 21
Coleman Timothy Lt	Salina Cem, Salina, NY 47
Colesworthy Nathaniel	Copps Hill Cem, Boston, MA 46

Abstract of Graves of Revolutionary Patriots

Coley William	Otselic, NY 16
Colfax William Brig Gen	Pompton, Passaic Co, NJ 26
Colflesh Henry	St Paul's Evan Luth Cem, Montgomery Co, PA 59
Colglazier David	Old Mill Cem, W of Salem, Washington Co, IN 72
Colgrove Jeremiah	South View Cem, North Adams, MA 45
Colgrove Jeremiah Esq	Southview Cem, North Adams, MA 15
Colgrove Joseph	Rose Rd, Sandisfield, MA 56
Colgrove Stephen	Pittsfield Cem, Pittsfield, Otsego Co, NY 72
Collamer Anthony Jr	Dunning St, Malta, NY 56
Collamore Enoch	Assinippi, Gilman Plains, MA 56
Collens Charles	Morris, CT 17
Colleny Thomas	Old Village Cem, Locke, Cayuga Co, NY 57
Collester John	New Center Cem, Blandford, MA 58
Collett John	Meth Cem, Shrub Oak, Westchester Co, NY 41
Collett Joseph	Old Pennsylvania Run Ch nr Bullitt Co, Jefferson Co, KY 25
Collette –	Hendricks Cem, 9 mi fr Thomaston, GA 32
Colley John	Maplewood Cem, Bennington, NH 45
Collidge Paul	Hillsboro Center Cem, Hillsboro, NH 34
Collier James	Greenfield Cem, sect 1 #18, Greenfield, Highland Co, OH 25
Collier James	Highland Co, OH 55
Collier Vines	Fam bur gr, 100 yd fr fam home, Oglethorpe Co, GA 34
Collin Robert Capt	Town Cem, Sandown, NH 33
Colline Clement	Copps Hill Cem, Boston, MA 46
Collings Edward Z	Newton Union Sloan Cem, West Collingswood, NJ 50
Collings Jonathan	Old North Cem, Truro, MA 49
Collings Joseph Z	Newton Union Sloan Cem, West Collingswood, NJ 50
Collins Abraham	Old Center Cem, Monterey, MA 41
Collins Albermarle	Friends Meeting Ground, Trenton, NJ 28
Collins Andrew	Wrightstown Friends Mtg Cem, Wrightstown, Bucks Co, PA 66
Collins Augustus	North Guilford Cem, North Guilford, CT 55
Collins Benjamin	Stiner's Cem, Lincoln Twp, Morrow Co, OH 55
Collins Benjamin	West Lawn Cem, Goffstown, NH 28
Collins Chedor Lagner	Sand Hill Churchyard, Unadilla, NY 71
Collins Clement	Copps Hill Bur Gr, Boston, MA 55
Collins Clement	Copps Hill, Boston, MA 56
Collins Daniel	Center Cem, Marlboro, NH 38
Collins Daniel	North Guilford Cem, North Guilford, CT 55
Collins Daniel	Old Cem, Gloucester, MA 47
Collins Edward	Old Newton Union Cem, W of Collingswood, Camden Co, NJ 35
Collins Edward	Waterford Twp, Gloucester, NJ 55
Collins Enoch	Salisbury Plains Bur Gr, Amesbury, MA 46
Collins Henry	Mount Rest Cem, Rosencrary, GA 29
Collins Henry	Newport, Lake Co, IL 16
Collins Henry	Rosencrans Cem, Waukegan, IL 28
Collins Isaac	Leeds, ME 18
Collins James	Burial Hill, Plymouth, MA 56
Collins James Capt	Greenfield Cem, OH 15
Collins James Staton	New Berne, Fairfax Co, no state 56
Collins John	Friendship Ch Cem, New Castle Co, DE 46
Collins John	Hillsdale Rural Cem, Columbia Co, NY 42
Collins John	Mars Hill Cem, Cobb Co, GA 52
Collins John	Mendon, NY 33
Collins John	Old North Cem, Truro, MA 49
Collins John	Portland, ME 16
Collins John	Pres Ch Cem, Chartiers Creek, Allegheny Co, PA 15
Collins Joseph	Northampton, Fulton Co, NY 15
Collins Joseph	Old North Cem, Truro, MA 49
Collins Joseph	Old Newton Union Cem, W of Collingswood, Camden Co, NJ 35
Collins Joseph	Winters Cem, Jay Co, IN 72
Collins Josiah	Pres Ch Cem, Kingston, Decatur Co, IN 72
Collins Lemuel	Cem nr Industry, Stark, ME 56

Collins Levi	McCafferty Cem, Rome, Macomb Co, MI 58
Collins Michael	Cem nr railroad station, Eastham, MA 49
Collins Moses	Rumney Marsh Cem, Revere, MA 41
Collins Nathaniel	Barkhamsted Center Cem, Barkhamsted, CT 59
Collins Philemon	North Anson, ME 15
Collins Pitman	Town Green (grave), Riverside Cem (stone), Guilford, CT 55
Collins Richard	Fam bur gr, nr Port Republic, NJ 23
Collins Robert Sr	Fam graveyard, fam farm, Franklin Co, KY 56
Collins Samuel	Old M E Ch Cem, Berkshire, NY 34
Collins Seth	Cem nr old Emery house, Chatham, MA 49
Collins Seth	West Hartford, CT 38
Collins Seth Capt	Old Cem, North Main St, West Hartford, CT 31
Collins Spencer	Bullitt, KY 56
Collins Stephen	Foster Lot, Historical Cem, Burlington, Boone Co, KY 70
Collins Stephen	West Lawn Cem, Goffstown, NH 29
Collins Thaddeus	Rose Cem, Rose, Wayne Co, NY 79
Collins Thomas	Nazareth Pres Ch Cem, Spartanburg Co, SC 70
Collins Thomas	Revolutionary War Cem, Salem, Washington Co, NY 78
Collins Thomas	Starr Cem, Ludlowville, NY 31
Collins Thomas Sr	Milford Meth Epis Cem, Kent Co, DE 46
Collins William	Cem on hill, E of Cold Brook Rd, Preble, NY 36
Collins William	Glenwood Cem, Collinsville, Madison Co, IL 77
Collins William	Old North Cem, Marlboro, NH 39
Collins William	Sodom Cem, Underwood, Scott Co, IN 73
Collins William	Stone Mills Cem, Orleans, Jefferson Co, NY 65
Collins William	Stone Mills or Collin Mills, NY 56
Collom Jonathan	Lumbrick Cem, E of Charleston, Coles Co, IL 72
Collyer Lemuel	North Dorchester Cem, Boston, MA 55
Colman John	Cem back of church, Templeton, MA 55
Colman Josiah	Cem, Milford, CT 56
Colson Christopher	Daniels farm, E of Willoughby, OH 26
Colson James	Bath Springs Cem, Union Co, IN 72
Colson James	Highland Cem, South Weymouth, MA 50
Colson Josiah	Highland Cem, South Weymouth, MA 50
Colson Thomas	Martin's Woods off Park Ave, South Weymouth, MA 50
Colt Benjamin	Village Cem, Hadley, MA 56
Colt Elisha	Old North Cem, Old Hartford, CT 19
Colt William	Pittsfield Cem, Pittsfield, ME 26
Colton David	Ira Hill, Ira, NY 56
Colton Samuel	Old Bloomfield Cem, Bloomfield, CT 55
Colton Thomas	Central Cem, Hartland, VT 51
Colver Elisha Esq	Fam Cem, North Lafayette Town, Milan, NY 21
Colver Nathaniel	East Hubbarton, VT 56
Colville John Sr	Hilltop Cem, farm, Buena Vista Rd, Licking Co, OH 56
Colvin Daniel	Chippenhook Cem, Clarendon, VT 23
Colvin Daniel	Fam Cem, nr Culpeper, VA 37
Colvin Joseph	Colvin, Coventry, RI 56
Colvin Levi	Chippenhook Cem, Chippenhook, VT 31
Colvin Levi Ens	Old Cem, Center, Rutland, VT 23
Colvin Noah	Rockland Cem, Scituate, Providence Co, RI 31
Colvin Peter	East Benton, Lackawanna Co, PA 15
Colvin Philip	Evergreen Cem, Factorville, PA 15
Colvin Reuben	Grandview Cem, North Bennington, VT 74
Colwall Hugh	Pres Ch Cem, Basking Ridge, NJ 47
Colwell Arthur	South Galway Cem, South Galway, Saratoga Co, NY 77
Colwell James	Gilead Cem, Carmel, Putnam Co, NY 57
Colwell Stephen	Gloucester, RI 38
Colwell William	Gilead Cem, Carmel, Putnam Co, NY 57
Combs Benjamin	Meth Epis Cem, Smyrna, Kent Co, DE 46
Combs Benjamin	On Combs Ferry Rd, ½ mi fr end, Clark Co, KY 55
Combs John	Nr Vicco, Perry Co, KY 50

Combs John	Poland Cem, Mahoning Co, OH	55
Combs Joshus	Warrensburg Cem, Warrensburg, NY	56
Comee David	The Old Cem, Gardner, MA	33
Comee David	The Old Cem, Gardner, MA	46
Comee Jonathan	Christ Ch Cem, Hopkinton, MA	46
Comegys Jesse	Fam Cem, nr Chestertown, Kent Co, MD	71
Comer John	Milo, Yates Co, NY	70
Comfort John	Old Brick Ch Cem, Montgomery, NY	48
Comfort Richard	Wellsburg Cem, Wellsburg, NY	32
Comingore Henry	Mud Mtg Hs, Mercer Co, KY	52
Comingore Henry Sr	Mud Mtg Hs Cem, Mercer Co, KY	22
Comingore John Sr	Mud Mtg Hs Cem, Mercer Co, KY	22
Comings Asa	Cummings Cem, Winthrop Rd, Augusta, ME	29
Comings John Dea	Metcalf Cem, Winthrop, ME	29
Comings Stephen	Old Litchfield Yard, Hampton, CT	31
Comins Samuel	Cem on Hinsdale farm, Hinsdale, NH	37
Commings Thomas	Knoxville, PA	52
Commons Robert	West Grove Cem, Wayne Co, IN	72
Como Francis	Town Cem, Sutton, NH	37
Compson Thomas	Parsippany Cem, Morris Co, NJ	32
Compton –	Fam land grant, nr Fairfax Court House, VA	48
Compton Ichabod	Haleyville Meth Cem, Cumberland Co, NJ	49
Compton Joseph	Bapt Ch Cem, Trenton, IN	56
Compton Joseph	Foothill Rd #2, plot 9, Bridgewater Twp, NJ	47
Compton Joseph	Prim Bapt Cem, Trenton, Butler Co, OH	55
Compton Richard	Compton-Castner Cem, Foothill Rd, Somerville, NJ	47
Compton Richard	McNeal, Gos Lot, Ovid, Seneca Co, NY	70
Compton Robert	Grantsville Cem, Grantsville, Garrett Co, MD	70
Compton Thomas	Parsippany Cem, Parsippany, Morris Co, NJ	59
Comrie Alexander	Colonial Cem, Johnson, NY	15
Comstock Abel	Lippitt Cem, Hartwick, Otsego Co, NY	71
Comstock Achilles	Yatesville Cem, Jerusalem, Yates Co, NY	69
Comstock Adam	Fam Cem, Argell land, Saratoga, NY	71
Comstock Anselm	Sweden, NY	15
Comstock David	Kirkland Ave Cem, Clinton, Oneida Co, NY	79
Comstock David	Prob Norwalk, CT	34
Comstock Jabes 2nd	Hadlyme, West Haddam, CT	56
Comstock James	Fam bur gr, nr Montville Station, VT	53
Comstock John	Cedar Grove Cem, New London, CT	57
Comstock John	Center Cem, New Milford, CT	55
Comstock John	Maple Grove Cem, Hoosick Falls, Hoosick, NY	36
Comstock Levi	West Cem, Webb prop, nr Burlington, VT	81
Comstock Peregrine	Muddy Brook Cem, Great Barrington, MA	45
Comstock Peter	Montville Cem, New London Co, CT	70
Comstock Raynsford	Exeter Cem, Exeter, Otsego Co, NY	72
Comstock Robert	Killed in Wyoming Massacre, Wyoming, PA	52
Comstock Samuel	Maple Grove Cem, Hoosick Falls, Hoosick, NY	36
Comstock Samuel	Riverview, East Haddam, CT	56
Comstock Samuel	West Yard Cem, Marlow, NH	25
Conant Amos	Irasburg, VT	35
Conant Benjamin	Conant priv yard, Turner, ME	29
Conant Benjamin	Fam Cem, Turner, ME	49
Conant Benjamin	Turner, ME	18
Conant Benjamin	Warwick Village, MA	31
Conant Caleb	Lyme Plain Cem, Lyme, NH	36
Conant Daniel	Lower Village Cem, Stow, MA	52
Conant Daniel	Old Bur Gr, Townsend, MA	48
Conant David	South Parish Cem, Bridgewater, MA	56
Conant Ezra	South Parish Cem, Bridgewater, MA	56
Conant George	Becket Center, Becket, MA	56
Conant Ivaas	Cem, East Hartford, CT	49

Conant Jeremiah	Pomfret, VT 23
Conant John	North Beverly Cem, North Beverly, MA 56
Conant John Jr	Summer St Cem, Bridgewater, MA 55
Conant Johnathan	Beverly, MA 55
Conant Josiah	Churchyard, Hollis, NH 39
Conant Josiah	Green St Cem, Gardner, MA 49
Conant Josiah	The Old Cem, Gardner, MA 33
Conant Lot	North Beverly Cem, North Beverly, MA 56
Conant Luther	Cem beside rd betw North Amherst & Shutesbury, MA 45
Conant Nathan	Old Bur Gr, Townsend, MA 48
Conant Peter	Lower Village Cem, Stow, MA 60
Conant Peter	Lower Village Cem, Stow, MA 52
Conant Phineas	Summer St Cem, Bridgewater, MA 55
Conant Zenas	South Parish Cem, Bridgewater, MA 56
Conaway Charles	Fam farm, 4 mi fr Scioto, Harrison Co, OH 55
Conaway John	Morgan Cem, Katy-Lincoln Dist, WV 42
Conaway Michael	Fam farm, 4 mi fr Scioto, Harrison Co, OH 55
Conaway Thomas	Welley Cem, Chatam Hill, nr Farmington, WV 42
Conch Ebenezer	Boyce Cem, Milton, Ulster Co, NY 78
Concklin Isaac	Van Cortlandville Cem, Peekskill, NY 41
Concklin John	Van Cortlandville Cem, Peekskill, NY 41
Conderman Adam	Fremont, Steuben Co, NY 57
Condict Abner	Pres Cem, Morristown, NJ 32
Condict Ebenezer	Pres Cem, Morristown, NJ 32
Condict Phillip	Pres Cem, Morristown, NJ 32
Condict Silas	Pres Cem, Morristown, NJ 32
Condict Zenas	Pres Cem, Morristown, NJ 32
Condit Abner	Morristown Pres Ch Cem, Morristown, NJ 78
Condit Amos	Pres Cem, Orange, NJ 32
Condit Daniel	Old bur gr, Orange, NJ 26
Condit David	Pres Cem, Orange, NJ 32
Condit Enoch	Pres Cem, Orange, NJ 32
Condit Jabez	Old Pres Cem, Morristown, NJ 50
Condit Japhia	Old bur gr, Orange, NJ 26
Condit Jeptha	Pres Cem, Orange, NJ 32
Condit Joel	Pres Cem, Orange, NJ 32
Condit John Dr	Old bur gr, Orange, NJ 26
Condit Jonathan	First Ch Cem, Orange, NJ 47
Condit Jonathan	Pres Cem, Orange, NJ 32
Condit Moses	Old bur gr, Orange, NJ 26
Condit Moses	Pres Cem, Orange, NJ 32
Condit Nathaniel	Pres Cem, Orange, NJ 32
Condit Philip Sr	1st Pres, Morristown, NJ 55
Condit Samuel	Old First Ch Cem, Newark, NJ 47
Condit Samuel	Old bur gr, Orange, NJ 26
Condit Simon	Pres Cem, Orange, NJ 32
Condit Simon	Trenton Cem, Condit, Trenton Twp, Delaware Co, OH 53
Condit Timothy	Old bur gr, Orange, NJ 26
Condon Redman	Farm, Scioto, S of Chillicothe, 3 mi N of Pike Co, OH 55
Cone Daniel	Center Cem, Peru, MA 52
Cone Daniel	Moodus, East Haddam, CT 56
Cone Daniel H	Center Cem, Winchester, CT 59
Cone Elijah	East Haddam Cem, Haddam, CT 59
Cone Elijah	Hadlyme, CT 54
Cone Elisha	Old Cove, East Haddam, CT 56
Cone George	Millington, East Haddam, CT 56
Cone Ichabod	Tully Village Cem, Onondaga Co, NY 57
Cone Israel	Millington, East Haddam, CT 56
Cone James	Bashan, East Haddam, CT 56
Cone Jared Maj	Cem nr Columbia Bridge, Columbia, NH 36
Cone Jonah	Millington, East Haddam, CT 56

Cone Joseph	Clam River Cem, Sandisfield, MA 56
Cone Joshua	Cong Cem, East Haddam, CT 56
Cone Oliver	Millington, East Haddam, CT 56
Cone Oliver	Mount Pleasant Cem, Shelby, NY 36
Cone Robert	Middletown Cem, Middletown, CT 59
Cone Roswell	Hadlyme, West Haddam, CT 56
Cone Sylvanus	Bashan, East Haddam, CT 56
Cone Timothy	Riverview, East Haddam, CT 56
Cone William	Millington, East Haddam, CT 56
Cone Zachariah	Townsend Cem, Andover, CT 55
Coneley Peter	Massacred nr mouth of Lechry Creek, Dearborn Co, IN 24
Coney Edward	Norwich Town Cem, Norwich, CT 18
Coney John	Portland Cem, Chautauqua Co, NY 15
Coney Joseph	Old Cem, Canton St, Sharon, MA 56
Confehr A	St Peter's, Mantzville, PA 49
Congdon James	Sugar Hill Cem, Wallingford Twp, Rutland Co, VT 55
Congdon Stephen	Congdon Hill, North Kingstown, RI 51
Conger Benjamin	Bapt Ground, lot #1, Stanford, Dutchess Co, NY 21
Conger Daniel	Pres Cem, Morristown, NJ 32
Conger David	Old Cem, Woodbridge, NJ 56
Conger David	Rockaway Pres Churchyard, Rockaway, Morris Co, NJ 80
Conger Reuben	Johnson farm, Westfall, Niles, NY 56
Conger Stephen	Clarksville, Montgomery Co, TN 24
Conger Uzziah	Ira Hill, Ira, NY 56
Congleton John	Old Pres Bur Gr, Pennsville, Salem Co, NJ 27
Conick John	Schuyler Lake Cem, Exeter, Otsego Co, NY 71
Conine Jeremiah	Old Perrysville Cem, Green Twp, Ashland Co, OH 55
Conkey Dick	Old Bur Gr, Salem, Washington Co, NY 58
Conkey Ezekiel	Nr Rittman, OH 25
Conkey James	Orwell, Shoreham, VT 15
Conkey Joshua	Old Bur Gr, Salem, Washington Co, NY 58
Conklin Benjamin Rev	Rawson Brook Cem, Leicester, MA 55
Conklin Cornelius	Old Huntington Cem, Huntington, Suffolk Co, NY 36
Conklin Cornelius Capt	Old Cem, Huntington, NY 15
Conklin David	Huntington, NY 15
Conklin David	Orange Twp, OH 18
Conklin Edward	North End Cem, Easthampton, NY 35
Conklin Elias	Kirkwood Cem, Kirkwood, Broome Co, NY 78
Conklin Ezra	Huntington, NY 15
Conklin Ezra	Old Huntington Cem, Huntington, Suffolk Co, NY 36
Conklin Hubbard	Old Huntington Cem, Huntington, Suffolk Co, NY 36
Conklin Isaac	5 Points Mission Farm Cem, Pomona, Rockland Co, NY 78
Conklin Isaac	New Hackensack Ref Ch Cem, New Hackensack, NY 70
Conklin Jacob	Berwyn Cem, LaFayette, Onondaga Co, NY 78
Conklin Jacob	Prospect Cem, Jamaica, Queens Co, NY 78
Conklin Jeremiah	Smithfield Cem, opposite Pres Ch, Dutchess Co, NY 66
Conklin Jeremiah	White Cem, Yorktown, NY 34
Conklin John	Friends Cem, Croton, NY 35
Conklin John	Jersey Hill Cem, S of Galway Village, Saratoga Co, NY 77
Conklin John	Meth Cem, Shrub Oak, Westchester Co, NY 41
Conklin John	Meth Ch Cem, Shrub Oak, Westchester Co, NY 36
Conklin John	Poughkeepsie Rural Cem, Poughkeepsie, NY 70
Conklin John	Riverside Cem, nr Kirkwood, Broome Co, NY 78
Conklin Joseph	Freetown Cem, Cortland Co, NY 36
Conklin Joseph	Maple Grove Cem, Horseheads, Chemung Co, NY 78
Conklin Lewis	Sherwood Fam Bur Gr, N of Suffern, Rockland Co, NY 78
Conklin Matthew	Fam Cem, Niles, NY 56
Conklin Matthew	Niles Cem, Bonnie Brae, nr Keonig's Point, Cayuga, NY 54
Conklin Richard	Old Cem, Huntington, NY 15
Conklin Richard	Old Huntington Cem, Huntington, Suffolk Co, NY 36
Conklin Samuel	Mount Hope Cem, Rochester, Monroe Co, NY 33

Conklin Selah — Old Huntington Cem, Huntington, Suffolk Co, NY 36
Conklin Stoddard — Horseheads Cem, Horseheads, NY 32
Conklin Thomas — Old Cem, Huntington, NY 15
Conklin Thomas — Stirling Cem, Greenport, Suffolk Co, NY 79
Conklin Thomas Dr — Buell, NY 35
Conklin Timothy — Old Huntington Cem, Huntington, Suffolk Co, NY 36
Conklin Timothy Col — Old Cem, Huntington, NY 15
Conklin Timothy Col — Old Huntington Cem, Huntington, Suffolk Co, NY 36
Conkling Benjamin — Boland Cem, Sharon, Litchfield Co, CT 66
Conkling Daniel — Rensselaerville, Rensselaerville, NY 32
Conkling Daniel — Rensselaerville, NY 33
Conkling Isaac — Pres Cem, Morristown, NJ 32
Conkling Stephen Jr — Pres Cem, Morristown, NJ 32
Conkling Stephen Sr — Pres Cem, Morristown, NJ 32
Conkwright Hercules — Clark, KY 56
Conn William Young — Sinking Spring Cem, Abingdon, VA 30
Conn William Young — Sinking Spring Cem, Abingdon, VA 29
Connable John — Old Cem, Burks Flat, Bernardston, MA 00
Connable Samuel — Old Cem, Burks Flat, Bernardston, MA 00
Connaly Arthur Sr — Old Augusta Stone Ch Cem, Ft Defiance, VA 62
Connant Rufus — Lyme Plain Cem, Lyme, NH 29
Connant Solomon — Town Cem, Canaan, NH 29
Connant William — Lyme Plain Cem, Lyme, NH 29
Connell Ebenezer — Fam Cem, Crown Point, Strafford, NH 71
Connelly John — Burke Co, NC 56
Connelly John — Columbia, MO 32
Connelly John — Harmony, Warren Co, NJ 39
Conner Benjamin — Town Cem, Greenland, NH 28
Conner Cornelius — Bethany Pres Ch Cem, nr Bridgeville, PA 16
Conner James — Baker's Cem, south Iredell Co, NC 49
Conner James — Hardin Cem, OH 53
Conner John — Friendship Ch Cem, New Castle Co, DE 46
Conner John — [no cem named], WV 42
Conner John King — Depot Hill Cem, Henniker, NH 32
Conner Moses — Colby Cem, Henniker, NH 32
Conner Richard — Clinton Grove Cem, Mt Clemens, MI 65
Connick William — Grave obliterated, Cincinnatus, Cortland Co, NY 36
Conning Andrew — Field Cem, 4 mi fr Slingerlands, Albany Co, NY 75
Connor Jeremiah — Tin Corner Cem, Tilton, NH 31
Connor Simeon — Boston Hill Cem, Andover, NH 31
Connor Terence — Priv Cem, Groves farm, nr Rome, IN 56
Connover Garrett — Owasco Rural Cem, Owasco, NY 56
Connover John — Owasco Rural Cem, Owasco, NY 56
Conover Elias — Brick Ch Cem, Freehold, NJ 47
Conover Garret — Fam farm bur gr, Vanderburg, Monmouth Co, NJ 78
Conover Garret — His farm, Adair Co, KY 49
Conover Garret Benjamin — Old Tennent Ch Cem, Tennent, NJ 47
Conover Jacob — Lower Salford Mennonite Cem, Montgomery Co, PA 59
Conover William — Dutch Ref Cem, Middletown, NJ 35
Conover William — Lippit Bur Gr, Middletown, Monmouth Co, NJ 78
Conoway Samuel — Fayette Cem, Fayette Co, PA 59
Conrad Cline — Marlboro Twp, Delaware Co, OH 18
Conrad Frederick — Wentz Ref Cem, Worcester, PA 15
Conrad Jacob — Moravian Cem, North Heidelburg, Berks Co, PA 57
Conrad Jacob — Zoar Cem, Mt Zion, Lebanon Co, PA 83
Conrad Jacob Sr — Fam prop, Pendleton Co, WV 42
Conrad Johan J — Zoar Cem, Mt Zion, Lebanon Co, PA 83
Conrad Johan Peter — Hamilton Ch Cem, Hamilton Twp, Northampton Co, PA 68
Conrad Joseph — North Heidelburg Ch Cem, North Heidelburg, Berks Co, PA 57
Conrad More — Dutch Ref Brick Ch Cem, Montgomery, Orange Co, NY 76
Conrad Nessle — Huron Cem, Huron Co, OH 40

Abstract of Graves of Revolutionary Patriots

Conrey John	Winn Cem, 9 mi N of Paris, Edgar Co, IL 52
Conroy John	Mount Hope Cem, Rochester, Monroe Co, NY 33
Conroy Samuel	Pine Hill Cem, Hollis, NH 39
Convarse Joseph	Wetherbee Hill Cem, Chesterfield, NH 39
Convers Elijah	Wilsonville Cem, Thompson, Windham Co, CT 24
Converse Benjamin	Westford Cem, Ashford, CT 55
Converse Israel	Randolph Center Cem, Randolph, Orange Co, VT 72
Converse Israel	Randolph Center Cem, Randolph, VT 33
Converse Israel Col	Randolph Center Cem, Randolph, VT 23
Converse James	Brookfield, MA 48
Converse Jeremiah	[no cem named], OH 17
Converse Jeremiah Rev	Darby Twp Cem, nr Plain City, Madison Co, OH 55
Converse Jesse	Stafford, Stafford, CT 56
Converse Josiah Capt	Fam Cem, Chesterfield, NH 38
Converse Jude	Lyme Plain Cem, Lyme, NH 36
Converse Luke	Old Cem, Spencer, MA 56
Converse Pain	Bridgeport, VT 56
Converse Robert	Old Center Cem, Marlboro, NH 39
Conway Henry	Maloney Cem, Smelser farm nr Greeneville, Greene Co, TN 74
Conway John	Green St Cem, Marblehead, MA 55
Conway Joseph	Fam Cem, St Louis Co, MO 59
Conway Richard	Kissinger Cem, nr Mooreland, Millville, Henry Co, IN 72
Conway Richard	Old Cem, betw Millville & Mooreland, Henry Co, IN 24
Conway Samuel Corp	Fam Cem, 7 mi E of Palmyra, MO 36
Conway William	Ovley Cem, 2 mi SE of Newark, Greene Co, IN 24
Conyes Jacob	Plattekill Cem, NY 15
Conyne John	Newkirk Plot, Rees farm, nr Fort Hunter, NY 36
Cooch Thomas Jr	Welsh Tract Bapt Ch Cem, nr Newark, New Castle Co, DE 36
Cooch Thomas Jr	Welsh Tract, ½ mi S of Newark, New Castle Co, DE 45
Cooch Thomas Jr	Welsh Tract Cem, New Castle Co, DE 46
Cooch Thomas Sr	Welsh Tract Bapt Ch Cem, nr Newark, New Castle Co, DE 36
Cooch Thomas Sr Col	Welsh Tract Ch Cem, Newark, New Castle Co, DE 41
Cooch Thomas Sr Col	Welsh Tract, ½ mi S of Newark, New Castle Co, DE 45
Cooch William Sr	Welsh Tract, ½ mi S of Newark, New Castle Co, DE 45
Cook Aaron	Old Ballou Ch Cem, Cumberland, RI 46
Cook Aaron	Sweetman Cem, Charlton, Saratoga Co, NY 78
Cook Aaron Capt	Old North Cem, Old Hartford, CT 19
Cook Abial	Wooley Hill, nr Garretsville, NY 71
Cook Absalom	Laurel or Carmel Cem, Rt 232 nr Laurel, Clermont Co, OH 74
Cook Absolom	Laurel Cem, nr Laurel, OH 53
Cook Amos	Buell, NY 35
Cook Amos	Little York Cem, Homer, NY 36
Cook Anthony	Fam Cem, Broadtop City, PA 56
Cook Asaph	North Monroeville Cem, North Monroeville, Huron Co, OH 55
Cook Asaph Sr	Granville Cem, Washington Co, NY 71
Cook Benajah	Fancher, nr Sunbury, Delaware Co, OH 70
Cook Benejah	Fancher Cem, Delaware Co, OH 52
Cook Benjamin	Fam bur gr, nr Sago, Franklin Co, VA 31
Cook Benjamin	Old Bur Cem, Kingston, MA 62
Cook Benjamine	Shady Grove Cem, Van Buren, Union Co, AR 15
Cook Burrell	His estate, Broad River, Fairfield Co, SC 40
Cook Chauncey	Erie Co, OH 26
Cook Chauncey	Oxford Twp, Erie Co, NY 15
Cook Daniel	Center Cem, Bellingham, MA 55
Cook Daniel	Frieden's, New Ringold, PA 49
Cook Daniel	Union Chapel Cem, Warren Co, NJ 35
Cook Daniel	Warwick Village Cem, Warwick Village, MA 30
Cook David	Canaan Court, Columbia Co, NY 56
Cook David	Center Cem, Bellingham, MA 55
Cook David	Hayground Cem, Bridgehampton, NY 35
Cook Ebenezer	Field opposite Wentworth place, Sandwich, NH 31

Cook	Edward	Fam Cem, Upper, Cleveland Co, NC 72
Cook	Eli	Weeks Mills Cem, New Sharon, ME 39
Cook	Elias	Old Hill, Newburyport, MA 56
Cook	Elihu	Village Hadley, MA 56
Cook	Elihu	West Torrington Cem, Torrington, CT 55
Cook	Elijah	Cook's Prairie, nr Homer, MI 56
Cook	Elijah B Sr	Fam Cem, Clarenden, NY 16
Cook	Elisha	East Otis Cem, Otis, MA 56
Cook	Elisha	Old Hadley Cem, Hadley, MA 54
Cook	Ellis	Hanover, NJ 29
Cook	Ellis	Hanover, Morris Co, NJ 32
Cook	Ellis	Pres Graveyard, Hanover, NJ 50
Cook	Enoch	Dummerston Center, VT 17
Cook	Ephraim	Cong Cem, Cheshire, New Haven Co, CT 24
Cook	Ephraim	Old Bur Gr, Arlington, MA 56
Cook	George	Grindstone Hill Ch Cem, Guilford Twp, Franklin Co, PA 56
Cook	Gideon	Moodus, East Haddam, CT 56
Cook	Hezekiah	Old Center, New Marlborough, MA 56
Cook	Isaac	Corey farm, Tiverton, RI 51
Cook	Isaac	Fam graveyard, nr Covington, Fountain Co, IN 72
Cook	Isaac	Lewiston Old Cem, Lewiston, NY 65
Cook	Jacob	East Otis Cem, Otis, MA 56
Cook	Jacob	Zion Luth Ch Cem, Montgomery Co, PA 59
Cook	James	Lyme Plain Cem, Lyme, NH 29
Cook	James	Olive Grove Bapt Ch Cem, Cleveland Co, NC 49
Cook	James Dea	East Mecca, OH 25
Cook	Joel Sr	Darling Cem, Orwell Twp, Bradford Co, PA 72
Cook	John	Clark Schoolhouse Cem, Edinburgh, Saratoga Co, NY 78
Cook	John	Cook Cem, Laurens, NY 31
Cook	John	Highland Cem, Newburyport, MA 78
Cook	John	Oakwood Cem, Joilet, GA 29
Cook	John	Oakwood Cem, Joliet, IL 15
Cook	John	Old West St Cem, Rutland, VT 51
Cook	John	Oneonta, NY 56
Cook	John	Toms River Cem, Toms River, NJ 51
Cook	John Capt	Island Creek Ch, 16 mi fr Sparta, Hancock Co, GA 40
Cook	John Capt	West Claremont Cem, Claremont, NH 50
Cook	John Jr	Torrington Cem, Torrington, CT 55
Cook	John M	Montezuma High Cem, Montezuma, NY 56
Cook	John W	Island Farms, Foster, RI 37
Cook	Jonathan	Center St, Newton, MA 56
Cook	Jonathan	Howell, Livingston Co, MI 56
Cook	Joseph	Butler Co, OH 55
Cook	Joseph	Harwinton, CT 56
Cook	Joseph	North Monroeville Cem, North Monroeville, Huron Co, OH 55
Cook	Joseph	Stonington, CT 32
Cook	Joshua	Findlay Twp, Mercer Co, PA 15
Cook	Joshua	Leverett-Cook Cem, Washington Co, GA 31
Cook	Josiah	Ancient Bur Gr, Kingston, MA 50
Cook	Josiah	Center Cem, Alstead, NH 37
Cook	Lemuel	Clarendon, NY 15
Cook	Lemuel	Roots Cem, Clarendon, NY 31
Cook	Levi	Mount Zion Cem, Whitman, MA 46
Cook	Lot	Sandwich Center Cem, Sandwich, NH 29
Cook	Luther	Sandwich Lower Corner Cem, Sandwich, NH 29
Cook	Moody	Campton Bog Cem, Campton, NH 36
Cook	Moses	Bronson Cem, Library Park, Waterbury, CT 55
Cook	Moses	Palisado Cem, Windsor, CT 55
Cook	Moses Bassett	Hagaman's Cem, MI 56
Cook	Nathan	South Butler Cem, Spring Lake, Conquest, Cayuga Co, NY 57
Cook	Nathaniel	His plantation, nr Alston, Fairfield Co, SC 41

Abstract of Graves of Revolutionary Patriots

Cook Nathaniel	Sweetman Cem, Charlton, Saratoga Co, NY	78
Cook Nicholas Capt	North Cem, Richmond, NH	36
Cook Noah	Center Cem, Westhampton, MA	53
Cook Noah	Lexington Cem, Lexington, OH	26
Cook Oliver Lt	Brattleboro, VT	17
Cook Pardon	North Bur Gr, Fall River, Freetown, MA	54
Cook Perez	Granby Cem, Granby, MA	56
Cook Peter	Fam lot, Wakefield, NH	25
Cook Reuben	Osceola, PA	15
Cook Richard	Fam Cem, Plainfield, Otsego Co, NY	77
Cook Robert	9 mi SW of Sparta, White Co, TN	74
Cook Robert	Ancient Bur Gr, Kingston, MA	50
Cook Robert	Evergreen Cem, Kingston, MA	26
Cook Robert	Groveland Cem, Scituate, MA	45
Cook Roswell	Oak Grove Cem, Delaware Co, OH	18
Cook Samuel	Lyme Plain Cem, Lyme, NH	29
Cook Samuel	Sweetman Cem, Charlton, Saratoga Co, NY	78
Cook Saul	Litchfield, ME	20
Cook Sears	South Billerica, MA	55
Cook Simeon	Amenia Bur Gr, 1 mi N of Amenia, Dutchess Co, NY	66
Cook Solomon	Cem nr railroad station, Eastham, MA	49
Cook Solomon	Kimball Hill Cem, Whitefield, NH	32
Cook Solomon	Old Cem, Provincetown, MA	54
Cook Stephen	Milford, MA	53
Cook Stephen	Pres Cem, Morristown, NJ	32
Cook Sylvanus	Ancient Bur Gr, Kingston, MA	50
Cook Thaddeus	Center Street Cem, Wallingford, CT	56
Cook Thomas	Friends Cem, Azalia, IN	48
Cook Thomas B	Guernsey Co, OH	53
Cook W H	Cook Cem, Etowah, TN	31
Cook William	Beverly, MA	55
Cook William	Old Cem, Crandall Rd, Tiverton, RI	35
Cook William	Pease Cem, Pompey Hill Cem, Pompey, Onondaga Co, NY	81
Cook William	Primitive Cem, Mexico, NY	15
Cook William J	Cornwell Cem, Scipio, Cayuga Co, NY	59
Cook Zebulon	Sweetman Cem, Ballston, Saratoga Co, NY	77
Cooke Consider Sr	Marksboro Cem, Warren Co, NJ	38
Cooke Elisha	Old Hadley Cem, Hadley, MA	46
Cooke Elisha Sr	Marksboro Cem, Warren Co, NJ	38
Cooke Hannah	St James Cem, Wilmington, NC	49
Cooke Isaac	Lewiston Cem, Lewiston, NY	33
Cooke Isaac	Pres Ch, Lewistown, NY	52
Cooke John	Ravenswood, WV	31
Cooke Nicholas	North Bur Gr, Providence, RI	55
Cooke Noah	Keene, NY	16
Cooke Perez Hadley	West Cem, Granby, MA	58
Cooke William Jr	Marksboro Cem, Warren Co, NJ	38
Cookendoffer Leonard	Oak Hill Cem, Washington, DC	20
Cookendorfer Leonard	Oak Hill Cem, Georgetown, DC	30
Cooksey Zachariah	Franklin Cem, Franklin Co, IN	73
Cookus Michael	Prob Reform Cem, Shepherdstown, WV	24
Coolbaugh John	Pres Ch Cem, Smithfield, VA	29
Coolbaugh John	Priv Cem, Middle Smithfield, Monroe Co, PA	57
Coolbaugh Moses	Wysox Cem, Wysox Twp, PA	72
Coolbaugh William	Unmarked, Shawnee, PA	51
Cooley Aaron	Town Cem, Landaff, NH	28
Cooley Abel	Springfield, MA	15
Cooley Abel	Valley Forge, PA	54
Cooley Abner	Pioneer-Forestville Hanover, Chautauqua Co, NY	72
Cooley Asahel	Coolville Cem, Coolville, OH	56
Cooley Asahel	Union Myers, Springport, NY	56

Cooley Daniel	West Center Cem, Granville, Hampden Co, MA 63
Cooley Jonathan	Old Town Bur Gr, Newburgh, Orange Co, NY 69
Cooley Thomas	East Sweden, NY 15
Cooley William	Bapt Cem, Shollenbarger Rd, Butler Co, OH 55
Cooley William	Old Cem, Granville Centre, MA 47
Coolidge Asa	Red Bridge Cem, Orange, MA 26
Coolidge Daniel	Sherborn No 2, Sherborn, MA 56
Coolidge James	The Old Cem, Gardner, MA 33
Coolidge James	The Old Cem, Gardner, MA 46
Coolidge Joel	South Cem, South Framingham, MA 48
Coolidge John	Dell Park, Natick, MA 56
Coolidge John	Plymouth, VT 56
Coolidge Joseph	Buried under Kings Chapel, Boston, MA 46
Coolidge Joseph	Old bur gr, Mt Auburn St & Washington St, Watertown, MA 45
Coolidge Samuel	Common St Cem, Watertown, MA 51
Coolidge Silas	Lamoine Corner Cem, Lamoine, ME 31
Coolidge Silas	Riverside Cem, Kingfield, Franklin Co, ME 83
Coolidge Silas	West Lamoine, ME 30
Coolidge William	Bolton Pan Cem, Bolton, MA 56
Coombs Anthony	Fosgate Cem, Winchester, NH 36
Coombs Caleb	Old Parish Cem, North Rochester, MA 59
Coombs Jezekiah	Lisbon, ME 18
Coombs John	Cornish Cem, Bowdoin, ME 45
Coombs John	Readfield, ME 20
Coombs John Dea	Growstown Cem, Brunswick, ME 39
Coombs John Jr	North Bellingham Cem, Bellingham, MA 46
Coombs Jonathan Sr	First Pres Ch Cem, Cranbury, NJ 76
Coombs Joseph Lt	South Thomaston Cem, Thomaston, ME 45
Coombs Joshua	Weaver (Combs) Cem, Warrensburg, Warren Co, NY 85
Coombs Simeon Rev	Hyannis Bapt Cem, Barnstable, MA 58
Coombs William	Bath, ME 39
Coombs William	Old Hill, Newburyport, MA 56
Coomes Francis	St Michael's Cem, Fairfield, Nelson Co, KY 46
Cooms John Sr	North Cem, Milford, MA 55
Coon Conrad	Cooperstown Junction, Milford, NY 71
Coon Israel	Mount Bethel Baptist, NJ 47
Coonly Frederick	Bur Gr, Stillwater, NY 41
Coonradt Henry	White Ch Cem, Brunswick, Rensselaer Co, NY 41
Coonradt John	[no cem named], NY 41
Coons Aaron	Old Pres, Bound Brook, NJ 47
Coons Adam A	Free Ground Old Cem, Ancram, Columbia Co, NY 74
Coons Henry Jr	Cole Cem, Saugerties, Saxton, NY 56
Coons Henry S	Vedder Ch Cem, Gallatan, Columbia Co, NY 74
Coons Matthias	White Ch Cem, Brunswick, Rensselaer Co, NY 41
Coons Philip	Old Melrose Cem, rd to Tomhannock Res, Schaghticoke, NY 38
Coop Horatio	Brossroads Cem, Bell Buckle, Bedford Co, TN 80
Cooper Aaron Lt	Cem on Hinsdale farm, Hinsdale, NH 37
Cooper Abraham	Sickletown Bur Gr, Pearl River, Rockland Co, NY 78
Cooper Adam	Cane Creek Bapt Ch Cem, Fairview, NC 49
Cooper Adam	Old part, Ref Ch Cem, Killinger, PA 56
Cooper Benjamin Col	Nr Cooper's Fort, New Hope, MO 15
Cooper Benjamin Col	On Bluff, 1 mi SW of Cooper's Old Fort, Howard Co, MO 23
Cooper Caleb	Oakland Cem, Sag Harbor, Long Island, Suffolk Co, NY 37
Cooper Caleb	Sag Harbor Cem, Sag Harbor, NY 31
Cooper Christian	Bloomingrove Rural Cem, N Greenbush, Rensselaer Co, NY 41
Cooper Daniel	Saucon Mennonite Cem, Coopersburg, Lehigh Co, PA 40
Cooper David	Duck Creek, Lawrence Co, PA 56
Cooper David	Hudson City Cem, Hudson, Columbia Co, NY 74
Cooper David	Old Rumford Cem, Rehoboth, MA 55
Cooper Elijah	Cem on Hinsdale farm, Hinsdale, NH 37
Cooper Enoch	Old North Cem, Agawam, MA 17

Cooper	Ezekial	Meth Epis Cem, St Clairsville, Belmont Co, OH 55
Cooper	Frederick	Frye Cem, Fallowfield Twp, Washington Co, PA 38
Cooper	George	Hollenbeck Cem, Wilkes-Barre, PA 52
Cooper	Gilbert	Brick Ch Cem, Monsey, Rockland Co, NY 78
Cooper	Gilbert T	Wesley Chapel Cem, Sherwoodville, Rockland Co, NY 78
Cooper	Henry	Hopewell Pres Ch Cem, New Bedford, PA 56
Cooper	Henry	South Church Cem, Bergenfield, NJ 54
Cooper	James	Fam Cem, 3 mi W of Gaffney, SC 27
Cooper	James	Fam farm, Coitsville Twp, Mahoning, OH 56
Cooper	Jan	Sickletown Bur Gr, Pearl River, Rockland Co, NY 78
Cooper	John	Asbury Meth Cem, Asbury, NJ 39
Cooper	John	Liberty Cem, Brown Co, OH 56
Cooper	John	Old Bethesda Ch Cem, McConnellsville, York Co, SC 56
Cooper	John	Revolutionary War Cem, Salem, Washington Co, NY 78
Cooper	John	South Ch Cem, Bergenfield, NJ 51
Cooper	John	South Ch Cem, Bergen Co, NJ 59
Cooper	John	Whiteside, Washington Co, NY 54
Cooper	John Price	Danby Cem, NY 15
Cooper	Joseph	Chester Cem, Orange Co, NJ 61
Cooper	Joseph	Humphrey Cem, Holland, Erie Co, NY 31
Cooper	Leonard Maj	His farm, N side of Kanawha River, WV 19
Cooper	Levi	Montowese Cem, North Haven, CT 15
Cooper	Malachi	Pleasant Run Cem, Rushville Noble Twp, Rush Co, IN 78
Cooper	Nathaniel	Center Cem, Alstead, NH 43
Cooper	Nathaniel	Northbridge Cem, Northbridge, MA 47
Cooper	Nathaniel	Old Bur Cem, Kingston, MA 62
Cooper	Noah	Old Kirk Yard, Attleboro, MA 15
Cooper	Obadiah	New Hackensack Ref Ch Cem, New Hackensack, NY 70
Cooper	Obariah A	Victory Rural Cem, Victory, NY 56
Cooper	Obediah	East Cem, Warrensville Heights, Cuyahoga Co, OH 55
Cooper	Reuben	Pres Cem, Morristown, NJ 32
Cooper	Richard	Burial Hill, Plymouth, MA 56
Cooper	Richard	North Ch Cem, Bergenfield, NJ 51
Cooper	Richard P	Old Hook Cem, Westwood, NJ 47
Cooper	Samuel	Taylor Cem, Bemis Heights Crossing, Stillwater, NY 41
Cooper	Samuel	Warm Springs Rd, Columbus, GA 56
Cooper	Samuel Maj	Christ Ch Cem, Alexandria, VA 27
Cooper	Seighton	Simpson Co, KY 54
Cooper	Spencer	Spring Grove, Cincinnati, OH 54
Cooper	Theunis	Sickletown Cem, Orangetown, Rockland Co, NY 56
Cooper	Thomas	Ancient Bur Gr, Kingston, MA 50
Cooper	Thomas	Conquest, NY 56
Cooper	Thomas	Old Kirk Yard, Attleboro, MA 15
Cooper	William	Horse Branch, Ohio Co, KY 56
Cooper	William	Huntington Twp, Brown Co, OH 15
Cooper	William	Whiteside, Washington Co, NY 54
Cooper	William	Yellow Mtg Hs Cem, Stillwater, NY 41
Coopernail	William	Stone Ch, Rhinebeck, Dutchess Co, NY 21
Coosard	Valentine	Rootstown, OH 26
Coots	James	Buffalo Pres Ch Cem, Guilford Co, NC 59
Cope	Jonathan Sr	Hebron Cem, Jefferson Co, IN 72
Copeland	Asa	Norton Cem, Norton, MA 45
Copeland	Jacob	New Cem, Stoddard, NH 27
Copeland	Jacob	Stoddard Cem, Stoddard, NH 46
Copeland	James	Ketoctin (Short Hill) Cem, Purcellville, Loudoun Co, VA 77
Copeland	John Sr	Duncan Creek Pres Ch Cem, Laurens Co, SC 70
Copeland	Jonathan	West Thompson, CT 16
Copeland	Jonathan 3rd	Old Graveyard, Bridgewater, MA 59
Copeland	Jonathan III	Pine Hill Cem, West Bridgewater, Plymouth Co, MA 82
Copeland	Moses	East Mansfield Cem, Mansfield, MA 55
Copeland	Nathaniel	Old Town Yard, Warren, ME 56

Copeland Samuel	Dexter Cem, Dexter, ME 25
Copeland Samuel	Dexter Cem, Dexter, ME 24
Copeland William	Mansfield Cem, Mansfield, MA 53
Copen Andrew	Granary Cem, Boston, MA 46
Copley Daniel	Center Cem, New Milford, CT 55
Copp David Lt Col	Lovell Lake Cem, Sanbornville, NH 45
Copp David Maj	Lovell Lake Cem, Wakefield, NH 28
Copp Solomon	Park Cem, Tilton, NH 31
Copp Thomas	Fam farm, nr Mohawk Point, Tilton, NH 36
Copp Timothy	Thorn Hill Cem, Marcellus, Onondaga Co, NY 75
Copper Richard	Old Bur Cem, Plympton, MA 58
Coppernoll Adam	Herkimer, NY 16
Coppernoll Richard	Stone-Arabia Cem, Stone-Arabia, NY 51
Coppernoll Richard Lt	Fam farm, Ephratah, Fulton Co, NY 41
Copple Daniel	Dutch Cem, Liberty Twp, Adams Co, OH 56
Coquillette Daniel	NYC, NY 56
Coquillette Daniel	New City, Rockland, NY 57
Cor Levi	West Litchfield, CT 56
Coray Anson	Killed in Wyoming Massacre, Wyoming, PA 52
Corbet Nathaniel	North Bur Gr, Rowe, Franklin Co, MA 54
Corbett Ichabod	South Hopedale Cem, Hopedale, MA 46
Corbett John	North Purchase Cem, Milford, MA 46
Corbett John Dr	North Bellingham Cem, Bellingham, MA 46
Corbett Robert	Corbettsville Cem, Corbettsville, Broome Co, NY 78
Corbin Amasa	South Lawn Cem, Williamstown, MA 33
Corbin Amasa	South Williamston, MA 15
Corbin Asa Lt	South Lawn Cem, Williamstown, MA 33
Corbin Asa Lt	South Williamston, MA 15
Corbin Asahel	Marcy Cem, Bradford, CT 55
Corbin Clement	Warren Heights Cem, Warren Twp, Bradford Co, PA 53
Corbin David	Quaker Cem, North Collins, NY 33
Corbin John	[no cem named], CT 19
Corbin John Esq	Priv plot, nr Elmwood Cem, Schaghticoke, NY 38
Corbin John Sr	Myers Cem, OH 53
Corbin Joshua	Cem, Dudley, MA 49
Corbin Lemuel	Dudley, MA 55
Corbin Lemuel	Dudley, MA 55
Corbin Peter	Old Colebrook Cem, Colebrook, CT 59
Corbin Stephen	Coopers Plains Cem, Erwin, Steuben Co, NY 80
Corbin Thomas	Bungay Cem, Woodstock, CT 55
Corbin Timothy	Fam Cem, Dudley, MA 53
Corbin William	Marcy Cem, Bradford, CT 55
Corbit William	Fam Cem, New Castle Co, DE 46
Corbly John	Garards Fort, Greene Co, PA 56
Cordell John Jr	Hiram Cem, nr Creve Couer Lake, St Louis Co, MO 77
Cordwell William	Poland, ME 18
Corey Abner	Pres Ch Cem, Rahway, NJ 76
Corey Bradock	Cem by church, Sag Harbor, NY 31
Corey Daniel	New Providence Pres Ch, New Providence, Union Co, NJ 77
Corey David	Ballston Cem, Ballston, Saratoga Co, NY 78
Corey Ebenezer	Columbia Twp, Bradford Co, PA 53
Corey Ebenezer	Pres Ch Cem, New Providence, NJ 56
Corey Ephriam	Salmon Hole Cem, Lisbon, NH 26
Corey Isaac	Old Cem, Sudbury, MA 47
Corey Isaac	Waverly Ave Cem, Patchogue, Suffolk Co, NY 79
Corey Jenks	Killed in Wyoming Massacre, Wyoming, PA 52
Corey John	Clark Schoolhouse Rd Cem, Edinburgh, Saratoga Co, NY 77
Corey Peleg	Fam Cem, S of Maple Grove Otisco, Onondaga Co, NY 78
Corey Rufus	Killed in Wyoming Massacre, Wyoming, PA 52
Corey Thomas	Becket farm, above Waterford, Washington Co, OH 56
Corey Timothy	Walnut St Cem, Brookline, MA 45

Abstract of Graves of Revolutionary Patriots

Corey William	Marion Village Cem, Marion, Wayne Co, NY 79
Corey William 5th	Fam bur gr, fam homestead, North Kingston, RI 53
Coriell David	Meth Cem, Plainfield, Union Co, NJ 24
Coriell David	Samptown Cem, South Plainfield, Middlesex Co, NJ 79
Corl Leonard	Mt Zion Cem, Union Twp, Bradford Co, PA 72
Corley Richard	Edgefield, SC 56
Corliss Elihu	Town Cem, Orford, NH 37
Corliss John	Second West Parish Cem, Haverhill, MA 31
Corliss Jonathan Lt	Cem betw Haverhill & Merrimac, NH 45
Corliss Samuel	Page Hill Graveyard, East Corinth, Orange Co, VT 72
Corn John	Massacred nr mouth of Lechry Creek, Dearborn Co, IN 24
Corn John Peter	Ebenezer Ch, E of Chimney Rock Hwy, Henderson Co, NC 49
Cornelius Elias Dr	Mahopac Falls Pres Ch Cem, Mahopac Falls, NY 35
Cornelius Henry	Hale's farm, Bradford Cos, PA 53
Cornelius Isaac	Wolf Creek, Slippery Rock Twp, PA 56
Cornelius John	White Mills Cem, Chatham, Columbia Co, NY 48
Cornell Abraham	Smith farm, South Westport, MA 55
Cornell Benoi	Ashford Hollow, Cattaraugus Co, NY 71
Cornell Gideon	Foster, RI 52
Cornell Gideon	Old Colony Bur Gr, Granville, OH 45
Cornell Gideon	Quaker Cem, Union Springs, Springport, NY 56
Cornell James	Thomas Cem, North Swansea, MA 54
Cornell Joseph	Blanchard Cem, Rathbun farm, East Greenwich, RI 35
Cornell Joseph	Blanchard Cem, Rathbun Farm, East Greenwich, RI 78
Cornell Joseph	Galway Village Cem, Galway, Saratoga Co, NY 77
Cornell Joseph	Millstone, NJ 32
Cornell Joseph J	Dry Creek Cem, Moravia, Cayuga Co, NY 57
Cornell Peter Jr	New Cem, Wilmington, MA 58
Cornell Richard	North Street Cem, Auburn, Cayuga Co, NY 65
Cornell Samuel	Highlands Cem, Smith Cove, Highland Mills, Orange Co, NY 63
Cornell Thomas	Elmwood Cem, Schaghticoke, Rensselaer Co, NY 38
Cornell William	Bainbridge Cem, Putnam Co, IN 70
Cornell William	Lakeview Cem, Penn Yan, NY 34
Corner Charles	Fleming Hill Cem, Fleming, NY 41
Cornett Roger	Cornettsville, KY 46
Cornick Thomas	South Ripley, KY 15
Corning Allen Capt	Upper Stepney Cem, Stepney, CT 33
Corning Uriah	Hamilton Ave Cem, Norwich, CT 18
Cornish Elisha	Hop Meadow Cem, Simsbury, CT 55
Cornish Elisha Jr	Hop Meadow Cem, Simsbury, CT 55
Cornish George	Hop Meadow Cem, Simsbury, CT 55
Cornish James	Hop Meadow Cem, Simsbury, CT 55
Cornish Joel	Howlett Hill Cem, Onondaga, Onondaga Co, NY 75
Cornish John	South Parish Bur Gr, Andover, MA 26
Cornish John	White Horse Manomet Cem, Plymouth, MA 57
Cornish William	Cong Ch Cem on Green, Middleboro, MA 55
Cornog John	Lower Merion Bapt Cem, Montgomery Co, PA 59
Cornwall Daniel	Cornwallville Cem, Durham, Greene Co, NY 65
Cornwall Joseph	Cornwell-Tilden Plot, New Lebanon, Columbia Co, NY 79
Cornwell Ashbell Sr	Aban Pres Ch Cem, Vails Mills, Mayfield, NY 41
Cornwell Benjamin	Public Cem, Cortland Co Farm, Truxton, Cortland Co, NY 36
Cornwell Elijah	Fam Cem, nr Monticello, GA 15
Cornwell William	Penn Yan Cem, Yates Co, NY 56
Cornwell William	Putnam Co, IN 16
Correll Philip	Mt Zion Cem, Rowan Co, NC 72
Corrington Archibald	Old Mount Horeb, NJ 47
Corry James	Battle of Kings Mountain, SC 52
Corsa Andrew	St John's Cem, Yonkers, NY 35
Corser David	Old Mtg Hs Cem, Webster, NH 34
Corson David	Town Cem, Milton Mills, NH 27
Corson Parmenas	Cape May Co, NJ 56

Cortelyn Simon	Brooklyn, NY 38
Cortelyon Simon	Barkeloo Cem, Brooklyn, NY 35
Cortelyou Hendrick	Ten Mile Cem, 2 mi fr Rocky Hill, Mercer Co, NJ 33
Corthell Sherebiah	Mount Zion Cem, Whitman, South Abington, MA 45
Cortright Christopher	Killed in Wyoming Massacre, Wyoming, PA 52
Cortright John	Killed in Wyoming Massacre, Wyoming, PA 52
Corttis Japheth	Upham-Corttis Yard, Thompson, CT 37
Corttis Japheth	Upham-Corttis Yard, Thompson, CT 29
Cortwright Moses	Vanetten Cem, Owasco, NY 41
Corwin Barnabas	Wilcox Cem, Locke, NY 56
Corwin Edward	Norwich Cem, Colegrove, PA 52
Corwin Henry	Aquebogue Cem, Aquebogue, Suffolk Co, NY 79
Corwin Jacob	Pres Ch Cem, Middle Island, Suffolk Co, NY 79
Corwin John Sr	Mattituck Parish Bur Gr, Southold, Suffolk Co, NY 58
Corwin Richard	Fam Cem, Brookhaven, NY 56
Corwin William	Pleasant Hill Cem, Chester, Morris Co, NJ 80
Cory David	Village Cem, Ballston Springs, Saratoga Co, NY 41
Cory David	Whippany, Morris Co, NJ 32
Cory Elnathan	Wilson's Graveyard, New Galilee, PA 17
Cory Joseph	Westfield Pres Cem, Westfield, NJ 32
Cory Joseph	Westfield Cem, Westfield, NJ 24
Cory Oliver	Fam Cem, nr Phoenix Mills, Middlefield, Otsego Co, NY 72
Cory Philip	Tiverton Cem,, RI 45
Cory Samuel	Bapt Cem, Scotch Plain, NJ 47
Cosby James	Falling Water Ch Cem, Hamilton Co, TN 31
Cosby James	Pitts farm, Hamilton Co, TN 24
Cosby James Dr	Farm, nr Dayton, TN 29
Cosier Benjamin	Greenwich Pres Cem, Greenwich, NJ 47
Cosier Benjamin	Newport Meth Cem, Cumberland Co, NJ 49
Costner Jacob	Philadelphia Ch Cem, Gaston Co, NC 56
Costner Jacob	Philadelphia Luth Ch Cem, Gaston Co, NC 59
Coston Bishop	Yorkshire, Cattaraugus Co, NY 71
Cotes John Capt	Spring Center Cem, NY 33
Cotheal Alexander	St James Epis Ch Cem, Edison, NJ 75
Cotheal Isaac	St James Epis Ch Cem, Edison, NJ 75
Cottle Isaac Jr	Augusta, ME 54
Cottle Silas	Chilmark Cem, Chilmark, MA 46
Cottle Warren	Oak Grove Cem, St Charles, St Charles Co, MO 66
Cotton Benjamin	Seville, OH 17
Cotton Benjamin	Truxton, Cortland Co, NY 18
Cotton Bybe Lake	Old Christ Churchyard, Bethel, Windsor Co, VT 72
Cotton Elisha	Hop Meadow Cem, Simsbury, CT 55
Cotton John	Mt Hope Cem, Swansea, MA 54
Cotton John	Priv Cem, Austintown, Mahoning Co, OH 55
Cotton John	Union Cem, Laconia, NH 29
Cotton Josiah Jr	Burial Hill, Plymouth, MA 56
Cotton Ralph	Cotton Graveyard nr Mt Sterling, Switzerland Co, IN 72
Cotton Rowland	Forest Hill, Wyoming Co, NY 54
Cotton Samuel Rev	Old Village Cem, Claremont, NH 50
Cotton Simon	Old Wheelock Yard, Putnam, CT 26
Cotton Theophilus	Burial Hill, Plymouth, MA 56
Cotton Thomas	Crowley's Junction Cem, Lewiston, ME 45
Cotton Thomas	East Cem, North Hampton, NH 31
Cotton Thomas	East Cem, North Hampton, NH 31
Cotton Ward	Forest Lawn Cem, Buffalo, NY 33
Cotton William	Cem, 1 mi fr Cotton Valley RR Station, Wolfeboro, NH 28
Cotton William	Cotton Cem, Portsmouth, NH 34
Cotton William	Seceder Ch (Portland Mills), Greene Twp, Parke Co, IN 71
Cotton William O	Hill Cem, Boxborough, MA 56
Cottrell Asa	North Cem, Worthington, MA 71
Cottrell Lebbeus	Reynolds Cem, Petersburg, Rensselaer Co, NY 51

Abstract of Graves of Revolutionary Patriots

Cottrill Thomas	Campbell farm, White Oak Creek, Brown Twp, OH	56
Cotz Christoff David	Dryland Cem, Northampton Co, PA	71
Cotz David	Dryland Union Ch Cem, Hecktown, Northampton Co, PA	40
Cotz David	Old Cem, Hecktown, Northampton Co, PA	21
Couch Benjamin	Old Mtg Hs Cem, Webster, NH	34
Couch Daniel	Johnson Cem, Hillsdale Co, MI	46
Couch Daniel	Milton Cem, Milton, Ulster Co, NY	78
Couch Ebenezer Capt	North Milton Cem, Saratoga Co, NY	41
Couch John	Hallowell Cem, Hallowell, ME	17
Couch John	Old Mtg Hs Cem, Webster, NH	34
Couch Jonathan	Redding Cem, Redding, CT	46
Couch Joseph	Old Mtg Hs Cem, Webster, NH	34
Couch Mellington	Randolph Co, IL	48
Couch Samuel	Clam River Cem, Sandisfield, MA	56
Couch Stephen	South Lee, MA	15
Couch Thomas	North Colebrook Cem, Colebrook, CT	59
Couch William	Union Cem, Portland Twp, Westfield, Chautauqua Co, NY	77
Coughlan Richard	Revolutionary War Cem, Salem, Washington Co, NY	78
Coughnet John Eberhard	Colonial Cem, Johnson, NY	15
Coughran Joseph	Old Cem, Grave Lost, Danville, IL	15
Coulbourne William	Pomphret, Somerset Co, MD	52
Coulter George	Lower Merion Bapt Cem, Montgomery Co, PA	59
Coulter James	Newton Union Sloan Cem, West Collingswood, NJ	50
Coulter James	Woodlawn Cem, Cambridge, Washington Co, NY	55
Coulter John	Union Station Cem, Union Twp, Licking Co, OH	41
Coulter Martin Jr	Grace Ref Ch Cem, Catawba Co, NC	59
Coulter Thomas	Cold Spring Cem, 10 mi SW of Georgetown, Sussex Co, DE	46
Coulter Thomas	Cool Spring Pres Cem, Lewes, Sussex Co, DE	71
Counce Samuel	Old Town Yard, Warren, ME	56
Council James	Fam Cem, Bladen Co, NC	60
Council James	Fam Cem, Council, Bladen Co, NC	59
Counkle Michael	Daugherty Cem, Jay Co, IN	72
Counkle Michel	Daughherty Cem, Jay Co, IN	25
Countryman John	Sand Hill Cem, Ft Plain, NY	56
Couper James	Pidgeon Run, nr Red Lion, DE	45
Couper James	Pigeon Run Cem, New Castle Co, DE	46
Coursen John	Yellow Frame Cem, Warren Co, NJ	38
Court John	Coleman Cem, Ira, NY	56
Courtis William	Old Burial Hill, Marblehead, MA	55
Courtney John	Paint Lick, Garrard, KY	56
Courtney Luke	Bapt Cem, Manahawkin, NJ	47
Courtright Abram Van C	Greencastle Cem, Fairfield Co, OH	55
Courtright Jacob	Old Clove Cem, Wantage, Sussex Co, NJ	79
Courtright Solomon	Peru Cem, Peru, OH	56
Courtwright Moses	Van Ettin Cem, Owasco, Cayuga Co, NY	55
Couse John	Old Cem, Newton, NJ	24
Couse John	Old Newton Cem, Newton, Sussex Co, NJ	79
Cousins Elisha	Hulls Cove Cem, Bar Harbor, Hancock Co, ME	27
Cousins Isaac	North Cem, Holliston, MA	74
Coutchman Henry	Brookside Cem, Preston Hollow, NY	33
Couter Henry	Sawmill Rd, Cem, Mendon, Monroe Co, NY	79
Couts Christian	Liberty Chapel Cem, nr Bucyrus, OH	52
Covel Isaac	Village Cem, Colebrook, NH	36
Covel James	Independence (Green's Corner) Cem, Allegany Co, NY	65
Covell Ebenezer	Chestnut Hill Cem, CT	28
Covell Jonathan	Fleming Hill Cem, Fleming, NY	41
Covell Samson	Covell Cem, Covell, CT	28
Covenhoven Edward	Old Dutch Cem, North Tarrytown, Westchester Co, NY	83
Covenhoven Garret	Fam bur gr, Green Co, KY	56
Covenhoven Gerrit	Conover farm bur gr, Vanderburg, Monmouth Co, NJ	78
Covenhoven Jacob	Schanck-Conover Bur Gr, Holmdel, Monmouth Co, NJ	78

Covenhoven Jacob Capt	[no cem named], NJ 27
Covenhoven John	Brick Ch Cem, Freehold, NJ 47
Covenhoven John Col	Brick Ch, Marlboro, NJ 27
Covenhoven Lewis	Old Tennent Ch Cem, Tennent, NJ 47
Covenhoven Rudolph C	Schanck-Covenhoven Bur Gr, NJ 47
Covenhoven Ruliff	Schanck-Conover Bur Gr, Holmdel, Monmouth Co, NJ 78
Covenhoven Ruliff	Schenck-Conover Bur Gr, Monmouth Co, NJ 26
Covenhoven William	First Pres Ch Cem, Cranbury, NJ 76
Covenhoven William	Sickletown Bur Gr, Pearl River, Rockland Co, NY 78
Covenhover Albert	Larrison's Corner Cem, Larrison's Corner, NJ 73
Covert Abraham	LeConte plot, Morris farm, nr Interlaken, Seneca Co, NY 59
Covert Daniel	Fam Cem, 6 mi NE of Charlestown, IN 15
Covert General	Old Ft Graveyard, Pioneer Park, Mercer Co, KY 52
Covert Tunis	McNeil Cem, Ovid Twp, Seneca, NY 57
Covey Walter	Stewarts Corners Cem, Venice, NY 58
Covey William	Upton Castle Cem, Butternuts, Saratoga Co, NY 77
Covington Francis	Fam Cem, 3 mi fr Washington, Rappahannock Co, VA 59
Covington Robert	Duncan Graveyard, Madison Co, KY 56
Cowan Benjamin	Head of Christiana Cem, nr Newark, New Castle Co, DE 60
Cowan David	Shafer Cem, Van Buren Twp, Lagrange Co, IN 64
Cowan Isaac	Horseheads Cem, Horseheads, NY 32
Cowan Isaac	Priv fam Cem, Sidney, ME 39
Cowan John	Cowan Station, Danville, KY 30
Cowan Joseph	Upper Octorara, Chester Co, PA 56
Cowan Mathias	Long Run Pres Ch Cem, nr Irwin, Westmoreland Co, PA 56
Cowan Thomas	Thyatira Pres Ch Cem, Rowan Co, NC 49
Coward Joseph	[no cem named], NJ 27
Cowden James	Greenlee Hill Cem, McDowell Co, NC 72
Cowden John	Farm, 1½ mi N of Mt Liberty, Knox Co, OH 55
Cowden Robert	Flagg Cem, Lancaster Co, PA 61
Cowden Samuel	Pres Cem, Lower Providence, PA 15
Cowden William	Aban Cem, fam farm, nr Pomfret, NY 58
Cowdery Jacob	Keno cem, Meigs Co, OH 55
Cowdin Robert	Mtg Hs Hill Cem, Princeton, MA 49
Cowdrey Nathaniel	Old Cem, Wakefield, MA 55
Cowdrey Nathaniel Jr	Old Cem, Church St, Wakefield, MA 45
Cowdrick John	Rosemont Cem, Hunterdon Co, NJ 54
Cowdry Ambrose	East Hartland Cem, East Hartland, CT 60
Cowdry Moses	East Hartland Cem, East Hartland, CT 62
Cowell David	Pres Ch Cem, Trenton, NJ 28
Cowell Ebenezer	First Pres Cem, Trenton, NJ 28
Cowell John	First Pres Ch Cem, Trenton, NJ 28
Cowell Samuel	Wrentham, MA 55
Cowen Calvin	Lisbon, ME 18
Cowen David	Van Buren Twp, Lagrange Co, IN 25
Cowen John	Seager Hill Cem, Conewango, Cattaraugus Co, NY 62
Cowen William	McCollum Cem, Wayne Twp, Clermont Co, OH 55
Cowenhoven Garret	Dutch Neck, NJ 32
Cowenhoven Lukes	Dutch Neck, NJ 32
Cowenhoven William	Hopewell Bapt Cem, Hopewell, NJ 32
Cowens William	McCollum Cem, Edenton, OH 53
Cowherd James	Green Co, KY 56
Cowing Asahel	Rochester, MA 55
Cowing David	Old Townsend Cem, Brewster Hill, SE Putnam Co, NY 57
Cowing Gathelus	Center Cem, Westhampton, MA 53
Cowing Gathelus	Westhampton Cem, Westhampton, MA 46
Cowing James	Sand Hill Cem, Geneva, Ontario Co, NY 86
Cowing James	Seneca, NY 15
Cowing Seth	Barlow Cem, Mattapoisett, MA 58
Cowing William	Clark's Grove Pres Ch Cem, Maryville, Blount Co, TN 76
Cowles Asa	West Lebanon Cem, West Lebanon, Columbia Co, NY 74

Abstract of Graves of Revolutionary Patriots

Cowles Elisha	Center Cem, Sheffield, MA	41
Cowles Elisha	East Hartland Cem, East Hartland, CT	60
Cowles Enos	South Amherst Cem, Amherst, MA	41
Cowles Isaac	Old Farmington Cem, Farmington, Hartford Co, CT	61
Cowles Joel	Ashley Cem, Oxford Twp, Delaware Co, OH	53
Cowles John	Meeting House Hill Cem, Durham, Greene Co, NY	83
Cowles Joseph	Town Hill Cem, New Hartford, Litchfield Co, CT	83
Cowles Josiah	Southington, CT	56
Cowles Moses	West Lebanon Cem, West Lebanon, Columbia Co, NY	74
Cowles Nathaniel	Barnard, Sheffield, MA	56
Cowles Noah	Old Cem, Austinburg, Ashtabula Co, OH	55
Cowles Reuben	West Cem, Amherst, MA	56
Cowles Samuel	Old Colebrook Cem, Colebrook, CT	59
Cowles Samuel	Rock Ledge, Berlin, CT	56
Cowles Simeon	West Cem, Amherst, MA	60
Cowles Solomon	Old Farmington Cem, Farmington, Hartford Co, CT	61
Cowles Solomon	Old Farmington Cem, Farmington, Hartford Co, CT	61
Cowles Thomas	Old Farmington Cem, Farmington, Hartford Co, CT	61
Cowles Timothy	Claremont, NH	21
Cowles Timothy	Smithville Center, NY	35
Cowley St Leger	Fam Cem, 1 mi N of Stamford, NY	63
Cowls David	West Cem, Amherst, MA	60
Cowls Eleazer	West Cem, Amherst, MA	60
Cowls Eleazer	West Cem, Amherst, MA	16
Cowls Oliver	West Cem, Amherst, MA	60
Cowls Simeon	Amherst, MA	15
Cox Abraham	Fam Cem, Heck farm, nr Lowesville, WV	27
Cox Albert S	Pres Ch Cem, east side, Flemington, NJ	26
Cox Benjamin	Willow View, Montgomery Co, OH	56
Cox Charles	Old Pres Cem, Grandin, NJ	35
Cox David	Fam farm, Rt 629, Baywood, Grayson Co, VA	56
Cox Ebenezer	Cem, Hope, ME	51
Cox Elisha	Old Cem, The Green, Middleboro, MA	50
Cox Elisha	Olney Cem, York Rd, Gaston Co, NC	56
Cox Enoch Sr	Old Quaker Cem, Galax, Carroll Co, VA	76
Cox Gabriel Col	Fam Cem, nr Bardstown, KY	31
Cox Hugh	Farmingdale, ME	20
Cox Isaac	Broad Run Cem, Lewis Co, WV	59
Cox Isaac	Matney farm, Noble Twp, Rush Co, IN	72
Cox Israel	Small Cem, Bristol, ME	31
Cox James	Yatesmont Cem, WV	30
Cox James	Yatesmont Cem, nr Ona, WV	29
Cox John	Bapt Cem, Hoosick Falls, NY	34
Cox John	Old fam plantation, nr Sparta, Alleghany Co, NC	74
Cox John New	Center, grave not located, OH	25
Cox Joseph	Washington, Mason Co, KY	72
Cox Michael	Fam Cem, nr West Liberty, Ohio Co, WV	58
Cox Nathaniel	Pretty Prairie Cem, Tippecanoe Twp, Tippecanoe Co, IN	70
Cox Paul	Old Pine Street Pres Cem, Philadelphia, PA	59
Cox Phillip	Fam Cem, Slab Creek, Ritchie Co, WV	50
Cox Phineas	Duncan farm, 12 mi W of Bowling Green, Warren Co, KY	57
Cox Ralph	Kings Station Cem, Wilton, Saratoga Co, NY	77
Cox Samuel	South Dorchester, Dorchester, MA	56
Cox Samuel	South Dorchester, Dorchester, MA	56
Cox Samuel Jr	South Dorchester, Dorchester, MA	56
Cox Seth	Fern Hill Cem, #22-R, West Parish, Pembroke, MA	40
Cox Thomas	Western Cem, West Lynn, MA	56
Cox Timothy	Handy Cem, West Woodstock, Windsor Co, VT	75
Cox William	Central, Beverly, MA	56
Cox William	Elbridge Rural Cem, Elbridge, Onondaga Co, NY	79
Cox William	Fern Hill Cem, #49-R, West Parish, Pembroke, MA	40

Cox William	Hillside Cem, Middletown, NY	68
Cox William	West Fairlee Cem, Fairlee, VT	46
Coxe John	Old Cem, 4 mi W of Lincolnton, NC	52
Coxe Thomas	Old Swedes, New Castle Co, DE	46
Coxe Thomas	Old Swedes, Wilmington, New Castle Co, DE	41
Coy David	Homer, Cortland Co, NY	36
Coy Edee (Edward)	Mt Hope Cem, Rochester, Monroe Co, NY	79
Coy Edward	Mount Hope Cem, Rochester, Monroe Co, NY	33
Coy Ephraim	Center Cem, Norfolk, CT	62
Coy Joseph	Shepard Settlement Cem, Skaneateles, Onondaga Co, NY	78
Coy William	Carver farm, Homeney Ridge, Switzerland Co, IN	72
Coy Willis	South Amherst, MA	15
Coykendall Benjamin	Ithaca City Cem, Ithaca, NY	15
Coykendall Harmon	Kingston Twp, Delaware Co, OH	18
Crabb Jeremiah Gen	Nr Derwood, MD	15
Cracraft Thomas	Shannon Cem, Mason Co, KY	55
Craddock Robert	Bowling Green Cem, Bowling Green, KY	26
Cradlebaugh John Rev	Grandview Cem, Rush Creek Twp, Fairfield Co, OH	55
Crady David Sr	Edlin Cem, nr Lyons Station, Larue Co, KY	55
Craft Thomas	Hillside Cem, E of Bazetta, OH	24
Crafts Ebenezer	Craftsbury, VT	54
Crafts Edward	Fam Cem, Benton, Yates Co, NY	78
Crafts Edward Dr	Colonial Cem, Derby, CT	15
Crafts Eleazer	Old Center Main Street Cem, Manchester, MA	48
Crafts Elezear	Old Cem, Washington St, Manchester, MA	45
Crafts Griffin Esq	Old Village Cem, nr Hartwick, NY	71
Crafts Joseph	Hartwick Seminary, Hartwick, NY	71
Crafts Moses	East Mansfield Cem, Mansfield, MA	55
Crafts Thomas	Middleboro, MA	15
Crage Abijah	Central Bur Gr, Auburn, MA	55
Cragin Benjamin	Old Village Cem, Temple, NH	28
Cragin Francis	Old Village Yard, New Ipswich, NH	29
Cragin John	Old Village Cem, Temple, NH	28
Cragin Samuel	Prospect Hill Cem, Uxbridge, MA	57
Cragin Simeon	Embden, ME	15
Craig Aaron	Lamington Pres Cem, Somerset Co, NJ	63
Craig David	Chatfield Cem, Greenfield, Saratoga Co, NY	77
Craig David	New Hope Congregation, Orange Co, NC	43
Craig David	Pres Ch Cem, Rahway, NJ	76
Craig Henry	Bethel Pres Cem, Upper York Co, SC	60
Craig James	Fam Cem, 1 mi E of Christiansburg, VA	38
Craig James	Fam Cem, nr Christiansburg, VA	36
Craig James	New Hope Congregation, Orange Co, NC	43
Craig James II	Augusta Co, VA	56
Craig James Jr	Christ Ch Cem, Philadelphia, Philadelphia Co, PA	78
Craig James Sr	Old Augusta Stone Ch Cem, Ft Defiance, VA	62
Craig John	Aban Cem, E of United Brethren Ch, Jacksonburg, OH	52
Craig John	Duncan Creek Ch, nr Clinton, SC	15
Craig John	East of Unit Brethren Ch Cem, Jacksonburg, OH	56
Craig John	Grasmere, Goffstown, NH	56
Craig John	Longtown Pres Cem, Ridgeway, SC	70
Craig John	Lower Brandywine Manor Pres Ch Cem, Chester Co, PA	75
Craig John	New Hope Congregation, Orange Co, NC	43
Craig John	Old Oxford Cem, Oxford, NJ	25
Craig John	Old Pickens Cem, Oconee Co, SC	70
Craig John	Oxford, Warren Co, NJ	35
Craig John	Thompson Cem, Northumberland, Saratoga Co, NY	77
Craig John Capt	Old Cem, Freeport, PA	15
Craig John S	Fletcher Meth Epis Cem, Harmony Twp, Clark Co, OH	55
Craig Joseph Sr	Cem, sect D, Lexington, KY	45
Craig Moses Jr	Lamington Pres Cem, Somerset Co, NJ	63

Craig Rodrick	Farm, W of Cadiz, Henry Co, IN 72
Craig Samuel Lt	Massacred nr mouth of Lechry Creek, Dearborn Co, IN 24
Craig Samuel Sr	Pine Grove Cem, nr Morgantown, Berks Co, PA 63
Craig Thomas	Fairview Cem, Allentown, Lehigh Co, PA 40
Craig Thomas Sr	Old Cem nr Hamden, Clinton Twp, Vinton Co, OH 55
Craig William	Center Twp, Columbiana Co, OH 56
Craig William	Morristown, OH 56
Craig William	Old Stone Ch, N of Staunton, Augusta Co, VA 36
Craige John	Grasmere Cem, Goffstown, NH 28
Craige Nathan	Greenville Bapt Cem, Leicester, MA 56
Craighead Alexander	1st Cem, Old Sugar Creek Ch, NC 49
Craighead George Col	Chartiers Hill Cem, PA 21
Craighead John Rev	Pres Ch Cem, Rocky Springs, PA 20
Craighead John Rev	Rocky Springs Pres Ch Cem, 6 mi fr Chambersburg, PA 19
Crain Clement	Charlestown, NH 15
Crain Joseph	Old Hanover Churchyard, Hanover, PA 59
Crain William	Salem Cem, Salem, OH 56
Craine Roger	Mentor Cem, Mentor, Lake Co, OH 55
Craine Roger	Mentor, Lake Co, OH 26
Cram Benjamin	Butterfly Cem, Hampton Rd, Exeter, NH 37
Cram Ephraim	Old Town Cem, N of Old Center Harbor Rd, Meredith, NH 29
Cram John	Cem, back of town hall, Pittsfield, NH 42
Cram Jonathan Col	Old Cem, Crossroad, Hampton Falls, NH 30
Cram Jonathan Col	Town Cem, Hampton Falls, NH 27
Cram Joseph	Butterfly Cem, Hampton Rd, Exeter, NH 37
Cram Samuel Partridge	Village Cem, Meredith Village, NH 29
Cram Samuel Tilton	Village Cem, Meredith, NH 37
Cram Theophilus	North Road Cem, Wilmot, NH 34
Cramer Isaac	Fam bur gr, New Gretna, Burlington Co, NJ 59
Cramer Isaac Jr	Fam bur lot, New Gretna, NJ 47
Cramer John	Dutch Ch, Rhinebeck Village, Dutchess Co, NY 21
Cramer Philip	Stone Ch, Rhinebeck, Dutchess Co, NY 21
Crammer John	Coles Cem, Towanda Twp, Bradford Co, PA 53
Crammer Noadiah	Coles Cem, Towanda Twp, Bradford Co, PA 53
Crammer Peter	German Cem, Waldoboro, ME 31
Crampton Luther	Old Summer Hill, North Madison, CT 54
Cramton Nevi	Tinmouth, VT 38
Crandall Abel	Hillside Cem, Champion, Jefferson Co, NY 41
Crandall Abner	Tibbetts farm, nr Troy, NY 34
Crandall Amariah	Middle Ridge Cem, Madison, OH 26
Crandall Christopher	Homer, Cortland Co, NY 36
Crandall Gideon	Old Cem, Norwich, VT 23
Crandall Jeremiah	Bapt Ch Cem, Delphi Falls, Onondaga Co, NY 81
Crandall Luke	Collins Center, NY 33
Crandall Peter	Bellmont Cem, Bellmont Allegany, NY 81
Crandall Samuel	Bapt Ground, lot #2, Stanford, Dutchess Co, NY 21
Crandell Richmond	North Thetford, VT 17
Crandon John	Greendale Cem, Lawrenceburg, Dearborn Co, IN 72
Crane Abia	Village Cem, Surry, NH 35
Crane Abiah	Center Cem, Alstead, NH 43
Crane Abraham	Old Cem, Wethersfield, CT 56
Crane Amariah	Cat Head Mt Cem, nr Benson, NY 52
Crane Amos	Bethel-Gilead Cem, Bethel, Windsor Co, VT 72
Crane Azariah	Caldwell Pres Cem, Caldwell, NJ 32
Crane Benjamin	Assonet Neck Rd Cem, Berkley, MA 55
Crane Benjamin 3rd	Old Pres Ch Cem, Westfield, NJ 55
Crane Benjamin Sr	Pres Ch Cem, Westfield, NJ 76
Crane Bernice	Assonet Neck Rd Cem, Berkley, MA 55
Crane Daniel	Benton Rural Cem, Benton Penn Yan, Yates Co, NY 80
Crane David	Connecticut Farms Pres Cem, Union, NJ 49
Crane David	Pres Cem, Newark, NJ 32

Crane Ebenezer	Assonet Neck Rd Cem, Berkley, MA 55
Crane Elihu II	Hope Cem, Wellsburg, Erie Co, PA 80
Crane Elisha	Clam River Cem, Sandisfield, MA 56
Crane Elisha	Union Dist Cem, North Killingsworth, CT 55
Crane Ezekial	Fam farm, Throop, NY 56
Crane Ezekial	Dutch Ref Brick Ch Cem, Montgomery, Orange Co, NY 76
Crane Ichabod	Pres Cem, Morristown, NJ 32
Crane Isaac	Old Cem, Milton, MA 56
Crane Isaac	Old bur gr, Newark, NJ 26
Crane Isaac	Sterling Village Cem, Sterling, NY 56
Crane Jacob	First Pres Churchyard, Elizabeth, NJ 52
Crane James	Case St Cem, Middlebury, VT 29
Crane James	First Pres Churchyard, Elizabeth, NJ 52
Crane James	Oakridge-Crane Cem, Springport, NY 56
Crane Jeremiah	Old Milton Cem, Milton, MA 46
Crane John	Assonet Neck Rd Cem, Berkley, MA 55
Crane John	First Pres Churchyard, Elizabeth, NJ 52
Crane John	Green Hill Cem, Amsterdam, NY 35
Crane John	Old Cem, McGraw, New Cem (stone), Cortland Co, NY 36
Crane John	Old bur gr, Newark, NJ 26
Crane John	Pres Cem, Morristown, NJ 32
Crane John	Westfield Cem, Westfield, NJ 24
Crane John	Westfield Pres Cem, Westfield, NJ 32
Crane John C	Hillside Cem, Madison, NJ 30
Crane John Caleb	Pres Cem, Orange, NJ 32
Crane John II	Pres Cem, Westfield, NJ 50
Crane John III	Pres Cem, Westfield, NJ 50
Crane Jonas	Caldwell Cem, Caldwell, NJ 32
Crane Jonas	Old bur gr, Newark, NJ 26
Crane Jonathan	First Pres Ch Cem, Newark, NJ 26
Crane Jonathan	Plymouth Cem, Plymouth, Chenango Co, NY 72
Crane Joseph	Old Cem, Wethersfield, CT 56
Crane Joseph	Old Wethersfield Cem, Wethersfield, CT 58
Crane Joseph	Pres Cem, New Providence, NJ 50
Crane Joseph	Pres Cem, Newark, NJ 32
Crane Josiah	Connecticut Farms Cem, Union Co, NJ 32
Crane Josiah Capt	Connecticut Farms Ch, Union, NJ 26
Crane Matthias	Old bur gr, Orange, NJ 26
Crane Moses	Parsippany Cem, Morris Co, NJ 32
Crane Noah	Armstrong Cem, Allendale, Wabash Co, IL 69
Crane Obadiah	Connecticut Farms Pres Cem, Union, NJ 49
Crane Oliver	Caldwell Pres Cem, Caldwell, NJ 32
Crane Rufus	Cem, East Windsor, CT 49
Crane Rufus	East Windsor Cem, East Windsor, CT 31
Crane Rufus	Scantic Cem, East Windsor, CT 27
Crane Samuel	Bur gr adjoining 1st Pres Ch, Caldwell, Essex Co, NJ 31
Crane Samuel	Pres Cem, Orange, NJ 32
Crane Samuel	South Parish Cem, Bridgewater, MA 56
Crane Silas	Bapt Cem, Manahawkin, NJ 47
Crane Silas	Lax Cem, Jerseyville, Jersey Co, IL 84
Crane Simeon	Mentz Ch Cem, Montezuma, Cayuga Co, NY 57
Crane Stephen	1st Pres Ch Cem, Elizabethtown, NJ 56
Crane Stephen Hon	First Pres Ch Cem, Elizabeth, NJ 30
Crane Stephen Jr	First Pres Churchyard, Elizabeth, NJ 52
Crane Thaddeus	North Salem Cem, North Salem, NY 56
Crane Timothy	Smith Cem, Charlton, Saratoga Co, NY 77
Crane Vose	Old Milton Cem, Milton, MA 46
Crane William	Bloomfield Cem, Bloomfield, NJ 47
Crane William	Milton Cem, Milton, MA 62
Crane William	[no cem named], NJ 24
Crane William	Newark, NJ 45

Abstract of Graves of Revolutionary Patriots

Crane Zadoc	Bur gr adjoining 1st Pres Ch, Caldwell, Essex Co, NJ	31
Cranmer John	Coles Cem, Towanda Twp, Bradford Co, PA	72
Cranmer Noadiah	Coles Cem, Towanda Twp, Bradford Co, PA	72
Crannell William W	Orig Arbor Hill Cem, now Albany Rural Cem, Albany, NY	58
Cranson Asa	His farm, nr Clockville, NY	15
Cranson Elisha	Spruce Corner Cem, Ashfield, MA	45
Cranston Amasa	Spring Hill Cem, Marlboro, MA	46
Cranston Elon	East Litchfield, CT	17
Cranston James	East Litchfield, CT	17
Cranston John	Cem, Wilson farm, N of Woodstock, OH	56
Cranston John	Smith Cem, Hancock, MA	46
Cranston John	Stephentown Cem, Stephentown, NY	33
Cranston Samuel	Sheridan, NY	15
Cranston Samuel	Sheridan Center Cem, Sheridan, Chautauqua Co, NY	72
Crapo Jonathan	Close St Cem, Sullivan Twp, Ashland Co, OH	55
Crapo Joshua	Hill Cem, Chesterville, ME	40
Crapo Peter	South Dartmouth, MA	53
Craps John	Fam Cem, 10 mi W of Dawson, Terrell Co, GA	25
Crapser John Jr	Providence Cem, Pleasant Plains, Clinton Co, NY	21
Crary Christopher	Curl Cem, Middleburg, Logan Co, OH	55
Crary Christopher	New London, CT	54
Crary Christopher	Union Co, OH	26
Crary John IV	Finney Bur Gr, Millcreek Twp, OH	82
Crary Nathan	Pierrepont Hill Cem, Pierrepont, St Lawrence Co, NY	75
Crary Nathan Sr	Burdatt's Corner, Rt 84, Groton Cem, Groton, CT	57
Crary Nathaniel Col	East Clarendon Cem, Clarendon, VT	24
Crary Nathaniel Col	East Clarendon Cem, Clarendon, VT	25
Crary William	Sugartown, Cattaraugus Co, NY	35
Cratty William	Edinburgh Cem, Scioto Twp, Delaware Co, OH	53
Craumer Jeremiah	Northfield Cem, Northfield, OH	56
Craven John	Congressional Cem, Washington, DC	71
Craven John	Palmer Ch, Rt 711, N of Ligonier, Westmoreland Co, PA	56
Crawford Andrew	Lakeview Cem, Jamestown, Chautauqua Co, NY	62
Crawford Andrew	Washington Co, PA	56
Crawford Archibald	Whitford Cem, Globerson's Corners, Saratoga Co, NY	41
Crawford Capt	Marion, SC	30
Crawford Charles	Prob his plantation bur gr, Beaufort Co, NC	15
Crawford Daniel	Dennison farm, Glen Wild, NY	30
Crawford Daniel	Whitford Cem, Saratoga Springs, Saratoga Co, NY	77
Crawford David	Bethany Ch Cem, Iredell Co, NC	60
Crawford David	Goodwill Cem, Montgomery, Orange Co, NY	78
Crawford David	Poplar Tent Ch Cem, nr Concord, Cabarrus Co, NC	75
Crawford Edward Jr	Falling Spring Pres Ch Cem, Chambersburg, PA	20
Crawford Edward Jr	Falling Spring Pres Ch Cem, Franklin Co, PA	19
Crawford George	Old Stone Ch, N of Staunton, Augusta Co, VA	36
Crawford Henderson J	Locust Grove Cem, Greenfield, Saratoga Co, NY	77
Crawford James	Galway Village Cem, Galway, Saratoga Co, NY	77
Crawford James	Goodwill Cem, Montgomery, Orange Co, NY	78
Crawford James	Hebron Cem, nr Madison, Jefferson Co, IN	16
Crawford James	Old Seceder Cem, Raynoldsburg, OH	26
Crawford James	Putney, VT	18
Crawford James Maj	Pine Creek Cem, PA	15
Crawford Jason	Virgil, Cortland Co, NY	36
Crawford John	Auburn Cem, N of Hillsboro, OH	15
Crawford John	Baldwin Fam Cem, nr Mt Sterling, Madison Co, OH	55
Crawford John	Fam Cem, Monroe Twp, OH	56
Crawford John	Meade, MI	56
Crawford John	Meade Cem, Meade, Macomb Co, MI	78
Crawford John	Meade Cem, Meade, MI	15
Crawford John	Old Augusta Stone Ch Cem, Ft Defiance, VA	62
Crawford John	Old Drawyers Ch Cem, DE	36

Crawford John	Old Drawyers Cem, Smyrna, DE 42
Crawford John	Old Hebron Ch Cem, nr Staunton, Augusta Co, VA 70
Crawford John	Old Hopewell Cem, Crawford Twp, Orange Co, NY 27
Crawford John	Old Cem, East Aurora, NY 32
Crawford John	White Clay Creek Ch Cem, New Castle Co, DE 46
Crawford John Capt	Falling Spring Ch Cem, Chambersburg, PA 21
Crawford John Capt	Oakham Cem, Oakham, MA 45
Crawford John Capt	Old Drawyers, New Castle Co, DE 46
Crawford John Rev	Asbury, NY 15
Crawford Jonathan	Woodlot, Pemigewasset River, Bridgewater, NH 29
Crawford Joseph	Massacred nr mouth of Lechry Creek, Dearborn Co, IN 24
Crawford Joseph	Pres Cem, Lower Providence, PA 15
Crawford Josiah Col	Falling Spring Ch Cem, Chambersburg, PA 21
Crawford Robert	North Side Cem, Sandown, NH 35
Crawford Robert	Old Waxhaws Cem, Lancaster Co, SC 70
Crawford Robert	White Clay Creek, nr Newark, New Castle Co, DE 42
Crawford Robert	White Clay Creek, nr Newark, New Castle Co, DE 45
Crawford Samuel	Warren Co, OH 56
Crawford Samuel	Washington Pike Pres Ch Cem, Knoxville, Knox Co, TN 74
Crawford Thomas	Plymouth & Bridgewater Bur Gr, MA 16
Crawford Thomas	Plymouth & Bridgewater Cem, Plymouth, NH 29
Crawford Thomas Capt	Fam bur gr, Bath, ME 25
Crawford Thomas Capt	Priv bur gr, Bath, ME 26
Crawford William	Bryant's Chapel, Wayne Co, IN 24
Crawford William	Bryant's Chapel Cem, nr Centerville, Wayne Co, IN 72
Crawford William	Burned by Indians, monument at Crawford, OH 52
Crawford William	Carey Assoc (Pioneer) Cem, Wyandot Co, OH 80
Crawford William	Crawford Cem, Union Co, IN 72
Crawford William	Crawford Cem, Alexandria, NH 35
Crawford William	Head of Christiana Cem, nr Newark, New Castle Co, DE 45
Crawford William	Meth Ch Cem, Shrub Oak, Westchester Co, NY 36
Crawford William	Shrub Oak Cem, NY 41
Crawford William Col	[no cem named], MO 32
Cray Benjamin	Bur Gr, Plainfield, CT 56
Crease Richard	Eustice St Cem, Roxbury, MA 46
Crediford Abner	Kennebunkport, ME 50
Cree William	Fam Cem, Ashton farm, nr Jefferson, PA 56
Creech Richard	Great Salkehatchie, Barnwell Co, SC 51
Creech William	Friendship Bapt Ch Cem, Barnwell Co, SC 51
Creed William	Prospect Cem, Jamaica, Queens Co, NY 78
Creekbaum Philip	Old Cem, Ripley, Union Twp, Brown Co, OH 39
Creemer Jacob	White Clay Creek Ch Cem, New Castle Co, DE 46
Creemer William	Woodbridge Pres Cem, NJ 49
Crehore John	Old Milton Cem, Milton, MA 46
Crehore Samuel	Old Milton Cem, Milton, MA 46
Crehore William	Old Milton Cem, Milton, MA 46
Creighton Moses	Stone Church Cem, WV 24
Cresap Daniel Jr	Glades, Glades Co, FL 56
Cresap Michael	Trinity Ch Cem, NYC, NY 56
Cresap Thomas	Fam plot, Oldtown, MD 56
Cresap Thomas	Oldtown, MD 75
Cresey Jonathan	Old West (Goodrich) Cem, Chesterfield, NH 36
Cresey Michael	Old West (Goodrich) Cem, Chesterfield, NH 36
Cressey Daniel	Bradford, NH 15
Cressey Daniel	Cem nr Ch, Bradford Center, NH 30
Cressey Daniel	Cem nr Ch, Bradford Center, NH 29
Cressey John	Rowley Cem, Essex, MA 48
Cressey Jonathan	West Cem, Rowe, Franklin Co, MA 54
Cressey Mark	Rowley Cem, Essex, MA 48
Creswell Andrew	Eusebia Pres Ch Cem, Maryville, Blount Co, TN 68
Creswell James	Cross Creek Dist Unit Pres Ch Cem, Colliers, WV 56

Crew Gideon	Minor Bur Gr, Granville Co, NC	49
Crews Joseph	Nr Big Island, Northern Bedford Co, VA	47
Crieutz Adam	Old Ref Cem, Milton, PA	59
Crim Adam	Fam Cem, Henderson, Herkimer Co, NY	41
Crim Adam	Fam Cem, Andrustown, NY	34
Crim Henry	Fam Cem, Brutus, NY	41
Crim Jacob	Fam Cem, Henderson, Herkimer Co, NY	41
Crim Jacob	Fam Cem, Andrustown, NY	34
Crim Paul	Fam Cem, Henderson, Herkimer Co, NY	41
Crim Paul	Fam Cem, Andrustown, NY	34
Crim Peter	Old Wood Cem, Woodbury, NJ	47
Crim Peter	Raders Cem, nr Timberville, VA	52
Crim Peter	Union Ch Cem, Middleway, WV	42
Crippen Reuben	Mt Everett, Egremont, MA	56
Crippen Roswell	Rutland Cem, Tioga, Tioga Co, PA	78
Crippen Silas	Cong Ch Cem, Worcester, NY	15
Cripps Matthes	White Clay Creek Ch Cem, New Castle Co, DE	46
Crips Mathew	Old Swedes, Wilmington, New Castle Co, DE	41
Crise Barnet	Richardson Cem, Cayuga Jct, Springport, NY	41
Crissey Ebenezer Jr	North Stamford Cong Ch Cem, Stamford, CT	68
Crissey William	North Stamford Cong Ch Cem, Stamford, CT	68
Crissman --	Fairview Cem, Altoona, PA	52
Crissman Josiah	Davis Cem, Davis, MI	15
Crist Christian	Hopewell Cem, Montgomery, Hamilton Co, OH	55
Crist David	Dutch Ref Brick Ch Cem, Montgomery, Orange Co, NY	76
Crist Henry Jr	Dutch Ref Brick Ch Cem, Montgomery, Orange Co, NY	76
Crist Stephen	Dutch Ref Brick Ch Cem, Montgomery, Orange Co, NY	76
Crist William	Dutch Ref Brick Ch Cem, Montgomery, Orange Co, NY	76
Cristy George	New Boston, NH	16
Critchfield Benjamin	Howard Twp, Know Co, OH	55
Critchfield John	Meth Epis Cem, Nashville, Holmes Co, OH	55
Critchfield John	Vevay Cem, Switzerland Co, IN	72
Critchfield Joseph	Old Jelloway Cem, Howard Twp, Knox Co, OH	55
Critchfield Joshua	Hocking Twp, Fairfield, OH	56
Critchfield Nathaniel	Old Jelloway Cem, Howard Twp, Knox Co, OH	55
Critchfield Nathaniel	Shrimplin Cem, (aban), 2 mi SW of Howard, OH	56
Critchfield William	Old Jelloway Cem, Howard Twp, Knox Co, OH	55
Critchlow James	Mount Nebo Cem, Whitetown, PA	15
Critchlow William	Slater farm, nr Whitetown, PA	15
Crites Jacob	Crooked Run UMC Cem, Dover Twp, New Philadelphia, OH	75
Crittenden Ichabod	Beach Plain, Sandisfield, MA	56
Crittenden John	Crittenden Cem, Chesterfield Twp, Macomb Co, MI	28
Crittenden Medad	Howland Cem, Conway, MA	53
Crittenden Richard	New Hope, IN	48
Crittenden Samuel	Howland Cem, Conway, MA	53
Crittenden Samuel Sr	Whitney-Crittenden Cem, Geneva, Ontario Co, NY	86
Crittenden Simeon	Buckland (Charlemont) Cem, Buckland, MA	56
Crittenden Simeon	Church Cem, Buckland, MA	56
Crittenden William S	Otis Center Cem, Otis, MA	28
Critz Hamon	Fam Cem, Patrick Co, VA	63
Crocker Charles	Old Cem, Mantua, OH	56
Crocker Cornelius	Lothrop's Hill Cem, Barnstable, MA	58
Crocker Daniel	United Cong Ch Cem, Barnstable, MA	55
Crocker David	Streetsboro, OH	26
Crocker David	Streetsboro, OH	53
Crocker Ebenezer	Fam Cem, betw Kinderhook & Chatham, Columbia Co, NY	42
Crocker Edmund	West Barnstable, MA	55
Crocker Eleazer	Center Cem, Carver, MA	58
Crocker Elisha	Lee Cem, Lee, MA	15
Crocker Francis	West Barnstable, MA	55
Crocker Heman	Center Cem, Carver, MA	58

Crocker Jacob Col	Paxton Cem, Haverhill, MA	28
Crocker Jeremiah	Center Cem, Henniker, NH	32
Crocker Job	Pitcher Village Cem, Pitcher, Chenango Co, NY	81
Crocker Joseph	Center (now Fairmont), Lee, MA	56
Crocker Joseph	Killed in Wyoming Massacre, Wyoming, PA	52
Crocker Joseph	West Barnstable, MA	55
Crocker Josiah	Plain Cem, Taunton, MA	41
Crocker Kenelm	Cem on Rt 6A, Sandwich, MA	56
Crocker Lemuel	Lakenham Cem, Carver, MA	59
Crocker Nathan	West Barnstable, MA	55
Crocker Oliver	Boland Cem, Sharon, Litchfield Co, CT	66
Crocker Richard	Salisbury Point Cem, Salisbury, MA	46
Crocker Roland	North Conway Cem, Conway, Carroll Co, NH	77
Crocker Samuel	Killed in Wyoming Massacre, Wyoming, PA	52
Crocker Timothy	Center Cem, Wareham, MA	55
Crocker Timothy	Old Bur Gr, Mill Rd, Falmouth, MA	64
Crocker William	Barnstable, MA	55
Crocker William	West Barnstable, MA	55
Crocker Winslow	Centreville Cem, Centreville, MA	46
Crocker Zacheus Capt	Sunderland Cem, Amherst, MA	41
Crocket Joshua Capt	Opechee Cem, Old Meredith, Laconia, NH	28
Crockett Andrew	Crockett Cem, Franklin, Williamson Co, TN	71
Crockett Anthony	National Cem, Frankfort, KY	58
Crockett Asa	Wayne Courthouse, WV	29
Crockett Asa	Wayne Courthouse, WV	30
Crockett David	D A R Cem, Sanbornton, NH	31
Crockett Ephriam	Auburn, ME	18
Crockett Hugh	Cem, 1 mi E of Shawsville, Hwy 637, VA	71
Crockett John	Nr His Home, Crockett's Cove, Wythe Co, VA	50
Crockett John	Old Waxhaws Cem, Lancaster Co, SC	70
Crockett Joseph	Fam bur gr, nr Nicholasville, Jessamine Co, KY	72
Crockett Nathaniel	Egbert Cem, Pleasant Twp, Seneca Co, OH	70
Crockett Samuel	Mt Sharon Cem, Springfield, Robertson Co, TN	74
Crockett William	Albia, Monroe Co, IA	42
Crockett William	Forest Cem, Albia, IA	27
Crockett William	Oak View Cem, Albia, IA	30
Crockett William Rev	Oakview, Albia, IA	56
Crocks William	[no cem named], OH	26
Croes John	Beneath chancel, Christ Ch, New Brunswick, NJ	46
Croff John	Ware Cem, Ware, MA	47
Croft Caleb	Walnut St, Brookline, MA	56
Croft James	Van Cortlandville Cem, Peekskill, NY	41
Croft John	Bird Cem, Locke, NY	16
Croft John	Bird Cem, Locke, NY	41
Croft Samuel	Walnut St, Brookline, MA	56
Crofut-Crawford Mark	Church Cem, Greenville, NY	45
Croker Joseph	West Genoa (Northville), Genoa, NY	56
Crom Adam	Seven Mile Creek, WV	30
Crom Adam	Seven Mile Creek, WV	29
Cromartie William	Fam plot, nr Elizabethtown, Bladen Co, NC	59
Cromartie William	[no cem named], MS	44
Crombie John	Forest Hill Cem, East Derry, NH	38
Crombie Samuel	Long Meadow Cem, Chester, NH	33
Cromer John	Avery Cem, Blue River Twp, Harrison Co, IN	62
Cromwell Philip	Aban fam Cem, nr Fultonville, Genesee Co, NY	80
Cromwell Richard	St Anne's Epis Ch Cem, Annapolis, Anne Arundel Co, MD	78
Croninger Joseph	Stark Co, OH	55
Cronk Garrett	Lisle Center Cem, Center Lisle, Broome Co, NY	78
Cronkhite Cornelius	Fordbush Cem, Minden, Montgomery Co, NY	65
Cronkleton Joseph	Fam farm, S of Stratford, Delaware, OH	55
Cronmiller Martin	Lewis Cem, Union Co, PA	15

Abstract of Graves of Revolutionary Patriots

Cronshore John	Brush Creek, Manor Road, PA 53
Crook Andrew	Village Cem, Piermont, NH 32
Crook Charles	Humphrey Cem, Holland, NY 33
Crook Henry	Candor Cem, Bulger, Washington Co, PA 74
Crook Samuel Lt	River Road Cem, Piermont, NH 32
Crook Thomas	East Aurora Cem, Aurora, NY 33
Crooker Elijah Capt	Bristol Mills, ME 39
Crooker Noah	Fullerton Yard Cem, South Woodstock, VT 65
Crooker Tilden	Church Hill Cem, Norwell, MA 59
Crooks Henry Sr	Candor Cem, Bulger, Washington Co, PA 73
Crooks James	Old Center Cem, Blandford, Hampden Co, MA 58
Crooks John	Old Center Cem, Blandford, Hampden Co, MA 58
Crooks Michael	Cottage Hill Cem, Brazil, Clay Co, IN 72
Crooks Thomas Col	Swagler Redstone Ch, Scenery Hill, Washington Co, PA 38
Crooks William	Tunkhannock, PA 17
Cropps John	[no cem named], GA 26
Cropsey Harmanus B	Morav Cem, Staten Island, NY 71
Crosby Abner	South East Cem, South East Twp, Putnam Co, NY 35
Crosby Eli	South East Cem, South East Twp, Putnam Co, NY 35
Crosby Elijah	Fam Cem, Rome Twp, Ashtabula Co, OH 55
Crosby Elkanah Capt	First Parish Unitarian Ch Cem, Brewster, MA 46
Crosby Enoch	Old Gilead Pres Ch Cem, Carmel, Putnam Co, NY 55
Crosby Hannah Mrs	Nr Broad River, 1 mi fr Hwy 215, NW Fairfield Co, SC 42
Crosby Isaac Lt	West Brattleboro Cem, Brattleboro, VT 30
Crosby Jaazanich Capt	Hebron Village Cem, Hebron, NH 36
Crosby James	First Parish Unitarian Ch Cem, Brewster, MA 46
Crosby Jesse	Phinney's Lane Cem, Centerville, Barnstable, MA 58
Crosby Joel	Evergreen Cem, Leominster, MA 47
Crosby John	Lee Cem, Lee, MA 15
Crosby John	Old Crosby Cem, Shelby Co, KY 26
Crosby John	Priv Cem, betw Simpsonville & Todd Hill, KY 50
Crosby John Capt	First Parish Unitarian Ch Cem, Brewster, MA 46
Crosby Joseph	Meadow View Cem, Amherst, NH 27
Crosby Joshua Capt	West Street Cem, Milford, NH 45
Crosby Joshua Jr	Old North Cem, Dorchester, MA 45
Crosby Josiah	Cem, Brewster, MA 49
Crosby Josiah Capt	Milford, NH 15
Crosby Levi	Hadlyme, West Haddam, CT 56
Crosby Moses	South East Cem, South East Twp, Putnam Co, NY 35
Crosby Nathan	Cem back of fire house, Carmel, Putnam Co, NY 36
Crosby Nathan	Nr Waukesha, WI 56
Crosby Obed Rev	Old Cem, S of center, Vernon, OH 24
Crosby Oliver	Billerica, MA 51
Crosby Richard	Nr Broad River, 1 mi fr Hwy 215, NW Fairfield Co, SC 42
Crosby Robert	Wilmington & Brandywine, New Castle Co, DE 46
Crosby Sampson	Milford, NH 15
Crosby Seth	First Parish Unitarian Ch Cem, Brewster, MA 46
Crosby Simon	Old Fredonia Cem, Pomfret, Chautauqua Co, NY 15
Crosby Sparrow	Park Ave Cem, Holden, MA 15
Crosby Thomas	Nr Broad River, 1 mi fr Hwy 215, NW Fairfield Co, SC 42
Crosby Timothy	Truxton, Cortland Co, NY 36
Crosby William	1st Parish Ch, Brewster, MA 55
Crosby William	Fam plantation, nr Fairfield Co line, SC 42
Crosby William	Milford, NH 15
Crose Philip C Sr	Bloomington, IL 15
Crose Phillip	Miller Cem, Randolph Twp, McLean Co, IL 78
Crosier John	Euclid Ave Cem, Cleveland, OH 52
Crosland Edward	Oak Ridge Cem, Bennettsville, SC 70
Crosley Moses	Warren Co, OH 55
Crosman Gabriel	Pleasant St Cem, Raynham, MA 55
Cross Abial	Old Cem, Salem Center, NH 28

Cross Abijah	Frye Hill, Methuen, MA 56
Cross Daniel	Methuen, MA 52
Cross David	North Becket, Becket, MA 56
Cross Ebenezer	Balltown Cem, Hanover, Chautauqua Co, NY 84
Cross Ebenezer	Evergreen Lawn Cem, Hanover Center, Chautauqua Co, NY 83
Cross Ichabod	Shaftsbury Center Cem, Shaftsbury Center, VT 72
Cross Jeduthan	Oakwood, Adrian, MI 56
Cross Jesse	Steven's Pasture, Northfield, NH 31
Cross Joel	South Parkman Cem, Parkman Twp, Geauga Co, OH 61
Cross John	Apulia Cem, Fabius, Onondaga Co, NY 75
Cross John	Glendy Bur Gr, Broadway St & Chase St, Baltimore, MD 15
Cross John	Hills Cem, Hudson, NH 30
Cross John	Mt Zion, Cedar Hill Pike, Hocking Twp, Fairfield Co, OH 55
Cross John	Steven's Pasture, Northfield, NH 31
Cross John	Town Cem, Landaff, NH 27
Cross Parker	Steven's Pasture, Northfield, NH 31
Cross Peter	Blodgett Cem, Hudson, NH 28
Cross Ralph Jr	Old Hill, Newburyport, MA 56
Cross Stephen	Highland Hill, Newburyport, MA 56
Cross Stephen	Williams Cem, Northfield, NH 36
Cross Thomas	Steven's Pasture, Northfield, NH 31
Cross Timothy	Port Crane Cem, Port Crane, Broome Co, NY 78
Cross Uriah	Georgetown Cem, Georgetown, Madison Co, NY 61
Cross William	Meeting House Hill, Methuen, MA 56
Cross Zachariah	Burnt Prairie Cem, Burnt Prairie, White Co, IL 65
Crossan John	Pres Cem, Red Clay Creek Ch, New Castle Co, DE 46
Crossman Abisha Rev	East Unity Cem, Unity, NH 35
Crossman Abner	Huntington Rural Cem, Huntington, Suffolk Co, NY 72
Crossman Abner	Lloyd Neck, Huntington, NY 15
Crossman Asahel	Foster, RI 53
Crossman James	Plain Cem, Taunton, MA 48
Crossman Josiah	Davis Cem, Ray Twp, Macomb Co, MI 78
Crossman Josiah	Washington, Macomb Co, MI 56
Crossman Robert	Plain Cem, Taunton, MA 48
Crossman Robert	Plain Cem, Taunton, MA 41
Crossman Simeon	Half Hollow Hills, Long Island, NY 15
Crossman William	Clarendon Flats, VT 31
Crossman William	East Clarendon Cem, Clarendon, VT 25
Crossman William	East Clarendon Cem, Clarendon, VT 24
Croston Gustavus	Cem in Romney, WV 68
Crouch Gerhart	Lower Salford Mennonite Cem, Montgomery Co, PA 59
Crounse Frederick Jr	Fam plot, fam farm, Guilderland, Albany Co, NY 75
Crounse Philip	Fam Cem, Comstock farm, nr Rt 154, Albany Co, NY 66
Crouse Adam	Bledsoe Fam Cem, Alleghany Co, NC 49
Crouse David Sr	Mt Lebanon Cem, Lebanon Co, PA 83
Crouse John Sr	Crouse's Chapel Cem, Green Twp, Ross Co, OH 55
Crouse Leonard	Aban Cem nr Komar house, Johnsville, Montgomery Co, NY 78
Crouse Leonard 1st	Aban Cem, 1 mi fr Kring's Bush School, Oppenheim, NY 41
Crow Abraham	Kemble Cem, Elkrun Twp, Columbiana Co, OH 57
Crow Charles Sr	Bush River Bapt Ch Cem, Newberry, Newberry Co, SC 77
Crow Elles	Pres Ch Cem, Woodbridge, Middlesex Co, NJ 75
Crow John	Mt Tabor Cem, Coal Center, Washington Co, PA 73
Crow Robert	Robinson's Cem, Roane Co, TN 24
Crow Robert	Robinson Cem, nr Webster, TN 23
Crow Samuel	1st Pres Ch Cem, Woodbridge, NJ 58
Crow Stephen	Mars Hill Cem, Jennings Mill Rd, Oconee Co, GA 68
Crow Thomas	Duncan Mem Cem, Floydsburg, Oldham Co, KY 57
Crow William	Crow Station, Danville, KY 30
Crow William	Kemble Cem, Elkrun Twp, Columbiana Co, OH 57
Crow William	Peoria, IL 15
Crow William	Priv Cem, nr Pottstown, Limestone Twp, IL 72

Abstract of Graves of Revolutionary Patriots

Crowden William	Nr Lebanon, KY 16
Crowder Philip	Crowder Cem, Illini Country Club Grounds, IL 30
Crowel Aaron	Dennis Cem, Rt 6 Yarmouth, MA 55
Crowell Aaron	Old bur gr, Orange, NJ 26
Crowell Abner	West Yarmouth Cem, Yarmouth, MA 46
Crowell Barzillia	Causeway Cem, Tisbury, Martha's Vineyard, MA 46
Crowell Christopher	Dennis Cem, Dennis, MA 33
Crowell Christopher	North Dennis Cem, Dennis, MA 46
Crowell Daniel	West Yarmouth Cem, Yarmouth, MA 46
Crowell David	Lapeer, Cortland Co, NY 36
Crowell Ebenezer	Pudding Hollow, Hadley, MA 55
Crowell Edmund	West Yarmouth Cem, Yarmouth, MA 46
Crowell Edward	Bur gr, First Pres Ch, Woodbridge, NJ 25
Crowell Edward	Center Cem, South Dennis, MA 49
Crowell Elisha	Center Cem, South Dennis, MA 49
Crowell Elkanah	West Yarmouth Cem, Yarmouth, MA 46
Crowell Gorham	West Yarmouth Cem, Yarmouth, MA 46
Crowell Jeremiah	Dennis Cem, Dennis, MA 33
Crowell Jeremiah	West Yarmouth Cem, Yarmouth, MA 46
Crowell John	Dennis Cem, Dennis, MA 33
Crowell John	Dennis Cem, Dennis, MA 33
Crowell John	West Yarmouth Cem, road to Hyannis, MA 51
Crowell Jonah	Union Cong Cem, Chatham, MA 49
Crowell Jonathan	Church Cem, South Dennis, MA 49
Crowell Joseph	Bur gr, First Pres Ch, Woodbridge, NJ 25
Crowell Joseph	Old Bur Gr, Mill Rd, Falmouth, MA 64
Crowell Joseph	West Yarmouth Cem, Yarmouth, MA 46
Crowell Lot	West Yarmouth Cem, Yarmouth, MA 46
Crowell Samuel	Bashan, East Haddam, CT 56
Crowell Solomon	West Yarmouth, MA 55
Crowell Sylvanus	West Yarmouth Cem, Yarmouth, MA 46
Crowell William	Dennis Cem, Dennis, MA 33
Crowford Samuel Capt	Inchahoe, NY 33
Crowl George Sr	Cath Cem, Dungannon, OH 56
Crowley Abraham	Williams St Cem, Mansfield, MA 55
Crowley James	3 mi W of Excelsior Springs, Washington Twp, Clay Co, MO 47
Crowley James	Excelsior Springs, MO 32
Crowley James	Fam Cem, 2 mi N of Randolph, MO 15
Crown Samuel	Bur gr, First Pres Ch, Woodbridge, NJ 25
Crownover Daniel	Spring Creek Cem, 3 mi N of Danville, Yell Co, AR 15
Crownover Robert	Pres Cem, Northumberland, PA 56
Croy Matthias Sr	Farmington Cem, Belmont Co, OH 52
Crozer John	East Fairfield Cem, Columbiana Co, OH 55
Crozier John	Euclid Cem, Cleveland, OH 56
Cruff Thomas	2 mi fr Hope Cem, Anthony Rd, Coventry, RI 37
Crum Jacob	Dunavin farm Cem, Chatham Center, Columbia Co, NY 79
Crum Johannes	Luth Ref Ch Cem, Schaefferstown, Lebanon Co, PA 83
Crum Martin	Dunavin farm Cem, Chatham Center, Columbia Co, NY 79
Crumbie James Lt	Old Cem, Rindge, NH 36
Crumbliss Thomas	Crumbliss, TN 23
Crumbliss Thomas	Kingston, Roane Co, TN 24
Crummitt James	Priv Cem, Wentworth's, Rollinsford, NH 31
Crump James	Cotton farm, 10 mi fr Albemarle, NC 56
Crumrine Michael	Old German Cem, Ellsworth, Mahoning Co, OH 55
Crutcher Henry	Randolph Co, IL 48
Cruttenden Abraham	Alderbrook Cem, Guilford, CT 55
Cruttenden Ichabod	North Beach Plain, Standishfield, MA 29
Cruttenden Timothy	Oakhill nr Saline, Washtenaw Co, MI 56
Cruzan Benjamin	Cross Plains Meth Epis Cem, Cross Plains, Ripley Co, IN 74
Cruzan Benjamin	Meth Ch Cem, Cross Plains, Ripley Co, IN 78
Cryder Tobias	Gingrich Menn Mtg Hs, North Cornwall Twp, Lebanon Co, PA 83

Crysel Jeremiah	Lone grave, Hwy 421W, nr North Wilkesboro, Wilkes Co, NC 76
Cubberly William I	Townhouse Cem, Berlin Twp, Delaware Co, OH 53
Cuddeback Benjamin	Port Jervis, NY 48
Cuddeback William A	Rural Valley Cem, Cuddebackville, Orange Co, NY 83
Cudworth Samuel	Old Cem, rear of Ch, Greenfield, NH 28
Cuerre Pierre	St Francis Xavier Cem, Vincennes, Knox Co, IN 72
Culberston Alexander	Rocky Spring Cem, Chambersburg, PA 46
Culbertson Alexander Jr	Old Town Cem, Zanesville, Muskingum Co, OH 55
Culbertson John	Lower Brandywine Manor Pres Ch Cem, Chester Co, PA 75
Culbertson Joseph Jr	Rocky Springs Pres Ch Cem, 6 mi fr Chambersburg, PA 19
Culbertson Josiah	Maysville Cem, nr Washington, Daviess Co, IN 72
Culbertson Robert	Culbertson-Elledge Cem, Laurens, SC 69
Culbertson Robert Capt	Rocky Spring Ch Cem, Franklin Co, PA 17
Culbertson Samuel	Salem Ch Cem, nr Blairsville, PA 56
Culbertson Samuel Jr	Rocky Springs Pres Ch Cem, 6 mi fr Chambersburg, PA 19
Cull Hugh	Elkhorn Cem, Wayne Co, IN 72
Culling Samuel	Cem on Clark Rd nr Rt 108, Victory, Cayuga Co, NY 57
Culp John	Woodlawn, Elmira, NY 33
Culver Amos	South Main St Cem, Naugatuck, CT 55
Culver Benjamin	Oswego Bitter Cem, Camillus, NY 56
Culver Bezaliel	West State St Cem, Athens, Athens Co, OH 55
Culver Daniel	Fleming Hill Cem, Fleming, NY 56
Culver Daniel	Fleming Rural Cem, Cayuga Co, NY 54
Culver Daniel	Prob The Boulder, VT 48
Culver Daniel Capt	The Boulder, Wells, VT 15
Culver David	Curl Cem, nr East Liberty, Logan Co, OH 55
Culver David	Fleming Hill Cem, Fleming, NY 41
Culver Edward	Stark Cem, Porter Twp, Delaware Co, OH 53
Culver John	Crum Elbow Cem, Hyde Park, Dutchess Co, NY 70
Culver John	Lyme, NH 16
Culver John	Lyme Plain Cem, Lyme, NH 29
Culver Jonathan	Bolton Hill Cem, Victor, Ontario Co, NY 77
Culver Jonathan	Boughton Hill Cem, Ontario Co, NY 33
Culver Joseph	Eddy Cem, Scipio, NY 41
Culver Samuel	Wells Village Cem, VT 48
Culver Samuel Sgt	Wells Cem, Wells, VT 15
Culver Thomas	North Branch Cem, nr Montpelier, VT 15
Culver Thomas	North Branch Cem, VT 20
Culver Timothy	Bradford Co, PA 55
Culver Timothy	Hornbrook Cem, Sheshequin Twp, PA 53
Cumen Minard	Dutch Ref Ch Cem, Belleville, NJ 27
Cumings Jonathan	Old Cem, Merrimack, NH 52
Cumings Thomas	Fairview, Westford, MA 56
Cumins Joshua	Williamsville Cem, Orange Twp, Delaware Co, OH 53
Cummings Archelaus Lt	New Cem, Temple, NH 35
Cummings Charles	Abington Cem, Abington, Washington Co, VA 78
Cummings Charles	Pres Ch Cem, Rocky Springs, PA 20
Cummings Charles	Rocky Springs Pres Ch Cem, 6 mi fr Chambersburg, PA 19
Cummings Charles Rev	New Town Cem, Old Churchyard, Sinking Spring, VA 30
Cummings Charles Rev	Old Ch (now Town) Cem, Sinking Spring, VA 29
Cummings David	Old Kirk Yard, Attleboro, MA 15
Cummings Eleazer Capt	Old Village Yard, New Ipswich, NH 29
Cummings Enoch	Mount Caesar Cem, Swanzey, NH 35
Cummings Harmon	Mountain Creek Bapt Ch Cem, Hwy 29S, Anderson Co, SC 76
Cummings John	Pres Cem, Beallsville, Monroe Co, OH 55
Cummings John Capt	Old Yard, Pine Ridge, Hancock, NH 29
Cummings John Lt	Old Pine Ridge Cem, Hancock, NH 32
Cummings Joseph	Old Cem, Canton St, Sharon, MA 56
Cummings Jotham	[no cem named] 16
Cummings Jotham	Lower Intervale Cem, Plymouth, NH 29
Cummings Nathaniel	Brighton Cem, Brighton, Monroe Co, NY 79

Cummings Nathaniel	Town Cem, Ashland, NH 29
Cummings Nehemiah	Mount Caesar Cem, Swanzey, NH 35
Cummings Robert	Fairmount Cem, Libertytown, Frederick Co, MD 77
Cummings Samuel	Cummings Cem, Winthrop Rd, Augusta, ME 29
Cummings Samuel	Old Cem, Canton St, Sharon, MA 56
Cummings Thomas	Fam Cem, nr Rome, Perry Co, IN 72
Cummings Thomas	Fam Cem, Topsfield, MA 46
Cummings Thomas	Maple Cem, Prospect, ME 28
Cummings Thomas Lt	Maple Cem, Prospect, ME 29
Cummings William	Old First Pres Ch Cem, Greensboro, NC 49
Cummings William	Washington Co, PA 38
Cummings William	Ye Old Cem, Shutesbury, MA 46
Cummins John	Guernsey Co, OH 53
Cummins John	Old Pennsylvania Run Ch nr Bullitt Co, Jefferson Co, KY 25
Cummins Nathan	Euclid Park Cem, Cleveland, OH 56
Cummins Peter	Ramsayburg Cem, Warren Co, NJ 38
Cummins Reynold K	Graceland Cem, Shelby Co, OH 53
Cummins Robert Dr	Mount Bethel Cem, Warren Co, NJ 38
Cummins William	Old Pennsylvania Run Ch nr Bullitt Co, Jefferson Co, KY 25
Cunn Samuel	Marysville Cem, Clark Co, IN 72
Cunnabel Samuel	Bernardston, Franklin Co, MA 56
Cunningham Alexander	West Lawn Cem, Goffstown, NH 28
Cunningham Arthur	Old Summerville Cem, Lancaster Co, SC 70
Cunningham Elizabeth	Greencastle Cem, Putnam Co, IN 24
Cunningham George	Bapt Ch Cem, Cullowhee, Jackson Co, NC 75
Cunningham Hugh	Oak Grove, Cem, Delaware Twp, Delaware Co, OH 53
Cunningham James	Bethel, Old Cem, Mead Twp, Key, OH 56
Cunningham James	Charlotte Co, VA 56
Cunningham James	Earlville, NY 15
Cunningham James	Farmington, MO 15
Cunningham James	Farm, 1 mi N of Reading, Hamilton Co, OH 55
Cunningham James	Old Swedes, New Castle Co, DE 46
Cunningham James	Old Cem, Peterborough, NH 29
Cunningham James	Old Cem, Charlton, Saratoga Co, NY 77
Cunningham James	Peterborough, NH 15
Cunningham John	Clark Co, KY 55
Cunningham John	Fam Cem, Hoodsvilly Rd, Baxter, WV 43
Cunningham John	Fam farm, S of Viola, TN 70
Cunningham John	Old Cem, Spencer, MA 56
Cunningham John	Sorrel Hill Cem, Van Buren, Onondaga Co, NY 75
Cunningham Nathaniel	Old Cem, Spencer, MA 56
Cunningham Nathaniel	Putnam Co, IN 16
Cunningham Richard	Bellbrook Cem, Sugarcreek Twp, Greene Co, OH 55
Cunningham Richard	Pres Cem, Newark, NJ 32
Cunningham Robert	Plum Twp, Allegheny Co, PA 15
Cunningham Robert M	Old Cem, Central Part, Tuscaloosa, AL 15
Cunningham Samuel	Belfast, ME 55
Cunningham Samuel	Lebanon Cem, Mifflin Twp, Allegheny Co, PA 71
Cunningham Thomas	Evans Cem, Huntington Twp, Brown Co, OH 56
Cunningham Thomas	Nr Smithville, Ritchie Co, WV 50
Cunningham William	Dixon Springs Cem, TN 23
Cunningham William	Dixon Springs, Trousdale Co, TN 24
Cunningham William	Harrisville, Ritchie Co, WV 50
Cunningham William	Old Cem, Spencer, MA 56
Cunningham William	Pyles fam bur gr, Oxford, AL 59
Cupples James	Bird Pres Cem, Mifflin Co, PA 21
Cuppy Abraham	Highland M E Ch Cem, Mt Pleasant, Jefferson Co, OH 78
Cuppy John	Fairfield Cem, Fairfield, now Fairborn, Greene Co, OH 55
Curd John	[no cem named], KY 50
Cureton James	Priv fam graveyard, Old Waxhaws, Lancaster, SC 50
Cureton John	Beaverdam Ch Cem, nr Clinton, Laurens Co, SC 52

Cureton John	Nr old Lester factory, nr Spartanburg, SC 51
Curhart Cornelius	Mansfield Cem, Washington, NJ 25
Curl William	Mt Olive Chapel Cem, Degraff, Logan Co, OH 55
Curr James Jr	Union, TN 23
Currence William	Nr Willis Creek, 17 mi fr Elkins, WV 30
Currey John	Sugg's Creek Cem, Mt Juliet, Wilson Co, TN 82
Currie Alexander	Church on the Green, Hackensack, NJ 55
Currie James Jr	Union Cem, Haywood Co, TN 24
Currie Richard	St David's Cem, Radnor, PA 15
Currier Amos	Loudon Center Cem, Loudon, NH 29
Currier Asa	Frye Hill, Methuen, MA 56
Currier Asa Capt	Town Cem, Newton, NH 32
Currier Daniel	Davisville Cem, Warner, NH 34
Currier Daniel	Mtg Hs Hill Cem, Methuen, MA 57
Currier David	Long Meadow Cem, Chester, NH 33
Currier Edward	North Road Cem, Wilmot, NH 34
Currier Ezra Capt	Old Cem, East Kingston, NH 28
Currier Gideon	Branch Cem, Raymond, NH 28
Currier Isaac	First Cem, Meredith, NH 29
Currier Jacob	Union Cem, Amesbury, MA 33
Currier James	George Hill Cem, Enfield, NH 36
Currier John	Union Cem, Amesbury, MA 46
Currier John Capt	Old Cem, East Kingston, NH 28
Currier John Capt	Old Cem, Salem Center, NH 28
Currier Jonathan	Durham, ME 18
Currier Jonathan	North Cem, Bow, NH 32
Currier Reuben	North Cem, Bow, NH 32
Currier Reuben	Old Cem, South Hampton, NH 30
Currier Richard Capt	Lockhaven Cem, East Enfield, NH 39
Currier Sargeant	1st Pres Ch, Euclid Ave, East Cleveland, Cuyahoga Co, OH 55
Currier Thomas	Town Cem, West Bath, NH 27
Currier Thomas	West End Cem, New London, NH 46
Currier Thomas Capt	West Park Cem, New London, NH 37
Currin James	2 mi fr Union Pres Ch, Haywood Co, TN 27
Currin James	2 mi fr Union Pres Ch, Haywood Co, TN 29
Curry James	Claverack Ref Ch Cem, Claverack, Columbia Co, NY 74
Curry James	Pres Cem, Norristown, PA 15
Curry James	Pres Cem, Montgomery Co, PA 52
Curry James	Randolph Co, IL 48
Curry James Jr	Marysville Cem, Union Co, OH 55
Curry James Sr	Paris Cem, Paris, KY 55
Curry John	Ochiltree, Knox Co, IN 54
Curry John	Preble Co, OH 52
Curry John	South Trenton, Oneida Co, NY 71
Curry Nicholas	Fam Cem, 10 mi SE of Gaffney, SC 27
Curry Richard	St David's Cem, Radnor, PA 52
Curry Richard	Van Cortlandville Cem, Peekskill, NY 41
Curry Richard Jr	Van Cortlandville Cem, Peekskill, NY 41
Curry Robert	[no cem named] 17
Curry Robert	Georgetown, OH 15
Curry Robert	Old Augusta Stone Ch Cem, Ft Defiance, VA 62
Curry Robert	Park Cem, Tilton, NH 35
Curry Samuel	Old bur gr, Newark, NJ 26
Curry Stephen	Van Cortlandville Cem, Peekskill, NY 41
Curry Thomas	Ebenezer Cem, Franklin Co, IN 72
Curry Thomas	Ebenezer Cem, Franklin Co, IN 70
Curry Thomas Capt	Center Cem, Canterbury, NH 28
Curry William	Brush Creek Cem, North Huntington, Westmoreland Co, PA 76
Curry William	Fam bur gr, Valois, NY 34
Curry William	Van Kirk Cem, Amwell Twp, Washington Co, PA 38
Curry William Sr	Milan Cem, Ulster Twp, PA 53

Curry William Sr	Milan Cem, Ulster Twp, Bradford Co, PA 72
Curser Benjamin	St John's Cem, Yonkers, NY 35
Curtice Isaac Palmer	Eastern Cem, Danbury, NH 36
Curtice Moses	Monegan Cem, Locke, Cayuga Co, NY 59
Curtice Stephen Sr	Old Cem, Danbury, NH 52
Curtico Ebenezer	Webster, NY 33
Curtis Abel	Center, Wolcott, CT 56
Curtis Abel	Stockbridge Cem, Stockbridge, MA 47
Curtis Abner	Cong Cem, Stratford, CT 56
Curtis Adam	Hancock Cem, Quincy, MA 54
Curtis Agur	Cong Cem, Stratford, CT 31
Curtis Andrew	Briggs Cem betw Middle Line Rd & Rt 20, Saratoga Co, NY 77
Curtis Andrew	Old bur place, Nichols Farms, Nichols, CT 33
Curtis Andrew	Union Cem, Stratford, CT 31
Curtis Benjamin	Mount Hope Cem, Rochester, Monroe Co, NY 33
Curtis Coleman	Blooming Grove Cem, Orange Co, NY 56
Curtis Daniel	Clark Cem, Pompey, Onondaga Co, NY 81
Curtis Daniel	Huron Cem, Huron, Erie Co, OH 43
Curtis Daniel	Old bur place, Nichols Farms, Nichols, CT 33
Curtis Daniel	Soule Cem, Sennett, NY 56
Curtis Daniel Jr	Christ John Cem, Orange, Schuyler Co, NY 86
Curtis David	Cong Cem, Stratford, CT 70
Curtis Ebenezer	West Cem, Douglas, MA 56
Curtis Eleazer	Belpre Twp, Washington Co, OH 16
Curtis Elihu	Cong Cem, Stratford, CT 31
Curtis Elijah	Cong Cem, Stratford, CT 31
Curtis Eliphalet Capt	Cem, Buell, NY 35
Curtis Elizah	Ashley Cem, South Galway, NY 57
Curtis Elnathan Maj	Stockbridge Cem, Stockbridge, MA 47
Curtis Everard	Old bur place, Nichols Farms, Nichols, CT 33
Curtis Felix	Galatia Cem, Herkimer Co, NY 36
Curtis Francis	Middlebury, NY 33
Curtis Isaac	Epis Bur Gr, Stratford, CT 31
Curtis Isaac	Huron, OH 15
Curtis Isaac	Stockbridge Cem, Stockbridge, MA 47
Curtis Israel Jr	Old Cem, Middleton, MA 45
Curtis Jabez	Cong Cem, Stratford, CT 31
Curtis James Capt	Bryant Cem, Webster, ME 29
Curtis James Capt	Webster, ME 18
Curtis Jeremiah	Millis, Millis-Medway, MA 56
Curtis Jeremiah	North St, Cong Ch Cem, Stamford, CT 68
Curtis Jeremiah Jr	Blair Cem, N of West Galway, Galway, Saratoga Co, NY 78
Curtis Jeremiah Judson	Epis Bur Gr, Stratford, CT 31
Curtis Job	1st Cong Ch Cem, Hanover Center, MA 54
Curtis Joel	Union, Stratford, CT 56
Curtis John	Cong Cem, Stratford, CT 31
Curtis John	Groveland, MA 55
Curtis John	Plantation Cem, Accomack Co, VA 63
Curtis John	South Milton Cem, South Milton, Ulster Co, NY 77
Curtis John Capt	Aban fam Cem, no stone, Barrytown Station, Red Hook, NY 21
Curtis John Capt	Fam Cem, Dudley, MA 40
Curtis John Lt	Fam Cem, Dudley, MA 40
Curtis Jonathan	Bow Wow Cem, Sheffield, MA 40
Curtis Jonathan	Briggs Cem betw Middle Line Rd & Rt 20, Saratoga Co, NY 77
Curtis Jonathan	Curtis Ridge Cem, Monroe Co, OH 66
Curtis Jonathan	Five Points, Mason Twp, Cass Co, MI 56
Curtis Jonathan	Hanover Center Cem, Hanover, NH 29
Curtis Jonathan Jr	Bow Wow Cem, Sheffield, MA 45
Curtis Joseph	Cong Cem, Stratford, CT 70
Curtis Joseph	Demet Cem, WV 24
Curtis Joseph	Millis, Millis-Medway, MA 56

Curtis Joseph	Mt Everett, Egremont, MA 56
Curtis Joseph	North Bur Gr, Wayland, MA 56
Curtis Joseph	Old Burial Hill, Marblehead, MA 55
Curtis Joshua	Ft Stanwick Cem, Oneida Co, NY 57
Curtis Joshua	Old Cem, Liberty St, Rockland, MA 55
Curtis Joshua Jr	Old Cem, Liberty St, Rockland, MA 55
Curtis Josiah	Cong Cem, Stratford, CT 31
Curtis Jotham	Five Points Cem, Adamsville, MI 31
Curtis Jotham	Five Points Cem, Chicago Rd, Mason Twp, Cass Co, MI 26
Curtis Lemuel	1st Cong Ch Cem, Hanover Center, MA 54
Curtis Lemuel	Windsor, Antrim, NH 15
Curtis Martin	Bantam, Litchfield, CT 56
Curtis Matthew	Newtown Village, Newtown, CT 56
Curtis Melzar	1st Cong Ch Cem, Hanover Center, MA 54
Curtis Nathan	Stockbridge Cem, Stockbridge, MA 47
Curtis Nehemiah	Center Cem, Harpswell, ME 56
Curtis Nehemiah	Cong Cem, Stratford, CT 31
Curtis Peleg Jr	Scituate Cem, Scituate, MA 47
Curtis Philip	Old Cem, Canton St, Sharon, MA 56
Curtis Reuben	South Cem, Parkman, Geauga Co, OH 55
Curtis Richard Rev	[no cem named], MS 44
Curtis Samuel	Ft Byron Old Cem, Mentz, NY 56
Curtis Samuel	Hancock Cem, Quincy, MA 54
Curtis Samuel	Kirkland Avenue Cem, Clinton, Oneida Co, NY 79
Curtis Samuel	North Hillsdale Meth Ch Cem, Hillsdale, Columbia Co, NY 77
Curtis Samuel	Old Cem, Port Byron, Mentz Twp, NY 41
Curtis Samuel Capt	Cong Cem, Stratford, CT 31
Curtis Samuel Sr	Hope Cem, Worcester, MA 17
Curtis Seth	Cartwright Cem, Sharon, Litchfield Co, CT 66
Curtis Sheldon	Elm St Cem, Ansonia, CT 55
Curtis Simeon	Old Cem, East Bridgewater, MA 56
Curtis Snow	Cong Ch Cem, Hanover Center, MA 53
Curtis Stephen	Antrim, NH 15
Curtis Stiles Capt	Cong Cem, Stratford, CT 31
Curtis Thomas	Fam Cem, Stockton, NY 15
Curtis Thomas	Fam Cem, Page St, Stoughton, MA 55
Curtis William	Old Cem, E Main St, Avon, MA 55
Curtis William	Standish Ch Cem, MA 46
Curtis Zarah Rev	View Cem, Mount Vernon, Knox Co, OH 55
Curtis Zebina	[no cem named] 17
Curtiss Giles	Maple Cem, Berlin, CT 56
Curtiss Samuel	South End Cem, Southington, CT 28
Curtiss Thomas	Center Cem, Norfolk, CT 62
Curtiss Zebulon	West Torrington Cem, Torrington, CT 55
Curts Lawrence	Loramie Valley Cem, Shelby Co, OH 53
Curts Thomas	Botkins Cem, Shelby Co, OH 53
Curtus Elihu	Flat Brook Cem, Canaan, Columbia Co, NY 74
Curtz Thomas	Fam Cem, Rt 6, 1 mi S of Botkins, Shelby Co, OH 55
Cushing Charles	Granary Cem, Boston, MA 46
Cushing Charles	Hingham Centre Cem, Hingham, MA 70
Cushing Daniel	Fam Cem, Dover, NH 50
Cushing David Col	High St Cem, South Hingham, MA 44
Cushing Elijah	Cem, #48-R, Natchez, LA 40
Cushing Elijah	Fern Hill Cem, #10-R, West Parish, Pembroke, MA 40
Cushing Isaac	Fern Hill Cem, Hanson, MA 59
Cushing Job Maj	Center Cem, Hingham, MA 45
Cushing John	Durham, ME 18
Cushing John	South Hingham Cem, MA 52
Cushing John	Webster, ME 18
Cushing John Dr	Grasmere Cem, Goffstown, NH 28
Cushing Jonathan	High Street Cem, Hingham, MA 70

Abstract of Graves of Revolutionary Patriots

Cushing Josiah	Fern Hill Cem, #23-R, West Parish, Pembroke, MA 40
Cushing Josiah	Rehoboth Village Cem, Rehoboth, MA 54
Cushing Lemuel	Tappan Ref Ch Cem, Rockland Co, NY 78
Cushing Moses	North Parish Bur Gr, Haverhill, MA 31
Cushing Nathaniel	Barlow Cem, Mattapoisett, MA 58
Cushing Nathaniel	Belpre Cem, Belpre, Washington Co, OH 55
Cushing Nathaniel	Fern Hill Cem, #24-R, West Parish, Pembroke, MA 40
Cushing Nathaniel I	Fam Cem, Mattapoiset, MA 46
Cushing Peter	Hingham Cem, Hingham, MA 70
Cushing Pyam	High St Cem, Hingham, MA 58
Cushing Seth	Little York Cem, Homer, NY 36
Cushing Seth	Old Cem, Plympton, MA 56
Cushing Theophilus	Fern Hill Cem, #5-R, West Parish, Pembroke, MA 40
Cushing Theophilus	High St Cem, Hingham, MA 51
Cushing Thomas	Granary Cem, Boston, MA 46
Cushing Wareham	Waltham, MA 53
Cushing William	Center, Pembroke, MA 56
Cushman Amaziah	Center Cem, Bellingham, MA 55
Cushman Andrew	Leeds, ME 18
Cushman Andrew	Old Burial Cem, Plympton, MA 57
Cushman Benjamin	Old Cem, Plympton, MA 56
Cushman Cephas	Duxbury, MA 18
Cushman Cephas	Old Hammond Cem, Mattapoisett, MA 45
Cushman Charles	Underneath Church, Burlington, VT 56
Cushman Ebenezer	Old Cem, Plympton, MA 50
Cushman Ebenezer	Old Bur Cem, Plympton, MA 58
Cushman Eliphalet	Marion Rd Cem, Middleboro, MA 55
Cushman Elisha	Ancient Bur Gr, Kingston, MA 50
Cushman Elkanah	Old Cem, Plympton, MA 50
Cushman Ephraim	North Amherst Cem, Amherst, MA 19
Cushman George	Mayflower Cem, Duxbury, MA 50
Cushman Gideon	Bapt Ch Cem, Hebron, ME 57
Cushman Isaac	Old Cem, South Middleboro, MA 56
Cushman Isaiah	Old Burial Cem, Plympton, MA 57
Cushman Jabez	Plymouth St, Middleboro, MA 56
Cushman Jacob	Old Cem, Plympton, MA 50
Cushman James	Ancient Bur Gr, Kingston, MA 50
Cushman Jonah	Becker Center, MA 29
Cushman Jonathan	Old Bur Cem, Kingston, MA 62
Cushman Joseph	Mayflower Cem, Duxbury, MA 58
Cushman Joseph	Old Cem, The Green, Middleboro, MA 50
Cushman Joseph	South Attleboro, MA 15
Cushman Joshua	Mayflower Cem, Duxbury, MA 62
Cushman Josiah	Old Cem, Plympton, MA 50
Cushman Mial	Wrecked off Chatham, MA 46
Cushman Noah	Old Cem, The Green, Middleboro, MA 50
Cushman Noah	Putnam Bur Gr, Middleboro, MA 46
Cushman Robert	Woolrich, ME 56
Cushman Samuel	Old Bur Cem, Plympton, MA 58
Cushman Samuel	Warrentown Cem, Middleboro, MA 55
Cushman Thomas	Old Cem, Plympton, MA 50
Cushman William	Old Cem, The Green, Middleboro, MA 50
Cushwa John	Faith Farm, nr Dry Run, Clearspring, Washington Co, MD 51
Cusick Nicholas Lt	Tuscarovas Reservation, NY 33
Custer Arnold	Hebron Cem, Jefferson Co, IN 72
Custer George	George's Cr German Bapt Ch, George's Twp, Fayette Co, PA 69
Custer Isaac	Wysox Cem, Wysox Twp, PA 53
Custer John Sgt	Liberty Cem, WV 24
Custer Paul	Old Town, Worcester Twp, Montgomery Co, PA 56
Custred William	Pine Creek Cem, PA 15
Cuthbertson John Capt	[no cem named], NC 17

Cuthbertson Joseph Jr   Pres Ch Cem, Rocky Springs, PA 20
Cuthbertson Joseph Sr   Pres Ch Cem, Rocky Springs, PA 20
Cuthbertson Samuel Jr   Pres Ch Cem, Rocky Springs, PA 20
Cuthbertson William   Cem nr South Mountain Institute, Burke Co, NC 60
Cutler Amos   Old Cutler Cem, Country Rd, VT 20
Cutler Ebenezer   Cem, Grafton, MA 49
Cutler Ebenezer   West Cem, Holliston, MA 74
Cutler Hodges   Willow Brook, Plainsfield, NH 56
Cutler Jacob   Pleasant Cem, Stoneham, MA 55
Cutler John   Chestnut Hill Cem, CT 28
Cutler John   West St Cem, Fair Haven, VT 36
Cutler Jonathan   Westfield Cem, Westfield, CT 28
Cutler Josiah   Forest Hill, Ann Arbor, MI 56
Cutler Manasseh Rev   Church Cem, Hamilton, MA 46
Cutler Moses   Center Cem, Grafton, MA 49
Cutler Nathan   Herrick Cem, Lewiston, ME 29
Cutler Nathan   Lewiston, ME 18
Cutler Nathan Dr   Old South Cem, Nashua, NH 34
Cutler Samuel   Arlington, MA 49
Cutler Samuel   Charlestown Cem, now Somerville, MA 49
Cutler Samuel Sr   Menotomy Cem, Arlington, MA 46
Cutler Silas   Bapt Cem, row 4, Templeton, MA 55
Cutler Silas   Bapt Common Cem, Templeton, MA 55
Cutler Simeon   Holliston Center, Holliston, MA 56
Cutler Simeon   Vine Lake, Medfield, MA 56
Cutler Thomas   Hudson Cem, Hudson, NH 45
Cutler Thomas   Lexington, MA 49
Cutler William   Old Town Cem, Plainfield, CT 15
Cutler William Capt   Meriden Cem, Plainfield, NH 29
Cutler Younglove   Watertown, CT 15
Cutright John   Buckhannon, WV 32
Cutter Ammi   Arlington, Menotomy, MA 30
Cutter Ammi   Menotomy Cem, Arlington, MA 29
Cutter Ammi   Old Cem, Arlington, MA 46
Cutter Ammi R   North Cem, Portsmouth, NH 34
Cutter Benjamin   New Cem, Temple, NH 35
Cutter Campyon   Bur gr, First Pres Ch, Woodbridge, NJ 25
Cutter Gershon   Old Bur Gr, Arlington, MA 56
Cutter John   Old Bur Gr, Arlington, MA 56
Cutter Jonathan   Lyme Plain Cem, Lyme, NH 36
Cutter Jonathan   Old Bur Gr, Arlington, MA 56
Cutter Kelcy   Bur gr, First Pres Ch, Woodbridge, NJ 25
Cutter Manasseh   Hamilton, MA 53
Cutter Nathan   Old Village Yard, New Ipswich, NH 29
Cutter Nehemiah   Old Bur Gr, Arlington, MA 56
Cutter Richard   Center Cem, Hudson, NH 28
Cutter Samuel   Bur gr, First Pres Ch, Woodbridge, NJ 25
Cutter Samuel   Old Bur Gr, Arlington, MA 56
Cutter Solomon   South Cem, Billerica, MA 55
Cutter Stephen   1st Pres Ch Cem, Woodbridge, NJ 58
Cutter Stephen   Bur gr, First Pres Ch, Woodbridge, NJ 25
Cutter Thomas   Hudson Cem, Hudson, NH 58
Cutter William   Old Bur Gr, Arlington, MA 56
Cutter William   Old Bur Gr, Arlington, MA 56
Cutter William Dea   Bur gr, First Pres Ch, Woodbridge, NJ 25
Cutting Francis Capt   Croydon Cem, Croydon, MA 44
Cutting Isaac   North Bur Gr, Wayland, MA 56
Cutting John   Old Wayland Cem, Old Sudbury Rd, Wayland, MA 55
Cutting Jonah   Guilford Center Cem, Guilford, VT 19
Cutting Jonathan   Old Cem, Sudbury, MA 47
Cutting Robert Dea   Old Wayland Cem, Old Sudbury Rd, Wayland, MA 55

Cutting William	Acton, MA 55
Cutting William	Woodlawn, North Acton, MA 56
Cutting Zaharia	Pease Cem, Pompey, Onondaga Co, NY 81
Cutting Zebedee	Lyme Plain Cem, Lyme, NH 29
Cutting Zebulon	Newport Cem, Newport, MA 44
Cutts William	Gibson Fam Cem, Jackson Twp, Hamilton Co, IN 72
Cuykendall Wilhemus	Owasco Rural Cem, Owasco, NY 56
Cuykensall Martin	Owasco Rural Cem, Owasco, NY 56
Cuyper Cornelius	Sickletown Bur Gr, Pearl River, Rockland Co, NY 78

D

Da Armas Christobal	St Louis Cem #1, New Orleans, LA 58
Dabney Austin	Mitchell plantation, Upson Co, GA 34
Daboll John	Fam lot, Providence Hwy, 1½ mi fr Groton Ferry, CT 51
Daboll John	South Cortland Cem, Cortlandville, Cortland Co, NY 36
Dacus Nathaniel	3 mi fr Simpsonville, Greenville Dist, SC 41
Dade Francis	Fam Cem, Rose Hill, Orange Co, VA 37
Dade Townshend Rev	Monocacy Cem, Beallsville, MD 15
Dadmun Daniel	Church Hill, Framingham, MA 56
Dadmun Elijah	Common Bur Gr, Marlboro, MA 49
Daggatt Benjamin	Attleboro Falls Cong Ch Cem, Attleboro, MA 55
Daggatt Daniel	Attleboro Falls Cong Ch Cem, Attleboro, MA 55
Daggatt Daniel	Old Rumford Cem, Rehoboth, MA 55
Daggatt Ichabod	Attleboro Falls Cong Ch Cem, Attleboro, MA 55
Daggatt James	Old Rumford Cem, Rehoboth, MA 55
Daggatt James Jr	Old Rumford Cem, Rehoboth, MA 55
Daggatt John	Old Rumford Cem, Rehoboth, MA 55
Daggatt John	Old Rumford Cem, Rehoboth, MA 55
Daggatt Levi	Old Rumford Cem, Rehoboth, MA 55
Daggatt Nathan	Old Rumford Cem, Rehoboth, MA 55
Daggett Arthur	Cat Cem, nr North Village, VT 20
Daggett Darius	Canoe Brook Cem, Westmoreland, NH 25
Daggett Ebenezer	Old Jordan Cem, Elbridge, Onondaga Co, NY 75
Daggett Joab	Old Kirk Yard, Attleboro, MA 15
Daggett John	Girard Cem, PA 21
Daggett John	Leicester Corners Cem, Leicester, VT 35
Daggett John Capt	Greene, ME 18
Daggett John Col	Old Kirk Yard, Attleboro, MA 15
Daggett John Col	Old Kirkyard Cem, Attleboro, MA 47
Daggett Nathan	New Vineyard Cem, nr West New Portland, Franklin Co, ME 61
Daggett Philip	Old Cem, North Haven, CT 15
Daggett Samuel Jr	Newark Cem, Arcadia, Wayne Co, NY 79
Daggett Samuel Sr	Mountain Cem, New Vineyard, Franklin Co, ME 83
Daggett William	Town Cem, Tisbury, MA 45
Dagley Thomas	Union Ridge Cem, White Co, IL 65
Dague Frederick	Fam farm Cem, Moundsville, Marshall Co, WV 78
Dague Mathias	Cem, 2 mi fr New Albany, OH 26
Dague Mathias	Rural Cem, 2 mi fr New Albany, Franklin Co, OH 55
Dagworthy John Gen	Old Epis Cem, Dagsboro, Sussex Co, DE 46
Dagyr John Adam	Western, West Lynn, MA 56
Dailey David	[no cem named], OH 26
Dailey David	Salmon Hole Cem, Lisbon, NH 27
Dailey Ebenezer	Canton Point, ME 31
Dailey John	Manchester Cem, Manchester, OH 56
Dailey John	Manchester Cem, the Village, Summit Co, OH 53
Dailey John	Mill Creek Cem, nr Utica, Venango Co, PA 37
Dain John	Durham, ME 18
Dains Asa	Keebaugh Cem, Orange Twp, Meigs Co, OH 68
Dains Caleb	Dains Ridge Cem, Lincoln Dist, WV 43
Dains Ephraim	Redford Cem, Wayne, MI 56
Dainwood Richard	Montezuma High St Cem, Mentz, NY 56
Dakin Amos	Pleasant View Cem, Mason, NH 70
Dakin Joshua	Old Orchard Cem, Hillsdale, Columbia Co, NY 79
Dakin Justus	Blodgett Cem, Hudson, NH 28
Dakin Preserved	Springfield Mtg Hs Bur Gr, Clinton, OH 53

Dakin Samuel	Old Bur Gr, Sudbury, MA 56
Dale Samuel	Lewisburg Cem, Lewisburg, PA 15
Dale Thomas	Fam Cem, Givan prop, nr Liberty, DeKalb Co, TN 72
Daley Charles	Peter's Creek Ch Cem, Library, Allegheny Co, PA 76
Dalliber John	Nr Syracuse, Onondaga Co, NY 35
Dalling Samuel Capt	North Cem, Portsmouth, NH 34
D'allinger —	Massacred nr mouth of Lechry Creek, Dearborn Co, IN 24
Dally Samuel	Bur gr, First Pres Ch, Woodbridge, NJ 25
Dalrymple David	Cem, Pittsfield, PA 52
Dalrymple James	St George's Cem, Saxonville, MA 56
Dalrymple Jesse	Pres Cem, Kingwood, NJ 35
Dalton Isaac	Parade Cem, Lower Warner, Warner, NH 35
Dalton John	Died on prison ship, Salisbury Plains Cem (stone), MA 46
Dalton Michael	Rye Center Cem, Rye, NH 29
Dalton Samuel	South Road Cem, Belmont, NH 36
Dalton William	Merryall Cem, Wyalusing, PA 53
Dalyrimple David	[no cem named], OH 25
Dam Joseph P	Old Kelly place, Province Rd, Barnstead, NH 28
Dame Abner	North Main St Cem, Rochester, NH 36
Dame Edward	Goshen, NH 50
Dame Edward	Goshen, NH 21
Dame George	Christ Ch Cem, Middlesex Co, VA 61
Dame George	His homestead, Durham, NH 35
Dame Jabez	Haven Hill Cem, Rochester, NH 46
Dame Joseph	Newington Cem, Newington, NH 59
Damewood Richard Capt	Old Cem, Montezuma, NY 41
Damon Abraham	Hambden Center, OH 26
Damon Benjamin	Amherst, NH 53
Damon Benjamin	Unitarian Ch Cem, Ashby, MA 49
Damon Daniel	Laurel Hill, Reading, MA 49
Damon David	Old Wayland Cem, Old Sudbury Rd, Wayland, MA 55
Damon David	Park St Cem, North Reading, MA 42
Damon Ebenezer	Park St Cem, North Reading, MA 42
Damon Ebenezer	Park St Cem, North Reading, MA 42
Damon Ebenezer	Park St Cem, North Reading, MA 42
Damon Ezra	Park St Cem, North Reading, MA 42
Damon Isaac	Bofat Cem, Chesterfield, MA 53
Damon Isaac	North Bur Gr, Wayland, MA 56
Damon Jabez	Laurel Hill, Reading, MA 49
Damon Jason	Old Cem, Bridgeport Cicero, Onondaga Co, NY 78
Damon Jonathan	Dawes Cem, Cummington, Hampshire Co, MA 63
Damon Joseph	Laurel Hill, Reading, MA 49
Damon Oliver	Town Cem, Fitzwilliam, NH 32
Damon Reuben	Scituate, MA 53
Damon Samuel	Laurel Hill, Reading, MA 49
Damon Samuel	Parker Hill Cem, Springfield, VT 33
Damon Thomas Jr	North Bur Gr, Wayland, MA 56
Damon Thomas Sr	North Bur Gr, Wayland, MA 56
Damon William	North Bur Gr, Wayland, MA 56
Damon Zadoc	Scituate, MA 54
Damp Frederick	Old Newtonville Ch Cem, Sicker Rd, Albany Co, NY 30
Dan Abaijah	Brookside Cem, Preston Hollow, NY 32
Dan Dana	Old Cem, Mahoning Ave, Warren, OH 25
Dana Amariah	Ireland St Cem, Chesterfield, MA 46
Dana Amariah	South Amherst, MA 15
Dana James	Lawyersville Cem, Seward, Schoharie Co, NY 74
Dana Nathaniel	Swan Point Cem, Providence, RI 75
Dana William	Pine Cem, West Lebanon, NH 27
Dana Williams	Old Bur Gr, Belpre, Washington Co, OH 55
Dane David	Center Cem, Hingham, MA 55
Dane Francis	Derby Center Cem, Derby, VT 55

Abstract of Graves of Revolutionary Patriots

Dane John	Old Cem, Greenfield, NH 36
Dane John	Opposite 1st Cong Ch, Hamilton, MA 56
Dane John Jr	Opposite 1st Cong Ch, Hamilton, MA 56
Dane Joseph	West Parish Bur Gr, Andover, MA 26
Danenhower Charles	Hood Cem, Germantown, PA 52
Danenhower George	Hood Cem, Germantown, PA 52
Danenhower George Ens	[no cem named], PA 19
Danford Enoch	Dunlap Cem, Colerain Twp, Hamilton Co, OH 55
Danford Peter	Belmont Ridge Cem, Alledonia, OH 56
Danforth David	Amherst, NH 56
Danforth David	Amherst, NH 51
Danforth David	North Anson, ME 15
Danforth David Lt	Old Cem, Washington Center, Washington, NH 33
Danforth Edward	Symond's Cem, Franklin, NH 30
Danforth Henry	Hodgdon Cem, Northfield, NH 31
Danforth John	Old Cem, Lynnfield Center, MA 55
Danforth John	Painesville, OH 26
Danforth Joseph	Union Cem, Laconia, NH 29
Danforth Joshua	Bushnell Cem, Sodus, Wayne Co, NY 79
Danforth Joshua	Old Cem, Monument Square, Saugus, MA 45
Danforth Moses Sr	Fam Cem, Tilton, NH 36
Danforth Oliver	Plain Cem, Taunton, MA 41
Danforth Samuel	First (Sadler) Cem, Greenfield, Saratoga Co, NY 78
Danforth William	River Dale Cem, Webster, NH 34
Danforth William Capt	Forest Hill Cem, East Derry, NH 38
Daniel Buckner	Heighton Hill Cem, nr Medora, Jackson Co, IN 72
Daniel David	[no cem named], OH 26
Daniel Frederick	Girtman prop, 1 mi N of Zebulon, Pike Co, GA 64
Daniel Henrich	St Peter's, Red Cross, PA 49
Daniel J K	Pleasant Gardens, nr Lone Jack, MO 36
Daniel James Cunningham	Greene Co, GA 56
Daniel Joseph	Christ Union Ch Cem, Shoenersville, Lehigh Co, PA 40
Daniel Joseph	Christ Union Ch, Schoenersville, Northampton Co, PA 22
Daniel Joseph	Needham, MA 50
Daniel Joseph Dea	Wellesley Village Cem, Wellesley, MA 40
Daniel Moses	Millis, Millis-Medway, MA 56
Daniel Nathaniel	Old Milton Cem, Milton, MA 46
Daniel Nehemiah	Quaker Cem, E of Morris, NY 71
Daniel William	Hamilton Co, OH 46
Daniel William	Keith's Cem, nr Boggstown, Shelby Co, IN 72
Daniel William	Sand Creek, Dearborn Co, IN 24
Daniell Jeremiah	Millis, Millis-Medway, MA 56
Daniell Jeremiah	Old Needham Cem, Needham, MA 47
Daniell Stephen	Center St Cem, Salem, MA 53
Daniells Nathaniel Jr	Pleasant St Cem, West Rutland, VT 71
Daniels Amariah	Palmyra, OH 53
Daniels Amariah	Ravenna, OH 26
Daniels Asa	East Medway (now Millis-Medway), MA 56
Daniels David	Pine Hill, South Mendon, MA 15
Daniels David	South Mendon Cem, Mendon, MA 46
Daniels David Jr	South Mendon Cem, Mendon, MA 46
Daniels David Jr	South Mendon, MA 15
Daniels Henry	Millis, Millis-Medway, MA 56
Daniels Henry Jr	Millis, Millis-Medway, MA 56
Daniels Increase	Lord Cem, Westmoreland, NH 25
Daniels James	Phillips Mill Bapt Ch, Washington, Wilkes Co, GA 80
Daniels Jeremiah	Old Bur Gr, Needham, MA 49
Daniels Jesse	Millis, Millis-Medway, MA 56
Daniels John	Trinity Cem, Swedesboro, NJ 28
Daniels Joseph	Center Cem, Stratford, NH 37
Daniels Joseph	Millis, Millis-Medway, MA 56

Daniels Joseph	Old Bur Gr, Needham, MA 49
Daniels Joseph	South Mendon Cem, Mendon, MA 46
Daniels Joseph	South Mendon, MA 15
Daniels Lemuel	Millis, Millis-Medway, MA 56
Daniels Moses	South Mendon, MA 15
Daniels Moses	South Mendon Cem, Mendon, MA 46
Daniels Nathan Jr	City Mill Cem, Franklin, MA 45
Daniels Randolph	Hillside Cem, Samptown, S Plainfield, Middlesex Co, NJ 77
Daniels Reuben	East Hartland Cem, East Hartland, CT 60
Daniels Starling	South Williamstown, MA 15
Daniels Sterling	South Lawn Cem, Williamstown, MA 33
Daniels William	Cleaver Cem, Marcy, Oneida Co, NY 82
Danielson Calvin	Prentis Cem, Gilbertsville, NY 32
Danielson John	Prentis Cem, Gilbertsville, NY 32
Danielson Levi	Old Cem, now plowed over, home place, Barrington, NH 41
Danielson Luther	Weldon Cem, Racine, Meigs Co, OH 55
Danielson Samuel	Westfield Cem, Westfield, CT 28
Danielson Samuel Capt	Westfield Cem, Killingly, CT 45
Danielson Timothy	Prentiss Cem, Butternuts, Gilbertsville, Otsego Co, NY 77
Danielson William	Westfield Cem, Westfield, CT 28
Danis Honore	St Francis Xavier Cem, Vincennes, Knox Co, IN 72
Danis Jerome	Randolph Co, IL 48
Danis Joseph	Randolph Co, IL 48
Danis Michael	Randolph Co, IL 48
Danks Robert	Center Cem, Southampton, MA 37
Dann Nathan	First Cong Ch Cem, Stamford, CT 68
Dann Squire	Simsbury Cem, High Ridge & Cross Rds, Stamford, CT 68
Dannaker Christian	Log Ch Cem, Napier Twp, Bedford Co, PA 80
Dannals Stacy	Old Beaver Cem, Beaver, PA 17
Dannehower George Ens	Hood's Cem, Germantown, PA 20
Daoran Alexander	Nr Boone's Trail, Trashoun, TN 29
Darbee Jedediah	Griffin's Wells Cem, Aurora, NY 33
Darby John	Bapt Cem, Scotch Plains, NJ 47
Darby John	Old Center Cem, Harvard, MA 56
Darby John P	Bapt Cem, Scotch Plains, NJ 48
Darby Samuel	Nelson Cem, Nelson, NH 46
Darby William	Allensville Cem, Vinton Co, OH 55
Darby William	Pres Ch Cem, Rahway, NJ 76
Darcy John	Pres Graveyard, Hanover, NJ 50
Darden George	4 mi fr Tuscaloosa, AL 15
Darden George Sr	Elbert Co, GA 56
Darden Jacob	Canady Cem, Brinson farm, Emanuel Co, GA 68
Darden John Jr	Stephen Heard Cem, Heardmont, GA 62
Dare John	Center Cem, Winchester, CT 60
Darke William Col	Old Renemous Cem, nr Duffields, WV 26
Darley George Jr	Riverside, Egremont, MA 56
Darling Benjamin	Collamer Cem, Manlius, Onondaga Co, NY 75
Darling Benjamin	Middleboro, MA 54
Darling Benjamin	Plymouth St, Middleboro, MA 56
Darling Benjamin	Tin Corner Cem, Tilton, NH 31
Darling Daniel	Killed in battle, MA 50
Darling David	Hillside Cem, North Adams, MA 46
Darling David	Virgil, Cortland Co, NY 36
Darling Ebenezer	Daville, CT 51
Darling Eilind	Wesley Denton Cem, Day, Saratoga Co, NY 78
Darling Henry Capt	Mount Hope Cem, Rochester, Monroe Co, NY 33
Darling Jabez	Killed in Wyoming Massacre, Wyoming, PA 52
Darling John	Chestnut Hill Cem, Millville, MA 46
Darling John	Cushing Cem, Woodstock, VT 46
Darling John	Cushing Cem, Woodstock, VT 65
Darling John	Meth Cem, South Woodstock, VT 65

Abstract of Graves of Revolutionary Patriots

Darling John	West Lebanon Cem, New Lebanon, Columbia Co, NY 79
Darling Joseph	Cushing Cem, Woodstock, VT 65
Darling Joseph	Cushing Cem, Woodstock, VT 15
Darling Joseph	Cushing Cem, Woodstock, VT 16
Darling Joseph	[no cem named], MI 19
Darling Joseph	Mayflower Cem, Duxbury, MA 58
Darling Joseph	Pine Grove Cem, Leominster, MA 47
Darling Joseph	Prosper Cem, Woodstock, VT 45
Darling Nathan	Old Cem, The Green, Middleboro, MA 50
Darling Pelatiah	Chestnut Hill Cem, Millville, MA 46
Darling Peter	Chestnut Hill Cem, Millville, MA 46
Darling Samuel	Center Cem, Bellingham, MA 55
Darling Thomas	Chestnut Hill Cem, Millville, MA 46
Darling Timothy Maj	Center Cem, Henniker, NH 32
Darling William	Fam Cem, Sutton, MA 52
Darlington John	Lower Brandywine Manor Pres Ch Cem, Chester Co, PA 75
Darr Abraham	German Ref Cem, Middletown, PA 55
Darr Conrad	German Ref Cem, Middletown, PA 55
Darrah Henry	Pres Cem, Deep Run, PA 56
Darrah James Lt	Old Graveyard, South Bedford, NH 34
Darrah Robert	Pine Crest Cem, Litchfield, NH 31
Darrin Daniel	Rogers Cem, outside Troupsburg, NY 58
Darrow Ammiras	Booneville, Oneida Co, NY 56
Darrow George	Mayville Cem, Mayville, Chautauqua Co, NY 76
Darrow John	New Concord Cem, Columbia Co, NY 42
Darrow Zaccheus	Corfu, NY 15
Darrow Zacheus	Corfu, NY 35
Dart David	Watrous Ames Cem, Vauxhall St, Waterford, CT 56
Dart Ebenezer	Wells Village Cem, VT 48
Dart Ebenezer	Wells Cem, Wells, VT 15
Dart Eliphalet	Village Cem, Surry, NH 35
Dart Joseph	Middle Haddam Cem, East Hampton, CT 55
Dart Nathaniel	Village Cem, Surry, NH 35
Dartt Josiah	Plain Cem, Weathersfield, VT 36
Darwin Ebenezer	Granby, MA 55
Darwin John	Fam plantation, York Co, SC 59
Dary John	Attleboro Cem, Attleboro, MA 48
Dates William	Parsell Cem, Lwasco, NY 58
Dates William	Parsell Cem, Owasco, NY 41
Daubenspeck George Sr	Squirrel Hill Cem, Clarion, Clarion Co, PA 57
Daubenspeck John Jacobs	Heidelberg Twp, Lehigh Co, PA 59
Daubert Henrich	Western Salisburg Old Cem, Lehigh Co, PA 40
Daugherty Andrew	First Cong Ch Cem, Stamford, CT 68
Daught John	Potter Hill Cem, Troy, NY 34
Daughtery William	Pine Twp, Mercer Co, PA 15
Davenpart Conrad	Killed in Wyoming Massacre, Wyoming, PA 52
Davenport Abraham Jr	Edge Hill Cem, Charlestown, Jefferson Co, WV 27
Davenport Abraham Jr	Edge Hill Cem, Charles Town, WV 26
Davenport Abraham Sr	Edge Hill Cem, Charles Town, Berkeley Co, WV 42
Davenport Abraham Sr	Fam Cem, Summit Point, Jefferson Co, WV 27
Davenport Abraham Sr	Fam bur plot, Summit Point, WV 26
Davenport Abraham Sr	Fam plot, Summit Point, WV 24
Davenport Abram Jr	Edgehill Cem, Charles Town, WV 24
Davenport Adam	Old Milton Cem, Milton, MA 46
Davenport Anthony Sims	Pleasant Valley Cem, Ross Co, OH 55
Davenport Benjamin	Needham Cem, Nehoiden St, Needham, MA 45
Davenport Charles	Dummerston Cem, Dummerston, VT 46
Davenport Charles	East Dummerston, VT 15
Davenport Charles Capt	Old Bur Gr, Newport, RI 39
Davenport Charles Jr	Dummerston Cem, Dummerston, VT 46
Davenport Cornelius	Pres Ch Cem, Oak Ridge, Morris Co, NJ 75

Davenport Ebenezer	Dorchester North, Boston, MA 56
Davenport Ebenezer	North Dorchester Cem, Boston, MA 55
Davenport Franklin Gen	Old Pres Cem, Woodbury, NJ 28
Davenport Isaac	North Dorchester Cem, Boston, MA 55
Davenport Jacobus	Eben Townsend Cem, Grahamsville, NY 33
Davenport James	North Dorchester Cem, Boston, MA 55
Davenport James Jacobus	Eben Twp Cem, Grahamsville, NY 32
Davenport John	Fam Cem, Summit Point, Jefferson Co, WV 27
Davenport John	Fam estate, WV 24
Davenport John	Fam estate, Summit Point, WV 26
Davenport John	North St, Cong Ch Cem, Stamford, CT 68
Davenport John	St John's Ch Cem, Portsmouth, NH 34
Davenport Joseph	West Branch Cem, Colrain, MA 45
Davenport Josiah	North Cem, Dorchester, MA 46
Davenport Moses	Old Hill Cem, Newburyport, MA 56
Davenport Noah	Stamford Cem, NY 35
Davenport Noah	Stamford Cem, Stamford, NY 32
Davenport Pardon	North Yard, Pomfret, CT 26
Davenport Peter	Union Cem, Stillwater, NY 41
Davenport Richard	Covington Cem, Covington Co, NY 64
Davenport Samuel	Estate (now Wiltshire place), nr Leetown, WV 26
Davenport Samuel	Fam Cem, Summit Point, Jefferson Co, WV 27
Davenport Samuel	North Dorchester Cem, Boston, MA 55
Davenport Samuel	Wiltshire Place, nr Leetown, WV 24
Davenport William	1 mi off main road, nr Mt Holly, NC 56
Davenport William	Lackey Cem, Whitinsville, MA 53
Davenport William	Old Milton Cem, Milton, MA 46
Daves John	Battlefield, Guilford, NC 56
David Eleazer	Bell farm, New Castle Co, DE 46
David Isaac	Lystra Ch Cem, Comer, Madison Co, GA 63
David John	Old Colonial Cem, Derby, CT 56
Davidson Abigail	East Farmington Cem, Farmington Twp, Trumbull Co, OH 55
Davidson Benjamin	Davidson River Cem, Pisgah Forest, NC 57
Davidson Benjamin	Davidson River Cem, Transylvania Co, NC 40
Davidson Benjamin Jr	Greenville Bapt Ch Cem, Leicester, MA 55
Davidson David	Pond Cem, Brookline, NH 36
Davidson Ephraim	Center Pres Ch Cem, Iredell Co, NC 49
Davidson James	Cem, Milford, CT 56
Davidson James	Scotch Cem, West Charlton, Saratoga Co, NY 78
Davidson James	Stockbridge Cem, Stockbridge, MA 47
Davidson James Dea	Old Cem on the Plains, Windham, NH 26
Davidson John	Cem, center of Boardman Twp, Mahoning Co, OH 55
Davidson John	Center Cem, Otis, MA 56
Davidson John	Fam Cem, nr Shady Dale, Jasper Co, GA 24
Davidson John	Fam Cem, Jasper Co, GA 22
Davidson John	Fam farm Cem, Mecklenburg Co, NC 49
Davidson John	First Pres Ch Cem, Cranbury, NJ 76
Davidson John	Reece Ch Cem, nr Columbia, TN 57
Davidson John	Reece Ch Cem, nr Columbus, Warren Co, MS 58
Davidson John Maj	Priv fam graveyard, Mecklenburg Co, NC 18
Davidson John Sr	Cem on the Plains, Windham, NH 34
Davidson Joseph	Farm Cem, Brushy Creek, nr Clarksburg, Harrison Co, WV 75
Davidson Joshua	Higginsport Cem, Brown Co, OH 55
Davidson Patrick	Amity Ch Cem, 10 mi N of Grove City, PA 56
Davidson Robert	First Pres Ch Cem, Cranbury, NJ 76
Davidson Samuel	Old Pres Ch Cem, Bedford Co, PA 80
Davidson Thomas	Center Cem, Grafton, MA 49
Davidson Thomas	Forest Hill Cem, East Derry, NH 38
Davidson Thomas	Galway Village Cem, Galway, Saratoga Co, NY 78
Davidson William	Bapt Cem, South Point, OH 43
Davidson William	Buncombe Cem, Buncombe, SC 59

Davidson William	Eckis Cem, Milton Twp, Mahoning Co, OH	55
Davidson William	First Pres Ch Cem, Cranbury, NJ	76
Davidson William	Lyme Plain Cem, Lyme, NH	36
Davidson William Lee	Hopewell Cem, Mecklenburg Co, NC	18
Davidson William Lee	Hopewell Pres Ch Cem, Huntersville, Mecklenburg Co, NC	78
Davidson William Lee	Hopewell Pres Ch Cem, Mecklenburg Co, NC	49
Davie Samuel Sgt	Clarktown Cem, South Barnstead, NH	28
Davies Marmaduke Sr	Meth Epis Cem, St Clairsville, OH	55
Davies William	Asbury Meth Epis, New Castle Co, DE	46
Davieson Charles	Old Cem, Peterborough, NH	29
Davinson Charles	Peterboro, NH	15
Davis Aaron	Poland, ME	18
Davis Aaron	West Topsham Cem, West Topsham, NH	45
Davis Abner	Woods Hole Cem, Falmouth, MA	68
Davis Allen	Hersey Cem, Minot, ME	43
Davis Allen	Hersey Cem, Minot, ME	42
Davis Amasa	Central Cem, Common, Boston, MA	46
Davis Amos	Greenwood Cem, East Parish, New Haverhill, MA	31
Davis Amos	Lewiston, ME	18
Davis Amos Maj	Buck Hollow Cem, Crown Point, NY	33
Davis Anne	Old fam Cem, Perry Twp, OH	26
Davis Arthur	Palmer St Cem, Somerset, MA	54
Davis Asa	Blodgett Cem, Hudson, NH	28
Davis Asa	Dobson Cem, Osborn farm nr Charlotte, Dickson Co, TN	83
Davis Asa Lt	Old Yard, Pine Ridge, Hancock, NH	29
Davis Azariah	Old 6th St Cem, Newark, Licking Co, OH	55
Davis Barnabas	Westfield Cem, Westfield, CT	28
Davis Benjamin	Center Cem, Hanover, NH	27
Davis Benjamin	North Parish Cem, Plaistow, NH	31
Davis Benjamin	Saxton River, Rockingham, VT	54
Davis Benjamin	St Paul's Epis Ch, Newburyport, MA	56
Davis Benjamin Sr	Little Pee Dee River Landing Cem, Marion Co, SC	70
Davis Bezaleel	Center Cem, Hanover, NH	27
Davis Caleb	Central Boston Common, Boston, MA	56
Davis Caleb	Davis Ridge Cem, Lincoln Dist, Marion Co, WV	40
Davis Caleb	Stony Brook, Long Island, NY	51
Davis Clement	Farm, road betw Lee Hill & Wadley's Falls, Lee, NH	39
Davis Conrod	Greenwich Cem, Warren Co, NJ	40
Davis Daniel	Acton, MA	55
Davis Daniel	Bowen Cem, Lavalette, WV	15
Davis Daniel	North Side Cem, Sandown, NH	35
Davis Daniel	Nr Bowen, WV	29
Davis Daniel	Nr Bowen, WV	30
Davis Daniel	Old Liming Cem, nr Cassville, Monongalia Co, WV	40
Davis Daniel	St Jacob's Ref Ch Cem, SE of Salem, OH	54
Davis Daniel	Thomas Cem, North Swansea, MA	54
Davis Daniel	United Cong Ch Cem, Barnstable, MA	55
Davis Daniel Capt	Fort Frey Cem, Beverly, Washington Co, OH	39
Davis David	Acton, MA	55
Davis David	Ch Cem, Paxton, MA	46
Davis David	Mansfield Second Pres Cem, Rockport, Warren Co, NJ	39
Davis David	Mansfield Second Pres Cem, Rockport, NJ	40
Davis David	Middle Island Pres Ch Cem, Brookhaven, Suffolk Co, NY	79
Davis David	Montgomery Bapt Cem, Montgomery Co, PA	59
Davis David	Montgomery Bapt Cem, Montgomery Co, PA	59
Davis David	Old North Bur Gr, Concord, NH	41
Davis David	Palmer St Cem, Somerset, MA	54
Davis David	Pughtown Cem, Gainesboro, Frederick Co, VA	51
Davis David Lt	Old fam Cem, road betw Lee Hook & Packer Falls, Lee, NH	39
Davis Davis	Fam homestead, nr Madison, Morgan Co, GA	59
Davis E	Cem, Oakvale, WV	52

Davis Ebenezer	Old Cem, Washington Center, Washington, NH 33
Davis Ebenezer Jr	Walnut Street Cem, Brookline, MA 56
Davis Ebenezer Lt	Old Cem, Rindge, NH 36
Davis Edmund	Old Hill Cem, Newburyport, MA 56
Davis Edmund	Park Ave Cem, Holden, MA 15
Davis Edward	Old Common Cem, Newport, RI 38
Davis Eleazer	Ye Old Burying Ground, Bedford, MA 55
Davis Elias	Fam Cem, Spafford, Onondaga Co, NY 75
Davis Elias	Old Hill Cem, Newburyport, MA 56
Davis Elijah	Acton, MA 55
Davis Elijah	Coram Cem, Brookhaven, Suffolk Co, NY 79
Davis Eliphalet	Old Cem, Gloucester, MA 55
Davis Elnathan	Coram Cem, Brookhaven, Suffolk Co, NY 79
Davis Enoch Sr	Crown Hill Cem, Salem, Washington Co, IN 72
Davis Enock Sr	Crown Hill Cem, Salem, IN 51
Davis Enos	Fam bur gr, Wabash Twp, Fountain Co, IN 72
Davis Ephraim	Old Cem, Washington Center, Washington, NH 33
Davis Ephraim Maj	Old Cem, Washington Center, NH 47
Davis Evan	Arnold Cem, Wilton, Saratoga Co, NY 78
Davis Ezekiel	Acton, MA 55
Davis Flint	Old Center Cem, Harvard, MA 56
Davis Francis	Malcomson farm, Hanover Hill, Jefferson Co, IN 72
Davis Francis	Old Town Cem, Falmouth, MA 58
Davis Francis	Parade Cem, Lower Warner, Warner, NH 35
Davis Francis Capt	Davisville Cem, Warner, NH 34
Davis George	Milton Cem, PA 16
Davis George	Sugaw Creek Cem, Mecklenburg Co, NC 60
Davis Goldsmith	Fam priv Cem, Brookhaven, Suffolk Co, NY 79
Davis Harry	St Paul's Luth Ch Cem, Red Hook Village, NY 21
Davis Henry	Beersheba Cem, SW of Gnadenhutten, Tuscarawas Co, OH 55
Davis Henry Sen	Tealtown, off Tealtown Rd, Union Twp, OH 56
Davis Hezekiah	Old Durham Epis Cem, Chicamauxen, Charles Co, MD 55
Davis Hezekiah H	Great Valley Pres Ch, Tredyffrin Twp, Chester Co, PA 75
Davis Increase	West Leebee Cem, Washington Co, ME 53
Davis Increase W	McCoy Cem, Old Gilmanton, Gilford, NH 28
Davis Isaac	Buck Cem, New Lisbon, Otsego Co, NY 72
Davis Isaac	Coram Cem, Brookhaven, Suffolk Co, NY 79
Davis Isaac	Durham, ME 18
Davis Isaac	Dutch Ch, Rhinebeck Village, Dutchess Co, NY 21
Davis Isaac	First Pres Ch Cem, Cranbury, NJ 76
Davis Isaac	Lower Merion Friends Bapt Cem, Montgomery Co, PA 59
Davis Isaac	Old Yard, Pine Ridge, Hancock, NH 29
Davis Isaac	Town Cem, Roxbury, NH 25
Davis Isaac	Under monument, Center of Acton, MA 53
Davis Isaac	Zarepath Cem #1, Zarepath, NJ 47
Davis Isaac Capt	Charlestown, NH 15
Davis Isham	Old Bapt Churchyard Cem, Franklin, NC 70
Davis Israel	Center Cem, Hubbardston, MA 26
Davis Israel	Old Bur Gr, Holden, MA 15
Davis Jacob	Farm, Center Harbor, NH 29
Davis Jacob	Old Town Hall Cem, Salisbury, CT 64
Davis Jacob	Pres Ch, Westfield, NJ 55
Davis Jacob Col	Elm St Cem, Montpelier, VT 15
Davis Jacob Col	Elm St Cem, VT 20
Davis James	Andover, MA 56
Davis James	Cem on fam farm, Pink Hill, Lenoir Co, NC 80
Davis James	Fam Cem, Fairfield Co, SC 70
Davis James	French Cem, nr Mount Sterling, KY 25
Davis James	New Hope Cem, Union Co, IN 72
Davis James	North Cem, Acton, MA 56
Davis James	North Parish Bur Gr, Haverhill, MA 31

Abstract of Graves of Revolutionary Patriots

Davis James	Nut Plains, Guilford, CT 55
Davis James	Old Bur Gr, Holden, MA 15
Davis James	Palmer St Cem, Swansea, MA 55
Davis James	Priv Cem, fam prop, Brookhaven, Suffolk Co, NY 79
Davis James	Town Cem, Barnstead, NH 28
Davis James	United Cong Ch Cem, Barnstable, MA 55
Davis James Capt	Fam Cem, nr Monticello, Fairfield Co, SC 40
Davis James I	Old Cutler Cem, Cutler, Washington Co, ME 79
Davis James Lt	Old Pine Ridge Cem, Hancock, NH 32
Davis Jesse	Bryant Cem, Webster, ME 29
Davis Jesse	Priv Cem, Edgehill, King George Co, VA 52
Davis Jesse	Priv Cem, old homestead, Lisbon, now Webster, ME 47
Davis Jesse	Webster, ME 18
Davis Jesse Sr Capt	Cem, back of grade school, Nelson, KY 31
Davis Job	Green St Cem, Marblehead, MA 55
Davis Joel	Cavendish, VT 16
Davis John	Acton, MA 55
Davis John	Ashland Co, OH 55
Davis John	Bailey's Mills Cem, Reading, VT 55
Davis John	Bethel Meth Epis Cem, Montgomery Co, PA 59
Davis John	Blue Spring Farm fam Cem, nr Mercersburg, PA 56
Davis John	Fam Cem, New Durham, NH 36
Davis John	Fam lot, New Durham, NH 15
Davis John	Frye Hill, Methuen, MA 56
Davis John	Glade Run Pres Cem, Middlesex Twp, Butler Co, PA 56
Davis John	Great Valley Bapt Ch, Tredyffrin Twp, Chester Co, PA 75
Davis John	Lumpkin, GA 29
Davis John	Marshall Cem, nr Coveyville, Saratoga Co, NY 78
Davis John	Maryville, TN 56
Davis John	New Concord Cem, Columbia Co, NY 42
Davis John	Oak Grove Cem, Falmouth, MA 46
Davis John	Old Newton Union Cem, W of Collingswood, Camden Co, NJ 35
Davis John	Old bur gr, Milton, NY 32
Davis John	Old fam Cem, Perry Twp, OH 26
Davis John	Piney Woods Bapt Ch, nr Palmetto, Fulton Co, GA 66
Davis John	St Peters Ch Cem, Spencertown, Columbia Co, NY 79
Davis John	Western Part of Wells, VT 48
Davis John	Woodland, Montgomery Co, OH 26
Davis John Capt	Bethel Mtg, Worcester Twp, Montgomery Co, PA 17
Davis John Capt	Eddington Bend, ME 31
Davis John Esq	Colonial Cem, Derby, CT 15
Davis John Esq	Great Valley Pres Ch, Tredyffrin Twp, Chester Co, PA 75
Davis John Gen	Greatly Valley Ch, PA 15
Davis John III	Pres Ch Cem, Westfield, NJ 76
Davis John Rev	Broad Run 7th Day Bapt Ch Cem, nr Jane Lew, WV 55
Davis John Sr	New Providence Pres Ch Cem, Maryville, Blount Co, TN 76
Davis John W	Beth Meth Ch Cem, Norwich, Muskingum Co, OH 78
Davis Jonas	North Cem, Acton, MA 56
Davis Jonathan	North Acton Cem, Acton, MA 55
Davis Jonathan	Old Village Yard, New Ipswich, NH 29
Davis Jonathan	Old West (Goodrich) Cem, Chesterfield, NH 36
Davis Jonathan	Springerville Cem, nr Connersville, Fayette Co, IN 72
Davis Jonathan	Springersville Cem, IN 15
Davis Jonathan 3rd	Shiloh Bapt Cem, Shiloh, NJ 26
Davis Jonathan Jr	United Cong Ch Cem, Barnstable, MA 55
Davis Joseph	Connecticut Farms Pres Cem, Union, NJ 49
Davis Joseph	Epis Cem, Beaufort, NC 52
Davis Joseph	Griffin farm, Flatbush, NY 15
Davis Joseph	Hollenbeck Cem, Wilkes-Barre, PA 52
Davis Joseph	Liller farm, nr Laureldale, Mineral Co, WV 65
Davis Joseph	New Pittsburg Cem, Randolph Co, IN 25

Davis Joseph	Old Town Bur Gr, Falmouth, MA	65
Davis Joseph	Stevens Cem, Annawan St, Rehoboth, MA	54
Davis Joseph	Tilden plot, New Lebanon, Columbia Co, NY	42
Davis Joseph	Tug Hill Cem, New Albion, NY	53
Davis Joseph	United Cong Ch Cem, Barnstable, MA	55
Davis Joshua	Churchyard, Hollis, NH	39
Davis Joshua	Greenfield Hill Cem, Fairfield, CT	62
Davis Joshua	Hartford, ME	31
Davis Joshua	Hillside Cem, Samptown, S Plainfield, Middlesex Co, NJ	77
Davis Joshua	Humphrey Cem, Holland, NY	33
Davis Joshua	New Burlington, Springfield Twp, OH	56
Davis Joshua	Ridgebury Cem, Slate Hill, Orange Co, NY	83
Davis Joshua	Turner, ME	18
Davis Josiah	Acton, MA	55
Davis Josiah	Duell's Corners Cem, Hamburgh, NY	33
Davis Josiah	Duels Corners Cem, Orchard Park, Erie Co, NY	15
Davis Josiah	New London Cem, New London, NH	37
Davis Lemuel	Old Cem, Milton, MA	56
Davis Lemuel	Wadsworth Cem, Sophronia Wadsworth Estate, NY	48
Davis Levi	Head of Christiana Cem, Newark, DE	59
Davis Lewis	Woodland Cem, Dayton, OH	56
Davis Llewellyn	Great Valley, Chester Co, PA	71
Davis Llewellyn	Great Valley Pres Ch, Tredyffrin Twp, Chester Co, PA	75
Davis Malatiah Col	Oak Bluffs Cem, Martha's Vineyard, MA	46
Davis Matthias	Old Cem, Huntington, NY	15
Davis Matthias	Old Huntington Cem, Huntington, Suffolk Co, NY	36
Davis Moses	Elmwood, Methuen, MA	56
Davis Moses	Folsom-Davis Cem, Lee, NH	41
Davis Moses	Forefather's Cem, Chelmsford, MA	46
Davis Moses	Highland, New Hill, Newburyport, MA	56
Davis Moses	Pine Grove Cem, Berwick, Columbia Co, PA	59
Davis Moses Esq	Davis Island, Edgecomb, ME	40
Davis Nathan	East Bethel Cem, Bethel, Windsor Co, VT	72
Davis Nathan	Westlawn, Westford, MA	56
Davis Nathan Jr	Rutland Cem, Rutland, MA	47
Davis Nathaniel	Blodgett Cem, Hudson, NH	28
Davis Nathaniel	Copley, OH	45
Davis Nathaniel	Copley, OH	15
Davis Nathaniel	Homochitte River Region, S of Natches, Adams Co, MS	57
Davis Nathaniel	Manorville Cem, Brookhaven, Suffolk Co, NY	79
Davis Nathaniel	Parker Hill Cem, VT	48
Davis Nathaniel Jr	Rutland, MA	53
Davis Nehemiah	Dover Twp, OH	26
Davis Nehemiah Rev	Nye Cem, Chauncey, Athens Co, OH	55
Davis Nicholas	Ancient Bur Gr, Kingston, MA	50
Davis Noah	[no cem named], OH	26
Davis Oliver	Princeton, MA	54
Davis Owen	Clifton Cem, NE of Clifton, OH	56
Davis Parley Gen	Montpelier, VT	15
Davis Paul	Falconer Ellicott Cem, Chautauqua Co, NY	70
Davis Peter Jr	Old Cem, nr fire station, Rutland, MA	46
Davis Philip	West Cem, Middlebury, VT	29
Davis Phineas	Lake Grove Cem, Suffolk Co, NY	34
Davis Reuben	Acton, MA	55
Davis Richard	6 mi S of Madison, Morgan Co, GA	59
Davis Richard	Hopkins Co, KY	51
Davis Richard	Phillips-Davis Cem, Mt Sinai, Suffolk, NY	82
Davis Richard	Union Co, OH	45
Davis Robert	Central Cem, Common, Boston, MA	46
Davis Robert	Fam Cem, Bowman, Elbert Co, GA	78
Davis Robert	Wythe Co, VA	54

Abstract of Graves of Revolutionary Patriots

Davis Samuel	Acton, MA 55
Davis Samuel	Chichester, NH 54
Davis Samuel	Dublin Cem, Norwich Twp, OH 26
Davis Samuel	Dublin Cem, Franklin Co, OH 55
Davis Samuel	Magnolia Cem, Chautauqua Co, NY 62
Davis Samuel	Old Parish Cem, Rockport, MA 37
Davis Samuel	Shiloh Bapt Cem, Shiloh, NJ 26
Davis Samuel E	Beauvoir, MS 44
Davis Samuel E	Hurricane Cem, Warren Co, MS 57
Davis Samuel Sgt	Head of Christiana Cem, nr Newark, New Castle Co, DE 45
Davis Septimus Lt	Beall farm, Ecton Pike, Clark Co, KY 45
Davis Silas	[no cem named], OH 25
Davis Silas	Whitford Cem, Globerson's Corners, Saratoga, NY 41
Davis Silas	Whitford Cem, Saratoga Springs, Saratoga Co, NY 78
Davis Simon	Fam Cem, Ellenboro, Rutherford Co, NC 76
Davis Simon	Massachusetts Cem, Princeton Depot, MA 49
Davis Solomon	Stone House, North Killingsworth, CT 55
Davis Squire	Cayuga-Lakeview Cem, Aurelius, NY 56
Davis Stephen	Clough Bapt Cem, nr Newtown, OH 56
Davis Stephen	Pittstown Cem, Pittstown, Rensselaer Co, NY 36
Davis Thomas	[no cem named] 17
Davis Thomas	Cross Creek Cem, Fayetteville, Cumberland Co, NC 80
Davis Thomas	Davis Yard, Shady Nook Rd, West Newfield, York Co, ME 74
Davis Thomas	Litchfield Rd, Hallowell-Farmingdale, ME 20
Davis Thomas	Old Bur Gr, Arlington, MA 56
Davis Thomas	Old Davis Cem, Waynesboro, Wayne Co, MS 86
Davis Thomas	Park Ave Cem, Holden, MA 15
Davis Thomas	Pittsylvania Co, VA 56
Davis Thomas	Wilsonville Yard, Thompson, CT 26
Davis Thomas Rev	Cem, Eastern Shore, MD 55
Davis Thomas W Rev	White Day Creek Cem, Monongalia Co, WV 55
Davis Timothy	Cem N of North Country Rd, Mt Sinai, Suffolk Co, NY 79
Davis Timothy	Hillside Cem, Townsend, MA 48
Davis Walter	9 mi N of Jackson, Jackson Twp, Jackson Co, OH 55
Davis Wells	Old Cem, Warner Village, NH 35
Davis William	Annisquam Cem, Annisquam, MA 46
Davis William	Bayside Cem, Potsdam, NY 30
Davis William	Cem, Youngsville, PA 52
Davis William	Dublin Cem, Dublin, Cheshire Co, NH 77
Davis William	Dutch Ch, Rhinebeck Village, Dutchess Co, NY 21
Davis William	Eddington Bend, ME 31
Davis William	Greenwood Cem, 60 ft fr entrance, Zanesville, OH 56
Davis William	Hardin Cem, OH 53
Davis William	Hillside Cem, E of Bazetta, OH 24
Davis William	Leonardsville Cem, Brookfield, Otsego Co, NY 72
Davis William	Pres Ch Cem, Rocky Springs, PA 20
Davis William	Priv Miller Cem, Brookhaven, Suffolk Co, NY 79
Davis William	Proctor Cem, AL 36
Davis William	Rocky Springs Pres Ch Cem, 6 mi fr Chambersburg, PA 19
Davis William	Salem Cem, Salem, Harrison Co, WV 55
Davis William	Shiloh Cem, Lancaster Co, SC 70
Davis William	Three Mile Creek, Avery Co, NC 49
Davis William	Three-Mile Creek Cem, Avery Co, NC 60
Davis William	White Day Creek, Monongalia Co, WV 42
Davis William	Whittle Fam Cem, Mecklenburg Co, VA 73
Davis William	Yankee St Cem, 3 mi S of Wilkesville, Vinton Co, OH 55
Davis William R	Waxhaws Pres Ch Cem, Lancaster Co, SC 70
Davis Zachariah	Pleasant View Cem, Mason, NH 70
Davis Zachariah	Thorn Grove Cem, Knoxville, Knox Co, TN 72
Davis Zebulon	Poland, ME 18
Davison Asa	Brock Bur Gr, Grafton, NY 53

Davison Ezra	Steward Cem, Grafton Center, NY	56
Davison John	Old Cem, Hamilton, MA	56
Davison John	Woods Cem, back of Hickory Grove, Otsego Lake, NY	71
Davison Joseph	South Yard, Brooklyn, CT	30
Davison Robert	Old Sand Hole Cem, Rockville Center, NY	56
Davison Robert	Sand Hill Cem, Lynbrook, NY	34
Davison Thomas	Chestnut Ridge Cem, Residence, Royalton, NY	33
Davisson Isaac	Green Lawn, sect 5 lot 93, S Charleston, Clark Co, OH	55
Davoe Anthony	Middle Village Cem, East Springfield, NY	33
Dawes Ebenezer	Ancient Bur Gr, Kingston, MA	50
Dawes Robert	Harlow Cem, Cummington, MA	55
Dawes Thomas	Kings Chapel Cem, Boston, MA	46
Dawes William	Kings Chapel Cem, Boston, MA	46
Dawkins Elisha Maj	Old home, nr Union, SC	17
Daws John Capt	Boothbay, ME	31
Dawson Benjamin	Culpeper, VA	56
Dawson Edward	Bryan farm, Tippecanoe Co, IN	72
Dawson Henry	Asbury M E Ch, 9 mi NE of Springfield, Clark Co, OH	55
Dawson Isaac	Mason Co, KY	55
Dawson James	Pidgeon Creek Cem, Somerset Twp, Washington Co, PA	46
Dawson James	Prob Four Mile Cem, W of Franklin Twp, Jackson Co, OH	55
Dawson Jeremiah	Fam Cem, 1½ mi fr Munfordsville, Hart Co, KY	58
Dawson John	Oakdale Cem, Urbana, OH	56
Dawson Joseph	Wilkes Co, GA	56
Dawson Robert Doyne	Monocacy Cem, Beallsville, MD	15
Dawson Titus	Beers Cem, Danby, NY	15
Dawson William	Old Cem, Charlton, Saratoga Co, NY	78
Day Abner	Old Yard, South Killingly, CT	29
Day Adonijah	Pres Cem, Lima, NY	17
Day Amasa Capt	Stockbridge Cem, Stockbridge, MA	47
Day Amos Jr	Connecticut Farms Pres Cem, Union, NJ	49
Day Benjamin	Fredericksburg, VA	29
Day Benjamin	Fredericksburg, VA	30
Day Benjamin	Old Day Bur Gr, Bristol, ME	45
Day Benjamin Maj	Fredericksburg, VA	31
Day Ebenezer	Rural Cem, Walpole, MA	45
Day Edward	DeWitt Cem, DeWitt Co, IL	36
Day Edward	Elmwood Cem (stone only), NY	57
Day Eli	Smith's Ferry, Holyoke, MA	56
Day Ephraim Dea	West Greece, Corners Cem, Monroe Co, NY	33
Day Fairathy	Springfield, MA	15
Day George	Island Creek Cem, Jefferson Co, OH	25
Day Isaac	Elm Grove Cem, Poquonock, CT	55
Day Isaac	Torrington Cem, Torrington, CT	55
Day Israel Col	Hillside Cem, Madison, NJ	30
Day Jacob	Indian Mound Cem, Moravia, NY	56
Day James	Crossroads Cem, CT	28
Day James	Dayville, CT	15
Day James	Holtshire, Orange, MA	30
Day Jeremiah	Williamsburg, OH	56
Day Joel	Elmwood Cem, Holyoke, MA	17
Day Joel Jr	Elmwood Cem, Holyoke, Hampden Co, MA	80
Day John	Birch Creek, Lemhi Co, ID	53
Day John	Conant Cem, Strong, Franklin Co, ME	83
Day John	Crossroads Cem, CT	28
Day John	Goodwin Chapel Bur Gr, Grocery Creek, Morgan Co, KY	51
Day John	Norton, Bristol Co, MA	56
Day John	West Lawn Cem, Williamstown, MA	33
Day John Capt	Dayville, CT	15
Day John Capt	Sugar Hill Cem, East Weare, NH	33
Day John D	Bantam, Litchfield, CT	56

Abstract of Graves of Revolutionary Patriots

Day John D	Laurel Cem, Rt 232, Monroe Twp, Clermont Twp, OH 57
Day John Lt	Elmwood Cem, Holyoke, MA 17
Day Jonathan	Dudley, MA 55
Day Jonathan	South Killingly Cem, South Killingly, CT 28
Day Jonathan Jr	Old Yard, South Killingly, CT 29
Day Joseph Capt	Elmwood Cem, Holyoke, MA 17
Day Lewis	Deerfield, OH 26
Day Liphaz	South Attleboro, MA 15
Day Loaminsh	South Attleboro, MA 15
Day Maj Aaron	McGraw Cem, Cortland, Cortland Co, NY 36
Day Moses	Pentucket Cem, Haverhill, MA 28
Day Nathaniel Jr	Riverdale Cem, Gloucester, MA 46
Day Nehemiah	Mendham, NJ 50
Day Nehemiah	Mendhime Cem, Morristown, NJ 28
Day Othniel	Whipple Hill Cem, Richmond, NH 36
Day Paul	Madison, NJ 49
Day Samuel	Fam Cem, fam farm, nr Good Hope, Ross Co, OH 55
Day Samuel	Medway Cem, Medway, MA 47
Day Samuel	Pres Cem, Morristown, NJ 32
Day Samuel	Wrentham Cem, Wrentham, MA 56
Day Standish	Handy Cem, West Woodstock, Windsor Co, VT 75
Day Stephen	Priv Cem, 1½ mi fr Grovetown, Columbia Co, GA 24
Day Thomas	West Thompson, CT 53
Day Thomas Stanley	Lovely St Cem, Avon, CT 35
Day Timothy	Beach Plain, Sandisfield, MA 56
Day Timothy	Deerfield Cem, Deerfield, OH 56
Day William	Barnard, Sheffield, MA 56
Day William	Old Town Bapt Ch Cem, Dallas Co, AL 35
Day William Capt	Hillside Cem, Madison, NJ 30
Day Zebrina	Gurn Spring Cem, Emersons Corners, Saratoga, NY 41
Dayoe Daniel	Deyoe Grounds, 1 mi fr Valley Falls, Pittstown, NY 36
Dayton Elias	First Pres Churchyard, Elizabeth, NJ 52
Dayton Ezekiel	Old Harmony Cem, Morris, Otsego Co, NY 71
Dayton Henry	Common Ground, Newport, RI 51
Dayton Henry Col	Old Cem, Newport, Newport Co, RI 31
Dayton Hezekiah	Hudson City Cem, Hudson, Columbia Co, NY 74
Dayton Isaac	Black Rock Cem, Black Rock, Erie Co, NY 66
Dayton Isaac	Newport, RI 53
Dayton Jeremiah	North End Cem, Easthampton, Long Island, NY 35
Dayton John Capt	South Cem, Easthampton, Long Island, NY 35
Dayton John Lt	South Cem, Easthampton, Long Island, NY 35
Dayton Jonathan	In vault, St Johns Churchyard, Elizabeth, NJ 52
Dayton Jonathan	Old Cem, North Haven, CT 56
Dayton Jonathan Capt	Old Cem, North Haven, CT 15
Dayton Jonathan Dr	First Pres Churchyard, Elizabeth, NJ 52
Dayton Michael	Ancient Bur Gr, Waterford, CT 66
Dayton Michael Capt	Watertown, CT 15
Dayton Nathan	Rensselaerville, Rensselaerville, NY 32
Dayton Samuel	North End Cem, Easthampton, Long Island, NY 35
Dayton Samuel	Watertown, CT 15
DeAngelis Pascal C	Holland Patent Cem, Oneida Co, NY 80
DeArmond James	DeArmond, TN 23
DeBaun David	Saddle River Cem, Saddle River, NJ 47
DeCamp Gideon Dr	Scotch Plains Cem, end of Lambert's Mill Rd, NJ 53
DeCamp James Eliphalet	Rahway Cem, Rahway, NJ 62
DeCamp John	Scotch Plains Cem, end of Lambert's Mill Rd, NJ 53
DeCamp Moses	Bethel Cem, Millville, Salman Rd, Butler Co, OH 55
DeCamp Norris	Fam Cem, Scotch Plains, Union Co, NJ 71
DeClark Jacobus	Clarkstown Ref Ch Cem, West Nyack, Rockland Co, NY 78
DeCou Isaac	Friends Meeting Ground, Trenton, NJ 28
DeFord John	Brookfield Center Cem, Fayette Co, OH 55

DeForest Abel	Rogers Hollow Cem nr Friends Ch, Unadilla, Otsego Co, NY 72
DeForest Nehemiah	Union Cem, Easton, CT 33
DeForest Samuel	Ballston-Crapo Cem, Collamer farm, Saratoga Co, NY 77
DeForst William	Cato-Meridan Cem, Cato, NY 56
DeFrees Joseph Hutten	Johnsons priv Cem, Piqua, Miami Co, OH 55
DeFreest David	Bloomingrove Rural Cem, North Greenbush, Rensselaer, NY 41
DeFreest John	Bloomingrove Rural Cem, North Greenbush, Rensselaer, NY 41
DeGolyer Joseph	Prospect Hill Cem, Gloversville, NY 41
DeGraffenreid Tscharner	Fam bur gr, Lunenburg Co, VA 63
DeGroots Jacob	Fam vault, Old Pres Cem, Bound Brook, NJ 47
DeGrove Adolph	Old Town Bur Gr, Newburgh, Orange Co, NY 69
DeHart Abraham	Sinks Grove fam Cem, Monroe Co, WV 51
DeHart John	Parsippany Cem, Morris Co, NJ 32
DeHart Peter	Three Mile Run Cem, NJ 47
DeHaven Jacob	Bapt Ch, Scott Co, KY 56
DeHoff George P	Columbiana Cem, Columbiana Co, OH 55
DeJarnette John	Anson Co, NC 55
DeLamattar Jacob	Florida Cem, Ref Ch, Minaville, Montgomery Co, NY 36
DeLano Ebenezer	Nequasset, South Cong Ch Cem, Woolrich, ME 56
DeLivaudais Joseph E	St Louis Cem #1, New Orleans, LA 68
DeLoach Francis	Northampton Cem, Halifax Dist, Northampton Co, NC 59
DeLoach Samuel Sr	Fam plot, Edgefield, SC 56
DeLoach William	Nr Antioch Ch, nr Logan-Todd Line, nr Clifty Creek, KY 55
DeMeritt Samuel	Pine Hill Cem, Dover, NH 43
DeMerritt John Maj	Fam Cem, fam estate, Cherry Lane, Madbury, NH 35
DeMoss John	Byer farm, Clay Twp, Decatur Co, IN 72
DeMoss Peter	Cem, Pendleton Co, KY 66
DeNoyelles John	Mt Repose Cem, Haverstraw, Rockland Co, NY 78
DePuy Benjamin	Owasco Rural Cem, Owasco, NY 56
DePuy Moses	Van Etten Cem, Owasco, NY 56
DePonde Abram	Fam bur gr, Hillcrest Spring Valley, Rockland Co, NY 78
DeRonde Henry	Fam bur gr, Hillcrest Spring Valley, Rockland Co, NY 78
DeRonde Jacob	Fam bur gr, Hillcrest Spring Valley, Rockland Co, NY 78
DeRonde Tobias	Waldron Cem, Grassy Point, Rockland Co, NY 78
DeSaussure Henry W Col	First Pres Ch, Columbia, SC 44
DeTernay Charles L	Trinity Ch Cem, Spring St, Newport, RI 75
DeTurck John	Priv Cem, fam farm (restored), Oley, PA 56
DeVeau Daniel	New Rochelle 1st Meth Ch, E Chester, Westchester Co, NY 55
DeVou Frederick	Carey farm, New Castle Co, DE 46
DeVou Isaac	Glasgow Rd nr Bear, New Castle Co, DE 46
DeWees Hezekiah	Ramah Pres Ch, NE of Huntersville, Mecklenburg Co, NC 77
DeWees William Lt	Greenwich Cem, Warren Co, NJ 40
DeWeese Joshua	Staunton Cem, Troy, Miami Co, OH 55
DeWitt Aaron	First Pres Ch Cem, Cranbury, NJ 76
DeWitt Abraham	Harmony, Warren Co, NJ 39
DeWitt Barnett	Harmony, Warren Co, NJ 39
DeWitt Charles Col	Old Hurley Bur Gr, Ulster Co, NY 36
DeWitt Cornelius D	Owasco Rural Cem, Skaneateles Twp, Onondaga Co, NY 41
DeWitt Garrett	Old Hurley Bur Gr, Ulster Co, NY 36
DeWitt Garrett Van Horn	Cem, Milford, CT 56
DeWitt Jacob	Sussex, NJ 39
DeWitt John	Frankfort Plains Cem, Sussex Co, NJ 29
DeWitt John	Frankford Plains Cem, Frankford Twp, Sussex Co, NJ 79
DeWitt John	Old Town Bur Gr, Newburgh, Orange Co, NY 69
DeWitt John	Owasco, NY 56
DeWitt Lucas	Oak Hill Cem, Weaver, NY 56
DeWitt Peter	First Pres Ch Cem, Cranbury, NJ 76
DeWitt Peter	Harmony, Warren Co, NJ 39
DeWitt Simeon	Albany rural Cem, Albany, NY 31
DeWolf Elisha	Fam Cem, fam farm, West Deerfield, MA 34
De Armond James	Fam Cem, Roane Co, TN 24

De Baun David	Upper Saddle River Cem, Bergen Co, NJ 49
De Baun Joseph	Grapevine Cem, 10 mi W of McAfee, Mercer Co, KY 31
De Berry Henry	Montgomery Co, NC 17
De Blane Louis Charles	Old Churchyard, St Martinville, LA 63
De Camp Ezekiel	Meth Cem, Plainfield, Union Co, NJ 24
De Camp James	Pres Ch Cem, Rahway, NJ 76
De Camp Lambert	Pres Ch Cem, Rahway, NJ 76
De Castorer John	Adams, NY 15
De Chalmette Ignance	St Louis Cem No 1, New Orleans, LA 63
De Favrot Don Pedro J	Old Cem, Highway Rd, nr LSU, Baton Rouge, LA 63
De Fever John	His farm, 3 mi fr Canmer, KY 31
De Forest Abel	Edmeston, Otsego Co, NY 71
De Forest David	Old Colonial Cem, Derby, CT 56
De Forest Gideon	Cem on roadside, S of Edmeston, Otsego Co, NY 71
De Freist Philip	Greenbush (De Friestville) Cem, Oneida Co, NY 65
De Golyer Joseph	Broadalbin Cem, Broadalbin, NY 32
De Groff Moses	Vanderbilt Place, Hyde Park, NY 21
De Groff Simeon	Albany rural Cem, Albany, NY 31
De Groot Freeman	[no cem named], NJ 24
De Gruy Jean Baptiste A	St Louis Cem #1, New Orleans, LA 59
De Hart Cyrus Capt	[no cem named], NJ 24
De Hart John	[no cem named], NJ 24
De Hart William	First Pres Ch, Morristown, NJ 24
De Haven John	Christ Swedes Cem, Montgomery Co, PA 59
De Haven Moses	Christ Swedes Cem, Montgomery Co, PA 59
De Haven Samuel	Old Swedes Ch Cem, Bridgeport, Montgomery Co, PA 52
De La Grange Myndert	Nr Voorheesville-Guilderland Center Rd, Albany Co, NY 66
De La Houssaye Louis	St Martinville Churchyard, St Martinville, LA 59
De La Ronde Pierre D	St Louis Cem #1, New Orleans, LA 58
De Lameter Isaac	Oran Pioneer Cem, Fayetteville, NY 49
De Launay James	City Cem, Milledgeville, GA 31
De Livaudais Balthazar	St Louis Cem #1, New Orleans, LA 58
De Luce Francis	In fam tomb, Hawes Cem, South Boston, MA 45
De Pauw Charles	Crown Hill Cem, Salem, Washington Co, IN 72
De Puy Abram	Van Etten Cem, Owasco, Cayuga Co, NY 57
De Soniat Du Fossat Guy	St Louis Cem #1, New Orleans, LA 59
De Soniat Guy	St Louis Cem #1, New Orleans, LA 58
De Spagne Peter	[no cem named], KY 50
De Turk Samuel	Exeter Twp, CT 56
De Verges Francois	St Louis Cem #1, New Orleans, LA 58
De Vou Isaac	Old Swedes, Wilmington, New Castle Co, DE 41
De Witt Barnett	Harmony, Warren Co, NJ 24
De Witt Paul	Hilton Cem, West Burlington, PA 16
De Witt Peter	Dutch Ch, Rhinebeck Village, Dutchess Co, NY 21
De Wolf Daniel	Eno Hill Cem, Colebrook, CT 60
De Wolf Levi	Morris, CT 17
De Wolfe Peter	Cem, Fowler, Trumbull Co, OH 30
Deacon Aaron	Pres Cem, Morristown, NJ 32
Deaderick David	Jonesboro, Washington Co, TN 24
Deadrick David	City Cem, TN 23
Deake Charles	Dake Fam Cem, Greenfield, Saratoga Co, NY 41
Deake Charles Jr	Fam Cem, Greenfield, Saratoga Co, NY 77
Deake Simon	Old Cem, Nottingham Square Rd, Epping, NH 30
Deake William Gould	Oak Hill-Picket Line Cem, Mt Morris, Livingston Co, NY 74
Deakins James	Fairfield Twp, Franklin, IN 71
Deakyne Thomas	Collin farm, New Castle Co, DE 46
Deal Daniel	St John's Luth Ch Cem, Montgomery Co, PA 59
Deal John	Pres Ch Cem, Frankford, PA 56
Deal William	St Paul's Luth Ch Cem, 1 mi NW of Newton, Catawba Co, NC 62
Dean Aaron	Omar Cem, Reed Twp, OH 26
Dean Abel	Taunton, MA 53

Dean Abiel	West Elm St, Raynham, MA	56
Dean Abiezer	Cem on Broadway, Taunton, MA	55
Dean Abijah	Stevens St, East Taunton, MA	56
Dean Abraham	South Salem Cem, Ross Co, OH	55
Dean Asa	Old Kirk Yard, Attleboro, MA	15
Dean Ashbel	Barnum Cem, Monkton, VT	56
Dean Benjamin	Assonet Cem, off Water St, Assonet, MA	56
Dean Benjamin	Benton Rural Cem, Benton, Yates Co, NY	64
Dean Benjamin	Canfield, OH	17
Dean Benjamin	Canfield, OH	18
Dean Benjamin	Pine Hill, Taunton, MA	49
Dean Clifford	West Elm St, Raynham, MA	56
Dean David	Chewick Cem, Chaplin, CT	55
Dean David	Newburg Cem, Lavenia Twp, Wayne Co, MI	31
Dean David	Newburg Cem, 4 mi E of Plymouth, MI	33
Dean David	Newburg, Wayne Co, MI	56
Dean Ebenezer	Center Cem, Plympton, MA	58
Dean Ebenezer	Durham, ME	18
Dean Ebenezer	Pinehill Cem, Taunton, Bristol Co, MA	86
Dean Ebenezer Jr	North Stamford Cong Ch Cem, Stamford, CT	68
Dean Ebenezer Jr	Pine Hill Cem, Taunton, MA	41
Dean Edward	Summer Street Cem, Taunton, MA	48
Dean Elijah	Center Cem, Mansfield, MA	55
Dean Elijah	Mahopac Falls, NY	35
Dean Elijah	Patterson, Putnam Co, NY	35
Dean Elijah I	Maple Ave Cem, Patterson, NY	58
Dean Enos	Oakland Cem, Taunton, MA	41
Dean Ephraim	Old Kirk Yard, Attleboro, MA	56
Dean Ephriam	Old Kirk Yard, Attleboro, MA	15
Dean George	Cem on Broadway, Taunton, MA	55
Dean Ichabod	Howland Cem, Conway, MA	55
Dean Isaac	Center Cem, Mansfield, MA	55
Dean Isaac	Old Dutch Cem, Kingston, Ulster Co, NY	85
Dean Isaac	Plain Cem, Taunton, MA	41
Dean Isaac 2d	Town Yard, Mansfield, MA	56
Dean Israel	Stevens St, East Taunton, MA	56
Dean Israel	Summer Street Cem, Taunton, MA	48
Dean Israel Capt	Pine Hill Cem, Taunton, MA	41
Dean James	Cem on Broadway, Taunton, MA	55
Dean James	Church St, Easton, MA	56
Dean Jeremiah	County Farm Cem, Unity, NH	34
Dean Job	Pine Hill Cem, Taunton, MA	41
Dean Job	West Elm St, Raynham, MA	56
Dean John	Austerlitz Cem, Columbia Co, NY	42
Dean John	Cornwall Cem, Cornwall, CT	22
Dean John	Ewing Ch Cem, nr Trenton, NJ	28
Dean John	Old Cem, Dedham, MA	56
Dean John	Old Cem, Hamilton, MA	56
Dean John	Old Cem, Dedham, MA	56
Dean John	Old Dutch Bur Gr of Sleepy Hollow, Tarrytown, NY	56
Dean John	Thomas Bur Gr, Pulteney, Steuben Co, NY	51
Dean John	Town Yard, Mansfield, MA	56
Dean John	Village Cem, Dedham, MA	56
Dean Joseph	Pine Hill Cem, Taunton, MA	41
Dean Joseph	West Elm St, Raynham, MA	56
Dean Josiah	Flat Brook Cem, Canaan, Columbia Co, NY	74
Dean Josiah	Village Cem, Galway, Saratoga Co, NY	77
Dean Josiah Capt	Village Cem, Galway, Saratoga Co, NY	41
Dean Lemuel	Plain Cem, Taunton, MA	48
Dean Lemuel	West Claremont Cem, Claremont, NH	50
Dean Lot	Old Stafford Cem, Furnace Hollow Rd, Stafford, CT	60

Dean Luther	Old Village Cem, Claremont, NH	50
Dean Micajah	Old Himrod Cem, Himrod, Milo, Yates Co, NY	78
Dean Nathan	Cem, W Main, Rt 123, Norton, MA	55
Dean Nathan	Plain Cem, Taunton, MA	41
Dean Nathaniel	Cem on Broadway, Taunton, MA	55
Dean Nathaniel	West Elm St, Raynham, MA	56
Dean Noah Lt	Pine Hill Cem, Taunton, MA	41
Dean Obed	Cem, Taunton, MA	34
Dean Philip	Cem, Taunton, MA	34
Dean Philip Jr	Stevens St, East Taunton, MA	56
Dean Richard	Stevens Cem, Annawan St, Rehoboth, MA	54
Dean Rufus	Plain Cem, Taunton, MA	41
Dean Samuel	Fair View Cem, Rockport, Cuyahoga Co, OH	55
Dean Samuel	North Stamford Cong Ch Cem, Stamford, CT	68
Dean Samuel	Sampson Chapel, Farmington, PA	56
Dean Samuel	St Peters Ch Cem, Spencertown, Columbia Co, NY	79
Dean Samuel	Unitarian Ch Cem, Dighton, MA	55
Dean Seth	Barnard, VT	16
Dean Silas	New Stafford Cem, Stafford, CT	60
Dean Stephen	West Elm St, Raynham, MA	56
Dean Thomas	Ambrose Cem, Monticello, Jasper Co, GA	59
Dean Thomas	Assonet Neck Rd Cem, Berkley, MA	55
Dean Ward Clark	Winter St Cem, Exeter, NH	40
Dean William	Dodge Cem, Pompey, Onondaga Co, NY	81
Dean William	Plain Cem, Taunton, MA	41
Dean William	Stony Brook Cem, Mansfield, MA	55
Deane Barnabas Jr	Gold St Cem, Old Hartford, CT	19
Deane Daniel Dea	Cong Ch Cem, Pine St, Norton, MA	55
Deane John Capt	Mansfield Cem, Mansfield, MA	47
Deane Walter	Kellogsville Cem, Ashtabula Co, OH	55
Dearborn Asahel	Lord's Hill Cem, Effingham, NH	32
Dearborn Ebenezer	Village Cem, Chester, NH	33
Dearborn Henry Gen	Mount Auburn, nr Boston, MA	17
Dearborn James	Old Davis Mtg Hs Cem, Effingham, NH	32
Dearborn James Jr	Davis Mtg Hs Cem, Effingham, NH	55
Dearborn Jeremiah	Old Yard, Kensington, NH	47
Dearborn John	East Cem, North Hampton, NH	51
Dearborn John	Hodgdon Cem, Northfield, NH	34
Dearborn John	Priv lot back of Kelsey house, Newmarket Plains, NH	35
Dearborn John	Village Cem, Chester, NH	33
Dearborn Joseph	Village Cem, Rumney, NH	36
Dearborn Joseph Freeze	Ring Swamp Cem, Hampton, NH	31
Dearborn Josiah	Hillside Cem, South Weare, NH	33
Dearborn Josiah Maj	Ring Swamp Cem, Hampton, NH	31
Dearborn Samuel	First Cem, Candia, NH	29
Dearborn Samuel	Old Yard, Kensington, NH	47
Dearborn Samuel	Town Cem, North Hampton, NH	33
Dearborn Shubael	Hodgdon Cem, Northfield, NH	34
Dearborn Shubael Sr	Williams Cem, Northfield, NH	35
Dearborn Simon	North Monmouth, ME	20
Dearborn Simon Jr	North Monmouth, ME	29
Dearborn Stephen Col	Long Meadow Cem, Chester, NH	33
Deardorf Abraham	[no cem named], OH	26
Deardorff Isaac	Lobach Cem, Latimore Twp, Tolland Co, CT	72
Deardorff Jacob	Cem on old Stover prop, Shady Grove, PA	56
Dearing James	Altavista, VA	30
Dearing James	Altavista, VA	29
Death Henry	Sherborn No 1, Sherborn, MA	56
Deatrick Peter	Fam Cem, Boone Twp, Harrison Co, IN	72
Deats Henry	La Boyteaux, Van Zandt & Hamilton Rd, Springfield, OH	56
Deats John	Martin's Creek Cem, Martin's Creek, Northampton Co, PA	66

Deaver Aquilla	Angel Hill Cem, Havre De Grace, MD	30
Debaun Joseph	Mercer Co, KY	52
Debel Alexander	Center Cem, Alstead, NH	37
Debra Jacobus	Miami, Morrow or Fayette Co, OH	45
Decamp James	Bethel Cem, Clermont Co, OH	55
Decarteret John/James	Copps Hill Cem, Boston, MA	57
Decatur Stephen Jr	St Peter's Ch Cem, Philadelphia, PA	52
Dech Jacob	Christ Union Ch Cem, Shoenersville, Lehigh Co, PA	40
Dech Jacob	Christ Union Ch, Schoenersville, Northampton Co, PA	22
Deck Frederick	Christ Luth Ch Cem, Stouchsburg, PA	56
Decker Abraham	Milton Twp, Ashland Co, OH	55
Decker Cornelius	Riverside Cem, Union, Broome Co, NY	38
Decker Daniel	Fam farm, Walpack Twp, Sussex Co, NJ	55
Decker David	Bingham, ME	16
Decker David	Moscow, ME	17
Decker Elisha	Fam farm, Delaware Twp, Pike Co, PA	56
Decker Evert	Brunswick Ch Cem, Shawangunk, Ulster Co, NY	67
Decker Godfried	St Peter's, Red Cross, PA	49
Decker Jacob	Riverside Cem, nr Elmira, NY	32
Decker Johannes 2d	Blooming Grove Cem, Precinct Shawangunk, NY	55
Decker Johannes Jacob	Walmer's Cem, Indiantown Gap, Lebanon Co, PA	83
Decker John Sr	Fam graveyard, Decker Twp, Knox Co, IN	72
Decker Joseph	Dutch Ref Brick Ch Cem, Montgomery, Orange Co, NY	76
Decker Joseph	Fam graveyard, Decker Twp, Knox Co, IN	72
Decker Josiah	New Clove Cem, Sussex, Sussex Co, NJ	79
Decker Josiah	Sussex, NJ	39
Decker Lawrence I	Copake Meth Ch Cem, Copake, Columbia Co, NY	79
Decker Luke	Fam graveyard, Decker Twp, Knox Co, IN	72
Decker Peter	Owasco Rural Cem, Owasco, NY	56
Decker Phillip	Dutch Ref Brick Ch Cem, Montgomery, Orange Co, NY	76
Declouet Alexandre F	St Martin of Tours Cath Ch Cem, St Martinville, LA	76
Declouet Andre F	St Martin of Tours Cath Ch Cem, St Martinville, LA	76
Dederick Christian	St Thomas Luth Ch Cem, Claverack, Columbia Co, NY	48
Dederick Gnysbert	Hill above West Camp, NY	15
Dederick Harmon	Friendship Ice House Farm, NY	15
Dederick Jacobus	Friendship Ice House Farm, NY	15
Dederick Matthias Capt	Field, SE of West Camp, NY	15
Dee Elijah	Old Davis Cem, Georgia, VT	78
Deeds George	Zoar Ch Cem, Caeser's Creek, OH	25
Deeds Thomas	Evansburg Epis Cem, PA	15
Deeds Thomas Sr	St James Cem, Germantown Rd, Montgomery Co, PA	52
Deefenbach Peter	Jacob's Luth Ch, 2 mi W of Pine Grove, Schuylkill Co, PA	37
Deems Mark	Priv fam Cem, West Pike Twp, Washington Co, PA	38
Deering James Capt	Fam Cem, Evington, VA	37
Deets George	Priv fam Cem, Hallam Twp, York Co, PA	52
Defen Peter	East Vincent German Ref Ch Cem, Chester, PA	52
Deforest David	Colonial Cem, Derby, CT	15
Deforest George	Rogers Hollow Cem, Unadilla, Otsego Co, NY	73
Degraff William F	Parsell Cem, Owasco, Cayuga Co, NY	65
Deheart Samuel	Strader Hill Cem, Concord Twp, Ross Co, OH	53
Dehuff John	Island Creek Cem, Jefferson Co, OH	41
Deibert Michael Jr	Zions Red Ch, Orwigsburg, PA	49
Deibert Michael Sr	Zions Red Ch, Orwigsburg, PA	49
Deibert Wilhelm	Zions Red Ch, Orwigsburg, PA	49
Deichman Johannes	Dryland Union Ch Cem, Hecktown, Northampton Co, PA	40
Deichman Johannes	Old Cem, Hecktown, Northampton Co, PA	21
Deiley Daniel	Allentown, PA	16
Deiley Daniel	Old Allentown Cem, Allentown, PA	17
Deiley Daniel	Old Cem, Tenth & Linden St, Allentown, Lehigh Co, PA	40
Deiley George	Western Salisburg Old Cem, Lehigh Co, PA	40
Deininger Adam	Bindnagle Ch Cem, N of Palmyra, Lebanon Co, PA	83

Deisinger Nicholas	Dutch Ref Cem, Bearytown, Seneca Co, NY	62
Deitrick John Balsar Sr	Luth Cem, Stover Town, Muskingum Co, OH	55
Delamater Benjamin	Now in Lakewood Cem, Jamestown, Chautauqua Co, NY	63
Delamater Jacobus	Claverack Ref Ch Cem, Claverack, Columbia Co, NY	74
Delamater Jeremiah	Claverack Ref Ch Cem, Claverack, Columbia Co, NY	74
Delance Delevan Sr	Essex, NY	15
Deland Daniel	South Wolfeboro Cem, betw Wolfeboro & Middleton, NH	27
Deland Obediah	Chestnut Ridge Cem, Monterey, MA	41
Delaney Daniel	Unmarked grave, ice factory lot, Paris, Bourbon Co, KY	27
Delaney William	Old Blountville Cem, Blountville, Sullivan Co, TN	73
Delano Abisha	Cornwall, Shoreham,, VT	15
Delano Amaziah	Gray Cem, Gray, ME	58
Delano Cornelius	Mayflower Cem, Duxbury, MA	58
Delano Gideon	Center Cem, Alstead, NH	37
Delano Jesse	North Duxbury Cem, Duxbury, MA	57
Delano Jonathan	Stowe Cem, Lamoille Co, VT	70
Delano Joshua	Ancient Bur Gr, Kingston, MA	50
Delano Nathaniel	Mayflower Cem, Duxbury, MA	62
Delano Oliver	Mayflower Cem, Duxbury, MA	50
Delano Philip	New Haven Cem, New Haven, Oswego Co, NY	64
Delano Samuel	Old Settler's Cem, Duxbury, NH	49
Delap James	Cem ½ mi fr Ingalls, Madison Co, IN	68
Delemater Benjamin	Dutch Ch Cem, Hyde Park, NY	21
Delena Thomas Sr	Boland Cem, Sharon, Litchfield Co, CT	66
Delevan Nathan	North Salem, MA	56
Delevan Timothy	Patterson, Putnam Co, NY	51
Dellinger Christian	Fam farm Cem, Madison Dist, Shenandoah Co, VA	72
Delong Francis	Van Buren Co, MI	15
Delong John	Eckis Cem, Jackson Twp, Mahoning Co, OH	55
Delong John Frederick	Zions Red Ch, Orwigsburg, PA	49
Delp Abraham	Fam bur place, Montgomery Co, PA	59
Delp Isaac	Fam bur place, Montgomery Co, PA	59
Delphane John	Frederick Co, MD	53
Delvee Peter	Warwick Village, MA	31
Demarest Cornelius	Saucher Tave's Bur Gr, Demarest, NJ	75
Demarest Daniel	Dumont, NJ	47
Demarest David	Cem adjoining Old North Ch, Dumont, NJ	31
Demarest David	Old French Bur Gr, New Bridge, NJ	55
Demarest David	South Ch Cem, Bergenfield, NJ	47
Demarest Hendrick	South Ch Cem, Bergenfield, NJ	47
Demarest Jacobus	French Cem, River Edge, NJ	47
Demarest Jacobus D	Cem adjoining Old North Ch, Dumont, NJ	31
Demarest James D Col	Westwood Cem, Westwood, NJ	31
Demarest James G	Moved fr aban Hillsdale Cem to Westwood, NJ	49
Demarest James J	Tappan Ref Ch Cem, Rockland Co, NY	78
Demarest James S	Fam farm, Oakland, NJ	47
Demarest Jan Rev	French Cem, River Edge, NJ	47
Demarest John	French Cem, River Edge, NJ	47
Demarest John	North Ch Cem, Dumont, NJ	62
Demarest Joseph	Auryansen Fam Cem, Closter, Bergen Co, NJ	82
Demarest Peter	French Cem, River Edge, NJ	47
Demarest Peter	South Ch Cem, Bergenfield, NJ	47
Demarest Peter D	Dumont, NJ	47
Demarest Petrus	French Cem, River Edge, NJ	47
Demarest Philip	Old Mill St Cem, Sodus, Wayne Co, NY	79
Demarest Phillip	Sodus Corners Cem, Wayne Co, NY	52
Demarest Ralph	South Ch Cem, Bergenfield, NJ	47
Demarest Samuel	South Ch Cem, Bergenfield, NJ	47
Demarest William	South Ch Cem, Bergenfield, NJ	47
Demary David	Old West Shelby Cem, Four Corners, Orleans Co, NY	76
Demary John	Rindge Cem, Rindge, NH	47

Demerit Daniel	Mt Repose Cem, Liberty, Waldo Co, ME 77
Demet Benajak	Fam Cem, WV 24
Deming Aaron	South Williamstown, MA 15
Deming Aaron	Southlawn Cem, Williamston, MA 55
Deming Andros	Cem nr Avon & Geneseo, NY 33
Deming Andrus	South Avon Cem, Avon, Livingston Co, NY 22
Deming Benjamin	Cem nr Avon & Geneseo, NY 33
Deming Chauncey	Old Farmington Cem, Farmington, CT 62
Deming Daniel	Hemlock Cem, Colebrook, CT 60
Deming Daniel	Sharon Cem, Sharon, Litchfield Co, CT 66
Deming Daniel	Stockton Cem, Stockton, NY 15
Deming David	Clam River Cem, Sandisfield, MA 56
Deming Davis	Bronson Cem, Vernon Center, NY 71
Deming Elijah	Clam River Cem, Sandisfield, MA 56
Deming Elijah Sgt	Center Cem, East Hartford, CT 19
Deming Gideon	West Hartford, CT 35
Deming Israel	Beckley Cem, Berlin, CT 57
Deming John	Clam River Cem, Sandisfield, MA 56
Deming John	West Center, West Stockbridge, MA 56
Deming Josiah	Wethersfield, CT 56
Deming Julius	East Litchfield, CT 17
Deming Lemuel	Old Cem, Wethersfield, CT 56
Deming Ozias	Clam River Cem, Sandisfield, MA 56
Deming Pownal Capt	Gold St Cem, Old Hartford, CT 19
Deming Prosper	Quaker Cem, nr village of Athens, Ontario, Can 51
Deming Richard	Old Cem, Wethersfield, CT 56
Deming Samuel	Waites Corners, nr Cambridge, NY 30
Deming Seth	Christian Lane, Berlin, CT 56
Deming Simeon	His farm, 2½ mi E of Watertown, Washington Co, OH 55
Deming Soloman	Sandisfield Cem, Sandisfield, MA 70
Deming Theron	West Hartford, CT 35
Deming Theron	West Hartford Cem, Hartford, CT 46
Deming William	Pleasant Valley Cem, Elizabethtown, NY 33
Demint Jarret	The Cabins Cem, Taylor farm, nr English, Carroll Co, KY 74
Demming William	Hawkins Cem, Genoa, NY 56
Demon Levi	Hartford, VT 17
Demond Moses	Danby Cem, NY 15
Demoranville Simeon	Acushnet Cem, Berkley, MA 55
Demoss Peter	[no cem named], VA 55
Demott Lawrence	Bonta Graveyard, Cove Springs, Mercer Co, KY 52
Demott Peter	Bonta Graveyard, Cove Springs, Mercer Co, KY 52
Dempsey Dennis	Charlestown, Chester Co, PA 52
Dempsey Dennis	Old Charlestown Cem, Charlestown Twp, Chester Co, PA 75
Demund William	Lamington Pres Cem, Somerset Co, NJ 63
Demune John	Old Cem, Mifflin Twp, OH 26
Demuth Christopher	Morav Cem, Gnadenhutten, Tuscarawas Co, OH 55
Demuth Gottlieb	Morav Cem, Gnadenhutten, Tuscarawas Co, OH 55
Denbo Elijah	Fam Cem, English, Crawford Co, IN 72
Deneen James	Ward Cem, Reily, OH 56
Deneger George	Luth Cem, Viewmonte, nr Germantown, Columbia Co, NY 42
Denham Cornelius	Allis Dist Cem, Conway, MA 53
Denham Obed	Bethel Meth Epis Cem, Main St, Tate Twp, Clermont Co, OH 55
Denier Jacob	Smith farm, nr Springtown, Ulster Co, NY 59
Denike John S Capt	Pleasant Mills, NJ 47
Denison Amos	North Stonington, CT 31
Denison Beebe	Fam Cem, Mystic, CT 70
Denison Beebe	Stonington, CT 31
Denison Daniel	Old Denison Yard, Mystic, CT 31
Denison Daniel	Old Denison Yard, Mystic, CT 31
Denison Elisha	Old Denison Yard, Mystic, CT 31
Denison George	Old Denison Yard, Mystic, CT 31

Abstract of Graves of Revolutionary Patriots

Denison Jabez	Beaver Meadow Cem, Leyden, Bernardston, MA	55
Denison John	Seceder Corners, Liberty Twp, PA	24
Denison John	Seceeder Corners Cem, Liberty Twp, Trumbull Co, OH	55
Denison Jonathan	Bapt Cem, Center Berlin, NY	46
Denison Nathan	Cem, Forty Fort, PA	52
Denison Robert	Stonington, CT	54
Denison William	Fam Cem, nr Adamsville, Salem Twp, Muskingum, OH	55
Denman Andrew	Priv Cem, nr Mill Bennington, Bennington, OH	55
Denman Christopher	Pres Ch Cem, Westfield, NJ	76
Denman Isaac	Lick Creek Cem, Harrisburg, Fayette Co, IN	79
Denman Samuel	Dalton Cem, Dalton, OH	56
Denman Thomas Jr	Old Pres Cem, Springfield, NJ	50
Denmark David	Watchung, NJ	48
Denmore John	Old Cem, Mifflin Twp, Franklin Co, OH	55
Denn Christopher	Riverside Cem, nr Elmira, NY	32
Dennard Jacob	Cem nr Jeffersonville, Twiggs Co, GA	60
Denne Samuel	Minot, ME	18
Dennen Samuel Jr	Minot, ME	18
Dennett David	Newington, NH	51
Dennett Ebenezer	Clough Cem, South Lewiston, ME	42
Dennett Moses	Barnstead Cem, NH	49
Dennett Moses	Fam lot, Foss farm, Barnstead, NH	29
Dennett Samuel	Fam lot, Dennett farm, Dayton, ME	47
Dennie Albert	North Cem, Portsmouth, NH	34
Dennie Nichols	New Cem, Mayfield, Fulton Co, NY	55
Dennies Samuel	Oldtown Cem, Springfield, Otsego Co, NY	78
Denning Job	Poland, ME	18
Denning Samuel	Poland, ME	18
Dennis Adonijah	Central, Hardwick, MA	56
Dennis Benjamin	Old Burial Hill, Marblehead, MA	55
Dennis Francis Borden	Broad St Cem, Salem, MA	56
Dennis James	Oak Hill Cem, Eldred, PA	52
Dennis John	Grant neighborhood, Litchfield, ME	20
Dennis John	Monroe Twp, Clermont Co, OH	56
Dennis John	Upper Fairfield Churchyard, Candor, Tioga Co, NY	80
Dennis John	Upper Fairfield Cem, Candor, NY	35
Dennis Jonas Capt	Old Bur Hill, Marblehead, MA	29
Dennis Joseph	St James, Staatsburgh, Hyde Park, NY	21
Dennis Moses	Hancock, NH	57
Dennis Moses	Jasper Cem, Jasper, Steuben Co, NY	80
Dennis Moses	Old Yard, Pine Ridge, Hancock, NH	29
Dennis Phillip	Old First Meth Ch Cem, West Long Branch, Monmouth Co, NJ	78
Dennis Samuel	Middle Village Cem, East Springfield, NY	33
Dennis Thomas	Rockwood, NY	41
Dennis William	Old Cem, Newport, RI	52
Dennison Asa	Warren Cem, Little Lakes, Warren, Herkimer Co, NY	41
Dennison Chauncey	Headquarters, CT	17
Dennison David	Freeport, ME	29
Dennison Ebenezer	Union Cem, Stillwater, Saratoga Co, NY	77
Dennison George	Brookfield, Madison Co, NY	56
Dennison George	Denison Cem, Mystic, CT	70
Dennison Isaac	Bay View Cem, Gloucester, MA	51
Dennison John	Village Cem, Walpole, NH	25
Dennison John	Walpole, NH	16
Dennison Jonathan	Dutch Ch, Rhinebeck Village, Dutchess Co, NY	21
Dennison Joseph	Hoyt Cem, Middle Grove Twp, Milton, Ulster Co, NY	77
Dennison Samuel	Pleasant St, West Rutland, VT	31
Dennison William	New Boston Cem, Mercer Co, IL	59
Denniss Samuel	Town Ground, East Springfield, NY	15
Denniston William	Little British Cem, Ulster Co, NY	59
Denny Alexander	Nr Franklin, Howard Co, MO	34

Denny Charles	Mokena, GA 29
Denny Charles	Old Cem, Mokena, IL 15
Denny Charles	Pioneer Memorial Cem, Mokena, IL 40
Denny Eligah	Mt Pleasant Cem, Old Mt Vernon Rd, Somerset, KY 39
Denny Isaac	Rawson Brook Cem, Leicester, MA 55
Denny James	Buffalo Pres Ch Cem, Guilford, NC 56
Denny Robert	Sharon Cem, nr Salem, Washington Co, IN 72
Denny Samuel	Mt Pleasant Cem, Kingston, Ross Co, OH 55
Denny Samuel	Putnam Co, IN 16
Denny Samuel Col	Rawson Brook Cem, Leicester, MA 46
Denny Thomas Jr	Rawson Brook Cem, Leicester, MA 58
Denny Walker	Washington Co, PA 38
Denny Walter	Jackson Cem, nr Benton Haw Patch, Elkhart Co, IN 72
Denny William	Priv Cem, nr Greencastle, Putnam Co, IN 72
Denny William	Putnam Co, IN 16
Denslow Benjamin	Cherry Valley Cem, East Springfield, NY 33
Denslow Elijah	Palisado Cem, Windsor, CT 55
Denslow Joseph	Cem, Bowdoinham, ME 55
Denslow Martin	Windsor Cem, fam lot, Windsor, CT 45
Densmoor Eliphalet	Hartland Cem, Hartland, VT 56
Densmore Eliphalet Capt	Old Cem, Washington Center, Washington, NH 33
Densmore John R	Densmore Hill, Hartland, VT 56
Dent John	Meth Epis Cem, East Richland, OH 56
Dent John Capt	Fairview Cem, nr Morgantown, WV 31
Denton Amos	Prospect Cem, Jamaica, Queens Co, NY 78
Denton D	Killed in Wyoming Massacre, Wyoming, PA 52
Denton Israel	Rogers Cem, Saratoga, Saratoga Co, NY 77
Denton Nehemiah	Cooksboro, Rensselaer Co, NY 35
Denton Preston	Fam Cem, nr Woodlawn Park, Saratoga, NY 41
Denton Preston	Miller Cem, Greenfield, Saratoga Co, NY 77
Denty Sophia Barker	Pohick Cem, VA 48
Denune John	Riverside Cem, nr Linden Heights, Franklin Co, OH 55
Denyke –	Hamonton, NJ 15
Depew Abraham	Van Cortlandville Cem, Peekskill, NY 41
Depew Henry	Van Cortlandville Cem, Peekskill, NY 41
Depew Isaac Sr	Depew's Chapel, Kingsport, TN 56
Depoy Christopher	Waugh's Hill, W of Austin, Concord Twp, Ross Co, OH 55
Depp William	Atkinson farm, nr Scaggs & Nobob Creeks, Barren Co, KY 45
Deppen Joseph	Priv Cem, nr Womelsdorf, PA 42
Deppen Peter	Hetzel's Church, Pine Grove Twp, PA 49
Depue Daniel	Milton Twp, Mahoning Co, OH 55
Depue Daniel	Priv fam Cem, Calno, Pahaquarry Twp, Warren Co, NJ 55
Derby Abner	¼ mi in woods, Summer St, Weymouth, MA 50
Derby Amos	Old South St Cem, Fitchburg, MA 39
Derby Eliab	Johnson farm, Westfall, Niles, NY 56
Derby Jonathan	Essex, NY 15
Derby Jonathan	Highland Cem, South Weymouth, MA 50
Derby Samuel	Cem on town common, Nelson, NH 35
Derby Simeon	Orford Cem, Orford, NH 37
Derby Thomas	Old Yard, Pine Hill, Hancock, NH 29
Derickson Peter	St James Cem, nr Marshallton, New Castle Co, DE 46
Dering Henry	Old Pres Cem, Morgantown, WV 40
Derr Carl	Old Cem, Freidensville, Lehigh Co, PA 40
Derr Jacob	Great Swamp, Trinity Ref Cem, Spinnertown, Lehigh Co, PA 40
Derrick Anthony	Priv Cem, Center Brunswick, Rensselaer Co, NY 41
Derrick Ephraim	Clarence, NY 33
Derrick Major	Mount Hope Cem, Dahlonega, Lumpkin Co, GA 25
Desch Adam	Lehigh Ch Cem, nr Alburtis, Lehigh Co, PA 40
Desch Jacob	Lehigh Ch Cem, nr Alburtis, Lehigh Co, PA 40
Descher Carl	Western Salisbury Old Cem, Lehigh Co, PA 40
Deschler David	Western Salisbury Old Cem, Lehigh Co, PA 40

Deschler Peter	Christ Union Ch Cem, Shoenersville, Lehigh Co, PA 40
Deschler Peter	Christ Union Ch, Schoenersville, Northampton Co, PA 22
Deshambs Louis	Orange Co, NC 56
Deshazer Henry	Green Johnson farm, Mackville Pike, Mercer Co, KY 52
Deshler Adam	Egypt, old Cem part, Lehigh Co, PA 40
Deshler Charles	Allentown Union & West End Cem, Lehigh Co, PA 40
Deshler Charles Col	Union Cem, Allentown, PA 16
Desillets Francois C	St Louis Cem #1, New Orleans, LA 77
Desilva Joseph	Gilboa Rural Cem, Gilboa, Schoharie Co, NY 74
Dessinger George	Ref Cem, Schafferstown, PA 67
Devalon Francis	Old Cem, Washington Courthouse, OH 56
Devendorf Henry	Battlefield Cem, Oriskany, NY 46
Devens Richard	Phipps St Cem, Boston, MA 47
Dever John	Nr Lucasville, Scioto Co, OH 55
Devereux John	Unitarian Yard, Marblehead, MA 56
Devinney Aaron	Myriah Ch Cem, Rd in Cornfield, Rutherford Co, NC 70
Devoe John	Atwater Cem, Homer, Cortland Co, NY 36
Devoe John	St John's Cem, Yonkers, NY 35
Devol Jonathan	Putnam Cem, nr Marietta, Washington Co, OH 55
Devon David	His farm, Monroe Twp, Perry Co, OH 55
Devore Nicholas	Fam Cem, Ripley, OH 15
Devose Nicholas	Union Twp, Brown Co, OH 56
Dew Arthur	Nr Lebanon, Wilson Co, TN 24
Dewald Johannes	Sumner Hill Ch, PA 49
Dewees Samuel	Manchester Cem, Carroll Co, MD 51
Dewett Barnett	Harmony Pres Cem, Warren Co, NJ 25
Dewey Barzalae	Old West St Cem, Rutland, VT 51
Dewey Daniel	Liberty Hill, Lebanon, CT 56
Dewey Daniel	Sheffield, MA 42
Dewey David	Mechanic St, Westfield, MA 56
Dewey David	North Manlius Center Cem, Onondaga Co, NY 51
Dewey Eliab	Mechanic St, Westfield, MA 56
Dewey Elijah	Pres Ch Yard, Owego, NY 34
Dewey Hugo	Mahawie Cem, Great Barrington, MA 28
Dewey Israel	Westfield, MA 56
Dewey John	Talcottville, NY 15
Dewey John	Trumbull, Lebanon, CT 56
Dewey Joseph	East Hill Rd Cem, Austerlitz, Columbia Co, NY 74
Dewey Josiah	Water St, Great Barrington, MA 56
Dewey Justin	Mahawie Cem, Great Barrington, MA 28
Dewey Martin	School St Cem, Lebanon, NH 27
Dewey Moses	Mechanic St, Westfield, MA 56
Dewey Oliver	Northampton, OH 45
Dewey Oliver	Northampton Cem, Summit Co, OH 15
Dewey Oliver	Northampton, OH 45
Dewey Russell	Mechanic St, Westfield, MA 56
Dewey Samuel	Cem, Allen Twp, sect 28, Hillsdale Co, MI 26
Dewey Samuel	South Allen Cem, Hillsdale Co, MI 30
Dewey Samuel	South Allen Cem, Hillsdale Co, MI 46
Dewey Samuel	South Allen Twp, Hillsdale Co, MI 56
Dewey Silas	Zions Hill Cem, Suffield, Hartford Co, CT 24
Dewey Simeon	Center Cem, Hanover, NH 27
Dewey Solomon	Whitesboro, NY 16
Dewey Stephen	Barnard, Sheffield, MA 56
Dewey William	Cem nr river, Hanover, NH 36
Dewing Hezekiah	Bungay Cem, Woodstock, CT 55
Dewing Timothy	Needham, MA 50
Dewitt Abraham	Lowther farm, Mount Marion, NY 15
Dewitt Charles	Blockhouse Cem, Berlin Twp, Delaware Co, OH 53
Dewitt John	Fam Cem, Dewitt, OH 42
Dewitt John Lucas Capt	Lowther farm, Mount Marion, NY 15

Dewitt Moses	New Clove Cem, Wantage Twp, Sussex Co, NJ 33
Dewitt Moses	Stowe Square, Lowville, NY 15
Dewitt Stephen	Second St Cem, Elmira, NY 33
Dewitt Thomas	Old Dutch Cem, Kingston, Ulster Co, NY 85
Dewitt Tjerck C	Old Dutch Cem, Kingston, Ulster Co, NY 85
Dewning James	Downing Cem, nr Magnolia, Stark Co, OH 45
Dewolf Benjamin	Old Cem, Johnstown, Harrison Twp, Licking Co, OH 55
Dewolfe Seth	Cheshire St Cem, Cheshire, CT 55
Dewolph Abda	West Andover Cem, Ashtabula Co, OH 55
Dexter Caleb	1st Parish Cem, Rochester, MA 58
Dexter Caleb	Salmon Hole Cem, Lisbon, NH 26
Dexter Constant	Rochester, 4 Corners nr Church, Rochester, MA 55
Dexter David	Barlow Cem, Mattapoisett, MA 58
Dexter David	Dover, VT 16
Dexter David Col	Old Village Cem, Claremont, NH 50
Dexter Elijah	1st Parish Cem, Rochester, MA 58
Dexter Elisha	Barlow Cem, Mattapoisett, MA 18
Dexter Elisha	Rochester Cem, Rochester, MA 56
Dexter Ephraim	Barlow Cem, Mattapoisett, MA 58
Dexter John	Barnstable, MA 55
Dexter John	Spring Hill Cem, Marlboro, MA 45
Dexter Joseph	Salmon Hole Cem, Lisbon, NH 60
Dexter William	Bell Rock Cem, Malden, MA 55
Deyarman Henry	Pres Ch Cem, Rocky Springs, PA 20
Deyarman Henry	Rocky Springs Pres Ch Cem, 6 mi fr Chambersburg, PA 19
Deyerle Peter	Fam Cem, western boundary of Roanoke Co, VA 73
Deyo Jonas	Delaware Co, OH 53
Deyo Simon	Kinderhook Cem, Columbia Co, NY 42
Deyoe James	Salisbury Cem, Crow Hill, Stillwater, NY 41
Deyoe Peter	Deyoe Grounds, 1 mi fr Valley Falls, Pittstown, NY 36
Deyoe Peter	Fam Cem plot, Saratoga, NY 41
Deyoe Peter Jr	School House Rd, Austerlitz, NY 71
Deyoe Richard	Priv Cem 4 mi W of Ghent Village, Rt 66, Columbia Co, NY 48
Dial Jeremiah	Crossroads Mtg Hs Cem, nr Bell Buckle, TN 78
Dial Martin	Fam Cem, Laurens Co, SC 56
Dial Martin	Fam Cem, Laurens Co, SC 70
Diamond John	Old Diamond Cem, Bond Co, IL 30
Diamond Thomas Smith	Albany rural Cem, Albany, NY 31
Diamond William	Old Cem, Peterborough, NH 29
Diamond William	Peterboro, NH 15
Dias Joseph	Causeway Cem, Tisbury, Martha's Vineyard, MA 46
Dibble Daniel	Torrington Cem, Torrington, CT 55
Dibble Ebenezer	Dunning St Cem, Malta, Saratoga Co, NY 77
Dibble Ebenezer Capt	Dunning St Cem, Malta, Saratoga Co, NY 41
Dibble George	Cornwall Cem, Cornwall, CT 22
Dibble Israel	Cornwall Cem, Cornwall, CT 15
Dibble John 2nd	Cornwall Cem, Cornwall, CT 22
Dibble Joseph	First Austerlitz Cem, S of Village, Columbia Co, NY 48
Dibble Moses Jr	Granby Center, Granby, CT 54
Dibble Sineus	North Guilford Cem, North Guilford, CT 55
Dibert John	Dilbert farm graveyard, Bedford Twp, Bedford Co, PA 80
Dibert Michael	Messiah Ch Cem, Bedford Co, PA 80
Dibert Michael Jr	Old Cem, Unionville, Neffs, Lehigh Co, PA 40
Dibrell Charles	Beulah Bapt Ch Cem, Mt Zion Rd, Union City, Obion Co, TN 74
Dick David	Fam Cem, White Plains, NY 35
Dick Henry	Ref Ch Cem, Germantown, Columbia Co, NY 41
Dick Herman	Snowberger farm, Roaring Spring, PA 52
Dick John	Ansel Cem, nr Somerset, KY 39
Dick Peter	Will's Cem, Mountain City, TN 29
Dick Samuel	Hamilton Co, OH 45
Dick Samuel M D	St John's Epis Cem, Salem, NJ 27

Dickens Tristam	Westerly, RI 15
Dickens Tristam	Westerly, RI 35
Dickens Tustum	Davis Bur Gr, Westerly, RI 48
Dickenson Consider	Deerfield, MA 55
Dickenson Daniel	Deerfield, MA 55
Dickenson Eliphalet	Deerfield, MA 55
Dickenson Francis	Cong Ch Cem, Worcester, NY 15
Dickenson John	Bapt Cem, Cape May Courthouse, NJ 29
Dickenson Thomas	Deerfield, MA 55
Dicker Gottrich	Sumner Hill Ch, PA 49
Dickerman Benjamin	North Cem, Dorchester, MA 46
Dickerman Griffith	Berger Bur Gr, Tillsylvania, VA 58
Dickerman Jonathan 1st	Mount Carmel Cem, Hamden, CT 31
Dickerman Peter	Pearl St Cem, Stoughton, MA 55
Dickerson Daniel	Rockaway, NJ 49
Dickerson Elijah	Salisbury Cem, Crow Hill, Stillwater, NY 41
Dickerson George	Rumley Twp, Harrison Co, OH 56
Dickerson John	Marling Cem, nr Hanover, Jefferson Co, IN 72
Dickerson Joseph	Fam Cem, nr Moneta, Bedford Co, VA 47
Dickerson Joseph	Old Cem, Rowley, MA 49
Dickerson Kinzer	Nr Danville, Vermilion Co, IL 40
Dickerson Peter	Pres Cem, Morristown, NJ 32
Dickerson Silas	Pres Cem, Morristown, NJ 32
Dickerson Walter	Fam bur gr, Lost Creek Twp, Vigo Co, IN 72
Dickey Adam	Nr Waits River, VT 56
Dickey David	Congruity Cem, Westmoreland Co, PA 56
Dickey Eleazer	Mt Solitude Cem, Monroe, Waldo Co, ME 76
Dickey Elias	[no cem named] 17
Dickey Elias	New Boston Cem, New Boston, NH 28
Dickey James	Antrim, NH 15
Dickey James	McFadden Graveyard, Clarendon, SC 62
Dickey James	Riverside Cem, Towanda, PA 53
Dickey James	State Hill Cem, 1 mi fr Mercersburg, PA 21
Dickey James	Sterling, MA 53
Dickey John	Old Bethany Ch Cem, Iredell Co, NC 51
Dickey Matthew	Forest Hill Cem, East Derry, NH 38
Dickey Moses	Bowman Cem, Elk Run Twp, Columbiana Co, OH 56
Dickey Robert	Stinson farm, Ross Co, OH 55
Dickey Robert	Village Cem, Chester, NH 33
Dickey Samuel	Elk Creek Cem, Madison Twp, Butler Co, OH 55
Dickey William	Fam Cem, Harrisburg, Fayette Co, IN 79
Dickey William	Friends Creek Cem, Argenta, Macon Co, IL 58
Dickinson Abraham	Dutch Ref Brick Ch Cem, Montgomery, Orange Co, NY 76
Dickinson Azariah	West Cem, Amherst, MA 16
Dickinson Benjamin	Hudson City Cem, Hudson, Columbia Co, NY 74
Dickinson Ebenezer	Old Hadley Cem, Hadley, MA 46
Dickinson Ebenezer	West Cem, Amherst, MA 16
Dickinson Eli	Granby, MA 55
Dickinson Elihu	Amherst, MA 15
Dickinson Elisha	West Cem, Amherst, MA 60
Dickinson Enos	South Amherst Cem, Amherst, MA 41
Dickinson Francis	East Worcester Cem, Worcester, Otsego Co, NY 74
Dickinson Griffith	Rt 685, 6 mi E of Gretna, Pittsylvania Co, VA 73
Dickinson Israel	Terrace Grove Cem, Pittsfield, MA 56
Dickinson Jesse	Fitch's Cem, Northumberland Co, PA 17
Dickinson Joel	North Cem, Hinsdale, NH 37
Dickinson John	Augusta Cem, Augusta, Bath Co, VA 59
Dickinson John	Friends Cem, Wilmington, New Castle Co, DE 36
Dickinson John	Old Hadley Cem, Hadley, MA 47
Dickinson John	West Cem, Amherst, MA 17
Dickinson John Lt	Adams, NY 15

Dickinson Jonothan	West Cem, Amherst, MA	60
Dickinson Joseph	Mount Caesar Cem, Swanzey, NH	35
Dickinson Moses	West Cem, Amherst, MA	41
Dickinson Nathan	West Cem, Amherst, MA	16
Dickinson Nathaniel	Beckley Cem, Berlin, CT	56
Dickinson Nathaniel	West Cem, Amherst, MA	41
Dickinson Nathaniel	West Cem, Amherst, MA	17
Dickinson Noah	West Cem, Amherst, MA	60
Dickinson Oliver	Milton, CT	17
Dickinson Reuben	Howland Cem, Conway, MA	53
Dickinson Reuben	Southeast Cem, Granville, Hampden Co, MA	63
Dickinson Simeon	Millington, East Haddam, CT	56
Dickinson Solomon	Upper Cincinnatus Cem, Cincinnatus, Cortland Co, NY	36
Dickinson Versel	Wyoming Cem, Wyoming, NY	33
Dickinson Versel	Wyoming Cem, Middlebury, Wyoming Co, NY	64
Dickinson Waitstill	Kingsville, Ashtabula Co, OH	18
Dickinson Waitstill	Kingsville, OH	15
Dickinson Waitstill A	West Cem, Granby, MA	58
Dickinson William	Fleming Hill Cem, Fleming, NY	41
Dickinson Zebulon	Lawrenceburg, IN	56
Dickman Isaac	Copps Hill Bur Gr, Boston, MA	45
Dickman William	[no cem named], MI	19
Dickson David	Priv Cem, nr Jonesboro, GA	32
Dickson David Capt	Field 5 mi fr Jonesboro, Clayton Co, GA	34
Dickson Henry	Dickenson Fam Cem, nr old courthouse, Russell Co, VA	63
Dickson James	Protestant Cem, Northeast, PA	56
Dickson John	Grand View Cem, Vigo Co, IN	25
Dickson Joseph	Rutherford Co, TN	24
Dickson Josiah	Now Walnut Grove Cem, Booneville, Cooper Co, MO	15
Dickson William	Old Swedes Pres Cem, Christiana, New Castle Co, DE	46
Didson Benjamin	Mayhew farm, Starks, Somerset Co, ME	70
Diedenderfer Gottfried	Trexlertown Cem, Trexlertown, Lehigh Co, PA	40
Diedenderfer Jacob	Trexlertown Cem, Trexlertown, Lehigh Co, PA	40
Diedenderfer John	Old Cem, Tenth & Linden St, Allentown, Lehigh Co, PA	40
Diederich Matheus	West Camp Cem, Ulster Co, NY	72
Diefenbach Peter	Jacob's Ch, Pine Grove Twp, PA	49
Diefenbaugh Jacob	Klopp Ch Cem, Hamlin, Lebanon Co, PA	83
Diefenderfer John	Allentown, PA	16
Diefenderfer John	Old Allentown Cem, Allentown, PA	17
Diefendorf Jacob	Herkimer Cem, Herkimer, NY	56
Diehl Frederick J	Pfoutz Marsh Creek Dunkard Cem, Adams Co, PA	72
Diehl Johannes	Howerter's Ch, Pitman, PA	49
Diehl Philip	Kager farm, nr Ellsworth, Mahoning Co, OH	56
Dienky Jacob	Heidelberg Ch Cem, Lehigh Co, PA	40
Dieter Adam	Zion's Stone Ch Cem, Kreidersville, Northampton Co, PA	40
Dieter John	Zion's Stone Ch Cem, Kreidersville, Northampton Co, PA	40
Dietrich John	Coleman's, Hubley Twp, PA	49
Diffendeffer David	St Stephen Ref Ch Cem, New Holland, PA	59
Diffenderfer David	Ref Ch Cem, New Holland, PA	56
Diffenderfer Jacob	Stephens Ref Ch Cem, New Holland, PA	56
Digges Dudley	Bluefield nr Williamsburg, VA	56
Diggins Oliver	Weathersfield Cem, Weathersfield, VT	46
Diggs Dudley	Monticello Cem, Glasgow, MO	34
Diggs Edward Col	Denbigh Ch, Warick Co, VA	38
Dike Adin	Cuyahoga Co, OH	46
Dike Anthony	Plymouth, MA	15
Dike Anthony	Sutton Center Cem, Sutton, MA	15
Dike Daniel	Sutton Center Cem, Sutton, MA	15
Dike James	Dike Yard, Thompson, Windham Co, CT	24
Dike Nicholas	Woodside Cem, Westminster, MA	53
Dike Thomas	Dike Yard, Thompson, Windham Co, CT	24

Abstract of Graves of Revolutionary Patriots

Dildine Abram	Yellow Frame Cem, Warren Co, NJ 38
Dilkes Aaron	Bethel Cem, Hurffville, Gloucester Co, NJ 49
Dilkes Andrew	Bethel Cem, Hurffville, NJ 45
Dilkes John	Bethel Cem, Hurffville, NJ 45
Dill —	Old Newton Cem, West Collingswood, NJ 51
Dill Boniet E	Oak Hill Cem, Youngstown, Mahoning, OH 55
Dill Daniel	St Paul's Ch Cem, Augusta, GA 16
Dill John	Wheeler Cem, Camillus, NY 56
Dill John T	Newton Union Sloan Cem, West Collingswood, NJ 50
Dill Mathew	Priv farm Cem, East Wheatfield Twp, Indiana Co, PA 56
Dill Robert	North St Cem, Auburn, NY 41
Dill Solomon	Dyer Cem, Canton, CT 55
Dill Thomas	Yellow Creek Pres Cem, Madison Twp, Columbiana Co, OH 57
Dillanay William	North Parish Bur Gr, Andover, MA 26
Dillard George	St Mark's Parish Cem, Culpeper, VA 56
Dillard James	Duncan Creek Pres Ch, Laurens, SC 56
Dillard John	Dillard Bapt Ch Cem, Dillard, GA 54
Dillard Mary Ramage	Duncan Creek Pres Ch, Laurens, SC 56
Dillaway John	Boston, MA 56
Dille Caleb	Knightstown Cem, Henry Co, IN 24
Dille Caleb	Old Graveyard, NE part of Knightstown, Henry Co, IN 72
Dille David	Euclid Park Cem vault, Euclid, Cuyahoga Co, OH 55
Dille Samuel	Fam Cem, Valley Pike, OH 56
Dillenback John	East Stone Cem, Arabia, NY 56
Dilley Ephraim Sr	Guernsey Co, OH 53
Dilley Samuel	Hubbard, OH 24
Dilliner August	Wolf's Cem, Dunkard Twp, Greene Co, PA 59
Dillinger Casper	Brumbaugh Cem, Martinsburg, PA 52
Dillinger Johannas	Zionsville Luth Cem, Shimersville, Lehigh Co, PA 40
Dillingham Edward	Village Cem, Sandwich, MA 56
Dillingham Jeremiah	Auburn, ME 18
Dillingham Jeremiah	Dillingham Hill, Auburn, ME 29
Dillingham John	Auburn, ME 18
Dillingham John	Dillingham Hill, Auburn, ME 29
Dillingham John	Village Cem, Sandwich, MA 56
Dillingham John Jr	Village Cem, Sandwich, MA 56
Dillingham William	Old Village Cem, Hartwick, Otsego Co, NY 71
Dillman Andrew	Sharon Cem, 2 mi E of Chatham, NE of Brooksville, KY 62
Dillon Jesse	Center Cem, Union Twp, Clinton Co, OH 56
Dillon Richard	East of Warrenton, Washington Parish, LA 68
Dilts Jacob	Tarason Corners, NJ 47
Dilts William	Pres Ch Cem, E side, Flemington, NJ 26
Dimick E	Town Cem, Madison, NH 29
Dimick John	Lyme Plain Cem, Lyme, NH 36
Dimick Moor	Tallmadge, Summit Co, OH 15
Dimick Moor	Talmadge, OH 45
Dimick Shubal	Lyme Plain Cem, Lyme, NH 36
Dimmick Benjamin	Fam Cem, Wilton, Saratoga Co, NY 77
Dimmick Edward	Uniondale, Susquehanna Co, PA 15
Dimmick Jabez	Old Town Cem, Falmouth, MA 58
Dimmick Joseph	Old Town Cem, Falmouth, MA 58
Dimmick Lot	Old Town Cem, Falmouth, MA 58
Dimmick Solomon	Town Hall Cem, Salisbury, CT 68
Dimmick Sylvanus	Lee Cem, Lee, MA 15
Dimmick Timothy	Nathan Hale Cem, South Coventry, Tolland Co, CT 55
Dimmock John	Old Town Cem, Falmouth, MA 58
Dimmuck Braddock	Old Town Cem, Falmouth, MA 58
Dimon Daniel	Old Bur Gr, Fairfield, CT 62
Dimon David	Old Bur Gr, Fairfield, CT 62
Dimon Jonathan	Old Epis Cem, Great Bend, PA 21
Dimond Isaac	Parade Cem, Lower Warner, Warner, NH 35

Dimond Jacob	Old Village Cem, Claremont, NH	50
Dingess Peter	Johnston Cem, Oakvale, Mercer Co, WV	42
Dingess Peter	Nr Oakvale, Mercer Co, WV	30
Dingie Samuel	Somers Todd Cem, NY	35
Dingley Abner	Fam Cem, North Duxbury, MA	50
Dingley Thomas	Winslow, MA	17
Dingley Thomas	Winslow Cem, Marshfield, MA	50
Dingman Andrew	Old Part, Delaware Cem, Dingmans Ferry, PA	51
Dingman Andrew Sr	Walpack, Sussex, NJ	56
Dingman Henry	West Hill Cem, Austerlitz, Columbia Co, NY	74
Dingman Rudolphus	West Ghent Ref Ch Cem, Hillsdale, Columbia Co, NY	74
Dings Adam	Cassayuna Lake Cem, Argyle, Washington Co, NY	56
Dings Adam	Fam Cem, Gallatin, NY	48
Dinkey Jacob Sr	Heidelberg Ch Cem, N Whitehall Twp, PA	56
Dinkey Jacob Sr	Heidleberg Ch Cem, N Whitehall Twp, York Co, PA	61
Dinkle Peter	Christ Luth Ch Cem, York, PA	51
Dinsmoor John Lt	Cem on Hill, Range Rd, Windham, NH	26
Dinsmoor Robert Dea	Cem on Hill, Range Rd, Windham, NH	26
Dinsmore Abel Capt	Conway Cem, Conway, MA	46
Dinsmore Elijah Capt	Intervale Cem, Intervale, NH	32
Dinsmore Elijah Capt	Intervale Cem, Intervale, NH	32
Dinsmore James	Buffalo Cem, Huntington, Washington Co, PA	68
Dinsmore James	New Providence, Morgan Co, AL	56
Dinsmore John	Cem on hill, Windham, NH	36
Dinsmore John	Dearborn pasture, Northfield, NH	31
Dinsmore John	Forest Hill Cem, East Derry, NH	38
Dinsmore John	Grasmere Cem, Goffstown, NH	28
Dinsmore Robert	Evergreen Cem, Bennington, NH	26
Dinsmore Robert	Long Meadow Cem, Chester, NH	33
Dinsmore Robert	Old Cem, above Corbetts Pond, nr Windham, NH	58
Dinsmore Samuel	Antrim, NH	15
Dinsmore Samuel	Old Yard, Northfield, NH	29
Dinsmore Samuel	Williams Cem, Northfield, NH	34
Dinsmore Thomas	North Anson, ME	15
Dinwiddie James	Caledonia Cem, Smith Rd 2 mi S of Henry, Henry Co, TN	77
Disant Benjamin	Fam priv bur gr, Montgomery Co, PA	59
Disbrow Asahel	West Settlement Cem, Ashland, Greene Co, NY	75
Dismukes Jessie	West Baldwin Co, GA	36
Disney George Capt	Old Town Cem, Newbury, MA	36
Dissinger George	Ref Cem, Schafferstown, PA	56
Dissinger John George	Luth Ref Ch Cem, Schaefferstown, Lebanon Co, PA	83
Dittman Johannes	Luth Ref Ch Cem, Schaefferstown, Lebanon Co, PA	83
Ditto Francis	Nr Tiffin, Seneca Co, OH	55
Ditzler Peter	Union Chapel Cem, Clark Co, IN	72
Divan John	Old Cem, nr Reading Center, Schuyler Co, NY	73
Diven William Capt	Van Cortlandville Cem, Peekskill, NY	41
Diver Daniel	[no cem named], OH	26
Divine James	Killed in Wyoming Massacre, Wyoming, PA	52
Divoll John 3rd	Old Pine Grove Cem, Leominster, MA	47
Divoll Oliver	Old Pine Grove Cem, Leominster, MA	47
Dix Benjamin	Maple Grove Cem, nr east town line, Barre, VT	20
Dix Benjamin	Nr Montpelier, VT	15
Dix Jacob 2nd	Old Cem, Wethersfield, CT	56
Dix Joseph	Pickett Cem, Portland, NY	15
Dixey John	Burial Hill, Plymouth, MA	56
Dixey Richard	Old Bur Hill, Marblehead, MA	30
Dixon Amos	Longview Cem, Stamford, CT	52
Dixon Andrew	Neffs Cem, Pultney Twp, Belmont Co, OH	55
Dixon George	Foster-Dixon, Foster, IN	
Dixon Jacob	Cross Road Cem, Gibsonia, PA	56
Dixon James	Cherry Valley Cem, Cherry Valley, Otsego Co, NY	74

Abstract of Graves of Revolutionary Patriots

Dixon James	Dixon-Wilson Cem, Mentz, NY 56
Dixon James	South Killingly Cem, South Killingly, CT 28
Dixon John	Fam Cem, nr Rising Sun, Ohio Co, IN 72
Dixon John	Fam Cem, 4 mi fr Rising Sun, Ohio Co, IN 25
Dixon Joseph	Grandview Cem, Terre Haute, Vigo Co, IN 72
Dixon Joseph	West Hill Cem, Sherburne, NY 16
Dixon Joshua	East Fairfield Cem, East Fairfield, OH 56
Dixon Marshall	Fam Cem, Tunkhannock, PA 67
Dixon Robert	East Ripley Cem, East Ripley, Chautauqua Co, NY 77
Dixon Thomas	Jamesville Cem, Jamesville, Onondaga Co, NY 78
Dixon William	Old Town Cem, Plainfield, CT 15
Dixon William	Red Oak Cem, nr Georgetown, Brown Co, OH 55
Dixon William	Waddells (now Spring Green) Cem, Lehmaster, PA 56
Dixon William Sgt	State Hill Cem, 1 mi fr Mercersburg, PA 21
Dixon Wynn	Fernwood Cem, Henderson, KY 73
Dizinger Nicholas	Dutch Ref Cem, Fayette, NY 15
Doak Benjamin	Lynn, MA 56
Doak Robert Col	Bethel Ch Cem, Augusta Co, VA 36
Doak Samuel Rev	Salem Ch Cem, TN 24
Doak Samuel Rev	Sales Ch Cem, TN 23
Doak William	Old Cem, Washington Co, PA 38
Doane Amos	Locust Grove Cem, Hampden, ME 52
Doane Elisha	Harwick Protestant Cem, Harwick, MA 45
Doane Elnathan	Cem, South East Twp, Putnam Co, NY 35
Doane Ephraim	Marston Cem, North Orrington, ME 31
Doane Ephraim	Marston Cem, East Orrington, ME 29
Doane Freeman	Cem off Airport Rd, Chatham, MA 56
Doane Hezekiah	Old Wellfleet, Duck Creek, Wellfleet, MA 55
Doane Isaiah	Cem nr railroad station, Eastham, MA 49
Doane John	Cem nr railroad station, Eastham, MA 49
Doane Jonathan	South Eastham Cem, Bridge St, Eastham, MA 55
Doane Nathaniel	Harwich Center Cem, Harwich, MA 55
Doane Oliver	Orrington Corner Cem, Orrington, ME 28
Doane Oliver	Orrington, ME 55
Doane Oliver	Orrington Corner Cem, Orrington, ME 29
Doane Samuel	Cem nr railroad station, Eastham, MA 49
Doane Samuel	South Eastham Cem, Bridge St, Eastham, MA 55
Doane Seth	Middle Haddam Landing Cem, Haddam, CT 46
Doane Timothy	Nr Cong Ch, Orleans, MA 49
Doane Zenas	Cem nr railroad station, Eastham, MA 49
Dobbin Lodowick	Wooden Cem, Northeast Geneva, NY 56
Dobbins David	Pleasant Hill Cem, Fulton, Fulton Co, KY 75
Dobbins Thomas	Delaneys Creek (Bapt Ch), Salem, IN 56
Dobbins William	Dobbins-Harrill Cem, Ellenboro, Cleveland Co, NC 80
Dobbins William	Old Ch Cem, Burlington, PA 16
Dobel John	Copps Hill Cem, Boston, MA 46
Dobel Joseph	[no cem named], MA 46
Dobson Henry Capt	Cecil Co, MD 19
Dockstader Frederick	Fonda, NY 15
Dockstader Marks	Fonda, NY 15
Dod Caleb Maj	Caldwell Pres Ch Cem, Caldwell, NJ 30
Dod Matthew	Pres Cem, Orange, NJ 32
Dodd Abel	Old Pres Cem, Caldwell, NJ 50
Dodd Amos	Dutch Ref Ch Cem, Belleville, NJ 27
Dodd Daniel	Old bur gr, Orange, NJ 26
Dodd David	Old bur gr, Orange, NJ 26
Dodd David	Ten Mile Ch Cem, 6 mi NE of Turkey, NC 58
Dodd James	Old bur gr, Orange, NJ 26
Dodd Jesse	Fam Cem, below Lynn, Winston Co, AL 51
Dodd John	Old Bur Gr, Holden, MA 15
Dodd John	Old bur gr, Orange, NJ 26

Dodd Joseph	Old bur gr, Orange, NJ 26
Dodd Matthias	Old bur gr, Orange, NJ 26
Dodd Timothy	Indian River Cem, Clinton, CT 55
Dodd Timothy	Zion Hill Cem, Hartford, CT 19
Dodd Uzal	Old bur gr, Orange, NJ 26
Doddridge Joseph	Cem nr Bedford, PA 45
Doddridge Phillip	Doddridge Chapel Cem, West End, Wayne Co, IN 62
Dodds Andrew	Fairview Cem, Scioto Twp, Delaware Co, OH 53
Dodds Thomas	White Oak Springs Cem, nr Connoquenessing, Butler Co, PA 76
Dodds William	Pres Ch, Centerville & Miamisburg Rd, Montgomery Co, OH 55
Dodge Abner	Rural Cem, Sedgwick, ME 54
Dodge Abraham	Highland, New Hill, Newburyport, MA 56
Dodge Abraham	Old Mill River, New Marlborough, MA 56
Dodge Ammi	Village Cem on hill, New Boston, NH 46
Dodge Amos	Kirkland Ave Cem, Clinton, Oneida Co, NY 79
Dodge Antipas	Grasmere Cem, Goffstown, NH 28
Dodge Barnabas	Opposite First Cong Ch, Hamilton, MA 56
Dodge Benjamin	New Boston Cem, New Boston, NH 28
Dodge Benjamin	New Boston, NH 16
Dodge Benjamin	Old Cem, McGraw, Cortland, Cortland Co, NY 36
Dodge Caleb	Beverly, MA 55
Dodge Caleb	Madison Co, OH 46
Dodge Daniel	West Auburn, MA 15
Dodge Daniel	Westfield Flats Cem, Roscoe, NY 17
Dodge David	Mentze Meth Epis Ch Cem, Montezuma, NY 56
Dodge Ebenezer	Woodland Cem, Keene, NH 32
Dodge Elijah	Village Cem, Winchester, NH 36
Dodge George	Middle Village Cem, East Springfield, NY 33
Dodge George	Town Ground, East Springfield, NY 15
Dodge George Jr	Hamilton, MA 52
Dodge Gideon	New Boston Cem, New Boston, NH 28
Dodge Gideon	New Boston, NH 16
Dodge Gideon Capt	Evergreen Cem, Bennington, NH 26
Dodge Henry	New Hackensack Ref Ch Cem, New Hackensack, NY 70
Dodge Isreal	Old Yard, Wareham, MA 49
Dodge Jacob	Dodge Row, Beverly, MA 28
Dodge Jacob	North Beverly Cem, back of church, Beverly, MA 46
Dodge Jacob Sr	Dodge's Row Cem, Dodge St, Beverly, MA 46
Dodge Jeremiah	Dodgeville Cem, New Lyme, Ashtabula Co, OH 55
Dodge Job	Old Center Cem, Jaffrey, NH 37
Dodge Joel	Evans Mills Cem, Leray, Jefferson Co, NY 42
Dodge John	Cem on the hill, Monterey, MA 41
Dodge John	Old Mill River, New Marlborough, MA 56
Dodge John	Randolph Co, IL 48
Dodge John	Robinson Cem, Clarendon, Orleans Co, NY 83
Dodge John Capt	Dodge Row, Beverly, MA 28
Dodge John Thorne	Dodge's Row, North Beverly, MA 54
Dodge Jonathan	North Beverly, Beverly, MA 56
Dodge Jonathan	Opposite First Cong Ch, Hamilton, MA 56
Dodge Luke	Old Cem, Hamilton, MA 56
Dodge Mial	Old Cem, Hamilton, MA 56
Dodge Nathaniel	Mound Cem, Marietta, Washington Co, OH 55
Dodge Nathaniel Brown	Maplewood Cem, Barre, VT 48
Dodge Nehemiah	Old Essex Cem, Essex, MA 48
Dodge Noah	Buell Cem, nr Canajoharie, NY 35
Dodge Oliver	Schantz Cem, 2 mi above Lowell, OH 56
Dodge Oliver Sr	Terrytown Cem, Terry Twp, PA 53
Dodge Paul	Old Cem, Newcastle, MA 50
Dodge Phineas	Rowley Cem, Essex, MA 48
Dodge Phinetas	Daws, NY 15
Dodge Richard	Colonial Cem, Johnson, NY 15

Abstract of Graves of Revolutionary Patriots

Dodge Richard	Dodge's Row, North Beverly, MA 54
Dodge Robert	Opposite First Cong Ch, Hamilton, MA 56
Dodge Seth	Fox Cem, West Dryden, NY 32
Dodge Shadrack	Edgewood Cem, Ashtabula, Ashtabula Co, OH 55
Dodge Simon	New Boston, NH 16
Dodge Simon	New Boston Cem, New Boston, NH 28
Dodge Solomon	Old Topsfield Pine Grove Cem, Hanover Center, MA 55
Dodge Solomon	Tinkham Cem, nr Four Corners, VT 20
Dodge Thomas	Beverly Cem, Beverly, MA 56
Dodge Thomas	Highland-New Hill, Newburyport, MA 56
Dodge Thomas	Maplewood Cem, Barre, VT 48
Dodge William	Beverly, MA 55
Dodge William	Old Cem, Hamilton, MA 56
Dodge William Lt	Bly Hill Cem, Newbury, NH 41
Dodson Charles	Cook farm nr Trammel, Allen Co, KY 57
Dodson John	Cem, Harveyville, PA 52
Dodson John	Finnytown Cem, Hamilton Co, OH 41
Dodson Thomas	Cem, Harveyville, PA 52
Dodson Tom	Fam Cem, East Freedom, PA 52
Dodson William	Three Forks Cem, Alexander Co, NC 49
Doe Andrew	Old Oxford Cem, Warren Co, NJ 38
Doe Joseph	Old Cem, Rockingham Junction, Newmarket, NH 35
Doe Nathaniel Jr	Cem, Vassalboro, ME 45
Doebler Abraham	Mt Lebanon Cem, Lebanon, PA 21
Doebler Abraham	Mt Lebanon Cem, Lebanon Co, PA 83
Doebler Heinrich A	Mt Lebanon Cem, Lebanon Co, PA 83
Dogan Henry	Stonewall Mem Cem, Manassas, Prince William Co, VA 80
Dogan Jeremiah	Mount Carmel Cem, Decatur Co, IN 25
Dogan Jeremiah J	Mt Pleasant Cem, Decatur Co, IN 72
Doggett Isaac	Village Cem, Dedham, MA 56
Doggett Noah	Old Granary Bur Gr, Boston, MA 56
Doggett Samuel	Village Cem, Dedham, MA 56
Doherty George Col	Shady Grove Cem, Jefferson Co, TN 24
Doherty George Col	Shady Grove Cem, TN 23
Dohorty John	Hopewell Pres Ch Cem, Mecklenburg Co, NC 49
Dohrman Arnold Henry	Union Cem, Steubenville, OH 25
Dolbier Benjamin	Freeman Ridge Cem, Freeman, Franklin Co, ME 83
Dolbier Benjamin	Freeman Ridge Cem, Freeman, ME 30
Dolbier Benjamin	Freeman Ridge, ME 15
Dole Amos	Marston Cem, East Orrington, ME 28
Dole Amos	Marston Cem, East Orrington, ME 29
Dole Belcher	Salisbury Plains Bur Gr, Salisbury, MA 46
Dole Isaiah	Old Cem, South Hampton, NH 30
Dole John	New London Cem, New London, NH 37
Dole Parker Sr	Shelburne Cem, Shelburne, MA 47
Dole Samuel	Town Yard, Grafton, NH 36
Doliber Peter	Old Bur Hill, Marblehead, MA 30
Dollar Reuben	Nr Meridian, MS 44
Dollbier Benjamin	Kingfield, ME 22
Dollinger John	St Peter's Ch, Pine Grove, PA 49
Dolliver Joseph	Cem on Rowley farm, Laurens, Otsego Co, NY 71
Dolliver Joseph Jr	Priv Cem, Laurens, NY 31
Dolliver Peter	Granary Cem, Boston, MA 46
Dolloff Phineas	Town Cem, New Hampton, NH 29
Dolloff Richard	Rumford Center Cem, ME 52
Dolloff Thomas	Marston Cem, Meredith, NH 28
Dolph Moses	Dunmore Cem, Scranton, PA 15
Dolsen Henry Van	Oak Grove Cem, 6 mi E of La Porte, IN 24
Domblaser Paul	Old Cem, Hecktown, Northampton Co, PA 21
Donaldson Altamount	Fenton, MI 15
Donaldson Charles	Fam Cem, Cheat Neck, WV 41

Donaldson Hugh Dr	Old Town Cem, Falmouth, MA 46
Donaldson John	Nr Nashville, TN 24
Donaldson John Jr	Davidson, TN 56
Donaldson Lothario	Raisin Twp Cem, Lenawee Co, MI 25
Donaldson Patrick	Fam Cem, Winchester, KY 66
Donaldson Richard	Raccon Pres Ch Cem, Robinson Twp, Washington Co, PA 72
Donaldson William	Charles Baber, Pottsville, PA 49
Donaldson William	Jarnagin Cem, Morristown, Hamblen Co, TN 71
Donally Andrew	Nr Charleston, Kanawha Co, WV 56
Donalson John	Barren River, KY 56
Donat Christian	St Thomas P E Cem, Whitemarsh, Montgomery Co, PA 63
Done Daniel	Monaghan Cem, Locke, Cayuga Co, NY 69
Donley James	Calvary Cem, Washington Twp, OH 56
Donnell Andrew	Buffalo Pres Ch Cem, Guilford Co, NC 49
Donnell George	Buffalo Pres Ch Cem, Guilford Co, NC 49
Donnell John	Buffalo Pres Ch Cem, Guilford Co, NC 49
Donnell Joseph	Buffalo Pres Ch Cem, Guilford Co, NC 59
Donnell Nathaniel	Philadelphia, PA 32
Donnell Robert	Buffalo Pres Ch Cem, Guilford Co, NC 49
Donnell Thomas	Kingston Cem, Decatur, IL 72
Donnelly Henry	Brighton Cem, South Rochester, NY 34
Donnelly Peter	Old Town Bur Gr, Newburgh, Orange Co, NY 69
Donnelly Thomas	Jamesville Cem, Onondaga Co, NY 70
Donnelly William	Old Cem, Mountain City, TN 29
Donovan Richard	Louden Park, Baltimore, MD 52
Donover Christopher Sr	Old Founders Cem, Cambridge, OH 53
D'onset Prince	Leeds, ME 18
Dood Abel	Millersburg, MO 23
Dooley Samuel	Mt Run Cem, Boone Co, IN 72
Doolittle Ambrose	Cheshire, CT 17
Doolittle Ambrose	Cong Cem, Cheshire, New Haven Co, CT 24
Doolittle Benjamin	Hillside Cem, Cheshire, CT 55
Doolittle Daniel	Old Cem, North Haven, CT 15
Doolittle David	Doolittle Hill Cem, Mehoopany, Wyoming Co, PA 67
Doolittle Ezra	Hillside Cem, Cheshire, CT 55
Doolittle George	Whitesboro, NY 16
Doolittle Obed	Woodtick, Wolcott, CT 56
Doolittle Uri	St Paul's Cem, Paris Hill, Oneida Co, NY 56
Doran Alexander	Nr Boone's Trail, Shouns, TN 27
Doran Alexander	[no cem named], TN 24
Dorcas John	Goodwill Cem, Montgomery, Orange Co, NY 78
Dorchester Alexander	Muscalonge Cem, Hounsfield, Jefferson Co, NY 41
Dorchester Reuben	Corfu, NY 35
Dorchester Reuben	Old Cem, Marcellus, Onondaga Co, NY 78
Doremus David	Saddle River Cem, Saddle River, NJ 45
Doremus Thomas	Dutch Ref Ch Cem, Belleville, NJ 27
Doremus Thomas	Montville, NJ 35
Dorene Jacob	Johnson's Crossroad, Monroe Co, WV 42
Dorey James	Lakeside School grounds, South Spring Valley, NY 70
Dorham Arnold Henry	Union Cem, Steubenville, OH 56
Dorman Amos	Protestant Cem, Ellington, CT 47
Dorman John	Lakeview Cem, Milo, Yates Co, NY 69
Dorman Timothy	East Boxford, MA 31
Dorn Jeremiah	Johnstown Cem, Johnstown, NY 63
Dornbach John	Frieden's, New Ringold, PA 49
Dornblaser Paul	Dryland Union Ch Cem, Hecktown, Northampton Co, PA 40
Dornrach William	Union Twp, PA 49
Dorr Beniah	Town Cem, Milton Hills, NH 27
Dorr Edward	Salisbury Point Cem, Salisbury, MA 46
Dorr Edward	White Mills Cem nr Old Meth Ch, Chatham, Columbia Co, NY 48
Dorr Hon Joseph Jr	Brookfield Cem, Brookfield, MA 46

Dorr Jonathan	Fam farm, Plummer's Ridge, Milton, NH 27
Dorr Matthew Sr	The Plains, Pioneer Cem, Athens Co, OH 52
Dorr Moses Capt	North Cem, Westmoreland, NH 36
Dorr Samuel	Lee Cem, Lee, MA 15
Dorrance George	Killed in Wyoming Massacre, Wyoming, PA 52
Dorrance George	Soule Cem, Sennet, Cayuga Co, NY 57
Dorrington John	Copps Hill Cem, Boston, MA 46
Dorsett Francis	Unknown spot, 1 mi E of Love's Creek Ch, Chatham Co, NC 49
Dorsett Joseph	Fam bur gr, Hazlet, NJ 50
Dorsey Charles	Fam Cem, Fromme farm, Jackson Twp, Champaign Co, OH 55
Dorsey Daniel	Lyons, NY 56
Dorsey John Hammond Jr	Oxford, Butler Co, OH 55
Dorsey John Worthington	St John's Cem, Howard Co, MD 55
Doten Ephraim	Bean Yard, Center Harbor, NH 29
Doten Ephriam	Old Burial Cem, Plympton, MA 57
Doten Jabez	Burial Hill, Plymouth, MA 56
Doten James	Burial Hill, Plymouth, MA 56
Doten Thomas	Burial Hill, Plymouth, MA 56
Doten William	Burial Hill, Plymouth, MA 56
Dotson Richard	Lower Arnolds Creek Cem, Doddridge Co, WV 58
Dotterer Michael	Beitolets Mtg Hs, nr Swamp, Montgomery Co, PA 56
Dotterer Michael	Bertolit's Mennonite Cem, Montgomery Co, PA 59
Dotterer Phillip	Saucon Mennonite Cem, Coopersburg, Lehigh Co, PA 40
Doty Barnabas Capt	First Town Cem, Grove farm, Center Village, VT 20
Doty Barnabee Capt	Nr Montpelier, VT 15
Doty Benjamin	Durham, NY 56
Doty Benjamin	Green River Cem, Hillsdale, Columbia Co, NY 74
Doty Benjamin	Maple Grove Cem, Candor, NY 35
Doty Danforth	Honeyville Cem, Adams Center, Jefferson Co, NY 41
Doty Daniel	Pres Ch Cem, Basking Ridge, NJ 47
Doty David	Boland Cem, Sharon, Litchfield Co, CT 66
Doty Dorus	North St Cem, Auburn, NY 41
Doty Ezra	Glenwood Cem, Lockport, NY 33
Doty Isaac	Cushing Cem, Woodstock, VT 65
Doty John	Alton, Bennington Twp, Shiawassee Co, MI 56
Doty John	Cushing Cem, Woodstock, Windsor Co, VT 75
Doty John Capt	First Town Cem, Grove farm, Center Village, VT 20
Doty John Capt	Nr Montpelier, VT 15
Doty Joseph	New Concord Cem, Chatham, Columbia Co, NY 74
Doty Peter	Chester Bapt Ch, Chester, OH 56
Doty Reuben	Flint Hill Cem, Pike, Wyoming Co, NY 64
Doubleday Benjamin	Copps Hill Cem, Boston, MA 46
Doubleday Seth	Drake farm, nr Cooperstown, Otsego Co, NY 73
Doucet Michael	St Martin of Tours Cath Ch Cem, St Martinville, LA 74
Doucet Pierre	Cath Cem, Opelousas, LA 63
Doud Peleg	Doud Hill Cem, PA 52
Doud Richard II	East Cem, Middletown, CT 52
Doudel Jacob	Christ Luth Ch Cem, York, PA 15
Dougan John	Earlham Cem, Wayne Co, IN 24
Dougan John	Earlham Cem, Wayne Co, IN 72
Dougherty Charles	Church Hill, Framingham, MA 56
Dougherty Thomas	Cap Civil, Ashe Co, NC 71
Dougherty William	Bank of White River nr Yorktown, Delaware Co, IN 72
Doughty Abner	Fam bur gr, nr Absecon, NJ 23
Doughty Absalom	Absecon Meth Epis Cem, Absecon, NJ 23
Doughty Christopher	Pittsburgh, Allegheny Co, PA 15
Doughty John	Pres Cem, Morristown, NJ 32
Doughty Stephen	Fam farm, Topsham, ME 25
Doughty Stephen	Fam farm, Topsham, ME 26
Doughty William	Pres Ch Cem, Basking Ridge, NJ 47
Douglas –	Massacred nr mouth of Lechry Creek, Dearborn Co, IN 24

Douglas Anthony	Berry Cem, nr Manteo, Dare Co, NC	49
Douglas Asa Jr	Canaan Center Cem, Columbia Co, NY	42
Douglas Asa Sr	Stephenson, NY	56
Douglas David	Ninth St Cem, Logansport, IN	24
Douglas David	Old Cem, nr Logansport, Cass Co, IN	72
Douglas Edward	Station Camp Creek, Sumner Co, TN	56
Douglas James	Alkire Cem, nr Mt Sterling, Pickaway Co, OH	55
Douglas James	Fayette, MO	32
Douglas James	Nr Coopers Fort, New Hope, MO	15
Douglas James	St Michael's Ch Cem, Trenton, NJ	28
Douglas John	Gloria Dei (Old Swedes) Ch, Philadelphia, PA	53
Douglas John	Nr Abingdon, VA	30
Douglas John	Nr Abingdon, VA	29
Douglas John	Old Swedes Ch Cem, Philadelphia, PA	51
Douglas John	Round Hill Cem, Monongahela, Washington Co, PA	75
Douglas John Gen	Old Town Cem, Plainfield, CT	15
Douglas John Jr	Fam Cem, Lakeville, MA	62
Douglas Levi	Twp Cem, Wyoming Co, WV	71
Douglass Barnard	North Conway, NH	56
Douglass Daniel Capt	West Rutland Cem, Rutland, VT	23
Douglass David	Pres Cem, Morristown, NJ	32
Douglass Edward	Fam Cem, Gallatin, TN	53
Douglass George	Old Waxhaw Cem, NC	17
Douglass James	Rain's farm, Howard Co, MO	15
Douglass Samuel	Cem nr Groveside, Rensselaer Co, NY	33
Douglass William	Greenfield Cem, Highland Co, OH	55
Douthett Hezekiah	Lebanon Cem, Mifflin Twp, Allegheny Co, PA	71
Dow Amos	Old Cem, Salem Center, NH	28
Dow Benjamin	Old Yard, Kensington, NH	47
Dow Benjamin Brown	Old Yard, Kensington, NH	47
Dow Daniel	College Springs, IA	42
Dow Ebenezer	Small yard, his farm, Meredith, NH	29
Dow Isaac	Fam bur gr, Rye, NH	39
Dow Jeremiah Capt	Old Cem, Salem Center, NH	28
Dow Jesse	Town Cem, Orange, NH	37
Dow John	Durham, ME	18
Dow John	Ring Swamp Cem, Hampton, NH	31
Dow John	River Road or Oil Mills Cem, Weare, NH	34
Dow John	Town Cem, Atkinson, NH	28
Dow Jonathan	Gordon Hill Cem, North Hampton, NH	55
Dow Jonathan	Old Yard, Kensington, NH	47
Dow Joseph	Brown Cem, Chichester, NH	29
Dow Joseph	Ring Swamp Cem, Hampton, NH	31
Dow Joseph Maj	Hampton Falls Cem, W of hill, Hampton, NH	26
Dow Josiah	Canterbury Center Cem, Canterbury, NH	29
Dow Josiah	Old Yard, Kensington, NH	47
Dow Lemuel	Center Cem, Hanover, NH	27
Dow Nathan	Lakeview Cem, Richfield, Otsego Co, NY	72
Dow Nathan	Old Yard, Kensington, NH	47
Dow Nathaniel	Old Yard, Kensington, NH	47
Dow Reuben Capt	Churchyard, Hollis, NH	39
Dow Salmon	Center Cem, Hanover, NH	27
Dow Samuel	Ring Swamp Cem, Hampton, NH	31
Dow Stephen	Churchyard, Hollis, NH	39
Dow Thomas	Arcade Village Cem, Arcade, Wyoming Co, NY	64
Dow Thomas	Old Atkinson, NH	51
Dow Thomas	Village Cem, Arcade, Wyoming Co, NY	19
Dow Zebulon	Lawrence Cem, North Epping, NH	35
Dowd Conner	Oak Grove Cem, Zaleski, Vinton Co, OH	55
Dowd Nathaniel	West Otis Cem, Otis, MA	56
Dowd Samuel	Strong Cem, Middlebury Twp, Knox Co, OH	56

Abstract of Graves of Revolutionary Patriots 265

Dowd Stephen	Bur Place, Town Hill Cem, New Hartford, CT 33
Dowden Clementius	Elmwood, Peoria, IL 56
Dowell George	Moore Cem, nr Elliottsville, Monroe Co, IN 72
Dower Samuel	Westfield Cem, Westfield, NJ 24
Dowers Conrad	Pleasant Hill Cem, nr Cross Plains, Ripley Co, IN 74
Dowers Jacob	Pleasant Hill Cem, nr Cross Plains, Ripley Co, IN 74
Dowey Robert	Fam Cem, Hwy 87, 9 mi E of Elizabethtown, Bladen Co, NC 75
Dowlar George	Danby Cem, NY 15
Dowling David	Old Neshaminy Pres Cem, Hartsville, Bucks Co, PA 65
Dowling James	Fam Cem, Darlington Co, SC 70
Dowling John	Fam Cem, Darlington Co, SC 70
Dowling Robert	Fam Cem, Darlington Co, SC 70
Dowling William	Nr Bamberg, SC 70
Down David	Greenfield Hill Cem, Fairfield, CT 62
Down Joseph	Laurel Hill Cem, Fitchburg, MA 55
Downer Eliphalet	Walnut Street Cem, Brookline, MA 56
Downer John	Towslee, Pownal, VT 56
Downer Joseph	School St Cem, Lebanon, NH 27
Downer Samuel	Westfield Pres Cem, Westfield, NJ 32
Downer Samuel Sr	Pres Ch Cem, Westfield, NJ 76
Downer Zaccheus	School St Cem, Lebanon, NH 27
Downer Zacheus	Utica, NY 16
Downey William Aston	Old Union Cem, Bowling Green, Warren Co, KY 72
Downing Daniel	Hogeboom farm, Hillsdale, Columbia Co, NY 42
Downing Frances	Home place, 3 mi fr town, W side of Lexington Pike, KY 20
Downing George	Killed in Wyoming Massacre, Wyoming, PA 52
Downing Hezekiah	[no cem named], CT 19
Downing James	Betw Waynesburg & Magnolia, Stark Co, OH 54
Downing John	Auburn, ME 18
Downing John	Bowers-Templeton Cem, nr Mt Pulaski, Logan Co, IL 78
Downing John	North Auburn, ME 29
Downing John	Raymertown Cem, Pittstown, Rensselaer Co, NY 37
Downing Michael	Fam Cem, Mt Sidney, Grassy Fork Twp, Jackson Co, IN 64
Downing Palfrey	South Parish Bur Gr, Andover, MA 26
Downing Samuel	Edenburgh Cem, Edenburgh, NY 70
Downing Stephen	Woodland Cem, Monroe, Monroe Co, MI 26
Downing Stephen	Woodland Cem, Monroe, Monroe Co, MI 27
Downing William	New Petersburg Cem, Highland Co, OH 55
Downs David	Sharon Cem, Sharon, Litchfield Co, CT 66
Downs Henry Jr	Providence, NC 56
Downs John	Cem, Milford, CT 56
Downs John Sr	Hopetown Cem, Green Twp, Ross Co, OH 55
Downs Jonathan	Fam Cem, Hwy 76, Laurens, Laurens Co, SC 77
Downs Noah	Wright Plot Cem, Monroe Co, NY 33
Dows Eleazer	Charlton, NY 54
Dowse Eleazer	Sherborn No 2, Sherborn, MA 56
Dowse John	Eustis St, Boston, MA 56
Dowse Joseph	Plain Cem, Sherborn, MA 48
Dowse Joseph	Plain Cem, Sherborn, MA 46
Dowse Joseph	Sherborn Cem, Sherborn, MA 45
Doxsee Thomas	Levers Cem, nr Brookfield, Stark Co, OH 55
Doying Daniel	Shipton Cem, Shipton, Quebec, Can 46
Doyle Barnabas	Catholic Cem, Doylesburg, PA 56
Doyle John	Randolph Co, IL 48
D'Oyley –	St Michael's Ch Cem, Charleston, SC 51
Drake Abraham	His farm, Meredith Hill, Meredith, NH 29
Drake Abraham	Niles, OH 24
Drake Abraham Col	Town Cem, North Hampton, NH 33
Drake Abraham Jr	North Hampton, NH 50
Drake Abraham Lt Col	Old Cem, Rye, NH 46
Drake Albrittain	Fam Cem, 10 mi S of Greenville, Muhlenberg Co, KY 59

Drake Andrew	Scotch Plains Bapt Ch Cem, Scotch Plains, NJ	55
Drake Archippus	Dry Pond Cem, Stoughton, MA	55
Drake Augustine	Windsor, CT	15
Drake Benjamin	North Monroeville, OH	15
Drake Benjamin	Van Cortlandville Cem, Peekskill, NY	41
Drake Cornelius	West Webster, Monroe Co, NY	34
Drake Cornet Abraham	Town Cem, North Hampton, NH	33
Drake Daniel	Pearl St Cem, Stoughton, MA	55
Drake Daniel Capt	Razor Hill Cem, Grafton, NH	35
Drake Elias	Riverside Cem, Union, Broome Co, NY	38
Drake Elihu	Palisado Cem, Windsor, CT	55
Drake Elijah	Owasco Rural Cem, Owasco, NY	56
Drake Elijah	Pearl St Cem, Stoughton, MA	55
Drake Elijah	Royal Oak Cem, MI	33
Drake Elijah	Royal Oak, MI	15
Drake Elisha	Royal Oak Cem, Royal Oak, MI	29
Drake Enoch	Hopewell, NJ	32
Drake Ensign Joshua	Van Cortlandville Cem, Peekskill, NY	41
Drake Ephraim	Middlesex Hillside Cem, Middlesex, NJ	24
Drake Ephraim	Samptown Cem, South Plainfield, Middlesex Co, NJ	80
Drake Francis	New Market Bapt Ch Cem, New Market, NJ	76
Drake Francis	Putnam Settlement, Bethany, Genesee Co, NY	65
Drake Garradus L	Oaklawn Cem, Sag Harbor, NY	56
Drake George	Stelton Bapt Ch Cem, Edison, NJ	76
Drake George	Stelton Bapt Ch Cem, Edison, NJ	75
Drake Gilbert Lt Col	Van Cortlandville Cem, Peekskill, NY	41
Drake Hezekiah	Boston, MA	53
Drake Isaac	Fam Cem, Perrin Rd, Silbey, Jackson Co, MO	76
Drake Isaac	Nr Buckner, MO	15
Drake Isaac	Spring Grove Cem, Cincinnati, Hamilton Co, OH	76
Drake James	County line, Reading Center, Steuben Co, NY	56
Drake James	Fam Cem, 10 mi S of Greenville, Muhlenberg Co, KY	59
Drake James	Lake Wesauking Cem, Wysox Twp, PA	53
Drake James	Old St John's Ch Cem, Richmond, VA	56
Drake James Maj	Floral Park Cem, Pittsfield, NH	28
Drake Jasper Capt	Van Cortlandville Cem, Peekskill, NY	41
Drake Jeremiah	Van Cortlandville Cem, Peekskill, NY	41
Drake John	Dry Pond Cem, Stoughton, MA	55
Drake John	North Easton Cem, Elm St, Easton, MA	55
Drake John	Old Newton Cem, Newton, Sussex Co, NJ	79
Drake John	Stelton Bapt Ch Cem, Edison, NJ	75
Drake John Jr	Dry Pond Cem, Stoughton, MA	55
Drake Jonathan	Rye Center Cem, Rye, NH	29
Drake Joseph	Middlesex Hillside Cem, Middlesex, NJ	24
Drake Joseph	Sampton Cem, South Plainfield, NJ	75
Drake Joseph	Van Cortlandville Cem, Peekskill, NY	41
Drake Joseph	Washington St Cem, Easton, MA	47
Drake Lemuel	Palisado Cem, Windsor, CT	55
Drake Lemuel	Windsor, CT	15
Drake Mills	Clam River Cem, Sandisfield, MA	56
Drake Nathan	Fam Cem, West Stoughton, MA	55
Drake Nathan	West Stoughton Cem, Stoughton, MA	31
Drake Nathan Jr	West Stoughton Cem, Stoughton, MA	31
Drake Noah	Cem, Newfield, CT	56
Drake Oliver	Leeds, ME	56
Drake Ovid	Mercer Plot, Canaan, Columbia Co, NY	79
Drake Perez	Draper Hill Cem, Westford, Otsego Co, NY	74
Drake Phineas	Zions Hill Cem, Suffield, Hartford Co, CT	24
Drake Richard	Cem, Milford, CT	56
Drake Samuel	Ring Swamp Cem, Hampton, NH	31
Drake Samuel	Samptown Cem, South Plainfield, Middlesex Co, NJ	79

Drake Samuel	Van Vliet farm, Stroud Twp, Monroe Co, PA 55
Drake Samuel Capt	Van Cortlandville Cem, Peekskill, NY 41
Drake Samuel Col	Northville Cem, Genoa, NY 41
Drake Simeon	Samptown Cem, South Plainfield, Middlesex Co, NJ 79
Drake Theodore	Pearl St Cem, Stoughton, MA 55
Drake Thomas	Bapt Ch Cem, Hopewell, NJ 51
Drake Thomas	Furnace Village Cem, South St, Easton, MA 47
Drake Thomas	Loudoun Cem, Loudoun Co, VA 61
Drake Thomas	North Easton Cem, Elm St, Easton, MA 55
Drake Thomas	Old School Bapt Churchyard, Hopewell, NJ 50
Drake Thomas Carlton	Deep Creek Ch, Emanuel Co, GA 68
Drake William	Dry Pond Cem, Stoughton, MA 55
Drake William	Ronemous Cem, Shepherdstown, WV 24
Drake William	Van Cortlandville Cem, Peekskill, NY 41
Drake William Col	Ronemous Cem, Duffields, Jefferson Co, WV 27
Drane James	Fam Cem, Prince Georges Co, MD 59
Drane James Jr	Zion Luth Cem, Accident, Garrett Co, MD 67
Drane William	On his plantation nr Dearing, GA 52
Draper Abijah	Village Cem, Dedham, MA 56
Draper David	Prospect Hill Cem, Uxbridge, MA 57
Draper Ichabod	West Cem, Amherst, MA 41
Draper James	Old Cem, Spencer, MA 56
Draper John	Dover Cem, Dover, MA 45
Draper John	Old Cem, Spencer, MA 54
Draper Johnathan	Hudson, Summit Co, OH 15
Draper Jonathan	Chapel St Cem, Hudson Village, Summit Co, OH 77
Draper Jonathan	Old Hudson Cem, Western Reserve campus, Summit Co, OH 53
Draper Jonathan	Old Hudson, OH 45
Draper Jonathan	South Cem, Bellingham, MA 55
Draper Joshua	Draper Hill Cem, Westford, Otsego Co, NY 75
Draper Nathan	Union Cem, Niles, OH 56
Draper Nathaniel	Old Village Cem, Claremont, NH 50
Draper Paul	Center St Cem, West Roxbury, MA 46
Draper Stephen	South Attleboro, MA 15
Dray Edward	Casterline Cem, S of Cortland, Trumbull Co, OH 55
Dreher George	Dansbury Cem, Lower Main St, Stroudsburg, Monroe Co, PA 68
Dreher Mathias	Zions Red Ch, Orwigsburg, PA 49
Dreher Peter	Zions Red Ch, Orwigsburg, PA 49
Dreibellis Martin	Union Cem, Schuylkill Haven, PA 49
Dreisbach Adam	Zion's Stone Ch Cem, Kreidersville, Northampton Co, PA 40
Dreisbach George	Zion's Stone Ch Cem, Kreidersville, Northampton Co, PA 40
Dreisbach Jacob	Zion's Stone Ch Cem, Kreidersville, Northampton Co, PA 40
Dreisbach Jacob Ens	Zion's Stone Ch, nr Kreidersville, PA 15
Dreisbach John J Jr	Zion's Stone Ch Cem, Kreidersville, Northampton Co, PA 40
Dreisbach John J Sr	Zion's Stone Ch Cem, Kreidersville, Northampton Co, PA 40
Dreisbach Simon	Kreidersville, PA 56
Dreisbach Simon Jr	Zion's Stone Ch Cem, Kreidersville, Northampton Co, PA 40
Dreisbach Yost Col	Zion's Stone Ch, nr Kreidersville, PA 15
Dreisbach Yost Jr	Zion's Stone Ch Cem, Kreidersville, Northampton Co, PA 40
Drennan John	Round Hill Cem, Monongahela, Washington Co, PA 75
Drennan John	Sugg's Creek Cem, Mt Juliet, Wilson Co, TN 82
Drennan William	Fleming County Cem, Fleming Co, KY 59
Dresher George	Fam priv grounds, Montgomery Co, PA 59
Dresser David	Rowley Cem, Essex, MA 48
Dresser David Capt	Stockbridge Cem, Stockbridge, MA 47
Dresser Elijah	Turner, ME 18
Dresser Elijah	Upper St Cem, Turner, ME 39
Dresser John	Dresser Hill, Charlton, MA 56
Dresser Reuben	Center Cem, Goshen, MA 51
Dresser Stephen	Stockbridge Cem, Stockbridge, MA 47
Drew Arthur	Nr Lebanon, TN 23

Drew Cornelius	Old Bur Gr, Kingston, MA	55
Drew Isaac	Mayflower Cem, Duxbury, MA	58
Drew James Jr	Ancient Bur Gr, Kingston, MA	50
Drew Job	Ancient Bur Gr, Kingston, MA	50
Drew John Lt	Nr Old Hodgdon Tavern, Barnstead, NH	28
Drew Samuel	Ancient Bur Gr, Kingston, MA	50
Drew Samuel	Huron Co, OH	46
Drew Seth	Ancient Bur Gr, Kingston, MA	50
Drew Seth	Evergreen Cem, Kingston, MA	26
Drew Stephen	Ancient Bur Gr, Kingston, MA	50
Drew Stephen	Fam Cem, fam farm, East Buckfield, ME	46
Drew Sylvanus	Mayflower Cem, Duxbury, MA	58
Drew Thomas	Field Cem, old rd betw Lowell St, Rochester & Dover, NH	36
Drew Thomas	Thompson St Cem, Halifax, MA	50
Drew William	Ancient Bur Gr, Kingston, MA	50
Drew Wilson	Union Grove Ch Cem, nr Herndon, Emanuel Co, GA	34
Drewer John	Pres Cem, Morristown, NJ	32
Driesbach Peter	Dryland Union Ch Cem, Hecktown, Northampton Co, PA	40
Driesbach Peter	Dryland Ch Cem, Hecktown, Northampton Co, PA	22
Drine George	New Tripoli, old graveyard, Lehigh Co, PA	40
Drisco James Capt	Point of Graves Cem, Portsmouth, NH	34
Driskel John	Topanemus, Monmouth Co, NJ	35
Dritt Jacob	York Co, PA	53
Driver Solomon	Main Street Cem, Manchester, MA	49
Driver Stephen	Broad St, Salem, MA	56
Drown Frederick	Burial Place Hill, Rehoboth, MA	54
Drown Jonathan	Rehoboth Village Cem, Rehoboth, MA	54
Drown Samuel	Old Cem, Rockingham Junction, Newmarket, NH	35
Drowne Benjamin Jr	Cem, Warren, RI	56
Drowne Nathanael	New Bedford Cem, New Bedford, MA	51
Druand Joseph Francis	Boquet Valley Cem, Elizabethtown, NY	56
Druary Zedekiah	Old Village Cem, Temple, NH	28
Drulliner Frederick	Hamilton Cem, Newcastle, St Joseph Co, IN	72
Drulliner Frederick	Newcastle Cem, St Joseph Co, IN	24
Drum Andrew	St Paul's Luth Ch Cem, Red Hook Village, NY	21
Drum Peter	Prospect Hill Cem, Guilderland, NY	32
Drum Philip	Zion's Stone Ch Cem, Kreidersville, Northampton Co, PA	40
Drumheller Nicholas	Himmel's Ch, Rebuck, PA	49
Drumm Philip	Stone Ch Cem, Kreidersville, Northampton Co, PA	22
Drummond James Jr	Silver Creek Cem, Clark Co, IN	25
Drummond James Jr	Silver Creek Cem, W of Charlestown, Clark Co, IN	72
Drummond John	Vischer's Ferry Cem, Vischer's Ferry, Saratoga Co, NY	77
Drury Asa	Boden Cem, Natick, MA	56
Drury Elisha	Church Hill, Framingham, MA	56
Drury Luke	Center Cem, Grafton, MA	49
Drury Moses	Town Cem, Fitzwilliam, NH	32
Drury Nathan	Church Hill, Framingham, MA	56
Drury Samuel Jr	Felchville, Natick, MA	56
Drury Thomas	Center Cem, Grafton, MA	49
Drury William	Park Ave Cem, Holden, MA	15
Dry William	St Philip's Ch Cem, Brunswick Co, NC	49
Dryden Artemas	Park Ave Cem, Holden, MA	15
Dryden James Jr	Rockbridge Cem, Rockbridge Co, VA	58
Dryden Nathaniel	Battle of Kings Mountain, SC	52
Dryden Thomas	Old Cem, Holden, MA	45
Dryer Samuel	Boughton Hill Cem, Ontario Co, NY	33
Dryer William	Briggs Corner Cem, Oak Knoll, Rehoboth, MA	54
Dryer William	Rockdale, West Stockbridge, MA	56
DuBOICE Barnet	Thompson St Cem, Catskill, Greene Co, NY	58
DuBOICE Cornelius	Old fam Cem, Catskill, Greene Co, NY	58
DuBOICE Joel	Fam Cem, Lower Grandview Ave, Catskill, Greene Co, NY	58

DuBOIS Cornelius	Old part, E Greenbush Cem, Schodack, Rensselaer Co, NY	57
DuBOIS Cornelius	Old Hurley Bur Gr, Ulster Co, NY	36
DuBOIS David	Pittsgrove Pres Bur Gr, Daretown, Salem Co, NJ	27
DuBOIS Jerediah	Pittsgrove Pres Bur Gr, Daretown, Salem Co, NJ	27
DuBOIS John Jr Lt	Old Hurley Bur Gr, Ulster Co, NY	36
DuBOIS Petrus	Old Hurley Bur Gr, Ulster Co, NY	36
DuPREE Jeremiah	Fam Cem, Pulaski, GA	62
Du Bois Isaac	Old Town Bur Gr, Newburgh, Orange Co, NY	69
Du Bois Koert	Friends Cem, Crum Elbow, Hyde Park, NY	21
Du Bois Lewis	Marlboro Cem, Marlboro, Ulster Co, NY	61
Du Bois Martin	Fitchburg Cem, Bunker Hill, Ingham Co, MI	17
Du Bois Matthew	Middle sect 3, Newburgh Cem, Newburgh, Wyoming Co, NY	61
Du Bourg Andrew Capt	City Cem, Milledgeville, GA	31
Du Fossat Guy De Soniat	St Louis Cem No 1, New Orleans, LA	63
Dubbs Heinrich	Mt Lebanon Cem, Lebanon Co, PA	83
Dubois Benjamin	Carlisle Cem, Warren Co line, Montgomery Co, OH	56
Dubois Benjamin	First Ref Ch of Freehold, Bradevelt, NJ	26
Dubois Joseph	St Francis Xavier Ch Cem, Vincennes, Knox Co, IN	77
Dubois Joshua	Old Dutch Cem, Kingston, Ulster Co, NY	85
Dubois Louis	Old Daretown Cem, Daretown, NJ	28
Dubois Mathias	Riverside Cem, Union, Broome Co, NY	38
Dubois Nicholas	First Pres Ch Cem, Trenton, NJ	28
Dubs Daniel	Great Swamp, Trinity Ref Cem, Spinnertown, Lehigh Co, PA	40
Dubs Oswald	Wildasin School House Bur Gr, Hanover Twp, PA	59
Duckworth John	First Pres Ch Cem, Morganton, Burke Co, NC	76
Duckworth John Sr	First Pres Ch Cem, Burke Co, NC	49
Ducrest Luis Armand	St Martin of Tours Cem, St Martinville, LA	72
Dudder Jacob Jr	Yellow Frame Cem, Warren Co, NJ	38
Dudley Amos	Alderbrook Cem, Guilford, CT	55
Dudley Benjamin	Douglass Center Cem, Douglass, MA	45
Dudley Benjamin	Old Yard Cem, Weston, MA	55
Dudley Benjamin Capt	Douglas Center, MA	16
Dudley David	Old Summer Hill, North Madison, CT	54
Dudley David	West Side, North Madison, CT	54
Dudley David 3rd	Rockland, North Madison, CT	54
Dudley Eber	Alderbrook Cem, Guilford, CT	55
Dudley George Capt	Stockbridge Cem, Stockbridge, MA	47
Dudley Gilman	Old fam farm, Sanbornton, NH	36
Dudley Isaac	Old Middlebury, OH	45
Dudley Isaac	Old Middlebury Cem, Akron, OH	15
Dudley Jared	North Guilford Cem, North Guilford, CT	55
Dudley Jared	North Guilford Cem, North Guilford, CT	55
Dudley John	Fam Cem, Brentwood, NH	27
Dudley John	[no cem named], IL	19
Dudley John	Naperville Protestant Cem, Naperville, IL	38
Dudley John Lt	Smith Mtg Hs Cem, Gilmantown, NH	38
Dudley Luther	North Guilford Cem, North Guilford, CT	55
Dudley Medad	North Guilford Cem, North Guilford, CT	55
Dudley Nathaniel	Alderbrook Cem, Guilford, CT	55
Dudley Paul	Douglass Center Cem, Douglass, MA	45
Dudley Paul	North Milford, ME	30
Dudley Samuel	Dunkard Mill Run, nr Farmington, Lincoln Dist, WV	43
Dudley Samuel	Leavitt-Dudley-Kimball Cem, Brentwood, NH	39
Dudley Samuel Ens	Fam Cem, Brentwood, NH	27
Dudley Thomas Gov	Roxbury, MA	51
Dudley William	Stockbridge Cem, Stockbridge, MA	47
Dudley Winthrop Capt	Dudley Rd Cem, Brentwood, NH	26
Duer John Sr	Covenenter's Cem, Jackson, Mahoning Co, OH	55
Duesler Marcus	Aban Cem, East Flanders land, Yonkers, Herkimer Co, NY	74
Duesler Marcus	Fulton Co, NY	41
Duff John	Glasgow Mem Cem, Glasgow, Barren Co, KY	73

Duff Samuel — Green Spring Cem, Washington Co, VA 64
Duffel James C — City Cem, Lynchburg, Campbell Co, VA 74
Duffield Thomas — Swartzwald, PA 56
Duffield William — Utica Cem, Venango Co, PA 56
Dugan Thomas — Martha Bell Cem, Randolph Co, NC 49
Dugan Thomas Col — Hood's Cem, Germantown, PA 20
Dugan Thomas Col — [no cem named], PA 19
Dugan William P — Greenville Cem, Soldiers Lot, N Main St, Darke Co, OH 55
Dugas Jean — St Martin of Tours Cath Ch Cem, St Martinville, LA 74
Dugger Julius C — Fish Springs, Carter Co, TN 24
Duhon Claude Dit A — St Martin of Tours Cath Ch Cem, St Martinville, LA 76
Duke Isaac — Loveless Cem, nr Colfax, Clinton Co, IN 73
Duke Matthew — Hendrick farm, nr Uvilla, WV 42
Dukes Joseph — Fam Cem, nr Branchville, SC 70
Dula William — Nr Yadkin River, Wilkesboro, NC 55
Dulaney Benjamin — Blountville Cem, Sullivan Co, TN 29
Dulaney John — Fam Cem, Fairfax Co, VA 56
Duley James — Old Quinn Cem, Iron Works Pike, KY 20
Duley James — Quinn Cem, nr Georgetown, Scott Co, KY 86
Dulin John — Congress Cem, Congress Twp, nr Congress Village, OH 25
Dulin John Sr — Congress Cem, Congress Twp, Wayne Twp, OH 55
Dull Christain — Ch of the Brethren Cem, Germantown, PA 65
Dumas Peter — Sterling Valley Cem, Sterling Valley, NY 41
Dumbleton John — Prospect Park Cem, Hamburgh, NY 33
Dumm Peter — Oldest Adelphia Cem, Colerain Twp, Ross Co, OH 55
Dummer Nathaniel — Hallowell, ME 17
Dummer Nathaniel — Hallowell, ME 15
Dumont Abram — Ref Cem, North Branch, NJ 47
Dumont Peter — Duke's Park #2, Raritan, NJ 47
Dumphy Thomas — Hubbard Cem, Weathersfield, VT 34
Dunagan Isaac — Mill Springs, KY 33
Dunaway William — Fam Cem, Bradford farm, Tignall, Wilkes Co, GA 77
Dunbar Abner — Greenville Bapt Cem, Leicester, MA 57
Dunbar Barnabas — Cem, Rt 106, West Bridgewater, MA 56
Dunbar Daniel — Old Town Yard, Warren, ME 56
Dunbar David — Fam Cem, Penobscot, Hancock Co, ME 76
Dunbar David Jr — Conner Cem, Penobscot, ME 55
Dunbar Ebenezer — Old Cem nr fairground, Brockton, MA 16
Dunbar Ebenezer — Old Forest Ave Cem, Brockton, MA 45
Dunbar Elijah — Canton Cem, nr Unitarian Ch, Canton, MA 59
Dunbar Hosea — Thompson St Cem, Halifax, MA 50
Dunbar Jesse — Fam Cem, East Neck Rd, Nobleboro, ME 58
Dunbar John — Huron Cem, Huron Co, OH 40
Dunbar Joseph — Thompson St Cem, Halifax, MA 58
Dunbar Melzar — Hingham, MA 54
Dunbar Nehemiah — Moore Cem, Greene, NY 35
Dunbar Peter — Old Cem, Bridgewater, MA 46
Dunbar Robert — Old bur gr, Newport, RI 39
Dunbar Thomas — Rawson Brook Cem, Leicester, MA 55
Dunbar William — Forest Cem, nr Natchez, Adams, Patriot, MS 74
Dunbar William — Layman, Washington Co, OH 56
Duncan Abraham — Valley Cem, Londonderry, NH 35
Duncan Charles — Madison Co, KY 56
Duncan David — Pittsburgh, PA 56
Duncan George — Nr Hardware River, Fluvanna Co, VA 73
Duncan George — Pres Ch Cem, Preble, NY 36
Duncan George — Stampers Creek Cem, Orange Co, IN 25
Duncan George — Stampers Creek Cem, Orange Co, IN 72
Duncan James — Antrim, NH 15
Duncan James — Trinity Ch Cem, Spring St, Newport, RI 75
Duncan James Capt — Pymatuning Prospect Hill Cem, Mercer Co, PA 15

Duncan James Lt	Milledgeville Cem, Milledgeville, Baldwin Co, GA	36
Duncan Jason Capt	Dummerston Center, VT	15
Duncan Jesse	Rockville Cem, Rockville, IN	59
Duncan John	Cranbury, NJ	47
Duncan John	Fam Cem, Bownan, GA	39
Duncan John	First Pres Ch Cem, Cranbury, NJ	76
Duncan John	Hill Cem, Londonderry, NH	35
Duncan John	Londonderry, NH	15
Duncan John	Marlboro Ch Cem, Troy Twp, Delaware Co, OH	53
Duncan John	New Providence Cem, Maryville, Blount Co, TN	62
Duncan John	New Providence Pres Ch Cem, Maryville, Blount Co, TN	76
Duncan John	Sangerfield, Oneida Co, NY	15
Duncan John	Trinity Ch Cem, Spring St, Newport, RI	75
Duncan John Col	Old Cem, Acworth, NH	34
Duncan John Sgt	Acworth Cem, Acworth, MA	44
Duncan Joseph	Bapt Ch, Barnwell, SC	51
Duncan Moses	Cave Springs Cem, Sarcoxie, Jasper Co, MO	80
Duncan Moses	Cave Springs Cem, La Belle, Lewis Co, MO	81
Duncan Robert	Webster, ME	18
Duncan Samuel Dr	Old Cem, West Bath, ME	55
Duncan William	Cem on Hill, Londonderry, NH	45
Duncan William Capt	Hill Cem, Londonderry, NH	35
Duncanson James	St George's Cem, Fredericksburg, VA	59
Dungan Elias	Southampton, Bucks Co, PA	57
Dungan Thomas	Hood Cem, Germantown, PA	52
Dunham A Col	Priv Cem, Lincoln Hwy, NJ	24
Dunham Abial Dea	North Road Cem, Truxton, Cortland Co, NY	36
Dunham Abiel Capt	Old Kirk Yard, Attleboro, MA	15
Dunham Ammi	Trask Cem, South Jefferson, ME	31
Dunham Asa Rev	Hidlay Ch, nr Light St, PA	15
Dunham Azariah	Fam Cem, Edison, Middlesex Co, NJ	79
Dunham Ben	Broad St, Salem, MA	56
Dunham Cornelius	Burnside Cem, Pemaquid Point, Bristol, Lincoln Co, ME	76
Dunham Cornelius	Fam Cem, Waterloo, Seneca Co, NY	65
Dunham Cornelius	West Abington Cem, Abington, MA	55
Dunham Daniel	Old Cem, Newport, Newport oC, RI	31
Dunham Daniel	Oran Pioneer Cem, Fayetteville, NY	49
Dunham David	Fam Cem, Edison, NJ	75
Dunham David	Fam priv Cem, Stelton, Middlesex Co, NJ	78
Dunham David	Lamington Pres Cem, Somerset Co, NJ	63
Dunham Ebenezer	Center Cem, Carver, MA	59
Dunham Edmund	Old Pres Ch Cem, Bound Brook, NJ	48
Dunham Elijah	Burial Hill, Plymouth, MA	56
Dunham Elijah	St James Epis Ch Cem, Edison, NJ	75
Dunham Elijah	St Peters Epis Ch Cem, Perth Amboy, NJ	76
Dunham Elisha	Pease Point Way, Martha's Vineyard, Edgartown, MA	48
Dunham Ephraim	Lexington Cem, Greene Co, NY	65
Dunham George	Carver Cem, Plymouth, Carver, MA	55
Dunham George	Wenham Cem, East Carver, MA	59
Dunham George Jr	Wenham Cem, East Carver, MA	59
Dunham Hezekiah	Bapt Ch Cem, Wilton, Saratoga Co, NY	77
Dunham Hezekiah	Moe Cem, South Victory Mills, Saratoga, NY	41
Dunham Isaac Rev	Lakenham Cem, Carver, MA	59
Dunham Israel	Old Cem, Plympton, MA	45
Dunham James	Ionia Cem, Vanburen, Onondaga Co, NY	75
Dunham James Maj	Van Lieu Cem, New Brunswick, NJ	28
Dunham Jeremiah	Old Cem, W of Camillus, NY	56
Dunham John	Cedar Grove Cem, 3 mi S of New Holland, Pickaway Co, OH	55
Dunham John	Old Kirk Yard, Attleboro, MA	15
Dunham John	Pres Cem, New Providence, NJ	47
Dunham John	Pres Ch Cem, Westfield, NJ	76

Dunham John	Wenham Cem, Carver, MA	58
Dunham Jonathan	Fam Cem, Dunham Twp, Washington Co, OH	55
Dunham Jonathan	Fam Cem, Edison, Middlesex Co, NJ	79
Dunham Jonathan	Fam Cem, Edison, Middlesex Co, NJ	79
Dunham Jonathan Jr	Wells Bur Gr, nr Battenville, NY	58
Dunham Jonathan Sr Rev	Piscataway Cem, Piscataway, NJ	58
Dunham Joseph	Brimfield Center Cem, Brimfield, MA	55
Dunham Joseph	Edgartown, MA	15
Dunham Joseph	Epis Ch Cem, Woodbridge, NJ	76
Dunham Joseph	New Cem, Edgartown, MA	46
Dunham Josiah	Handy Cem, West Woodstock, Windsor Co, VT	75
Dunham Lewis Ford	Van Liew Cem, Old Pres sect, New Brunswick, NJ	75
Dunham Moses	Cox Cem, Hartford, ME	31
Dunham Robert	Dunham Bluff Plantation Cem, Marion Co, SC	70
Dunham Samuel	Salisbury Cem, Crow Hill, Stillwater, NY	41
Dunham Samuel	Valley Home Cem, Windham Twp, PA	53
Dunham Silas	Carver Cem, Carver, MA	56
Dunham Silvanus	Wenham Cem, East Carver, MA	59
Dunham Sylvanus	Old Cem, Carver, MA	47
Dunham Thomas	Bethel Cem, Bethel, Windsor Co, VT	58
Dunham Thomas	Fairview Cem, Bethel, Windsor Co, VT	72
Dunham William	On Rt 106, East Mansfield, MA	56
Dunkel George Garret	Dunckel (Freysbush) Cem, Montgomery Co, NY	65
Dunkel Peter	Dunkel's Ch Cem, Berks Co, PA	59
Dunkel Peter Jr	Dunckel (Freysbush) Cem, Montgomery Co, NY	65
Dunkin John Jr	Green Springs Ch Cem, Abingdon, VA	70
Dunklin Joseph	Fam Cem, Bersley Dist, SC	54
Dunlap Adam	Antrim, NH	15
Dunlap Alexander	Red Oak Cem, nr Georgetown, Brown Co, OH	55
Dunlap Ephraim	Chippenhook Cem, Clarendon, VT	24
Dunlap Ephriam	Chippenhook Cem, Clarendon, VT	25
Dunlap Hugh	City Cem, nr Courthouse, Paris, Henry Co, TN	77
Dunlap James	Oriskany Cem, Cherry Valley, NY	56
Dunlap James	Pittsgrove Pres Cem, Pittsgrove, NJ	47
Dunlap James	Village Cem, Chester, NH	33
Dunlap John W	Cherry Valley, NY	56
Dunlap Joseph	Oak Grove Cem, Delaware Co, OH	18
Dunlap Patti Frank	Plantation, Anson Co, NC	15
Dunlap Robert 300 ft fr Rt 65 nr Forst Rd, Middletown, OH		56
Dunlap Robert	Maumee, Wood Co, OH	55
Dunlap Robert	Mercer Cem, Cornish, NH	30
Dunlap Samuel	Farm, N of Utica, OH	56
Dunlap William	Cherry Valley, NY	56
Dunlap William	Fam lot, Lexington, KY	56
Dunlevy Anthony 2d	Red Oak Ch Cem, Brown Co, OH	56
Dunlevy Francis	Lebanon Cem, Warren Co, OH	55
Dunlevy Mary Craig	Old Bapt Cem, Lebanon, Warren Co, OH	45
Dunlop James	Bellefonte Cem, Bellefonte, Centre Co, PA	78
Dunn Benjamin	St James Epis Ch Cem, Edison, NJ	75
Dunn Clawson	Middlesex Hillside Cem, Middlesex, NJ	24
Dunn Clawson	Samptown Cem, South Plainfield, Middlesex Co, NJ	80
Dunn Elinor M	Indiana Univ campus, Bloomington, Monroe Co, IN	72
Dunn Elinor M Brewster	Indiana Univ, Bloomington, Monroe Co, IN	24
Dunn George	Morriton Pres Cem, Montgomery Co, PA	52
Dunn George Lt	Pres Cem, Norristown, PA	15
Dunn Henry	Salisbury Cem, Crow Hill, Stillwater, NY	41
Dunn Hugh	St James Epis Ch Cem, Edison, NJ	75
Dunn James	Colonial Cem, Johnstown, NY	63
Dunn James	Fam Cem, nr Cheatview, Union Dist, Monongalia Co, WV	40
Dunn James	Old Greenville Ch, nr Ware Shoals, SC	53
Dunn James Capt	Portland, NY	15

Abstract of Graves of Revolutionary Patriots

Dunn James Jr	Chelmsford, MA 55
Dunn Jeremiah	St James Epis Ch Cem, Edison, NJ 75
Dunn Joel	Seventh Day Bapt Cem, New Market, NJ 24
Dunn John	St James Epis Ch Cem, Edison, NJ 75
Dunn Jonathan	Felchville, Natick, MA 56
Dunn Joshua	Durham, ME 18
Dunn Josiah	Poland, ME 56
Dunn Levi	Killed in Wyoming Massacre, Wyoming, PA 52
Dunn Nahun	Priv Cem, Lincoln Hwy, Stelton, NJ 47
Dunn Peter	Providence Cem, Mercer Co, KY 52
Dunn Reuben	Old Cost Graveyard, nr Wright Field, Dayton, OH 50
Dunn Samuel	Plymouth, Wayne Co, MI 56
Dunn Samuel	Upper Indiana Cem, Vincennes, Knox Co, IN 72
Dunn Samuel	Woodbridge Pres Ch Cem, Woodbridge, NJ 76
Dunn Simon	Long Creek Bapt Ch Cem, nr Gastonia, Gaston Co, NC 76
Dunn Thomas	Narrowsburg Cem, Sullivan Co, NY 52
Dunn Thomas	Nr Carey, OH 53
Dunn Timothy	East Cem, Smyrna, NY 16
Dunn William	Dunnston Cem, PA 21
Dunn William	Killed in Wyoming Massacre, Wyoming, PA 52
Dunne William	Second St Cem, Elmira, NY 33
Dunnell David	Cambridge Cem, Cambridge, NY 46
Dunnet Christian	St Thomas Epis Ch Cem, Montgomery Co, PA 59
Dunning Andrew	Harpswell Center, Harpswell, ME 56
Dunning Benjamin	Harpswell Center, Harpswell, ME 56
Dunning Isaac	Tashua, Trumbull, CT 56
Dunning James	Malta Cem, Malta, Saratoga Co, NY 42
Dunning John Gen	Dunning St Cem, Malta, Saratoga Co, NY 41
Dunning Josiah	Pleasant View Cem, Williamson, NY 69
Dunning Lewis	West Genoa Cem, Genoa, Cayuga Co, NY 57
Dunning Michael	Dunning St Cem, Malta, Saratoga Co, NY 41
Dunning Michael	Malta Cem, Malta, Saratoga Co, NY 42
Dunning Robert	Maquoit Cem, Brunswick, ME 56
Dunning Silas	Melrose Rd Cem, Owasco, Cayuga Co, NY 65
Dunphey James	Ashtabula Co, OH 46
Dunscomb Daniel	Greenburgh Pres Ch Cem, Greenburgh, NY 34
Dunscomb Ed Capt	Danby, NY 15
Dunseth James	Massacred nr mouth of Lechry Creek, Dearborn Co, IN 24
Dunspaugh Philip	Mellenville Union Cem, Claverack, Columbia Co, NY 79
Dunster Jason	Pleasant View Cem, Mason, NH 39
Dunworth George	Westford Hill Cem, Ashford, CT 55
DuplessiS	Danby, NY 15
Dupue David	Highland Cem, block 85 lot 1, Ypsilanti, MI 64
Dupuy William	His home, Greenville Rd, nr Hopkinsville, KY 15
Duran John	Mount Evergreen, Jackson Co, MI 56
Duran Matthew	Durham, ME 18
Durand John Capt	Mount Evergreen Cem, Jackson, MI 25
Durand Samuel	Cheshire, CT 17
Durand Samuel	Cong Cem, Cheshire, New Haven Co, CT 24
Durand Samuel	Hillside Cem, Cheshire, CT 58
Durant Amos	South Parish Bur Gr, Andover, MA 26
Durant Henry	Old Rembert Cem, Sumpter Dist, SC 59
Durant Joseph Francis	Pleasant Valley Cem, Elizabethtown, NY 33
Durant Joshua	Aldrich Cem, Weathersfield, VT 36
Durant Joshua	Aldrich Cem, Weathersfield, VT 42
Durel Juan Bautista	St Louis Cem No 1, New Orleans, LA 63
Durell Jean Baptiste	St Louis Cem, New Orleans, LA 74
Durfee Gideon	Lakey farm, East Palmyra, Wayne Co, NY 54
Durfee Hon Thomas	Oak Grove Cem, Fall River, MA 46
Durfee Joseph Lt Col	North Cem, Fall River, MA 46
Durfee Lemuel	Fam bur gr, farm 2 mi N of Palmyra, Wayne Co, NY 79

Durfee Lemuel	Fam bur gr, farm, 2 mi N of Palmyra, NY	51
Durfee Richard	Oak Grove, Fall River, MA	55
Durfey Daniel	St James Ch Cem, Wilmington, NC	49
Durgin Benjamin	Fam farm, rd betw Lee Hill & Epping, Lee, NH	39
Durgin Gershom	Boston Hill, Andover, NH	31
Durgin James	Fam Cem, Strafford, NH	38
Durgin John Lt	Town Cem, Sanbornton, NH	29
Durgin Josiah	Priv fam Cem, Lee, NH	34
Durham Asa	Freetown, Cortland Co, NY	36
Durham Charnal	Nr Dutchman's Creek (Ridgeway), east Fairfield Co, SC	42
Durham John	Bellevue Cem, Danville, Boyle Co, KY	81
Durham John	Grove Cem, Belfast, Waldo Co, ME	78
Durkee Andrew	Soule Cem, Sennett, NY	56
Durkee Andrew	South Yard, Hampton, CT	31
Durkee Andrew	West Galway Cem, West Galway, Saratoga Co, NY	77
Durkee Bartholomew	His farm, nr Pomfort, Windsor Co, VT	55
Durkee Benjamin	Augusta Cem, Augusta, Oneida Co, NY	58
Durkee Daniel	East Homer Cem, Homer, NY	36
Durkee Ebbe	East Cem, Deakesburg, OH	53
Durkee Ebbe	[no cem named], OH	26
Durkee John	Center Cem, Hanover, NH	27
Durkee John	Norwich Town Cem, Norwich, CT	18
Durkee Nathan	School St Cem, Lebanon, NH	27
Durkee Nathaniel Maj	Old Redwine Ch Cem, Jasper Co, GA	22
Durkee Robert	Killed in Wyoming Massacre, Wyoming, PA	52
Durkee Robert	North Newport Cem, Newport, NH	32
Durkee Soloman Sgt	South Farnham, OH	15
Durkee Solomon	South Farman, Ashtabula, OH	18
Durkee Thomas Lt	Center Cem, Hanover, NH	27
Durkee Timothy	Cem, Royalton, VT	56
Durst John	Durst (Dust) Cem, Uvilla Bakerton, Jefferson Co, WV	78
Durwin Amos	East side, Pittsfield-Williamstown Rd, Lanesborough, MA	55
Duryea Charles	Reber Hill Cem, SW Corner, 6 mi NE of Circleville, OH	56
Duryea Garret	Blooming Grove Cem, Orange Co, NY	56
Duryea John	Elmont Cem, Elmont, Queens Co, NY	80
Duryea John	Prospect Cem, Jamaica, Queens Co, NY	78
Duryee John Rev	Bur gr adjoining 1st Pres Ch, Caldwell, Essex Co, NJ	31
Duseaux Peter	Luth Cem, Barren Hill, PA	52
Duseaux Peter	St Paul's Evan Luth Cem, Montgomery Co, PA	59
Dusenberry Duten	Van Cortlandville Cem, Peekskill, NY	41
Dusenberry William	Adams Corners Cem, Adams Corners, Putnam Co, NY	36
Dusenberry William	On hill midway betw Somerset & Fultonham, Perry Co, OH	55
Dusenberry William Sr	St Paul's Ch Cem, New York City, New York Co, NY	78
Dusenbury Charles	Pres Ch Cem, White Plains, NY	36
Dusenbury Henry	Old Mansfield Cem, Washington, NJ	57
Dusenbury Henry	Pres Ch Cem, White Plains, NY	36
Dusenbury Henry	Pres Ch Cem, White Plains, NY	36
Dusenbury John Capt	Old French Cem (now under buildings), Peoria, IL	17
Dusenbury Richard	Albany Rural Cem, Albany, NY	30
Dushane Cornelius	St Georges, New Castle Co, DE	46
Dustin David	Canaan St Cem, Canaan, NH	36
Dustin David	Dustin Yard, Sanbornton, NH	29
Dustin Ebenezer	Lockhaven Cem, Enfield, NH	38
Dustin John	Surrey, NH	51
Dustin Moody Ens	West Claremont Cem, Claremont, NH	50
Dustin Moses Capt	First Cem, Candia, NH	29
Dustin Peter	Cem on Hill, Range Rd, Windham, NH	26
Dustin Timothy	West Claremont Cem, Claremont, NH	50
Dustin William Lt	Hillside Cem, South Weare, NH	33
Duston David	Town Cem, Salem, NH	41
Duston Peter	Cem on the hill, Windham, NH	46

Dutch Samuel	Winter St Cem, Exeter, NY 15
Dutcher Elias	Round Top Cem, Cairo, Greene Co, NY 59
Dutcher John	Middle Village Cem, East Springfield, NY 33
Dutcher John	Town Ground, East Springfield, NY 15
Dutcher Ruluff Capt	Dutcher's Bridge Cem, CT 31
Dutton Amasa	Center, Lebanon, CT 56
Dutton Asa	Dummerston Center, VT 15
Dutton Benjamin	Hillsborough Cem, Hillsborough, NH 46
Dutton David	Windham Cem, Windham, VT 45
Dutton Ephriam	Ludlow, VT 15
Dutton Jacob	Francestown Cem, Francestown, NH 28
Dutton Jacob	Town Cem, Francestown, NH 27
Dutton John	Epis Cem, Oxford, CT 37
Dutton Joseph	Fairview, Westford, MA 56
Dutton Moses	Village Cem, Sherman, Chautauqua Co, NY 61
Dutton Oliver	Meredith Village Cem, Meredith, Delaware Co, NY 71
Dutton Oliver Dr	Cong Ch Cem, Ludlow Center, MA 55
Dutton Salmon	Village Cem, Cavendish, VT 36
Dutton Thadeus	Haun farm Cem, E of Van Hornesville, Herkimer Co, NY 41
Dutton Thomas	Old Center Cem, Jaffrey, NH 37
Dutton Thomas	Old Cem, Jaffrey, NH 28
Dutton Timothy	Quinipiac Cem, Plantsville, CT 15
Dutton Titus	St James Churchyard Cem, Hyde Park, NY 70
Duvall Gabriel	Beall farm, Glenn Dale, Prince Georges Co, MD 48
Duvall Jeremiah	Fam Cem, Broad Top Twp, Bedford Co, PA 80
Duvall William	Mill Creek Cem, Concord Twp, Delaware Co, OH 53
Dwelle Abner Capt	Greenwich, NY 15
Dwelle Joshua	1st Cong Ch Cem, Hanover Center, MA 55
Dwight Elijah	Mahaiwe, Great Barrington, MA 56
Dwight Hamlin Capt	South Lawn Cem, Williamstown, MA 33
Dwight Henry William	Stockbridge Cem, Stockbridge, MA 47
Dwight Joseph Jr	Upper Cincinnatus Cem, Cincinnatus, Cortland Co, NY 36
Dwight Seth	Vine Lake, Medfield, MA 56
Dwinal Aaron	Lisbon, ME 18
Dwinal Amos	Webster, ME 18
Dwindell Stephen	North Bennington, VT 52
Dwinel Henry	County Bridge Cem, Millbury, MA 56
Dwinell John	Old Topsfield Pine Grove Cem, Hanover Center, MA 55
Dwinell Thomas	Ash Swamp (West Kenne) Cem, Keene, NH 32
Dwinnell Benjamin	Court Street Bur Gr, Keene, NH 16
Dwyer Ezra	Greenwich, NY 15
Dyckman Abraham Lt	Pres Ch Cem, Yorktown, NY 34
Dyckman William	Paw Paw, Jackson, MI 56
Dye Andrew Sr	Pleasant Hill Cem, Troy, OH 56
Dye Brown	Old fam Cem, fam prop, nr Elberton, Elbert Co, GA 66
Dye Enoch	Washington, PA 55
Dye Ezekiel	Old Cem, Renrock, Noble Co, OH 56
Dye John	Day farm, 3 mi E of Georgetown, Brown Co, OH 55
Dye John	First Pres Ch Cem, Cranbury, NJ 76
Dye John	Pleasant Twp, Ripley, OH 15
Dye Joseph	First Pres Ch Cem, Cranbury, NJ 76
Dye Peter	First Pres Ch Cem, Cranbury, NJ 76
Dye William	First Pres Ch Cem, Cranbury, NJ 76
Dyer Amherst	Waites Corners, nr Cambridge, NY 30
Dyer Bela	Mount Zion Cem, Abington, MA 45
Dyer Benjamin	Canton St Cem, Canton, CT 55
Dyer Benjamin	Wiswell Cem, West Townshend, VT 34
Dyer Charles	Burial Hill, Plymouth, MA 56
Dyer Christopher	Mount Zion Cem, Abington, MA 45
Dyer Christopher	Scotland Cem, Bridgewater, MA 46
Dyer Christopher Lt	Mount Zion Cem, Abington, MA 45

Dyer Daniel	Canton St Cem, Canton, CT 55
Dyer Daniel	Canton St Cem, Canton, CT 15
Dyer Edward	Waites Corners, nr Cambridge, NY 30
Dyer Elisha	Reed Creek Ch, Hart Co, GA 27
Dyer Elkanah	South Lewiston Cem, ME 48
Dyer Ephraim	Priv Cem back of Hann House, E Sullivan, Hancock Co, ME 56
Dyer George	Clarendon Flats, VT 31
Dyer Jacob	Mount Zion Cem, Abington, MA 45
Dyer James	Red Bridge Cem, Orange, MA 26
Dyer John	Old Cem, Smithfield (Providence), RI 56
Dyer John	Pleasant Cem, Bridgewater, MA 55
Dyer Joseph	Fam Cem, Canton, CT 15
Dyer Joseph	Mount Zion Cem, Abington, MA 45
Dyer Joseph	Old Cem, The Green, Middleboro, MA 50
Dyer Peter	Dyer Hill Cem, South Braintree, Braintree, MA 55
Dyer Samuel	Quidnesset Mem Cem, N Kingstown, Kent Co, RI 63
Dyer Solomon	Old Cem, The Green, Middleboro, MA 50
Dyer Thomas	Old North Cem, Truro, MA 49
Dyer Thomas	Pompey Hill Cem, Pompey, Onondaga Co, NY 81
Dyer Thomas	Pratt Dist Yard, Southbridge, MA 29
Dyer William Capt	Commanding a scouting detachment, VT 24
Dyer William Capt	[no cem named], VT 25
Dygert William	Frankfort, Herkimer, NY 56
Dyke Nicholas Col	Westminster Cem, Westminster, MA 45
Dykeman Abraham	Pres Ch Cem, Yorktown, NY 41
Dykerman Joseph	Dykerman's Station, NY 51
Dykman Hezekiah	South East Cem, South East Twp, Putnam Co, NY 35
Dysart Cornelius Dr	Hopewell Pres Ch, Mecklenburg Co, NC 43
Dysart James	Hopewell Pres Ch, Mecklenburg Co, NC 43
Dysart John	Drucilla Cem, Old Fort, NC 70
Dysart William	Hopewell Pres Ch, Mecklenburg Co, NC 43
Dyson John	Beverly, MA 55

About the Author

Patricia Law Hatcher, CG, FASG is a Certified Genealogist, a trustee of the Association of Professional Genealogists, and in 2000 was elected a Fellow of the American Society of Genealogists. A popular lecturer and instructor, she has spoken at many national conferences. Her articles have appeared in over a dozen publications and she has written *Producing a Quality Family History* (Ancestry, 1996); *Barren County, Kentucky, Deeds 1798–1813* (Pioneer Heritage Press, 1998); and the genealogical portion of *A Rhoads Family History, The Family and Ancestry of Jay Roscoe Rhoads* (Newbury Street Press, 2001).

These volumes were her first major genealogical publications.

www.ingramcontent.com/pod-product-compliance
Lightning Source LLC
Chambersburg PA
CBHW051040160426
43193CB00010B/1007